S0-AZP-738

MASTER Active Directory™ VISUALLY™

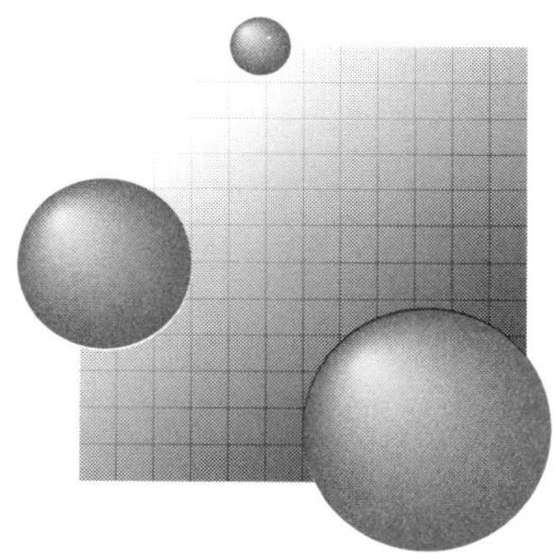

by Curt Simmons

IDG's 3-D Visual™ Series

From

maranGraphics™

IDG Books Worldwide, Inc.
An International Data Group Company
Foster City, CA • Indianapolis • Chicago • New York

Master Active Directory™ VISUALLY™

Published by
IDG Books Worldwide, Inc.
An International Data Group Company
919 E. Hillsdale Blvd., Suite 400
Foster City, CA 94404
www.idgbooks.com (IDG Books Worldwide Web Site)

Library of Congress Catalog Card No.: 00-105128

ISBN: 0-7645-3425-4

Printed in the United States of America

10 9 8 7 6 5 4 3

1V/RZ/QX/ZZ/IN

Distributed by CDG Books Canada Inc. for Canada; by Transworld Publishers Limited in the United Kingdom; by IDG Norge Books for Norway; by IDG Sweden Books for Sweden; by IDG Books Australia Publishing Corporation Pty. Ltd. for Australia and New Zealand; by TransQuest Publishers Pte Ltd. for Singapore, Malaysia, Thailand, Indonesia, and Hong Kong; by Gotop Information Inc. for Taiwan; by ICG Muse, Inc. for Japan; by Intersoft for South Africa; by Eyrolles for France; by International Thomson Publishing for Germany, Austria and Switzerland; by Distribuidora Cuspide for Argentina; by LR International for Brazil; by Galileo Libros for Chile; by Ediciones ZETA S.C.R. Ltda. for Peru; by WS Computer Publishing Corporation, Inc., for the Philippines; by Contemporanea de Ediciones for Venezuela; by Express Computer Distributors for the Caribbean and West Indies; by Micronesia Media Distributor, Inc. for Micronesia; by Chips Computadoras S.A. de C.V. for Mexico; by Editorial Norma de Panama S.A. for Panama; by American Bookshops for Finland.

For corporate orders, please call maranGraphics at 800-469-6616.

For general information on IDG Books Worldwide's books in the U.S., please call our Consumer Customer Service department at 800-762-2974. For reseller information, including discounts and premium sales, please call our Reseller Customer Service department at 800-434-3422.

For information on where to purchase IDG Books Worldwide's books outside the U.S., please contact our International Sales department at 317-572-3993 or fax 317-572-4002.

For consumer information on foreign language translations, please contact our Customer Service department at 1-800-434-3422, fax 317-572-4002, or e-mail rights@idgbooks.com.

For information on licensing foreign or domestic rights, please phone +1-650-653-7098.

For sales inquiries and special prices for bulk quantities, please contact our Order Services department at 800-434-3422 or write to the address above.

For information on using IDG Books Worldwide's books in the classroom or for ordering examination copies, please contact our Educational Sales department at 800-434-2086 or fax 317-572-4005.

For press review copies, author interviews, or other publicity information, please contact our Public Relations department at 650-653-7000 or fax 650-653-7500.

For authorization to photocopy items for corporate, personal, or educational use, please contact Copyright Clearance Center, 222 Rosewood Drive, Danvers, MA 01923, or fax 978-750-4470.

Screen shots displayed in this book are based on pre-released software and are subject to change.

Trademark Acknowledgments

Permissions

U.S. Corporate Sales

Contact maranGraphics
at (800) 469-6616 or
fax (905) 890-9434.

U.S. Trade Sales

Contact IDG Books
at (800) 434-3422
or (650) 653-7000.

ABOUT IDG BOOKS WORLDWIDE

Welcome to the world of IDG Books Worldwide.

IDG Books Worldwide, Inc., is a subsidiary of International Data Group, the world's largest publisher of computer-related information and the leading global provider of information services on information technology. IDG was founded more than 30 years ago by Patrick J. McGovern and now employs more than 9,000 people worldwide. IDG publishes more than 290 computer publications in over 75 countries. More than 90 million people read one or more IDG publications each month.

Launched in 1990, IDG Books Worldwide is today the #1 publisher of best-selling computer books in the United States. We are proud to have received eight awards from the Computer Press Association in recognition of editorial excellence and three from Computer Currents' First Annual Readers' Choice Awards. Our best-selling *...For Dummies®* series has more than 50 million copies in print with translations in 31 languages. IDG Books Worldwide, through a joint venture with IDG's Hi-Tech Beijing, became the first U.S. publisher to publish a computer book in the People's Republic of China. In record time, IDG Books Worldwide has become the first choice for millions of readers around the world who want to learn how to better manage their businesses.

Our mission is simple: Every one of our books is designed to bring extra value and skill-building instructions to the reader. Our books are written by experts who understand and care about our readers. The knowledge base of our editorial staff comes from years of experience in publishing, education, and journalism — experience we use to produce books to carry us into the new millennium. In short, we care about books, so we attract the best people. We devote special attention to details such as audience, interior design, use of icons, and illustrations. And because we use an efficient process of authoring, editing, and desktop publishing our books electronically, we can spend more time ensuring superior content and less time on the technicalities of making books.

You can count on our commitment to deliver high-quality books at competitive prices on topics you want to read about. At IDG Books Worldwide, we continue in the IDG tradition of delivering quality for more than 30 years. You'll find no better book on a subject than one from IDG Books Worldwide.

oducts worldwide. Further information about the company can be

John Kilcullen
Chairman and CEO
IDG Books Worldwide, Inc.

Eighth Annual Computer Press Awards 1992

Ninth Annual Computer Press Awards 1993

Tenth Annual Computer Press Awards 1994

Eleventh Annual Computer Press Awards 1995

IDG is the world's leading IT media, research and exposition company. Founded in 1964, IDG had 1997 revenues of $2.05 billion and has more than 9,000 employees worldwide. IDG offers the widest range of media options that reach IT buyers in 75 countries representing 95% of worldwide IT spending. IDG's diverse product and services portfolio spans six key areas including print publishing, online publishing, expositions and conferences, market research, education and training, and global marketing services. More than 90 million people read one or more of IDG's 290 magazines and newspapers, including IDG's leading global brands — Computerworld, PC World, Network World, Macworld and the Channel World family of publications. IDG Books Worldwide is one of the fastest-growing computer book publishers in the world, with more than 700 titles in 36 languages. The "...For Dummies®" series alone has more than 50 million copies in print. IDG offers online users the largest network of technology-specific Web sites around the world through IDG.net (http://www.idg.net), which comprises more than 225 targeted Web sites in 55 countries worldwide. International Data Corporation (IDC) is the world's largest provider of information technology data, analysis and consulting, with research centers in over 41 countries and more than 400 research analysts worldwide. IDG World Expo is a leading producer of more than 168 globally branded conferences and expositions in 35 countries including E3 (Electronic Entertainment Expo), Macworld Expo, ComNet, Windows World Expo, ICE (Internet Commerce Expo), Agenda, DEMO, and Spotlight. IDG's training subsidiary, ExecuTrain, is the world's largest computer training company, with more than 230 locations worldwide and 785 training courses. IDG Marketing Services helps industry-leading IT companies build international brand recognition by developing global integrated marketing programs via IDG's print, online and exposition pr
found at www.idg.com.

1/26/00

maranGraphics is a family-run business located near Toronto, Canada.

At maranGraphics, we believe in producing great computer books – one book at a time.

maranGraphics has been producing high-technology products for over 25 years, which enables us to offer the computer book community a unique communication process.

Our computer books use an integrated communication process, which is very different from the approach used in other computer books. Each spread is, in essence, a flow chart – the text and screen shots are totally incorporated into the layout of the spread. Introductory text and helpful tips complete the learning experience.

maranGraphics' approach encourages the left and right sides of the brain to work together – resulting in faster orientation and greater memory retention.

Above all, we are very proud of the handcrafted nature of our books. Our carefully-chosen writers are experts in their fields, and spend countless hours researching and organizing the content for each topic. Our artists rebuild every screen shot to provide the best clarity possible, making our screen shots the most precise and easiest to read in the industry. We strive for perfection, and believe that the time spent handcrafting each element results in the best computer books money can buy.

Thank you for purchasing this book. We hope you enjoy it!

Sincerely,
Robert Maran
President
maranGraphics

Please visit us on the Web at:
www.maran.com

CREDITS

Acquisitions, Editorial, and Media Development

Project Editor
Darren Meiss

Acquisitions Editor
Martine Edwards

Associate Project Coordinator
Lindsay Sandman

Senior Copy Editor
Ted Cains

Proof Editor
Dwight Ramsey

Technical Editor
Indika Boteju

Permissions Editor
Carmen Krikorian

Associate Media Development Specialist
Megan Decraene

Editorial Manager
Rev Mengle

Media Development Manager
Heather Heath Dismore

Editorial Assistant
Candace Nicholson

Production

Book Design
maranGraphics

Project Coordinator
Valery Bourke

Layout
York Graphics Service, Inc.

Special Art
Craig Dearing, Deborah Naor

Proofreaders
York Production Services, Inc.

Indexer
York Production Services, Inc.

Special Help
Steve Arany
Angie Hunckler
Clint Lahnen
Shelley Norris
Mary Jo Richards
Brent Savage
Kathie Schutte

General and Administrative

IDG Books Worldwide, Inc.: John Kilcullen, CEO

IDG Books Technology Publishing Group: Richard Swadley, Senior Vice President and Publisher; Walter R. Bruce III, Vice President and Publisher; Joseph Wikert, Vice President and Publisher; Mary Bednarek, Vice President and Director, Product Development; Andy Cummings, Publishing Director, General User Group; Mary C. Corder, Editorial Director; Barry Pruett, Publishing Director

IDG Books Consumer Publishing Group: Roland Elgey, Senior Vice President and Publisher; Kathleen A. Welton, Vice President and Publisher; Kevin Thornton, Acquisitions Manager; Kristin A. Cocks, Editorial Director

IDG Books Internet Publishing Group: Brenda McLaughlin, Senior Vice President and Publisher; Sofia Marchant, Online Marketing Manager

IDG Books Production for Branded Press: Debbie Stailey, Director of Production; Cindy L. Phipps, Manager of Project Coordination, Production Proofreading, and Indexing; Tony Augsburger, Manager of Prepress, Reprints,and Systems; Laura Carpenter, Production Control Manager; Shelley Lea, Supervisor of Graphics and Design; Debbie J. Gates, Production Systems Specialist; Robert Springer, Supervisor of Proofreading; Trudy Coler, Page Layout Manager; Troy Barnes, Page Layout Supervisor, Kathie Schutte, Senior Page Layout Supervisor; Michael Sullivan, Production Supervisor

Packaging and Book Design: Patty Page, Manager, Promotions Marketing

The publisher would like to give special thanks to Patrick J. McGovern, without whom this book would not have been possible.

About the Author

Curt Simmons, Microsoft Certified Systems Engineer (MCSE) and Microsoft Certified Trainer (MCT), is a Windows expert who spends his most of his time writing technical books. Curt has been working closely with Windows 2000 and the Active Directory since beta 1 was released, and he is author of a dozen high-level computing books on Microsoft technologies. Curt lives in a little Texas town outside of Dallas with his wife and daughter, and you can visit him on the Internet at `curtsimmons.hypermart.net`.

Author's Acknowledgements

I would like to thank everyone at IDG Books, especially Martine Edwards and Darren Meiss. Thanks to Martine for the opportunity to write this book, and a big thanks to Darren for all his time and effort. I would, as always, like to thank my agent, Margot Maley, for always pursuing opportunities on my behalf. Finally, thanks to my wife Dawn for her constant patience and support when I spend too many hours hammering the computer keys.

I UNDERSTANDING ACTIVE DIRECTORY

II WINDOWS 2000 NETWORKING

III PLANNING THE ACTIVE DIRECTORY

WHAT'S INSIDE

IV INSTALLING ACTIVE DIRECTORY

V USERS, GROUPS, COMPUTERS

VI DOMAINS AND TRUSTS

VII ACTIVE DIRECTORY SITES

VIII IMPLEMENTATION

1 UNDERSTANDING ACTIVE DIRECTORY

1) INTRODUCTION TO ACTIVE DIRECTORY

2) TCP/IP BASICS

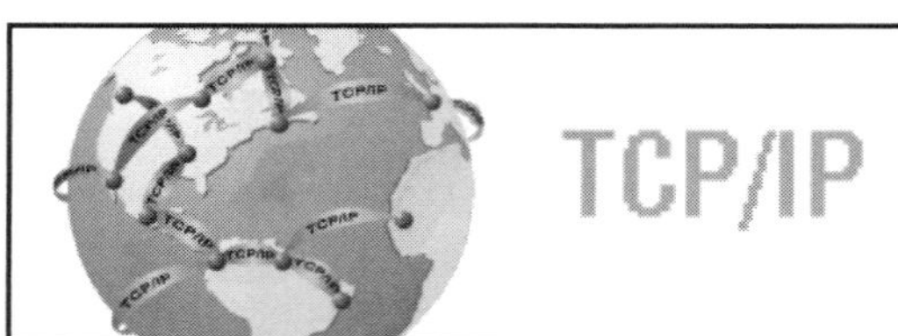

2 WINDOWS 2000 NETWORKING

3) THE WINDOWS 2000 SERVER NETWORKING INTERFACE

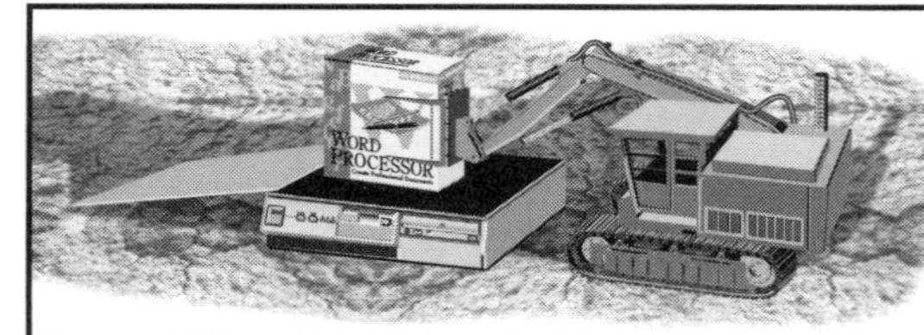

TABLE OF CONTENTS

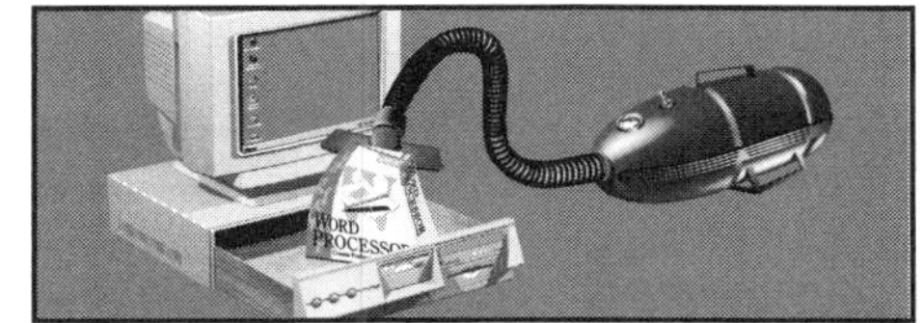

4) CONFIGURING DHCP

5) CONFIGURING WINS

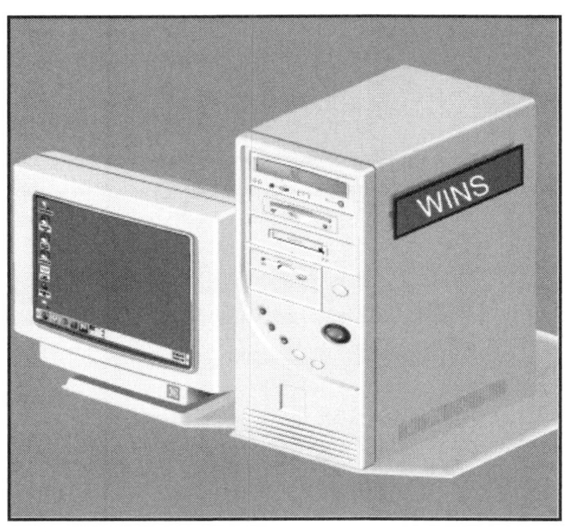

6) CONFIGURING DNS

7) ROUTING AND REMOTE ACCESS SERVICE

3 PLANNING THE ACTIVE DIRECTORY

8) PLANNING THE ACTIVE DIRECTORY NAME

TABLE OF CONTENTS

9) PLANNING THE ACTIVE DIRECTORY DOMAINS

10) PLANNING THE OU STRUCTURE

4 INSTALLING ACTIVE DIRECTORY

11) INSTALLING ACTIVE DIRECTORY

12) USING THE MMC

13) SEARCHING THE ACTIVE DIRECTORY

5 USERS, GROUPS, COMPUTERS

14) CREATING AND MANAGING USER ACCOUNTS

PLEASE ENTER YOUR PASSWORD

15) CREATING AND MANAGING GROUP ACCOUNTS

TABLE OF CONTENTS

16) CREATING AND MANAGING COMPUTER ACCOUNTS

17) CREATING AND MANAGING OUS AND OBJECTS

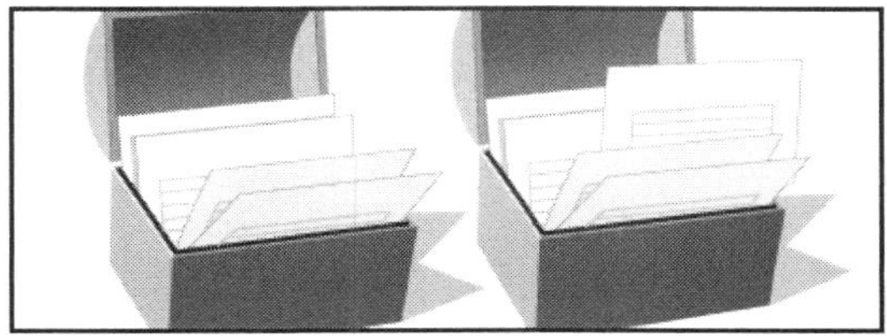

18) MANAGING ACTIVE DIRECTORY DOMAIN CONTROLLERS

6 DOMAINS AND TRUSTS

19) ACTIVE DIRECTORY REPLICATION CONCEPTS

20) USING THE ACTIVE DIRECTORY DOMAINS AND TRUSTS CONSOLE

21) MANAGING DOMAINS AND TRUSTS

7 ACTIVE DIRECTORY SITES

22) MANAGING ACTIVE DIRECTORY SITES

23) CONFIGURING ACTIVE DIRECTORY SITE COMMUNICATIONS

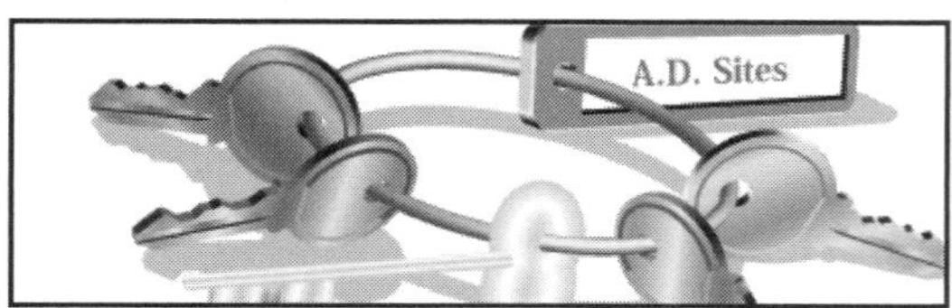

TABLE OF CONTENTS

8 IMPLEMENTATION

24) ACTIVE DIRECTORY SECURITY MANAGEMENT

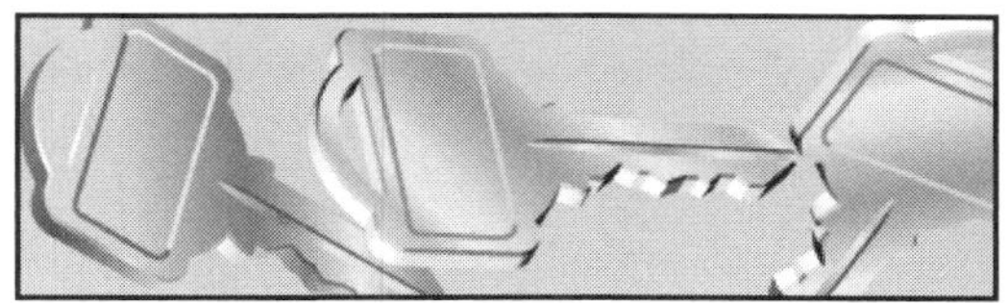

25) GROUP POLICY

26) PUBLISHING ACTIVE DIRECTORY RESOURCES

27) ACTIVE DIRECTORY SCHEMA

28) MAINTAINING THE ACTIVE DIRECTORY

APPENDIX A) COMMON GROUP POLICY CONFIGURATION

APPENDIX A) COMMON GROUP POLICY CONFIGURATION Continued

NO
ACCESS

TABLE OF CONTENTS

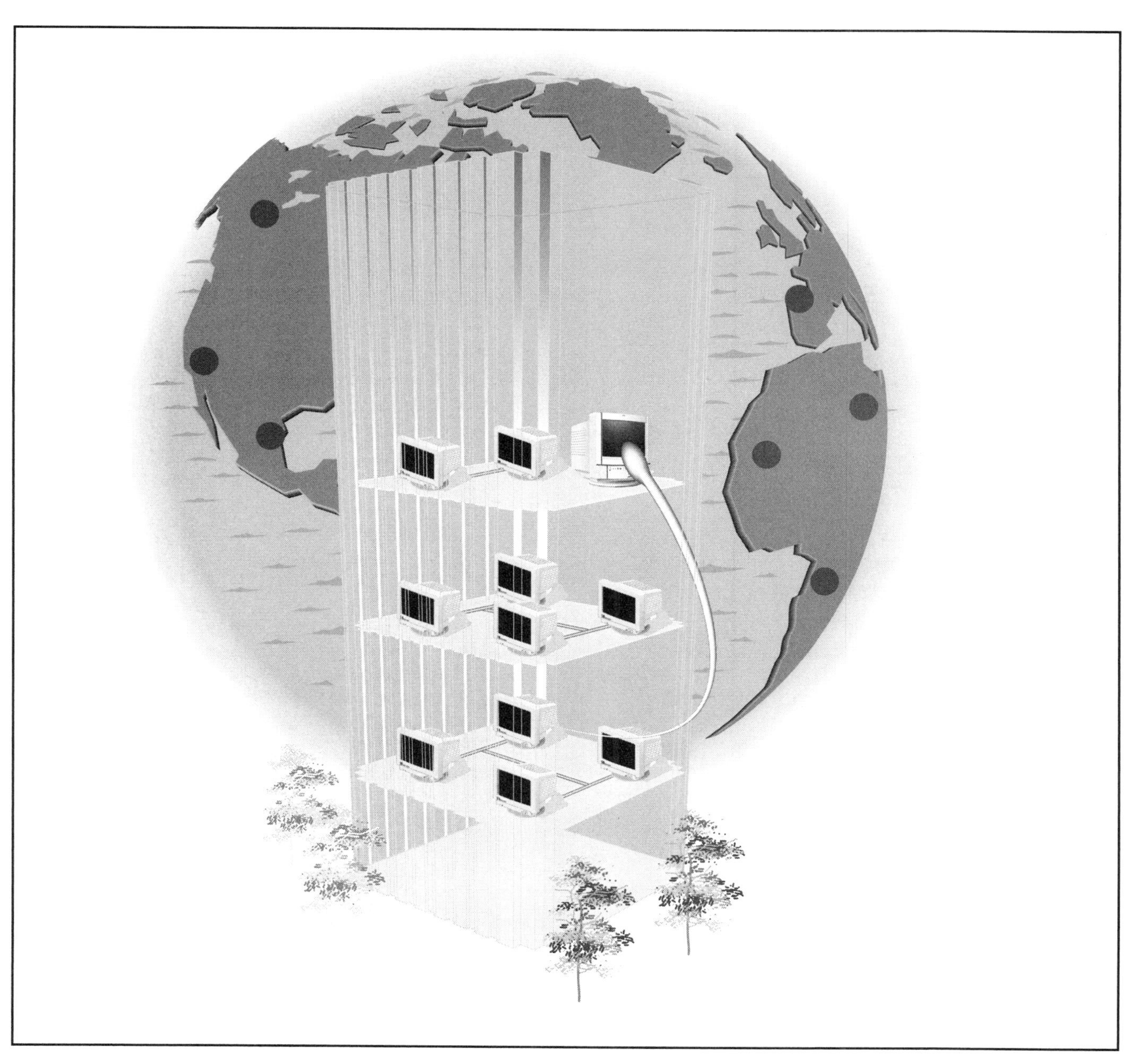

SECTION I

1) INTRODUCTION TO ACTIVE DIRECTORY

2) TCP/IP BASICS

UNDERSTANDING ACTIVE DIRECTORY

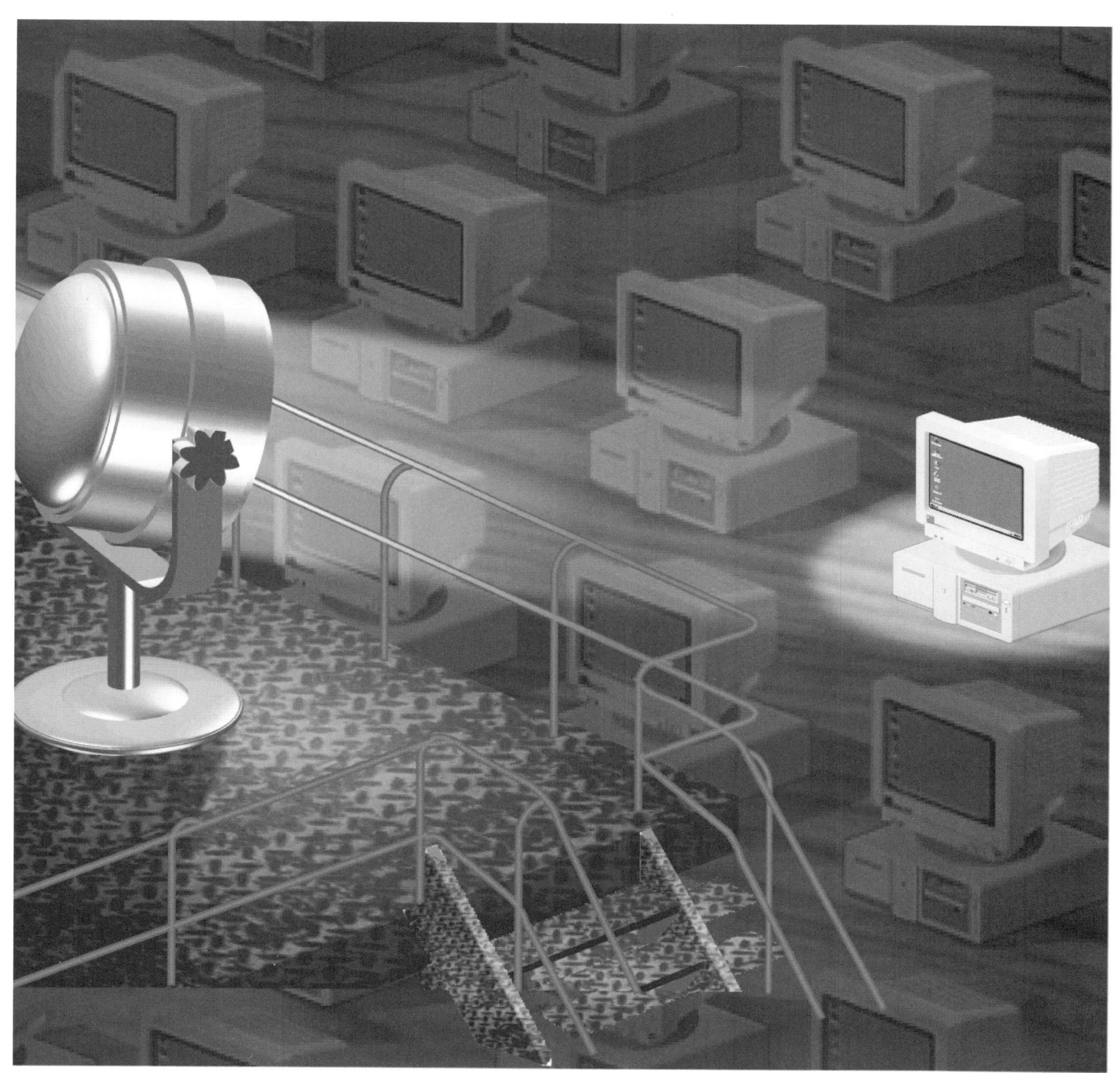

ACTIVE DIRECTORY TECHNOLOGY

If you have been in the computing and network environment at all during the past two years, you have heard a thing or two about the Active Directory. Some of what you have heard is probably true—a lot is probably not. This book can help you make sense of it all and master the Active Directory through a visual approach. But before you get into the details of installing and configuring the Active Directory, you need to know some conceptual information so that it all makes sense. Chapters 1, 2, and 3 show you the conceptual and background information you need to know to implement, configure, and support the Active Directory.

What is a directory?

The term *directory* has received a lot of use (and abuse!) in computing environments in the last several years. As computing environments have become larger and more complex, the need to organize information so that network users can locate the information they need has become increasingly important. By definition, a *directory* is an information storage location that uses a systematic scheme, or *namespace*, to organize the information. A common example is the telephone book. All information in a telephone book is stored by city/region, last name, and then first name. By referencing a particular name in a particular city/region, you can find that person's telephone number. The phone book uses a namespace in that all names are organized in alphabetical order using the last and first name. If the telephone book did not follow a namespace—in other words, if some names listed were by first name, some by last, some by nicknames, and some by address—you would never find what you needed.

What is the Active Directory?

The Active Directory is Microsoft's answer to directory services. The Active Directory's purpose is to organize information about real network objects—such as users, shares, printers, applications, and so forth—so that users can find the resources they need. Through the Active Directory, users do not have to keep track of which server holds which resource, or where a particular printer resides. The Active Directory lists the information, is completely searchable, and provides users a standard folder interface so that they can find what they need on the network.

The Active Directory is also designed to provide a single point of administration for network administrators. Instead of having to manage multiple servers that hold multiple resources, the administrator can find all the directory information located in the Active Directory, and that information can be replicated to all Windows 2000 domain controllers. Resource access, security permissions, and user and group accounts are all centrally located in one place.

Understanding the features of the Active Directory

The Active Directory contains many features and options, but you should understand the big picture and design goals first. The following list explains the major features and design goals of the Active Directory:

- **Scalability**: The Active Directory is highly scalable, which means it can function in small networking environments or global corporations. The Active Directory supports multiple stores and can hold more than one million objects per store. A store is a major grouping of Active Directory objects—and the Active Directory even supports multiple stores.
- **Extensibility**: The Active Directory is extensible, which means that you can customize it to meet the needs of an organization.

- **Security**: The Active Directory is integrated with Windows 2000 security, allowing administrators to control access to objects.
- **Seamlessness**: The Active Directory is seamlessly integrated with the local network and the intranet/Internet.
- **Open Standards**: The Active Directory is based on open communication standards, which allow integration and communication with other directory services, such as Novell's NDS.
- **Backward Compatibility**: Although Windows 2000 operating systems make the most use of the Active Directory, the Active Directory also works with earlier versions of Windows. This feature allows the implementation of the Active Directory to be taken one step at a time while still maintaining a functioning network.

Understanding domains and domain controllers

If you have worked with Windows NT at all, you should be familiar with the concepts of domain and domain controllers. A *domain* is a logical grouping of users, computers, and resources. In actuality, the domain is a security boundary that enables administrators to control the resources in that domain and keep unauthorized users out of the domain. The Active Directory is built through the domain. Domain controllers are the servers that manage the domain. *Primary domain controllers (PDC)* and *backup domain* no longer exist in Windows 2000; all the domain controllers simply act as peers. Through trust relationships, the Active Directory is replicated using multimaster replication, which means that all domain controllers are responsible for maintaining the Active Directory and replicating changes to other domain controllers. You learn more about managing trusts in Windows 2000 later in this book.

DNS and the Active Directory

Domain Name System (DNS) is the most widely used directory namespace in the world. Each time you use the Internet, you are finding URLs by using DNS. DNS takes a *Uniform Resource Locator (URL)*, such as `www.microsoft.com`, and resolves the URL into a TCP/IP address, such as 131.107.2.200, which is required for communication on the Internet. Because computers must have the TCP/IP address to communicate, and users need the language-based names to communicate, the job of DNS is to resolve the two.

The Active Directory is integrated with DNS, and the naming schemes used in the Active Directory are DNS names. For example, corp.com is a valid DNS name and can also be used as a Windows 2000 domain name. With DNS as the locator service in the Active Directory, the local area network (LAN) becomes more seamless with the Internet and an intranet. Corp.com can be an Internet name or a local area name, and `Jwilliams@corp.com` can be both an Internet e-mail address and a username in the local network. This structure enables you to find items on your network in the same manner you find them on the Internet.

Windows 2000 also supports *Dynamic DNS (DDNS)*, a new addition to the DNS standard. DDNS can dynamically update a DNS server with new or changed values, which had to be manually updated in the past. Because name records can be dynamically updated, pure Windows 2000 networks no longer need to use Windows Internet Naming Service (WINS). In mixed environments, however, WINS is used for backwards compatibility with older versions of Windows. You can learn all about WINS and DNS in Chapters 5 and 6.

ACTIVE DIRECTORY TECHNOLOGY

CONTINUED

Understanding LDAP

DNS is the namespace used in the Active Directory, and *Lightweight Directory Access Protocol (LDAP)* is how you access the Active Directory.

To understand LDAP, you need a brief history lesson. The X.500 standard is a directory specification that introduced *Directory Access Protocol (DAP)* to read and modify the directory database. DAP is an extensible protocol in that it can handle directory requests and changes, as well as directory security. However, DAP places much of the processing burden on the client computers and is considered to be a high overhead protocol. LDAP, which is not defined within the X.500 specification, was developed to overcome the weaknesses of DAP. LDAP is an open standard, which means that it can be used by anyone wishing to develop a directory service and is not restricted to X.500 directories like DAP is. Another major difference is that LDAP is not a client-based service. The service runs on the server and the information is returned to the client. The Active Directory is not an X.500 directory, but it supports the information model without requiring systems to implement the X.500 overhead. The result is an LDAP-based directory that supports high levels of interoperability.

LDAP is widely supported on the Internet. If you have participated in newsgroups or searched the World Wide Web with a search engine, you more than likely have used LDAP. This open standard is directly supported in the Active Directory so that users can find the resources they need.

THE STRUCTURE OF THE ACTIVE DIRECTORY

The Active Directory is designed in a hierarchy structure, and before installing and implementing the Active Directory, you must have a firm understanding of the structure as well as the components that make up the Active Directory. You may see these components as terms that you need to learn, but you must also know how these components or terms relate to each other and how they fit into the hierarchy.

In this chapter, you begin with the smallest component in the hierarchy and work your way up to the top of the hierarchy. This section gives you a complete view of the Active Directory's structure.

Object

An Active Directory *object* represents a physical object of some kind on the network. Common Active Directory objects are users, groups, printers, shared folders, applications, databases, contacts, and so forth. Each of these objects represents something tangible on the network.

Each object contains attributes. An *attribute* is a quality that helps define the actual object. For example, a user object could have attributes of a username, actual name, and e-mail address. Attributes for each kind of object are defined in the Active Directory. The attributes define the object itself and enable users to search for the particular object. Technically attributes are called "metadata"—which is simply "data about data"—and are a portion of the Active Directory "schema," which defines what objects and object attributes can be stored in the Active Directory.

THE STRUCTURE OF THE ACTIVE DIRECTORY CONTINUED

Attributes

Name - Comp3874
Role - Workstation
OS - Windows 2000

Computer Object

*Each object has attributes that define the object.

Organizational unit

An *organizational unit (OU)* is like a file folder in a file cabinet. The OU is designed to hold objects (or even other OUs). It contains attributes like an object, but it has no functionality on its own. As with a file folder, its purpose is to hold other objects. As the name implies, an OU helps you organize your directory structure. For example, you could have an accounting OU that contains other OUs, such as Accounts Payable and Accounts Receivable, and inside those OUs can reside objects, such as users, groups, computers, printers, and so forth.

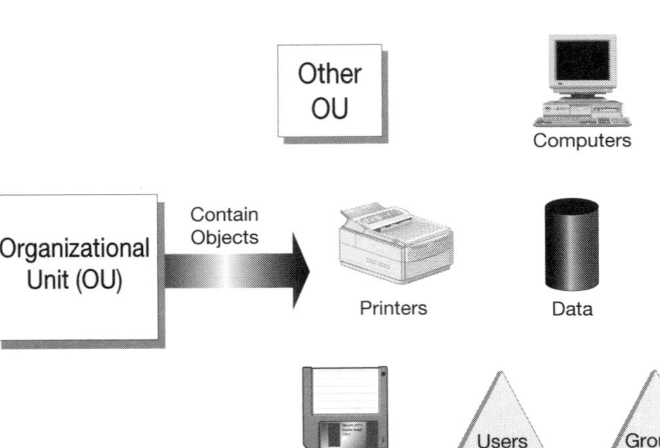

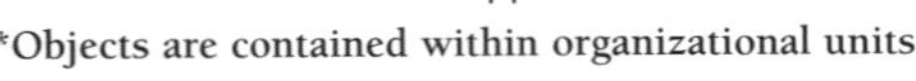

*Objects are contained within organizational units.

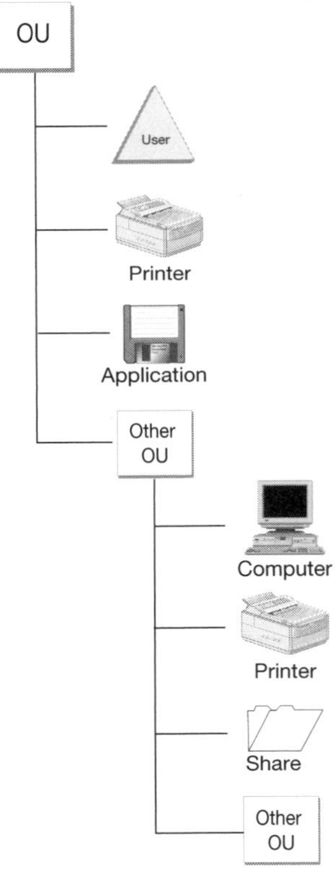

*This is a hierarchy view of the OU and objects within it.

Domain

By definition, a *domain* is a logical grouping of users and computers. The domain typically resides in a localized geographic location, but this is not always the case. In reality, a domain is more than a logical grouping—it is actually a security boundary of a Windows 2000 or NT network. You can think of a network with multiple domains as being similar to a residential neighborhood. All the homes make up the neighborhood, but each home is a security boundary that hold certain objects inside and keeps others out.

A domain is like a house in a neighborhood. Each domain can have its own security policies and can establish trust relationships with other domains. The Active Directory is made up of one or more domains. Domains contain a *schema*, which defines what objects are stored in the domain. The Schema defines objects by classes (such as a Users class, a Computers class, and so on) and all objects belonging to a class are called "instances" of that class. You can learn more about the Active Directory schema in Chapter 27.

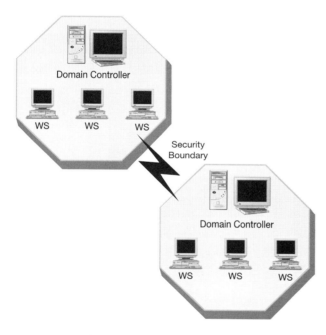

*Each domain serves as a security boundary.

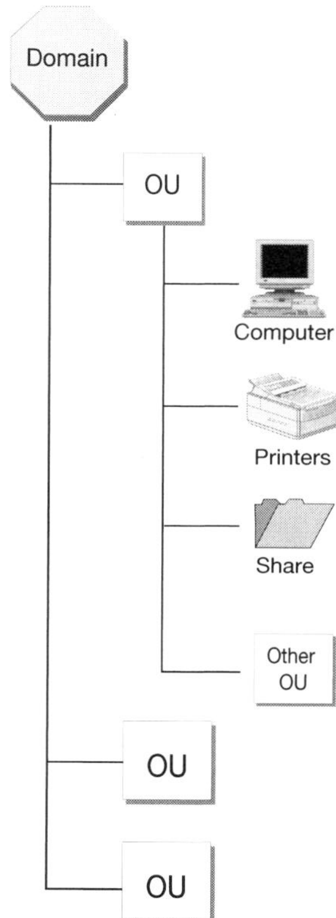

*The domain sits at the top of the hierarchy.

THE STRUCTURE OF THE ACTIVE DIRECTORY CONTINUED

Tree

The hierarchy structure of the domain, organizational units, and objects is called a *tree*. The objects within the tree are referred to as *endpoints* while the OUs in the tree structure are *nodes*. In comparison to a physical tree, you can think of the branches as OUs or containers and the leaves being objects—an object is the natural endpoint of the node within the tree.

Domain trees

A *domain tree* exists when several domains are linked by trust relationships and share a common schema, configuration, and global catalog. Trust relationships in Windows 2000 are based on the Kerberos Security protocol. Kerberos trusts are transitive. In other words, if Domain 1 trusts Domain 2 and Domain 2 trusts Domain 3, then Domain 1 trusts Domain 3. The Active Directory automatically configures trust relationships within the same tree and forest. You can learn more about trust relationships in the Active Directory in Chapter 21.

A domain tree also shares a contiguous namespace. A contiguous namespace follows the same DNS naming hierarchy within the domain tree. For example, if the root domain is corp.com and DomainA and DomainB exist in a domain tree, the contiguous namespace for the two would be domaina.corp.com and domainb.corp.com. If Domain A resides in corpjp.com and Domain B resides in the corp.com root, then the two would not share a contiguous namespace.

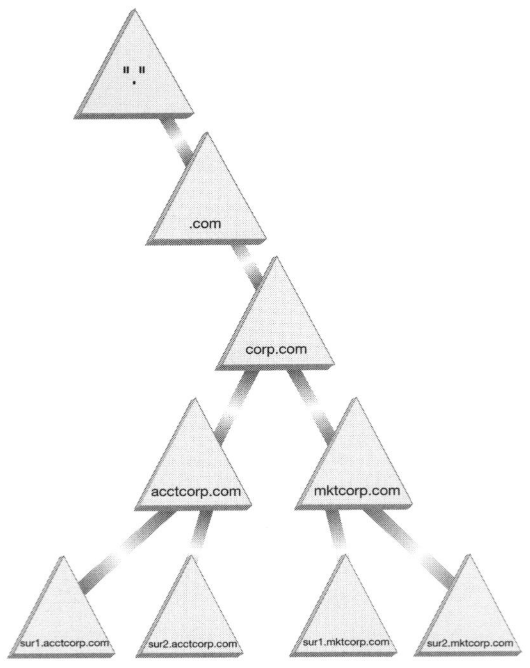

*This is an example of a contiguous namespace.

Forest

A *forest* is one or more trees that do not share a contiguous namespace. The trees in the forest do share a common schema, configuration, and global catalog, but the trees do not share a contiguous name space. All trees in the forest trust each other through Kerberos transitive trusts. In actuality, the forest does not have a distinct name, but the trees are viewed as a hierarchy of trust relationships. The tree at the top of the hierarchy normally refers to the tree. For example, corp.com, production.corp.com, and mgmt.corp.com form a forest with corp.com serving as the forest root.

Site

A *site* is not actually considered part of the Active Directory hierarchy, but it is configured in the Active Directory for replication purposes. A site is defined as a geographical location in a network containing Active Directory servers with a well-connected TCP/IP subnet. *Well-connected* means that the network connection is highly reliable and fast. Administrators use the Active Directory to configure replication between sites. Users do not have to be aware of site configuration. As far as the Active Directory is concerned, users only see domains.

How the structure appears to administrators and users

As an administrator, you view the structure of the Active Directory through the administrative tools that you can explore in detail later in Chapters 14 through 21. From the tools, you can see the structure through the domains, OUs, and objects that are a part of the Active Directory.

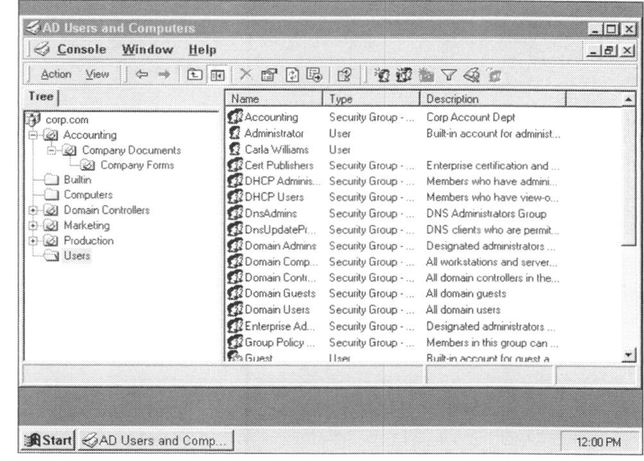

*Administrators can view the tree structure of the Active Directory.

Users browse the Active Directory by accessing it in My Network Places. Users see a folder view for the domain and organizational units within the domain. The objects then reside in their respective OUs. Primarily, users find resources by performing LDAP searches instead of browsing (see Chapter 13).

THE STRUCTURE OF THE ACTIVE DIRECTORY CONTINUED

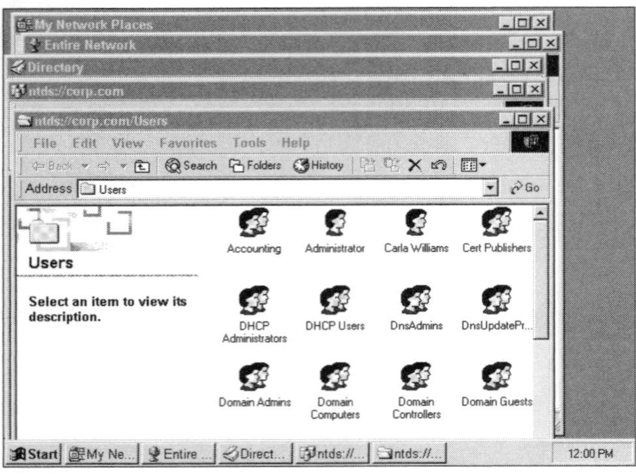

*Users can see a folder view of the Active Directory.

Active Directory names

In the Active Directory, every object, such as users, groups, computers, printers, and so forth, has a unique name. Four kinds of names are assigned to each object.

First, each object has a *distinguished name (DN)*. The DN is unique from all other objects and contains the full information needed to retrieve the object. The DN contains the domain where the object resides and the path to the object. The DN is made up of these attributes (or qualities):

- Domain component name (DC)
- Organizational unit name (OU)
- Common name (CN)

For example, if you wanted to access a document called "Company mission" that resides in a particular domain, the DN may read:

/DC=com/DC=mycompany/OU=acct/CN=documents/CN=Company Mission

By using the DN, the Active Directory can begin at the top of the domain and work its way down to the actual folder or document.

Second, the Active Directory uses *relative distinguished names (RDN)*. The RDN is the part of the DN that defines the actual object, called an attribute. This is the CN, or common name. Fortunately, all you need to know to search for objects are common names. You don't have to know or use the DN, and the DN itself is normally hidden from the users.

Third, the Active Directory uses *globally unique identifiers (GUID)*, which are unique 128-bit numbers. The GUID is assigned to an object when it is created in the Active Directory and it never changes.

And fourth, Active Directory objects can be identified by *user principal names (UPN)*, which are short, friendly names that look like an e-mail address, such as jwilliams@corp.com.

The major point to remember is that the Active Directory provides the DN, RDN, GUID, and UPN for objects to ensure uniqueness, ease of location for LDAP queries, and ease of use for users.

Global catalog

The purpose of LDAP is to allow network users to search and find objects in the Active Directory. In order for this to happen, certain Active Directory domain controllers, called "global catalog servers" maintain a *global catalog*.

The global catalog enables users and applications to find objects in the Active Directory by searching for particular attributes. The global catalog holds a partial replica of the objects and their most common attributes. When a user performs a search operation to find an object, the global catalog looks for that attribute and returns matches to the user.

The Active Directory replication builds and maintains the global catalog, and through the held replica, users can locate resources in any domain or OU in the tree or forest.

WHY YOU NEED TO KNOW ABOUT TCP/IP FOR THE ACTIVE DIRECTORY

TCP/IP *(Transmission Control Protocol/Internet Protocol)* is the de facto standard for Internet communication. TCP/IP is the protocol that allows all communication on the World Wide Web to take place, and over the years, TCP/IP has become more popular as the protocol of choice in LAN and WAN environments.

The Active Directory is integrated with TCP/IP in that all directory replication between domain controllers occurs using TCP/IP. In fact, Windows 2000 is designed for TCP/IP networks. In order to understand and implement the Active Directory, you do need at least a general understanding of TCP/IP. If you are already immersed in a TCP/IP network, then this chapter serves as a good review. If you are new to Windows networking, then this chapter is just what you need to understand the basics of TCP/IP.

WHAT IS TCP/IP?

TCP/IP is a protocol that was originally developed by the Department of Defense. Basically, TCP/IP provides a set of rules that govern how computers communicate with each other over a network. Just as people have to speak the same language to communicate with each other, computers must also communicate in the same language, or *protocol*. TCP/IP is considered a suite of protocols because it is made up of many protocols that provide the vast communication functionality we now enjoy in networking environments and on the Internet. In fact, over 100 protocols are in the TCP/IP suite. The following list points out some of the most common ones:

- *Transmission Control Protocol (TCP)* provides connection-oriented communication.
- *Internet Protocol (IP)* manages routing and network traffic.
- *File Transfer Protocol (FTP)* manages file transfer and remote directory management.
- *Hypertext Transfer Protocol (HTTP)* is the Internet standard for the delivery of HTML documents.
- *Simple Network Management Protocol (SNMP)* manages network devices and monitors network events.
- *Simple Mail Transfer Protocol (SMTP)* provides messaging (e-mail) services.
- *User Datagram Protocol (UDP)* provides connectionless communication.
- *Network News Transfer Protocol (NNTP)* provides newsgroup services.
- *Telnet* provides terminal emulation for remote connections.
- *Address Resolution Protocol (ARP)* resolves IP address to hardware (MAC) addresses
- *Internet Control Management Protocol (ICMP)* provides error control
- *Lightweight Directory Access Protocol (LDAP)* provides directory access capabilities

TCP/IP COMPONENTS

Just as a language has certain components, such as words, grammar, and syntax, the TCP/IP protocol contains components that enable each computer on a TCP/IP network to function and communicate on the network. You must configure three major TCP/IP components on TCP/IP computers: the IP address, subnet mask, and default gateway.

IP address

Each computer on a TCP/IP network must have a unique IP address. The IP address identifies that computer on the network and the address must be unique (no two computers can have the same IP address. You can think of an IP address as being similar to a postal address, which is uniquely identified by city, state, zip code, then by street address, then by the person's name. These address qualities enable the postal system to delivery a piece of mail to a particular person at a particular address. A computer's IP address enables the network to deliver communication to that particular computer.

Each IP address is 32 bits long, and is divided into 4 bytes. Each byte is referred to as an octet. A typical IP addresses looks like this: 131.107.2.200. In order to understand IP addressing, you have to start thinking in binary math. Computers see data in terms of ones and zeroes. In essence, a stream of network data is simply made up of ones and zeroes that the computer interprets. One (1) represents "on" and zero (0) represents "off."

Binary numbers are calculated by counting from the right to the left of a series of binary digits. Each bit counts twice as much as the previous bit. In other words, the first bit equals 1, the second bit equals 2, the third bit equals 4, and so forth. In an IP address, there are 8 bits, so the eighth bit is equal to 128:

128 64 32 16 8 4 2 1

In binary math, the bits are added together to determine the numerical value. For example, if all bits in the octect are turned "on," then the numerical value is 255. In other words, 11111111 in binary is equal to 128+64+32+16+4+2+1, which equals 255.

If all the bits are "off," then the binary representation is 00000000 which is equal to 0+0+0+0+0+0+0+0, which equals 0. Using this scheme, you can represent any number between 0 and 255.

For example, what is binary value of 10? Remember that the bits in the octet must be turned on or off to equal the number ten. In the binary octet, the number 10 is represented as 00001010, which equals 0+0+0+0+8+0+2+0, which equals 10.

An IP address is made up of four octets that are separated by periods. A typical IP address you may assign to a computer would be 10.2.0.4. In binary, the computers see this address as:

00001010 00000010 00000000 00000100

Network Computer

My IP address is 10.2.0.4
Other computers on the network communicate with me by using this IP address.
They see my IP address in binary, which is 00001010 00000010 00000000 00000100

You cannot simply assign computers on your network any IP address you choose. The IP addressing scheme you use must be defined by classes and subnets. Just as everyone in a certain town has the same addressing properties of city, state, and zip code, the IP addresses must belong to certain classes and subnets. An isolated LAN or WAN can determine a class of addresses and appropriate subnet masks to use for their network, but for proper Internet communication, many networks choose to obtain IP addressing from Network Solutions, which is the organization that handles all of the Internet's domain name and IP address assignment.

Each IP address identifies both the network in which the computer (or node, such as a router) resides and the actual computer or node itself. These are called the network ID and host ID. The three major groupings of IP addresses are called classes. The following list gives you an overview of the three classes:

- **Class A:** Class A addresses have a beginning octet from 1 to 126. Network Solutions assigns the first octet and the network administrator assigns the three remaining octets. Class A networks were developed for large networks and obtaining a Class A address today is very difficult. Class A networks can support up to 16,387,064 hosts. Also, the address range of 127 is reserved for TCP/IP troubleshooting and is called a *loopback address*.
- **Class B:** Class B networks have the first octet assignment from 128 to 191. Network Solutions assigns the first and second octet numbers and the network administrator assigns the last two. Class B networks can support up to 64,516 hosts.
- **Class C:** Class C networks use 192 through 255 for the first octet. Network Solutions assigns the first three octets and the network administrator assigns the final octet. Class C networks can only support up to 254 hosts.

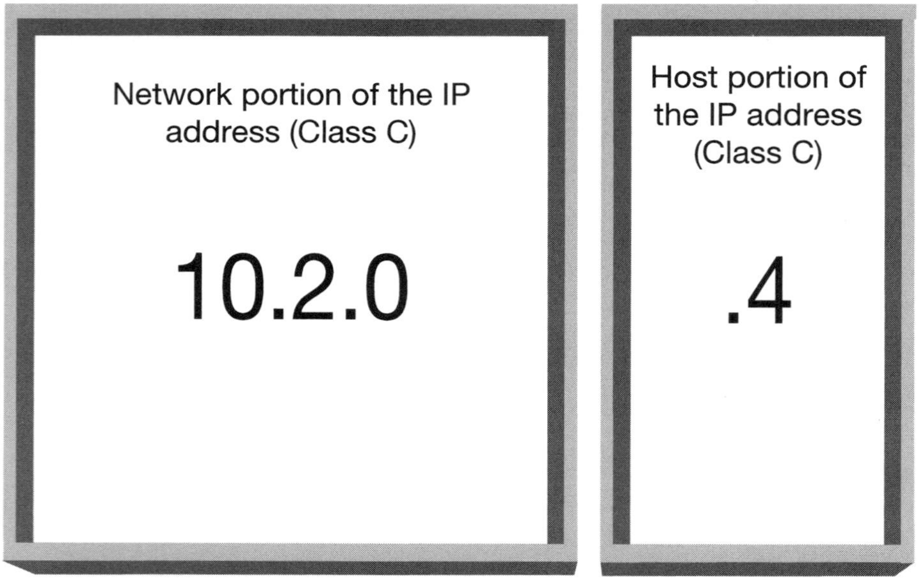

Subnet mask

The second component of IP addressing is the *subnet mask*. As mentioned in the previous section, part of the IP address points to the actual network while another portion of the IP address points to the actual computer or node (host). The subnet mask hides, or masks, part of the IP address to keep the network ID and the host ID separated. Subnet masks enable you to break your network into *subnets*, which can provide you more available IP addresses and further organize your network. Also, subnetting controls reduces overall network traffic. Each IP address assigned to a client must include at least a default subnet mask. For Class A networks, the default subnet mask is 255.0.0.0. For Class B networks, the default subnet mask is 255.255.0.0 and for Class C networks, the default subnet mask is 255.255.255.0.

The process of subnetting a network and assigning a proper mask for a subnet is often a difficult task and is beyond the scope of this book. But to understand the basics of TCP/IP, do remember that at least a default subnet mask is required.

Default gateway

The last component of IP addressing is the default gateway. A *default gateway*, or *router*, is the IP address of the router that leads out of the subnet. You can think of the default gateway as the "road that leads out." Client computers use the default gateway to communicate with computers on different subnets. A default gateway is not a required component of client IP configuration, but if gateways are in use in your network, the client computers must know the IP address of the gateway(s) for communication to take place with different network segments.

TCP/IP MANAGEMENT TECHNOLOGIES

If people could speak and think in binary math, they could seamlessly communicate with computers. But humans are language-based creatures while computers "think" in terms of math. You would have a very difficult time remembering the IP address of each computer you wanted to access on the network. It's much easier to remember ServerD as opposed to 131.107.2.200. So, people contact servers and computers using a friendly, language-based name, but computers must contact each other using the actual IP address. In order for the two worlds to mix, any friendly, language-based names must be resolved to IP addresses so that computers can communicate with each other. For this to happen and to ease the burden of IP address resolution and assignment, several services are available.

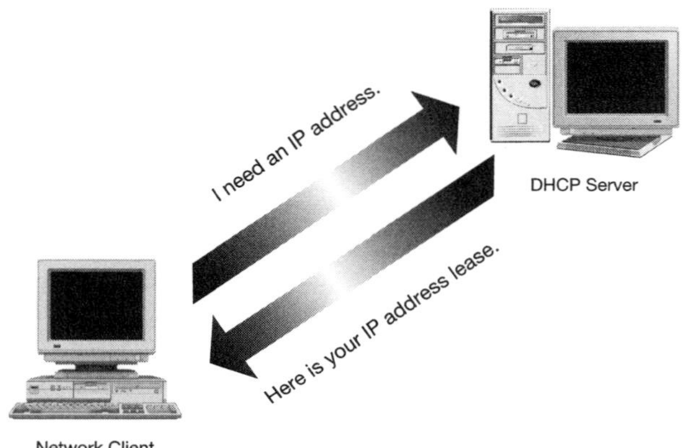
I need an IP address.
DHCP Server
Here is your IP address lease.
Network Client

Dynamic Host Configuration Protocol (DHCP)

DHCP is a server service that dynamically assigns IP addresses and IP address information (such as the default gateway) to network clients. Traditionally, TCP/IP had the reputation of having high overhead because each client had to be assigned a unique IP address. Imagine having to manually assign IP addresses to 1,000 network clients without making a mistake! DHCP solves this problem by automatically handling client IP assignment. DHCP works by *leasing* an appropriate and unique IP address to network clients for a specified period of time. DHCP makes certain that no duplicate addresses are assigned so that all clients can have connectivity. This process is invisible to users and requires little intervention on the part of network administrators. You can learn more about DHCP in Chapter 4.

Windows Internet Naming Service (WINS)

WINS resolves NetBIOS computer names to IP addresses. A NetBIOS name is a friendly, language-based computer name. Because computers must communicate using a computer's IP address and not its NetBIOS name, WINS maps NetBIOS names to their corresponding IP address. This way, you can name your computer "Joe's Laptop" instead of an IP address like 131.107.2.200. WINS maintains a database that keeps track of this information. WINS clients contact a WINS server to find the information that "MyComputer" equals 131.107.2.200. The client can then use the IP address to communicate with Joe's Laptop. This process is invisible to users and requires little intervention from administrators. WINS is not necessary in pure Windows 2000 environments, but is provided for backward compatibility. Windows 2000 computers use DNS for name resolution, so WINS will slowly phase out over the next several years. You can learn more about WINS in Chapter 5 and DNS in Chapter 6.

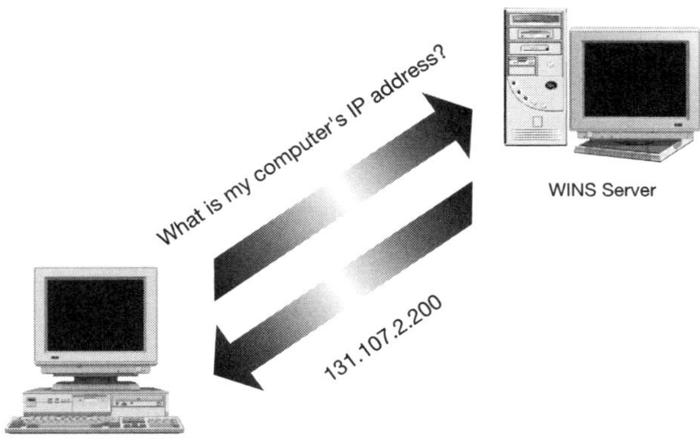

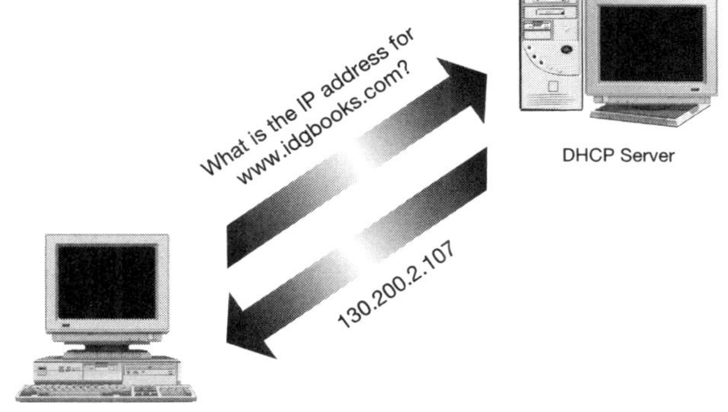

Note: DNS resolution usually requires a number of servers. Each server resolves a portion of the domain name.

Domain Name System (DNS)

DNS resolves fully qualified domain names (FQDN) to IP addresses. Just as WINS resolves friendly NetBIOS names to IP addresses, DNS resolves domain names, such as `www.microsoft.com`, to its appropriate IP address. This process enables you to communicate with computers on the Internet (and now in Windows 2000 networks) using friendly domain names instead of IP addresses. In the past, DNS was a static mapping contained in HOSTS files, which is simply a text file that lists the host name to IP address mapping. Now, Dynamic DNS (DDNS) can respond to and update changes that occur. You learn more about DNS and its place in Windows 2000 in Chapter 6.

TCP/IP UTILITIES

TCP/IP contains a number of command line utilities that help you gain information about the TCP/IP configuration of your computer and troubleshoot connectivity problems. The following sections tell you about the three most common utilities.

Ping

You can use *Ping* to test connectivity with both your computer and remote computers. Ping enables you to perform a test using a computer's IP address, NetBIOS name, or DNS name. You can perform a *loopback* test on your own computer to make sure your TCP/IP software is initializing properly. This test checks your computer to make certain TCP/IP is operational. To perform a loopback test, simply type **ping 127.0.0.1** at the

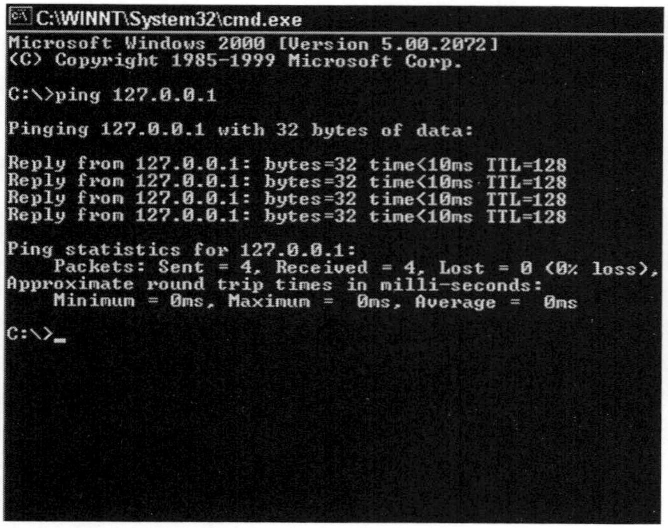

```
C:\WINNT\System32\cmd.exe
Microsoft Windows 2000 [Version 5.00.2072]
(C) Copyright 1985-1999 Microsoft Corp.

C:\>ping 127.0.0.1

Pinging 127.0.0.1 with 32 bytes of data:

Reply from 127.0.0.1: bytes=32 time<10ms TTL=128
Reply from 127.0.0.1: bytes=32 time<10ms TTL=128
Reply from 127.0.0.1: bytes=32 time<10ms TTL=128
Reply from 127.0.0.1: bytes=32 time<10ms TTL=128

Ping statistics for 127.0.0.1:
    Packets: Sent = 4, Received = 4, Lost = 0 (0% loss),
Approximate round trip times in milli-seconds:
    Minimum = 0ms, Maximum =  0ms, Average =  0ms

C:\>_
```

command line and press Enter. To test a remote computer, type **ping** *(IP address, NetBIOS name, or DNS name)* at the command line and press Enter. The ping test to a remote computer checks it to make certain TCP/IP is functioning properly. If you cannot contact a remote computer, ping is a good way to determine if the computer is "down" or if some other communication problem exists.

Netstat

Netstat provides TCP/IP statistics and current connection information. This utility is useful to get a close look at your current connections and find out about potential problems. Netstat comes with a number of switches you can use to refine the information returned to you. Simply type **netstat ?** at the command line to learn more.

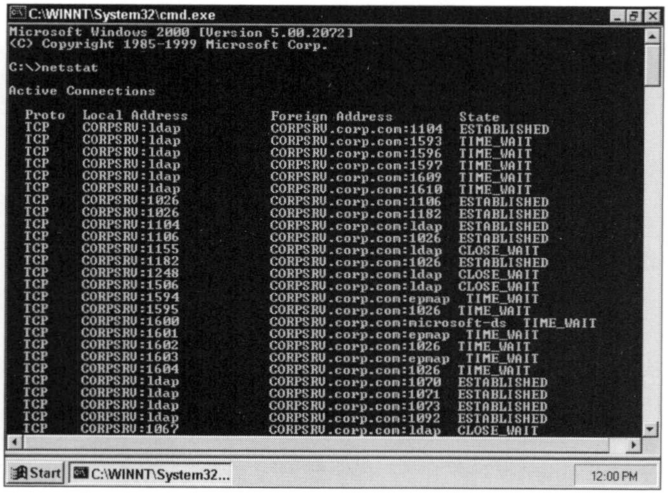

```
C:\WINNT\System32\cmd.exe
Microsoft Windows 2000 [Version 5.00.2072]
(C) Copyright 1985-1999 Microsoft Corp.

C:\>netstat

Active Connections

  Proto  Local Address          Foreign Address        State
  TCP    CORPSRV:ldap           CORPSRV.corp.com:1104  ESTABLISHED
  TCP    CORPSRV:ldap           CORPSRV.corp.com:1593  TIME_WAIT
  TCP    CORPSRV:ldap           CORPSRV.corp.com:1596  TIME_WAIT
  TCP    CORPSRV:ldap           CORPSRV.corp.com:1597  TIME_WAIT
  TCP    CORPSRV:ldap           CORPSRV.corp.com:1609  TIME_WAIT
  TCP    CORPSRV:ldap           CORPSRV.corp.com:1610  TIME_WAIT
  TCP    CORPSRV:1026           CORPSRV.corp.com:1106  ESTABLISHED
  TCP    CORPSRV:1026           CORPSRV.corp.com:1182  ESTABLISHED
  TCP    CORPSRV:1104           CORPSRV.corp.com:ldap  ESTABLISHED
  TCP    CORPSRV:1106           CORPSRV.corp.com:1026  ESTABLISHED
  TCP    CORPSRV:1155           CORPSRV.corp.com:ldap  CLOSE_WAIT
  TCP    CORPSRV:1182           CORPSRV.corp.com:1026  ESTABLISHED
  TCP    CORPSRV:1248           CORPSRV.corp.com:ldap  CLOSE_WAIT
  TCP    CORPSRV:1506           CORPSRV.corp.com:ldap  CLOSE_WAIT
  TCP    CORPSRV:1594           CORPSRV.corp.com:epmap  TIME_WAIT
  TCP    CORPSRV:1595           CORPSRV.corp.com:1026  TIME_WAIT
  TCP    CORPSRV:1600           CORPSRV.corp.com:microsoft-ds  TIME_WAIT
  TCP    CORPSRV:1601           CORPSRV.corp.com:epmap  TIME_WAIT
  TCP    CORPSRV:1602           CORPSRV.corp.com:1026  TIME_WAIT
  TCP    CORPSRV:1603           CORPSRV.corp.com:epmap  TIME_WAIT
  TCP    CORPSRV:1604           CORPSRV.corp.com:1026  TIME_WAIT
  TCP    CORPSRV:ldap           CORPSRV.corp.com:1070  ESTABLISHED
  TCP    CORPSRV:ldap           CORPSRV.corp.com:1071  ESTABLISHED
  TCP    CORPSRV:ldap           CORPSRV.corp.com:1073  ESTABLISHED
  TCP    CORPSRV:ldap           CORPSRV.corp.com:1092  ESTABLISHED
  TCP    CORPSRV:1067           CORPSRV.corp.com:ldap  CLOSE_WAIT
Start  C:\WINNT\System32...                                 12:00 PM
```

Ipconfig

Ipconfig is a popular utility that gives you additional information about your current settings, such as the IP Address, Subnet Mask, Default Gateway, and DNS, WINS, and DHCP servers. You can type **ipconfig** at the command line to get this information, or you can type **ipconfig /all** at the command line to have complete information returned to you. This information will include all of your computer's IP configuration information, such as DHCP lease, MAC (Media Access Control) address, and so forth. As with Netstat, you can type **ipconfig ?** to view the available switches to refine the information returned.

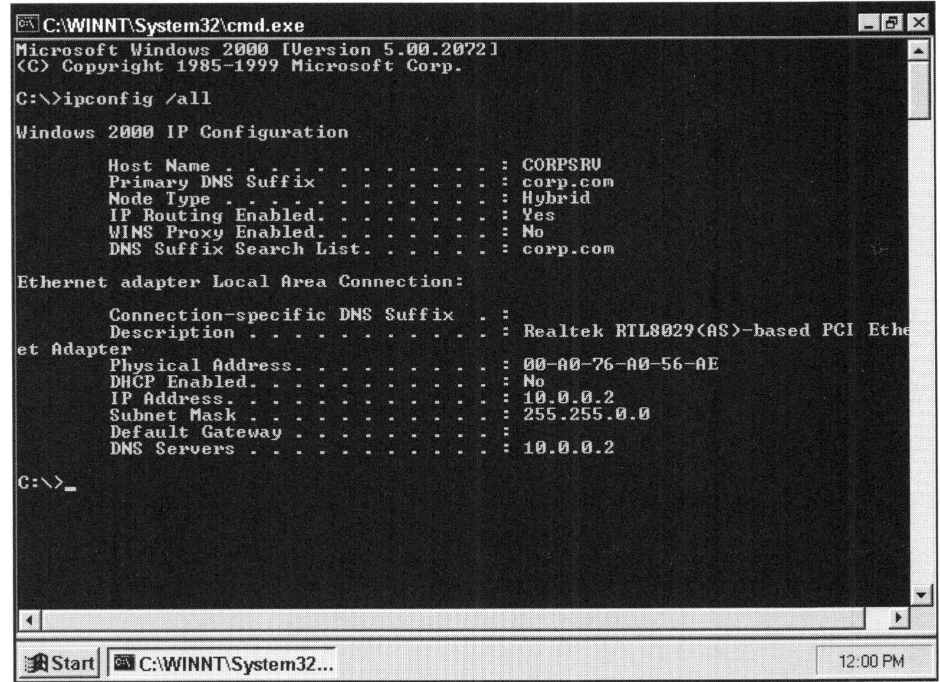

SECTION II

3) THE WINDOWS 2000 SERVER NETWORKING INTERFACE

4) CONFIGURING DHCP

5) CONFIGURING WINS

6) CONFIGURING DNS

7) ROUTING AND REMOTE ACCESS SERVICE

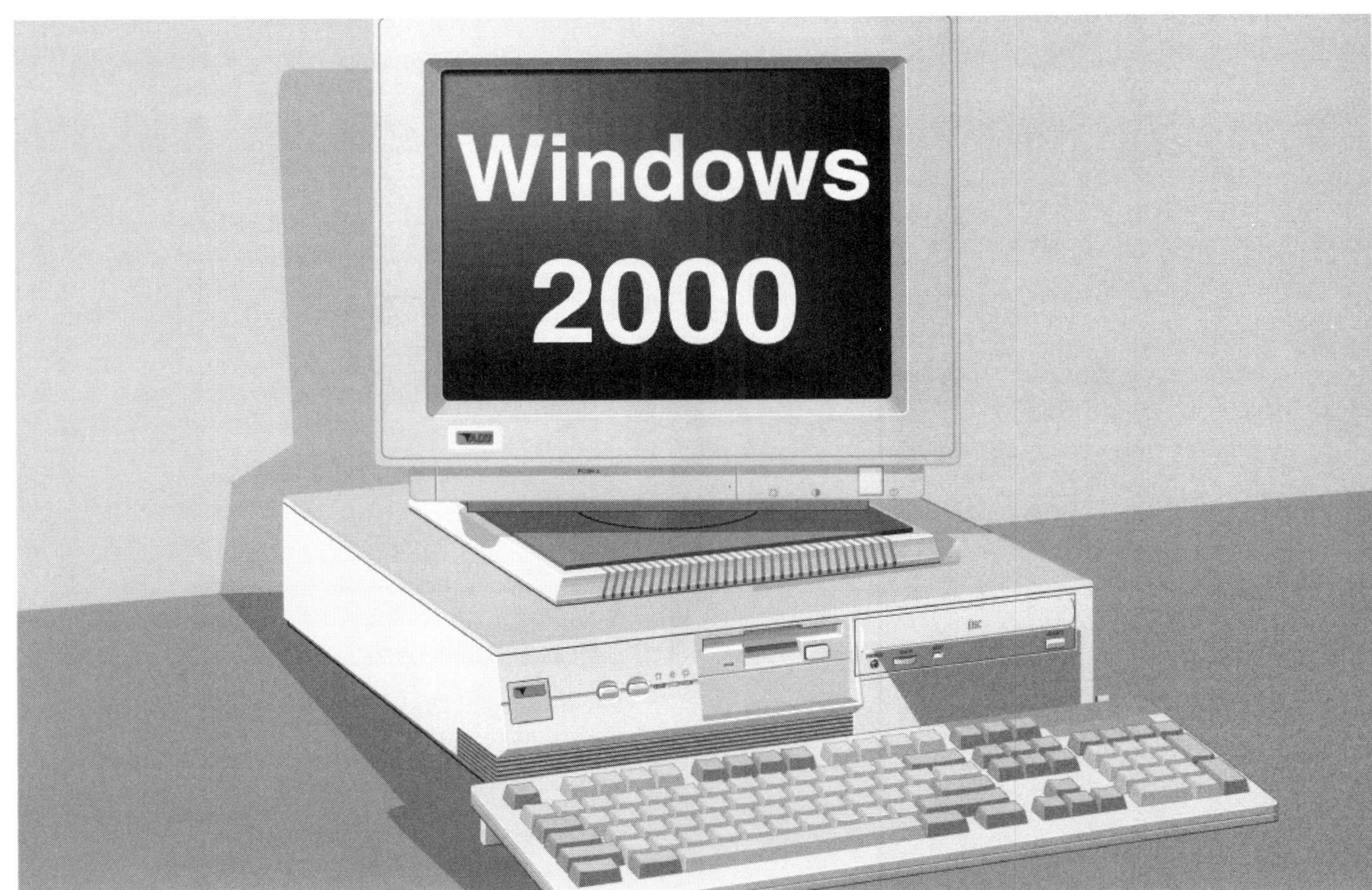

ACCESSING ADMINISTRATIVE TOOLS AND CONTROL PANEL

Before you install and configure Active Directory, you need to have a good handle on the location and configuration of several networking items in Windows 2000 Server.

Windows 2000 Server is a complex operating system that offers a variety of technologies, tools, and services. For the Active Directory, you are primarily going to use the networking interfaces to configure your server as necessary for your network environment. The two major locations for accessing networking tools and services are the Start menu and Control Panel. The tools that are installed with Active Directory appear in these locations. You also have the option to install and configure many networking components through a new program called "Configure Your Server," which is available in the Administrative Tools folder. Configure Your Server provides you a graphical interface that looks similar to a Web page.

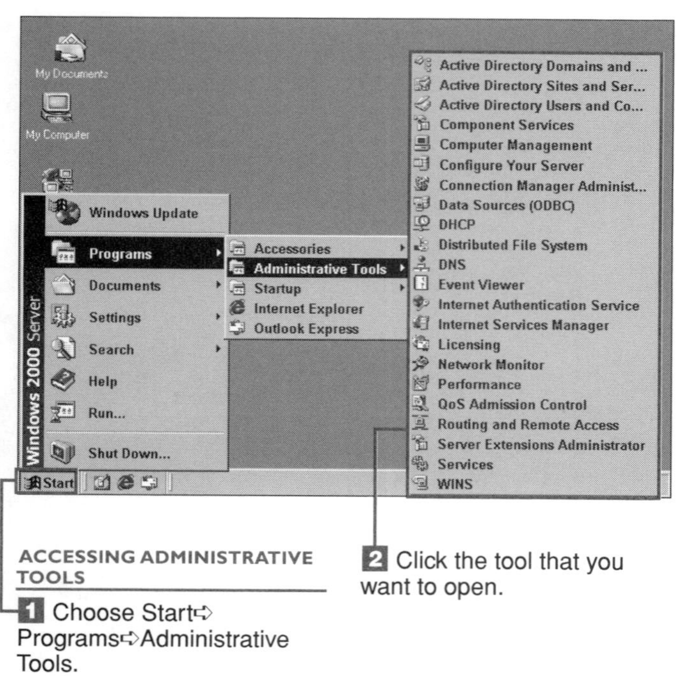

ACCESSING ADMINISTRATIVE TOOLS

1 Choose Start⇨Programs⇨Administrative Tools.

■ The Administrative Tools submenu appears.

2 Click the tool that you want to open.

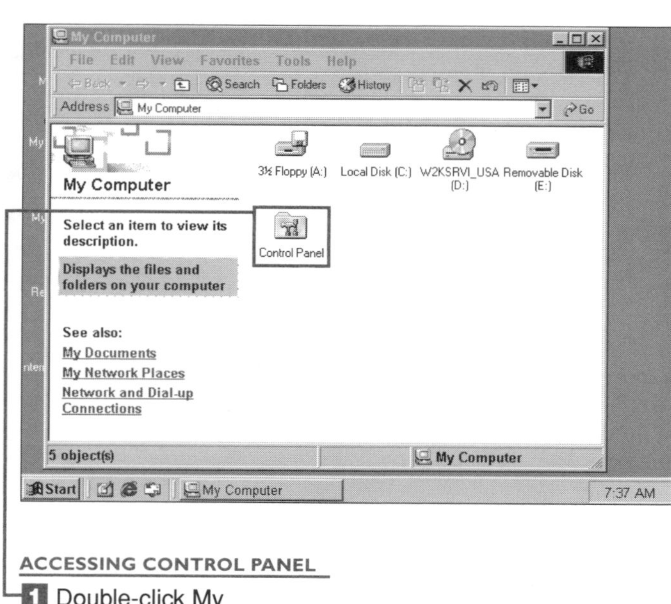

ACCESSING CONTROL PANEL

1 Double-click My Computer on the desktop, and then double-click Control Panel.

Is there a difference between using the Start menu or Control Panel?

No. All administrative tools that are available appear in the Start menu under Administrative Tools. Shortcuts to these tools also appear in the Control Panel Administrative Tools folder.

What are some of the most common administrative tools?

Aside from the Active Directory tools that will appear once you install the Active Directory, the following points out some of the most common administrative tools, many of which you may recognize from NT Server 4.0:

- DNS—allows you to configure DNS on your server.
- Internet Services Manager—allows you to configure your server to be a web server.
- Licensing—allows you to manage server and client licensing.
- Performance—opens Performance Monitor.
- WINS—allows you to configure WINS on your server
- DHCP—allows you to configure DHCP on your server
- Services—enables you to manage the various server services that are running.

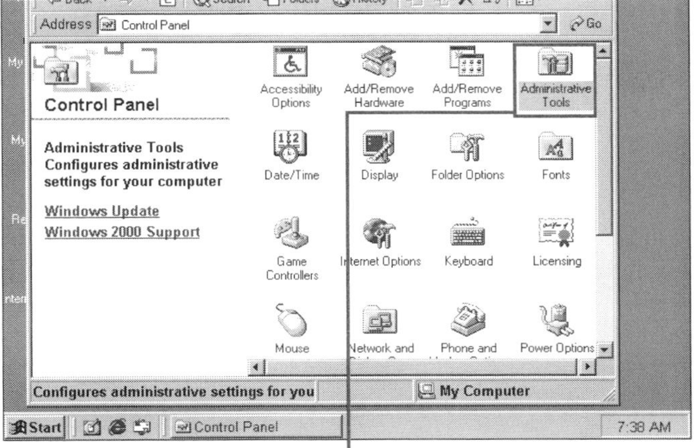

■ Control Panel contains a number of configuration tools.

2 Double-click the Administrative Tools folder.

■ The Administrative Tools window shows all the available tools.

USING THE CONFIGURE YOUR SERVER TOOL

Depending on the design of your network, you may need to add and remove networking components from time to time. Windows 2000 contains a number of services and protocols that you can use on your network.

One way that you can add or remove networking components is to use the Configure Your Server tool. This interface, which looks and acts similar to a Web page, contains menus and links for the various server components you may need to configure. This tool is particularly helpful for services or server configuration that is somewhat unfamiliar to you.

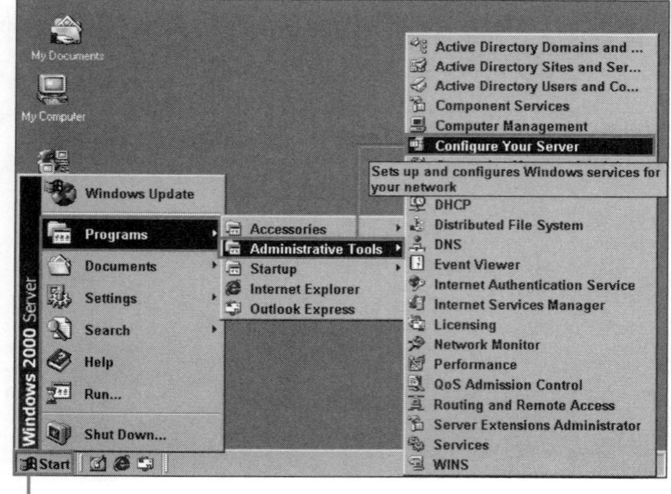

1 Choose Start⇨Programs⇨Administrative Tools⇨Configure Your Server.

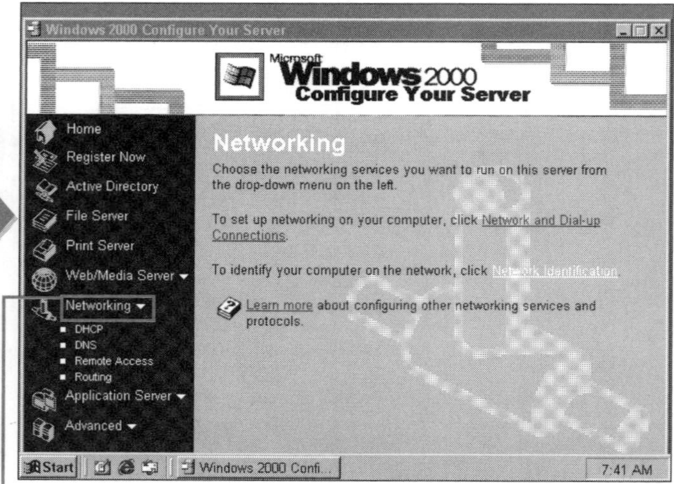

2 Click Networking.

■ The menu expands and also gives you a general networking screen. You can install any of the services in the left pane by clicking them.

What happens if I decide to install networking components from this interface?

- You can install any components through the Configure Your Server interface by clicking the subject in the left pane and then clicking the service you want to install. This action begins the installation wizard for that particular component.

What options are available in Configure Your Server?

- The Configure Your Server tool contains expandable categories, such as Active Directory, File Server, Print Server, Networking, and so forth. Under each category, various components and services appear. For example, under the Networking category, DHCP, DNS, Remote Access, and Routing appear.

Is there another way to install networking components in Windows 2000 Server?

- Yes. You also use Add/Remove Programs in Control Panel to configure Windows components. See the next page for more information.

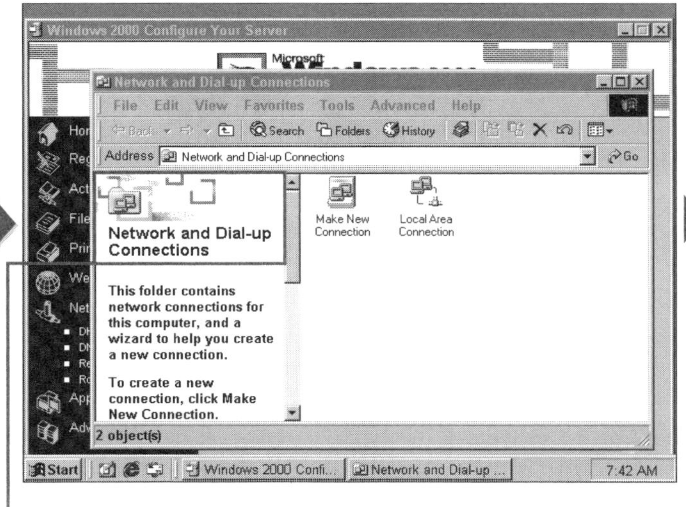

3 If you click the Network and Dial-Up Connections link in the right pane, the Network and Dial-Up Connections window appears.

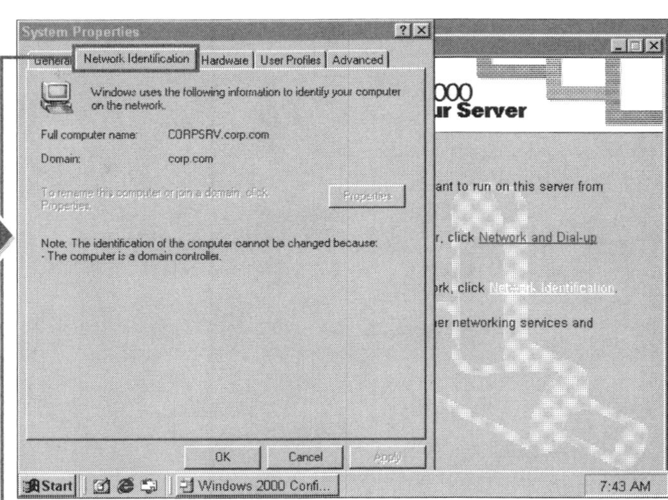

4 If you click the Network Identification link, your server's identification tab appears.

USING ADD/REMOVE PROGRAMS

Aside from the Configure Your Server tool, another way to install networking components in Windows 2000 Server is to use Add/Remove Programs in Control Panel. The Add/Remove programs feature now enables you to configure Windows components as well. If you are adding or removing a lot of components, you may find this interface easier to use than the Configure Your Server interface. The Add/Remove Windows Components feature does not present you with a graphical interface and information about each component. A wizard appears that allows you to select what you want to install or uninstall. You can use either Add/Remove Windows Components or Configure Your Server. Both tools provide the same functionality—one is simply more graphical than the other. In fact, the Configure Your Server tool still launches the same type of interface as the Add/Remove Windows Components tools when you choose to install or uninstall a service. The Add/Remove Windows Components simply allows you to bypass the graphical interface in Configure Your Server.

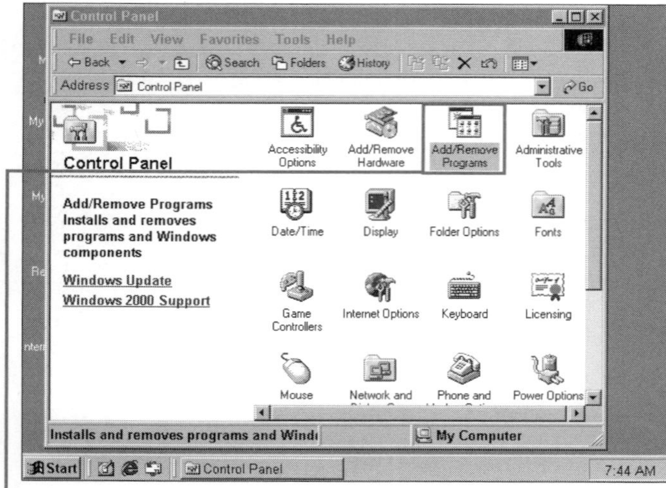

1 Open Control Panel, and then double-click Add/Remove Programs.

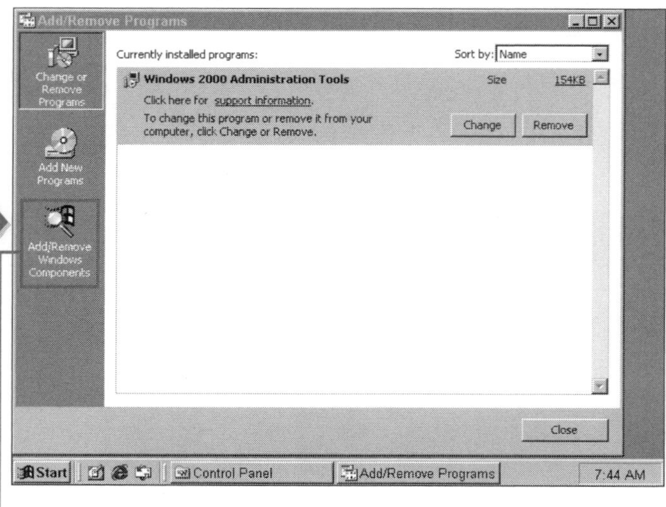

2 Click the Add/Remove Windows Components icon.

What can you do with Add/Remove Programs?

- You can use the Add/Remove Programs feature to change or remove existing programs on your server, add new programs, or add or remove Windows components. This single interface for all of these actions enables you to manage your system more effectively and easily. You can also learn more about the existing programs on your system and the amount of memory each of them uses.

Can I add or remove several Windows components at one time?

- Yes. You can add or remove Windows components at one time without having to walk back through the wizard for each instance. However, some components require you to complete various wizards and reboot your system, so adding or removing components one at a time may be best to avoid problems or confusion.

■ The Windows Components Wizard begins.

3 Click Next to continue.

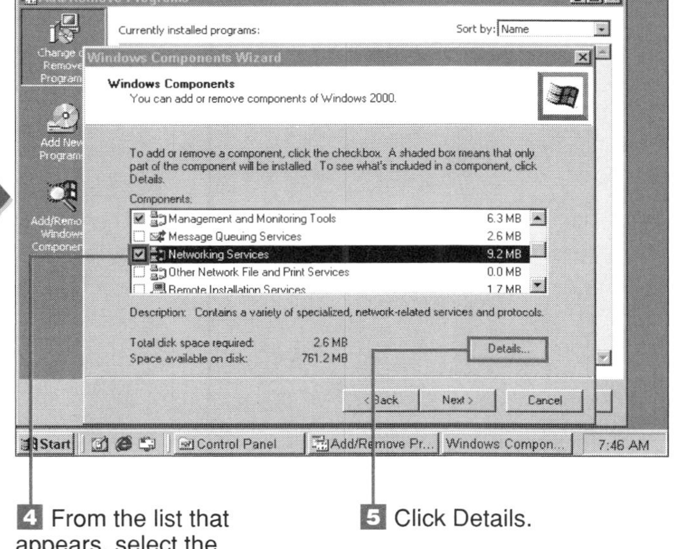

4 From the list that appears, select the component you want to add or remove.

5 Click Details.

CONTINUED

USING ADD/REMOVE PROGRAMS

CONTINUED

Under each category of components to add or remove, you may see additional components to select. If the Details button is available for the component, click it to see exactly what components you can add or remove. The major components you can add or remove are:

- **COM Internet Services Proxy**—enables Distributed Component Object Model (DCOM) to travel over HTTP through Internet Information Services (IIS)./o
- **Domain Name System (DNS)**—resolves fully qualified domain names to IP addresses (see Chapter 6).
- **Dynamic Host Configuration Protocol (DHCP)**—dynamically assigns IP addresses to network clients (see Chapter 4).
- **Internet Authentication Service**—enables authentication of dial-up users.
- **QoS (Quality of Service) Control Service**—enables you to specify the quality of network connections.
- **Simple TCP/IP Services**—installs simple TCP/IP services (such as Echo and Discard).
- **Site Server ILS Services**—scans TCP/IP stacks and updates directories with the most current user information.
- **Windows Internet Naming Service (WINS)**—resolves NetBIOS names for clients (see Chapter 5).

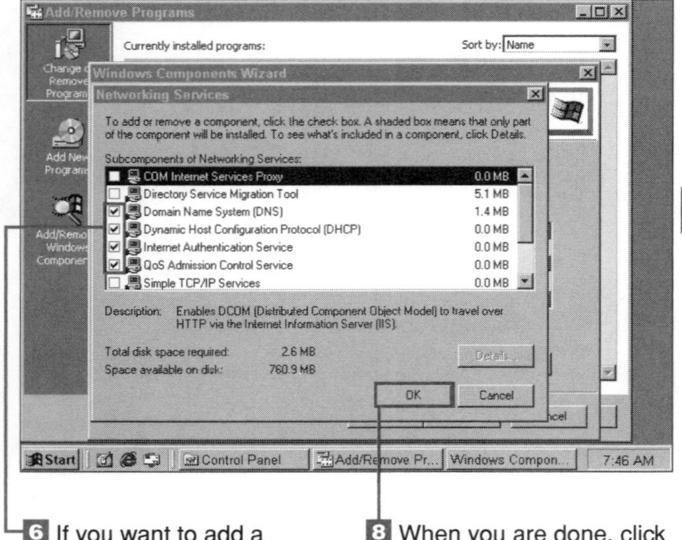

6 If you want to add a component, click the check box next to the component.

7 If you want to remove an existing component, clear the check box next to it.

8 When you are done, click OK.

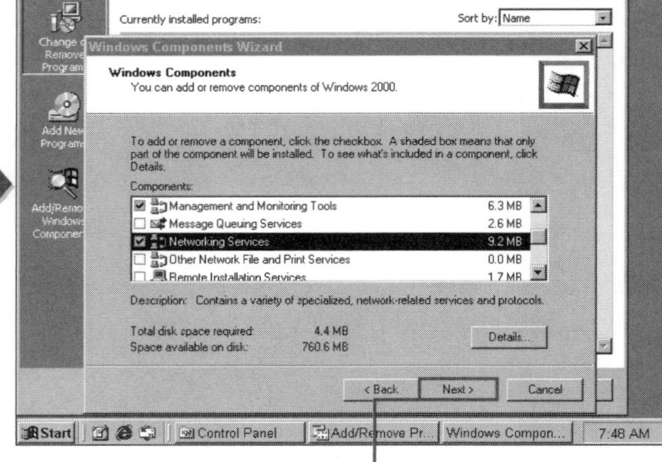

9 Click Next to continue.

TIPS

Can I both add new components and remove existing components at the same time?

- Yes. Simply check or clear the check box next to each component that you want to add or remove. If you check the check box, the component is added. If you clear the check box, the component is removed.

Will I need the Windows 2000 Server CD-ROM?

- Depending on the component you choose to add while using the Add/Remove Windows Components option, your system may need to copy files from the installation CD-ROM. Putting the CD-ROM into your drive before beginning any component addition is a good idea.

How do I know if I have enough disk space for an installation?

- The installation wizard provides the total disk space required for a component or service and the available space on your disk. Before installing a component, simply check the required space against your available disk space to determine if you have enough room on your hard disk.

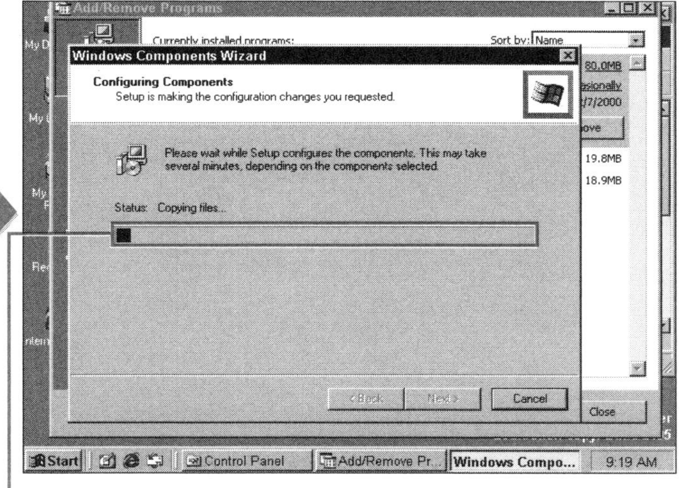

■ Setup copies files and installs the component. The status bar indicates the level of completion.

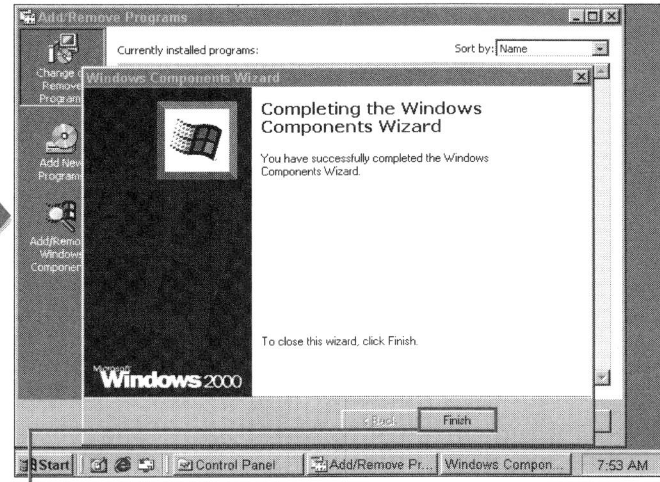

10 Click Finish to complete the configuration.

■ Depending on the component, you may be prompted to reboot your computer.

USING MY NETWORK PLACES

My Network Places replaces Network Neighborhood in Windows 2000 Server. You will find that My Network Places offers more features and provides network users with a way to access the Active Directory. My Network Places allows you to configure network connections, such as local area connections, VPN connections, ISDN connections, or simply dial-up connections. All of this can be done with the Add Network Place Wizard. You can also use My Network Places to Browse the network and the Active Directory. In Windows NT and 9*x*, Network Neighborhood was primarily used for network browsing. In other words, you could find a particular server on your network that contained a particular resource. In Windows 2000, My Network Places is primarily used to configure different network connections. Due to the advanced features of the Active Directory, browsing is seldom necessary because the Active Directory contains resource pointers so you do not have to browse the network.

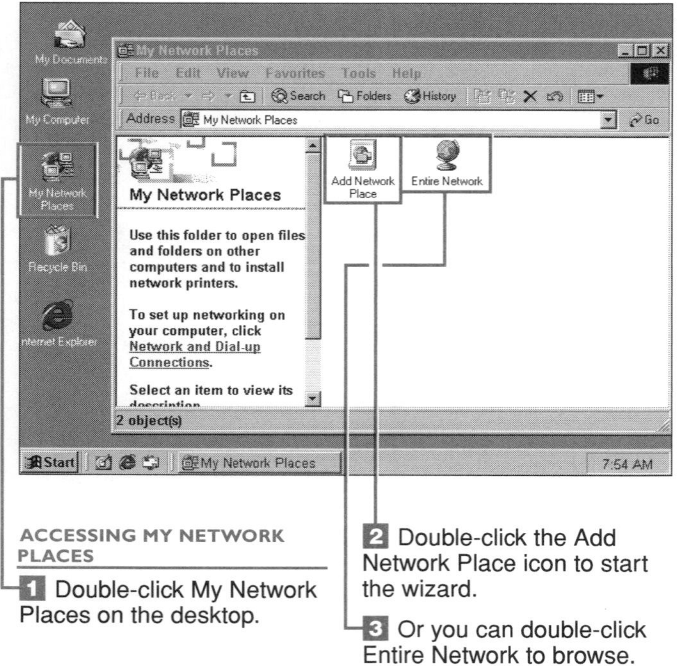

ACCESSING MY NETWORK PLACES

1 Double-click My Network Places on the desktop.

2 Double-click the Add Network Place icon to start the wizard.

3 Or you can double-click Entire Network to browse.

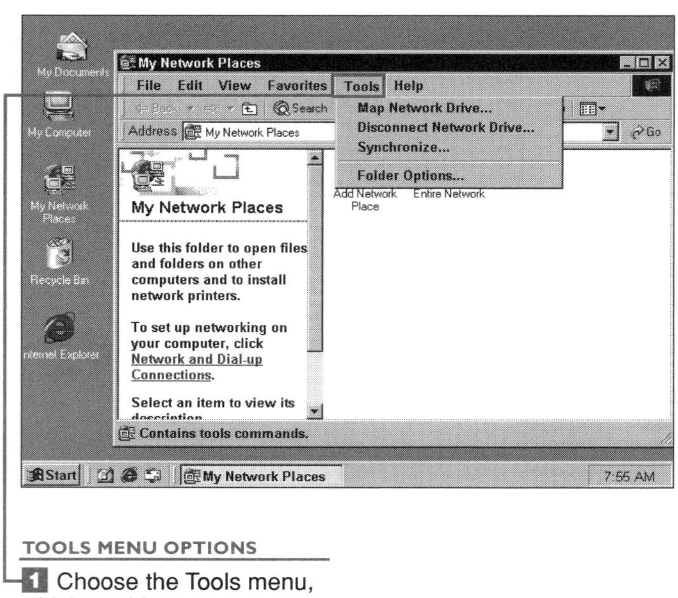

TOOLS MENU OPTIONS

1 Choose the Tools menu, which enables you to map a network drive, disconnect a network drive, synchronize, or access folder options.

How can I use My Network Places to find printers on my network?

You can use the search feature to locate printers on your network. In My Network Places, double-click Entire Network, and then click the Search for Printers link in the left pane. This action opens the search window where you can type the name of the printer you would like to find.

How can I map a network drive using My Network Places?

A network drive connects your computer to another computer by assigning a drive letter. You can then use the connection as though the drive exists on your local computer. You can map a network drive by opening My Network Places, clicking the Tools Menu, and then clicking Map Network Drive. You are prompted to enter the location of the network drive, such as \\server2\documents, and the drive letter you want to assign.

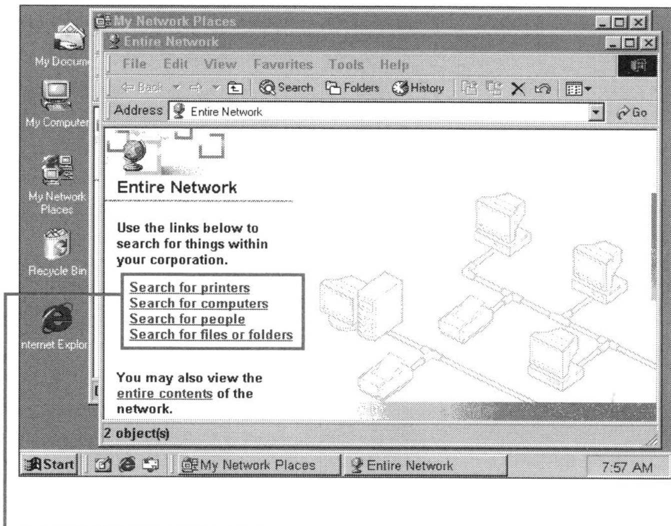

ACCESSING THE ENTIRE NETWORK

1 By double-clicking Entire Network, you can choose to search for printers, computers, people, or files. Click the Entire Contents link to view the entire contents of the network.

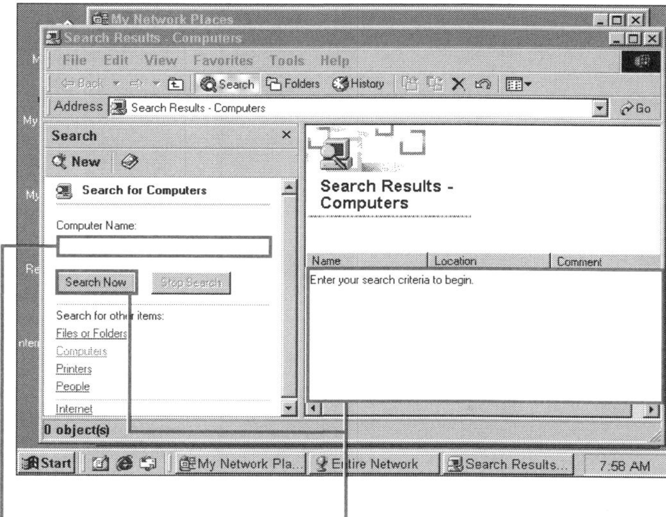

SEARCHING THE ENTIRE NETWORK

■ If you click one of the search links, this window appears.

1 Type the name of the object you want to search for.

2 Click Search Now.

■ The results for your search appear in the right-hand pane.

CONTINUED

USING MY NETWORK PLACES CONTINUED

You can use My Network Places to browse the Active Directory or the domain(s) available.

The Active Directory contains the OUs for the domain that you select and the objects within those OUs. Active Directory users can then browse the directory for the objects they need, such as users, groups, printers, folders, applications, and so forth. Take note that the Active Directory contains powerful search features, so user browsing is not the preferred method of finding Active Directory resources. In new Active Directory environments, users may need to be trained so they can effectively and quickly locate the Active Directory resources they need without having to browse the directory itself.

You can also browse the domain. This feature is the same as in Network Neighborhood in Windows NT, where you can browse the various computers in the domain and the resources they offer. However, users can more easily find the resources they need through the Active Directory.

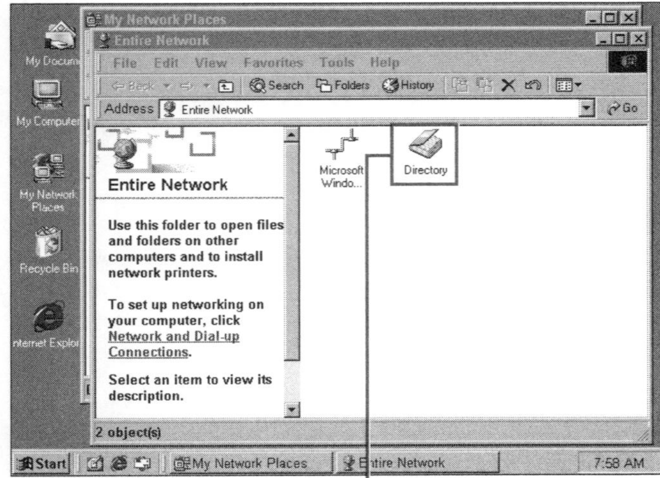

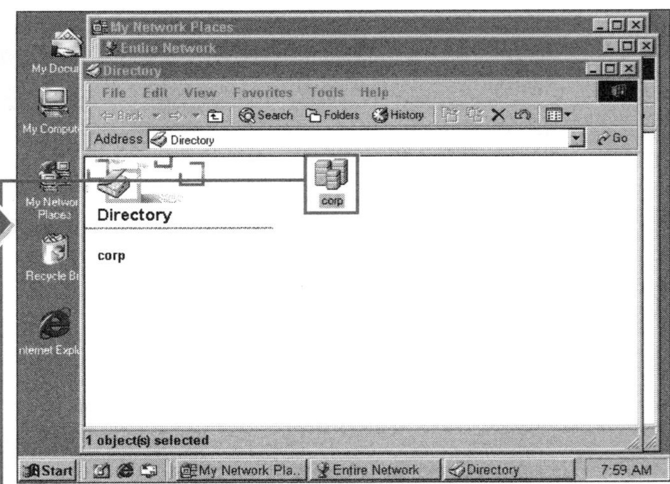

BROWSING THE NETWORK

1 Open Entire Network and then click the Entire Network link in the left-hand pane.

■ The contents of your network appear in the window.

2 Double-click Directory to make the available domains appear.

3 Double-click the domain you want to view.

Can users see everything about the Active Directory objects?

- Certain attributes of the objects held in OUs are available for network users to view. What users can view often depends on how the objects are defined in their Properties.. For example, users can browse a list of other users and obtain general information about another user, such as e-mail address and phone number. You learn more about these features in later chapters.

Can network users find Active Directory resources without browsing?

- Yes. The Active Directory natively supports the LDAP protocol, which allows users to query the directory database. Through this powerful search feature, users can perform full text searches to find the resources desired. Browsing is provided for backwards compatibility and is not the preferred method of resource discovery.

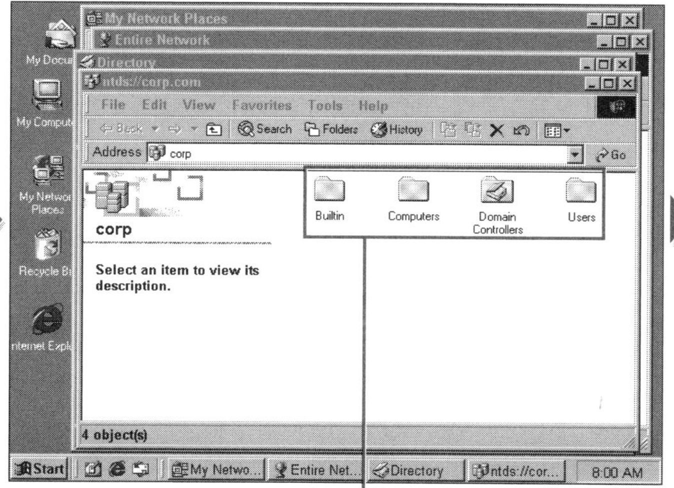

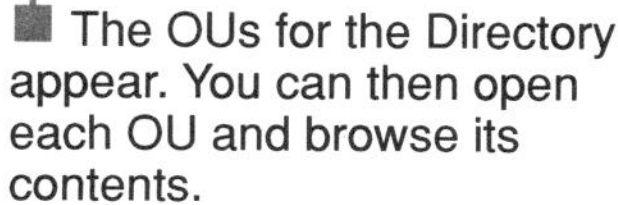

■ The OUs for the Directory appear. You can then open each OU and browse its contents.

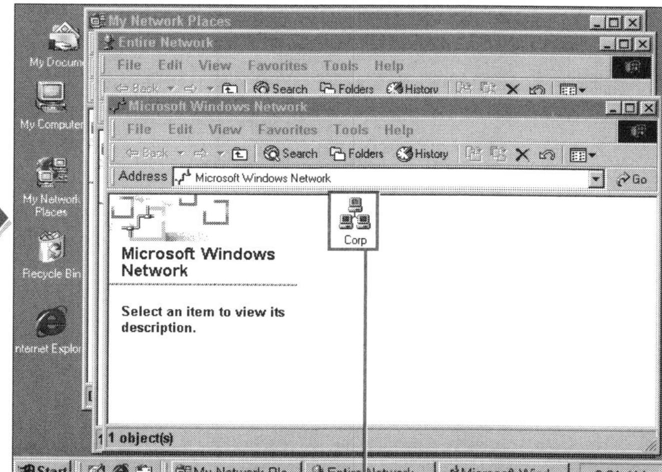

■ If you double-click Microsoft Network in the Entire Network window, you can then open the domain and browse the actual computers within the domain.

ADDING A NETWORK PLACE

A *network place* is a location on the network where you can store documents. This network place can be a shared folder on a computer, a Web folder on the Internet, or even an FTP site where documents can be stored.

After you add the network place, it appears in the My Network Places folder.

My Network Places makes it easy for you to add a network place by providing an Add Network Place wizard. The wizard enables you to enter the desired network place or browse your network to find the network place that you want to add. The Add Network Place feature is particularly helpful in environments that use Web and FTP servers for storage. You can use My Network Places to establish a connection to these locations that is reconnected each time you logon to the network. This way, the network place you configure is always available.

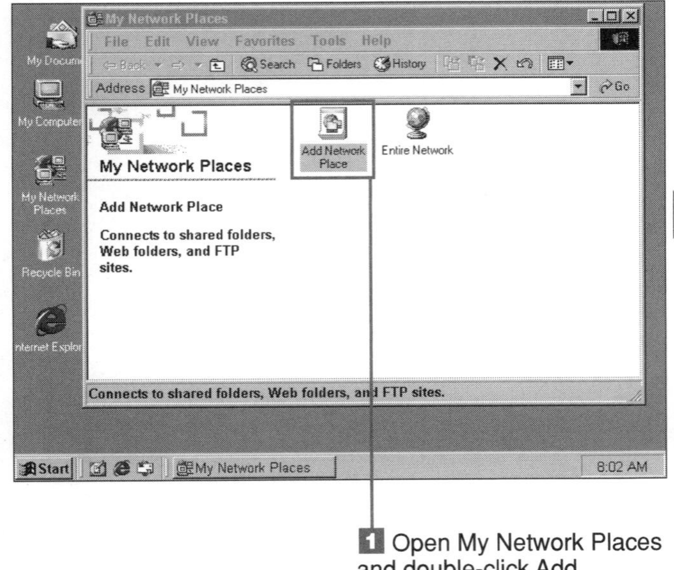

1 Open My Network Places and double-click Add Network Place.

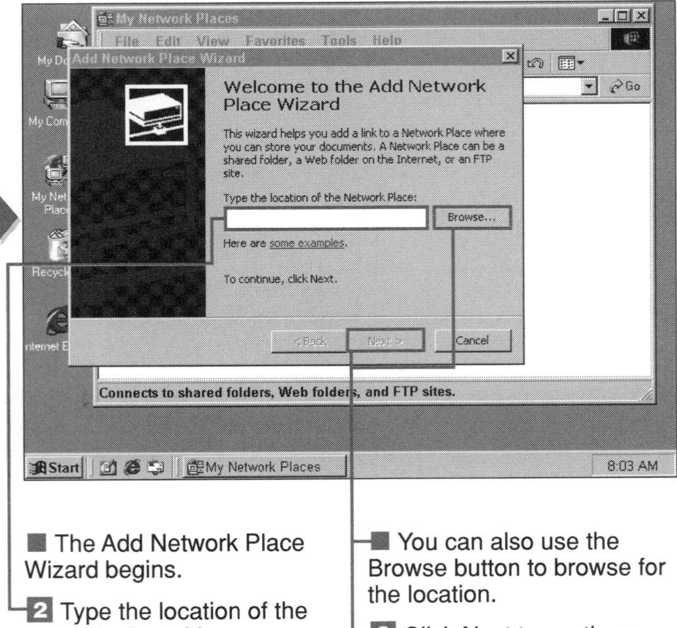

■ The Add Network Place Wizard begins.

2 Type the location of the network place. You can use a UNC path or a URL.

■ You can also use the Browse button to browse for the location.

3 Click Next to continue.

Why would you use this interface to connect to a URL?

One of the goals of Windows 2000 server is to provide seamless integration with the local network and the Internet. You can define a network place on the Internet or an intranet just as easily as on a local network computer by creating a network place. After you establish the network place, you can use the network place as though it resides on your local computer. If you use modem dial-up access, however, you need a dial-up connection each time you access the network place.

Why is the FTP Site option available?

In environments where Web servers reside, network clients may be assigned a folder on an FTP server where they can store documents. You can use the Add Network Place Wizard to establish a network connection to an FTP site. Once you establish the network place, the connection is reestablished each time you logon to the network. This allows you to use the FTP connection as though the folder resides on your local hard drive.

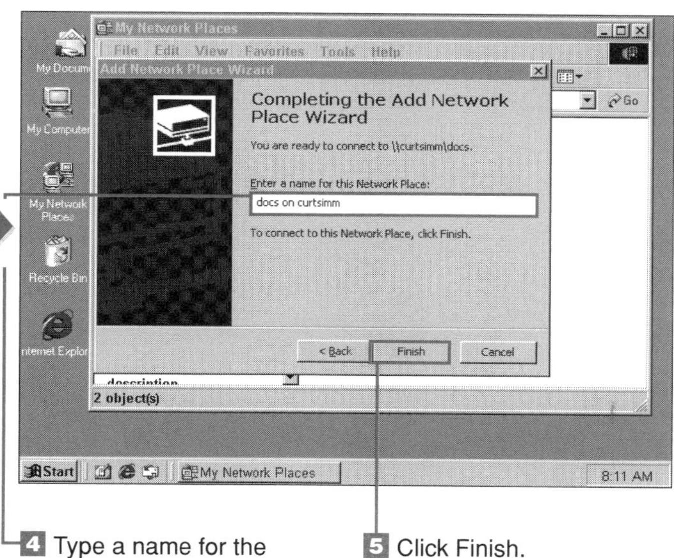

4 Type a name for the network place.

5 Click Finish.

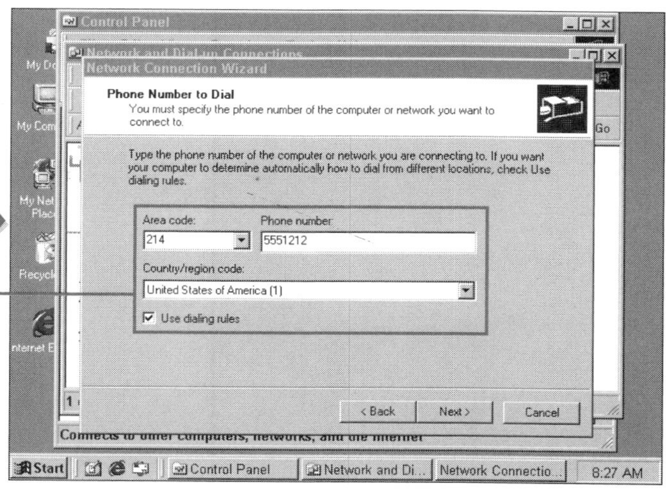

■ If you are connecting to a Web folder, you may be prompted for the dialing information or username and password for the connection.

ESTABLISHING AND CONFIGURING CONNECTIONS

Windows 2000 enables you to configure various connections for your system. You can both establish new connections and configure existing connections using the Network and Dial-up Connections folder located in Control Panel.

By using the Make New Connection Wizard, you can configure a variety of connections, such as dial-up to the Internet, dial-up to a private network, VPN, or parallel port connection, or you can even accept other connections.

After you configure the desired connection(s), the connections remain on your computer and you can use them to connect with various servers. You can easily establish desired connections by using the Make New Connection wizard. This wizard enables you to configure a variety of connection types, such as modem or ISDN, Virtual Private Network (VPN), serial, parallel, and even infrared connections.

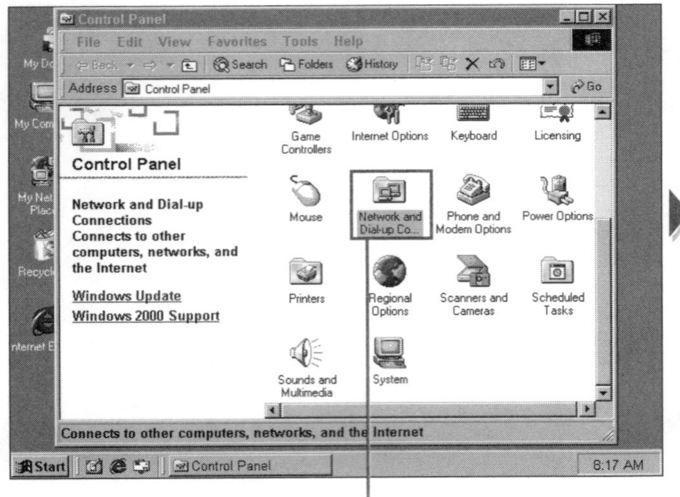

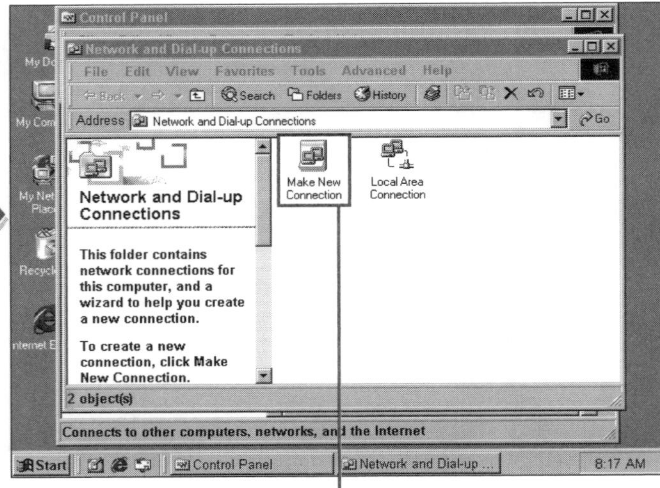

1 Open Control Panel, and then open Network and Dial-up Connections.

■ The Network and Dial-up Connections window opens containing your current connections and a wizard to make new connections.

2 To create a new connection, double-click the Make New Connection icon.

Is there another way to access the Network and Dial-up Connections folder?

- Yes. Instead of using Control Panel, you can also right-click My Network Places and click Properties. This action also opens the Network and Dial-up Connections folder.

Can I use the connection wizard to create a PPTP connection?

- Yes. To create a "PPTP" connection, or Virtual Private Network (VPN), select this option on the selection screen in the wizard. The wizard then asks you questions to configure the VPN connection. A VPN connection uses the Internet to transmit data to a remote computer. This is accomplished by making local area network data appear as PPP data over the Internet. In most cases, the data transmitted over the Internet is encrypted.

What about local area connections?

- Local area network (LAN) connections automatically appear in the Network and Dial-Up Connections folder if a Network Interface Card (NIC) is attached to your computer. You can right-click the Local Area Connection icon in the window and click Properties to configure it.

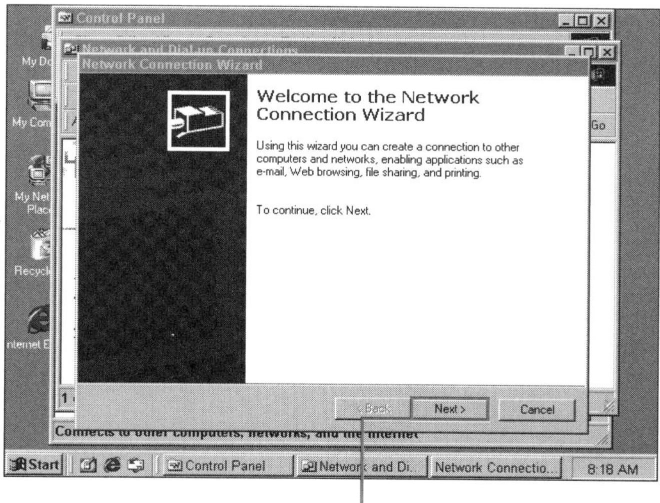

■ The Network Connection Wizard begins.

3 Click Next to continue.

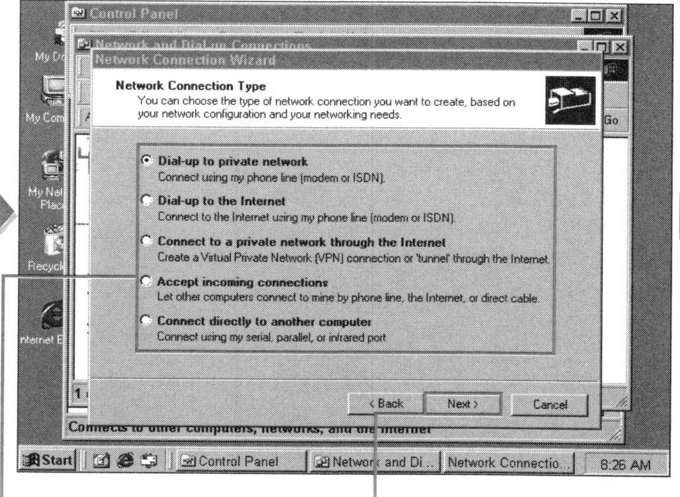

4 Select the type of connection you would like to make by clicking the appropriate radio button.

5 Click Next to continue.

CONTINUED

ESTABLISHING AND CONFIGURING CONNECTIONS CONTINUED

After you launch the Network Connection Wizard and select the type of connection you want to create, the wizard asks you to input additional information pertinent to the new connection. You may be asked to enter server names and username and password information for remote network connections.

In Windows 2000, you can also share connections with other users. In most cases, the wizard asks you if you want to share the connection or not. If you choose not to share the connection, you can still share it later if you wish. This is a powerful feature of Windows 2000. For example, a small office can have one Windows 2000 computer (server or Professional) configured with an ISDN adapter. This connection can then be shared so that other Windows 2000 computers in the office can use the ISDN connection. You can also share modem connections in the same manner.

After you create connections, you can further configure them by accessing their Properties sheets.

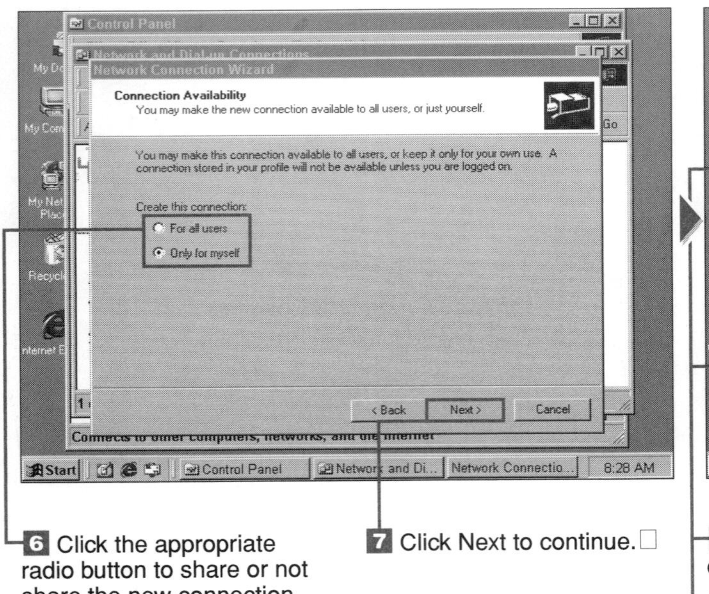

6 Click the appropriate radio button to share or not share the new connection.

7 Click Next to continue.

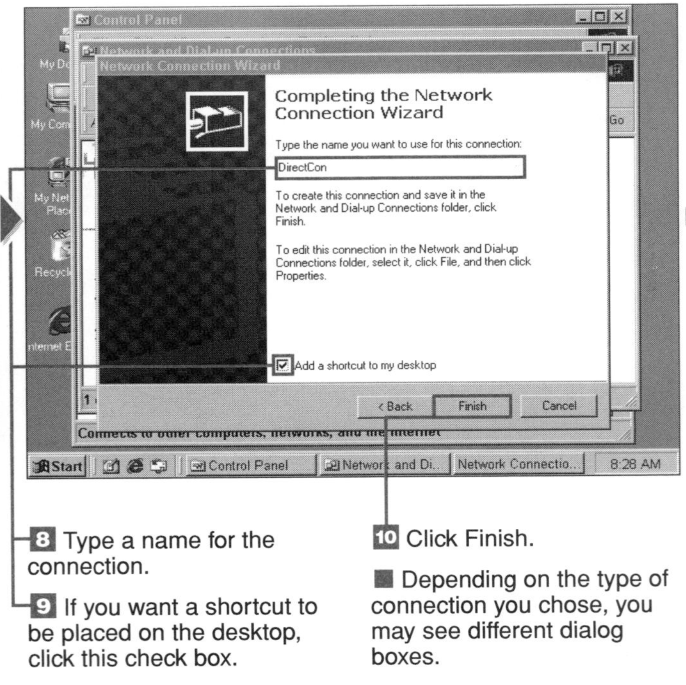

8 Type a name for the connection.

9 If you want a shortcut to be placed on the desktop, click this check box.

10 Click Finish.

■ Depending on the type of connection you chose, you may see different dialog boxes.

Can I share a dial-up connection?

- Yes. You can share a dial-up connection, such as an Internet connection, so that other users can access your dial-up connection and use it. This feature is an easy way for a small office or home network to use one modem connection.

Can I create shortcuts to may connections?

- Yes. The final screen of the wizard gives you the option of creating a shortcut on your desktop. You can also create a shortcut to your desktop by right-clicking the connection and selecting to create a shortcut.

Can I share my modem connection so that it dials on demand?

- Yes. When you configure your dial-up connection, simply click the Enable On-Demand Dialing button on the Internet Connection Sharing window. When you make this selection, the modem will automatically establish a dial-up connection when another user attempts to use the shared connection. Once the dial-up link is established, the user can use the connection just as though it were established on his or her computer.

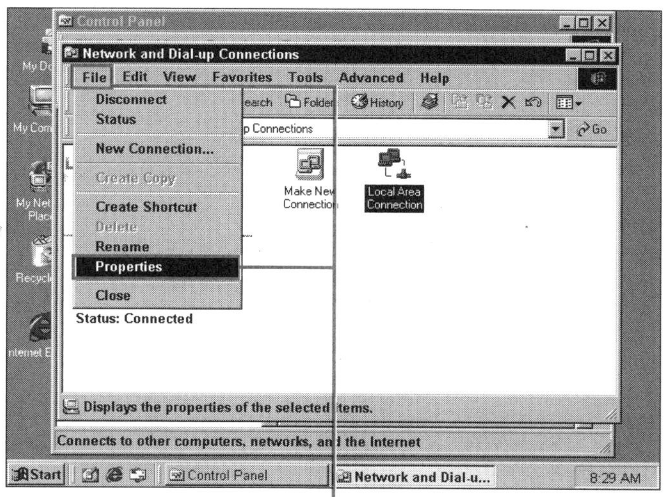

■ After you establish the connection, you can further configure it by accessing its Properties sheet.

11 In Network and Dial-up Connections, select the Local Area Connection, and then choose File⇨ Properties.

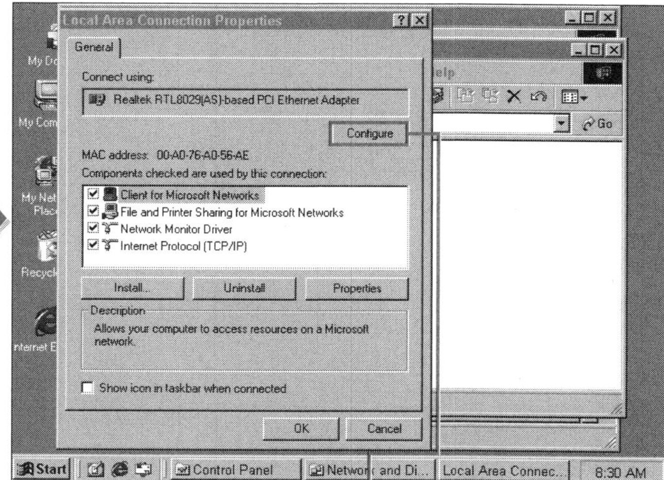

■ The Local Area Connection Properties sheet appears.

12 Click Configure to configure your Network Interface Card.

CONTINUED

ESTABLISHING AND CONFIGURING CONNECTIONS CONTINUED

You can use the Properties sheets for your local area connection to configure properties for your Network Interface Card (NIC). One of the most important features available to you through the Properties sheets is the Troubleshooter. If you are having problems with the NIC, you can launch the Troubleshooter, which opens a section of Windows 2000 help files so you can attempt to solve the problem.

The Advanced tab allows you to adjust various properties for the NIC. For example, the line speed property typically is available. You can use the Value drop-down menu to select the type of line speed that is available to the NIC, such as TP Half Duplex, TP Full Duplex, and so on.

You can also use the Properties sheets to learn more about the NIC's driver and update the driver if an update is available. This tab makes it easy for you to update your NIC driver as changes become available without having to uninstall and reinstall the NIC itself. Most hardware devices in Windows 2000 contain the Update Driver option.

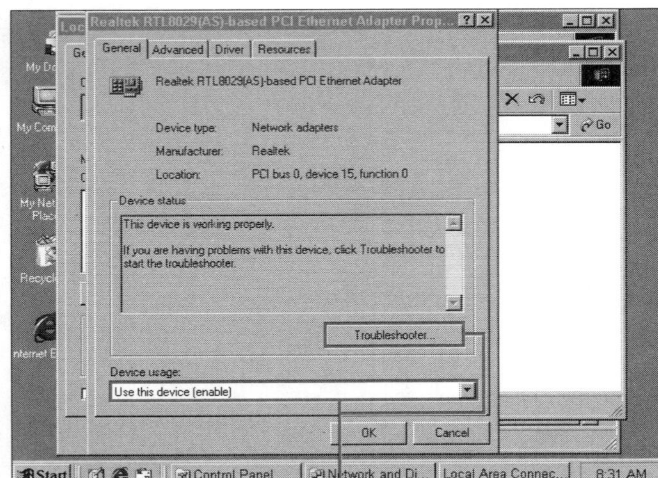

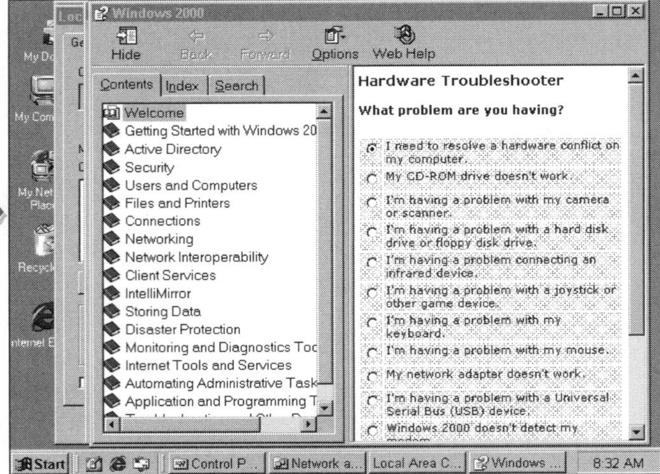

■ The Properties sheets for the NIC appears. The General tab gives you the status of the device.

13 Click the Device Usage drop-down box to either enable or disable the device.

14 Click Troubleshooter to launch the troubleshooting help files if you are having problems with the device.

■ The Troubleshooter window appears. Use the troubleshooter to walk through a series of steps to attempt to isolate the problem.

TIPS

When should I use the Troubleshooter?

- Any time you have problems with your NIC, such as slow performance or an inability to connect, you can use the Troubleshooter. You select the problems you are having from a list and the Troubleshooter attempts to offer possible solutions to the problem.

I have a new NIC driver. What is the easiest way to update the driver?

- Access the Properties dialog box for the NIC and click the Driver tab. At the bottom of the window, click the Update Driver button. Follow the instructions to update the driver. Most hardware devices in Windows 2000 can be updated in this manner.

Do I need to manually configure the line speed for my NIC?

- In most cases, the line speed is automatically configured when the NIC is installed. The line speed is dependent on the NIC itself—in other words—you can not simply select the line speed you want. The NIC has to be able to support the selected speed. See your NIC's documentation for more information about the line speed it can support.

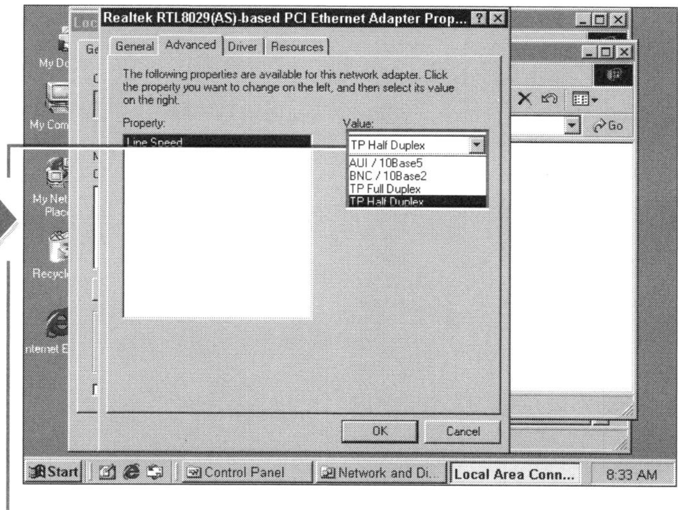

■ The Advanced tab enables you to change various properties for the NIC.

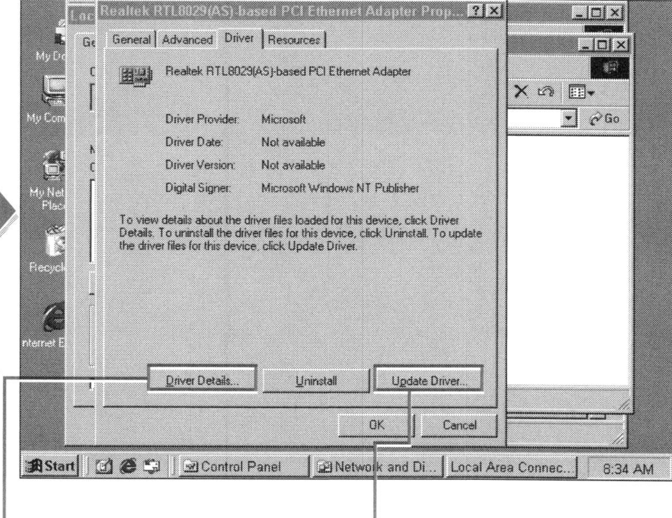

15 Click Driver Details.

■ The Driver tab of the NIC Properties dialog box lists the driver that is currently in use for the NIC.

CONTINUED

ESTABLISHING AND CONFIGURING CONNECTIONS CONTINUED

Finally, the Resources tab on the NIC Properties sheets tells what system resources are currently in use by the NIC. These settings will typically give you an Input/Output range and Interrupt Request number. A particularly helpful feature of this tab is the Conflicting Device List at the bottom of the window. This section reports any resource conflicts with other devices. For example, if another device was also configured to use IRQ 9, the conflict would appear in the list. Because Windows 2000 is plug and play compliant, it does a good job of managing devices and the resources they use without intervention from the administrator or use.

Aside from configuring setting for your NIC, you can access other Properties dialog boxes for the services that you have running. On the Local Area Connection Properties page, select any component that is installed, and then click the Properties button to further configure properties that are available for the component. The list includes both services and protocols that are currently available on your server.

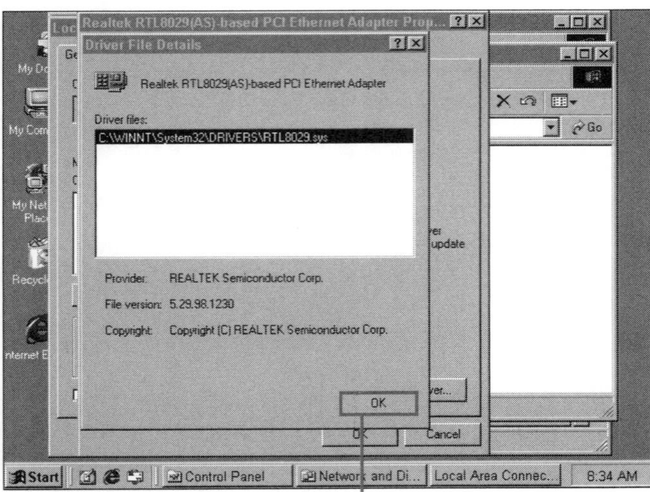

■ The Driver File Details window tells you more about the driver.

16 Click OK when you are done.

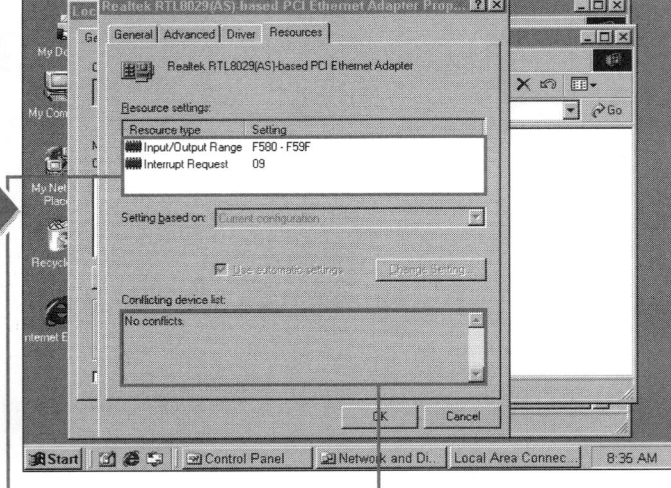

■ The Resources tab of the NIC Properties dialog box gives you the resource settings, such as the I/O Range and IRQ, for the NIC.

■ The Conflicting device list at the bottom of the window reports any resource conflicts with the device.

How can I reduce the amount of memory used for file sharing?

- To reduce or minimize the amount of memory used for file and printer sharing, select File and Printer Sharing for Microsoft Networks in the Local Area Connection Properties dialog box, and then click the Properties button. Click the Minimize memory used button and click OK.

How can I change the configuration of TCP/IP?

- You can access the Properties dialog box for any service or protocol from the Local Area Connection Properties page. Simply select Internet Protocol (TCP/IP), and then click Properties. The Properties dialog box appears and you can adjust the configuration as needed. Remember that TCP/IP settings should be planned carefully for each network server. Typically, all domain controllers should be issued a static IP address that does not change. Clients can be issued IP addresses by a DHCP Server.

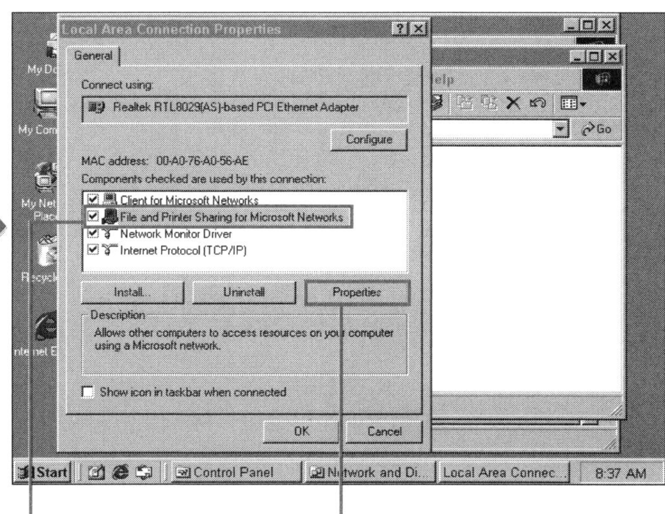

17 Return to the Local Area Connection Properties dialog box and click File and Printer Sharing for Microsoft Networks.

18 Click Properties.

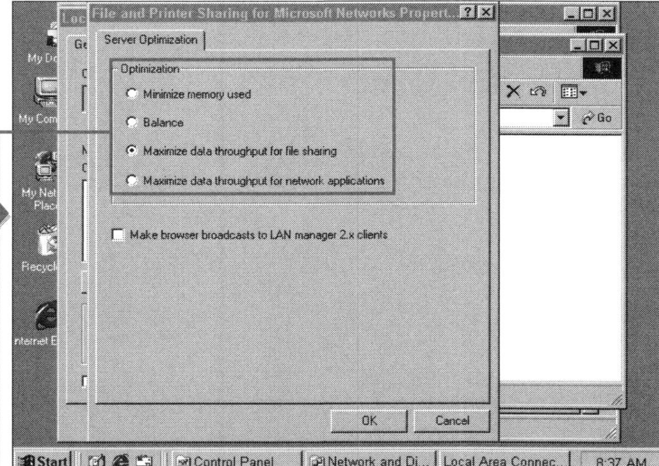

19 Adjust optimization settings, if desired, by clicking the appropriate radio button.

- The default setting of Maximize data throughput for file sharing provides the best performance for file sharing.

INSTALLING OR REMOVING CLIENT, SERVICE, OR PROTOCOL FOR A NIC

You can also use the Local Area Connections Properties dialog box to install or remove a client, service, or protocol. If you have used Windows 98, this interface will be familiar to you. To remove an item, simply select it and click the Remove button. To install a new item, click the Install button. This action prompts you to select a client, service, or protocol. After you make your selection, you are then provided a list of components that you can install. After you install a new item, you can access its Properties sheets by selecting the item and clicking the Properties button. This interface is useful because all protocols services, and clients for a particular NIC can configured in one location. Depending on the client, protocol, or service you decide to install, you may be prompted for you Windows 2000 Server CD-ROM so that files can be copied to your system.

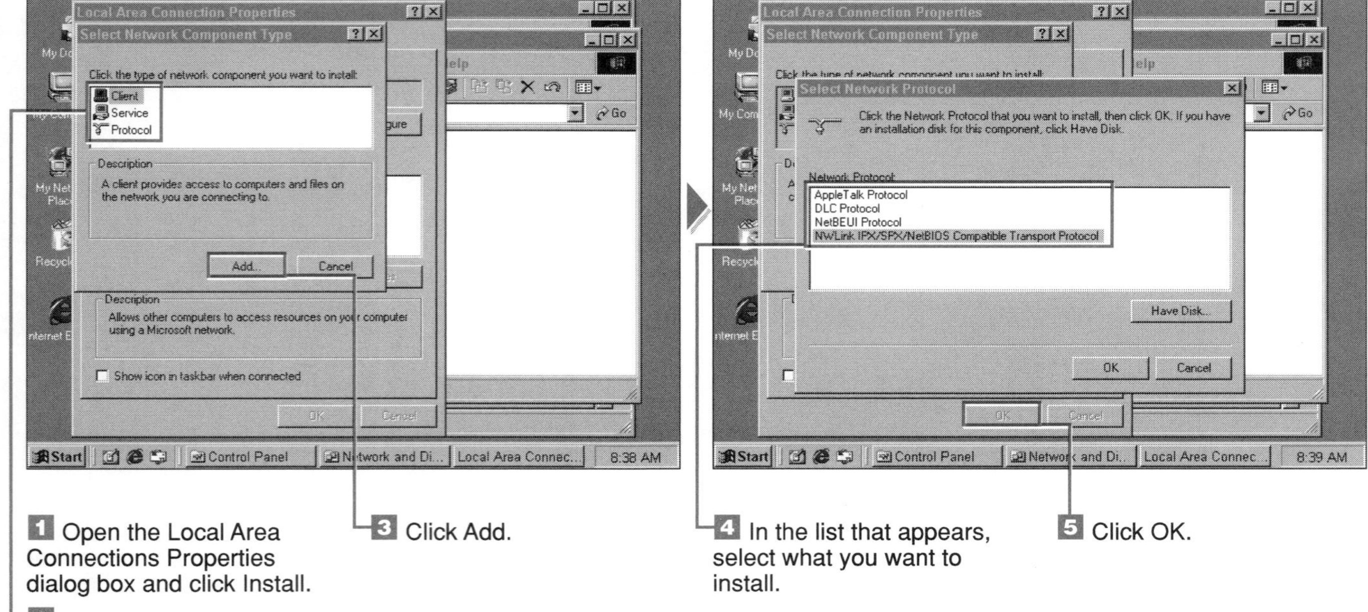

1 Open the Local Area Connections Properties dialog box and click Install.

2 Select either Client, Service, or Protocol.

3 Click Add.

4 In the list that appears, select what you want to install.

5 Click OK.

TIPS

How can I remove an unneeded protocol?

- To remove an unneeded protocol, simply select the protocol in the Local Area Connection Properties dialog box and click the Remove button.

Do all components have properties pages?

- No. Some components, such as NetBEUI, do not have configurable properties. In this case, the Properties button is grayed out because there is no Properties dialog box to access.

Why would I need to add a protocol?

- Protocols are simply "rules of communication behavior." In order for two people to communicate, they have to speak a language that is understood by both. You can think of a protocol as the language that a computer uses to communicate with another computer. Depending on the clients in your network, you may need to install additional protocols. For example, Novell Netware clients require the NWLink protocol to communicate with Microsoft clients, and Apple Macintosh clients require the AppleTalk protocol.

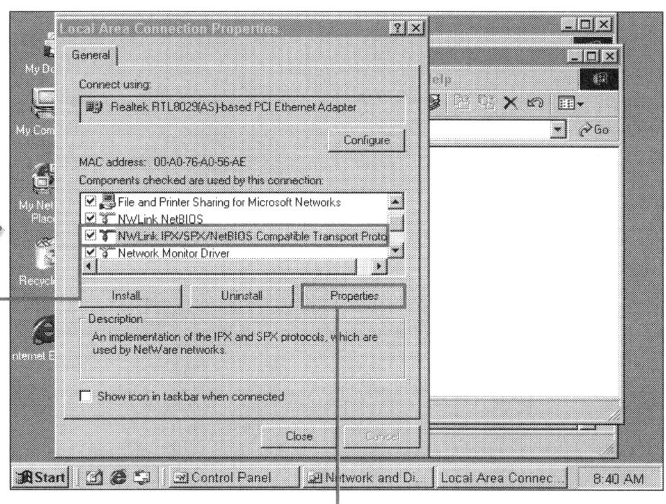

■ The new protocol, service, or client now appears in the list.

6 Select the item

7 Click Properties.

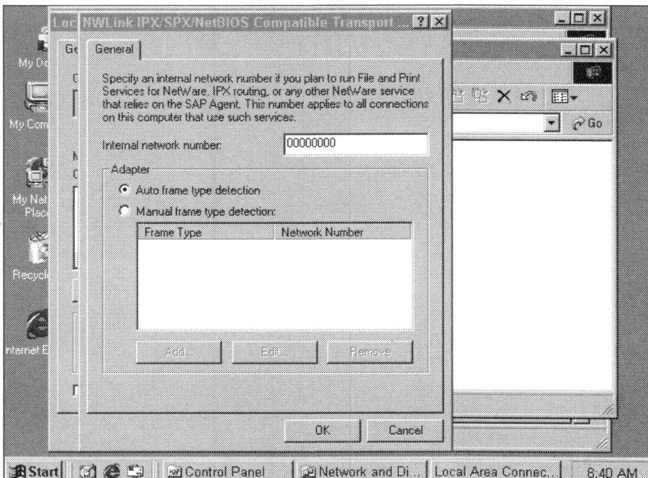

8 The Properties sheet appears for the item, and you can configure it as desired.

CONFIGURING REMOTE NETWORK CONNECTION PROPERTIES

Just as you can configure the Properties for a Local Area Connection, you can also configure various properties for remote network connections, such as dial-up connections or ISDN connections. You access the connection's properties by right-clicking the connection in the Network and Dial-up Connections window and clicking Properties, or you can use the File menu.

Depending on the connection you select, you have a number of properties sheets for remote connections. The General tab presents you with dial-up hardware you are using, such as a modem or ISDN adapter. You can click the Configure button to adjust the properties of the device itself. You also have the option of entering additional phone numbers that can be dialed for the connection and to use dialing rules. You can click the Rules button to configure the dialing rules you wish to use, such as local area code options or dialing long distance with a "1".

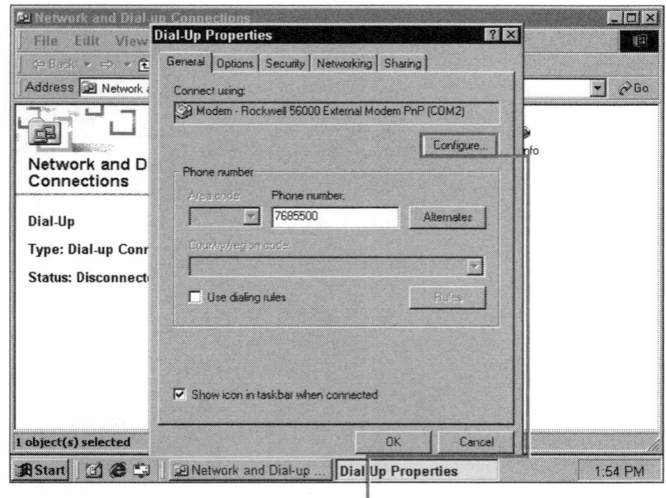

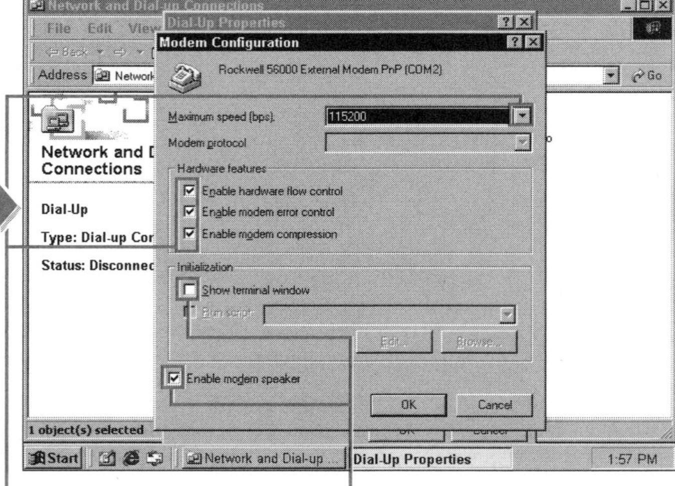

1 Select Dial-Up and choose File⇨Properties.

2 Click Configure to configure your modem or ISDN hardware.

3 Click this drop-down box to adjust the modem's maximum speed as needed.

4 Click the appropriate check boxes to enable hardware features.

■ These features are normally selected by default.

5 Click this check box to show a terminal window.

6 Click this check box to enable the modem speaker.

What is hardware flow control?

- Hardware flow control allows the modem to control the stream of data. The modem can tell the remote access software when the line is congested or clear so the remote access software knows when to send data. Hardware flow control increases throughput and reduces the possibility of errors because data is not sent when the line is congested.

What is modem error control?

- Modem error control allows the remote access software to perform a cyclical redundancy check (CRC) on blocks of data to check for errors. When errors occur, the data can be retransmitted.

What is modem compression?

- Modem compression allows the modem to compress data before it is sent to another modem. This feature reduces the number of bytes transmitted and consequently reduces the transmission time.

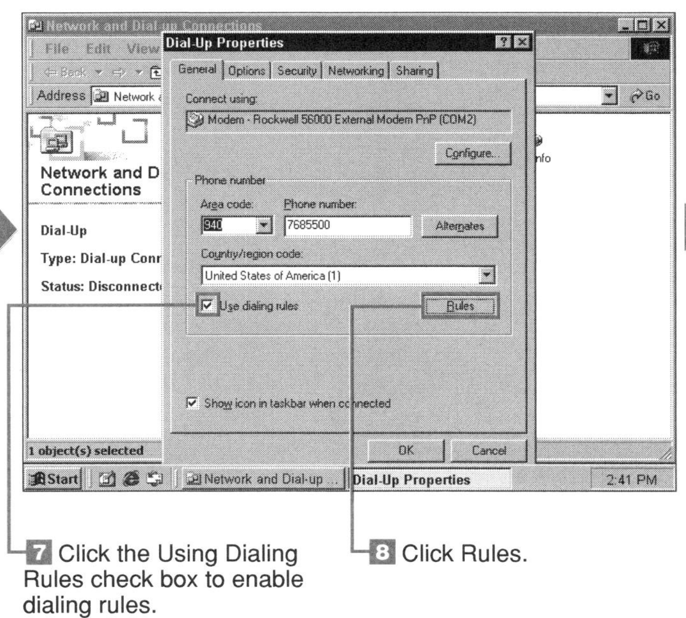

7 Click the Using Dialing Rules check box to enable dialing rules.

8 Click Rules.

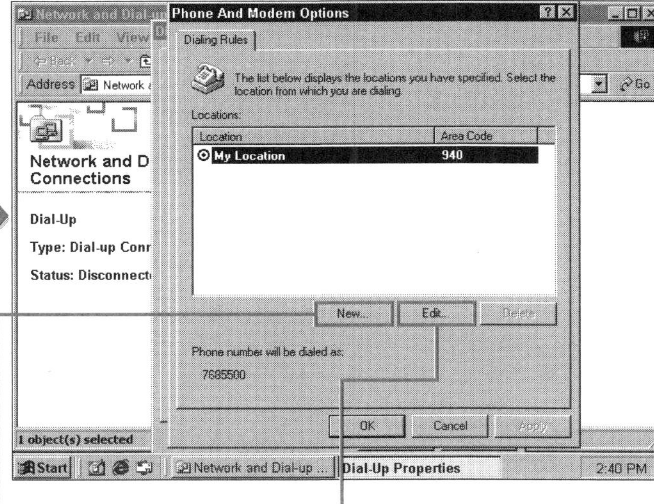

9 Click New to create a new Dialing Rule.

10 Click Edit to make adjustments to existing dialing rules.

11 Click OK when you are finished.

CONTINUED

CONFIGURING REMOTE NETWORK CONNECTION PROPERTIES CONTINUED

On the Options tab, you can configure a number of options that determine how your dial-up sessions occurs. You can select the appropriate check box to display a progress bar during connection, prompt for a username and password, include the Windows logon domain, or prompt for a phone number. You can also use the Options tab to configure the dial-up attempts and how re-dial occurs. The X.25 allows you to enter the dial-up information required for X.24 networks.

The Security tab allows you to set dial-up security options. If you select the Typical radio button, you can select the kind of connection authentication you want to use. The options are allow unsecured password, require secure password, or use smart card. If you choose to use secure authentication, you have the options of selecting to automatically use your Windows logon name and password or require data encryption.

If you click the Advanced settings button, you have the option to select advanced security protocols.

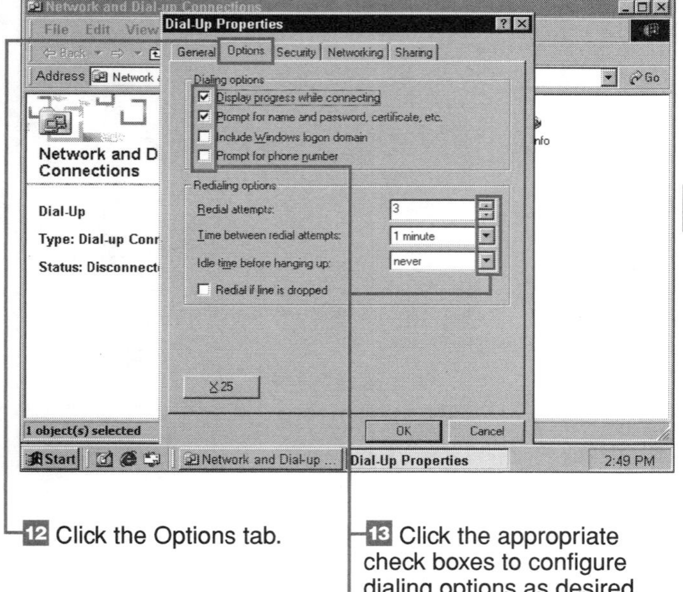

12 Click the Options tab.

13 Click the appropriate check boxes to configure dialing options as desired.

14 Click these drop-down boxes to configure redialing options.

15 Click the Security tab.

■ The Typical radio button is selected by default.

16 Select the desired security setting using the drop-down box.

17 If you want to specify custom settings, click the Advanced radio button.

18 Then click Settings to configure advanced security options.

TIPS

What advanced security features can I set?

The advanced security features allow you to employ a number of advanced authentication methods for a greater level of security. First, you can click the Use Extensible Authentication Protocol (EAP) radio button, which allows you to use a smart card or a digital certificate to logon. Next, you can click the allow these protocols radio button, which allows you to use PAP, SPAP, CHAP, MS-CHAP, or MS-CHAP V2

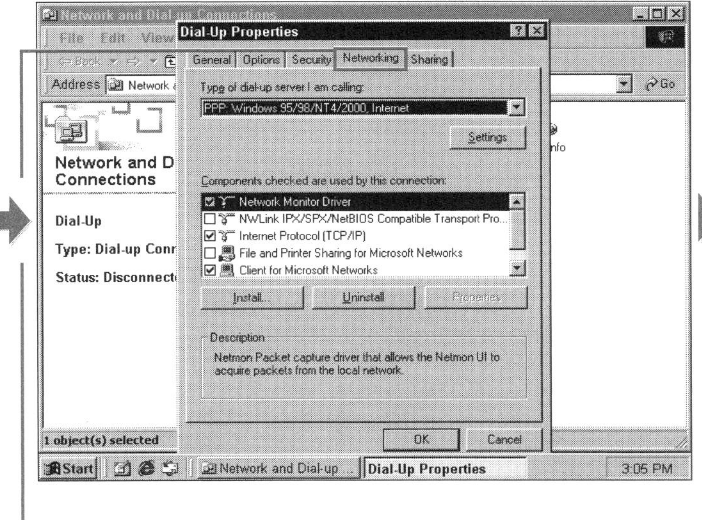

19 Click the Networking tab.

■ Use this tab to make general dial-up settings for the components used by the connection.

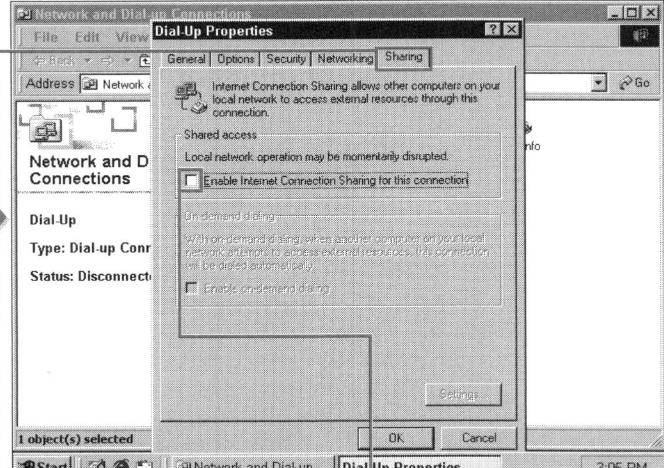

20 Click the Sharing tab.

21 Click this check box to enable connection sharing for this connection.

INTRODUCTION TO DHCP

Dynamic Host Configuration Protocol (DHCP) is used to dynamically assign IP addresses to network clients. DHCP is a TCP/IP standard that eliminates the need for manual TCP/IP address assignment. Before the use of DHCP, each client on a TCP/IP network had to be manually assigned a static IP address, subnet mask, and default gateway. Because each network client must have a unique TCP/IP address, the possibility of errors and network problems was great. With the wide usage of TCP/IP as a network protocol, administrators would be overwhelmed with IP address configuration and problems without DHCP. DHCP is an extension of the BOOTP protocol that enables diskless workstations to automatically configure TCP/IP. With the use of DHCP, the DHCP server automatically assigns the IP address and other TCP/IP information to clients so that administrators do not have to worry about automatic assignment and duplicate address problems.

How DHCP assigns IP addresses

A DHCP server automatically leases an IP address to network clients when the client logs on to the network. Because each network client must have a unique IP address, the DHCP server leases an IP address from a pool of available IP addresses. This ensures that no network clients receive the same IP address. When a client logs on, a process with the DHCP server occurs in order to assign the IP address. There are four steps to this process:

1. The process begins when the client sends a broadcast message that looks for a DHCP server. This is a DHCPDISCOVER request. The discover message contains the client computer's name and MAC address so that the DHCP server can respond to the request.

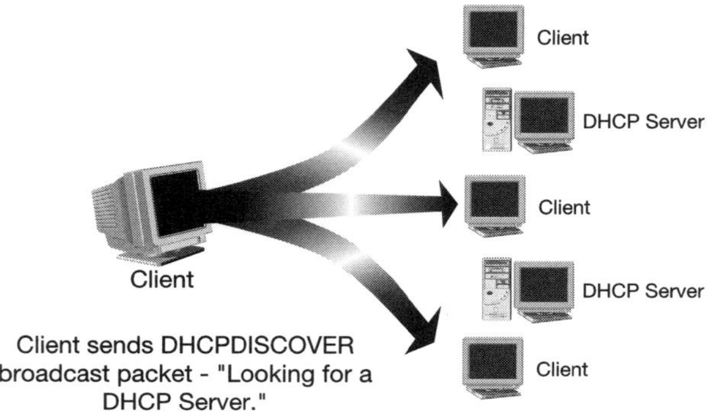
Client
DHCP Server
Client
DHCP Server
Client
Client
Client sends DHCPDISCOVER broadcast packet - "Looking for a DHCP Server."

2. The DHCP server answers the DHCPDISCOVER request by making a lease offer to the client. This is called the DHCPOFFER. The DHCP server reserves an IP address for the client in case the client accepts the offer. If multiple DHCP servers respond to the client, the client will only accept one offer. Offers not accepted are then rescinded and offered to other clients as needed.

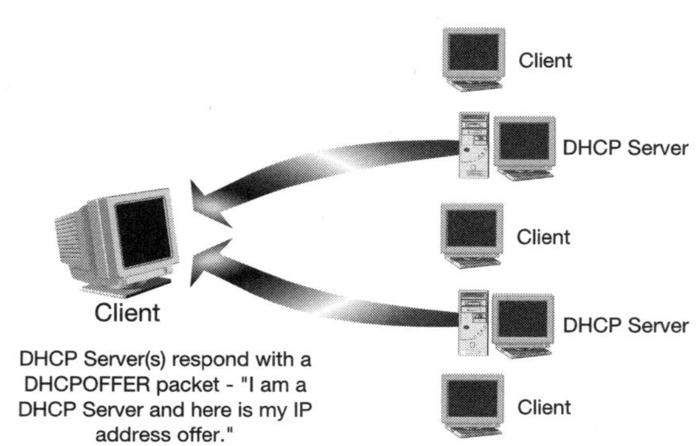
Client
DHCP Server
Client
DHCP Server
Client
Client
DHCP Server(s) respond with a DHCPOFFER packet - "I am a DHCP Server and here is my IP address offer."

3. The client accepts the DHCPOFFER request from one of the DHCP servers by sending a broadcast message for a particular server. This is called DHCPREQUEST. Other DHCP servers that have made an offer rescind their offers.

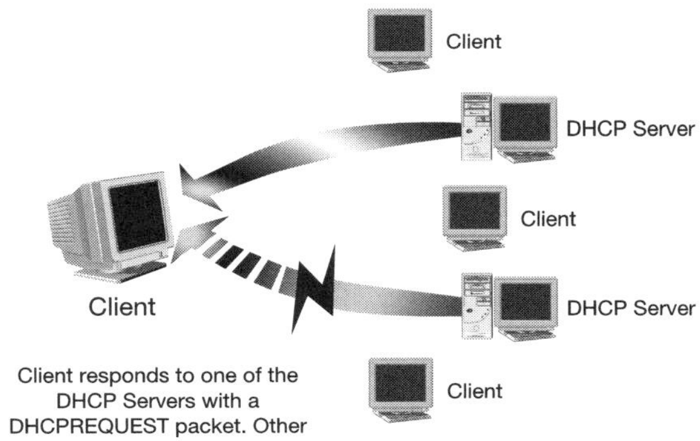

4. Finally, the DHCP server whose offer was accepted sends an acknowledgement message with a valid IP address and lease time information. This is called the DHCPACK, which is the server acknowledgement message and the IP address assignment to the client. The client then becomes a DHCP client and can fully participate in the TCP/IP network.

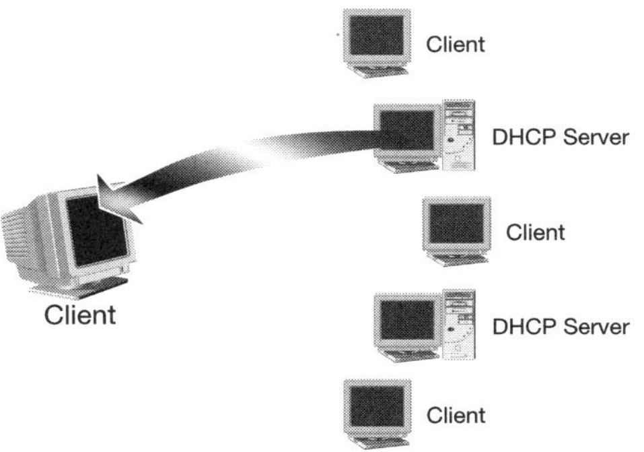

DHCP terms you need to know

In order to use and implement DHCP in your network, you need to understand the following terms. You see these terms throughout the rest of this chapter as you configure DHCP.

- **Address Pool:** An address pool is the addresses in a scope that are available for lease.
- **Exclusion Range:** An exclusion range is a group of addresses in the scope that are not available for lease. These are reserved for servers, routers, and other communication components on the network.
- **Lease:** The DHCP lease is the amount of time a client can keep an IP address before it expires.
- **Reservation:** A reservation is used to assign a particular IP address to a particular client so that the client always has the same IP address. Reservations are normally used for hardware devices, such as routers, that need a static address.
- **Scope:** A DHCP scope is the full range of IP addresses that are available for leasing for a particular DHCP server.
- **Superscope:** A superscope is a grouping of scopes used to support logical IP subnets that exist on one IP subnet.

INSTALLING DHCP

Any Windows 2000 server, whether it's a domain controller or member server, can be a DHCP server. Many administrators choose to use member servers to handle the DHCP functions in order to decrease the domain controller's workload. Generally, you should have at least one DHCP server on each subnet in your network.

In mixed environments, you can still use Windows NT 4.0 servers as DHCP servers as well. Client computers running Windows 2000 and earlier versions of Windows (such as NT and Windows 9*x*) can contact a Windows NT DHCP server for obtaining an IP address. Refer to the Windows NT documentation for how to install and configure DHCP.

To install DHCP on a Windows 2000 server, you use the Add/Remove Programs feature in Control Panel. You can also use the Configure Your Server program in Administrative Tools.

1 Open Control Panel and double-click Add/Remove Programs.

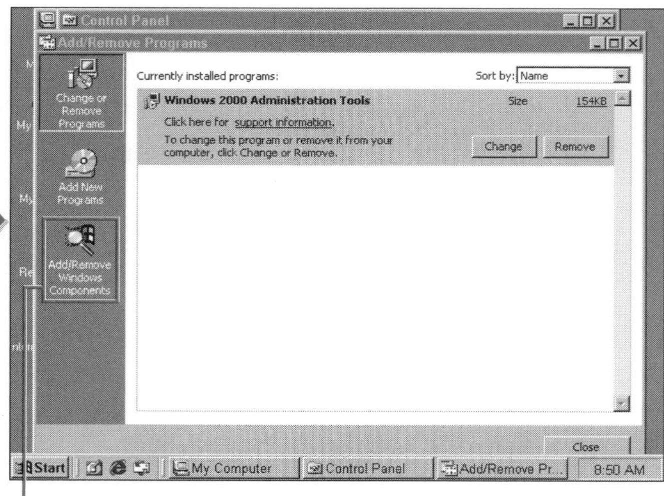

2 Click Add/Remove Windows Components.

TIPS

Is there another way to install DHCP?

- Yes. You can also install DHCP by choosing Start⇨Programs⇨Administrative Tools⇨Configure Your Server. Click the Networking link in the left pane, and then click DHCP. Follow the instructions that appear on your screen.

Can a Windows 2000 Professional computer function as a DHCP server?

- No. You can install DHCP on any Windows 2000 server or Windows 2000 Advanced Server, but Windows 2000 Professional computers cannot function as DHCP servers. You can also use Windows NT 4.0 Server computers as DHCP servers in Windows 2000 networks, but no versions of earlier Windows clients, such as NT or 9*x* can function as DHCP servers.

Does Windows 2000 include an auto-IP-addressing feature?

- Yes. Windows 2000 server includes an auto-addressing feature that allows clients to automatically assign an IP address to themselves if a DHCP server is not available or present. This feature is primarily designed for use in small networks so that TCP/IP can be used without configuring DHCP.

■ The Windows Components Wizard appears.

3 Click Next to continue.

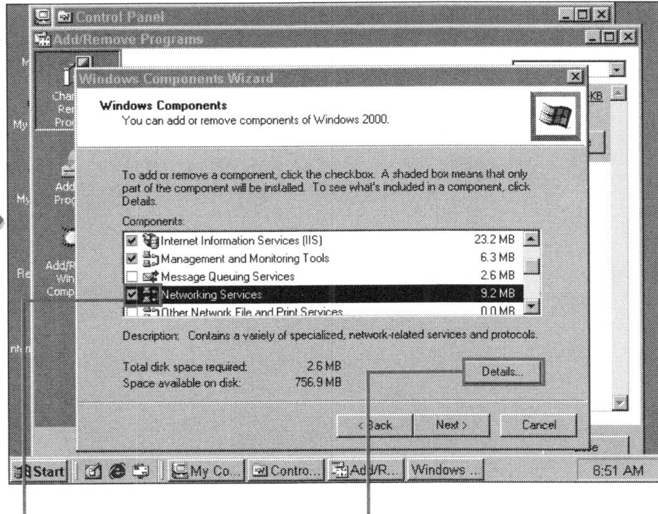

4 Select Networking Services.

5 Click Details.

CONTINUED

INSTALLING DHCP CONTINUED

As with other networking components, you install the DHCP service by selecting it from the Networking Services options. You can also use the Configure Your Server program that is available in the Administrative Tools folder. This particular service does not present you with a configuration wizard during the installation. You can simply install the service first, and then you can configure the service after the installation is complete.

After the installation is complete, the DHCP server does not become active on your network until you authorize it and configure it. Authorization allows the DHCP service to lease IP addresses to network clients, and the Active Directory provides authorization. The authorization feature provides an extra measure of security. Because all DHCP servers must be authorized with the Active Directory, an unauthorized DHCP server cannot come online and begin issuing IP addresses. See the next section to learn how to authorize the DHCP server.

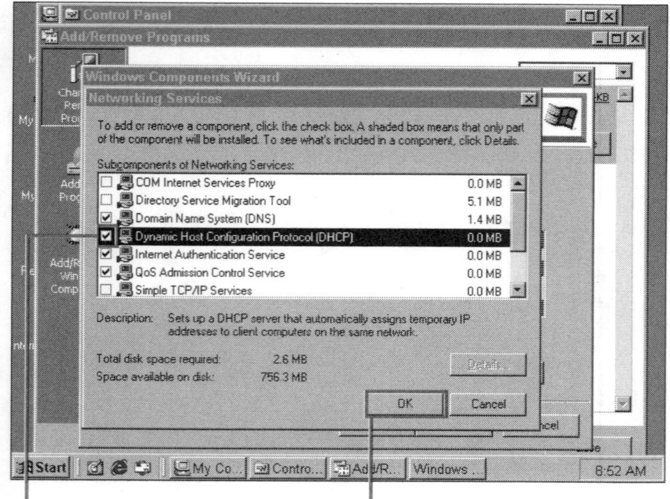

6 Click the Dynamic Host Configuration Protocol check box.

7 Click OK.

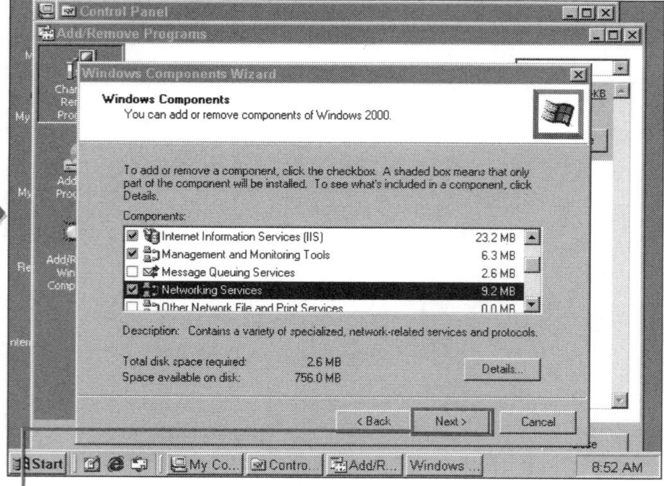

8 Click Next to continue.

TIPS

Will I need to know the scope information for my network during installation?

- No. You can install the DHCP service first, and then you need to authorize and configure it after the installation is complete.

Can I install other networking components when I am installing DHCP?

- Yes. If you would like to install other networking components as well, simply select the components you want to install by clicking their check boxes. Windows 2000 lets you install several components at one time.

Why doesn't the DHCP server begin functioning automatically?

- In order for DHCP to work, you have to configure certain components of the service. You need to create a scope that gives the service the IP address range that it can lease from, and a pool of addresses that it can actually lease. The server also has to be authorized by the Active Directory to lease IP addresses to clients.

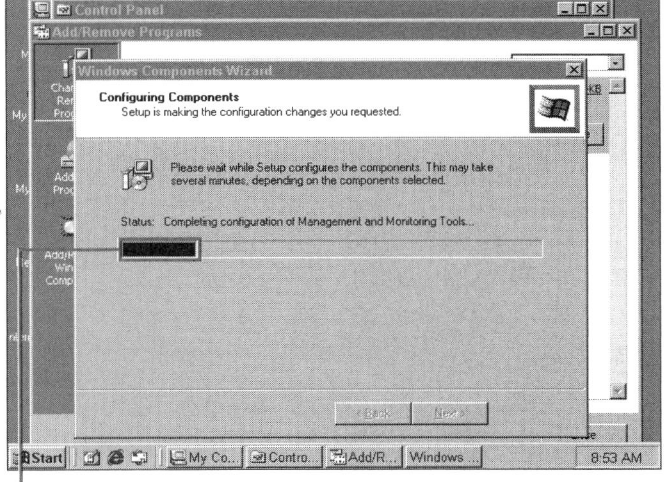

■ The system installs DHCP. The status bar indicates the level of completion.

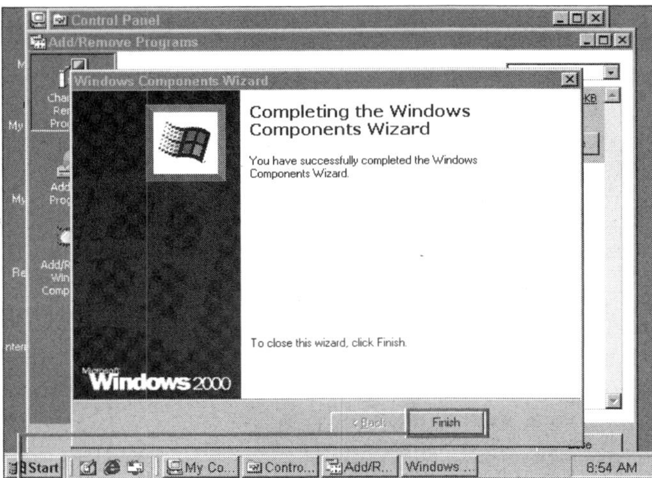

9 Click Finish to finish installing DHCP.

AUTHORIZING THE DHCP SERVER

The DHCP server does not become active when the installation is complete because it must be authorized first. Authorization occurs by adding the server to the authorized DHCP servers in the Active Directory. This authorization process prevents unauthorized, or *rogue*, DHCP servers from leasing IP addresses.

The Active Directory determines if the server can be authorized to participate on the network and lease IP addresses to clients. If you are installing DHCP on a domain controller, you may not have to authorize it manually, but you have to authorize member servers. To complete this action, you must be logged on with an account that is a member of the Enterprise Administrators group for the enterprise where you are adding the server. Authorization is a safety feature that enables you, as the administrator, to control the DHCP servers that function on your network.

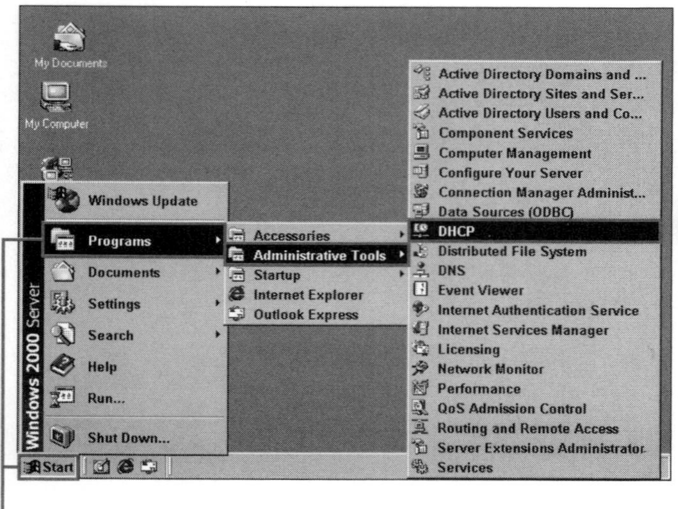

1 Click Start⇨Programs⇨Administrative Tools⇨DHCP.

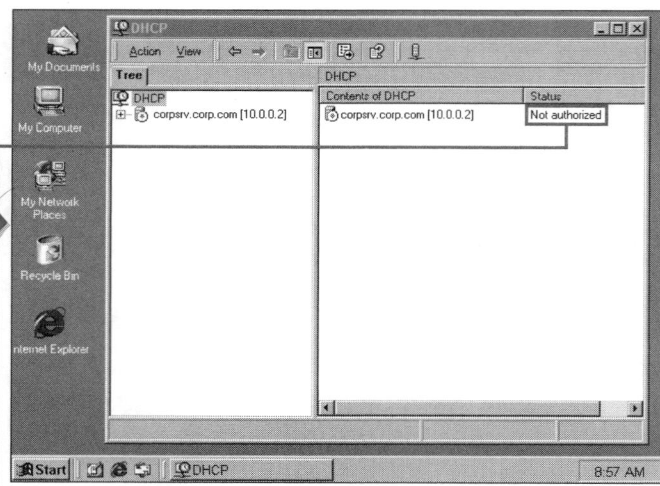

■ The MMC snap-in appears. Notice that the server is not yet authorized.

What is a rogue DHCP server?

A rogue DHCP server is one that is not authorized to lease IP addresses to clients. DHCP servers must be authorized by the Active Directory in order to prevent any server on the network from issuing IP addresses from invalid scopes. The authorization process prevents other users who have access to a server from installing the DHCP server and assigning inappropriate IP addresses to clients. This action may prevent those clients from gaining network connectivity. The Active Directory determines if the server is authorized to participate by checking both the server and the administrator's permissions.

What permission do I need to authorize a server?

Your user account must be a member of the Enterprise Administrators group in order to authorize a DHCP server in an Enterprise environment. This feature prevents a user or administrator who is not an Active Directory administrator from bringing a DHCP server online.

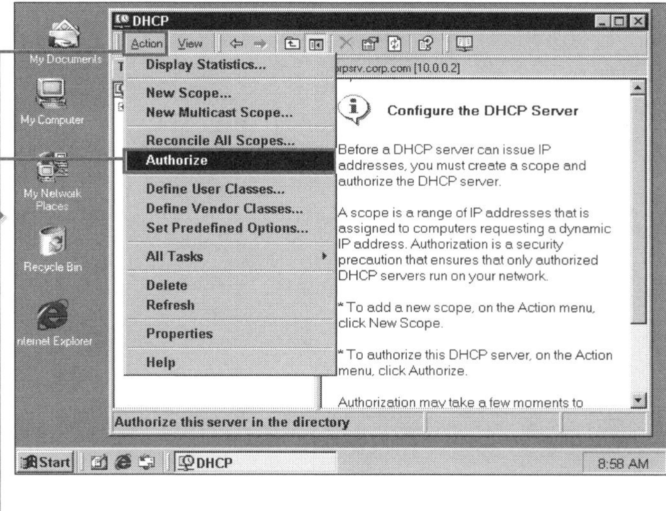

2 Choose Action➪Authorize.

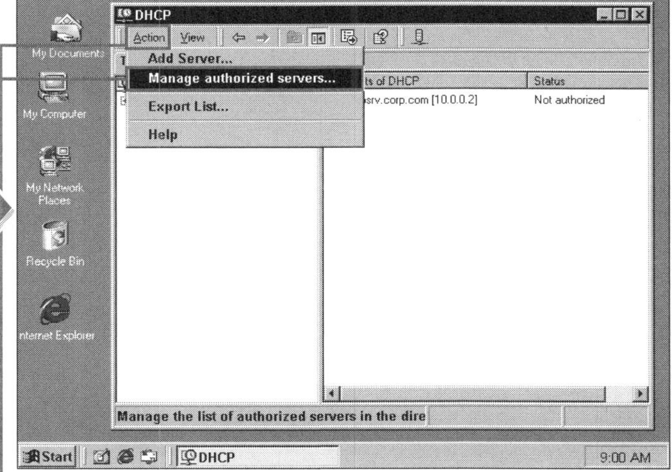

3 To authorize several servers, choose Action➪Manage Authorized Servers.

CONTINUED

AUTHORIZING THE DHCP SERVER

CONTINUED

If you select the server in the MMC snap-in and then use the Console menu, you can authorize that particular server. You can also use the snap-in to authorize (or unauthorize) other servers as well. This feature enables you to manage all DHCP servers from one location. This snap-in feature is particularly useful in environments where one person administers many DHCP servers. Instead of having to visit each machine, you can manage them all from one location after the initial installation is complete. From the single location, you can configure individual scopes, review performance, add new servers, and remove servers that you no longer want to function as DHCP servers.

In order to authorize the server, you need to know the server's IP address. All domain controllers should be configured with a static IP address and subnet mask that does not change.

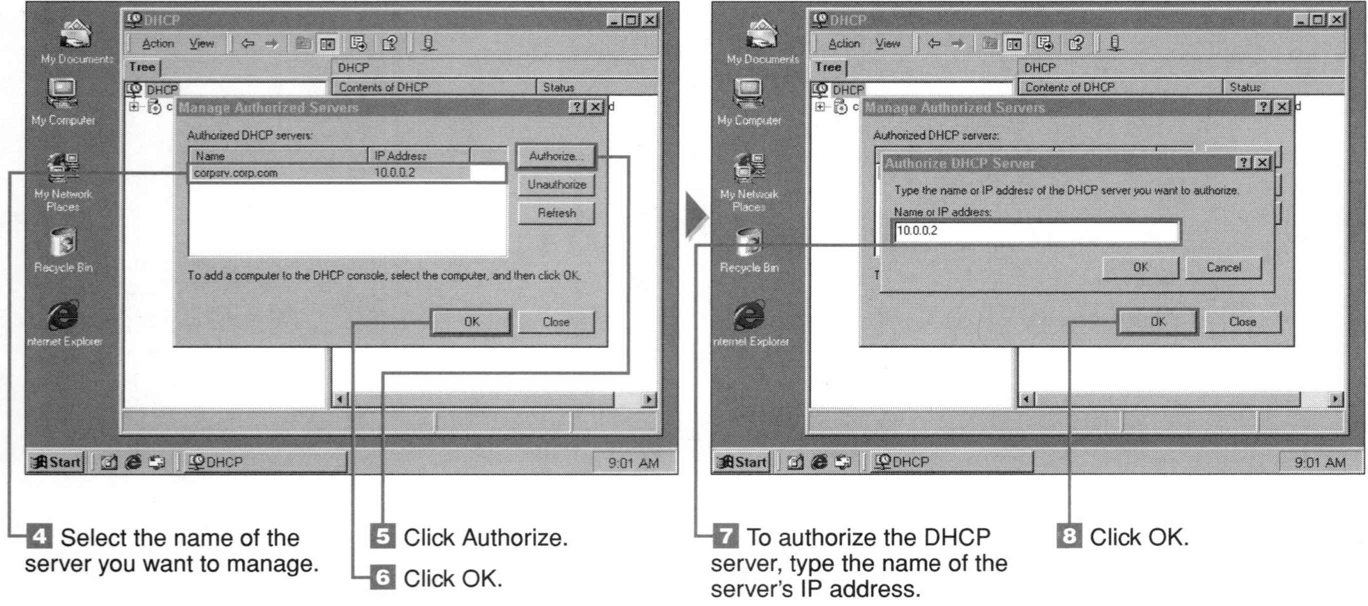

4 Select the name of the server you want to manage.

5 Click Authorize.

6 Click OK.

7 To authorize the DHCP server, type the name of the server's IP address.

8 Click OK.

Can DHCP assign IP addresses to other servers?

✔ All servers, whether they are DHCP servers or not, should be assigned a static IP address. You can enter the static IP address by accessing the TCP/IP Properties dialog box. You should not use DHCP to dynamically assign servers IP addresses.

Can Windows 9*x* computers receive a DHCP lease from a Windows 2000 DHCP server?

✔ Yes. You can use the TCP/IP Properties dialog box to configure Windows 9*x* computers to receive an IP address automatically. Windows 9*x* computers can receive this address and log on just as they could with Windows NT. To configure this feature, access the TCP/IP Properties dialog box for the computer. On that screen, you can either enter a manual IP address, subnet mask, and default gateway, or you can click the radio button that says, "Obtain an IP address automatically." Click this button to enable DHCP for the client. When the client logs on, it attempts to contact a DHCP server for an IP address.

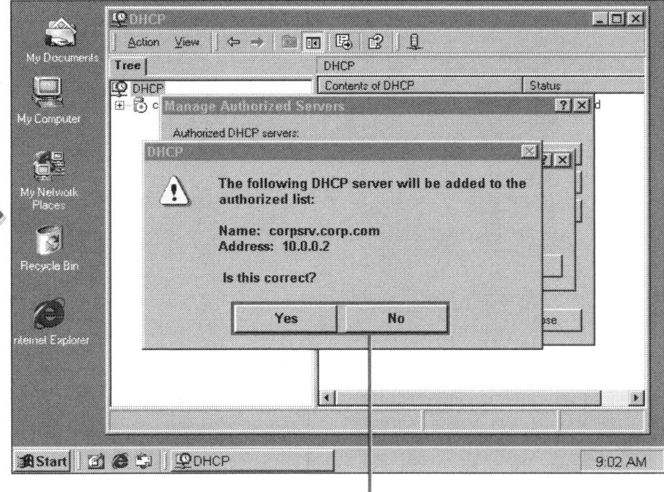

■ A notification appears with the name and IP address of the server.

9 Click the Yes button to authorize the DHCP Server or No to cancel.

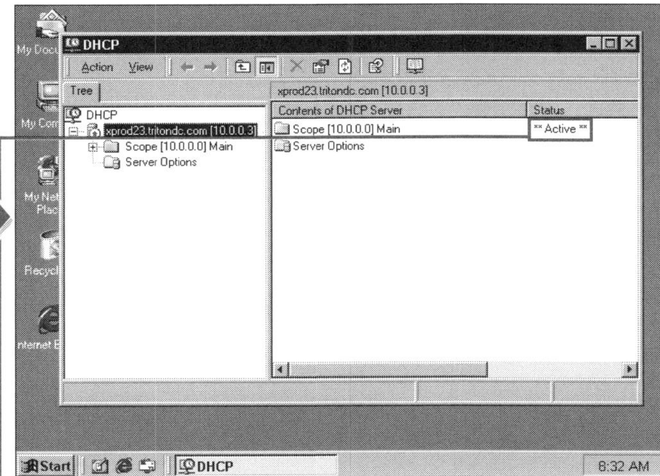

■ The server is now authorized and its status appears as Active.

CREATING SCOPES

A *scope* is the total group of IP addresses for a particular subnet. Before creating a scope, you need to know what the starting and ending IP addresses of the scope are. This action determines the number of IP addresses that are in the scope and which IP addresses can be leased to clients. You also need to know the subnet mask for the IP subnet. When the lease is made to the client, the client is provided with both an IP address and the correct subnet mask for the IP subnet. Each subnet must have only one scope.

The scope should contain all IP addresses that can be used in that subnet. This does not mean that all IP addresses within the scope must be available for lease. You can reserve address for other uses and create static mappings. The leftover addresses are then used for leasing purposes.

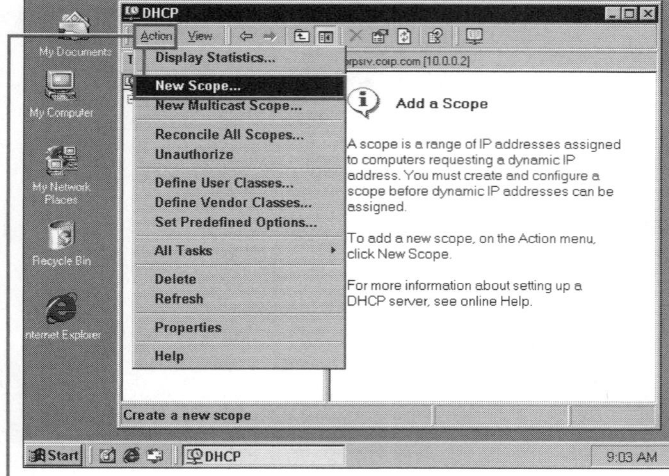

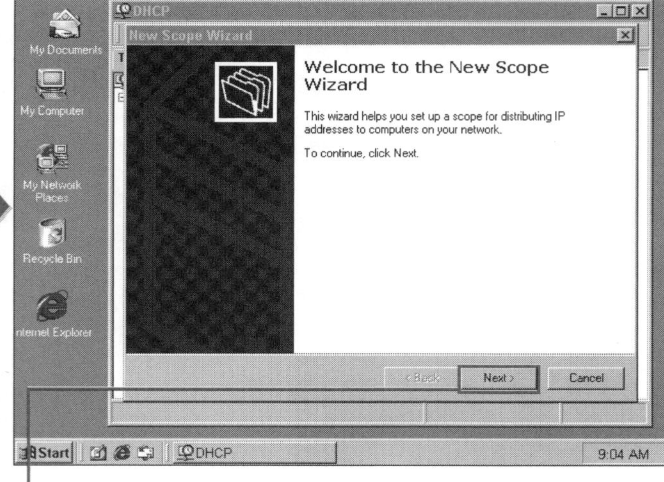

1 Select the server, and then choose Action⇨New Scope.

■ The New Scope Wizard appears.

2 Click Next to continue.

TIPS

How can I determine what IP addresses I should configure for the scope?

- You need to consult your network's configuration data to determine which IP addresses are available for the particular subnet where you are installing the DHCP server. Most TCP/IP networks use subnets to segment the network so that it is more manageable. Before implementing DHCP, make certain that you have planned your scope(s) so that they don't overlap with other DHCP servers.

Does a single scope apply to the entire network?

- No. A scope is configured for each individual subnet on the network. The server(s) then uses the addresses in the scope to lease IP addresses to clients on that subnet, with the exception of those addresses within the scope that have been reserved. Each subnet should have only one scope.

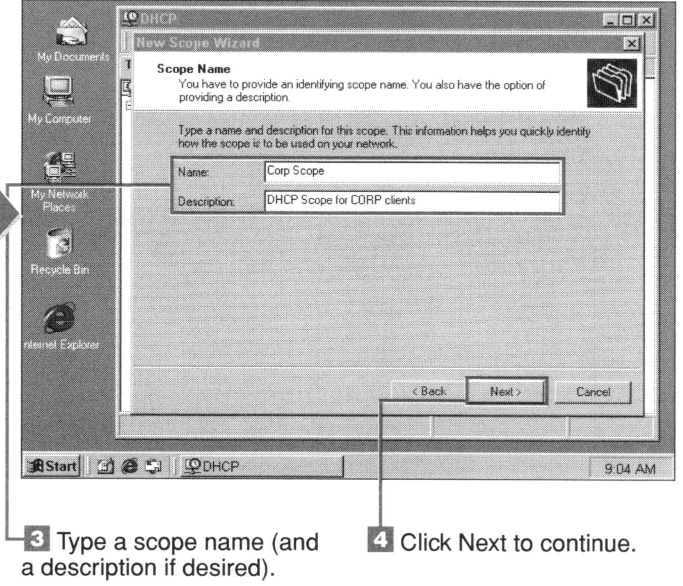

3 Type a scope name (and a description if desired).

4 Click Next to continue.

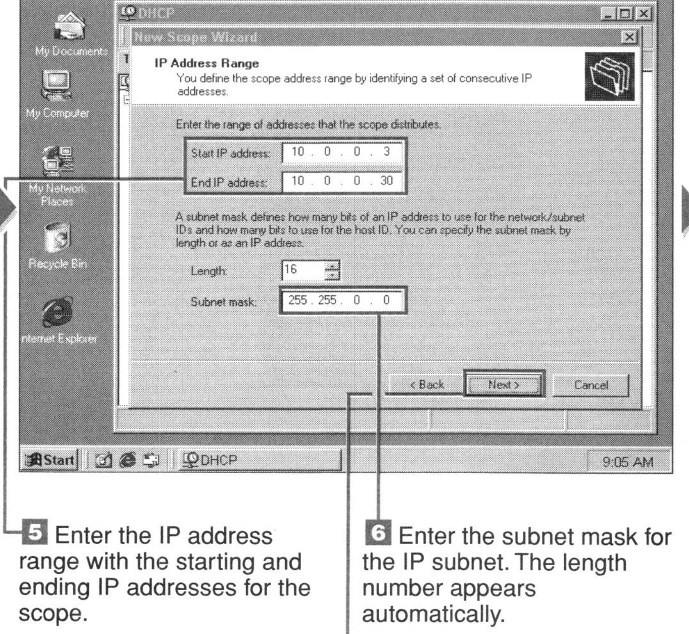

5 Enter the IP address range with the starting and ending IP addresses for the scope.

6 Enter the subnet mask for the IP subnet. The length number appears automatically.

7 Click Next to continue.

CONTINUED

CREATING SCOPES CONTINUED

An *exclusion range* is a range of IP addresses that exist in the scope but are not available for lease to clients. Exclusion ranges enable you to assign static IP addresses to servers using the excluded IP addresses. The excluded IP addresses still exist in the subnet scope, but they are never offered to clients for lease. You can then use these excluded addresses for static assignment. Exclusion ranges are particularly helpful because you can use DHCP to keep your static IP assignment organized. Because the complete IP address range is in the scope, the exclusion range allows you to use the scope as a means of assigning static addresses. This makes your job as an administrator easier and helps keep you organized.

During scope creation, you also have the option to configure other aspects of the scope. You can determine the default gateway (router) by entering the static IP address for it. This information is also sent to the DHCP clients so that they can access information on other subnets. The default gateway allows clients to communicate with other subnets by sending IP traffic to the appropriate subnet.

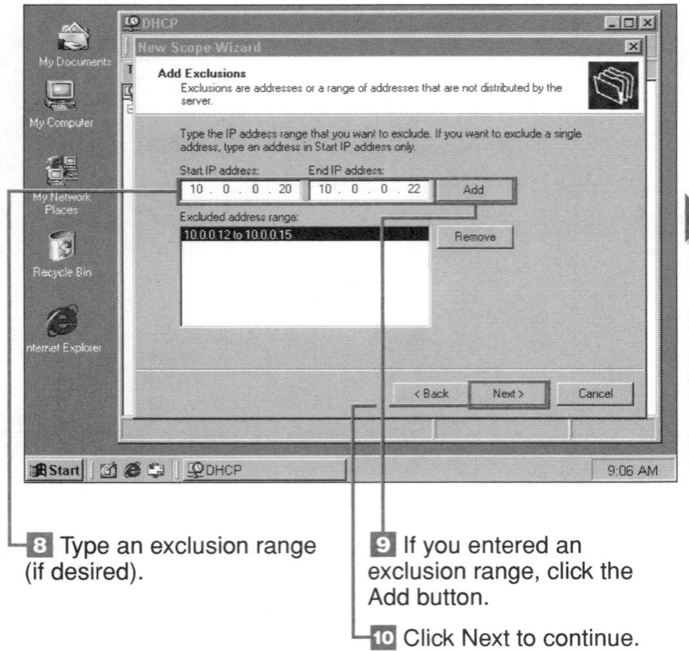

8 Type an exclusion range (if desired).

9 If you entered an exclusion range, click the Add button.

10 Click Next to continue.

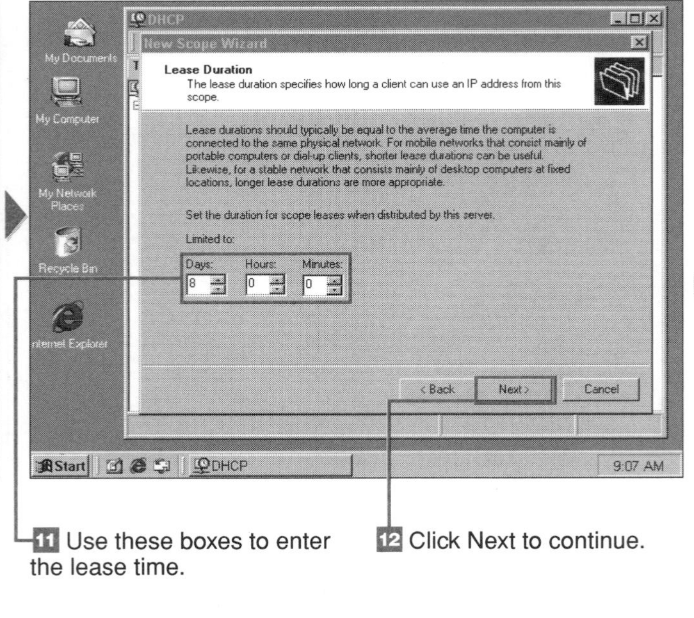

11 Use these boxes to enter the lease time.

12 Click Next to continue.

Can there be more than one gateway?

- Depending on your network configuration, you may have more than one gateway. You can think of the gateways as roads that lead out of the local subnet. The gateway allows communication to take place between different subnets. The gateway IP address refers to the router that can pass IP traffic onto another subnet. By providing the IP address of the gateway, clients can send packets bound for a different IP subnet directly to the gateway.

How many IP addresses can I include in the exclusion range?

- You can exclude as many IP addresses from the scope as desired by using the exclusion range. However, any excluded addresses are never available to clients for lease, so the general rule of thumb is to keep your exclusion range as small as possible.

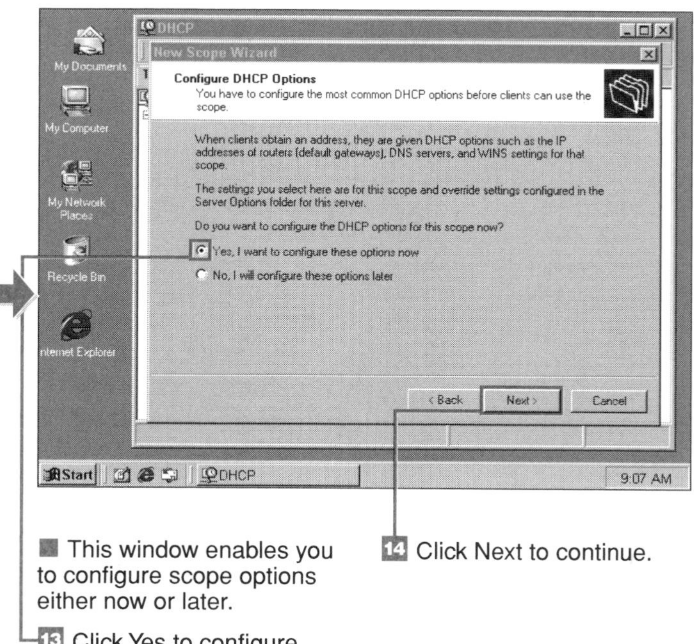

■ This window enables you to configure scope options either now or later.

13 Click Yes to configure now.

14 Click Next to continue.

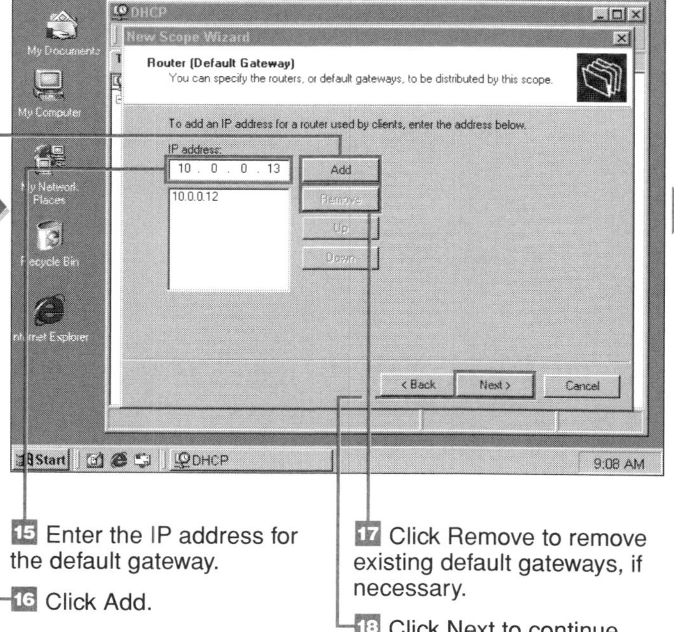

15 Enter the IP address for the default gateway.

16 Click Add.

17 Click Remove to remove existing default gateways, if necessary.

18 Click Next to continue.

CONTINUED

CREATING SCOPES CONTINUED

Along with the default gateway for the subnet, the DHCP server can also send IP address information for DNS and WINS servers. DNS resolves fully qualified domain names for the network while WINS resolves NetBIOS names. As with other IP address information, you can enter the DNS and WINS server addresses in the clients' TCP/IP Properties dialog boxes, but allowing the DHCP server to provide this information to the client is much easier.

After you complete the wizard, you are asked if you would like to activate the scope. You must activate the scope before it can be used and before IP addresses can be leased to network clients. You can choose not to activate the scope, but you must remember that a scope has to be activated before it can be used to lease IP addresses. If you want to further configure DHCP or other server components, you may choose not to activate the scope until you are finished with configuration.

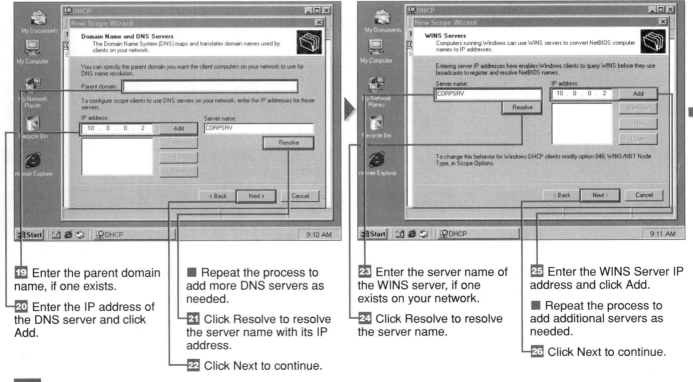

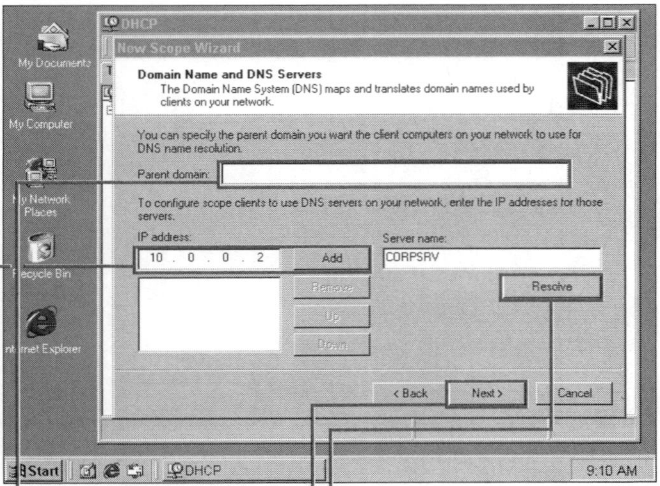

19 Enter the parent domain name, if one exists.

20 Enter the IP address of the DNS server and click Add.

■ Repeat the process to add more DNS servers as needed.

21 Click Resolve to resolve the server name with its IP address.

22 Click Next to continue.

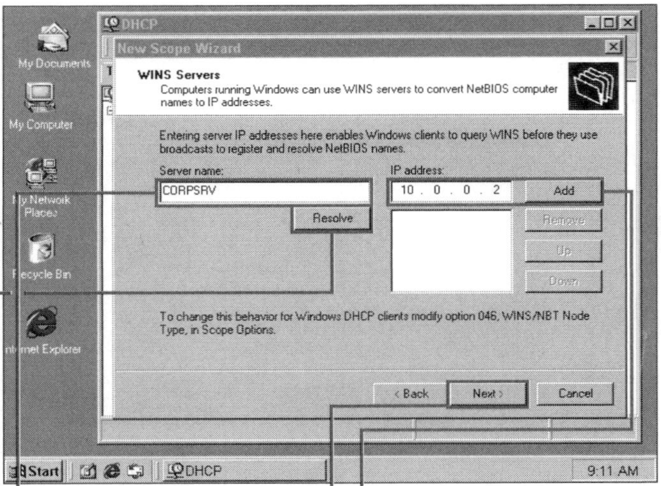

23 Enter the server name of the WINS server, if one exists on your network.

24 Click Resolve to resolve the server name.

25 Enter the WINS Server IP address and click Add.

■ Repeat the process to add additional servers as needed.

26 Click Next to continue.

What does DNS do?

✔ DNS (Domain Name System) resolves domain names to IP addresses. For example, the name server1.corp.com represents an IP address of server1 in the corp domain. DNS resolves server1.corp.com to an IP address, such as 10.0.0.2 so that communication can take place. You can learn more about DNS in Chapter 6.

What does WINS do?

✔ WINS (Windows Internet Naming Service) resolves NetBIOS names to IP address. This allows each computer to have a friendly name, such as Server1. WINS resolves the friendly name to its corresponding IP address so that communication on the network can take place. If you have a network with only Windows 2000 computers, you do not need WINS. See Chapter 5 to learn more about WINS.

Do I have to provide the IP addresses of the DNS and WINS servers?

✔ No. You are not required by DHCP to provide this information, but remember that the DNS and WINS IP-addressing information is returned to clients. Client computers can still discover the IP addresses of the DNS and WINS servers if they are not provided in a DHCP lease. This is accomplished through broadcast messages which increases your network traffic. The preferred method is to provide this information through DHCP.

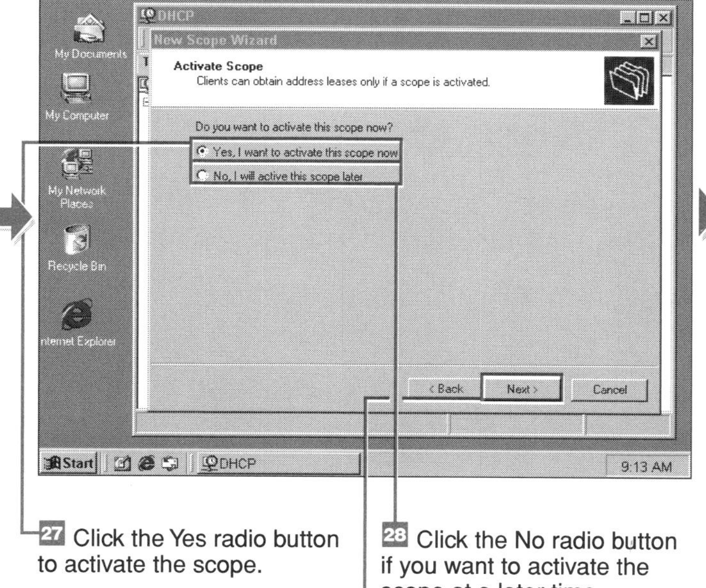

27 Click the Yes radio button to activate the scope.

28 Click the No radio button if you want to activate the scope at a later time.

29 Click Next to continue.

30 Click Finish to finish creating the scope.

CREATING SUPERSCOPES

As mentioned previously, a network subnet has one scope. However, you can use *superscopes* to group multiple scopes under one name. This allows you to extend the number of IP addresses you can use in a subnet by making several scopes appear as one. This solution is often used with multinets. A *multinet* is a single network segment where multiple, logical IP networks exist. This is an administrative solution to extend the network segment without creating additional subnets.

A superscope also enables you to support clients on the far side of the DHCP or BOOTP relay agent. As with any aspect of DHCP configuration, you should plan carefully before using superscopes to make certain that this organizational feature benefits the configuration of the subnet and the network in general. Although superscopes and multinets are effective, they should be planned carefully to avoid confusion and ensure communication interoperability.

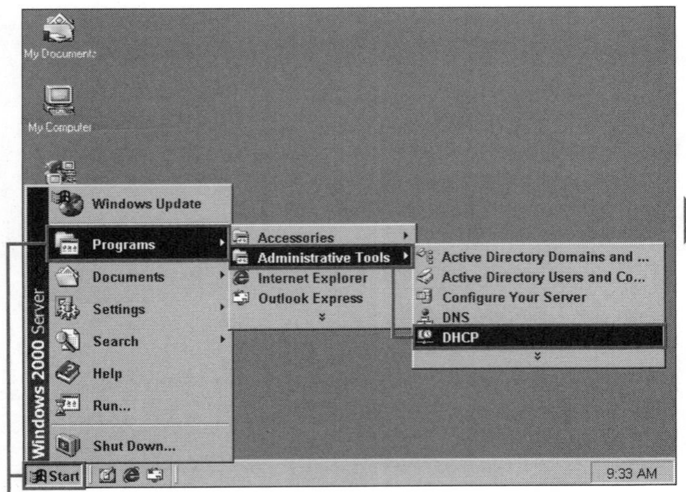

1 Click Start⇨Programs⇨Administrative Tools⇨DHCP.

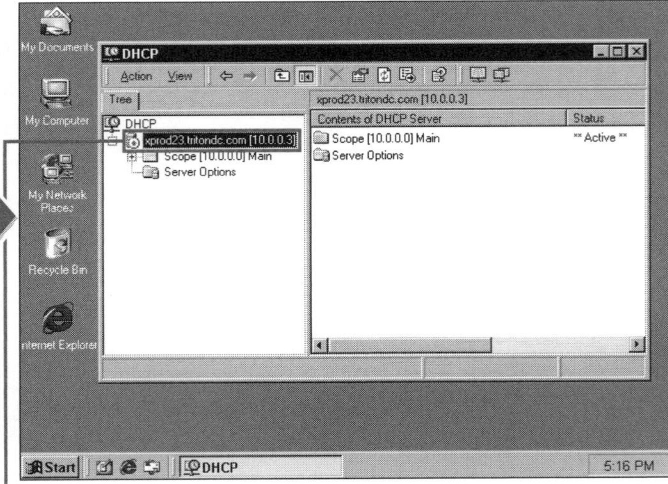

2 Select the server where you want to create a new superscope.

How many scopes are contained in a superscope?

Every superscope must contain at least one scope, but normally they contain two or more. No exact limit exists for the number of scopes a superscope can hold, but at some point, the superscope can become more problematic than helpful. The superscope is used to contain several scopes so they appear as one scope on your subnet, which is done for administrative purposes. You may find it helpful to think of a superscope as a large file folder that holds several smaller file folders. The large file folder does not have any functionality on its own, but is designed to contain the other file folders. A superscope is an organization solution to hold other scopes so that they appear as one. As with most implementations, superscopes require planning and careful thought to make certain that they benefit the design or needs of your subnet.

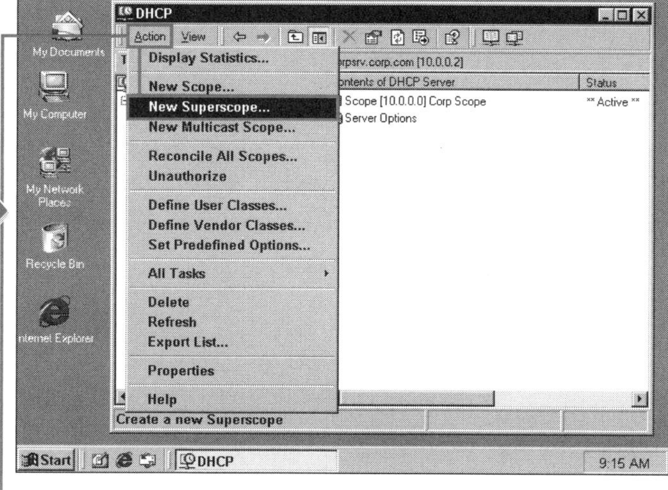

3 Choose Action⇨New Superscope.

■ The New Superscope Wizard appears.

4 Click Next to continue.

CONTINUED

CREATING SUPERSCOPES CONTINUED

You can use superscopes to solve several potential problems in multinet environments. The following list points out some of the major solutions superscopes can provide:

- When an address pool is nearly depleted because of growth and the full range of IP addresses for the subnet are nearly depleted, the superscope can solve this problem by providing a multinet approach. With this feature, you can expand the subnet "logically" through a multinet.
- You can use a superscope to slowly migrate client computers to a new scope that has been configured for the subnet.
- You can use a superscope so that two DHCP servers on the same physical network can manage separate logical IP networks.

The multinet and superscope solutions are effective solutions in environments where certain subnets or even networks need to be extended so that more IP addresses are available. Once again, careful planning is very important.

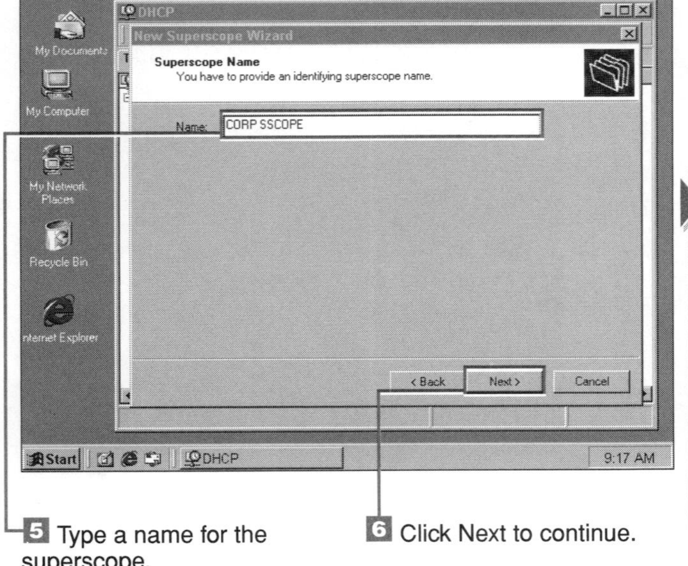

5 Type a name for the superscope.

6 Click Next to continue.

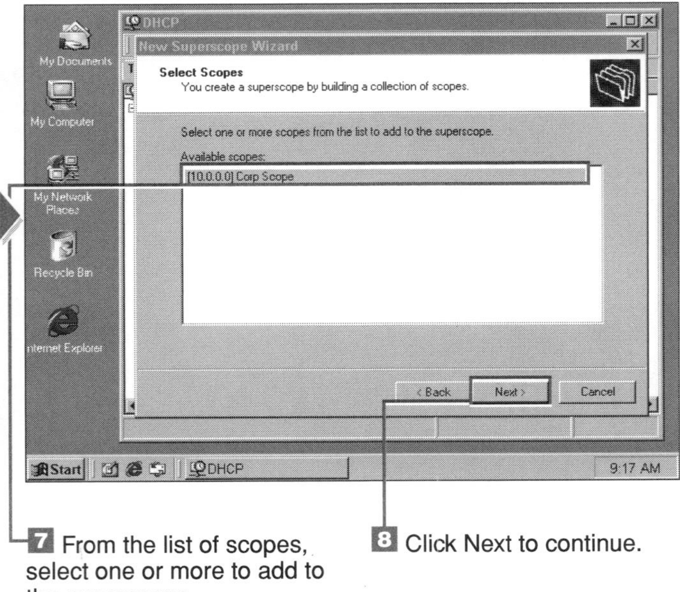

7 From the list of scopes, select one or more to add to the superscope.

8 Click Next to continue.

How can a superscope allow more than one scope on a subnet?

- The superscope makes several scopes appear as one scope. Because the scopes are grouped as one, DHCP can manage all scopes as one and ensure that duplicate IP addresses are not being leased. The superscope is a solution to use more than one scope on a particular subnet.

Why would you use a multinet?

- A *multinet* is an organizational solution that enables you to group a collection of computers together within a subnet or network so that the computers appear as if they are on a separate segment. This lets you organize the network segment into several logical IP networks without having to further subnet the segment. You can use multinets as a method of extending the subnet or breaking down the organization so that you can more easily manage it. You should plan carefully before implementing superscopes or multinets.

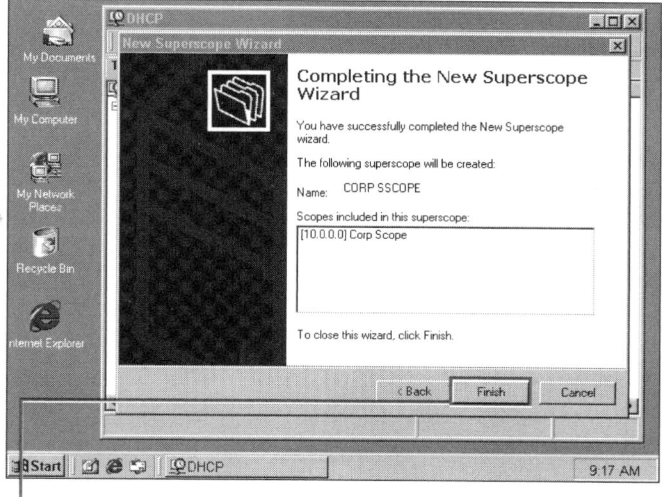

9 Click Finish to complete the wizard.

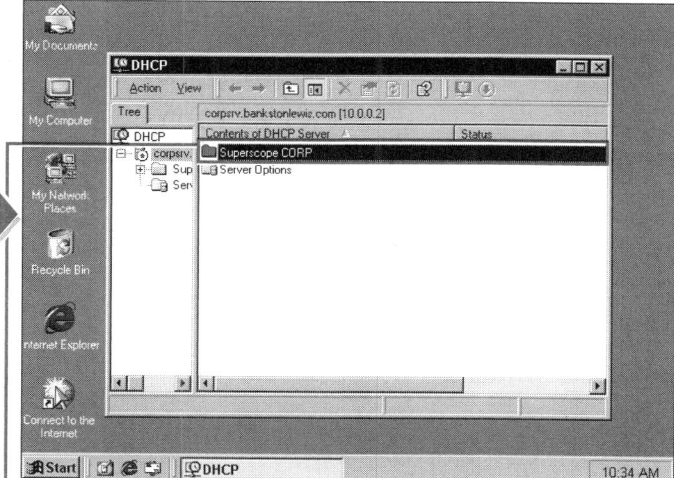

■ The new superscope now appears in the console.

CREATING MULTICAST SCOPES

Multicasting is the process of sending messages to multiple clients. In much the same way that you can send a single e-mail to several people, multicasting allows a group of network clients to appear as one client. This is accomplished using multicast addresses, which are Class D addresses (224.0.0.0 to 239.255.255.255). The entire Class D is reserved for multicasting and can be used on your network without IP address conflicts.

Multicast DHCP (MDHCP) is an extension of the typical DHCP services. MDHCP and DHCP work together but are considered separate services. Clients that participate in multicasting, however, must have a normal, leased IP address from the DHCP server. In other words, a client cannot be an MDHCP client and not a DHCP client. The multicasting functionality must work within the normal DHCP configuration. As you consider and plan a multicast implementation, this is important information to keep in mind.

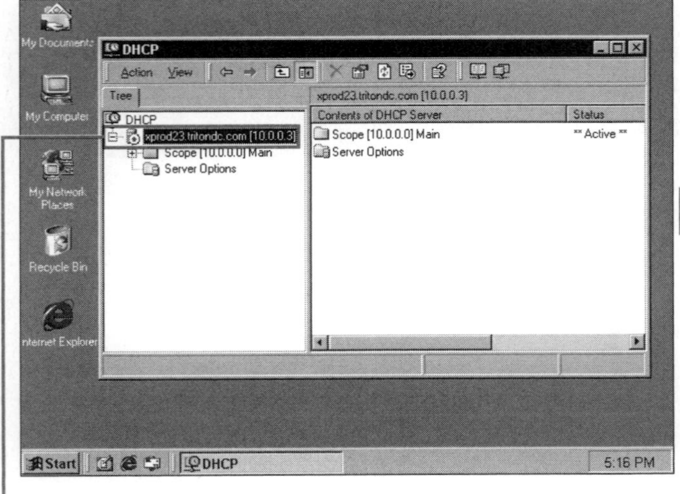

1 Select the desired server.

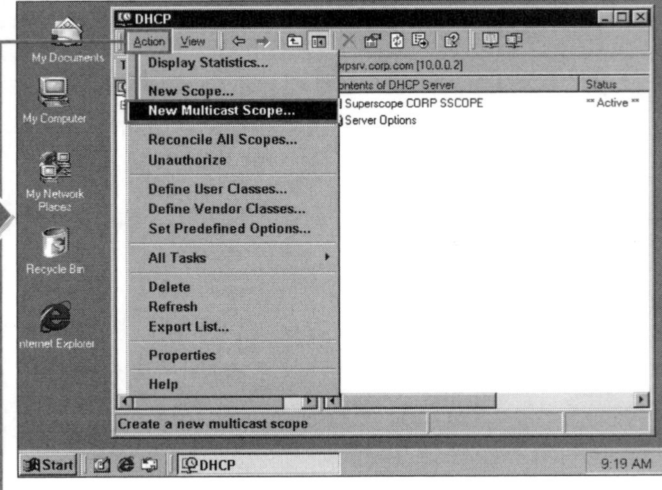

2 Choose Action⇨New Multicast Scope.

What is a Class D address?

IP address are defined by class. Class A, B, and C are typical IP address classes that you can use for network and Internet communication. Class D is a class created and reserved for multicasting. Class D is defined by the address range of 224.0.0.0 through 239.255.255.255. Multicast clients must be assigned an IP address that falls within that range.

Can computers be both DHCP and MDHCP clients?

Yes. Typical DHCP clients receive a DHCP lease, but clients that you want to include in the multicast group also receive an IP address for multicasting purposes. The two IP addresses are not interrelated and do not interfere with each other. In order for multicasting to work, the multicast client must also be a DHCP client. In this case, the client receives both a typical network IP address for normal communications and a multicast IP address for multicast communication.

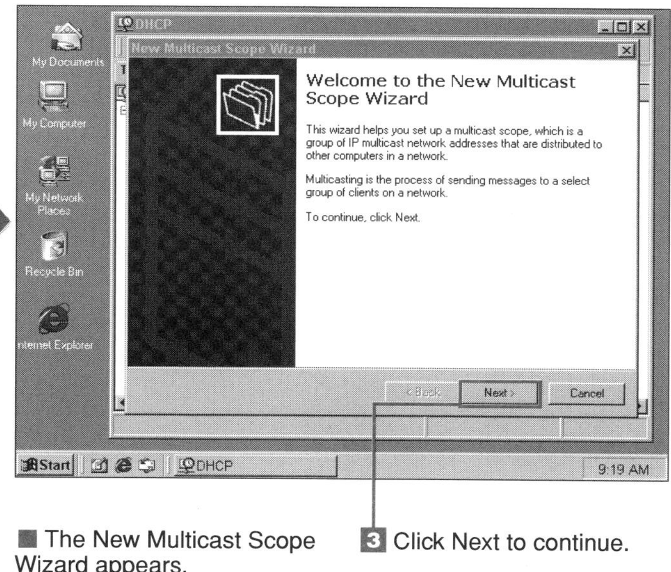

■ The New Multicast Scope Wizard appears.

3 Click Next to continue.

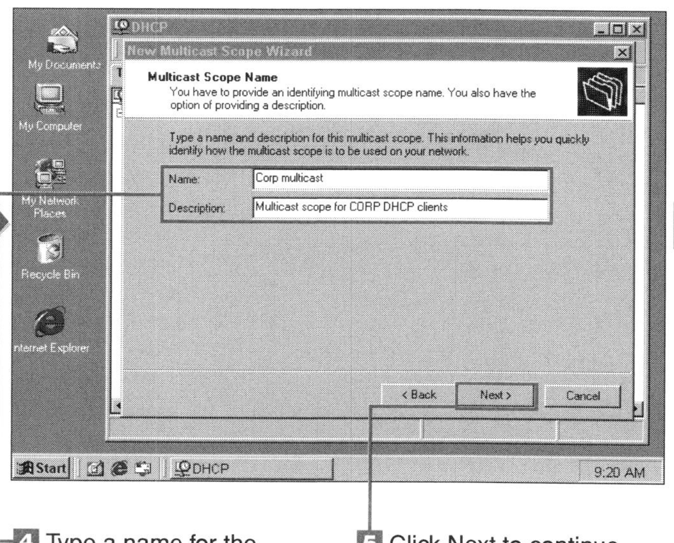

4 Type a name for the multicast scope(and a description if desired).

5 Click Next to continue.

CONTINUED

CREATING MULTICAST SCOPES
CONTINUED

As with a typical DHCP scope, you can set an exclusion range for the scope. The exclusion range enables you to assign static multicast IP addresses to certain clients that you choose. In some situations, you may choose for certain computers or hardware to receive a static multicast address. This is particularly useful for network clients that also receive a static DHCP IP address. The exclusion range, however, must leave enough multicast IP addresses available in the scope to lease to all the clients desired.

As with a standard DHCP lease, you can adjust the lease time. The default lease time for multicast addresses is for 30 days. Because multicasting is a feature of typical IP address leasing for network communication, the lease time is longer, and this default configuration is best under most circumstances.

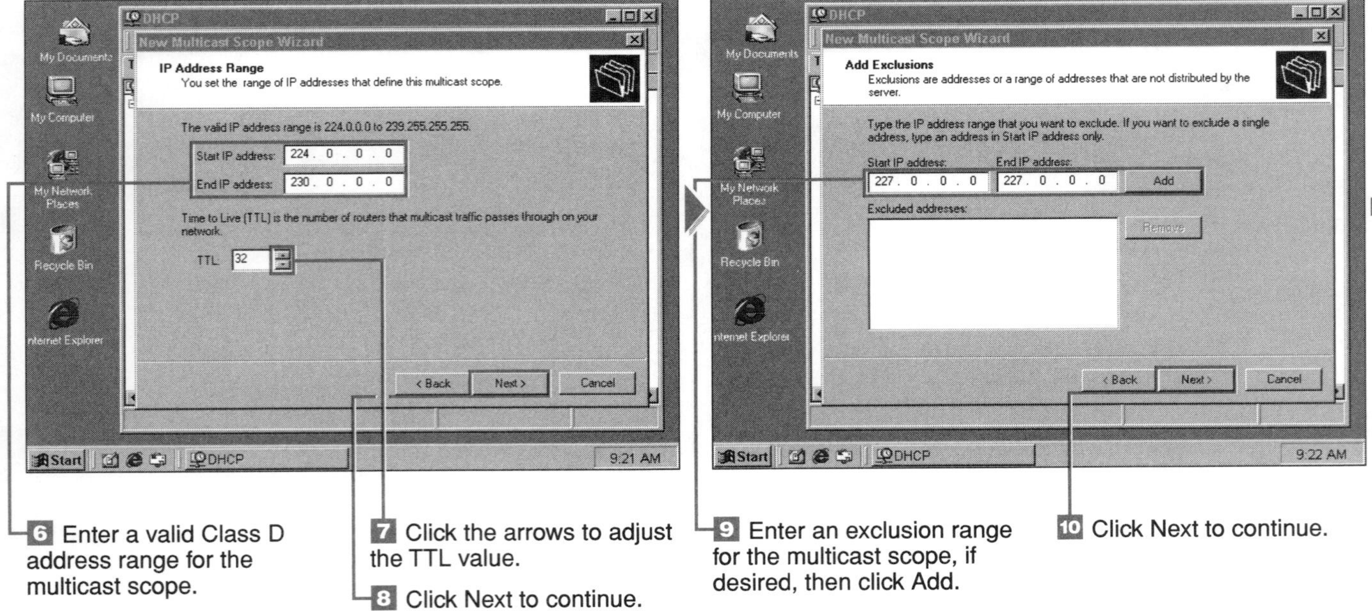

6 Enter a valid Class D address range for the multicast scope.

■ You can change the TTL if needed. The default is 32.

7 Click the arrows to adjust the TTL value.

8 Click Next to continue.

9 Enter an exclusion range for the multicast scope, if desired, then click Add.

10 Click Next to continue.

TIPS

Should I make the lease time shorter?

You can define any multicast lease time that you would like. However, unless you have a specific reason for changing the default, the 30 lease is sufficient. Due to the nature of multicasting, you do not need shorter lease times for security purposes, and as long as you have multicast IP addresses available in the pool, you should not need a shorter lease time.

Why can't I just assign a static multicast address to all my multicast clients.

You could assign a static multicast address to your multicast clients so that all clients have a static address. However, this manual configuration requires a lot of planning and implementation time on your part because you have to manually assign a multicast address to each client. Also, there is a great chance of errors or duplicate addresses that are difficult to track down. MDHCP is designed to remove this administrative burden from you, so letting MDHCP manage the multicast leases is best.

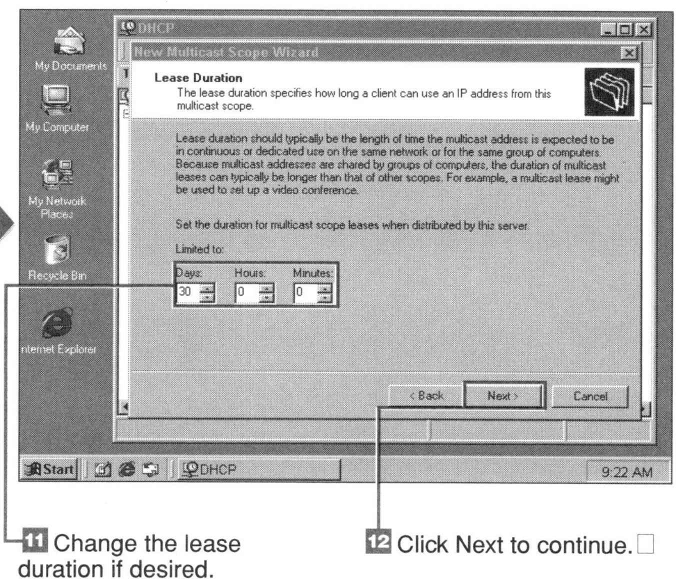

11 Change the lease duration if desired.

■ The default is 30 days.

12 Click Next to continue.

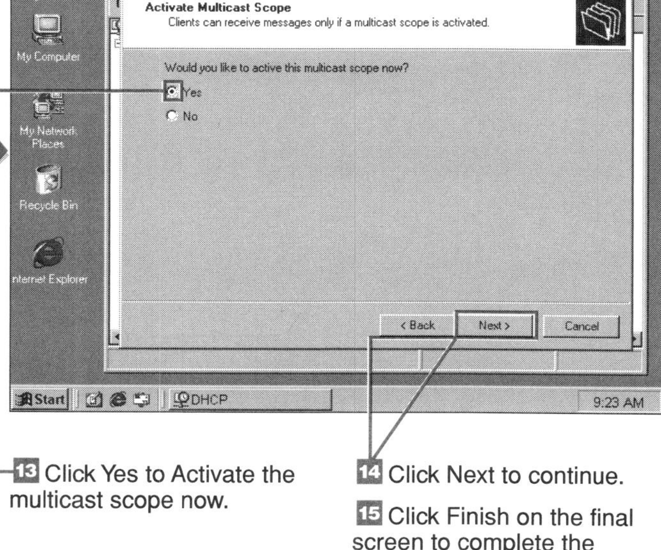

13 Click Yes to Activate the multicast scope now.

14 Click Next to continue.

15 Click Finish on the final screen to complete the wizard.

MANAGING SCOPES

Several options within the MMC console's Action menu can help you manage scopes.

First, you can reconcile the scopes. If you suspect that there are missing IP addresses within the scope that should be available, you can run the Reconcile command. This action checks the database for consistency. If discrepancies exist, a dialog box appears listing the discrepancies; if no discrepancies exist, a message box tells you that the scope is consistent.

You can also use the Action menu to deactivate a scope. When you deactivate a scope, the DHCP server can no longer use that scope to lease IP addresses to client computers. You could use the deactivation for a number of purposes, especially if you have designed a new scope that you want to implement. Remember that a subnet can only contain one DHCP scope.

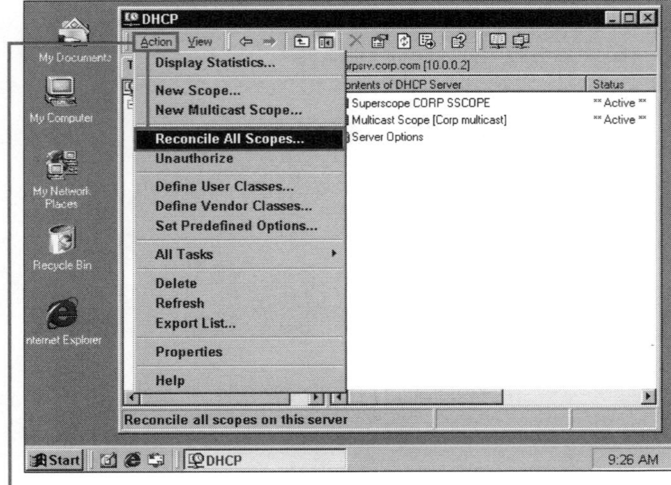

RECONCILING A SCOPE

1 Select the scope you want to manage in the console, and then choose Action⇨Reconcile All Scopes to check for inconsistencies.

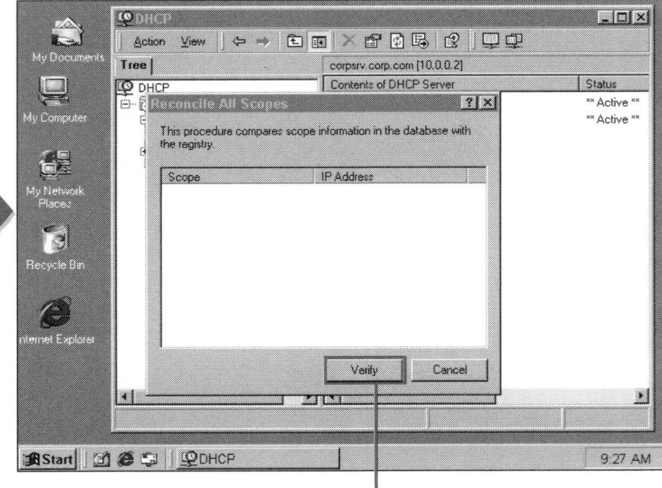

■ The Reconcile All Scopes dialog box appears.

2 Click Verify to continue.

TIPS

When should I run the Reconcile option?

- You can run the Reconcile scope option anytime you think problems with the DHCP scope may exist. If clients are having communication problems or are not receiving IP addresses from the server, you should reconcile the scope to look for any problems. Also, you may choose to reconcile the scope on a regular basis as a preventive tool in case problems are developing in the DHCP database.

Would overlapping scopes create problems?

- Yes. When planning your network scopes, it is important that scopes do not overlap with each other. Overlapping scopes would allow DHCP servers to lease duplicate IP addresses on different network segments. Depending on your network configuration, scopes could overlap if the subnet mask that applies to the scopes is different. As with most implementations, planning is of key importance.

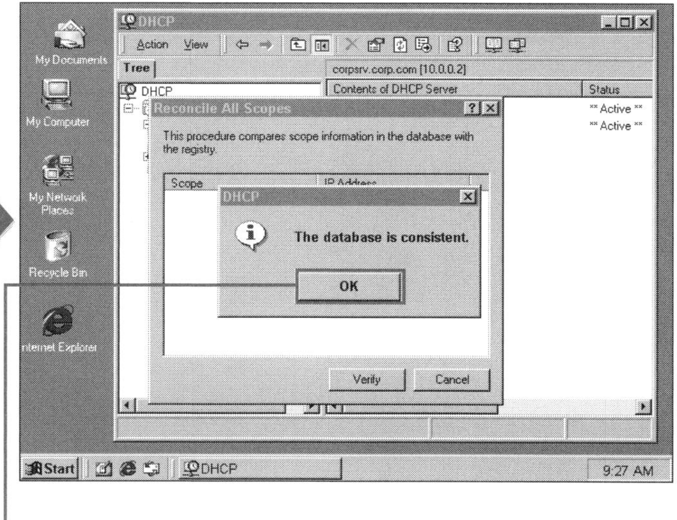

3 Click OK

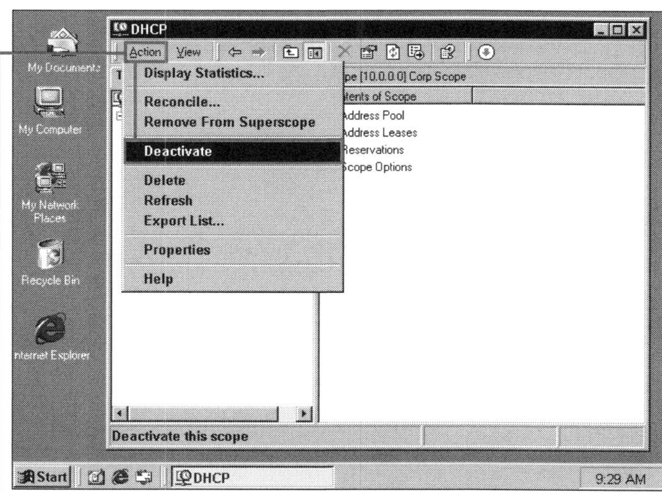

DEACTIVATING A SCOPE

1 To deactivate a scope, select the scope in the console and choose Action⇨Deactivate.

CONTINUED

MANAGING SCOPES CONTINUED

If you deactivate a scope, the scope still exists and remains configured, but it is not active in the Active Directory and cannot be used for leasing. You can reactivate the scope after you deactivate it.

You can also choose to delete a scope that you no longer need. If the scope is a part of a superscope, you receive a message telling you that the scope will also be removed from the superscope. If the scope is the only scope left in the superscope, you receive a message telling you that the superscope will be deleted as well. Remember that a superscope is an organizational method that typically contains several scopes. A superscope cannot exist without child scopes, and so if you remove the last scope within the superscope, you must delete the superscope also.

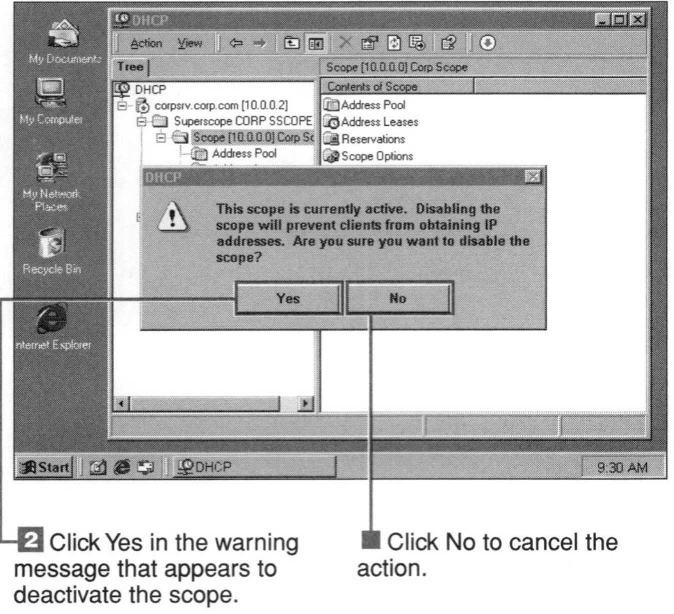

2 Click Yes in the warning message that appears to deactivate the scope.

■ Click No to cancel the action.

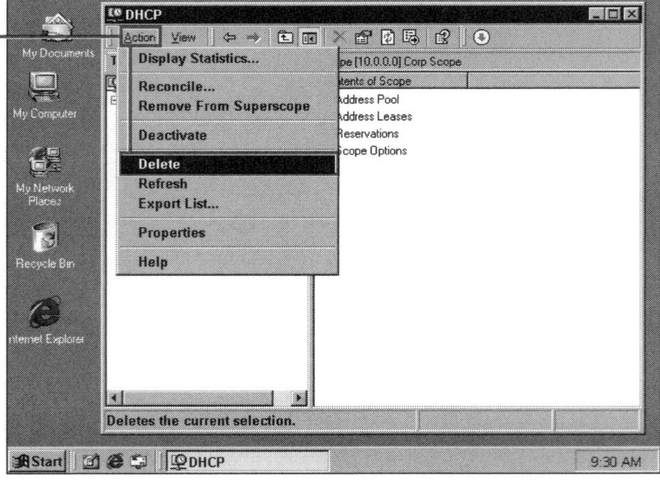

DELETING A SCOPE

1 Select the scope you want to delete in the console tree, and then choose Action⇨Delete.

Why would I want to deactivate a scope?

- The Deactivate command enables you to stop using a particular scope without deleting it. You may want to deactivate a scope for a number of reasons. First, you could deactivate the scope for troubleshooting purposes. In this case, the scope still exists, and you do not have to reconfigure the scope when you want to bring it online again. Also, you may choose to begin using a new scope, so you deactivate the old one. Deactivating the scope enables you to keep it in case you decide to use it again, or you can keep it until you are certain that you want to delete it.

Can't I keep a superscope without any child scopes configured for later use?

- No. Think of the superscope as a container. Without anything in the container, the superscope cannot function. The DHCP Manager does not allow you configure or keep a superscope that does not have at least one child scope.

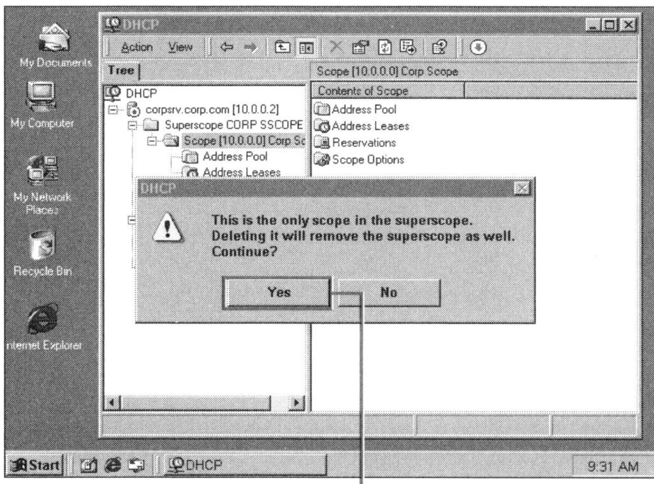

■ A warning message appears if this is the only scope in the superscope.

2 Click Yes to continue the delete.

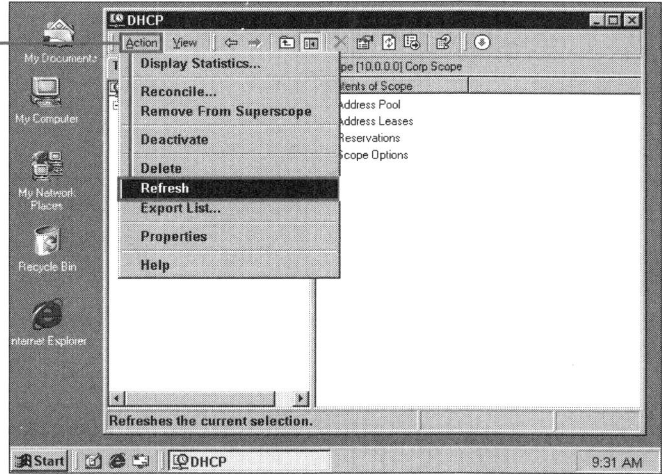

REFRESHING A SCOPE

■ You can refresh any scope by selecting it in the console tree.

1 Choose Action⇨Refresh.

CONFIGURING SCOPE PROPERTIES

You can access the Properties dialog boxes of each scope to further configure it. The Properties dialog box for a standard DHCP scope contain three tabs.

On the General tab, you can change the scope range by changing the starting and ending IP addresses, and you can also enter a new lease time value. These features make it easy for you to change the scope without having to create a new one.

On the DNS tab, you can determine if you want DHCP to dynamically update client name to IP address mappings in the DNS. These options are enabled by default when Active Directory is in use, and you should allow the default settings to remain for optimal performance. You can learn more about the functionality of Dynamic DNS in Chapter 6.

The Advanced tab enables you to also assign IP addresses to BOOTP clients, if they exist on your network. If you choose to allow the DHCP server to lease IP addresses to BOOTP clients, then you need to configure a lease expiration time for the BOOTP clients as well.

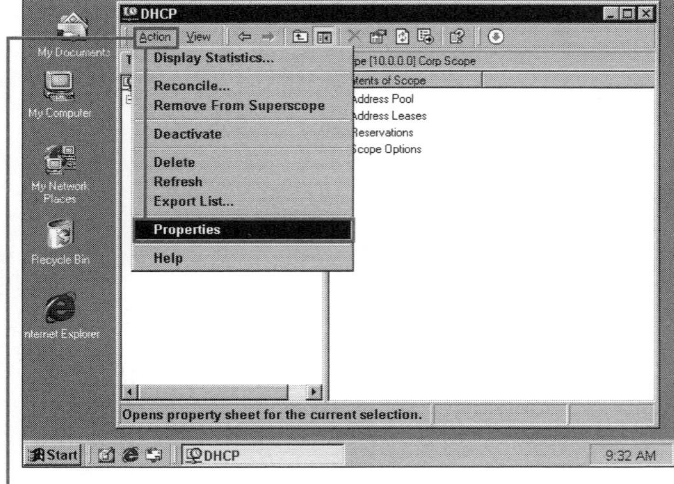

1 Select the scope in the console tree, and then choose Action⇨Properties.

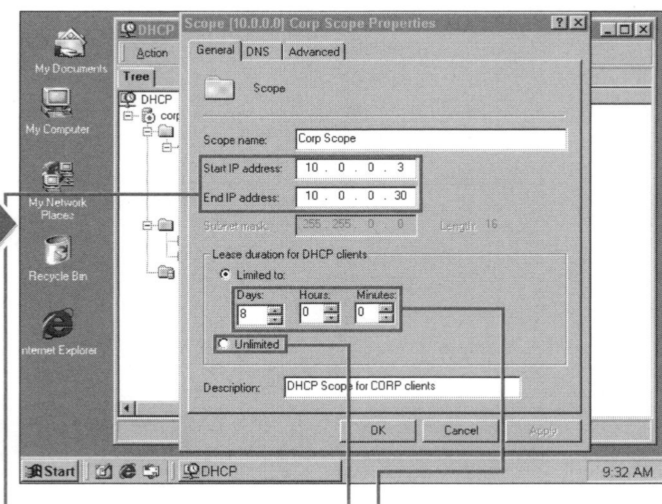

2 Use the General tab to reconfigure the scope by changing the starting and ending IP addresses as needed.

3 You can change the lease duration by entering a new value for the lease.

4 Or, you can click the Unlimited button to allow no time limit for the lease.

Should I allow unlimited lease time?

- You can allow DHCP clients to keep their IP addresses for an unlimited amount of time by selecting the option on the General tab. In large networks, this is usually not a good idea. This option allows the client to keep an IP address, even if the client is no longer on a particular subnet. As a result, a number of IP addresses cannot be leased to other clients because they are "locked up" by nonexistent clients on the network. In small environments, where the number of IP addresses available to lease is not an issue, the Unlimited option works fine.

What is a BOOTP client?

- A BOOTP client is a diskless workstation that receives operating system information from the server. DHCP originated from BOOTP. If you are using BOOTP clients on the network, you can use DHCP to dynamically assign the BOOTP clients an IP address, just as you would a normal network client.

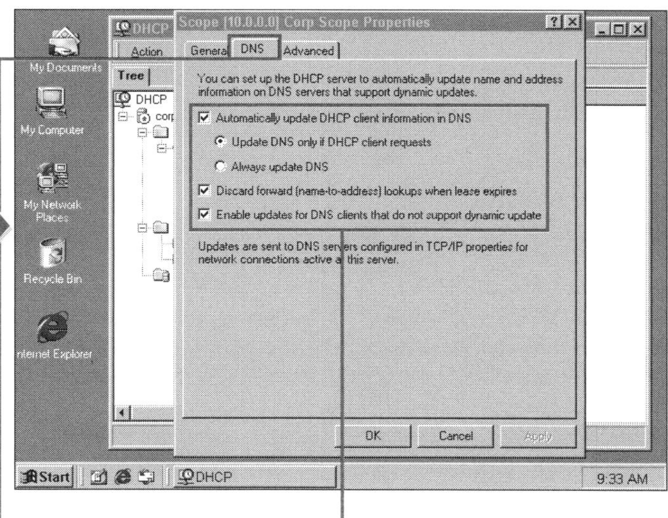

5 Click the DNS tab.

■ This tab enables you to automatically update client lease information in DNS.

6 Click the appropriate check boxes to enable the features you want.

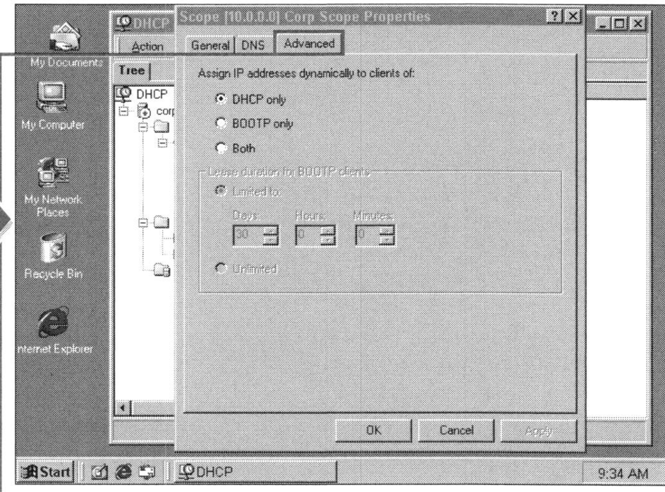

■ On the Advanced tab, you can choose which clients you would like to assign IP addresses to. You can click either DHCP, BOOTP, or both. If you use BOOTP clients on your network, enter an IP address lease time as well.

ADDITIONAL SCOPE CONFIGURATION

You can expand any scope you want to administer to see the Address Pool, Address Leases, Reservations, and Scope Options containers. These containers enable you to easily view the current IP addresses that have been leased to clients, the reservations within the scope that are made, and the IP addresses that are available for lease.

If you select the Address Pool container, the starting and ending IP addresses for the pool appear in the right console pane. You can use the Action menu to add a new exclusion range for the scope if desired.

If you select the Address Leases container, the clients and IP addresses lease appear in the right console pane so that you can see which client has been issued which IP address.

If you select the Reservations container, you can see the reservations that exist, and you can use the Action menu to create new reservations.

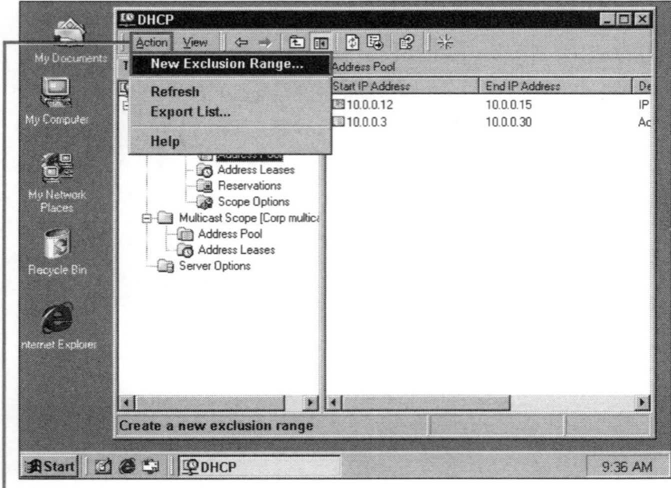

1 To expand the scope you want to administer, select Address Pool, and choose Action⇨New Exclusion Range.

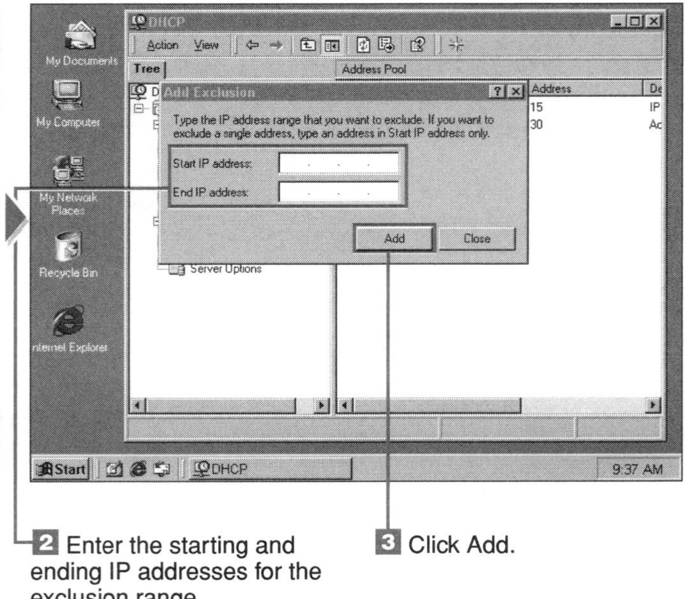

2 Enter the starting and ending IP addresses for the exclusion range.

3 Click Add.

Why would I want to add or change the exclusion range?

- Because networks are not static entities, you need to change some of your scope options from time to time. You may need to add or change exclusion ranges based on the number of IP addresses you need to exclude from the leasing process. This gives you a pool of IP addresses that you can statically assign to servers or other hardware that need static addresses.

What does a reservation do?

- A reservation sets aside an IP address that would normally be leased to a particular client. This ensures that the client always receives the same IP address. To configure the reservation, you need the client's name and MAC address, as well as the IP address that you want to reserve. After you complete the reservation, that client always has the same IP address.

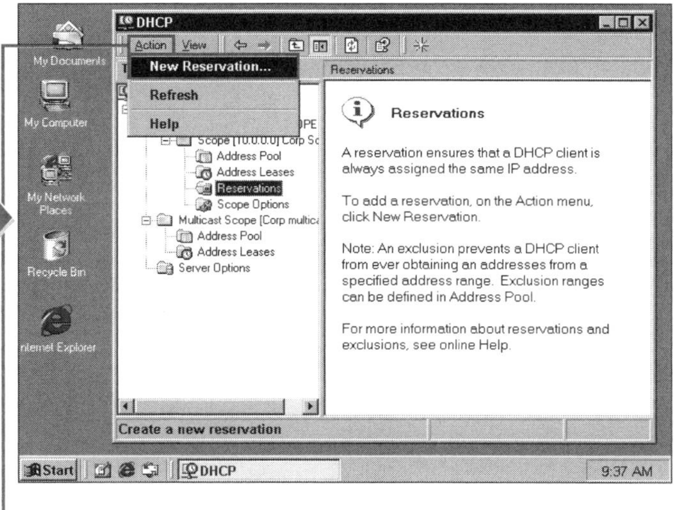

4 Select the Reservations container, and then choose Action⇨New Reservation.

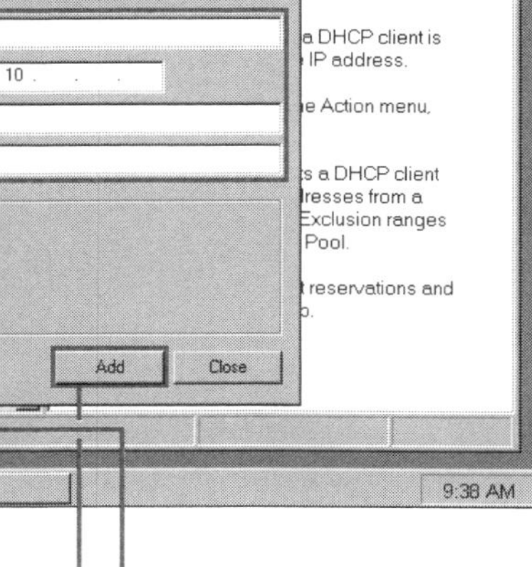

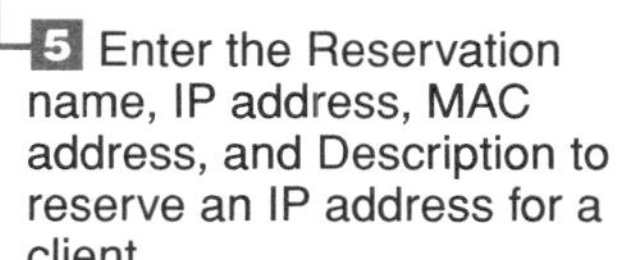

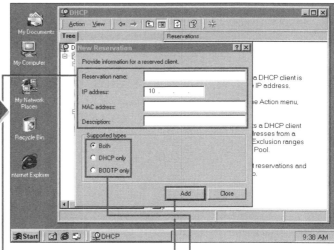

5 Enter the Reservation name, IP address, MAC address, and Description to reserve an IP address for a client.

6 Click the appropriate radio button for the reservation for either DHCP, BOOTP, or both.

7 Click Add.

CONTINUED

ADDITIONAL SCOPE CONFIGURATION
CONTINUED

You can define additional scope options by selecting the Scope Options container and choosing Action⇨Configure Options.

As in Windows NT, DHCP in Windows 2000 enables you to configure a number of additional options, depending on the services installed on your network. You can use the options to have DHCP return additional information to clients for particular servers. For example, if you are using Log Servers, Cookie Servers, other Name Servers, and so forth, DHCP can return this information to the clients along with their IP addresses.

You can also select different kinds of vendor and user classes to configure additional DHCP options. You can configure DHCP Standard Options, Microsoft Options, Microsoft Windows 2000 Options, or Microsoft Windows 98 Options, as well as user classes, such as the Default User class, Dynamic BOOTP class, or RRAS class.

The standard options are configured by default, so make certain that you have specific reasons for making changes to the DHCP options and that you are certain the changes will benefit your network clients.

8 Select the Scope Options container and choose Action⇨Configure Options.

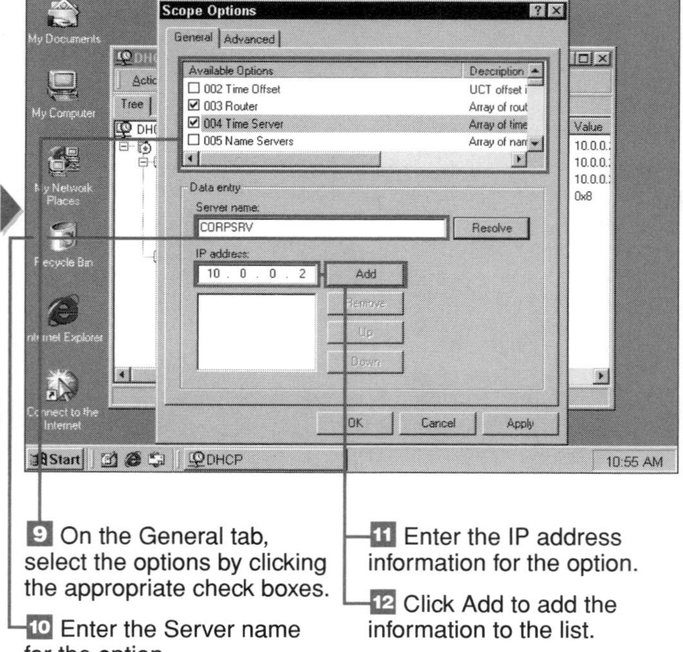

9 On the General tab, select the options by clicking the appropriate check boxes.

10 Enter the Server name for the option.

11 Enter the IP address information for the option.

12 Click Add to add the information to the list.

I want the IP address information for a finger server returned to clients. Can I configure this in DHCP?

- Yes. A *finger* server retrieves information about a user on a computer running the finger service. In environments where the finger service is used, you can have the IP address of the finger server returned to client computers with their IP address lease. You can select the option on the General tab and enter the server's name and IP address. When clients are assigned an IP address, the finger server's IP address is returned to the client as well.

Do I need to configure any of these options if I use simple DHCP services?

- No. The standard options are configured by default, so you do not need to make option changes unless you have specific needs. Microsoft has taken great care to ensure that the default options are configured automatically and are all that are needed for most DHCP implementations. You should plan carefully before changing these default options.

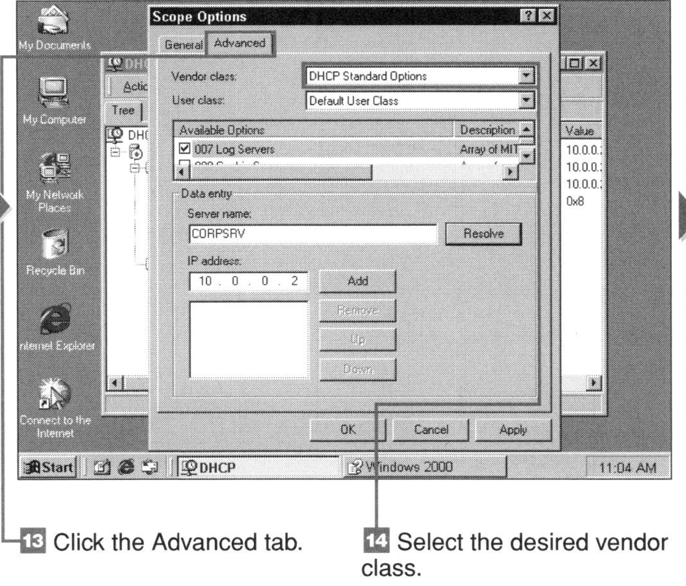

13 Click the Advanced tab.

14 Select the desired vendor class.

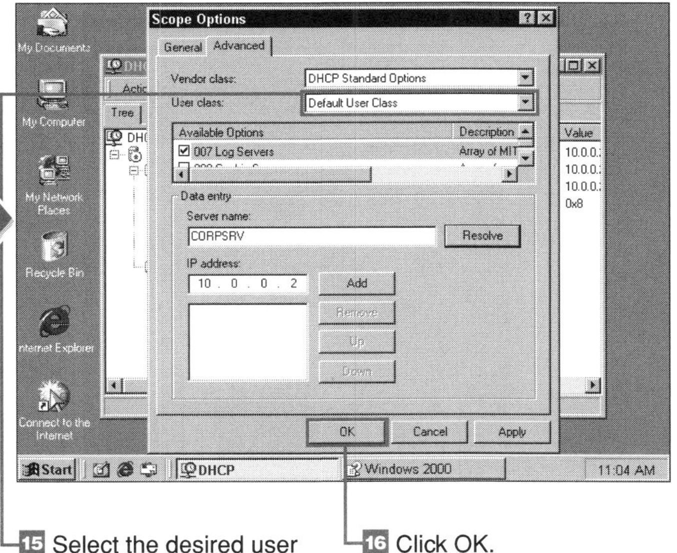

15 Select the desired user class.

16 Click OK.

MANAGING DHCP SERVERS

Aside from managing the scopes that you create, you can also perform several actions to manage and configure the DHCP server.

If you select the server you want to manage, you can choose the Action menu to see the options you have.

You can display the server statistics. A window appears that gives you a variety of statistical information about the DHCP servers functions and leasing. The statistics provided can help you determine the overall performance and functionality of your DHCP server, and you can use the statistics to see the number of IP addresses and renewals the server is handling.

You can also define user classes for the DHCP server. This is the same information you can configure for individual scopes. You can select an available class and add it for configuration. Generally, the default options are all you need, so you should plan carefully before implementing any of the additional user class options.

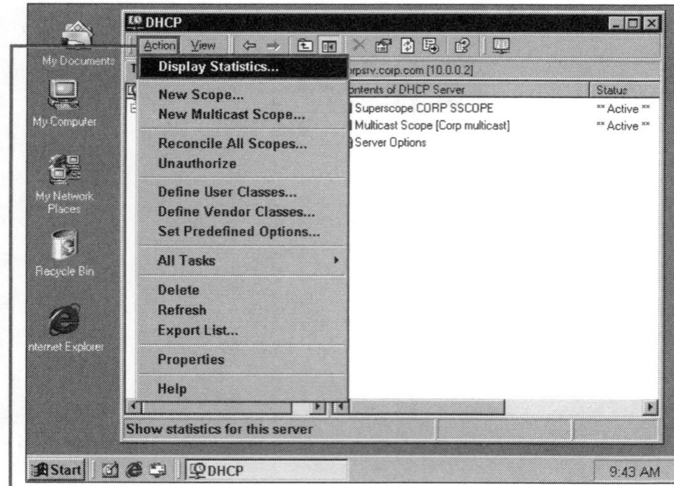

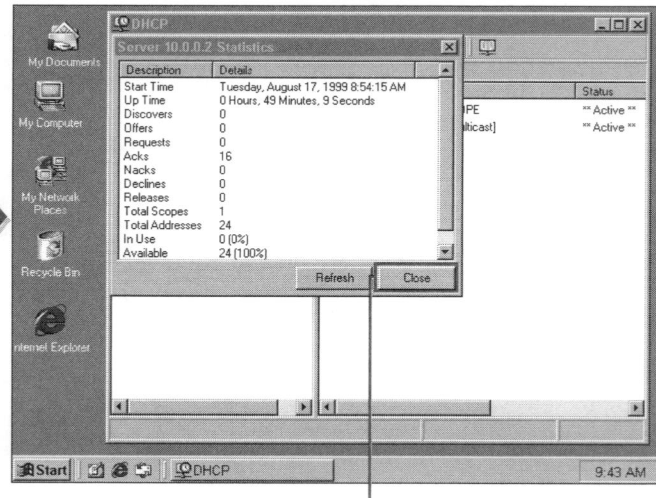

DISPLAYING STATISTICS

1 Select the desired server, and then choose Action⇨Display Statistics.

■ A window appears showing the statistics.

2 Click Close when you are done viewing the statistics.

Does the statistics dialog box tell me how many IP addresses are currently available for lease?

- Yes. Scroll to the bottom of the window and you can see an "Available" category. In the category, you see the actual number of available IP addresses that can be leased and a percentage of the addresses that are available for the scope. You can use this information to see how many IP addresses are available on an average basis. A low availability may indicate that your scope is too small (not enough IP addresses for lease) and may need to be expanded.

What is the RRAS user class?

- The RRAS user class defines addressing information for users who remotely dial into the network using remote access. DHCP can provide dial-in clients with an IP address and other addressing information just as those clients who are physically connected to the network.

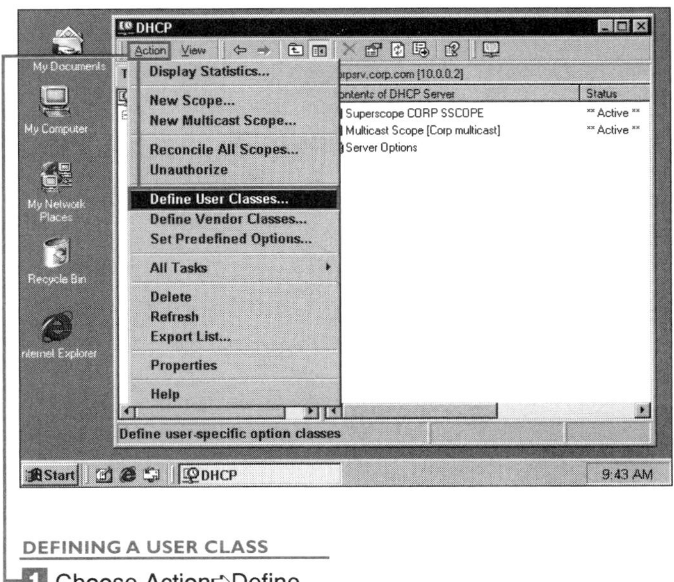

DEFINING A USER CLASS

1 Choose Action⇨Define User Classes.

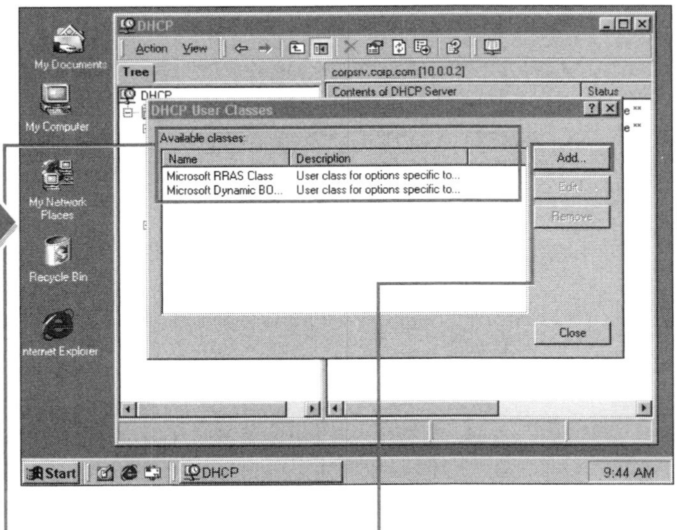

2 Select the class that you want to add from the list.

3 Click Add.

CONTINUED

MANAGING DHCP SERVERS CONTINUED

You can define both user and vendor classes for the DHCP server by choosing those options in the Action menu.

When you choose to add either a user class or vendor class, you need to enter the class name, description, and ID information as needed for that class. You can review the Microsoft documentation on your Windows 2000 Server CD-ROM for more detailed information about adding and using additional vendor classes. The default options are normally all you need, so you should carefully evaluate the addition of user or vendor classes to make certain the additions will benefit the DHCP functionality on your network. Keep in mind that DHCP automatically configures the needed options for Microsoft networking and Microsoft clients, so the addition of vendor and user classes is only necessary for unique networking situations.

You can also use the Action menu to set the predefined options, which are automatically configured by the DHCP service.

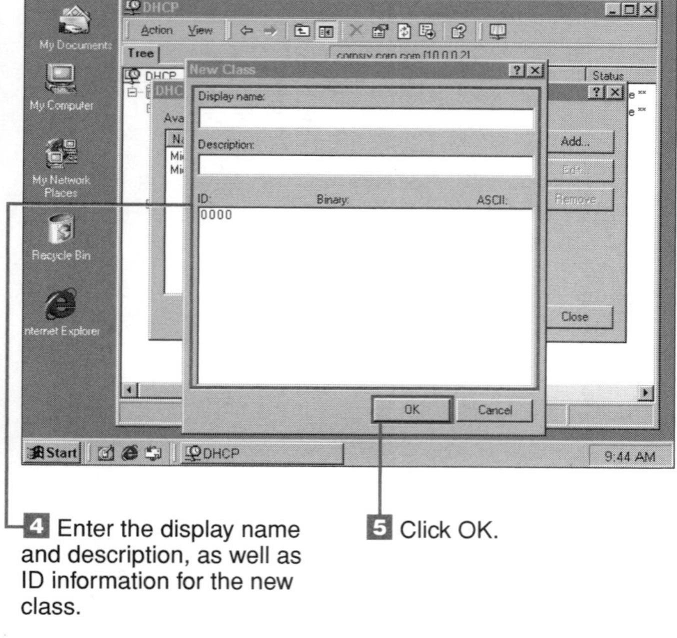

4 Enter the display name and description, as well as ID information for the new class.

5 Click OK.

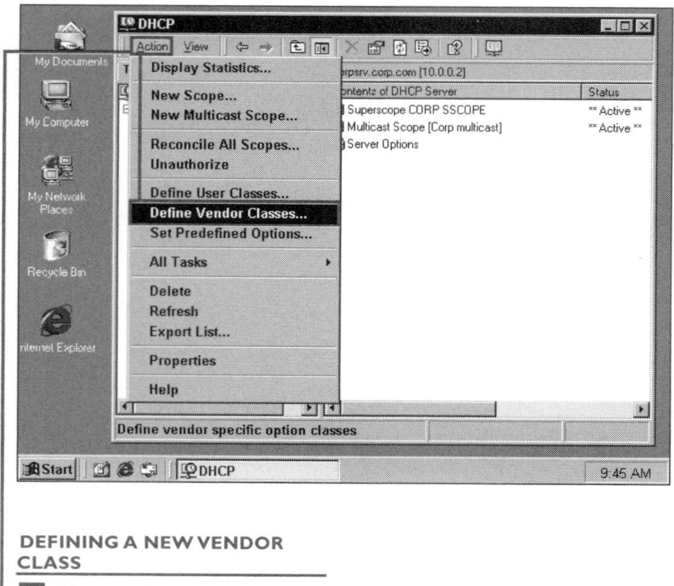

DEFINING A NEW VENDOR CLASS

1 Choose Action⇨Define Vendor Classes.

Do I need to define additional user and vendor classes?

- Typically, you do not need to define additional user and vendor classes. However, depending on the configuration of your network and your needs, you may find some of these user and vendor classes particularly helpful to service the needs of certain clients. You should carefully consider your need for these classes, however, and make certain the service they provide will be beneficial. The necessary options for Microsoft clients are automatically configured by DHCP, so in typical Microsoft networks, you do not have to worry about configuring additional user and vendor classes.

What are predefined options?

- Predefined options are the user and vendor class options that are automatically configured. You can change these options by adding new ones, deleting existing options, or editing existing options. In general, this is not an action you need to perform for most implementations of DHCP.

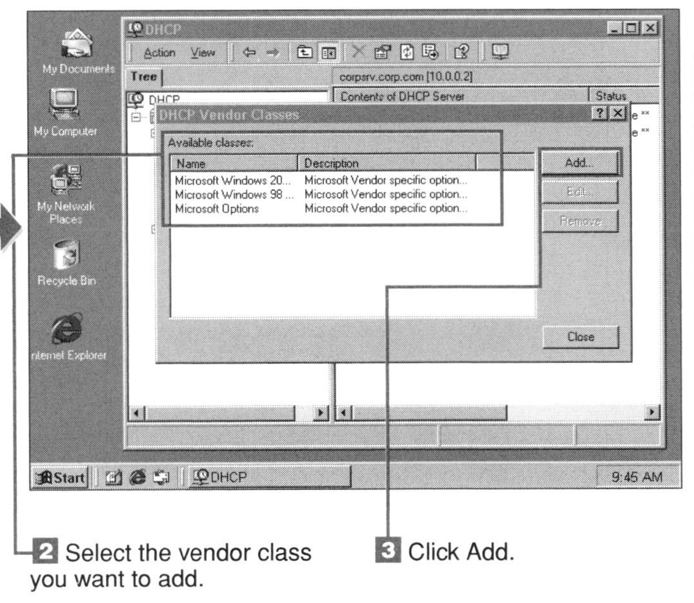

2 Select the vendor class you want to add.

3 Click Add.

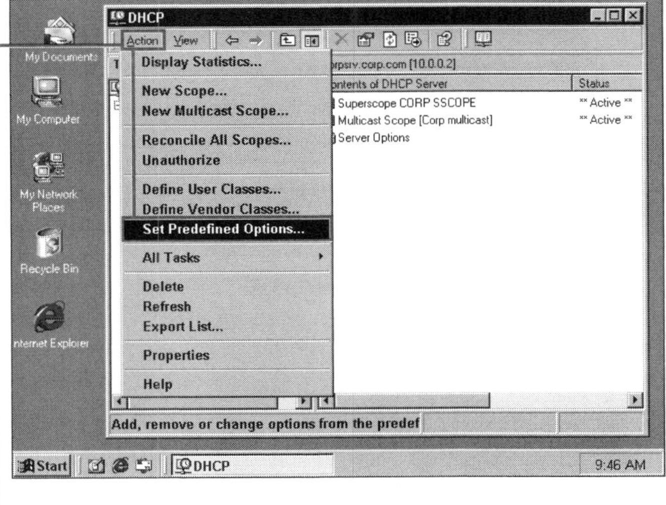

SETTING PREDEFINED OPTIONS

1 Choose Action⇨Set Predefined Options.

CONTINUED

MANAGING DHCP SERVERS CONTINUED

The Set Predefined Options command on the Action menu enables you to adjust the settings for the options that are defined by default in DHCP.

You can add, edit, or delete a class option as needed. You should consider carefully the need and result of making changes to the default class options. Generally, the default options are all you need and are configured appropriately. If you have specific reasons to make changes to the default options, consult the documentation on the Windows 2000 Server CD-ROM before proceeding.

You can also use the All Tasks feature to start, stop, or restart the DHCP service on a particular server. This feature enables you to easily manage the server service on all your DHCP servers from one central location. Keep in mind that any time you stop the DHCP service, the DHCP server cannot lease IP addresses to clients.

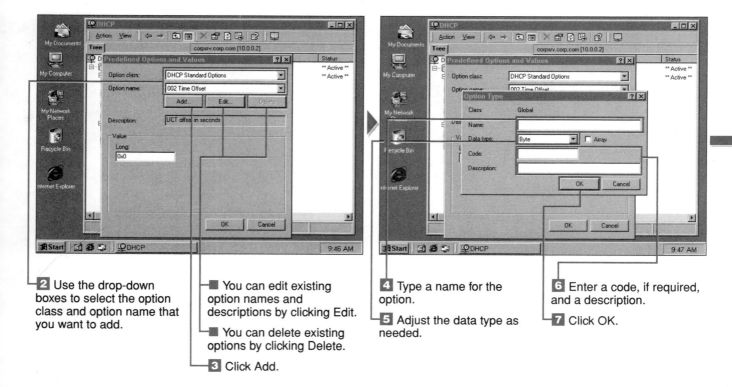

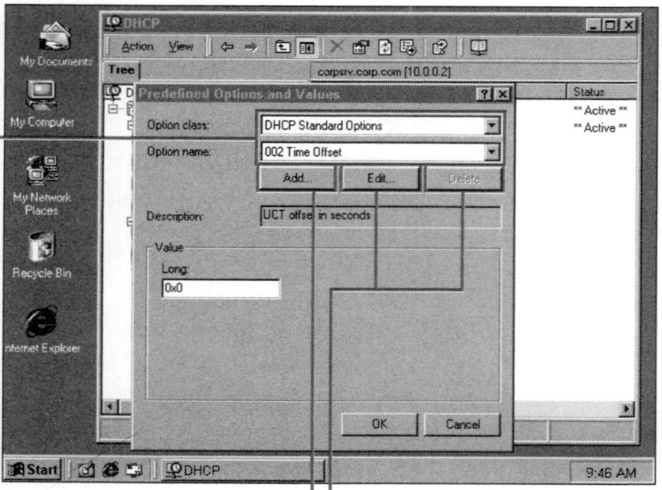

2 Use the drop-down boxes to select the option class and option name that you want to add.

■ You can edit existing option names and descriptions by clicking Edit.

■ You can delete existing options by clicking Delete.

3 Click Add.

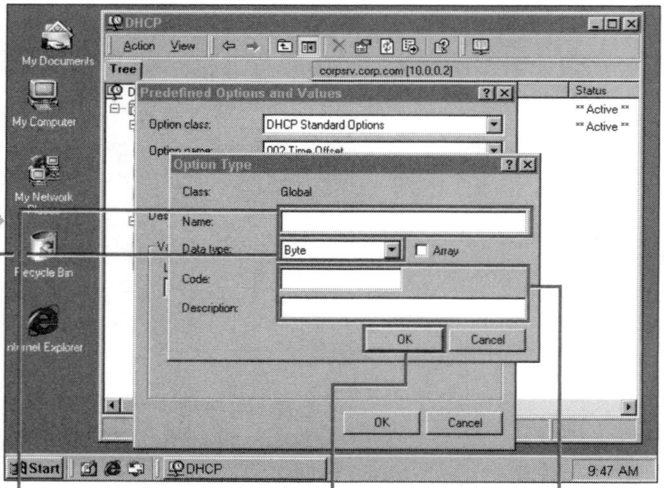

4 Type a name for the option.

5 Adjust the data type as needed.

6 Enter a code, if required, and a description.

7 Click OK.

Why would I want to stop the DHCP service?

- You may need to stop the DHCP service in certain instances. For example, if you are having a problem with the DHCP service or if you are having problems with the server itself, you can stop the DHCP service until you resolve the problem. After you stop the service, however, network clients cannot receive IP addressing from that particular server.

Does stopping the service affect the scope?

- No. You can stop the DHCP service without affecting your scope configuration. Because the service is stopped, no new IP addresses can be leased until the service restarts, but stopping the server does not change or remove the scope. This feature enables you to perform additional configuration or troubleshooting tasks for that particular scope.

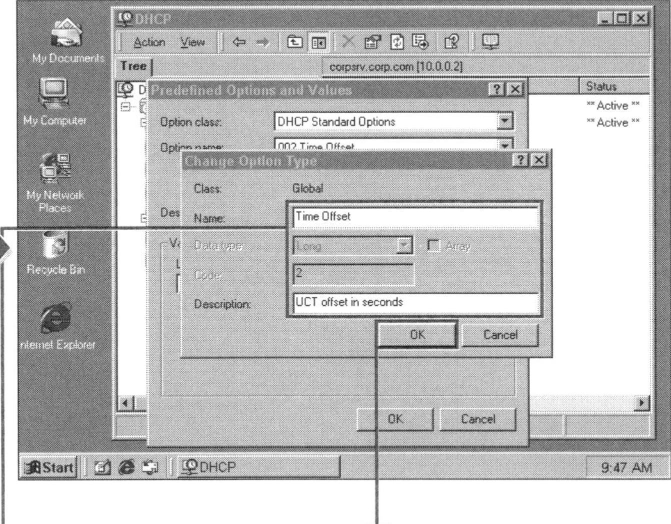

■ If you click Edit from the Predefined Options and Values dialog box, this window appears, enabling you to make changes to the name and description of the option.

8 Click OK.

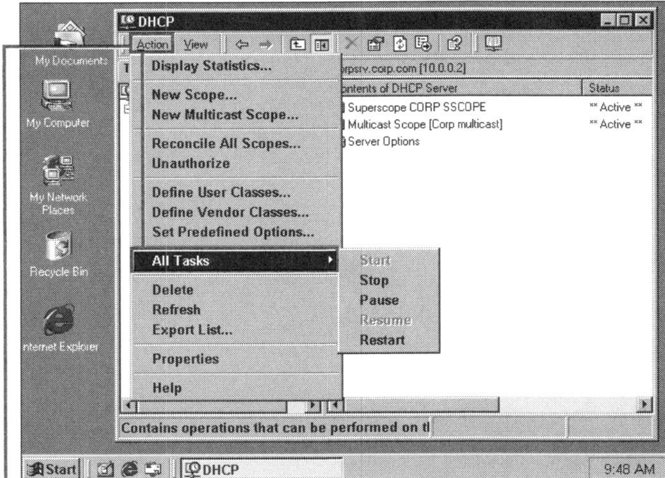

STARTING, STOPPING, OR RESTARTING THE DHCP SERVICE

1 Choose Action⇨All Tasks and then choose the desired action.

CONTINUED

MANAGING DHCP SERVERS CONTINUED

As with the scope, you can manage the DHCP server's properties, which enables you to configure how your server performs and the background actions that occur.

On the General tab, you can choose to update the server's DHCP statistics at certain time intervals that you enter. You can also enable DHCP audit logging and show the BOOTP table folder if desired. DHCP audit logging is available by default, but you can choose not to use audit logging if desired.

The DNS tab is the same as the one in the scope properties. The default options are already configured so that updates can be dynamically sent to DNS. You should not change the dynamic DNS ability.

Finally, the Advanced tab enables you configure the number of times DHCP should perform a conflicting detection before leasing an IP address to the client. You can also change the default audit log path and DHCP database path if desired.

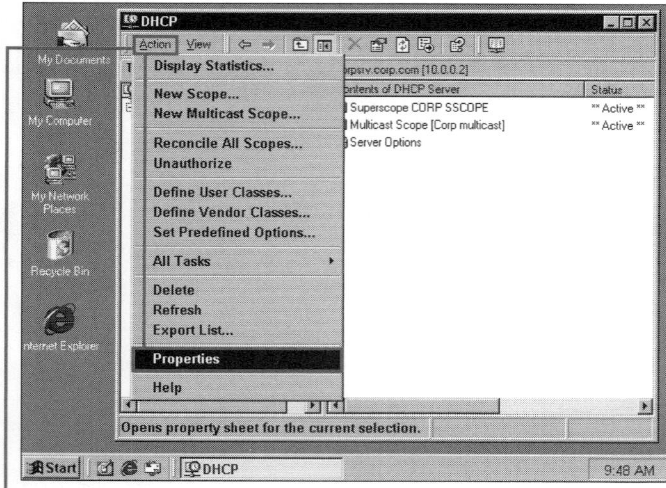

2 To configure the server s properties, choose Action➪Properties.

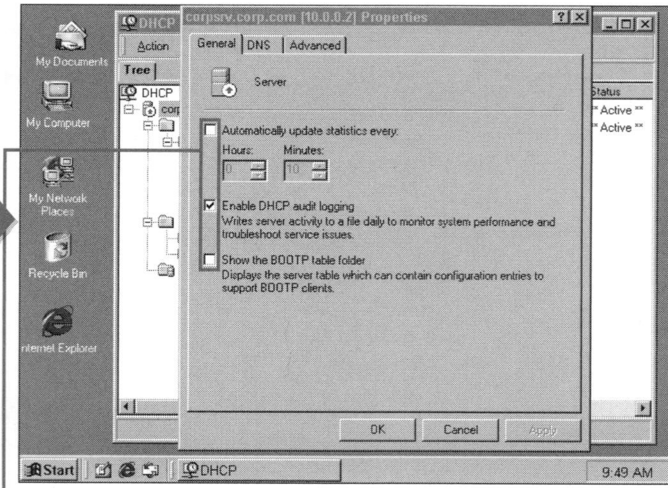

3 On the General tab, click the appropriate check boxes to make changes to the statistics update, enable the DHCP audit logging, or show the BOOTP table folder.

What is conflict detection?

You can let DHCP check for an IP address conflict before leasing the IP address to the client. The DHCP server attempts to detect the IP addresses that are leased and whether the new lease will create a conflict with another client. Because some clients have static IP addresses or are not DHCP clients, this feature reduces the possibility of IP address conflicts. This action is useful, but you may experience slower lease times by allowing DHCP to detect address conflicts too many times before leasing the IP address.

What does the Bindings button do?

If you click the Bindings button, you can adjust the LAN connection(s) that DHCP uses to communicate with network clients. This feature is useful if your server has more than one network interface card (NIC). The NIC, sometimes called a network adapter card, packages network data and sends it over the network cable. Each computer on a network contains a NIC.

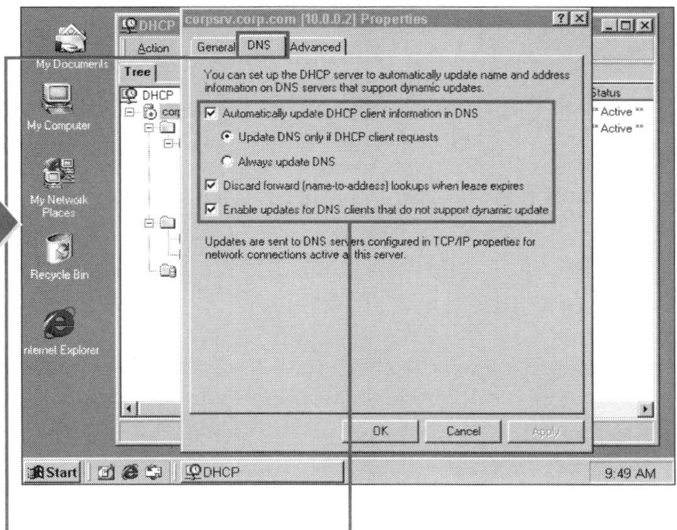

4 Click the DNS tab.

■ The DNS tab is the same as you have seen for scope properties.

5 Click the appropriate check boxes to make changes, or simply accept the defaults.

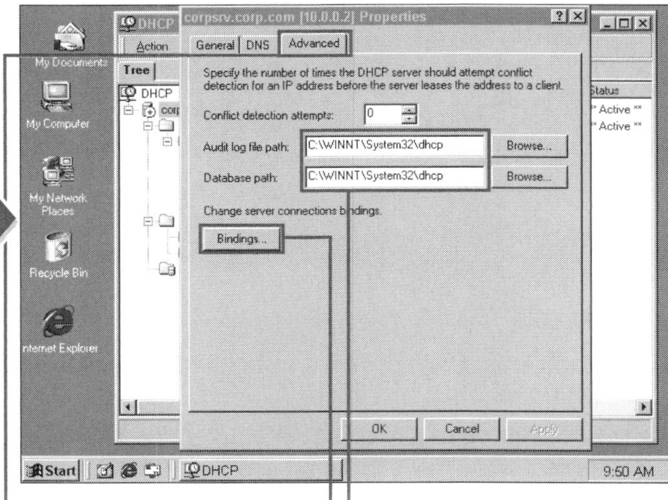

6 Click the Advanced tab.

7 If desired, change the default location of the audit log file and database path.

■ You can also change the server's connection bindings by clicking Bindings.

INTRODUCTION TO WINS

In networks that use the NetBIOS naming method to communicate, WINS (Windows Internet Naming Service) is responsible for resolving NetBIOS computer names to IP addresses. NetBIOS enables you to assign up to 15 characters as "friendly" names, such as Workstation2 or wk2. In a TCP/IP network, these friendly names have to be resolved to IP addresses so that communication on the network can occur.

In Windows 2000 networks, name resolution occurs through DNS, so WINS is provided in Windows 2000 for backward compatibility with previous Windows operating systems. In a network where all servers and client computers run Windows 2000, you do not need WINS. In most cases, however, networks contain a mix of operating systems, so WINS will continue to be a part of administrators' lives for some time into the future.

Who are WINS clients?

The following operating systems can be WINS clients:

- Windows 2000
- Windows 9*x*
- Windows NT 3.5 or later
- Windows for Workgroups 3.11 running TCP/IP-32
- Microsoft Network Client version 3.0 for MS-DOS with real-mode TCP/IP driver
- LAN Manager 2.2c for MS-DOS

How does WINS work?

WINS clients register their NetBIOS names and IP addresses with a WINS server. The WINS server's job is to maintain the database that maps the NetBIOS names to the IP addresses. When clients attempt to communicate with each other, the WINS server is queried for the name-to-IP address mapping.

When a WINS client starts, it registers its name and IP address with the WINS server. When this information changes, such as a new DHCP lease, the client updates its name-to-IP address mapping with the WINS server. When a WINS client needs to contact another WINS client, the resolution request—instead of a broadcast message—is sent to the WINS server. The WINS server resolves the request and returns the IP address information to the client. The client can then use the IP address to communicate with other clients.

WINS database records are temporary, so like DHCP, the WINS client has to renew its lease with the WINS server. When a client shuts down, it sends a name release to the WINS server so that the WINS server has the latest browse list.

You can configure the DHCP server to send the WINS server's IP address to the clients when an IP lease is made. This way, client computers do not have to use a broadcast message to discover the IP address of the WINS server (which reduces traffic on your network). You can learn more about DHCP in Chapter 4.

Workstation 2
128.143.7.226

INSTALLING WINS

As with other networking components in Windows 2000, you can install WINS by accessing Add/Remove Programs in Control Panel. You can also use the Configure Your Server program that is available in the Administrative Tools folder or from the Start menu.

Keep in mind that pure Windows 2000 networks use DNS for name resolutions, so WINS is unnecessary. If your network uses a mixture of Windows 2000 operating systems as well as earlier versions of Windows, such as NT and 9*x*, then you need to use WINS.

Before installing WINS, you should make certain that the WINS server has a static IP address, subnet mask, and default gateway (optional). If you are using DHCP, you should also configure DHCP to return the WINS server name and the IP address to clients with their IP lease. See Chapter 4 for more information about configuring DHCP.

1 Double-click Add/Remove Programs in Control Panel.

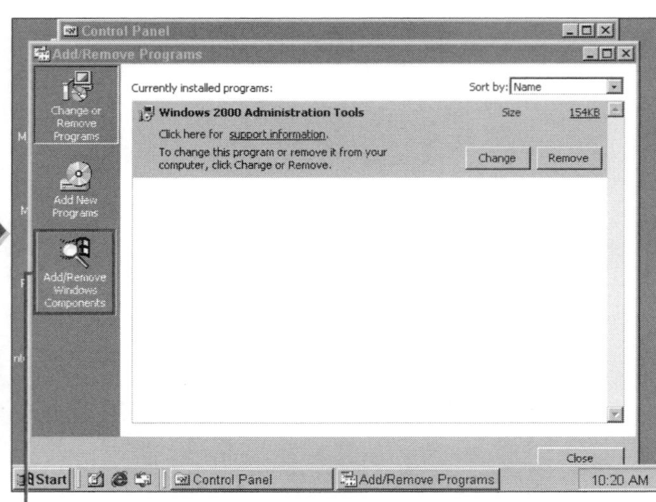

2 Click Add/Remove Windows Components.

Is there another way to install WINS?

✔ Yes. You can use the Configure Your Server tool by choosing Start⇨Programs⇨ Administrative Tools⇨Configure Your Server. Click the Networking link in the left pane and click WINS to begin the installation.

Can a DHCP server also be a WINS server?

✔ Yes. You can use the same server to run DHCP and WINS, and this is not an uncommon configuration. You should include the server's IP address for the WINS configuration so that clients contact the DHCP/WINS server for name resolution, just as they would if they were separate servers.

Can a domain controller be a WINS server?

✔ Yes. Your domain controller(s) can provide the WINS service. However, depending on the configuration and size of your network, you may want to use servers other than domain controllers to handle the WINS service. Doing so reduces the load on your domain controllers and improves their performance.

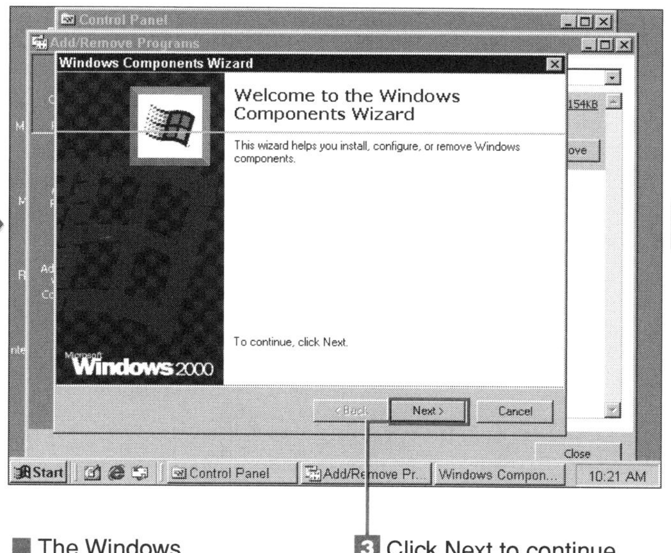

■ The Windows Components Wizard begins.

3 Click Next to continue.

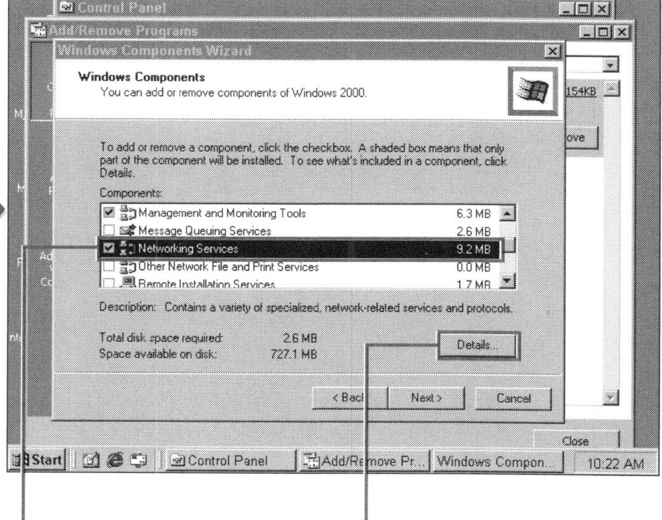

4 Select Networking Services in the list.

5 Click Details.

CONTINUED

INSTALLING WINS CONTINUED

If you have non-WINS clients on your networks, you can configure static name-to-IP address mappings for those clients and include them in the WINS database. This feature allows WINS clients to query the database to discover the name-to-IP address mapping for the non-WINS clients. By using this feature, you no longer need to use LMHOST files to keep track of non-WINS clients.

After the installation is complete, you need to configure and set up the WINS server. WINS configuration is generally easy, and Windows 2000 does most of the configuration work for you by configuring default options that are standard in most networks. Typical default options include subnet mask and default gateway mappings. Keep in mind that once your network runs only Windows 2000 computers, WINS will no longer be necessary and can be removed from your servers. Refer to the following sections to configure your WINS server.

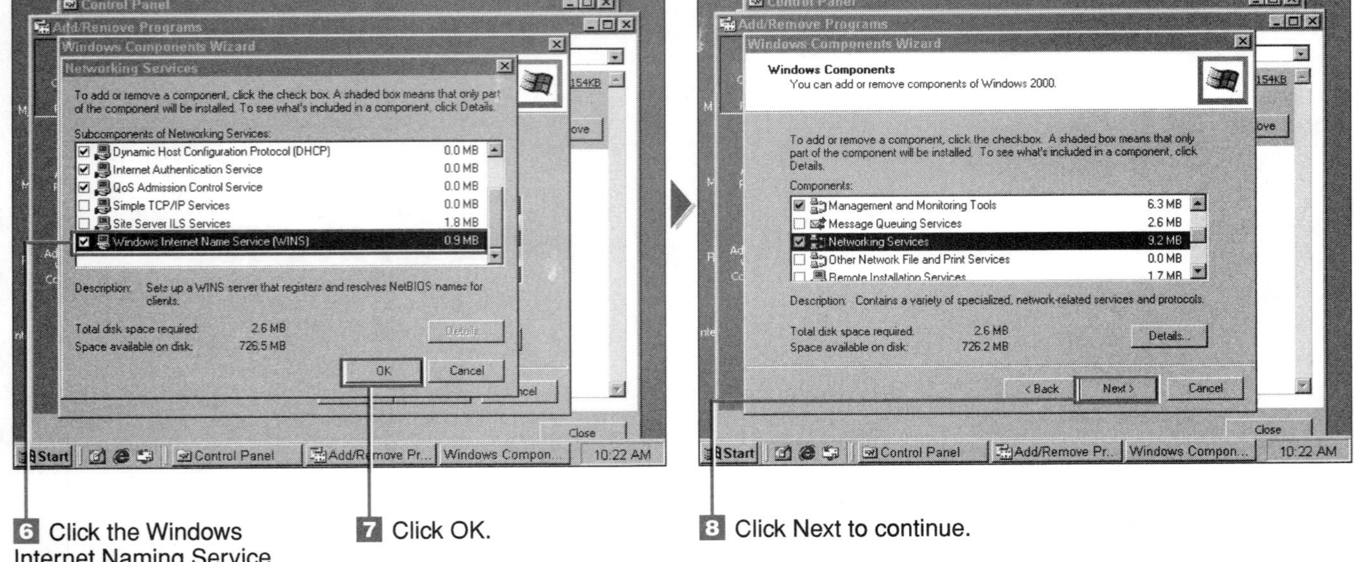

6 Click the Windows Internet Naming Service (WINS) check box.

7 Click OK.

8 Click Next to continue.

Do I have to configure WINS during the installation?

No. The installation places the service on your server. After the installation is complete, you must configure the service for operation.

Can I install other networking services when I install WINS?

Yes. You can select other networking components at the same time you install WINS and perform the installations together. Other networking components may present you with configuration wizards to complete before the installation takes place.

Can Windows NT servers on my network be WINS servers?

Yes. You can use your Windows NT servers to function as WINS servers, just as you did before implementing Windows 2000. Windows 2000 clients, NT clients, and Windows 9*x* computers can contact a WINS server for name resolution. In many mixed environments, Windows NT servers and Windows 2000 member servers are assigned the task of handling WINS and even DHCP. This feature reduces the load placed on domain controllers.

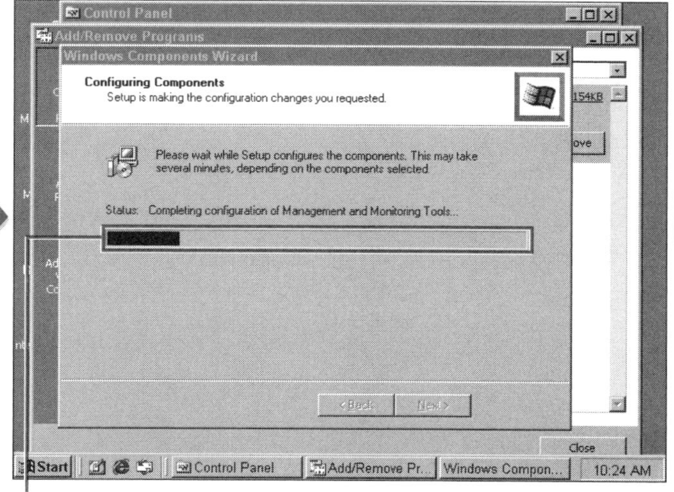

■ The system installs WINS. The status bar indicates the level of completion.

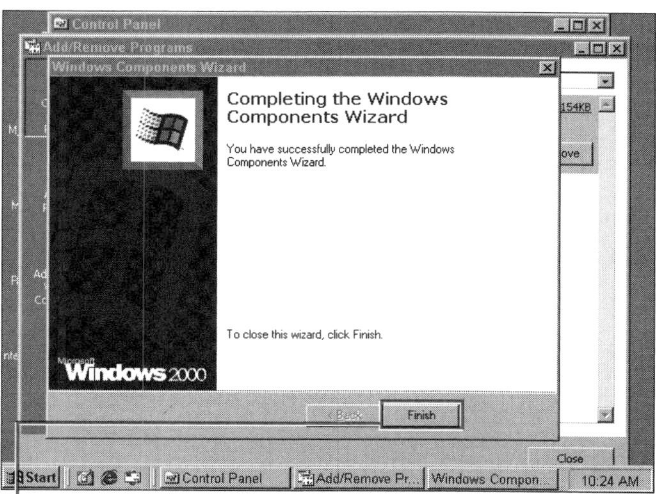

9 Click Finish to complete the wizard.

CONFIGURING WINS GENERAL PROPERTIES

As with other tools in Windows 2000 Server, the WINS manager is an MMC snap-in that enables you to configure and manage the local WINS server or other WINS servers in your network.

Of course, you must install WINS before you can configure it. See the previous section for information on installing WINS. After you open the WINS snap-in, you see a green arrow next to the server name. This arrow denotes that the WINS service is connected and running. At this point, you can configure the WINS server to perform as you desire.

You can also use this interface to administer all WINS servers on your network by simply adding other WINS servers to the interface. This feature enables you to manage your WINS environment from one location without having to physically visit each WINS server. In most cases, Windows 2000 allows administrators to load all servers for WINS, DHCP, DNS, and other components into a single MMC interface where they can all be configured together. This a great benefit for administrators who manage certain services rather than particular servers.

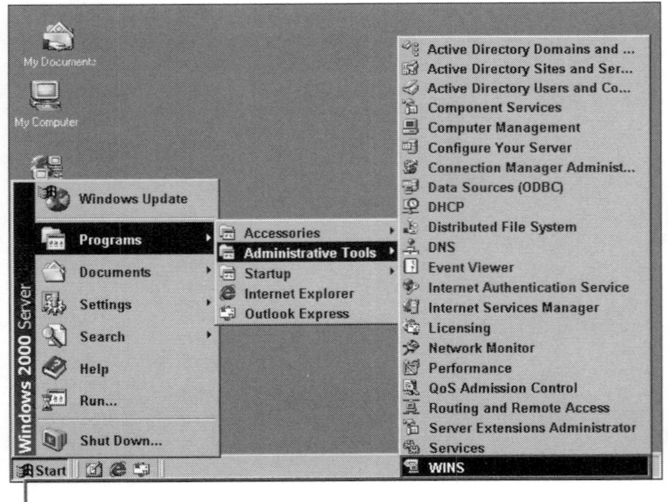

1 Choose Start⇨Programs⇨Administrative Tools⇨WINS to open the MMC snap-in.

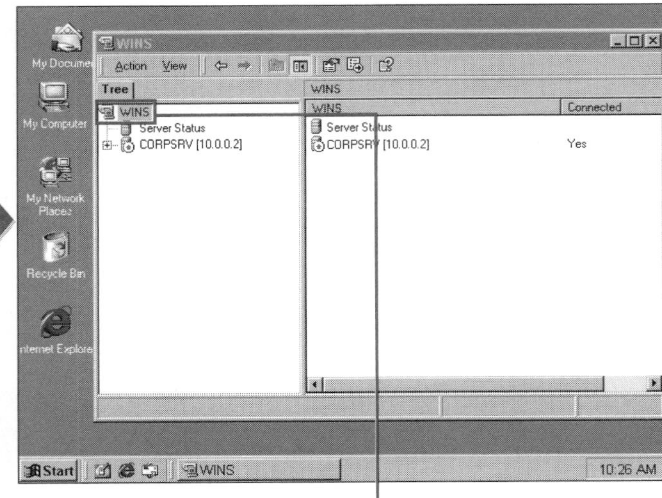

■ The snap-in opens.

2 Select WINS at the top of the console tree.

Can I manage all WINS servers on my network from this single snap-in?

- Yes. Assuming you have proper permissions, you can add all the WINS servers on your network to the snap-in so that you can administer all the servers from one location. This feature makes it easy for you to manage your total WINS environment.

Can I use a Windows NT 4.0 workstation for the WINS server?

- No. Only servers, such as Windows 2000 or Windows NT, can function as WINS servers. You cannot install the WINS server service on Windows 2000 Professional, Windows NT Workstation, or Windows 9*x* computers.

Can I manage both WINS and DHCP servers from the same MMC interface?

- Yes. You can create a custom interface by manually loading the two MMC snap-ins. Then, you can save the new MMC so that you can use it over and over. See Chapter 12 to learn more about using the MMC.

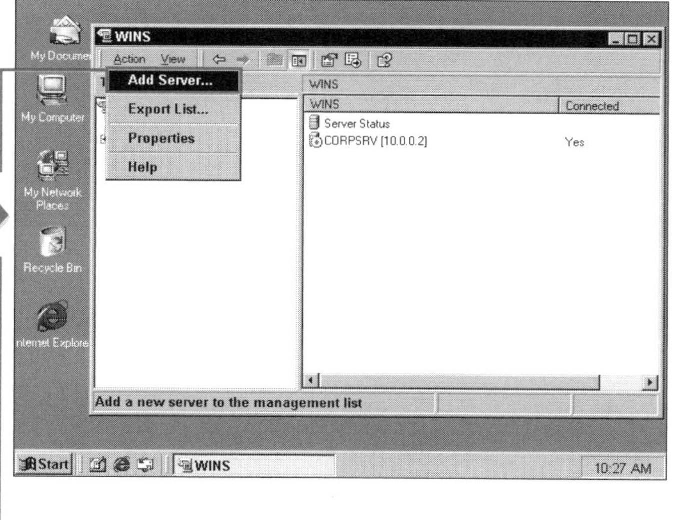

3 Choose Action⇨Add Server.

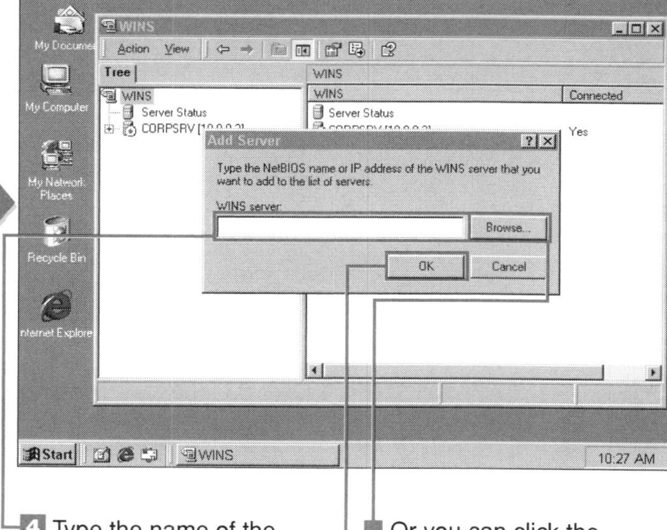

4 Type the name of the WINS server you want to administer.

■ Or you can click the Browse button to browse for the server.

5 Click OK.

CONTINUED

CONFIGURING WINS GENERAL PROPERTIES CONTINUED

You can use the Action menu to perform standard operations, such as exporting the MMC list or obtaining help from the Windows 2000 help files. The Export List option allows you to save the WINS database file as a text file that you can read.

You can also access the Properties for WINS through the Action menu. From the General tab of the Properties dialog box, you can choose to have the WINS servers displayed in the snap-in by name or IP address. You can also have the WINS snap-in show the DNS name of the WINS servers, and you can choose to validate the cache of the WINS servers at startup. These different features enable you to manage the WINS servers in a way that's best for you and your networking environment.

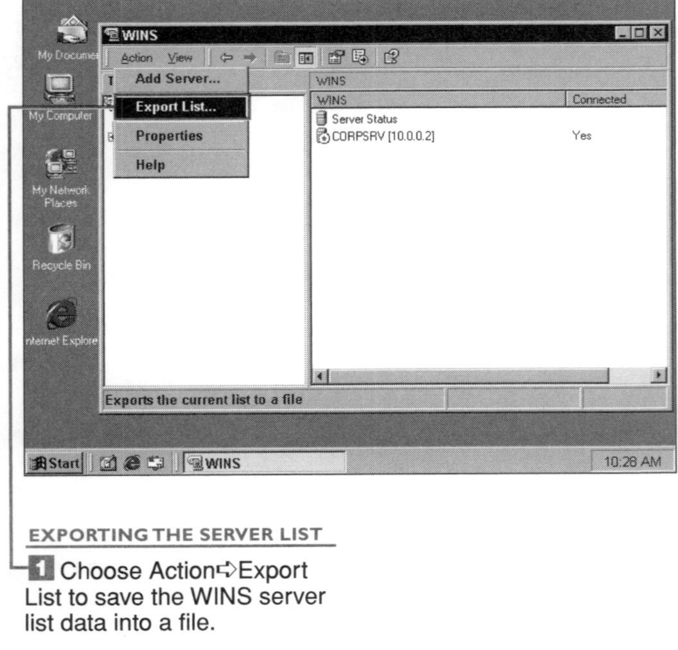

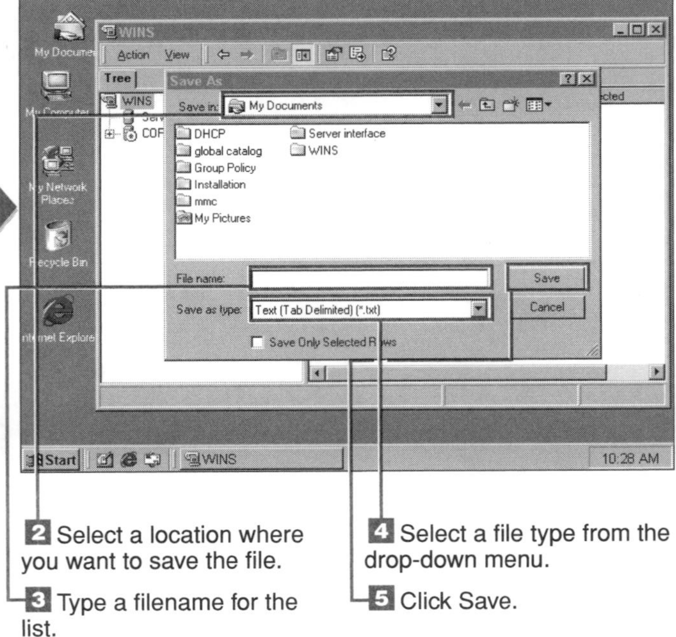

EXPORTING THE SERVER LIST

1 Choose Action⇨Export List to save the WINS server list data into a file.

2 Select a location where you want to save the file.

3 Type a filename for the list.

4 Select a file type from the drop-down menu.

5 Click Save.

Should I validate the WINS cache at startup?

- This option is not enabled by default because additional startup time is required to validate the WINS cache. You probably do not need this feature enabled, but if you do not mind the longer startup time, it is a good preventive feature.

Why does the snap-in enable you to view the servers by their DNS name?

- Because DNS is an integrated and integral part of Windows 2000, you can choose to set up your snap-in view so that the DNS name for each server is displayed. As Windows 2000 is more heavily implemented, administrators and users begin to see their servers and computers through the DNS naming scheme. This option simply makes your configuration easier to view after you are comfortable with the DNS names of your WINS servers.

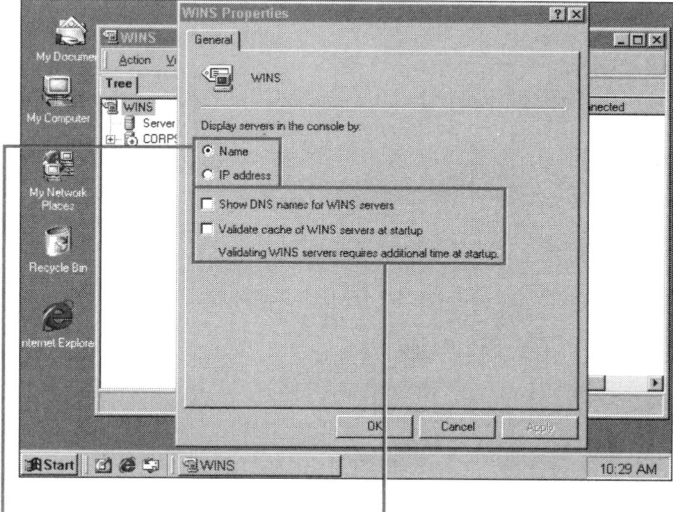

CONFIGURING GENERAL PROPERTIES

1 Select WINS and choose Action⇨Properties to view general WINS properties.

2 Click the appropriate radio button to show the servers either by name or IP address.

3 Click the appropriate check boxes to show the DNS names of the WINS servers and to validate the cache of WINS servers at startup.

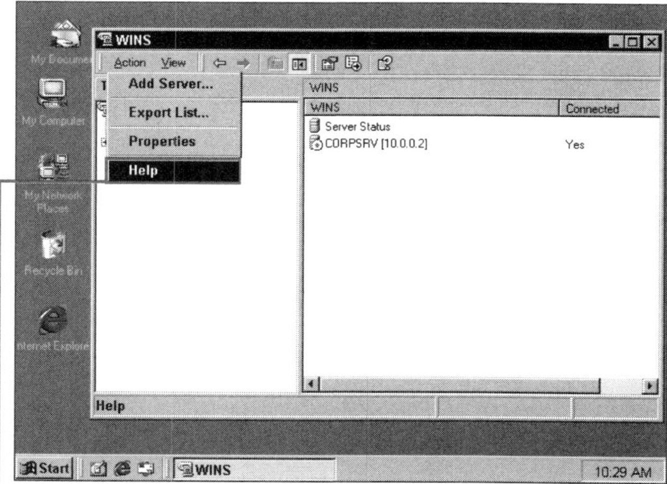

ACCESSING HELP

1 Choose Action⇨Help to open the Windows 2000 help files on WINS topics.

CHECKING SERVER STATUS

The WINS snap-in contains a server status icon that enables you to check the status of a server. When you click the Server Status icon, the WINS server is displayed in the right pane with a green icon telling you that it's running. If a server is not running, the icon tells you that the server is not running and is displayed with a red icon. You can adjust the time between server status updates; the default is every five minutes. In most cases, the default setting is best. If you lower or increase the five-minute interval, you may see performance problems or a lack of timely data on the performance of your WINS servers. If you lower the status update to one minute, for example, the server has to update its status every 60 seconds while also performing the many other tasks assigned to it. Although you want timely data to be displayed in the Server Status, you also do not want your server to work harder than necessary.

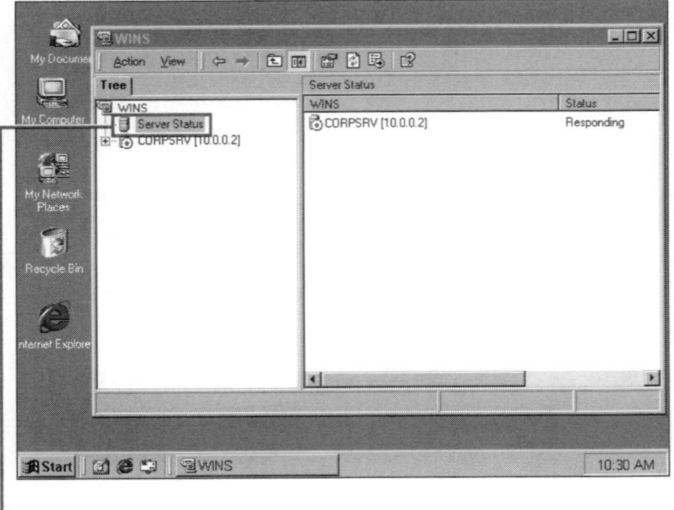

1 Select Server Status in the Console tree.

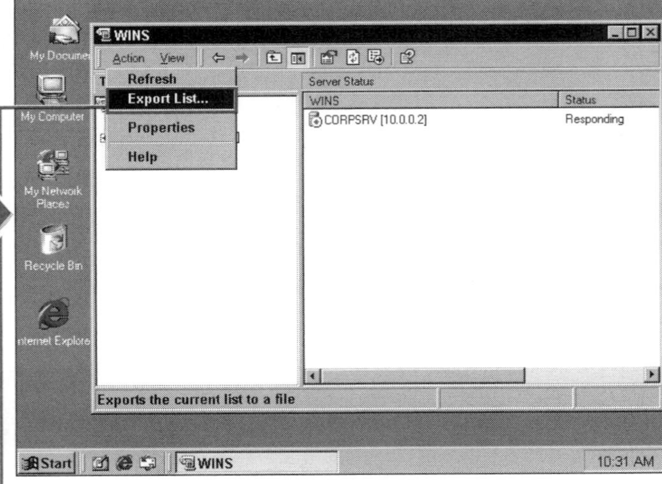

2 If you want to save the WINS database list to a file, choose Action⇨Export List.

Should I lower the frequency of status updates?

✓ The status updates are performed every five minutes by default. You can lower this value so that updates occur more often, or you can increase it so they do not happen as often. If you lower the value, the update checks perform more often, which increases the amount of time the server spends performing updates. If you increase the time too much, however, the status information will not be current.

What is the purpose of the server status icon in the console?

✓ The server status icon in the console enables you to quickly see the status of your WINS servers in the details pane. If you suspect that one of your WINS servers is not running, you can simply click the server status icon to determine if a server is down. If so, you can identify which server is down and then troubleshoot the problem.

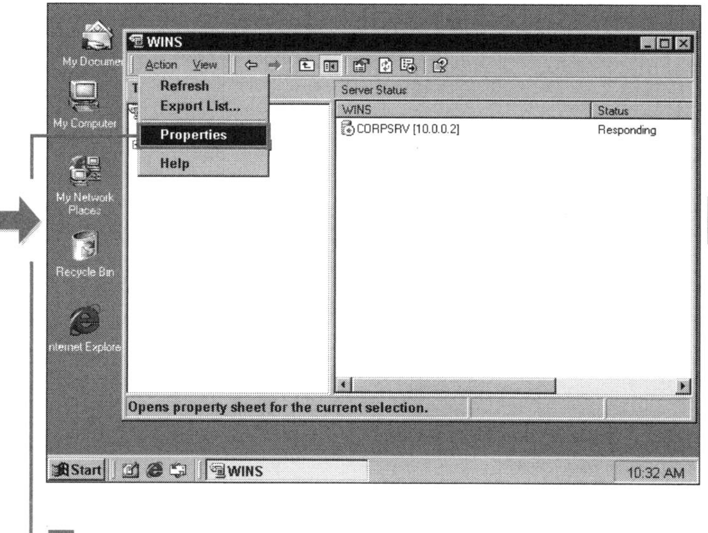

3 Choose Action⇨Properties.

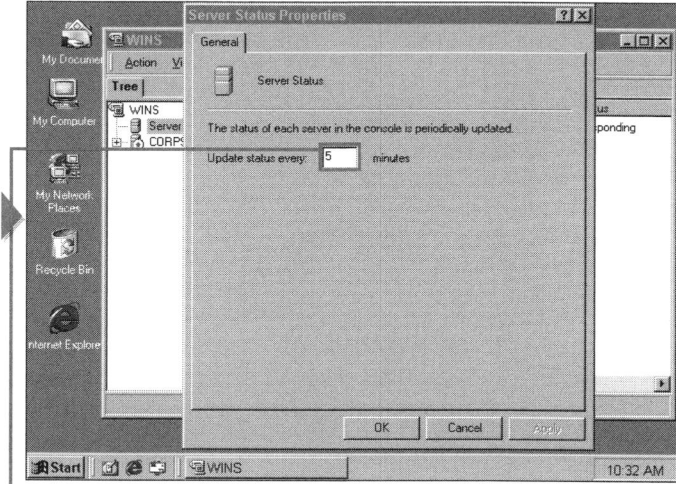

4 Type a new value to change the periodic update of the server status.

MANAGING THE WINS SERVER

You can check your server's performance by accessing the server's statistics. The statistical information returned to you includes information on replication with other WINS servers, the total number of name resolution queries, the records found and not found for queries, the total name reservation releases, as well as the number of WINS registrations. You can use this information to determine if the server is behaving in a satisfactory manner. You also have the option of resetting the current reading and refresh the statistics so that you can receive accurate, timely information.

The server statistics information is a good way to determine how well your server is performing and if the server seems to be handling the registration and query load that network clients place on it. As a WINS administrator, you should get in the habit of checking your server's status from time to time. This action can help you find existing problems and determine if future problems are developing.

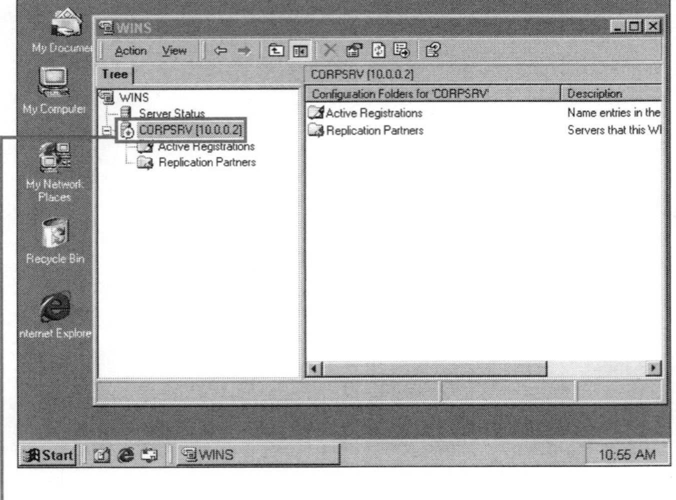

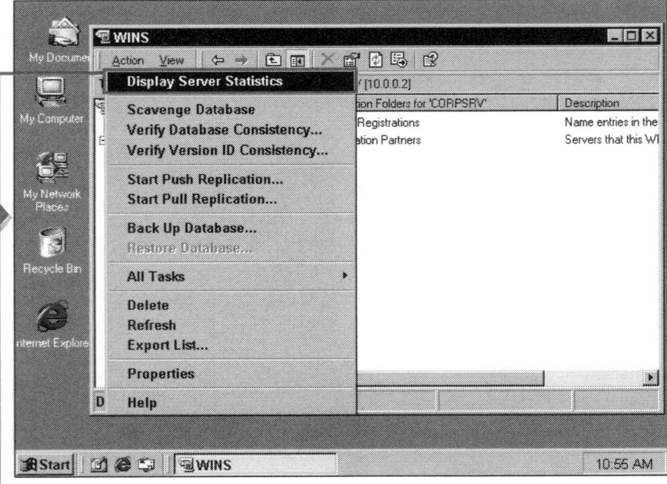

DISPLAYING SERVER STATISTICS

1 Select the WINS server that you want to manage from the console tree.

2 Choose Action⇨Display Server Statistics.

Where can I find information about queries received by the WINS server?

- The server statistics give you information about the queries that are sent to the WINS server. From the statistics file, you can see the total number of queries, the records that were found, and the records that were not found. If you want to gain statistical information for a specific time period, you can reset the statistics record and view the statistics again after a period of time has passed.

I need to know when a particular WINS server started. How can I find this information?

- You can learn the start time of the WINS server by clicking the WINS server in the console and then choosing Action⇨Display Server Statistics. At the top of the list, you see an entry called Server start time. In the details column, the start time is displayed by date and time.

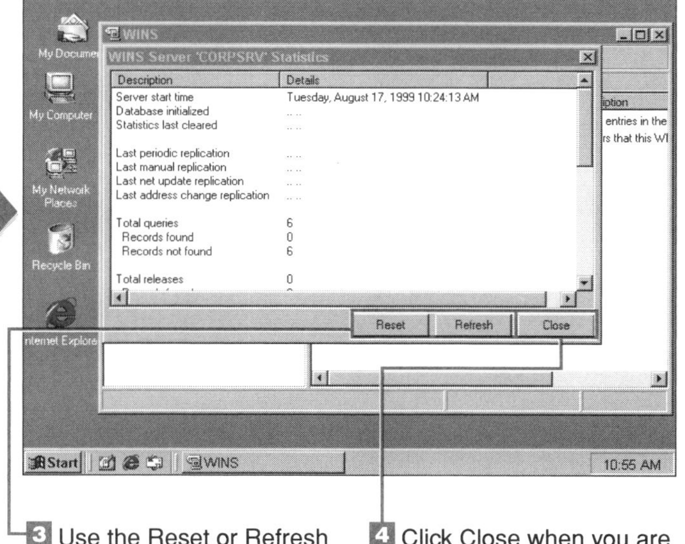

3 Use the Reset or Refresh buttons as necessary.

4 Click Close when you are done.

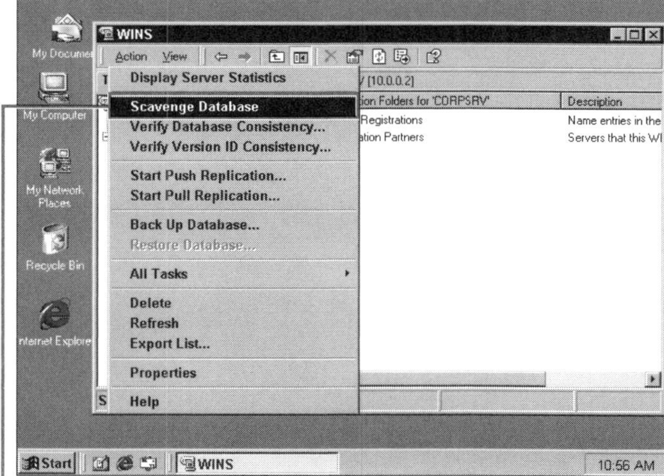

SCAVENGING THE DATABASE

1 Choose Action⇨Scavenge Database.

CONTINUED

MANAGING THE WINS SERVER
CONTINUED

You perform a number of operations by using the Action menu. First, you can scavenge the WINS database. As with all databases, the WINS database collects information that becomes outdated. Periodically, WINS needs to remove this outdated information, and this process is known as *scavenging*. You don't need to force scavenging using the Action menu unless you have specific reasons for wanting to clean the database—WINS will do this automatically through the settings on the Name Record tab in the server's Properties sheets (which you learn about later in this chapter.) If you do manually scavenge the database, you should know that the process is very CPU- and network-intensive, so you should scavenge only during nonpeak hours.

You can also use the Action menu to run a check for consistency. This task helps maintain database integrity among the WINS servers. In other words, the check determines if the database is consistent among all the WINS servers. The process is automatically scheduled, but you can force it to run using the Action menu. As with the database scavenge, the process is CPU-intensive.

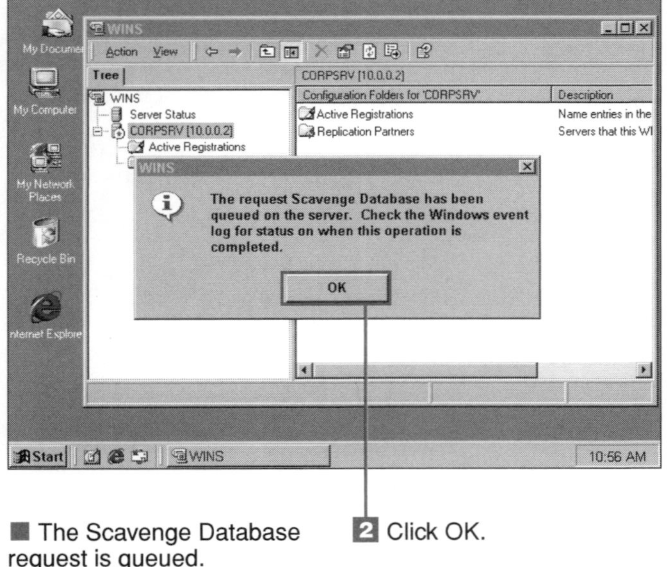

■ The Scavenge Database request is queued.

2 Click OK.

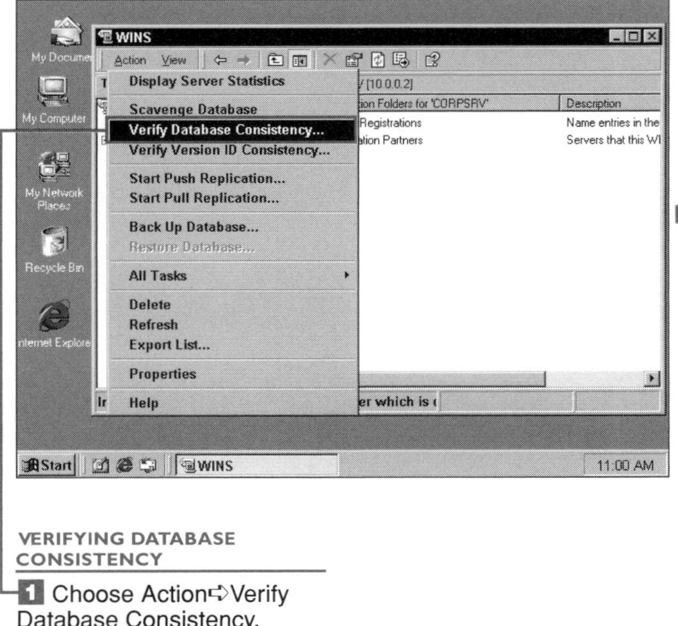

VERIFYING DATABASE CONSISTENCY

1 Choose Action⇨Verify Database Consistency.

How much time does scavenging take?

- Depending on the size of your network, the amount of WINS traffic, and the last time the database was scavenged, the process may take some time to complete. You can still work with your server while the process is running, but you will notice a performance hit. Scavenging the database during off-peak hours is always best.

How does the WINS server know if all databases are consistent?

- The consistency check allows the WINS server to compare its database records with other WINS servers. The server finds and corrects inconsistencies so that the database is identical on all servers. This process is also CPU- and network-intensive.

When is a good time to run a consistency check?

- Because consistency checking is both CPU- and network-intensive, you should try to perform the process during nonpeak hours. This includes both nonpeak hours for the server as well as the network. Typically, a good time to run consistency checking is at the end of a business day or early in the morning before business activities commence.

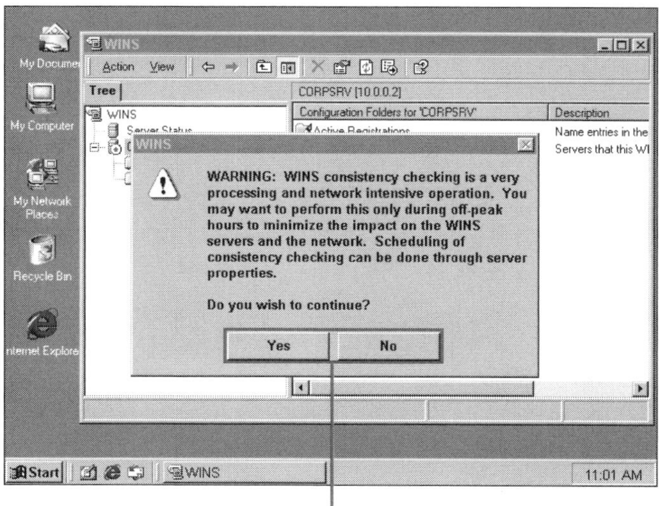

■ A Warning message tells you that consistency checking is very CPU- and network-intensive.

2 Click Yes to continue or No to exit.

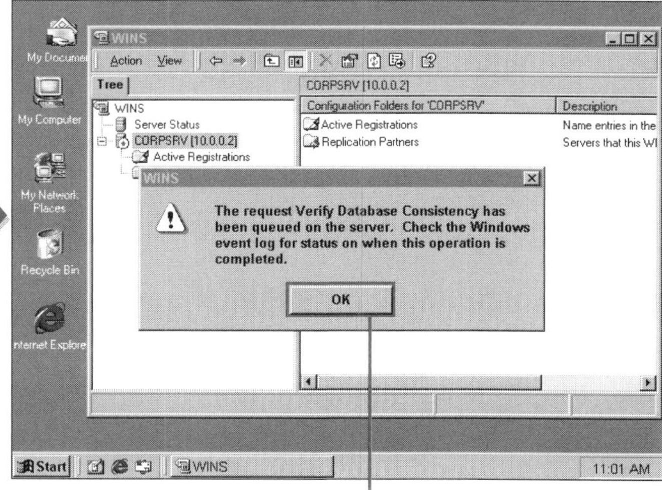

■ If you click Yes, a message appears telling you that the database consistency check has been queued on the server.

3 Click OK.

CONTINUED

MANAGING THE WINS SERVER

CONTINUED

You can also use the Action menu to check version number consistency. This check makes certain that each WINS server has the correct version number, which ensures that all servers have been tested for consistency. Each consistency check records a version number for the consistency check.

Your server can tell if all WINS servers have been checked by examining the consistency numbers. This action is performed by the WINS server to check that each server has the highest consistency number. To do this, the WINS server where you run the check pulls the owner-version map from the WINS servers on your network and then checks the map for the highest version number. If all numbers are the same, each WINS server has been tested for consistency. When you run this check, a dialog box appears telling you the results or problems.

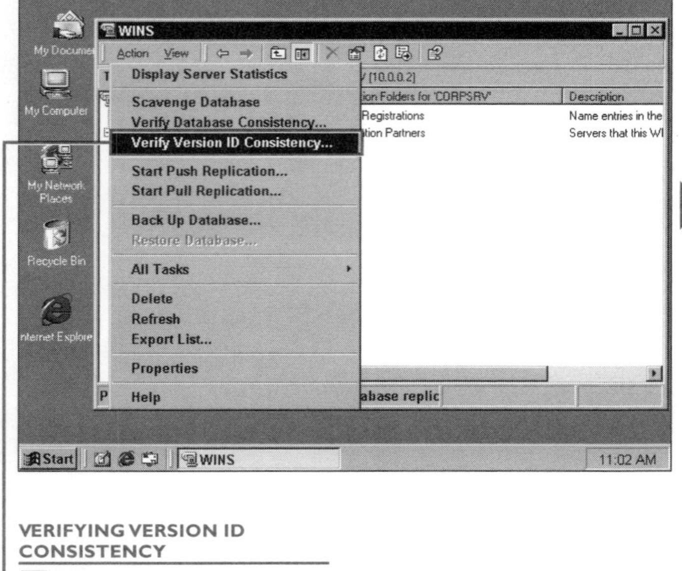

VERIFYING VERSION ID CONSISTENCY

1 Choose Action⇨Verify Version ID Consistency.

■ A message appears telling you that the operation may take a long time.

2 Click Yes to continue or No to cancel.

Does the version check operation take a long time?

- Depending on the size of your network, the operation can take some time because the WINS server has to pull the owner-version maps and then compare the version numbers. If only a few WINS servers are on your network, then the process does not take an inordinate amount of time. However, if you have many servers, it can be a long process. The number of servers, network speed and congestion, and server processing power all affect the amount of time a version check takes.

Do I need to run a version check regularly?

- No. A version check allows you to make certain that all servers have been checked for consistency. The version allows your server to check each server to make certain each server has the correct version number. If you think a server has not been checked or there is a problem communicating with a particular server, then you should run a version check.

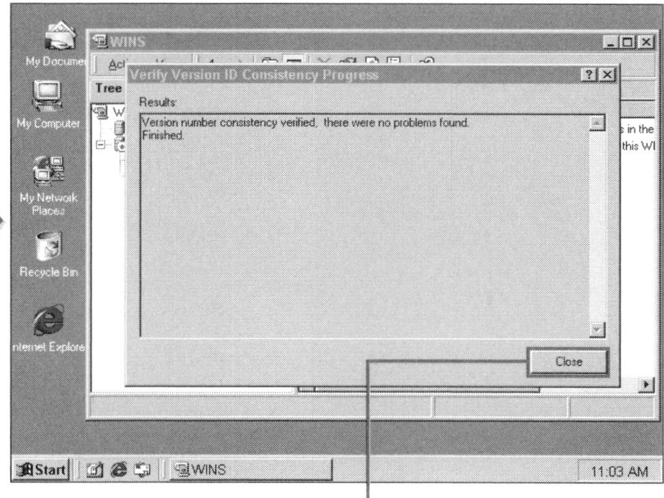

■ A window displays the results when the check is complete.

3 Click Close.

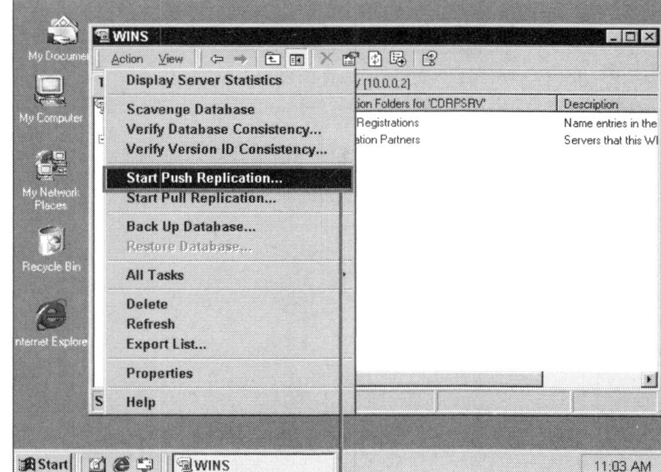

PERFORMING A PUSH REPLICATION

■ See the section "Managing Replication Partners" for more information.

1 To start a push replication, choose Action➪Start Push Replication.

CONTINUED

MANAGING THE WINS SERVER
CONTINUED

After replication is set up, WINS database replication among all WINS servers is managed automatically by WINS. However, you can use the Action menu to manually force replication. You have the option of using either a pull or push replication trigger. The *pull trigger* enables you to enter the name of a WINS server you want to pull replication from and start the pull. The *push trigger* allows you to push replication to other WINS servers. WINS replication functions in a partner design where one partner is a pull partner while the other is a push partner. This design allows effective replication between the two because one pushes changes while the other requests changes.

You can also use the Action menu to manually back up the WINS database. By default, the backup path is the root folder on your volume, such as C:\. You can change this, however. The WINS backup file is called Wins/mdb.

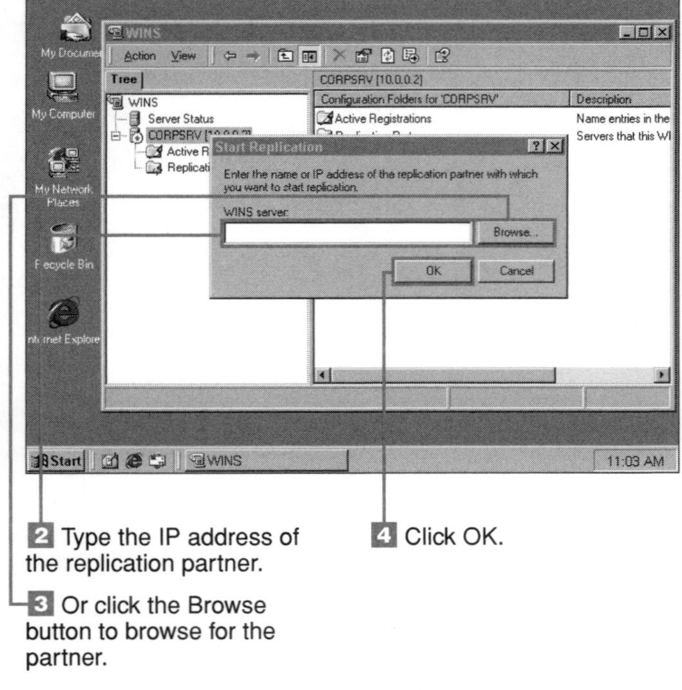

2 Type the IP address of the replication partner.

3 Or click the Browse button to browse for the partner.

4 Click OK.

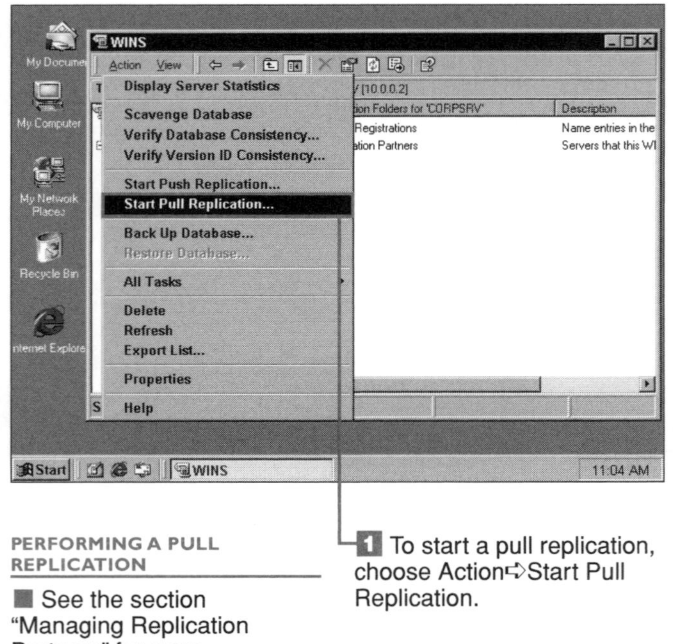

PERFORMING A PULL REPLICATION

■ See the section "Managing Replication Partners" for more information.

1 To start a pull replication, choose Action⇨Start Pull Replication.

Does a push or pull replication trigger interrupt the WINS server(s) operations?

- No. Replication occurs in the background and the process does not hinder the work of the WINS servers. You may see a performance decrease among the servers during the process, but they are still operational. If you need to use a push or pull replication trigger, you should wait until nonpeak network hours, which are typically early in the morning or late in the evening when network traffic and server requests are low.

Can I save the backup file in any location on your volume?

- Yes, you can browse to any location on your volume to save the WINS backup file. If you do not store the backup file in the default location, you should keep records so that you know exactly where the WINS database file, along with other database files, is stored. Many administrators choose to store backup files on other hard drives or even removable media.

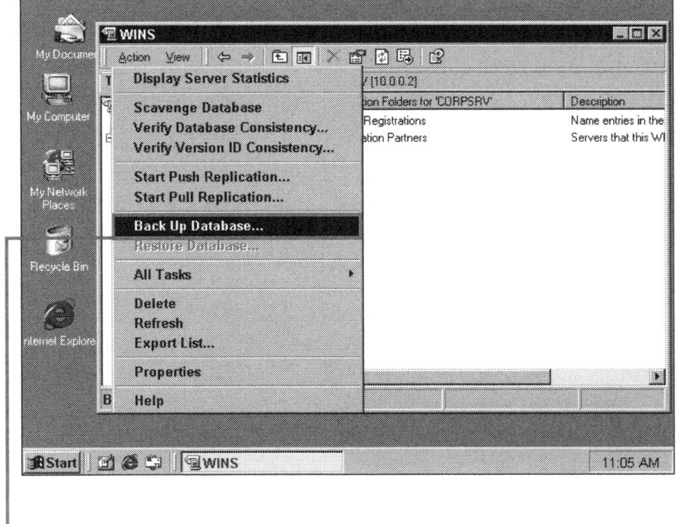

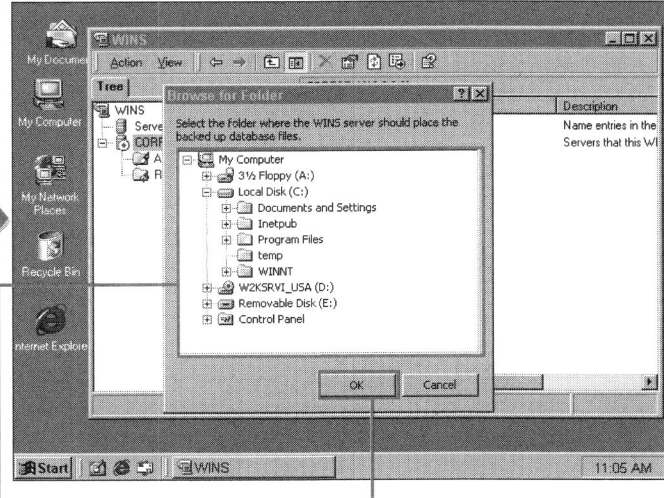

BACKING UP THE DATABASE

1. To back up the database, choose Action⇨Back Up Database.
2. Browse to the backup folder you want to use.
3. Click OK.

CONTINUED

MANAGING THE WINS SERVER CONTINUED

The Action menu's All Tasks feature enables you to stop, start, restart, pause, and resume the WINS server. In some cases, such as troubleshooting, you may need to stop or restart the service. Through this menu item, you can easily accomplish this task.

The WINS server also has Properties sheets that you can access from the Action menu. On the General tab, you can configure the time between statistic updates. The default is ten minutes, but you can change this as desired. You can also specify a location for the WINS backup file and configure the server to backup the database whenever the server shuts down. When you select this option, your server may take longer to shut down because the database has to be backed up, but the option is a good fault tolerance method so that you always have a backed-up copy of the database when you restart your server.

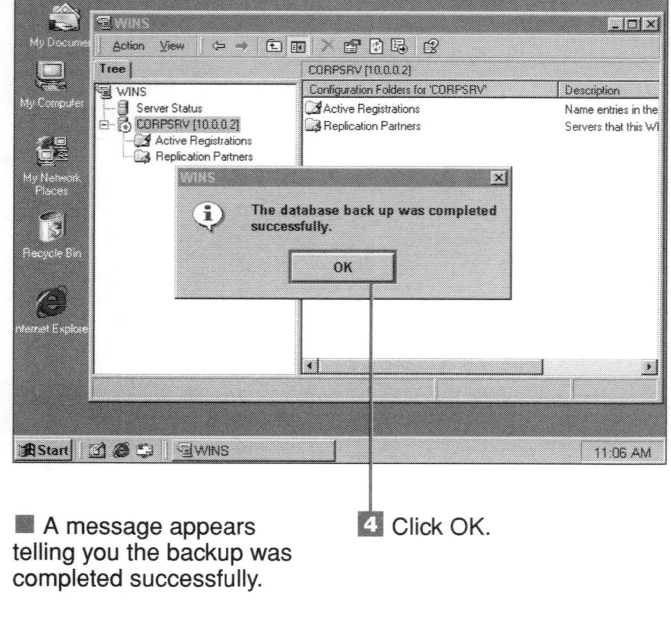

■ A message appears telling you the backup was completed successfully.

4 Click OK.

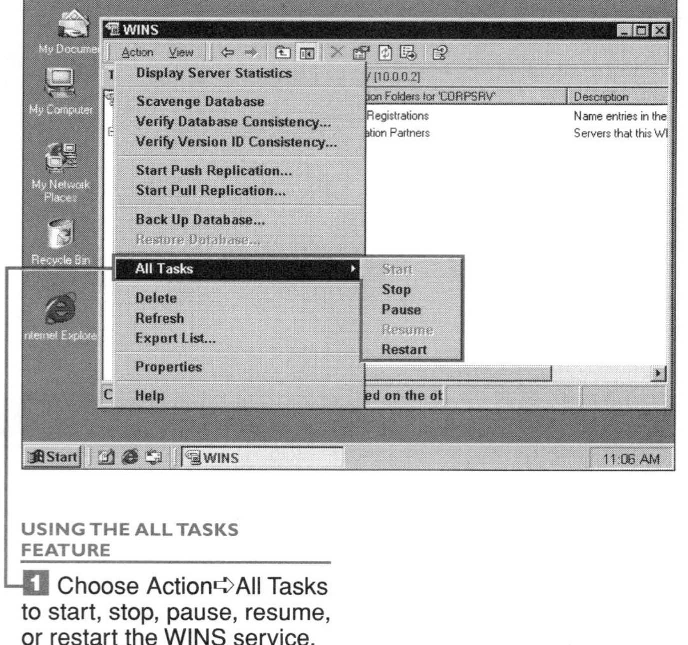

USING THE ALL TASKS FEATURE

1 Choose Action⇨All Tasks to start, stop, pause, resume, or restart the WINS service.

TIPS

Should I change the statistic update time?

- The default time is ten minutes, which gives you accurate information about the WINS server's performance. You can lower the time if desired, but this causes the server to do more update checks. If you increase the time, you may not receive as accurate statistical information as desired. The default setting is best, so make sure that you have a specific reason to change it before doing so.

Should I have the server back up the database each time it shuts down?

- Using the General tab in the Properties dialog box, you can tell the WINS server to back up the database every time the server shuts down. This option is not enabled by default, but it is a good safety measure. This action, however, may slow the time it takes to shut down the server.

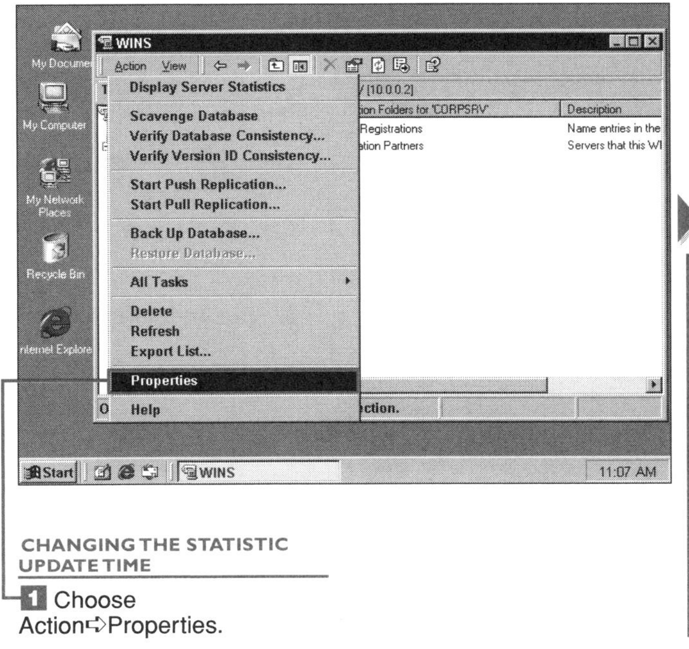

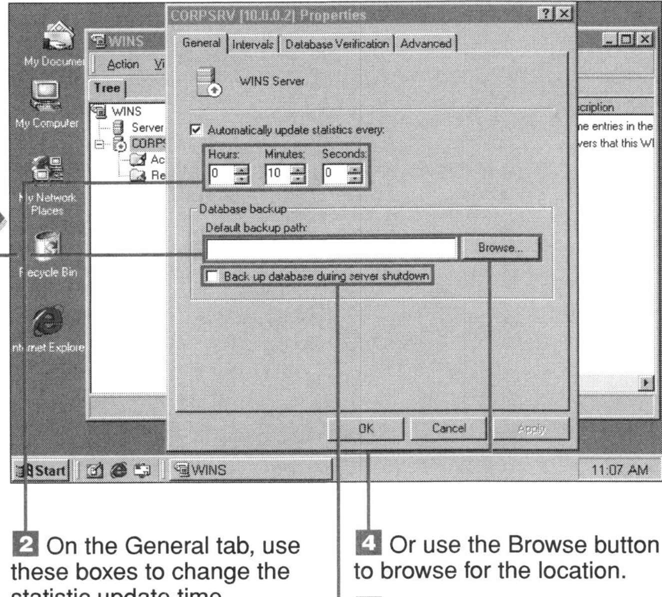

CHANGING THE STATISTIC UPDATE TIME

1 Choose Action⇨Properties.

2 On the General tab, use these boxes to change the statistic update time.

3 Enter a location for the backup path.

4 Or use the Browse button to browse for the location.

5 Click here to back up the database every time the server shuts down.

CONTINUED

MANAGING THE WINS SERVER
CONTINUED

On the Intervals tab, you can adjust the name record settings, such as the renew interval, extinction interval, extinction timeout, and verification interval. These settings control the rate at which records are renewed, deleted, and verified.

On the Database Verification tab, you can configure database verification to occur at certain intervals. If you enable this option, the default is every 24 hours. You can also change the number of records that are verified in each period, with the default being 3,000.

The Advanced tab enables you to configure logging options as desired. *Burst handling* is also configured on this tab. Burst handling allows the server to write database changes to a temporary file called jet.log in order to improve performance. This way, if there are many requests for updates from clients, the server can handle them all by using the temporary log until all the changes can be written to the actual database. You should allow the server to use burst handling; otherwise, clients have to requery the server during high update request times.

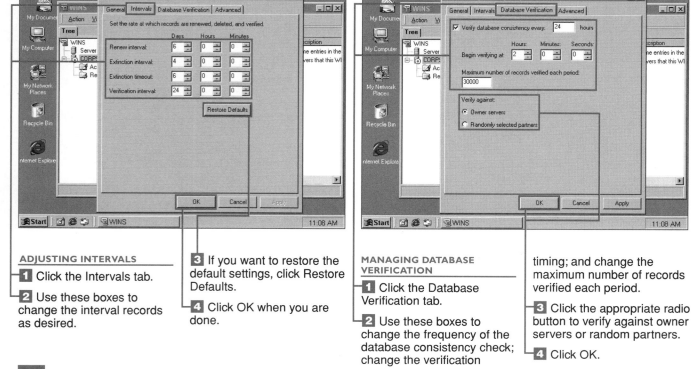

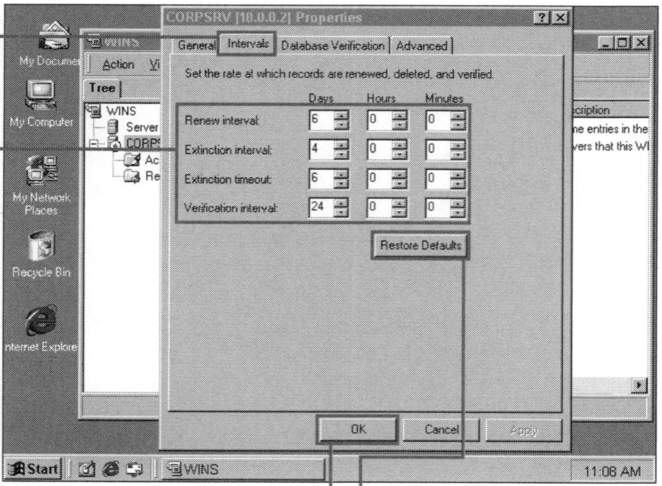

ADJUSTING INTERVALS

1 Click the Intervals tab.

2 Use these boxes to change the interval records as desired.

3 If you want to restore the default settings, click Restore Defaults.

4 Click OK when you are done.

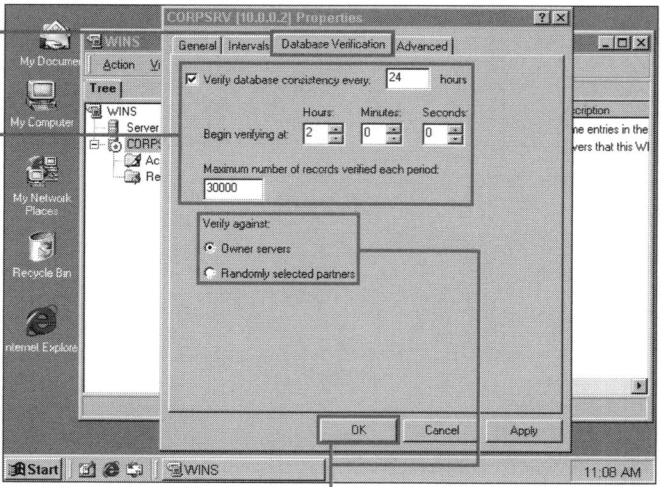

MANAGING DATABASE VERIFICATION

1 Click the Database Verification tab.

2 Use these boxes to change the frequency of the database consistency check; change the verification timing; and change the maximum number of records verified each period.

3 Click the appropriate radio button to verify against owner servers or random partners.

4 Click OK.

What are the burst settings I can choose from?

The burst handling settings enable you to tell the server how many requests can occur before burst handling takes effect. Each setting allows a certain number of name registrations or refresh requests in the *burst queue* before burst handling begins. You have four settings to choose from (the default setting is Medium):

- **Low:** 300 registrations and name refresh requests in the burst queue before burst handling begins
- **Medium:** 500 registrations and name refresh requests in the burst queue before burst handling begins
- **High:** 1,000 registrations and name refresh requests in the burst queue before burst handling begins
- **Custom:** Enter the desired number of registration and name refresh requests in the burst queue before burst handling begins.

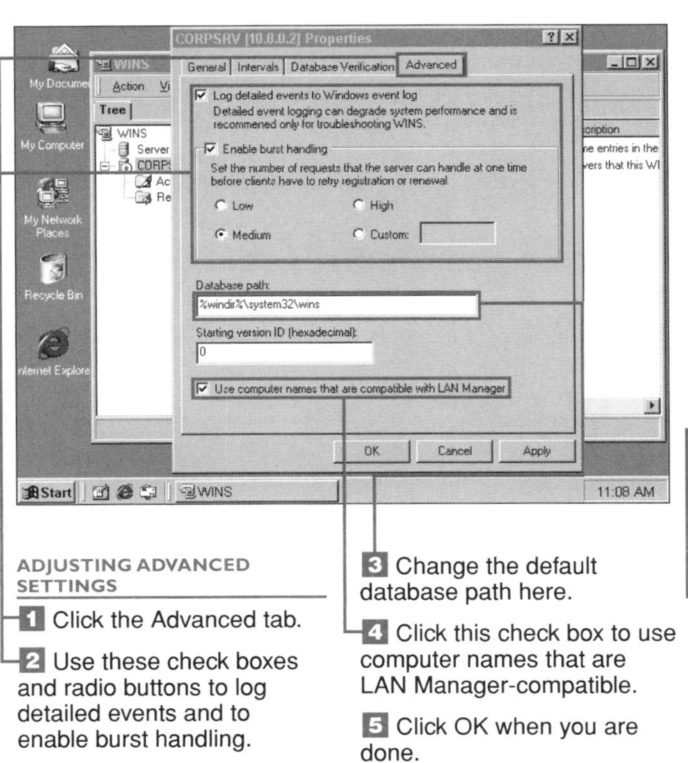

ADJUSTING ADVANCED SETTINGS

1 Click the Advanced tab.

2 Use these check boxes and radio buttons to log detailed events and to enable burst handling.

3 Change the default database path here.

4 Click this check box to use computer names that are LAN Manager-compatible.

5 Click OK when you are done.

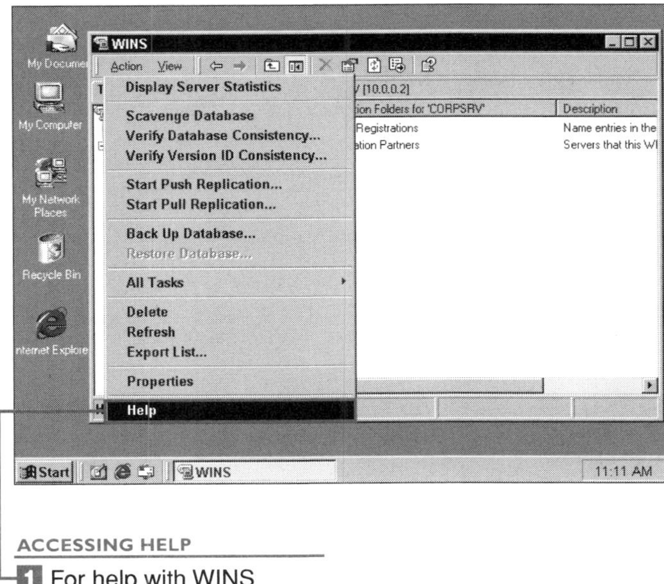

ACCESSING HELP

1 For help with WINS server management, choose Action⇨Help.

MANAGING REGISTRATIONS

The Registrations container in the console tree enables you to perform several actions concerning the current WINS registrations.

First, you can find records that currently exist. You can find a record by searching for the name of the record (or closest match) or for the record's owner. To find a record by the owner, you search all WINS servers for the record, or you can search a particular owner, which allows you to select a server from the list and run the search. The owner search allows to WINS database to find records for certain WINS server owners. Note that an owner search can be network-intensive because the search requires downloading databases from remote WINS servers. Depending on the size of the databases and network traffic conditions, the process can consume a lot of network bandwidth.

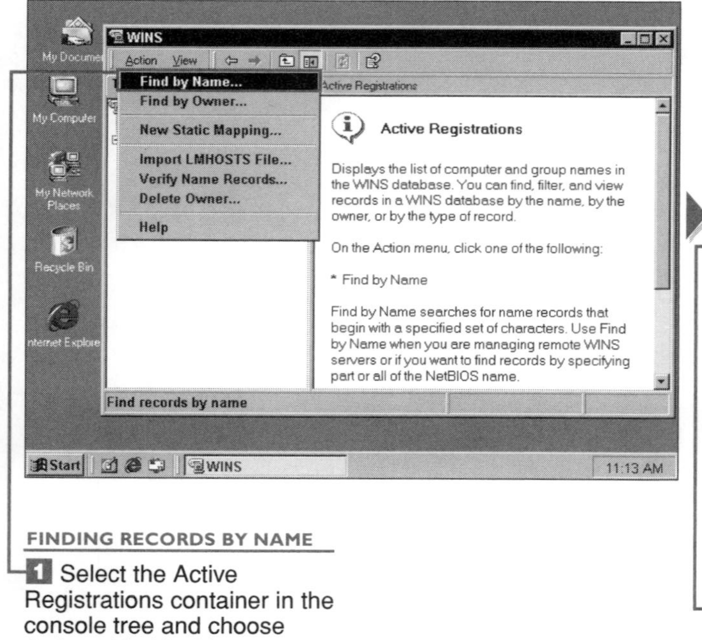

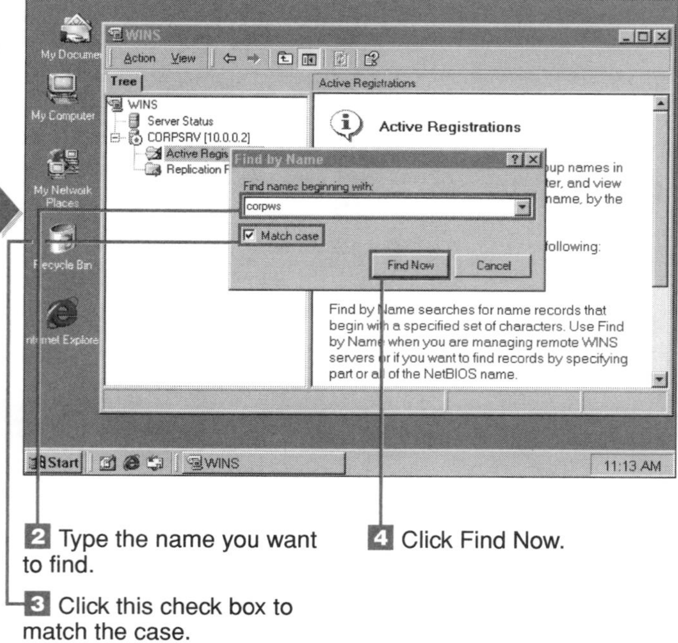

FINDING RECORDS BY NAME

1 Select the Active Registrations container in the console tree and choose Action⇨Find by Name.

2 Type the name you want to find.

3 Click this check box to match the case.

4 Click Find Now.

TIPS

If I search by owner, are all registration records returned?

Yes. The owner search pulls all the WINS registration records for all WINS servers or for a particular server, depending on which action you select. After the list appears in the details pane of the snap-in, you can browse the list to find the record that you want to view.

How does the Find by Name function work?

The Find by Name function enables you to search for particular name records through a set of characters. You enter the name you want to search for, and the WINS server uses the search entry to find all NetBIOS names that closely match your request.

Can I filter a Find by Owner function?

Yes. You can refine a Find by Owner search by filtering the search so that it only provides the types of records you want returned. You can filter the search by using the Record Types tab and checking or unchecking your desired returns.

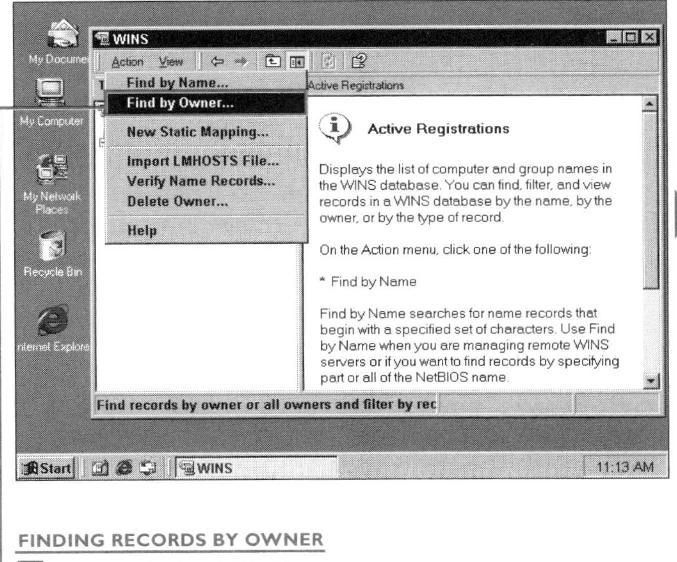

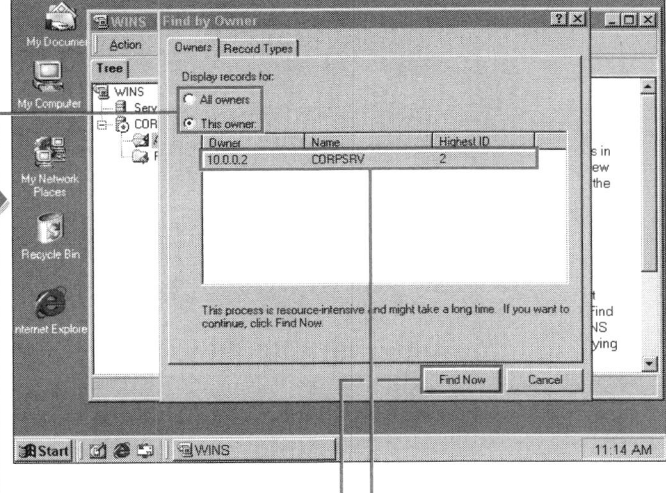

FINDING RECORDS BY OWNER

1 Choose Action⇨Find by Owner.

2 Click either the All Owners or This Owner radio button.

3 If you click This Owner, select an owner from the list.

4 Click Find Now.

CONTINUED

MANAGING REGISTRATIONS CONTINUED

From the Registrations container, you can also click the Action menu to define a static mapping and to import an LMHOST file.

You use the static mapping feature to create static name-to-IP address mappings in the WINS database. This mapping is replicated to all other databases and overwrites any conflicting records. You can use the static mapping only for non-WINS clients or clients that cannot dynamically register with the WINS database.

You can also import an LMHOSTS file into the WINS database. An LMHOSTS file is a static file that contains NetBIOS-to-IP address mappings. The import feature is used to preserve these mappings within the WINS database. Although LMHOSTS files are not typically used any longer, this feature is helpful if you have a static list of name-to-IP address mappings in an LMHOSTS file that you want to import into the WINS database.

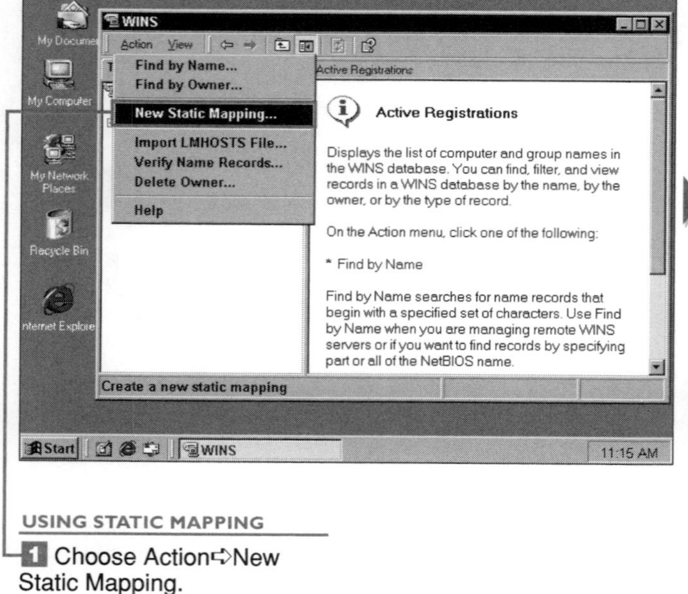

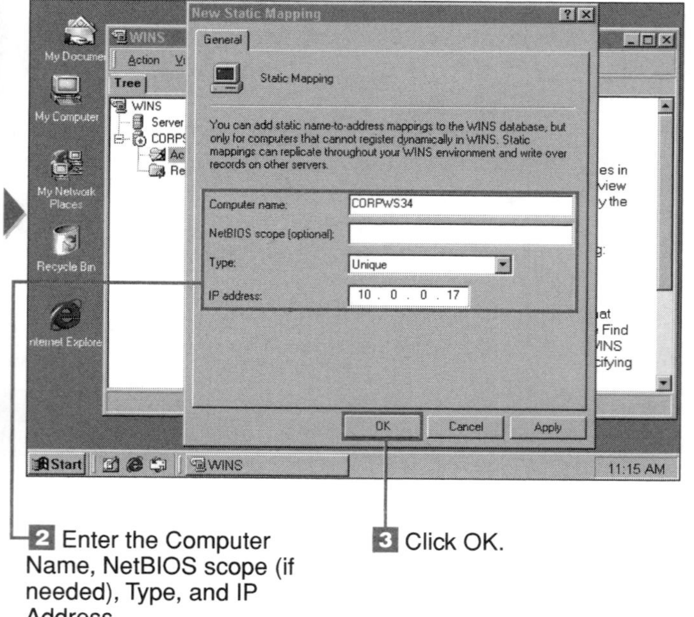

USING STATIC MAPPING

1 Choose Action⇨New Static Mapping.

2 Enter the Computer Name, NetBIOS scope (if needed), Type, and IP Address.

3 Click OK.

Why can't I create a static mapping for a normal WINS client?

- The static mapping feature is designed for non-Windows clients that cannot dynamically register their NetBIOS name and IP address with the WINS server. WINS clients automatically perform this action and attempt to update their mapping information as it both changes and expires.

How does an LMHOSTS file work?

- An LMHOSTS file is simply a text file that lists a computer's NetBIOS name and that computer's IP address. When resolution needs to occur, the computer can check the LMHOSTS file to find the NetBIOS name of the computer and resolve that name to an IP address. Although you do not need to use LMHOSTS files in a WINS network, Windows 2000 allows you to import them into the WINS database so they can be used. This is particularly helpful for static mappings you have already configured.

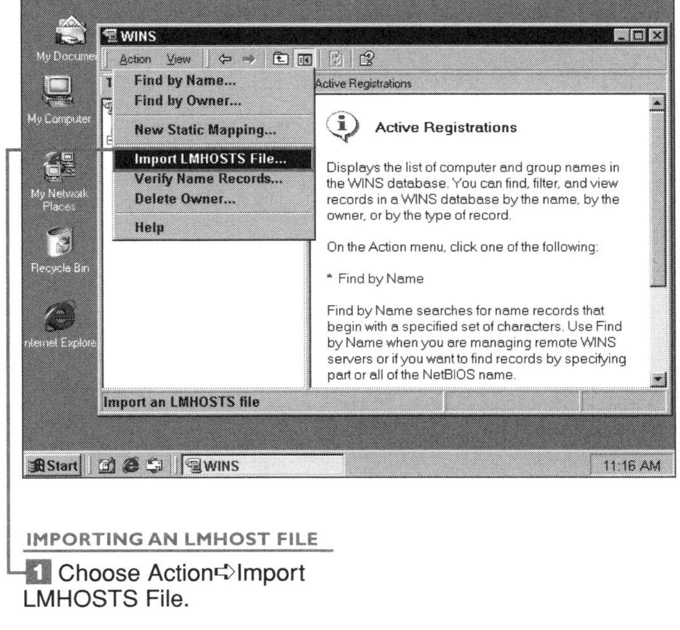

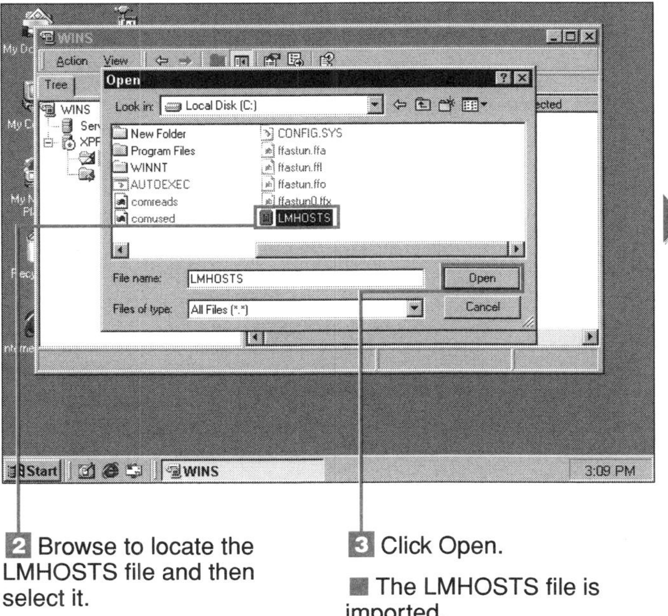

IMPORTING AN LMHOST FILE

1 Choose Action⇨Import LMHOSTS File.

2 Browse to locate the LMHOSTS file and then select it.

3 Click Open.

■ The LMHOSTS file is imported.

CONTINUED

MANAGING REGISTRATIONS CONTINUED

Finally, the Registrations container Action menu enables you to verify name records and also delete owners.

The Verify Name Records option allows you to verify a set of name records on specific servers. To perform this action, you either select a file or create a list of name records that you want to verify. Then, you select either a server or a list of servers by IP address to verify the records on. The record verification feature checks the records that you specify and verifies if the records are valid in the WINS database. When you perform the check, you also have the option of verifying all name records with all partners of the servers that you select.

You can also delete an owner. The owner deletion removes the selected owner and all the owner's records. You have the option to delete the owner from the server only or to replicate the deletion to all other WINS servers. This action creates a *tombstone marker*, which is then replicated to the other servers. A tombstone is simply a marker that a record has been deleted. The tombstone remains until all WINS servers have received the deletion request, and then the tombstone is removed.

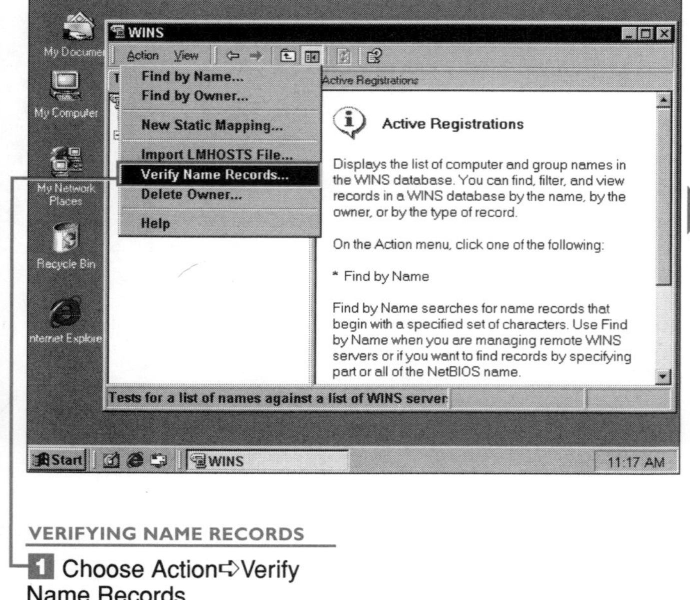

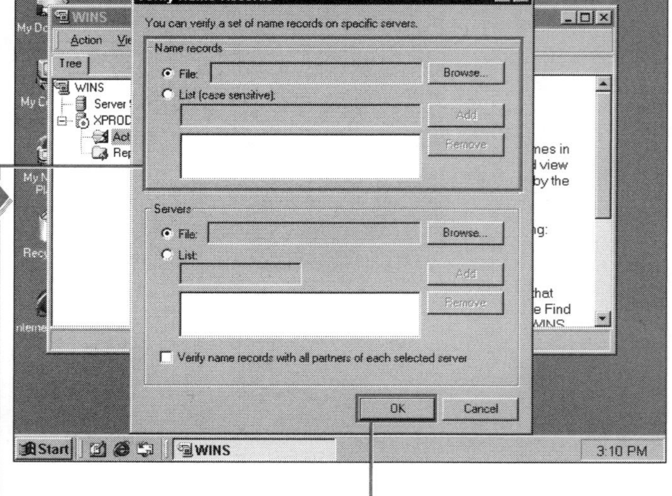

VERIFYING NAME RECORDS

1 Choose Action⇨Verify Name Records.

2 Enter the information in these boxes to verify the name records on specific services.

■ You can verify a particular file or a list.

3 Click OK after you enter the information.

Why would I want to verify a name record?

- The name record feature enables you to check the WINS registrations for a particular name record. The verification returns information to you about the registration. This tool is particularly useful for troubleshooting WINS registration problems or issues.

What does the tombstone do?

- When you delete an owner, you can delete the owner on a particular server or have the deletion replicated to other servers. If the deletion is replicated, a tombstone, which is a marker, is replicated so that other servers know the owner has been deleted. Each server holds the tombstone until all servers receive the deletion request. After all servers receive the tombstone, the owner and all records for that owner are deleted. The tombstone method is an effective way to make certain that servers receive the deletion request before actual deletion takes place.

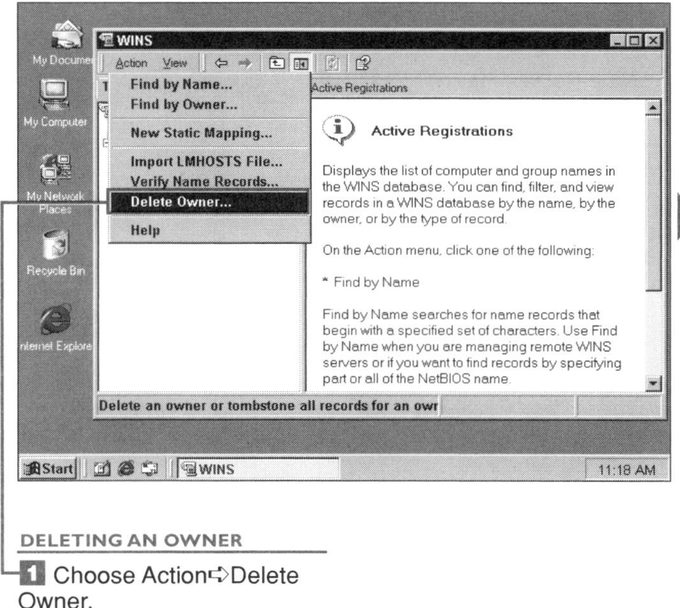

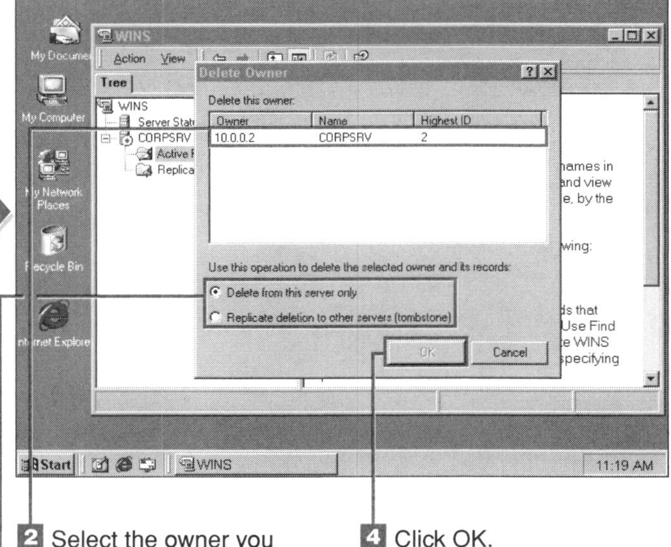

DELETING AN OWNER

1 Choose Action⇨Delete Owner.

2 Select the owner you want to delete.

3 Click the appropriate radio button to either delete from this server only or to replicate deletion to other servers (tombstone).

4 Click OK.

MANAGING REPLICATION PARTNERS

WINS replication ensures that all WINS server databases are replicated so that each server has an accurate copy. Replication occurs through the use of replication partners. This enables you to structure replication so that each server has a partner closest on the network for replication. For replication to work, each WINS server must be configured to have at least one replication partner. This design ensures that all records and changes are replicated to all WINS servers. Partners can either be push or pull partners, or they can be both push and pull. The push/pull partner offers the best performance and is the default configuration.

Replication occurs on a set schedule, but you can use the Action menu to force replication if desired. Generally, allowing the schedule to handle the replication requests is usually best unless you have a specific reason to force the replication.

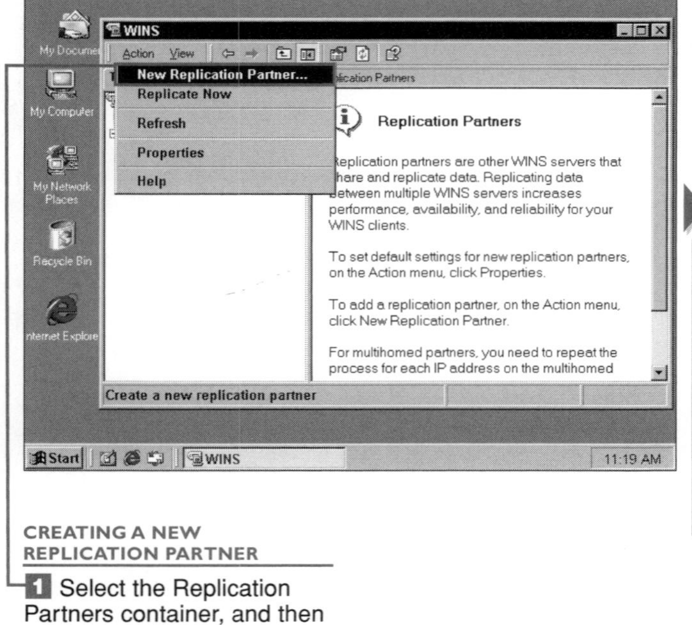

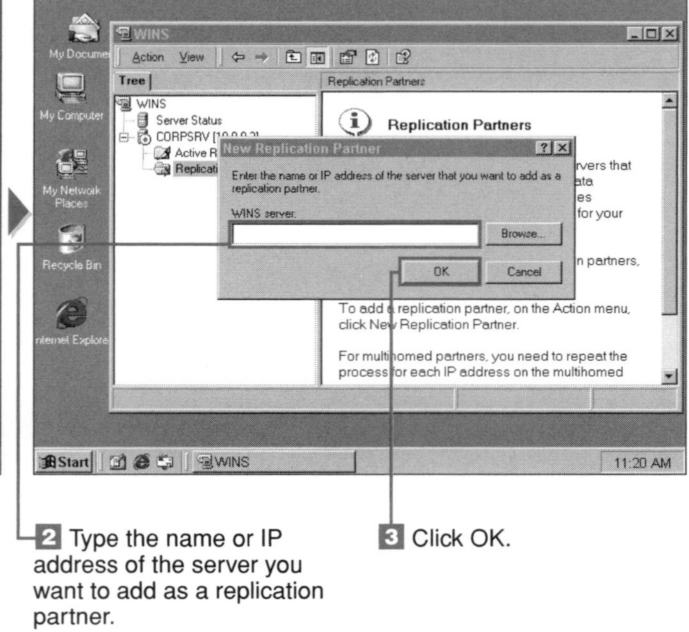

CREATING A NEW REPLICATION PARTNER

1 Select the Replication Partners container, and then choose Action⇨New Replication Partner.

2 Type the name or IP address of the server you want to add as a replication partner.

3 Click OK.

TIPS

Is replication really necessary?

Replication ensures that your WINS servers have each other's data. This action maintains one WINS database so that clients can be serviced from any WINS server. If multiple WINS servers are used in your network, replication is a necessary component of the WINS functionality to ensure that you have the best performance and reliability for WINS operation.

Why would I force replication?

Generally, you do not need to force replication among partners. Replication occurs automatically and the replication partners maintain a replication schedule. However, in some cases, especially if you have replication concerns, you may want to force WINS replication to attempt to resolve any accessibility problems WINS clients may be experiencing.

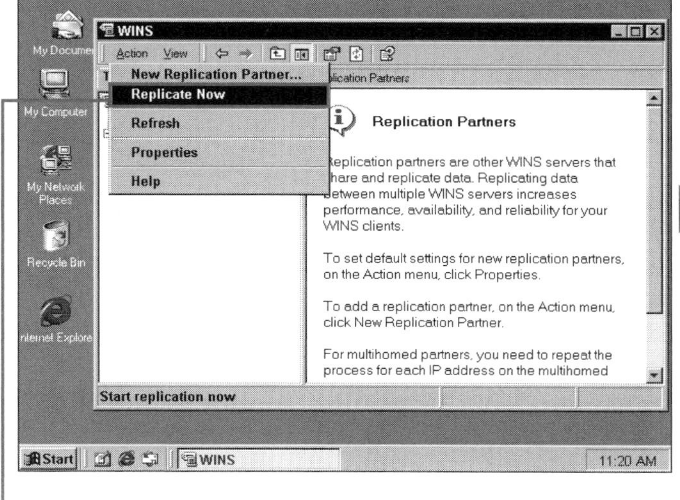

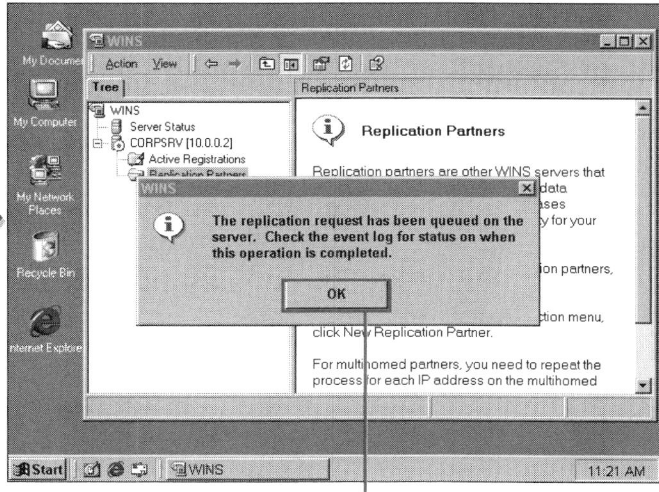

FORCING REPLICATION

1 To force replication, choose Action⇨Replicate Now.

■ A message tells you that the replication request has been queued.

2 Click OK.

CONTINUED

MANAGING REPLICATION PARTNERS
CONTINUED

You can configure the partner replication by accessing the properties sheet, which has four tabs.

On the General tab, you can choose whether or not to replicate only with partners. This action is selected by default and should not be changed unless you have specific reasons for doing so. You can also choose to overwrite unique static mappings at this particular server. This allows the server to overwrite the static records when they conflict with a new name registration.

On the Push Replication tab, you can configure push replication to occur at startup or when the address changes, which informs pull partners of the database status when an address changes in the mapping record. You can also determine the number of changes in version ID that must occur before replication—the default is 0. And you can choose whether to use persistent connections for replication with push partners.

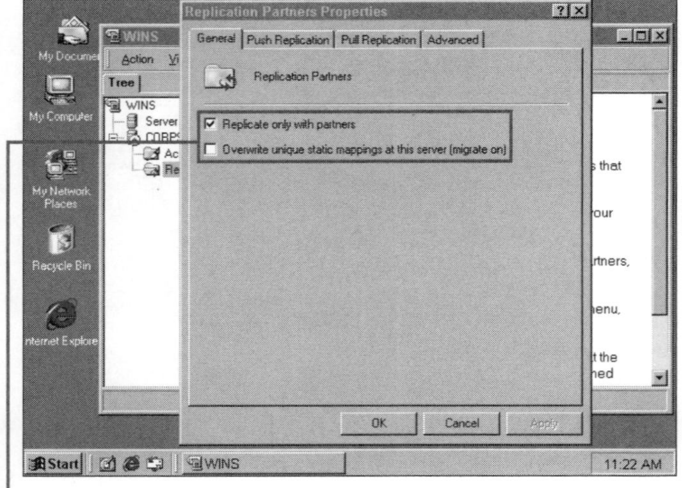

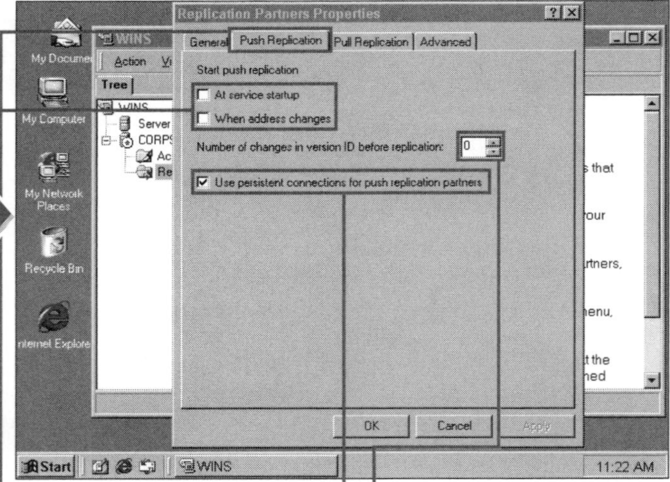

CONFIGURING PARTNER REPLICATION

1 On the General tab, you can select Replicate with partners only and Overwrite unique static mappings at this server by selecting the check boxes.

2 Click the Push Replication tab.

3 Click the appropriate check boxes to enable push replication at startup and/or when the address changes.

4 Enter a value here if you want a specific number of version ID changes before replication occurs.

5 Click this check box to use a persistent connection for push replication partners.

What options does the Pull Replication tab offer?

On the Pull Replication tab, you can configure the start time of the replication. You can set the time in hours, minutes, and seconds, when the pull replication should begin. If the values are set to 0: 0: 0, then no automatic pull replication occurs. You can also configure the replication interval, which is the amount of time in days, hours, and minutes that should pass between each pull replication. You can also choose to start replication at service startup and to use a persistent connection for all pull replication partners.

What options does the Advanced tab offer?

On the Advanced tab, you can choose to block records for certain owners. This feature enables you to block other WINS servers from having their records replicated to your WINS servers. You also have the option to enable automatic partner configuration. This method is designed for small networks and allows the WINS server to use a broadcast approach to automatically configure itself with a partner for replication.

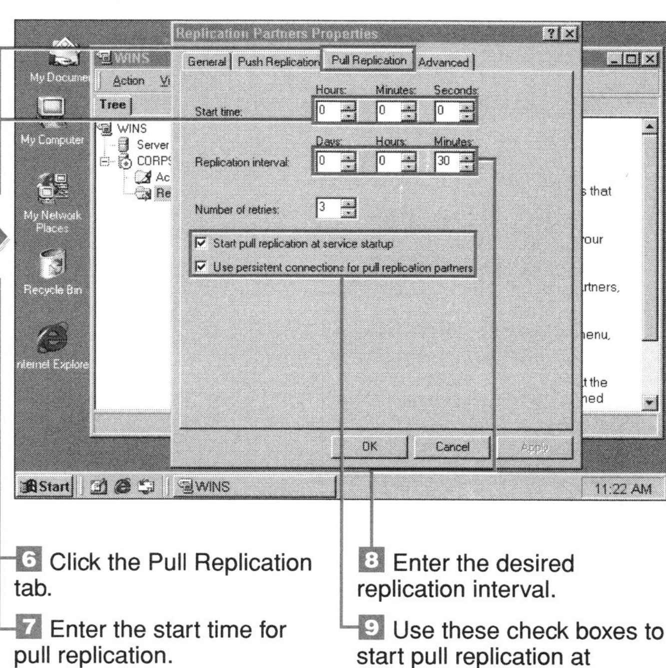

6 Click the Pull Replication tab.

7 Enter the start time for pull replication.

8 Enter the desired replication interval.

9 Use these check boxes to start pull replication at service startup and to use persistent connections for pull partners.

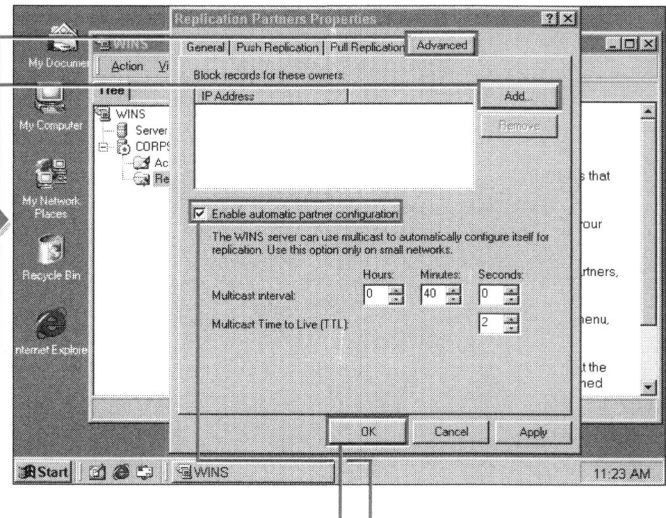

10 Click the Advanced tab.

11 Click Add to block certain records for particular owners so that they are not replicated.

12 Click this check box to enable automatic partner replication using multicast.

13 Click OK to save any changes.

DOMAIN NAME SYSTEM OVERVIEW

To effectively plan, implement, and maintain the Active Directory, you work with *Domain Name System* (DNS). DNS is an industry standard for resolving host names to IP addresses and IP addresses to host names. DNS is the primary naming system of choice in Windows 2000 networks. Why? Because DNS is widely used, accepted, and highly extensible. Every time you use the Internet, the URL you type in your browser is resolved to an IP address by DNS.

DNS is fully integrated with Windows 2000 and the Active Directory, and public domain names like `www.microsoft.com` can also be private names on your network. `JohnD@corp.com` is an e-mail address on the Internet and also a username in the Active Directory. With DNS as the naming structure in the Active Directory, users have to learn only one naming convention for the local network and Internet, and the use of DNS on the local network provides a more seamless approach to combining the local network and the Internet, as many organizations are doing today.

In order to effectively implement the Active Directory, you must have a firm understanding of DNS concepts and how to configure your Windows 2000 server as a DNS server. To fully understand DNS, you must first understand the DNS namespace.

DNS namespace

A *namespace* is any area that can be resolved. A telephone book is namespace in that all persons are listed by last name, first name, and address. By accessing this information, you can "resolve" the name into a telephone number. No matter who you want to call, you use the same process over and over to resolve different persons to different numbers.

DNS functions in much the same way. DNS is structured in such a way that `www.infoseek.com` or `www.ucla.edu` can be resolved to an IP address. Remember that computers on a TCP/IP network can communicate using only an IP address—friendly names must be resolved. DNS can accomplish this because all names are structured in a hierarchical fashion based on different domains.

The hierarchical structure of DNS is built on the DNS tree. At the top of the DNS tree is the root domain, called the Internet root. This is represented by a period.

Next in the tree is the first-level domain. First-level domains are made up of large divisions of names that you see at the end of the DNS name. Common examples are com, edu, net, gov, mil, org, and even foreign country initials such as jp (for Japan) and au (for Australia).

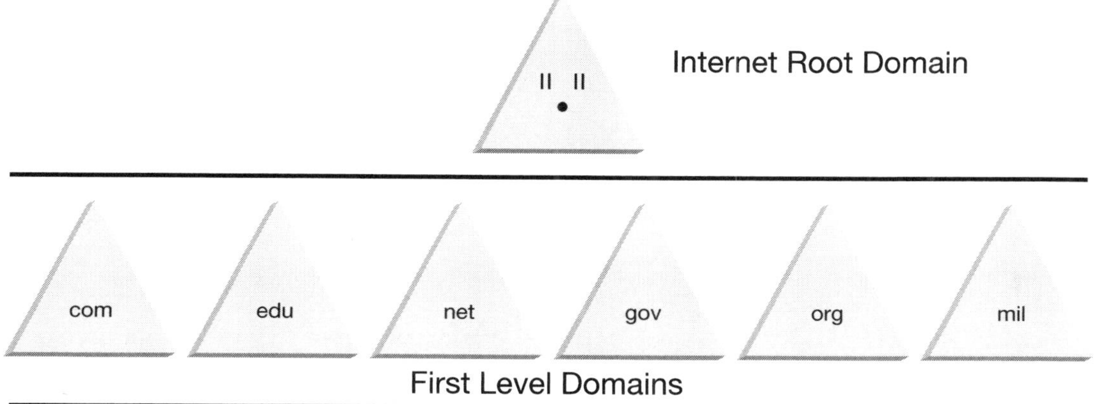

Next in the tree is the second-level domain. The second-level domain represents some business or organization and is normally a friendly name that users can recognize.

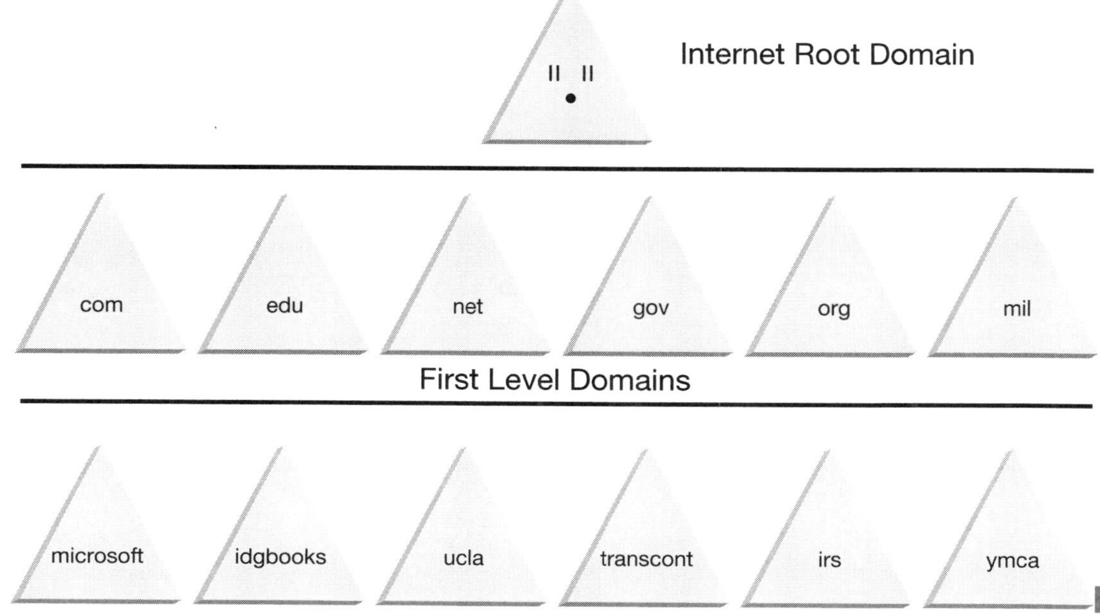

CONTINUED

DOMAIN NAME SYSTEM OVERVIEW
CONTINUED

Next, some domains may contain *subdomains* that further divide the second-level domain. These subdomains, also called *child domains* and *grandchild domains*, may be different divisions or groups within the second-level domain company.

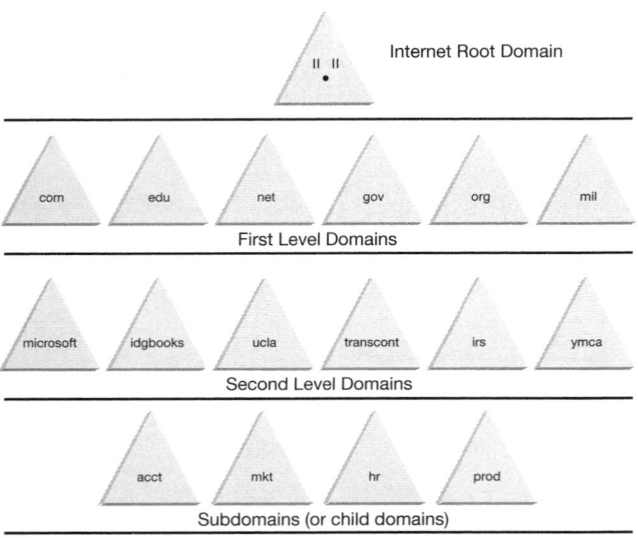

When resolution reaches a host—which is a computer within the domain—the DNS name is said to be a *Fully Qualified Domain Name.*

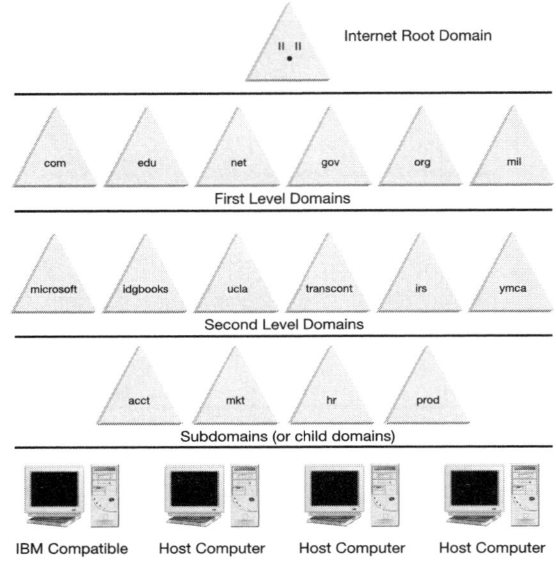

Host Computers. A Fully Qualified Domain Name can be resolved for the top of the tree down to the host computer.

Much like how the postal system can deliver a piece of mail to your home by resolving the zip code, state, city, street address, and then your name, DNS can resolve host names to IP address by resolving the root domain, first-level domain, second-level domain, subdomains (if present), and the host. In the example in Figure 6-6, any computer can reach Server12 by allowing DNS to resolve it to its IP address.

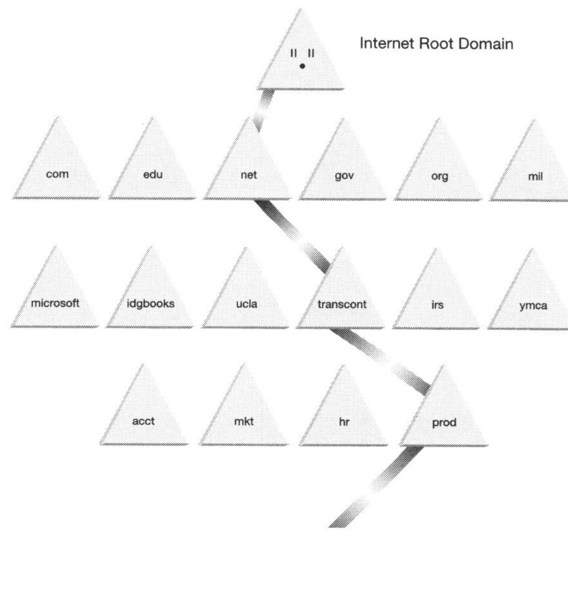

Understanding name resolution

Fully Qualified Domain Names (FQDN) must be resolved to IP addresses in order for network communication to occur. The DNS name resolution process is performed by resolving each domain in FQDN, beginning at the top of the hierarchy and working its way down. On your network, a DNS server may be able to check its database file and resolve a FQDN to an IP address. On the Internet, this process normally requires several servers. Different DNS servers must resolve each potion of the DNS name until the host is eventually reached and an IP address can be returned. This process is called a *forward lookup query.*

First, a computer requests a resolution for a FQDN — for example, `server12.prod.transcont.net`. The client sends the request to a local DNS server for resolution. If the DNS server does not have authority over the domain `corp.com`, then it has to go through a resolution process with other servers, beginning with an Internet root server. The DNS server asks the Internet root server for the IP address of a "com" server to begin the resolution process.

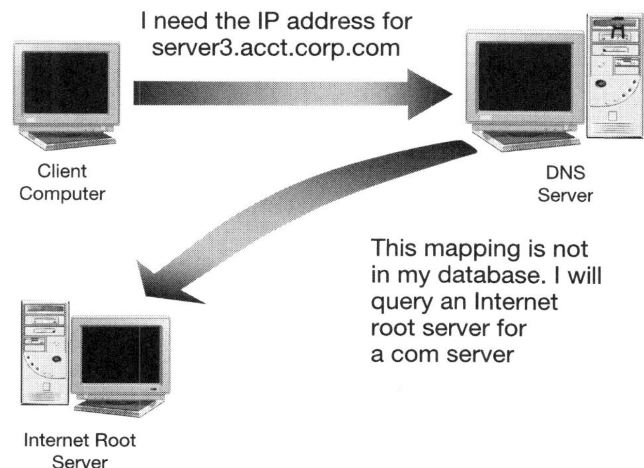

The Internet root returns the IP address of a com server, and then the DNS server contacts this server for the IP address of a "corp" DNS server. The com server checks its database and returns the IP address of a transcont DNS server.

CONTINUED

DOMAIN NAME SYSTEM OVERVIEW
CONTINUED

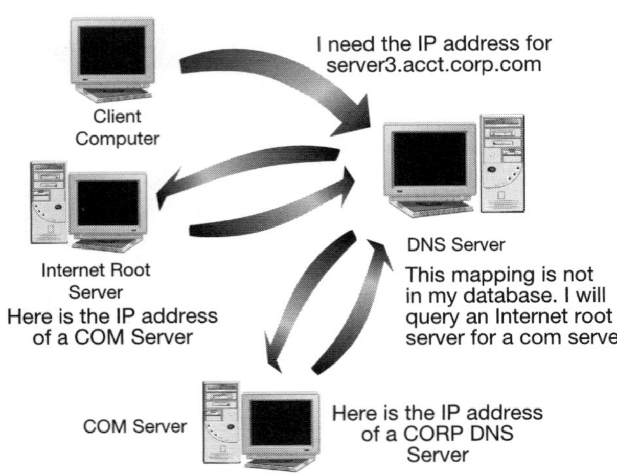
I need the IP address for server3.acct.corp.com
Client Computer
Internet Root Server
Here is the IP address of a COM Server
DNS Server
This mapping is not in my database. I will query an Internet root server for a com server
COM Server
Here is the IP address of a CORP DNS Server

The DNS server then queries the transcont DNS server for the IP address of a prod DNS server. The prod DNS server checks its database and returns the IP address to the DNS server.

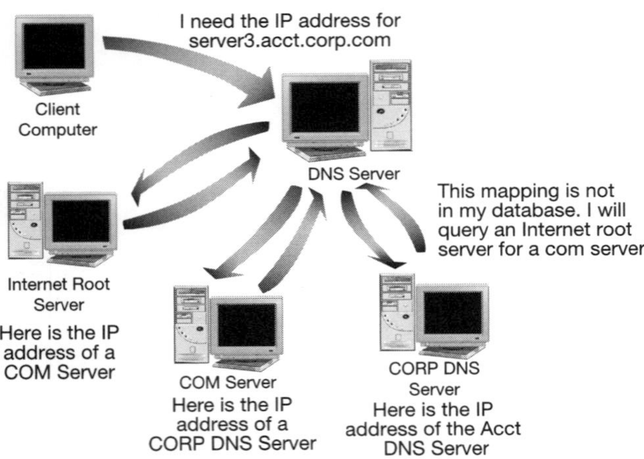
I need the IP address for server3.acct.corp.com
Client Computer
DNS Server
This mapping is not in my database. I will query an Internet root server for a com server
Internet Root Server
Here is the IP address of a COM Server
COM Server
Here is the IP address of a CORP DNS Server
CORP DNS Server
Here is the IP address of the Acct DNS Server

The DNS server then queries the prod DNS server for the IP address of Server12. The acct DNS server checks its database and returns the IP address of Server12 to the DNS server.

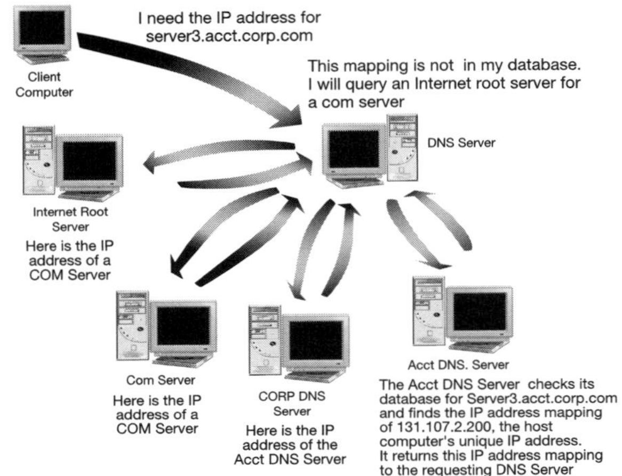
I need the IP address for server3.acct.corp.com
Client Computer
This mapping is not in my database. I will query an Internet root server for a com server
DNS Server
Internet Root Server
Here is the IP address of a COM Server
Com Server
Here is the IP address of a COM Server
CORP DNS Server
Here is the IP address of the Acct DNS Server
Acct DNS. Server
The Acct DNS Server checks its database for Server3.acct.corp.com and finds the IP address mapping of 131.107.2.200, the host computer's unique IP address. It returns this IP address mapping to the requesting DNS Server

The DNS server then returns the IP address mapping to the client computer. The client computer can now establish a TCP/IP communication session with the server using the server's IP address.

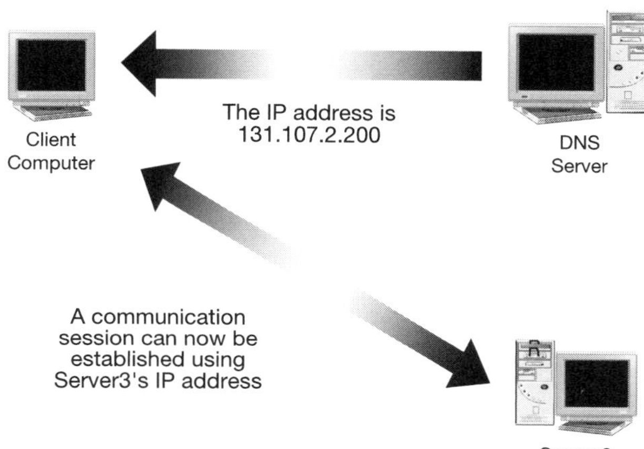
Client
Computer
The IP address is
131.107.2.200
DNS
Server
A communication
session can now be
established using
Server3's IP address
Server 3

This process can resolve any FQDN, and the entire process is invisible to the user.

Understanding DNS zones

A final DNS concept you should understand is DNS zones. *Zones* are used to subdivide administrative duties. A zone is a discreet and contiguous portion of the DNS namespace. Due to administration needs, zones provide a way to *partition* the namespace so that it can be managed by different persons. For example, you company may have divisions, such as "production" and "administration." In order to help IT administrators, the network can be divided into a "production zone" and an "administrative zone." This feature allows different groups of administrators to handle the DNS tasks in each zone.

Each DNS zone contains at least one DNS server that contains the DNS database for that zone. The DNS server can resolve name-to-IP-address queries for that zone. The main DNS server in the zone holds the *primary zone database file*. If other DNS servers are in the zone, they contain a *secondary zone DNS database file*. The secondary zone database file is a copy of the primary zone database file and it cannot be updated. Only changes to the primary zone database file can be made, and then the secondary zone database files are updated by a replication process known as *zone transfer*. Because only one DNS server can hold the primary zone database file and make changes to the file, that server is said to have *authority* over the zone. This DNS server may be referred to as the *authoritative DNS server* for the zone. Because of the zone transfer process, additional DNS servers can be used in the zone to help with FQDN queries, but only one DNS server is authoritative.

INSTALLING DNS

You can install the DNS service in the same manner as you install other networking components in Windows 2000 Server. You can use the Add/Remove programs feature in Control Panel and then access the Add/Remove Windows Components button to add the service. Or you can add the DNS service by using the Configure Your Server application in Administrative Tools.

You should note that you are prompted to install DNS when you install the Active Directory, but you can install it ahead of time to configure the DNS service if desired. If not, the Active Directory installation prompts you—, then setup can automatically install the service and perform a basic setup of DNS. You cannot install the Active Directory without installing DNS, and after you install the Active Directory, your server automatically becomes a domain controller. You can think of the Active Directory and DNS as partners—the Active Directory uses the DNS service to resolve domain names to IP addresses and it is an integrated part of the Active Directory.

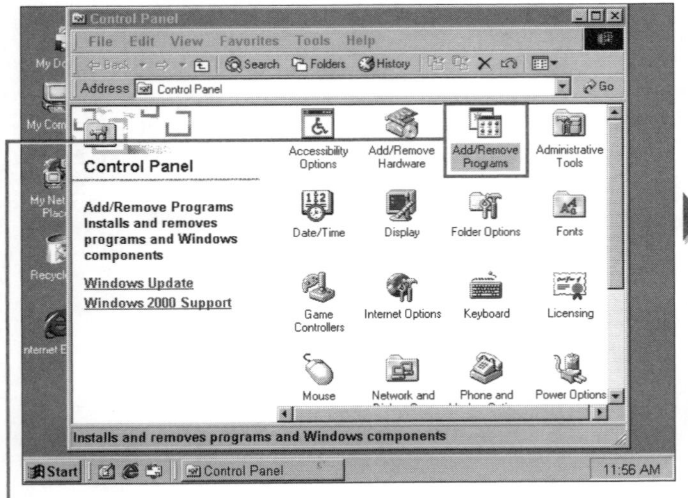

1 Open Control Panel and double-click Add/Remove Programs.

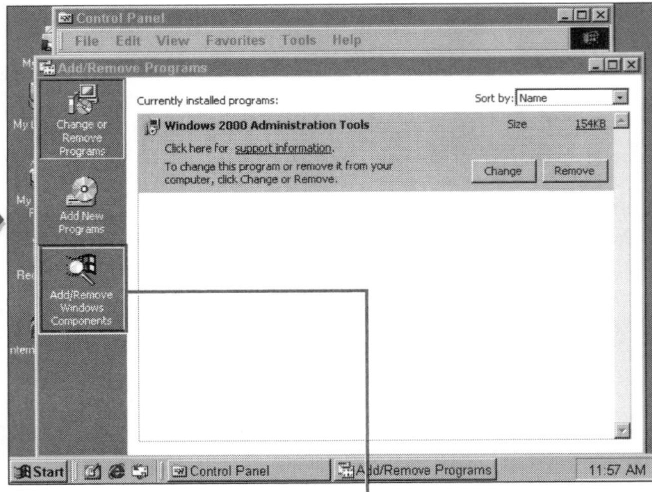

■ The Add/Remove Programs window appears.

2 Click Add/Remove Windows Components.

Do I need to set up the DNS service before installing the Active Directory?

No. The Active Directory installation automatically prompts you to install an initial configuration using the information you enter into the Active Directory installation wizard. However, you can choose to install and set up the service before you install the Active Directory if desired.

Can I have a Windows 2000 domain controller that does not run the Active Directory?

No. The act of installing the Active Directory automatically promotes a server to domain controller status. The act of removing the Active Directory automatically demotes a server from domain controller status. You cannot have a Windows 2000 domain controller that does not run the Active Directory.

■ The Windows Components Wizard appears.

3 Click Next to continue.

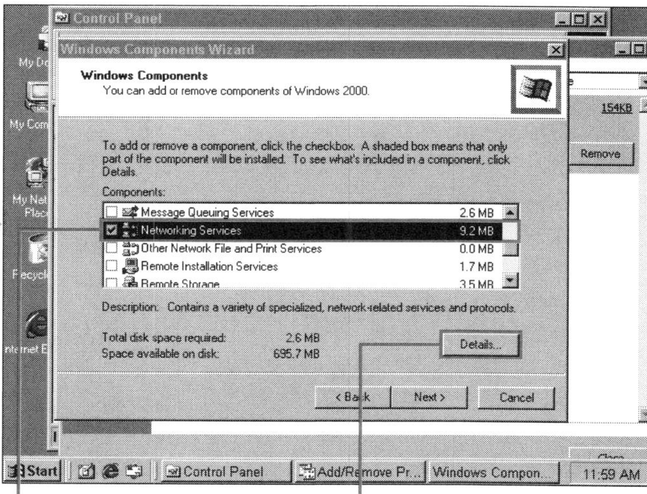

4 Select Networking Services.

5 Click Details to see what is included in a component.

CONTINUED

INSTALLING DNS CONTINUED

There is no difference between using Add/Remove Programs in Control Panel to install the service and using the Configure Your Server program in Administrative Tools. If you want to use the Configure Your Server program, simply choose Start⇨Programs⇨ Administrative Tools. In the left pane, expand Networking and click the DNS Service link to start the installation.

After the installation is complete, you need to configure the DNS server for service on your network. DNS is not automatically set up and configured upon installation as some of the other networking components are, so you have to configure it so that it functions appropriately in your network. Also, once installation is complete, you are not prompted to start a configuration wizard. The installation simply ends, and then your next step is to access the DNS Management console and begin the configuration process. The next section shows you how to configure the DNS service.

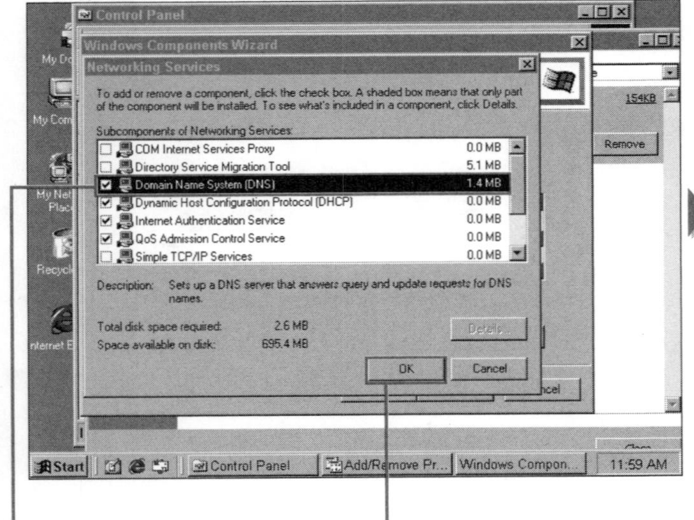

6 Click the Domain Name System check box.

7 Click OK.

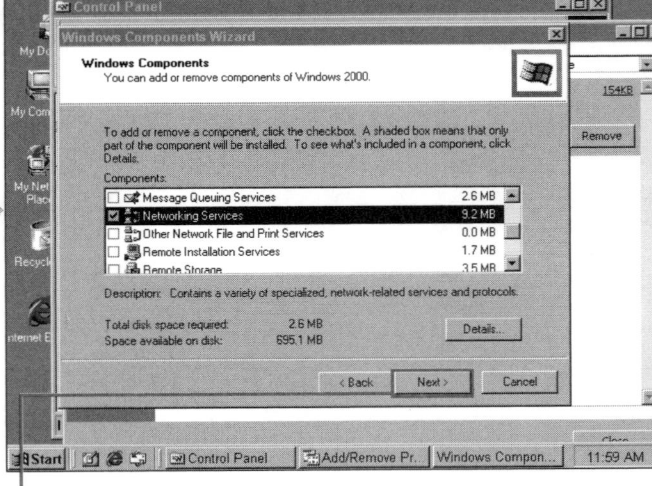

8 Click Next to continue.

Why does Windows 2000 Server provide two different ways to install components?

- These options are provided for administrative ease and user preference. You can install most major components in Windows 2000 Server through either Add/Remove Programs or the Configure Your Server program. You can perform many other tasks in Windows 2000 in several ways. No right or wrong way exists to configure your server—just pick which one works best for you.

Can I configure the DNS service at a later time?

- Yes. You can install any networking component and configure the component at a later time if desired. You should note that the DNS service will not be active and cannot resolve FQDNs to IP addresses until you configure the service.

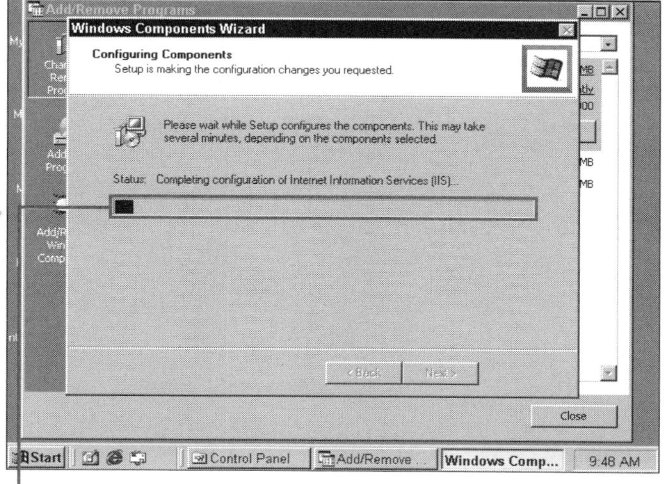

■ The system installs DNS. The status bar indicates the level of completion.

9 Click Finish to complete the DNS installation.

SETTING UP DNS

After you install the DNS service, you have to set up the service for use. You can find the service in Administrative tools, which you can access from either the Start menu or Control Panel. When you open the DNS manager, the name of your server appears in the left console pane and a note about configuring the DNS service appears in the right pane. Fortunately, Windows 2000 provides a wizard to help you set up your DNS service.

Before setting up the service, you need to take a look at your current network configuration and where your server falls within the configuration. In other words, you need to know which zone your server will service and what other zones are around your zone. Consult your network documentation to implement DNS so that it can service the needs of your particular zone.

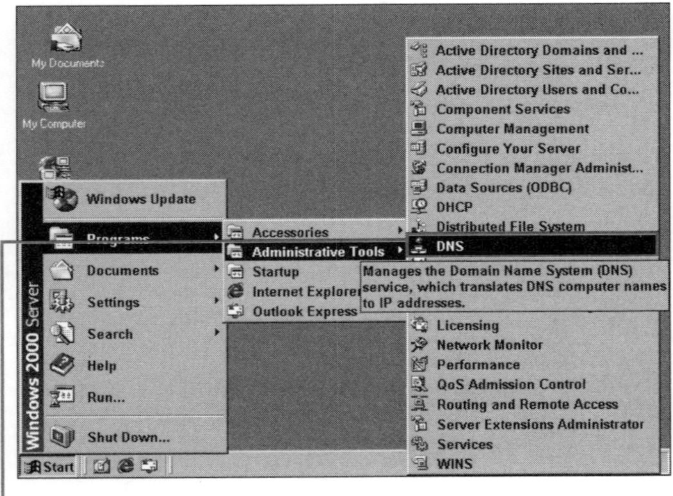

1 Choose Start⇨Programs ⇨Administrative Tools ⇨ DNS.

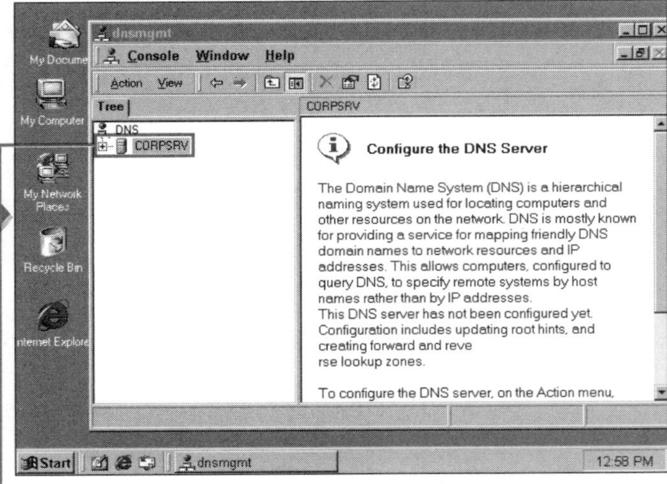

■ The DNS Manager opens showing your server icon in the left pane and a note in the right pane about configuring the server.

What is a zone?

- A *zone* is an area of the DNS namespace that is segmented for administrative purposes. This zone method enables you to run different DNS servers on your network that service the needs of particular groups. For example, if you had an `hr.corp.com` division and an `acct.corp.com` division in your network, each of these could function as DNS zones. They apply to a discreet portion of the namespace and you can set up different DNS servers to manage each zone. This feature keeps query traffic more localized on the network because all computers within a zone have to contact a DNS zone server for queries.

Why is a wizard provided to set up DNS?

- Windows 2000 includes wizards for most tasks that require several steps or several "pieces" that must be configured. The wizard makes certain you enter all the information needed to appropriately configure the service.

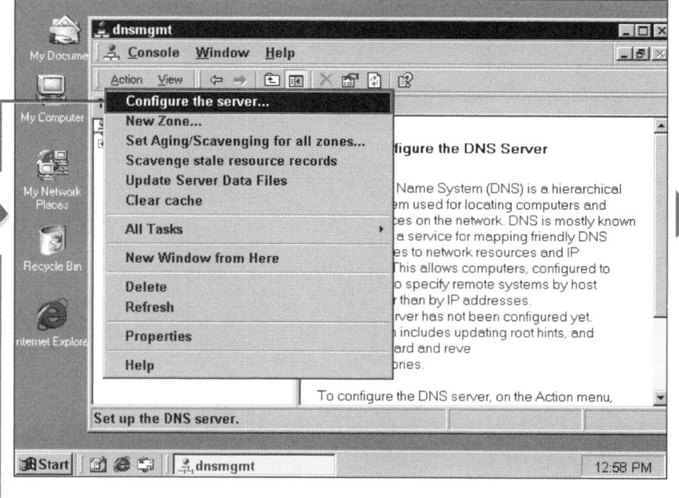

2 Choose Action ⇨ Configure The Server.

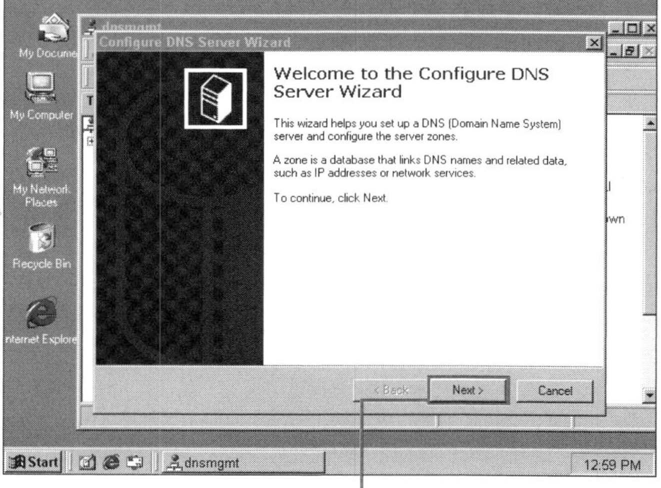

■ The Configure DNS Server Wizard appears.

3 Click Next to continue.

CONTINUED

SETTING UP DNS CONTINUED

The Configure DNS Server Wizard asks you a number of questions to determine what place the DNS server has on the network. DNS needs to know if this is the first DNS server on the network. If it is not, then you have to enter the IP address of a known DNS server that currently exists.

You also need to decide whether you want to set up a forward lookup zone. You should allow DNS to create the forward lookup zone because this zone is used to forward and resolve IP to name mappings. The wizard recommends that you allow the service to create the forward lookup zone.

You also need to select the type of zone you want to create. You have the options of Active Directory integrated or a primary or secondary zone. An *Active Directory integrated zone* stores new zone database information in the Active Directory and provides secure updates to the database file. A standard *primary zone* stores the database file in a text file on the server so that the zone database information can be exchanged with other DNS servers that use text-based storage.

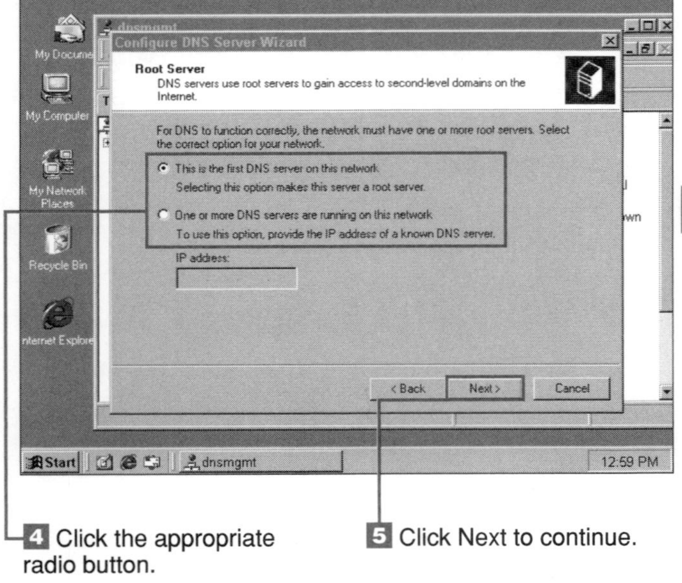

4 Click the appropriate radio button.

5 Click Next to continue.

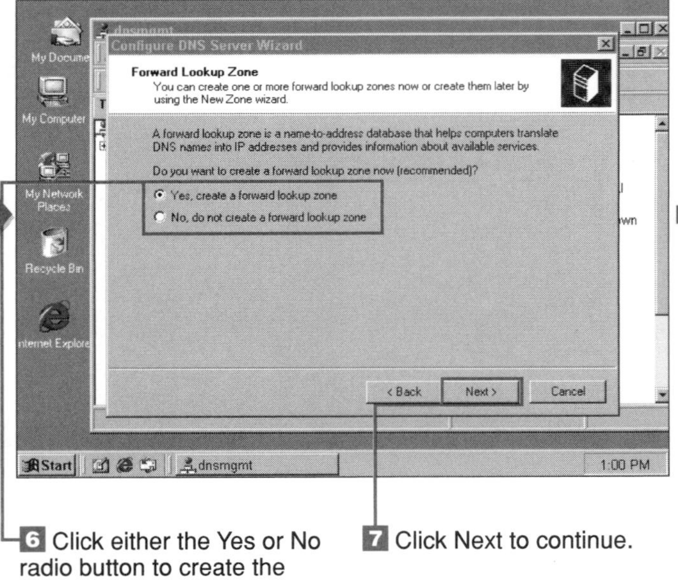

6 Click either the Yes or No radio button to create the forward lookup zone.

7 Click Next to continue.

Why do I need a forward lookup zone?

- A forward lookup zone resolves host names to IP address. The forward lookup zone allows the DNS server to "forward" host name to IP address resolution requests to other DNS servers in other zones and service local DNS queries.

Should my zone be Active Directory integrated?

- An Active Directory integrated zone enables you to integrate the DNS database files with the Active Directory. The Active Directory supports Dynamic DNS (DDNS) so that changes to the database file can be dynamically written. In the past, this was a manual process by editing the database text file. In most cases where the Active Directory is implemented, you should install your DNS servers so that they are integrated with the Active Directory.

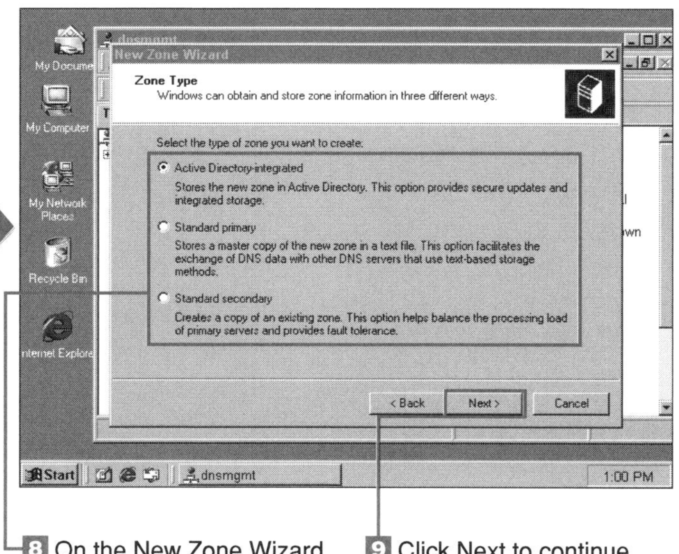

8 On the New Zone Wizard window, click the appropriate radio button to install the Zone type desired.

9 Click Next to continue.

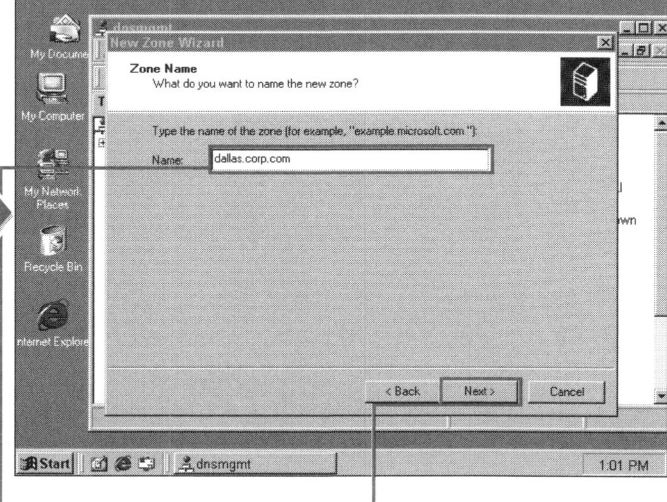

10 Type the name of the zone.

11 Click Next to continue.

CONTINUED

SETTING UP DNS CONTINUED

The standard *secondary zone* simply creates a copy of the existing zone database file. You can use this option for load-balancing purposes if your server is a secondary server in an existing zone.

You also need to enter a zone name. You should make certain that the zone name you enter is appropriate for your network design. Refer to your network documentation to determine the appropriate zone name.

You have the option of creating a *reverse lookup zone*. A forward lookup zone resolves a host, such as `server2.corp.com` to an IP address. A reverse lookup zone resolves the IP address to the DNS name, such as `131.107.2.00 = server2.corp.com`. Creating a reverse lookup zone is important for name resolution, but it is not required during the initial configuration. You can always add reverse lookup zones later using the New Zone Wizard. The zone selection window appears again so that you can choose to add the reverse lookup zone to the Active Directory or use it as a primary or secondary zone. The wizard also prompts you to enter how the reverse zone is identified, either by IP address or DNS name.

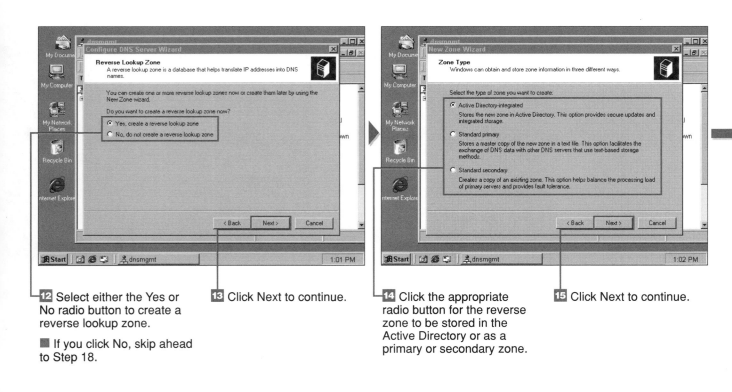

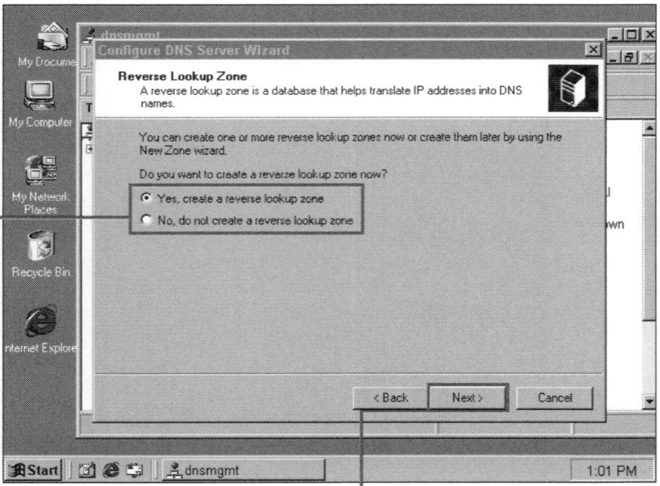

12 Select either the Yes or No radio button to create a reverse lookup zone.

■ If you click No, skip ahead to Step 18.

13 Click Next to continue.

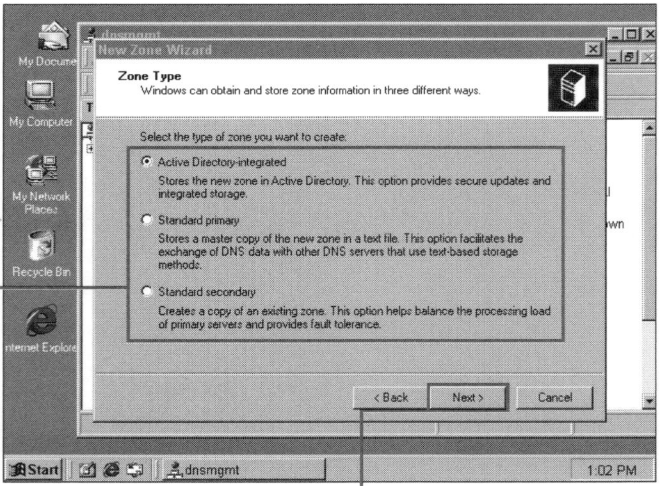

14 Click the appropriate radio button for the reverse zone to be stored in the Active Directory or as a primary or secondary zone.

15 Click Next to continue.

Do I need a reverse lookup zone?

- A reverse lookup zone simply allows a standard DNS resolution query to function in "reverse." Normally, a DNS name is sent to the DNS server for resolution to the IP address. The reverse lookup zone allows an IP address to be sent to DNS server to discover the DNS name of the host. Depending on your network, reverse lookup zones are not always necessary; however, they are easy to configure and for full DNS functionality, having them available is a good idea.

When I get to the end of the wizard, can I make changes if I made a mistake?

- You can always use the wizard's Back button to return to previous wizard screens and make changes. If you have already finished the wizard, you can manually make configuration changes within the DNS Manager. The following sections show you how to manage the different configuration tasks concerning the DNS server and the DNS zones.

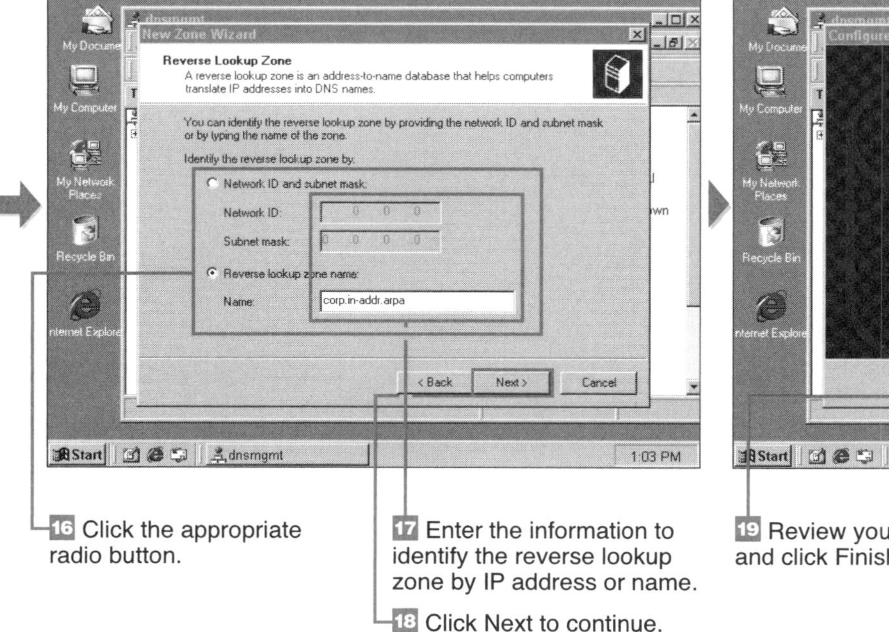

16 Click the appropriate radio button.

17 Enter the information to identify the reverse lookup zone by IP address or name.

18 Click Next to continue.

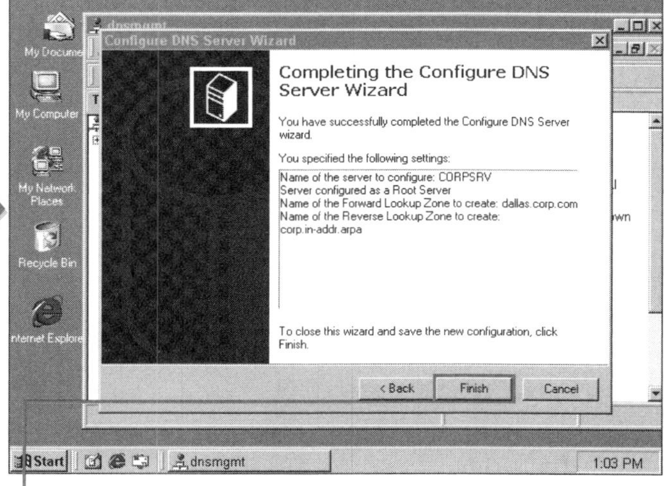

19 Review your selections and click Finish.

MANAGING DNS SERVER TASKS

As with most networking service consoles, such as WINS and DHCP, you can connect to other DNS servers. This feature enables you to easily manage a set of DNS servers from one location without having to physically visit each machine.

Typically, depending on the design of your organization, an administrator may be in control of all DNS servers for a particular zone. Remember that there is one primary DNS server per zone and any number of secondary DNS servers per zone. The secondary DNS servers provide load balancing for resolution request. Through this one interface, you can manage all the DNS servers, which makes your job as an administrator much easier.

To connect to another DNS server, simply use the Action menu and enter the name or IP address of the DNS server. After the connection is made, the server's icon appears in the console.

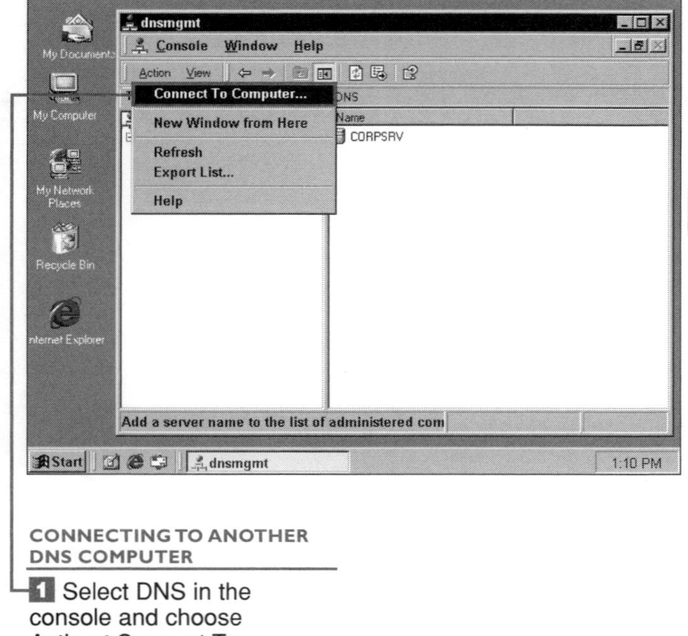

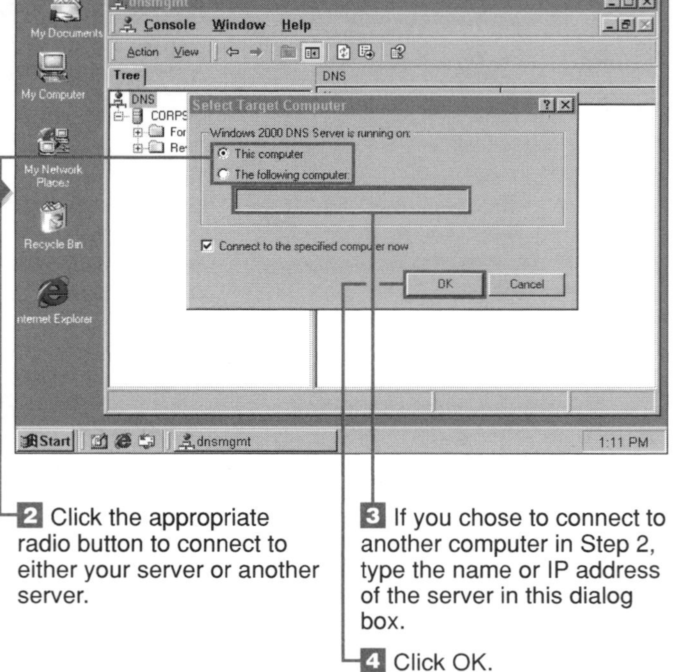

CONNECTING TO ANOTHER DNS COMPUTER

1 Select DNS in the console and choose Action⇨Connect To Computer.

2 Click the appropriate radio button to connect to either your server or another server.

3 If you chose to connect to another computer in Step 2, type the name or IP address of the server in this dialog box.

4 Click OK.

When you configured the DNS service, you made some decisions about forward lookup zones and reverse lookup zones. These zones help you control DNS on your network and make certain that host names can be resolved to an IP address or that IP addresses can be resolved to DNS names.

Zones also help you segment your network for administrative purposes. When you create zones, you must install a DNS server that will be authoritative for that zone. You can also use secondary DNS servers for the zone to help with load balancing.

You can easily add new zones to your server by using the New Zone Wizard. To perform this action, simply access the Action menu for the server and select New Zone. After you do this, the New Zone Wizard begins and you can create new zones as needed. This is the same wizard that you use when you set up DNS.

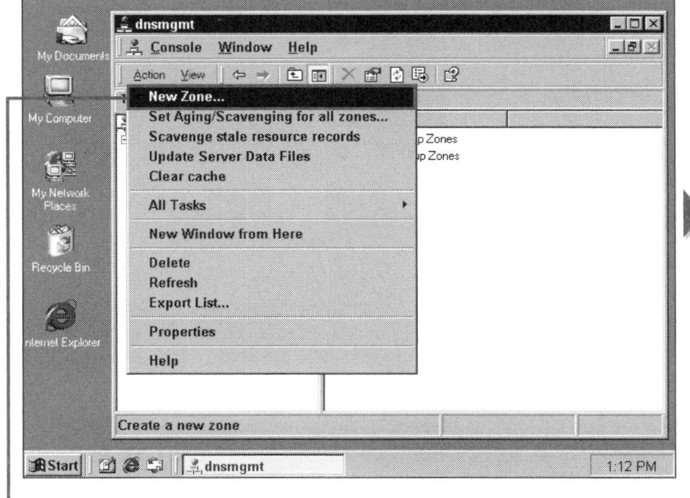

ADDING NEW ZONES

1 Select the server in the console and choose Action⇨New Zone.

■ The New Zone Wizard appears.

■ Refer to the section Setting Up DNS for more information on completing the New Zone Wizard.

CONTINUED

MANAGING DNS SERVER TASKS CONTINUED

You can use the Action menu to clear the DNS server's cache. Remember that a cache is simply a temporary storage location that holds DNS temporary records. Clearing the cache allows you to remove those records so new records can be immediately cached.

You can also run a process that helps you keep a clean DNS database. This process, known as *scavenging*, cleans old records out of the database to make certain the database is up-to-date.

First, you can set the properties for scavenging by accessing Set Aging/Scavenging for all zones on the Action menu. The properties sheet enables you to configure the DNS server to scavenge stale resource records. Then, you can set the no-refresh and the refresh interval. The no-refresh interval is the time between the most recent refresh of a record timestamp and time when it can be refreshed. The default setting is seven days. The refresh interval is the time between the earliest moment when a record timestamp can be refreshed and the earliest moment when the record can be scavenged. The default is also seven days.

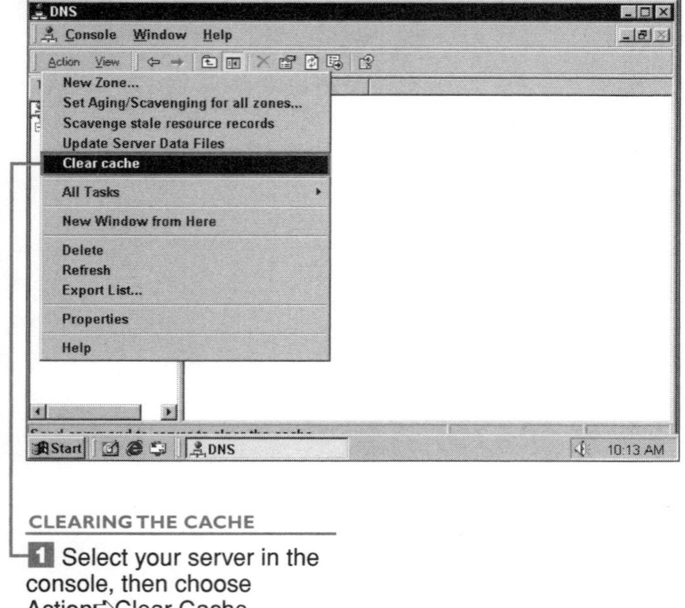

CLEARING THE CACHE

1 Select your server in the console, then choose Action⇨Clear Cache.

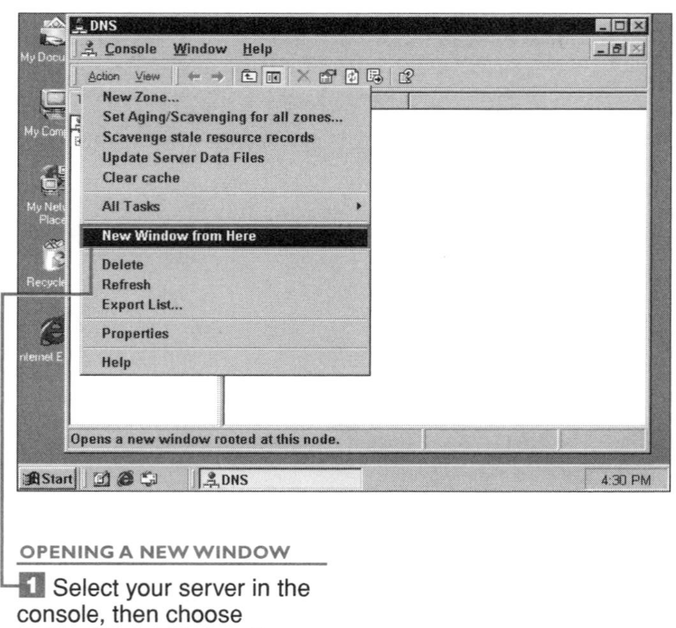

OPENING A NEW WINDOW

1 Select your server in the console, then choose Action⇨New Window From Here.

Why do I need to scavenge the database?

- As with any database, the DNS database can collect clutter over time. The clutter in the database is the old DNS records that have expired. The scavenge operation cleans these old records out of the database, which keeps your database free of unnecessary records.

How often should the database be scavenged?

- Under normal circumstances, the default setting of seven days for scavenge records is sufficient. You do not need to manually scavenge the database on a regular basis, unless you have specific reasons to believe the database needs to be cleaned. Windows 2000 DNS automatically scavenges the database every seven days, which under most circumstances is all you need.

How does scavenging affect performance?

- As with any system, the more "clutter" that is removed, the more likely the DNS service will perform better. By removing unneeded and old records, the DNS database will be clean of outdated information.

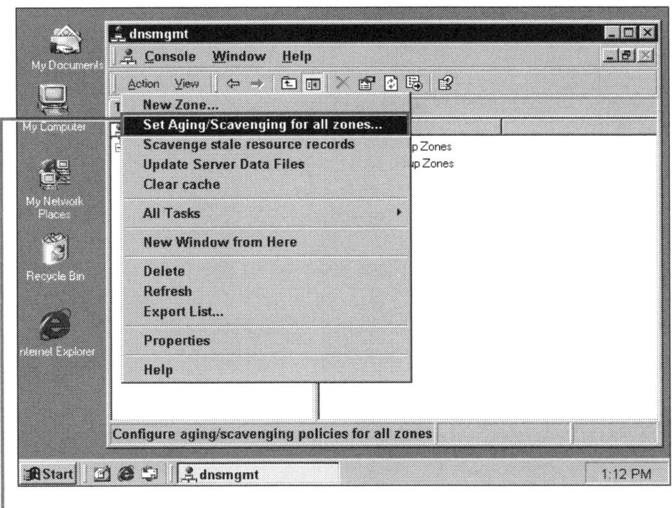

CHOOSING THE AGING AND SCAVENGING SETTINGS

1 Select the server in the console and choose Action⇨Set Aging/Scavenging For All Zones.

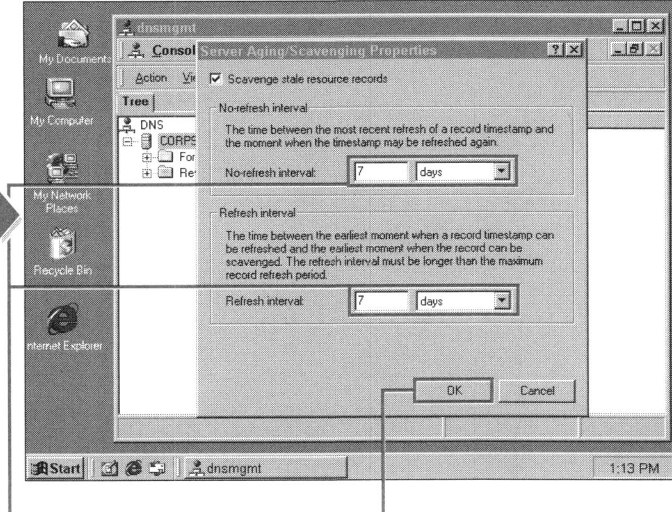

2 Adjust the no-refresh interval as desired.

3 Adjust the refresh interval as desired.

4 Click OK.

CONTINUED

MANAGING DNS SERVER TASKS
CONTINUED

You can manually update the DNS server's database files, if desired, by using the Action menu and choosing Update Server Data Files. Data files are normally updated to the database at predefined intervals and when the server is shut down, but you can choose to manually update the files as desired. This action causes the DNS service to write all changes to the zone data files immediately.

As with most MMC snap-in tools, you can also choose to stop, start, pause, and restart the DNS service by clicking the Action menu and accessing the All Tasks feature. In case of server maintenance or problems, you can pause or stop the service while the problem is being resolved. When you do this, the server is not available to answer name resolution queries, but other DNS servers in the zone can take on the query load while the server is offline.

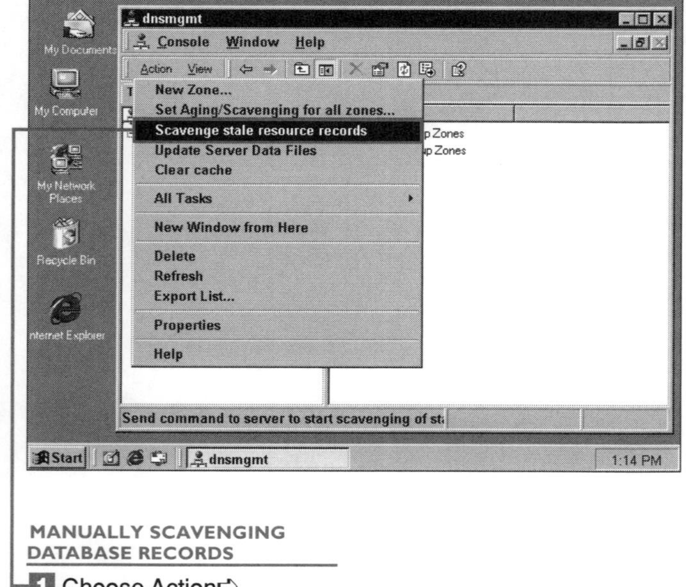

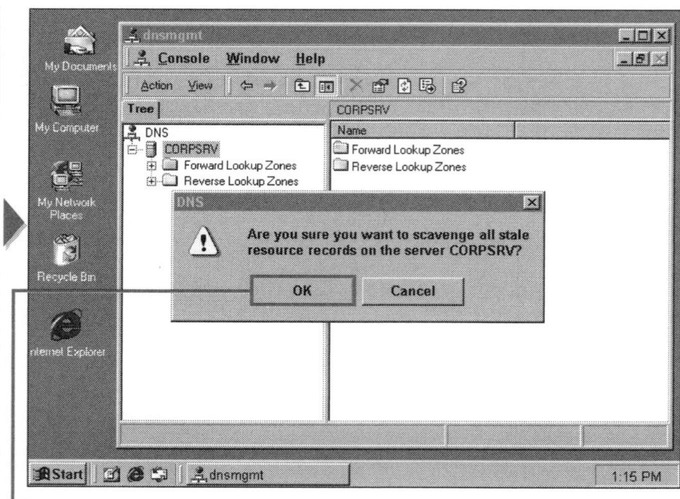

MANUALLY SCAVENGING DATABASE RECORDS

1 Choose Action⇨Scavenge Stale Resource Records to manually scavenge records.

2 Click OK to continue the scavenge operation.

Do I need to update the server's database files manually?

- No. The DNS server automatically updates its server database files on a periodic basis, so manually updating the files is not a task you need to perform as a part of your administrative duties. However, the option is provided for you in the case of major changes to the DNS database. If a number of changes occur, you can use the Update Server database files option to manually update the database so those changes can go into effect immediately. As with most options in DNS, the server handles the tasks automatically, or you can manually force them as the need arises.

What happens when I pause the DNS service?

- When you pause the DNS service, the service is taken offline and is not available to clients. Client DNS query requests will have to be fulfilled by other DNS servers. The pause option is particularly useful if you are having problems with the server. You can take the server offline until the problems are resolved, then resume the DNS service.

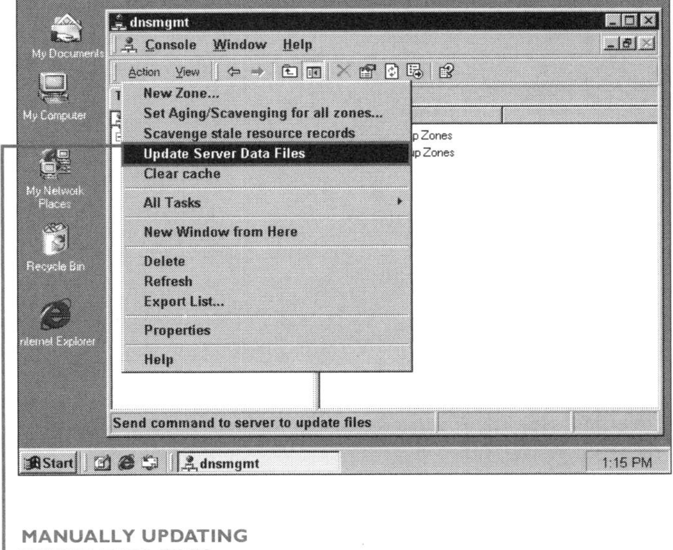

MANUALLY UPDATING SERVER DATA FILES

1 Choose Action⇨Update Server Data Files to perform the manual update.

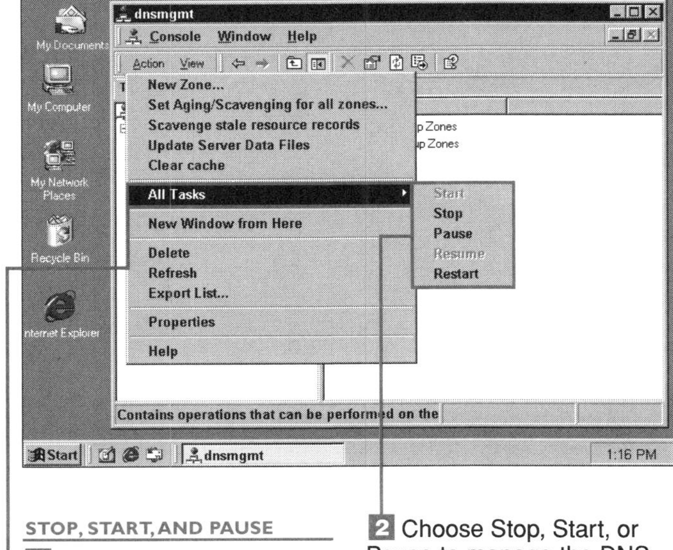

STOP, START, AND PAUSE

1 Choose Action⇨All Tasks.

2 Choose Stop, Start, or Pause to manage the DNS service.

CONFIGURING SERVER PROPERTIES

You access the DNS server properties sheets to configure the various DNS functions that you want your server to perform.

Depending on the needs of your network, you may want to restrict a DNS server so that it only listens for query requests on certain IP addresses. This feature allows you to use a DNS server for a specific group of clients. You can enable this option, or simply allow the DNS server to listen on all IP addresses on the Interfaces tab.

The Forwarders tab enables you to configure *forwarders*—which is a DNS service that is configured to provide recursive service for other DNS servers. The forwarder helps other DNS servers resolve a DNS name request that cannot be resolved by forwarding the request to other DNS servers. If your server is the root DNS server, the forwarders options is not available because it is the root server.

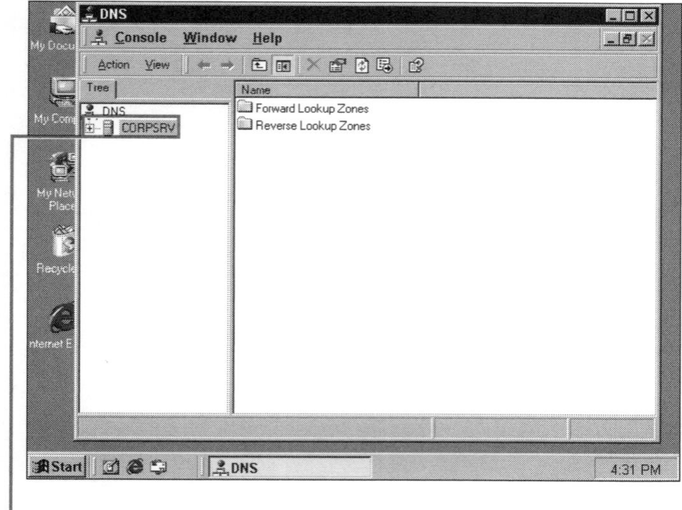

1 Select the desired server in the console.

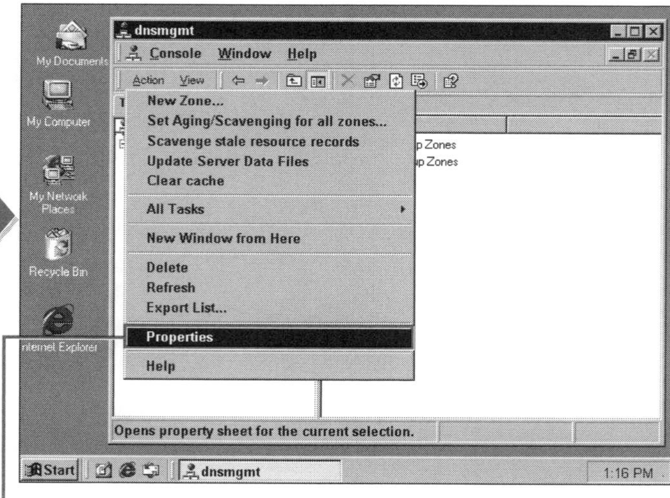

2 Click Action⇨Properties.

Why would I want to use the Interfaces tab to limit the IP addresses the server listens to?

- In networks where many DNS servers are in use, you may want to specify that a particular DNS server listen only to DNS queries from particular IP addresses. This feature enables you to restrict the DNS server so that it concentrates on a particular group of clients and only seeks to resolve queries for that group.

On my server, the Forwarders option is not available because it is a root server. Why?

- Forwarders help resolve any DNS queries that cannot be answered by the DNS server. They do this by forwarding the request to up-stream servers within the namespace. Because your server is a root server, it resides at the top of the namespace, and therefore there is nowhere to forward queries to.

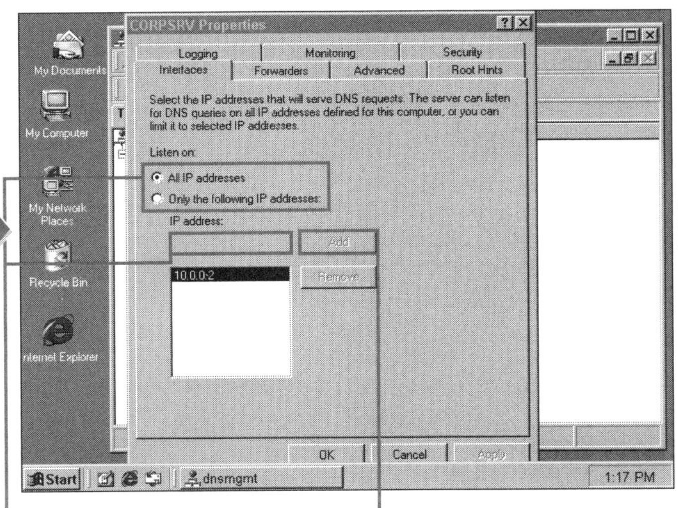

3 Click the appropriate radio button to specify what address the server listens to.

4 If you selected the Only The Following IP Addresses radio button in Step 2, type the desired IP addresses.

5 Click Add if you want to add an IP address.

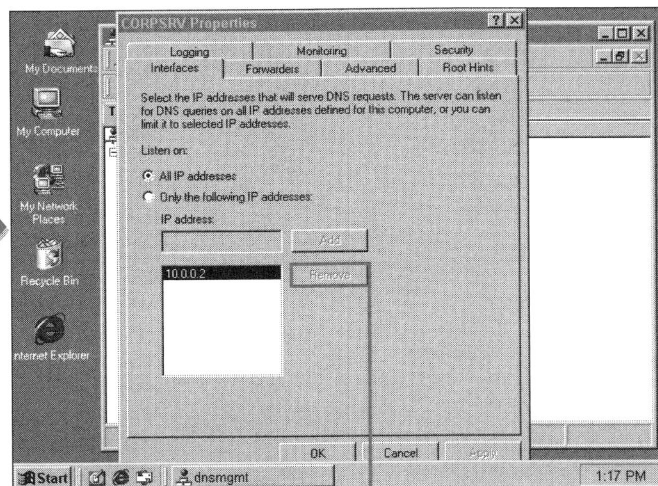

6 Click Remove if you want to remove an unwanted IP address.

CONTINUED

CONFIGURING SERVER PROPERTIES

CONTINUED

The Advanced tab gives you several options that may help your server perform with other DNS servers more effectively, such as BIND Secondaries, enable round robin, and enable netmask ordering (all of which are selected by default.) The name checking drop-down menu determines how the DNS server checks names and the kind of names it checks. You have the following options:

- **Strict RFC**—strictly enforces the use of RFC compliant rules for all DNS names. Non-RFC names are treated as errors.
- **Non-RFC**—any names that are not RFC compliant can be used.
- **Multibyte**—uses the Unicode 8-bit translation encoding scheme.
- **All Names**—allows all names to be used with the DNS server.

The All Names and Non-RFC options are the most lenient and provide the greatest amount of interoperability between DNS servers.

You can also alter the way DNS retrieves its zone data information at startup. You have the options of Active Directory and Registry, From Registry, or From File.

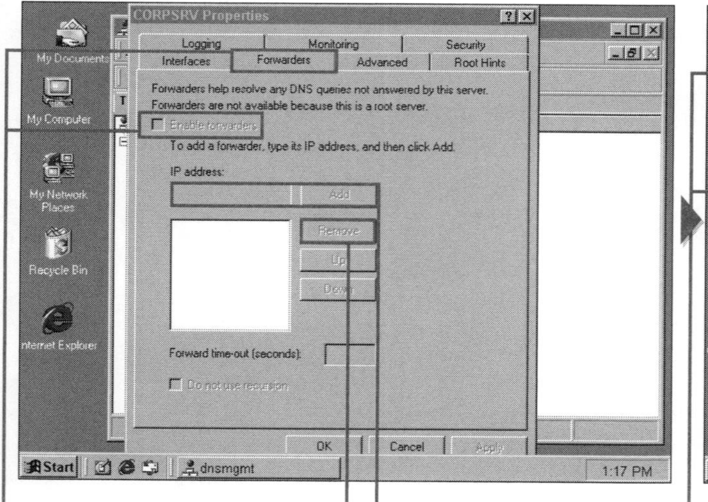

7 Click the Forwarders tab.

8 Click this check box to enable forwarders. If the option is unavailable or you choose not to enable forwarders, skip to Step 11.

9 Add IP addresses of forwarders by typing them in this box and clicking Add.

10 To remove an IP address, select the desired address and click Remove.

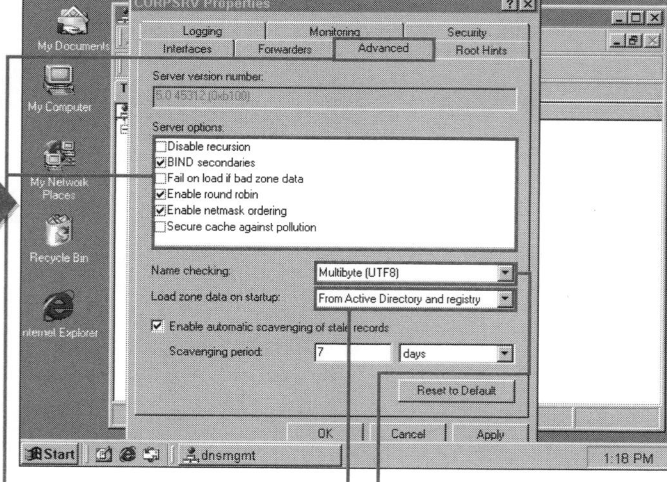

11 Click the Advanced tab.

12 Click the appropriate check boxes to enable different server options.

13 Click this drop-down list to change the default name-checking mechanism.

14 Click this drop-down list to change how the zone data is loaded when the server starts.

Which name checking option should I use?

- The three name checking options are provided so you can control the DNS naming schemes in your network. For example, you can provide a loose structure so that all names are checked by your DNS server, or you can tightly restrict the name so that only strict RFC naming can be used. The other options fall in-between these two extremes. The default option is Multibyte.

How should I load zone data?

- For Active Directory integrated DNS servers (on an Active Directory network), the load zone data should come from the Active Directory and Registry option. This ensures that your server DNS files are integrated with the Active Directory and other DNS servers on your network.

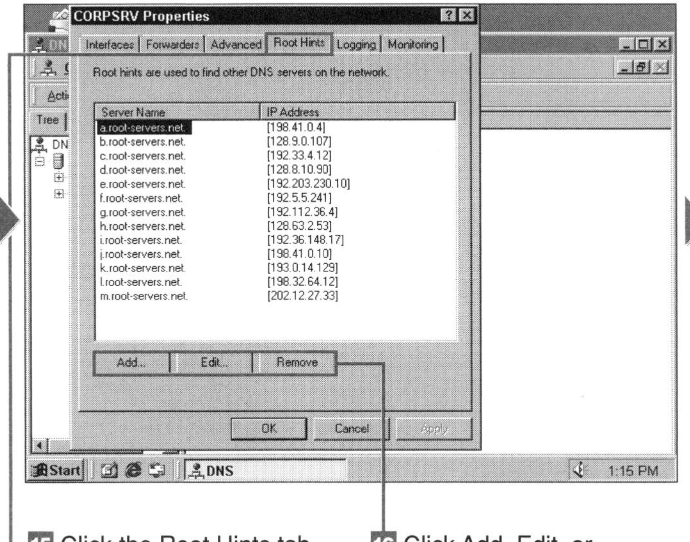

15 Click the Root Hints tab.

16 Click Add, Edit, or Remove to manage root hints for this server.

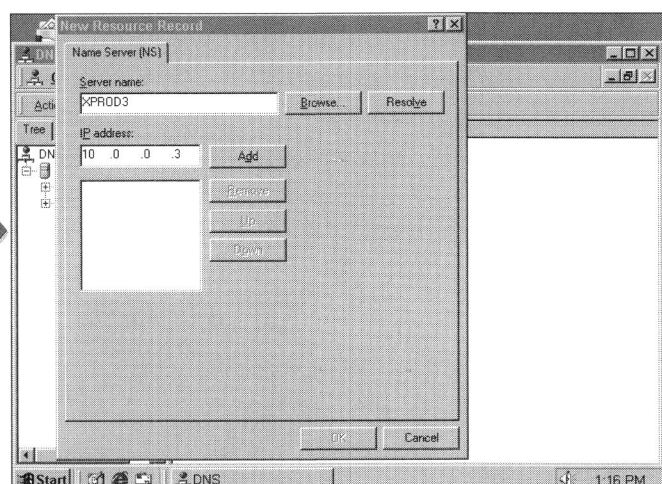

■ If you click the Add button, you can use this window to select a Root Hint server.

CONTINUED

CONFIGURING SERVER PROPERTIES

CONTINUED

Root hints are used by DNS servers to help the servers find other DNS servers that manage subdomains or domains at a higher place in the DNS namespace. The root hints allow a zone authoritative server to find the servers above it in the domain hierarchy for name resolution. The Root Hints tab contains a list of servers that are configured by default from the cache.dns file. You can use the Root Hints tab to edit this file so that it points to certain DNS servers that should be used to for name resolution at higher levels in the hierarchy. If your server is the root server on your network, then this option is naturally not available because your server is at the top of hierarchy.

As with many server services in Windows 2000, you can log a number of DNS events that can help you solve problems. Use the Logging tab to select the desired events.

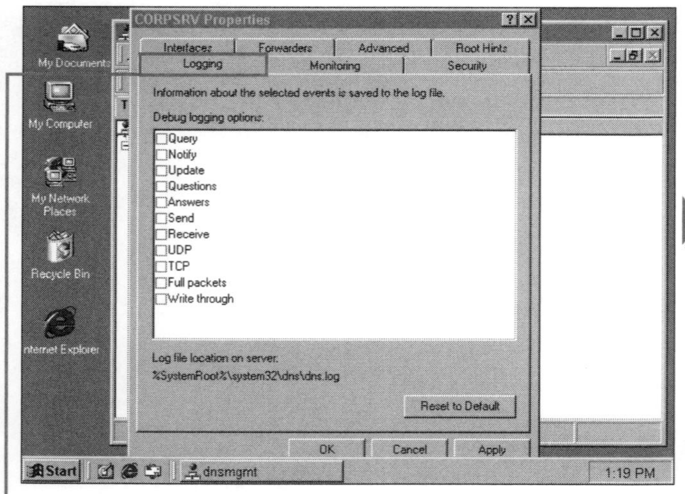

17 Click the Logging tab.

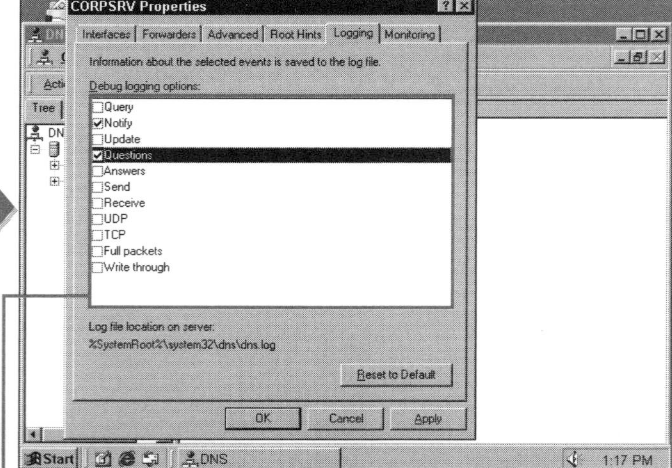

18 Click the appropriate check boxes for the information you want saved to a log file when events occur.

What are the available Logging Options?

Logging options allow you to track different kinds of data within DNS:

- **Query**: Logs all queries received from clients
- **Notify**: Logs all notification messages received from other DNS servers
- **Update**: Logs all dynamic updates received
- **Questions**: Logs the contents of the question part of each DNS query message
- **Answers**: Logs the contents of the answer part of each DNS query message
- **Send**: Logs the number of DNS query messages sent by the DNS service
- **Receive**: Logs the number of DNS query messages received by the DNS service
- **UDP**: Logs the number of DNS requests received on a UDP port
- **TCP**: Logs the number of DNS requests received on a TCP port
- **Full Packets**: Logs the number of full packets written and sent
- **Write Through**: Logs the number of packets written through the DNS service and back to the zone

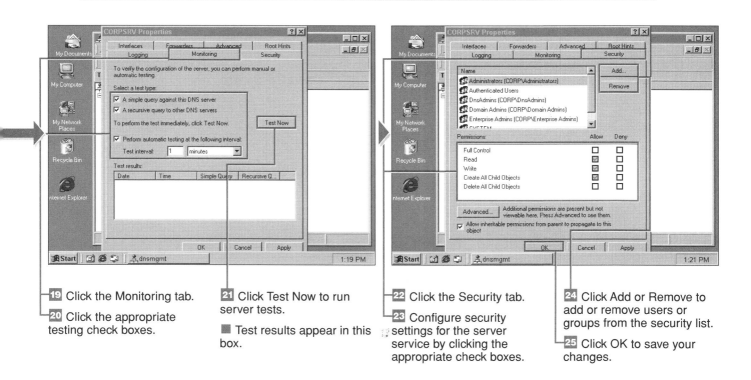

19 Click the Monitoring tab.

20 Click the appropriate testing check boxes.

21 Click Test Now to run server tests.

■ Test results appear in this box.

22 Click the Security tab.

23 Configure security settings for the server service by clicking the appropriate check boxes.

24 Click Add or Remove to add or remove users or groups from the security list.

25 Click OK to save your changes.

MANAGING ZONE DATA

You can administer each zone that you create by managing the zone database file for the server as well as resource records.

First, by using the Action menu, you can choose to manually update the Server Data File. This action manually forces a zone transfer so that the server's database file is updated. You don't need to do this under normal circumstances because changes to the primary zone database file are automatically sent to secondary DNS servers. However, if several changes have occurred, then you can choose to manually force the update.

You can also choose to completely reload the zone database file instead of update it. This option, which is accessible from the Action menu, removes the previous record and replaces it with a new copy of the primary zone database file.

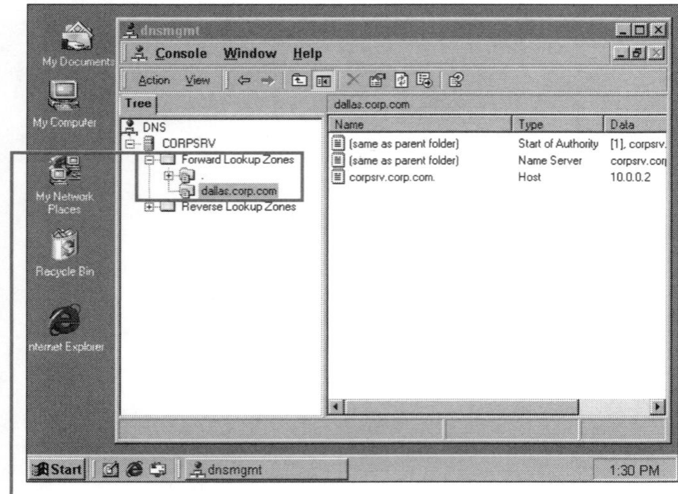

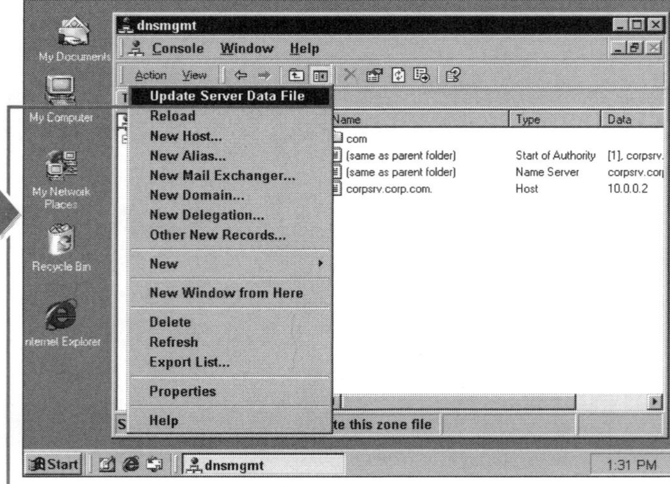

MANUALLY UPDATING THE SERVER DATA FILE

1 Expand the Forward and/or Reverse Lookup Zones Containers and select the zone you want to administer.

2 Choose Action➪Update Server Data File.

■ This action manually updates the database file.

Why do I have the option to update or reload the zone database file? Isn't this operation automatic?

- The zone database files are updated at regular intervals, which ensures that each DNS server has accurate database records so that client queries can be resolved. As with most operations that automatically occur in Windows 2000, you also have the capability to force the action to occur. This allows you to always have control over the operating system services. In case there are problems with the server or a number of DNS changes occur, you can manually reload the database file or manually update the database file.

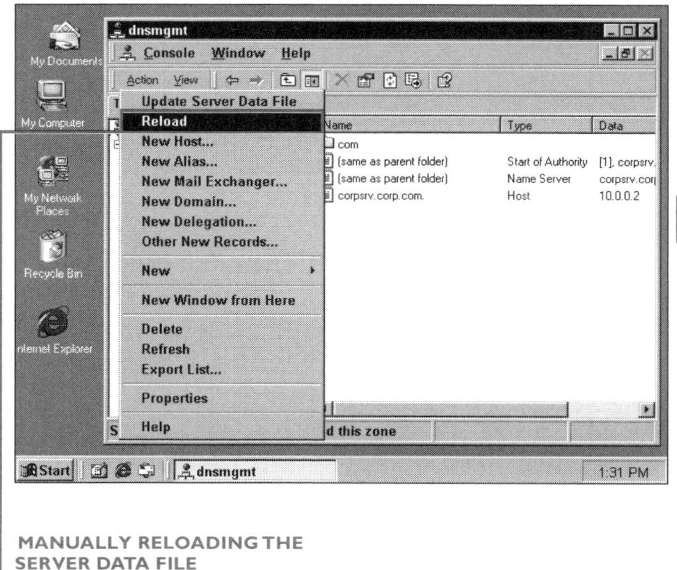

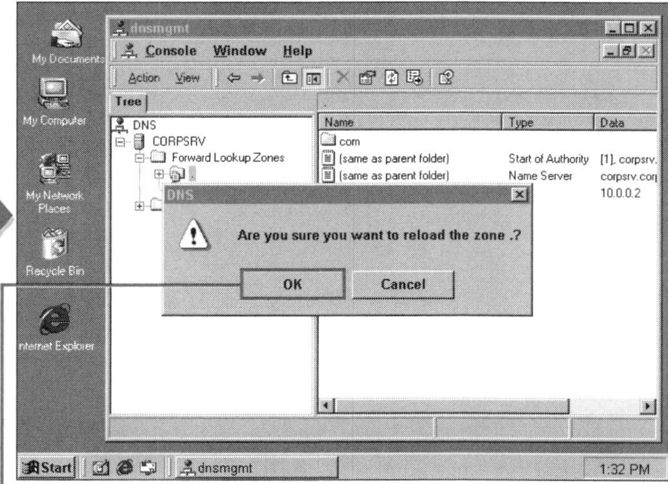

MANUALLY RELOADING THE SERVER DATA FILE

1 Choose Action⇨Reload.

2 Click OK to reload the zone data file.

MANAGING ZONE RESOURCE RECORDS AND DELEGATION

Managing Zone Resource Records

Each zone database file contains any number of resource records. A resource record is simply an entry in the database—a record—that the DNS can use to help resolve certain queries and resolutions. When a zone is created, two records are created by default—the Start of Authority (SOA) and the Name Server (NS). The SOA defines which server in the zone is the authoritative server. The NS records lists all the DNS servers operating in the zone. Besides these two default records, you can add several records as needed.

First, you can add a *host* record (A). An A record provides a host to IP address mapping for a forward lookup zone. With this resource record, the DNS server can access the A record and forward unresolved queries to the forward lookup zone host. Next, you can create an *alias* (CNAME). A CNAME record, which stands for "canonical name," allows a host to have an alternate name.

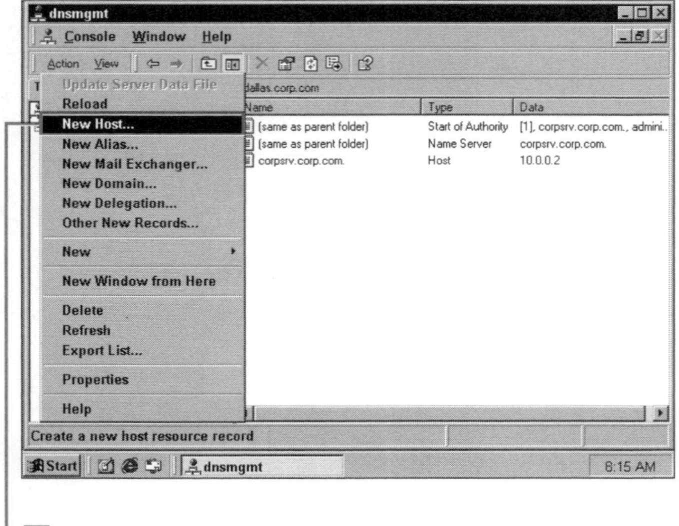

1 Select the zone in the console you want to administer and choose Action⇨New Host.

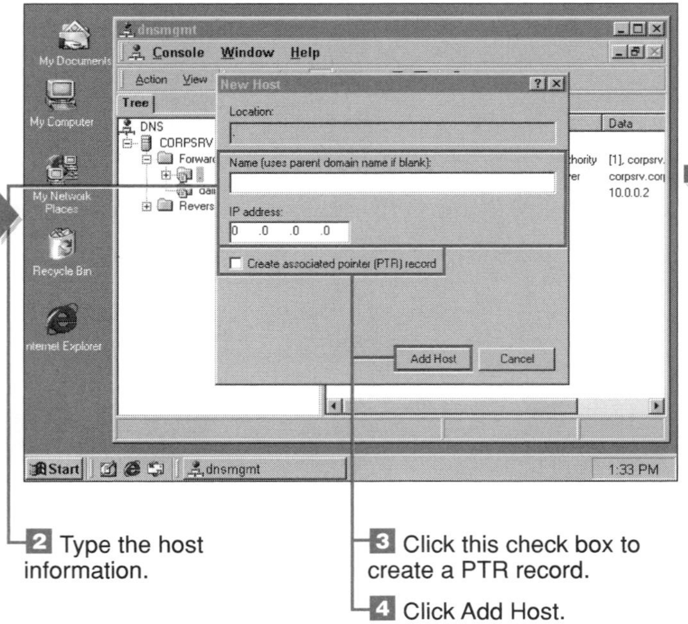

2 Type the host information.

3 Click this check box to create a PTR record.

4 Click Add Host.

TIPS

Why do I need to use A records?

A records are helpful for your DNS server to easily identify another server in a forward lookup zone. By accessing the A record, the DNS server knows exactly where to send query requests for forward lookup. In multiple zone environments, A records improve query performance, so you should use them when necessary. You also have the option of creating a "pointer record" (PTR) when you create an A record. A PTR record points to another portion of the namespace and can be used to resolve an IP address to a host name.

Why would I use a CNAME record?

A CNAME record allows a DNS server to have multiple "names." The CNAME record gives the server a canonical name, which can be used in situations where round-robin resolution requests are needed. For example, one CNAME record can contain several servers, or several CNAME records can point to one particular server.

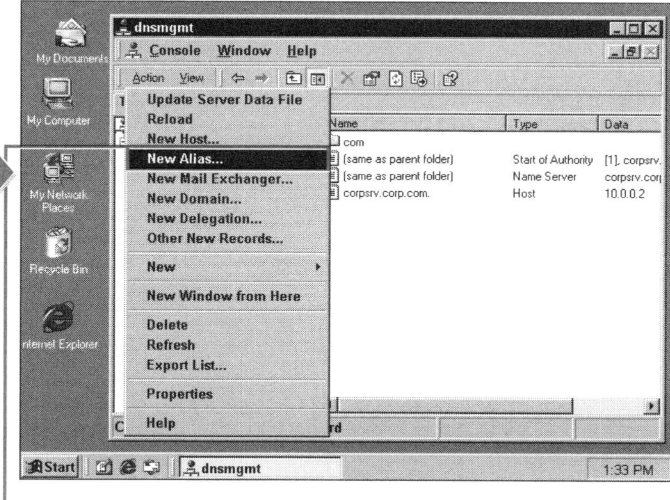

5 Choose Action⇨New Alias.

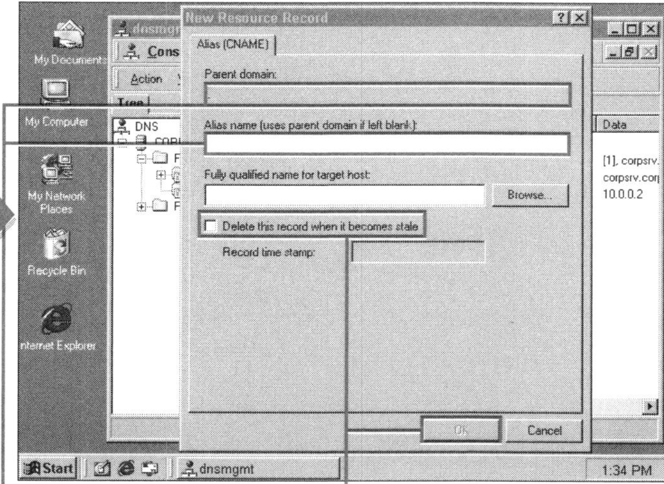

6 Type the alias name for the target host.

7 Type the fully qualified name for the target host.

8 Click this check box to delete the record when it becomes stale.

9 Click OK.

MANAGING ZONE RESOURCE RECORDS AND DELEGATION

New Mail Exchanger and New Domain Records

You can also create a Mail Exchanger (MX) record. The MX record identifies a mail server with a particular host or domain. With the addition of the MX record, mail addressed to either the host or the domain is sent to the mail server that you specify when you create the resource record. You also have the option of setting the mail server priority. This is a two-digit number that you can enter when you create the record that determines the priority of the mail servers over others. This enables you to set a mail server that has the highest priority over a host or domain.

You can also add a new domain to the zone. This feature is not a resource record function but is provided for ease of administration. After you add the domain, the DNS server(s) in the zone begins servicing the new domain.

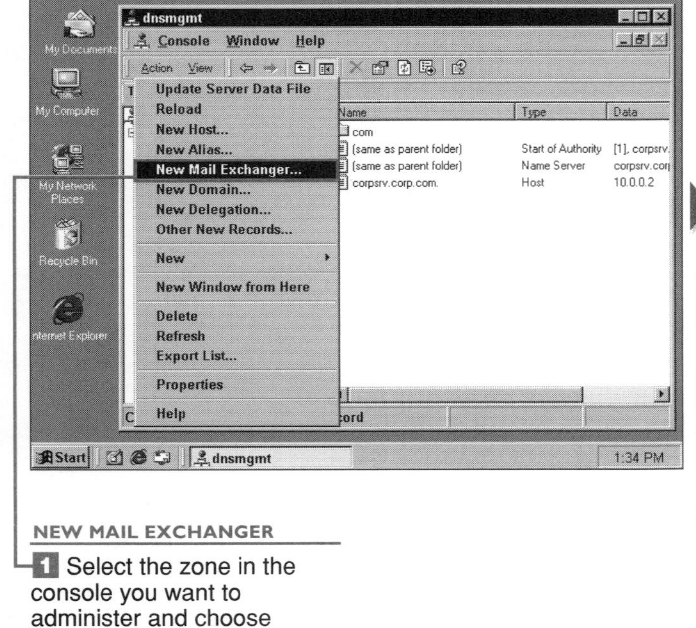

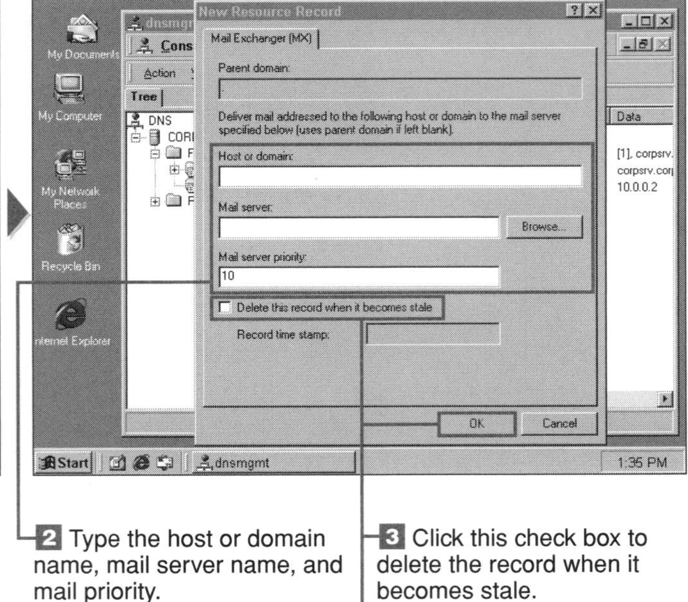

NEW MAIL EXCHANGER

1 Select the zone in the console you want to administer and choose Action⇨New Mail Exchanger.

2 Type the host or domain name, mail server name, and mail priority.

3 Click this check box to delete the record when it becomes stale.

4 Click OK.

Why should I use MX records?

- MX records help you identify particular mail servers within the zone in the DNS database. This feature allows DNS to prioritize the mail servers for use within the zone. MX records are particularly useful in environments that use a number of mail servers within different DNS zones. By creating the MX records, your DNS server can easily keep track of the location of the mail servers.

What happens when I add a new domain?

- By selecting a particular zone in the console and using the Action menu, you can add a new domain to a zone. Remember that zones and domains are not related in terms or organization. A business may have four domains but only two zones. You can choose to add a domain to a zone so that domain becomes a part of the DNS zone and is serviced by DNS servers within the zone.

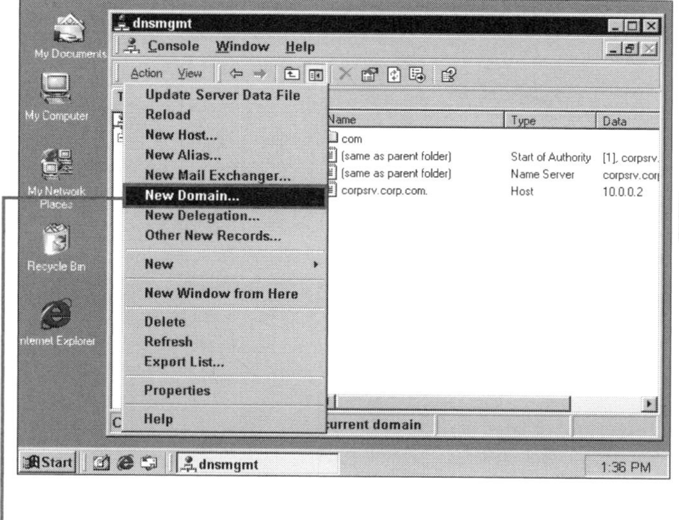

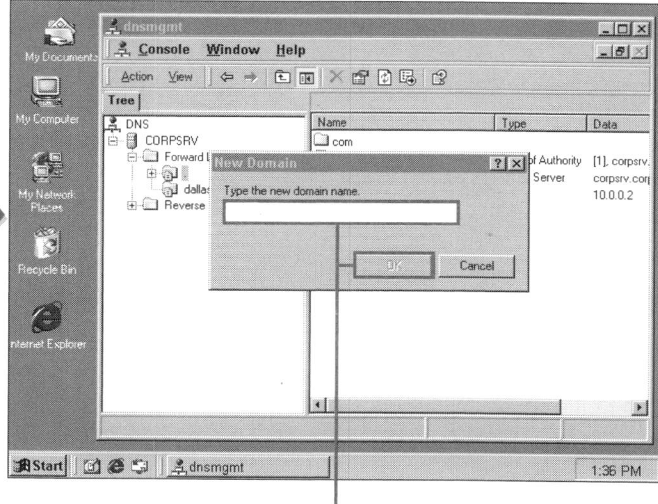

NEW DOMAIN

1 Choose Action⇨New Domain.

2 Type the name of the New Domain.

3 Click OK.

MANAGING ZONE RESOURCE RECORDS AND DELEGATION

Zone Delegation

As with many Windows 2000 components, both within the Active Directory and the operating system, you can delegate control. Delegation means that you allow another user, group, or computer to control some object, group, process, or service. Delegation is a concept you learn to use throughout the rest of the book in relation to Active Directory objects, OUs, services, and so on.

You can choose to delegate control of a zone to another DNS server in another zone. This action allows another DNS server(s) to have authority of a particular zone. When you perform this action, however, you must also create delegation records in the other DNS zones that point to the DNS servers that have authority over the new zone. This allows the transfer of authority to take place and provides a correct reference to the other DNS servers that the zone has been delegated to.

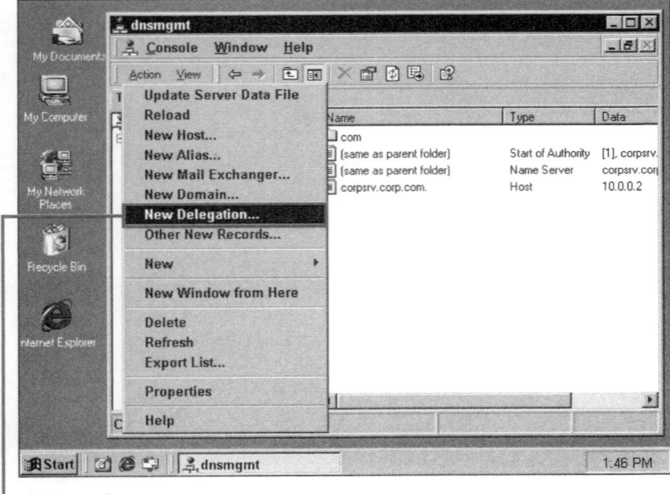

1 Select the appropriate zone in the console and choose Action⇨New Delegation.

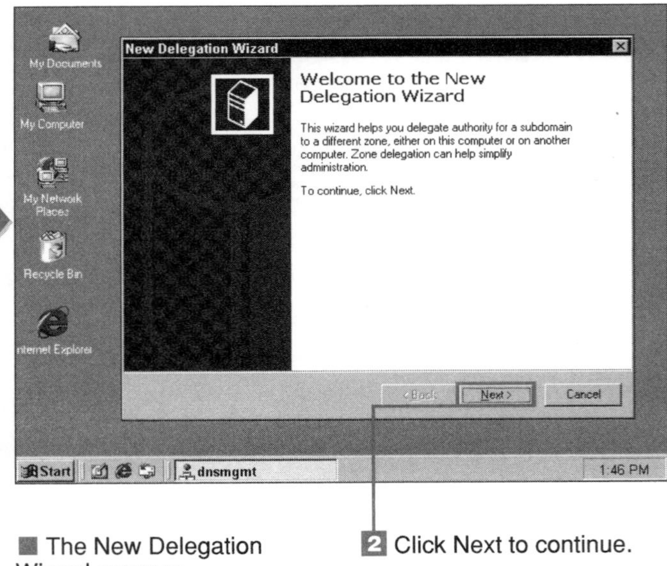

■ The New Delegation Wizard appears.

2 Click Next to continue.

Do I really need to delegate a zone?

✓ Keep in mind that delegation is powerful tool in Windows 2000 that allows you, as the administrator, to delegate duties or tasks to other individuals. By delegating portions of your administrative tasks, you can lower the amount of senior administrative overhead.

Who should be delegated tasks?

✓ Obviously, you must exercise caution and careful planning when delegating tasks or administrative duties to other people. The delegates must have the technical skills and knowledge to be able to complete the tasks. As with many issues in a networking environment, training and planning are of key importance.

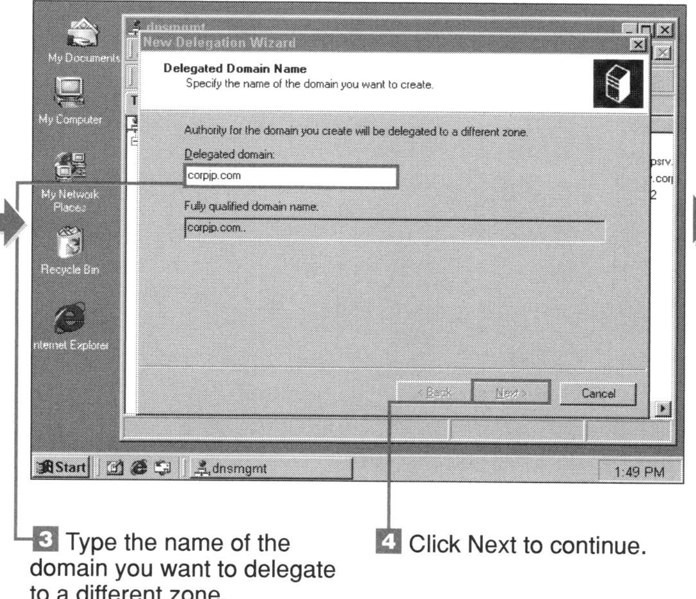

3 Type the name of the domain you want to delegate to a different zone.

4 Click Next to continue.

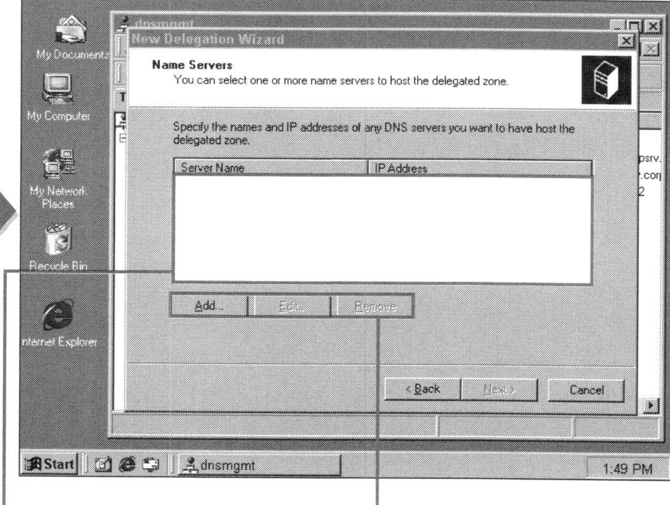

5 Select the names and IP addresses of any DNS server that you want to host the delegated zone.

6 Click Add, Edit, or Remove to manage the list, then complete the wizard for the delegation to take effect.

CONFIGURING ZONE PROPERTIES

The properties sheets for each zone enables you to configure the zone to operate within your environment. As with other server services, you can pause and change the type of service (such as Active Directory integrated) by using the General tab. This feature is particular useful for troubleshooting purposes. An important aspect of the General tab is the dynamic updates section. Windows 2000 supports Dynamic DNS (DDNS) so that database updates can be performed dynamically and not manually by the administrator. The General tab enables you to configure dynamic updates by allowing them, not allowing them, or using only secure updates. In an Active Directory environment, the zones should be allowed to perform dynamic updates.

You can use the Start of Authority tab (SOA) to manage the SOA record on your server.

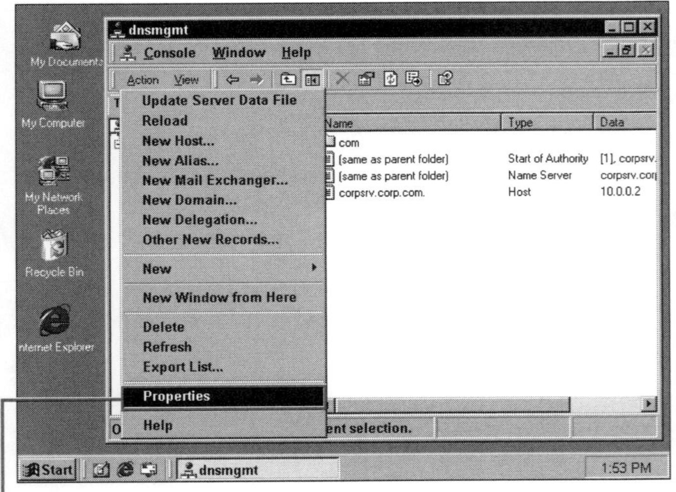

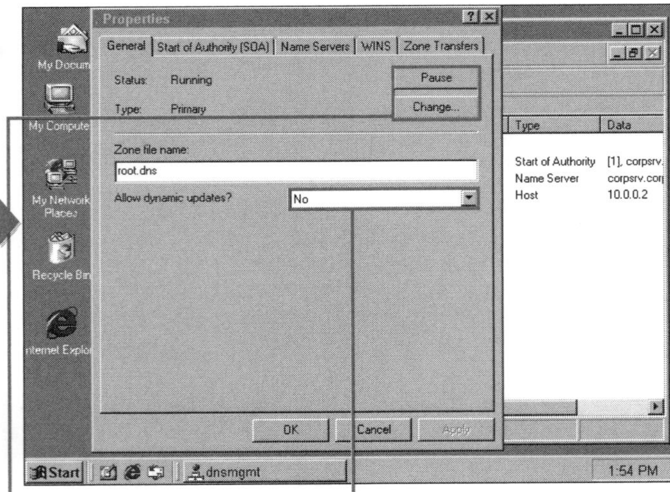

1 In the console, select the zone that you want to administer and choose Action⇨Properties.

2 Click these buttons to either pause the zone or to change the type of zone.

3 Use this drop-down list to select whether or not to use dynamic updates and the type of update.

TIPS

What is the SOA?

- The Start of Authority is a resource record that defines which server is authoritative for a zone. The SOA tab allows you to make adjustments this record as necessary. You can change the primary server that holds the SOA record, and you can even change the responsible person who manages the SOA on that server. The important point about this option is you can make major changes to your server's DNS configuration without having to delete your zones and start all over. This is, of course, a very important feature of Windows 2000.

What is the Name Servers tab?

- Like the SOA tab, the Name Servers tab lists the NS records that are configured for the zone. This list tells you which servers are in the zone and available for the zone. You can use the add, edit, and remove buttons on the Name Server tab to manage the list as desired.

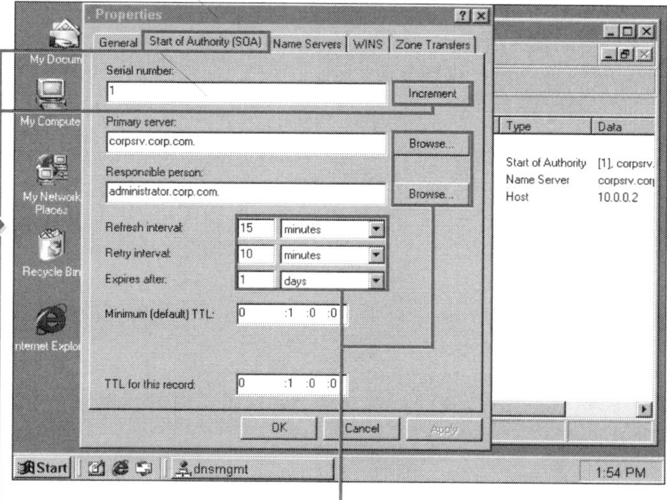

4 Click the Start of Authority (SOA) tab.

5 Click Increment to adjust the serial number, if necessary.

6 Click the appropriate Browse button to adjust the primary server and responsible person fields, if necessary.

7 Adjust the Refresh, Retry, and Expires After, if necessary.

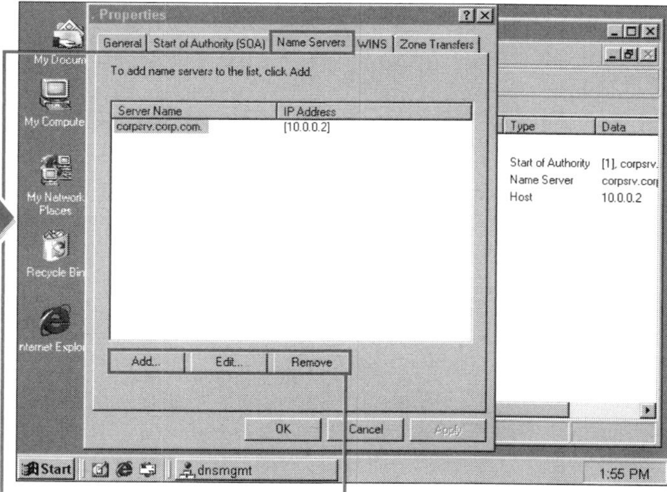

8 Click the Name Servers tab.

9 Use the Add, Edit, or Remove buttons to adjust the name servers in the list.

CONTINUED

CONFIGURING ZONE PROPERTIES
CONTINUED

The WINS tab enables you to use a WINS forward lookup to resolve NetBIOS names. DNS resolved domain names to IP addresses while WINS resolves NetBIOS names to IP addresses. The WINS lookup feature allows the DNS server to query the WINS server(s) that you specify to lookup a name in the WINS database that the DNS server cannot resolve. This feature is useful in mixed Windows 2000 environments where both DNS and WINS are in use. On the WINS tab, simply click the check box to enable the WINS lookup and then provide the IP address(es) of the WINS server(s).

On the Zone Transfers tab, you can choose to allow zone transfers. A zone transfer updates the secondary DNS servers with the primary zone database file. Remember that the secondary DNS servers in the zone receive a copy of the primary zone database file. Only the primary DNS zone database file can be updated. After the primary zone files is updated, the secondary servers will get the database file from the primary zone server.

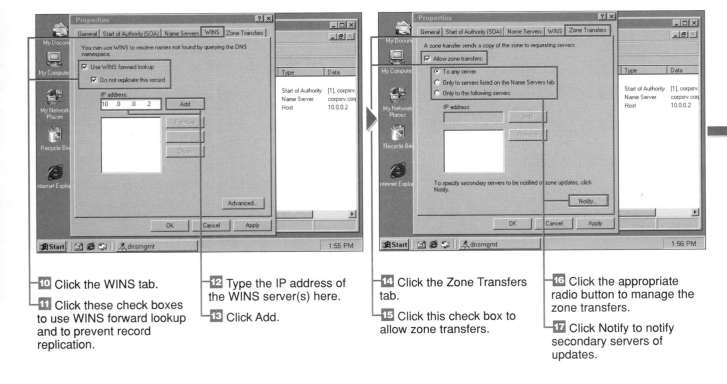

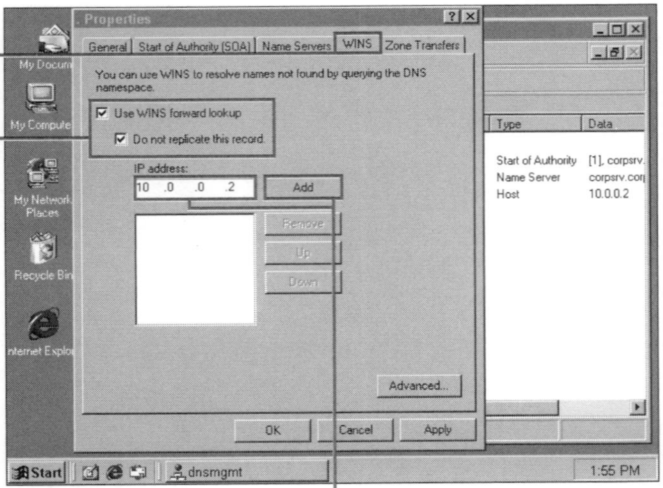

10 Click the WINS tab.

11 Click these check boxes to use WINS forward lookup and to prevent record replication.

12 Type the IP address of the WINS server(s) here.

13 Click Add.

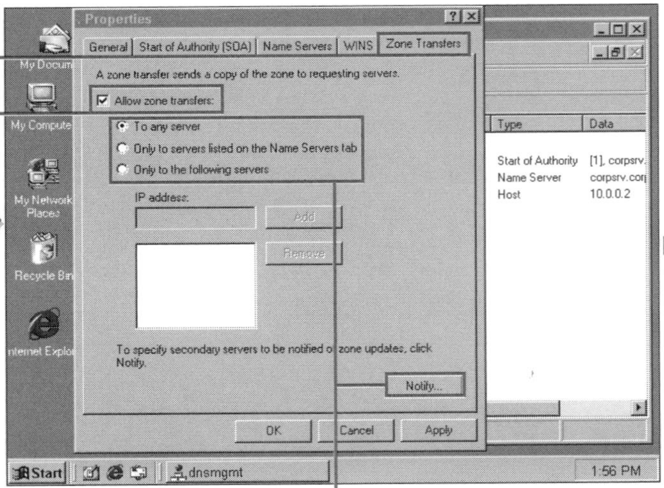

14 Click the Zone Transfers tab.

15 Click this check box to allow zone transfers.

16 Click the appropriate radio button to manage the zone transfers.

17 Click Notify to notify secondary servers of updates.

What is a zone transfer?

✓ The updates to the secondary DNS servers occurs through a process known as ***zone transfer***. Without the zone transfer process enabled, secondary DNS servers in the zone will not be automatically updated when the DNS database changes. You can choose to allow zone updates to any server in the zone, only the servers listed in the Name Servers tab, or you can configure the server list manually by adding them on the Zone Transfers tab. To add a name server to the list, simply enter the IP address of the name server and click Add. When you choose this option, only the servers you specify in the list receive zone transfers.

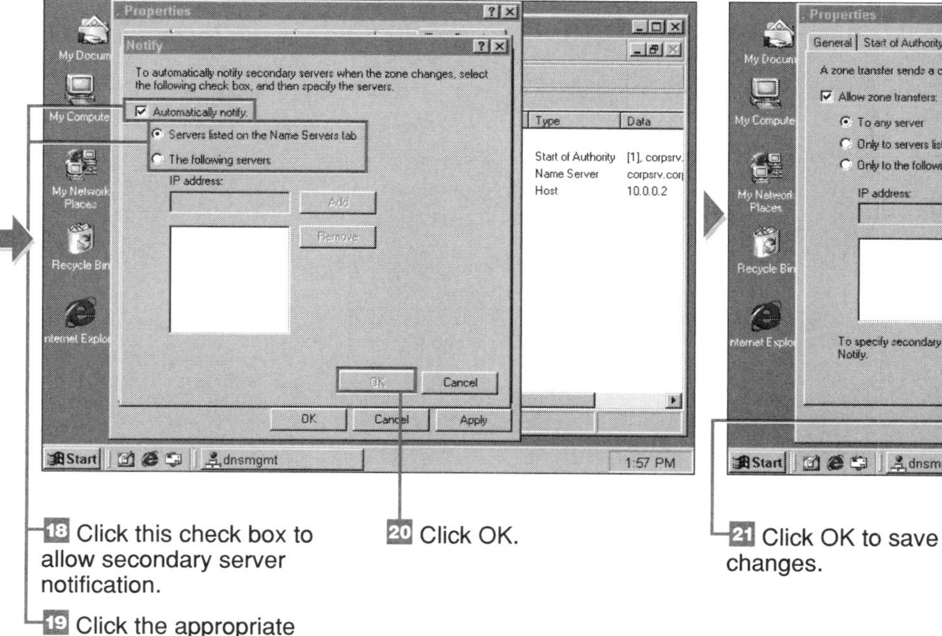

18 Click this check box to allow secondary server notification.

19 Click the appropriate radio button to specify the servers to be notified.

20 Click OK.

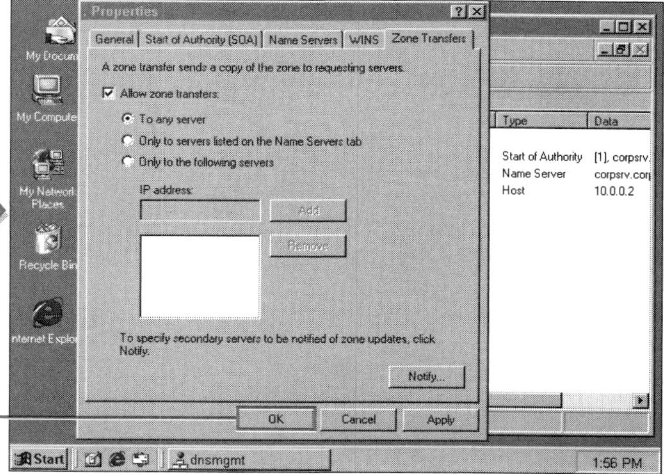

21 Click OK to save your changes.

ENABLING REMOTE ACCESS SERVICE

Remote Access Service (RAS) allows remote network clients to establish a remote connection with a RAS server. After the connection is established, RAS clients function just like locally connected network clients—they can browse the network, access resources, and perform all tasks available through a local connection. A RAS client can perform all these actions, if they are allowed to by RAS configuration, and they can use the Active Directory.

Although RAS is not technically a part of the Active Directory's operation, I include it in this book because of its networking nature and growing usage. As more users become mobile, users will access RAS more often. RAS in Windows 2000, formerly called Routing and Remote Access Service (RRAS) in Windows NT, is an integrated part of the operating system and is installed by default when you install Windows 2000 Server. In order to configure your server to be a RAS server, you have to enable RAS and configure it so it provides the functionality needed.

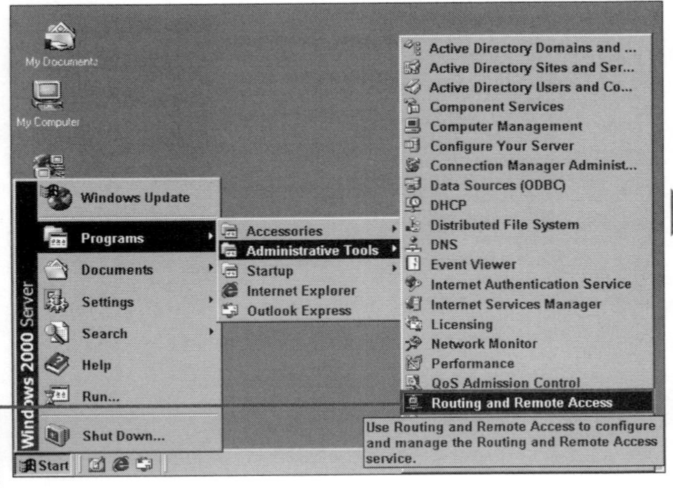

1 Click Start⇨Programs⇨ Administrative Tools⇨Routing and Remote Access.

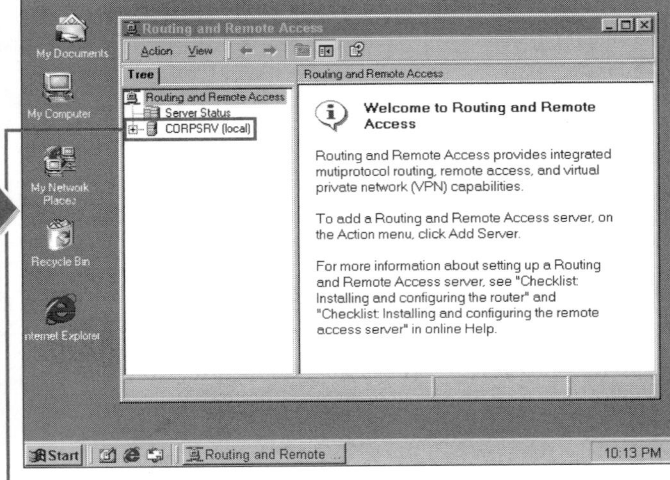

■ The RAS snap-in appears with your server icon and a note about enabling RAS.

Why is RAS installed by default?

- Windows 2000 expects you to use RAS. With the distributed nature of networks today and the mobility of users, most network environments need to use RAS to give remote network clients access to the network. Windows 2000 installs the service by default, but you can remove it from the system by using Add/Remove Programs in Control Panel if desired.

Do I have to enable RAS?

- RAS exists in your operating system, but it is not configured or enabled. If you want to use your Windows 2000 server as a RAS server, then you need to configure and enable RAS.

If I enable RAS, can I later remove it from my server?

- RAS is installed by default on your operating system. If you configure RAS for use, then later decide not to use the server as a RAS server, you can disable the service. See the next section to find out how to disable RAS.

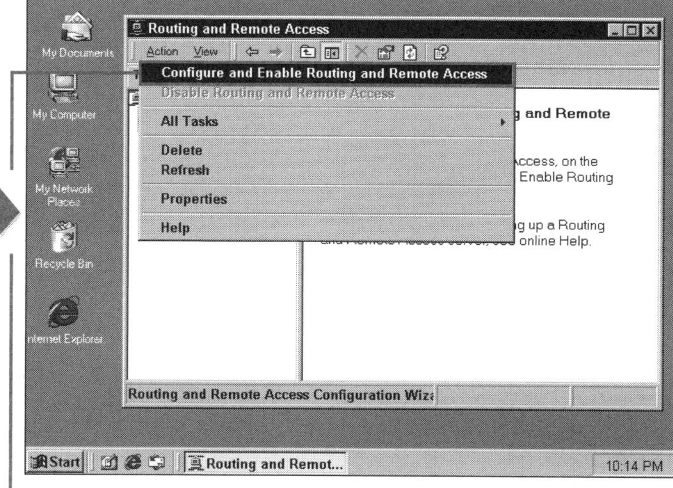

2 Select your server, and then click Action⇨Configure and Enable Routing and Remote Access.

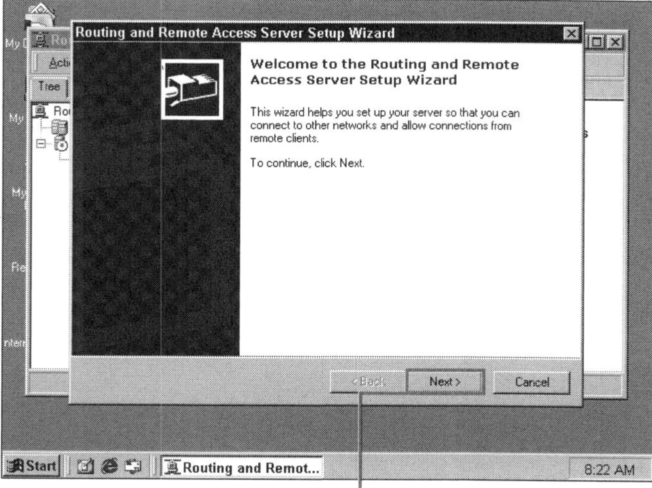

■ The Routing and Remote Access Configuration Wizard begins.

3 Click Next to continue.

CONTINUED

ENABLING REMOTE ACCESS SERVICE

CONTINUED

To enable and configure RAS, you use the Action menu for your server. A wizard appears that guides you through the configuration process. As you configure RAS, you need to make some important decisions.

First, you can choose to allow your server to function as a router, for either the local network or for both local and remote networks (LAN and WAN). A router passes TCP/IP traffic to different subnets so that communication among subnets can occur. By selecting the check box, your server can function as a router and help manage network traffic.

Next, you have to click a check box to enable remote access. This allows remote clients to gain access to the local network through your server. These two features together enable you to configure your server for both routing and RAS, or as one or the other.

Next, you have to select which external adapters (such as NICs, modems, ISDN, and so on) are configured for routing and remote access. The options allow you to enable all external devices, enable all devices for routing only, enable all devices for remote access only, or choose to configure your devices individually.

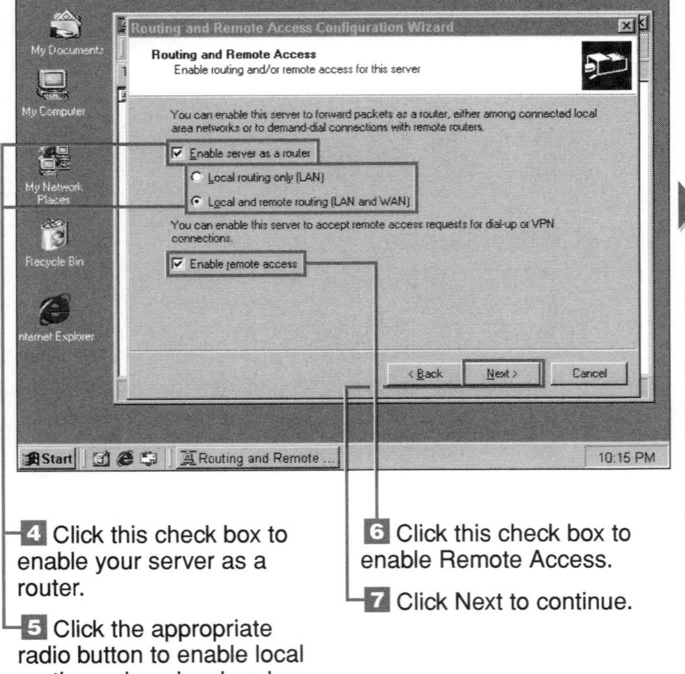

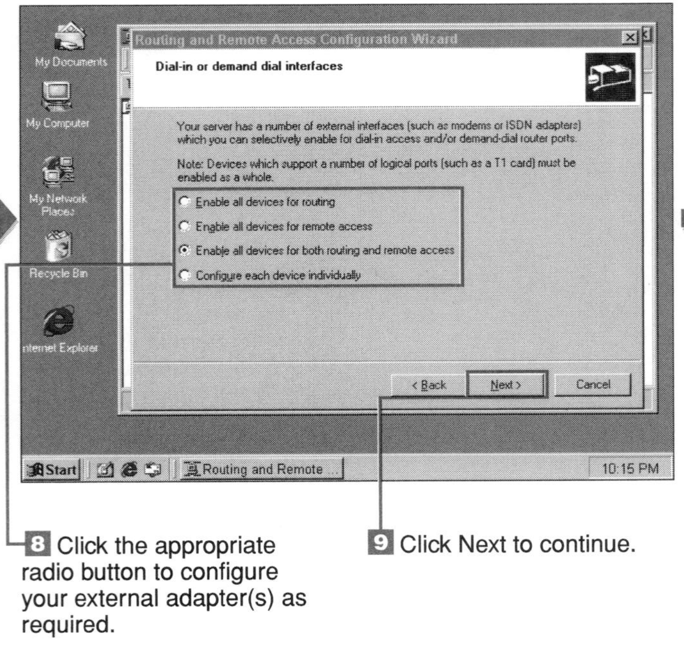

4 Click this check box to enable your server as a router.

5 Click the appropriate radio button to enable local routing only or local and remote routing.

6 Click this check box to enable Remote Access.

7 Click Next to continue.

8 Click the appropriate radio button to configure your external adapter(s) as required.

9 Click Next to continue.

What authentication and encryption methods should I use?

- First, you can choose all methods. This allows clients to submit their passwords to the RAS server for authentication using any authentication method available, including clear text. Obviously, this choice is not very secure. You can also choose to use only methods that secure the users' passwords, which basically means that passwords must be encrypted. This feature is more secure, but may cause problems for some network clients. You can fine-tune these features after you configure the RAS server, and policies that you implement on your network also drive the configuration as well.

Which protocol and access features should I use?

- Next, you select the protocol that RAS users must use to connect to the RAS server. This is normally TCP/IP. You also select whether to allow RAS clients to access only the RAS server or the entire network. The entire network feature is less secure, but it gives the RAS users the most access to Active Directory and network resources.

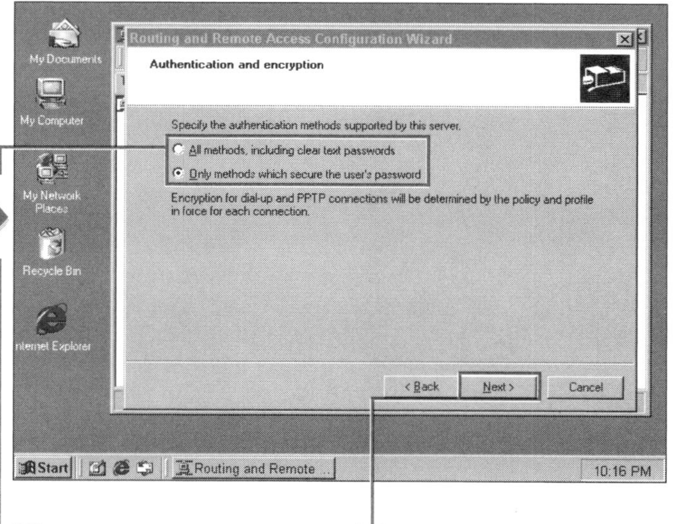

10 Click the appropriate radio button to allow either all methods of authentication or only secure methods.

11 Click Next to continue.

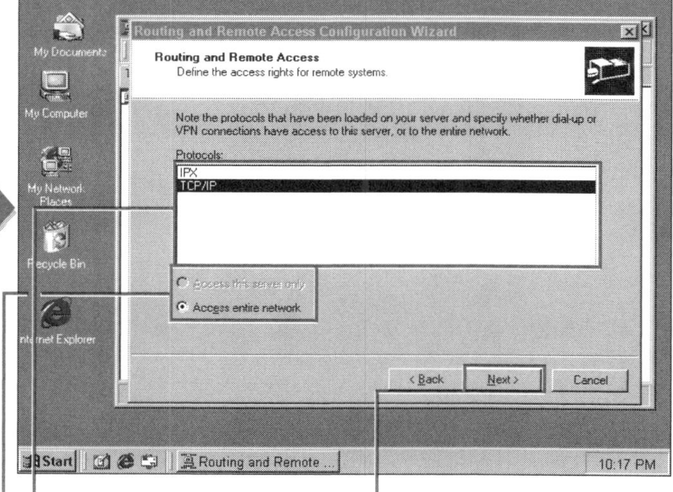

12 Select the protocol clients use for dial-up connections.

13 Click the appropriate radio button for either Access this server only or Access entire network.

14 Click Next to continue.

CONTINUED

ENABLING REMOTE ACCESS SERVICE

CONTINUED

Next, you decide whether you want RAS clients to use DHCP or whether you want to define a static IP address pool.

As you may recall, DHCP leases IP addresses to client computers so that they can participate on a TCP/IP network. This feature enables client IP configuration to occur automatically and without the administrative-intensive task of manual IP address assignment. You can configure RAS so that RAS clients are authenticated by the RAS server and then receive a DHCP IP lease from a DHCP server. However, some network environments choose to provide a static pool of IP addresses that can be assigned to RAS clients. This is a security feature to prevent RAS clients from being completely integrated into the network. If you choose this option, then the RAS wizard asks you to create a pool of IP addresses for RAS client leases. Obviously, you must supply a pool of IP addresses that are appropriate for your network and also supply an appropriate subnet mask.

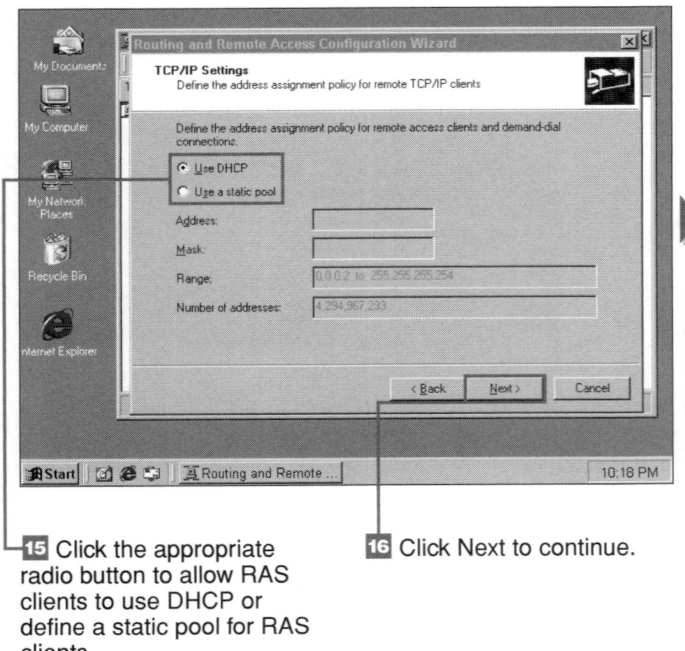

15 Click the appropriate radio button to allow RAS clients to use DHCP or define a static pool for RAS clients.

16 Click Next to continue.

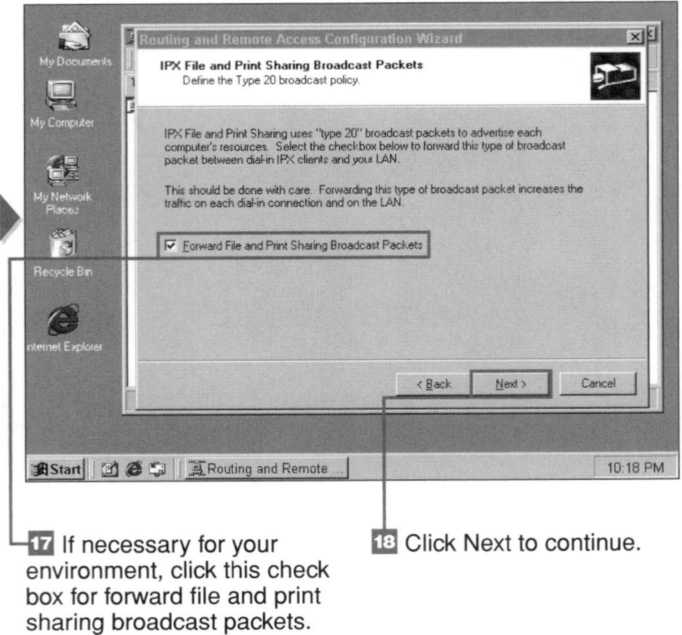

17 If necessary for your environment, click this check box for forward file and print sharing broadcast packets.

18 Click Next to continue.

When you reach the final wizard screen, you see several pieces of information that are important to note.

First, if you enabled routing and/or remote access, you can manage further configuration from the RAS snap-in. The wizard configures the basic details, but you will most likely need to perform further configuration to enable the RAS server to function as desired.

Next, the wizard informs you that user settings are managed through the Active Directory, which you learn about in Chapters 14 and 15. Also, policies based on site, domain, and OU levels may be applied so they affect RAS settings. Group Policies are a powerful feature of Windows 2000 and the Active Directory that gives you more administrative control and prevents many end-user problems. You can learn more about policies in the Active Directory in Chapter 25.

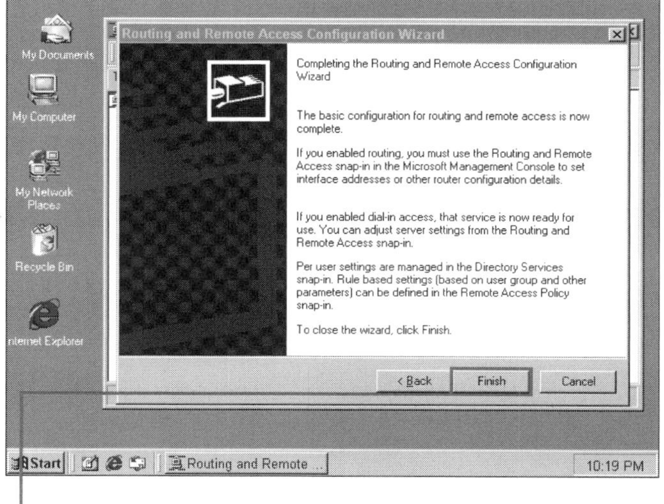

19 Click Finish complete the process.

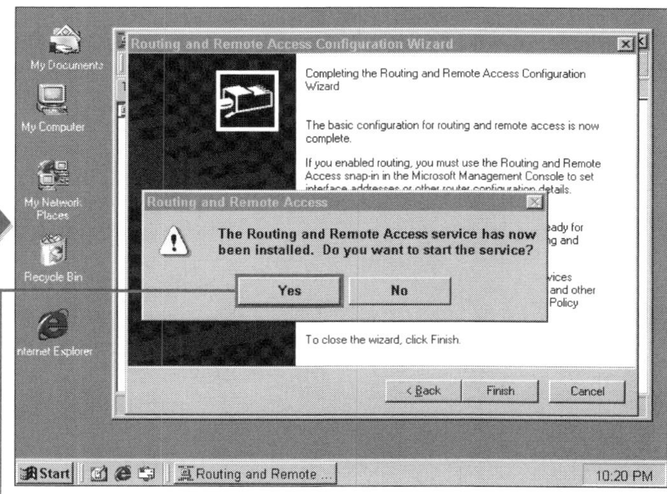

20 Click Yes to start the service.

DISABLING RAS

RAS is installed on your server by default. However, you must enable it in order for your server to become a RAS Server. Just as you can enable the RAS service, you can also disable it.

There are a number of reasons for disabling the RAS service. A major reason is a change in the role your server plays on the network. As networks grow and change, servers are often moved to different locations or are reconfigured to perform a different set of tasks. If the time comes when you no longer want your server to authenticate dial-in clients through RAS, you can disable the service. After the service is disabled, clients can not dial-in and be authenticated by the server, but will have to use other RAS servers that may be available. Before disabling the RAS service, make certain that you have a specific reason for doing so and make certain that other RAS servers are available to clients.

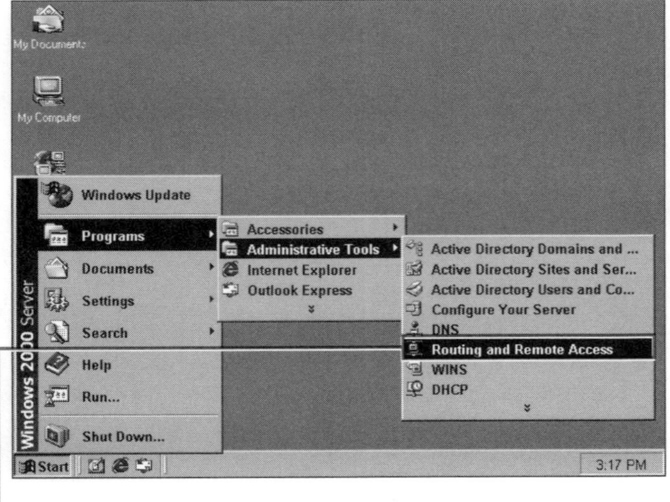

1 Choose Start⇨Programs⇨Administrative Tools⇨Routing and Remote Access.

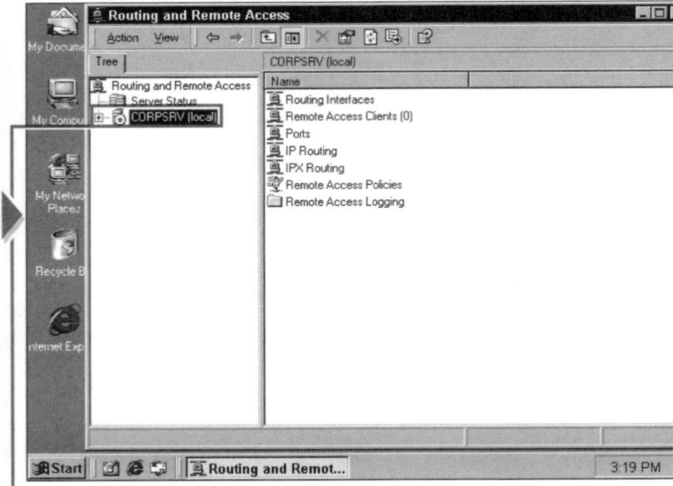

2 Select the server in the console for which you want to disable RAS.

TIPS

If I disable RAS, can I re-enable it?

✔ Yes. As with many services in Windows 2000, you can easily disable or re-enable RAS as necessary. This feature allows you to permanently take a RAS server offline so that the service is no longer available to clients, or you can take the service offline temporarily while you perform troubleshooting or system configuration. However, if you disable it, the service prompts you to re-run the setup wizard in order to start the service again. Generally, you should avoid disabling the RAS service unless you plan to permanently do so in order to avoid additional configuration.

If I disable RAS, are all of my previous settings removed?

✔ Yes. If you disable the RAS service, you can always re-enable it later. However, you will be prompted to re-configure the service through setup wizard. You cannot disable the service and preserve the previous settings.

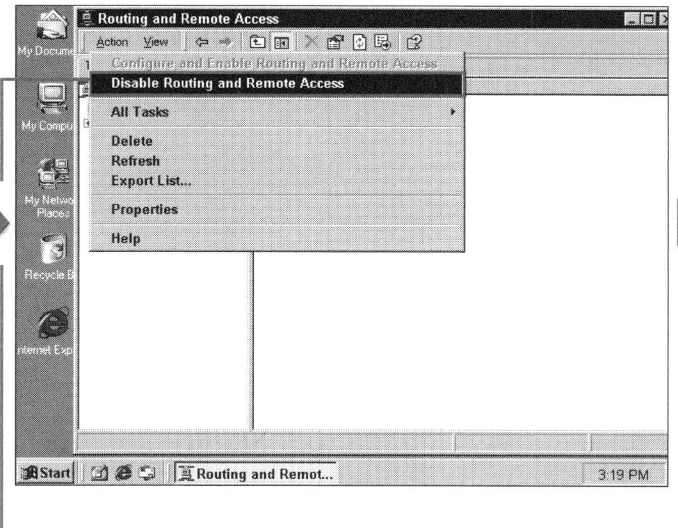

3 Choose Action⇨Disable Routing and Remote Access.

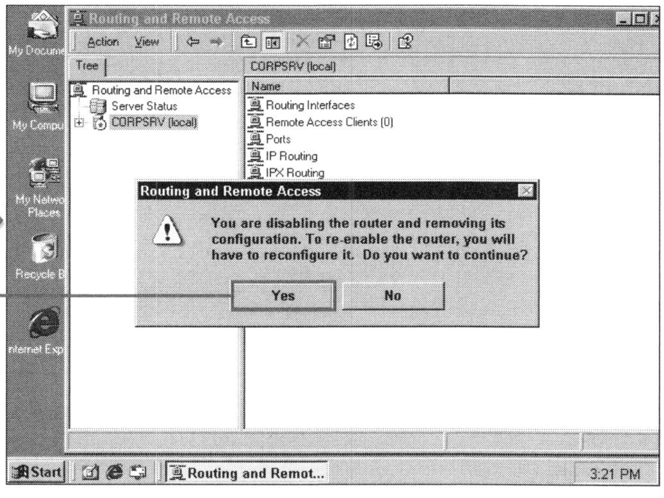

4 Click Yes to confirm that you want to disable RAS.

EXAMINING BASIC RAS OPTIONS

As with other networking components in Windows 2000 Server, you have the option to manage your RAS server from within the RAS console, but you can also add other RAS servers (and routing servers) to the console for management. This feature makes it easy for you, as the administrator, to manage all your RAS servers from one central location. Instead of having to physically visit each machine, you can load each server into one console and manage them all from one location.

You can also adjust the Refresh rate for all RAS servers loaded into the console. By default, RAS servers are refreshed every 60 seconds, but you can change this value as needed. After you make a change, this value affects all RAS servers in your RAS console. Typically, the 60-second interval is enough and you should not need to change this setting, unless you have specific reasons for lowering the refresh rate.

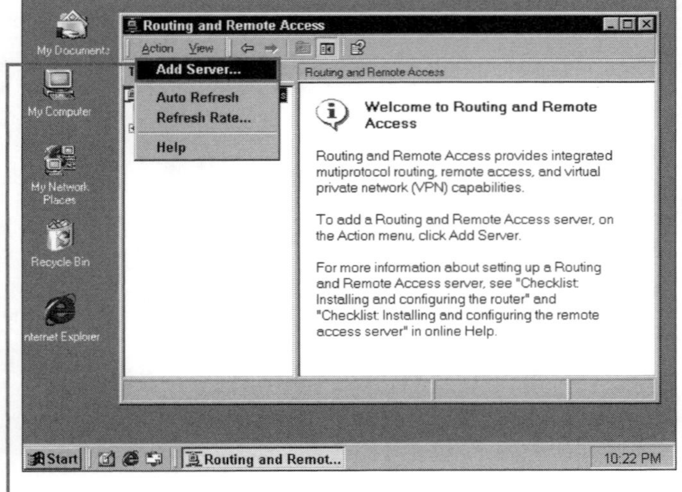

1 Select RAS in the console, and then choose Action⇨Add Server.

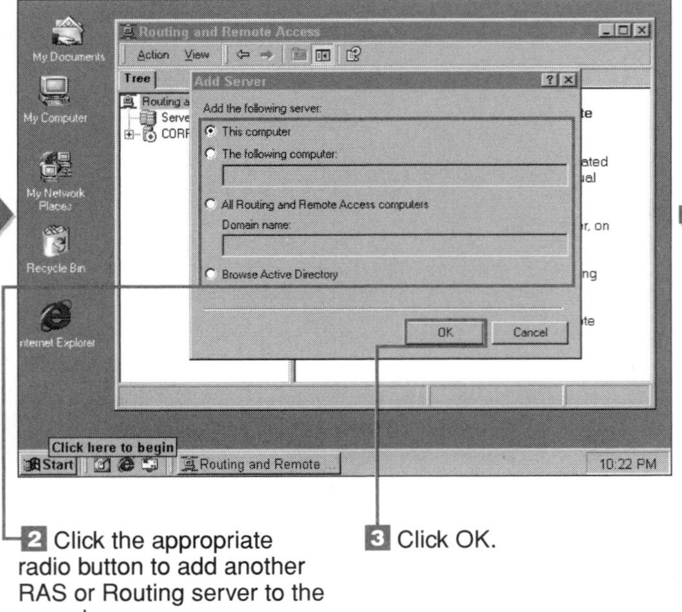

2 Click the appropriate radio button to add another RAS or Routing server to the console.

3 Click OK.

What permission do I need to manage all RAS servers on my network from my server?

- One person can manage most networking components from one location. This design allows your network to have a RAS administrator whose main job focus is to manage all the RAS servers and make certain they are working properly for your environment. This manager needs to be a member of the Enterprise Admins group so that he or she can authoritatively control other servers in the Enterprise. With this permission, the RAS administrator can manage all RAS servers from his or her own server.

Do I ever need to lower the refresh rate?

- By default, the refresh rate is every 60 seconds. You might need to lower the refresh rate for troubleshooting purposes, but for the most part, the default setting is all you need.

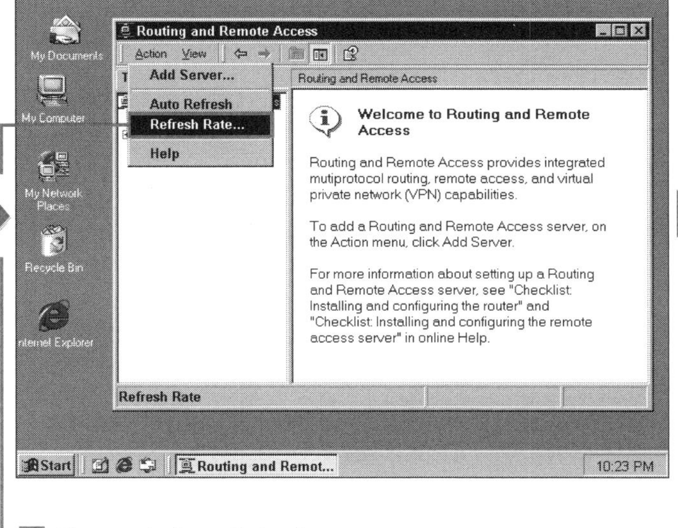

4 Choose Action⇨Refresh Rate.

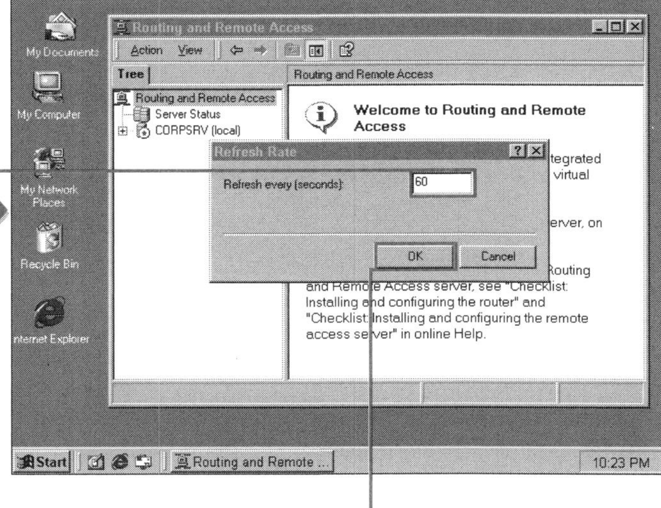

5 Adjust the Refresh Rate as desired.

6 Click OK.

EXPLORING SERVER PROPERTIES

The good thing about most wizard setups is that you can change the configuration later. In other words, the decisions you make during the initial setup are not "written in stone." You can make changes to that configuration without rerunning the wizard. RAS is no exception.

By accessing the properties sheet for the RAS server, you can make a number of configuration changes.

First, the General tab enables you to change the role the RAS server plays. You can either enable or disable the computer as a router, RAS server, or both, just as you did during setup.

The Security tab enables you to choose between Windows authentication for clients or RADIUS authentication. You can also select between the Windows accounting provider and the RADIUS Accounting provider. This feature allows you to use RADIUS servers in your network. For the security options, you can click the Configure button and select a number of options, which are explained on the next page.

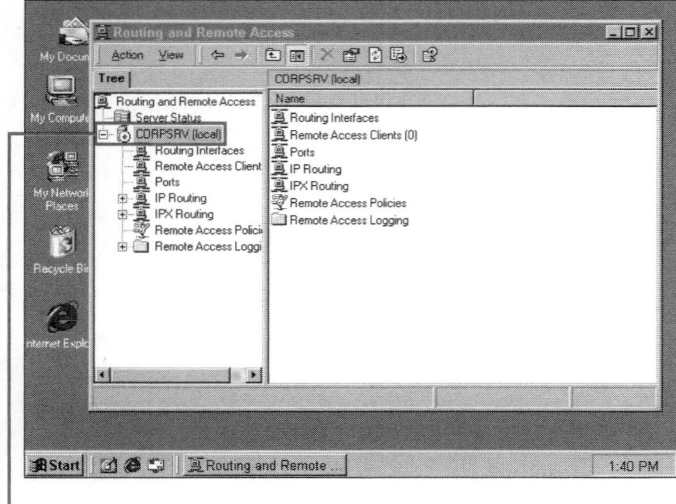

1 Select the server that you want to administer.

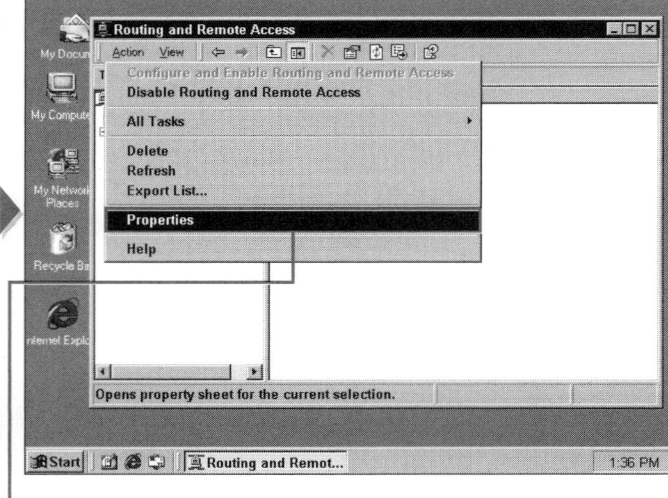

2 Choose Action⇨Properties.

What authentication methods can I choose?

You can choose the following authentication choices, listed from most secure to least secure:

- Extensible Authentication Protocol (EAP)—This protocol allows the use of third-party authentication software and is also used for Smart Card logon.
- MS-CHAP v2—This generates encryption keys during RAS authentication negotiation.
- MS-CHAP—This is the previous version that provides secure logon.
- CHAP—CHAP is Challange Handshake Authentication Protocol, an early version of MS-CHAP that provides secure logon.
- Shiva Password Authentication Protocol (SPAP)—This is used by Shiva clients connecting to a Windows 2000 RAS server. SPAP is more secure than clear text, but less secure than CHAP.
- Unencrypted password (PAP)—Unencrypted passwords are send in clear text—no encryption required.
- Unauthenticated access – Unauthenticated access allows a user to access the network without authentication. Obviously, this provides no security.

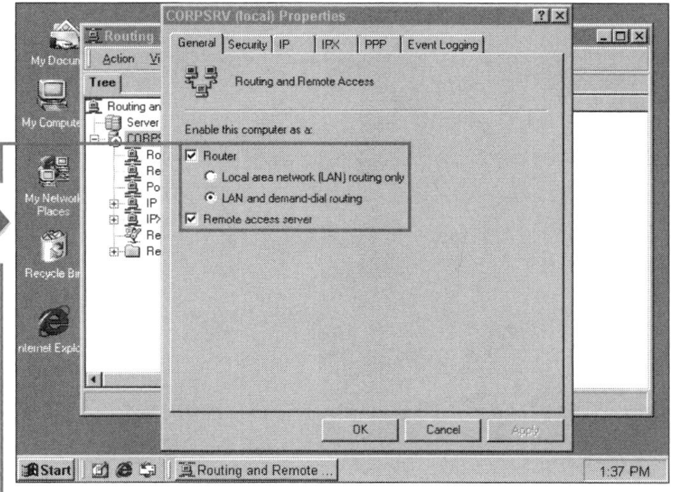

3 Click the appropriate check boxes to change the configuration of the RAS server.

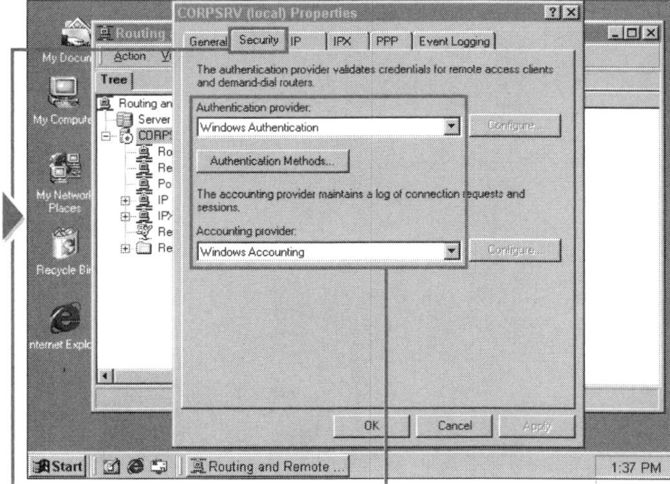

4 Click the Security tab.

5 Click the drop-down boxes to make changes to the Authentication and/or Accounting provider.

CONTINUED

EXPLORING SERVER PROPERTIES

CONTINUED

On the IP tab, you can make the desired configuration changes for your RAS clients who access the RAS server via a TCP/IP connection. First, you have the option to allow or not allow remote systems running IP. You also have the option to allow IP clients, once authenticated, to access the entire network or only the RAS server. Also, you have the option to use either DHCP or a static address pool for client IP address lease. You configured this option during RAS setup, but you can change it here if desired.

The IPX Clients allows client computers running IPX/SPX to be authenticated by the RAS server. As with the IP tab, you can either allow or disallow IPX clients, and you can choose whether IPX clients can access only the RAS server or the entire network.

For IPX clients, you have the option to define the network numbers the clients use to communicate, or you can allow the network numbers to be allocated automatically. IPX clients must have a proper network number to communicate on the network.

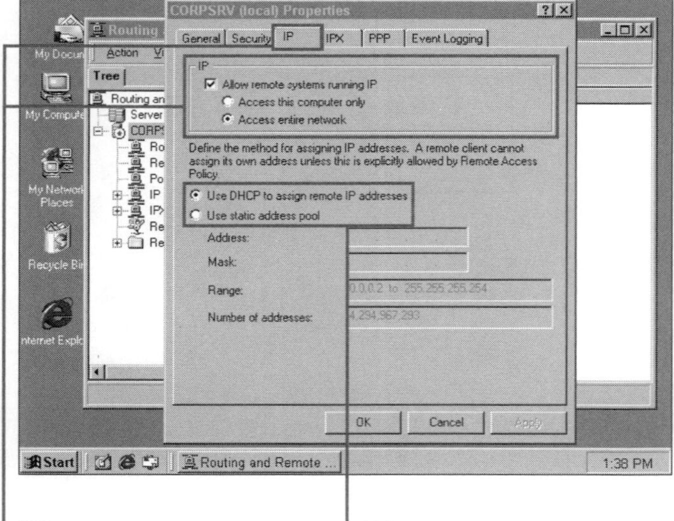

6 Click the IP tab.

7 Click the appropriate check box and radio button to make changes to your IP configuration.

8 Change the IP lease assignment to use either DHCP or a static address pool by clicking these radio buttons.

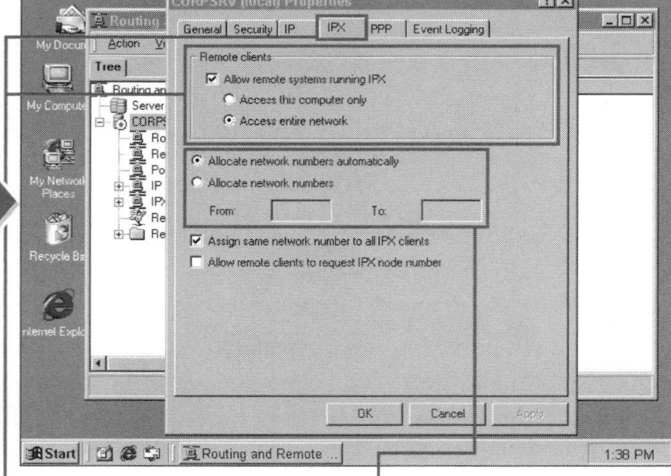

9 Click the IPX tab.

10 Change the IPX client usage by allowing or disallowing IPX clients by clicking the check box and appropriate radio button.

11 Adjust the network numbers allocation either automatically or manually using these radio buttons.

On the PPP tab, you have some different options when using the Point to Point Protocol. First, you can allow *multilink* connections. Multilink allows you to use several modems or adapters to increase bandwidth. With the multilink option, you can choose to use dynamic bandwidth control using BAP or BACP. BAP is Bandwidth Allocation Protocol and BACP is Bandwidth Allocation Control Protocol. Both of these allow the multilink connection to automatically drop or add PPP links as needed by the traffic flow. You can also choose to choose Link Control Protocol (LCP) extensions and software compression to help control PPP connections.

The Event Logging tab enables you to determine what events you want logged in the event log. You can choose from errors only or errors and warnings, you can log the maximum amount of information, you can disable all event logging, and you can enable PPP logging.

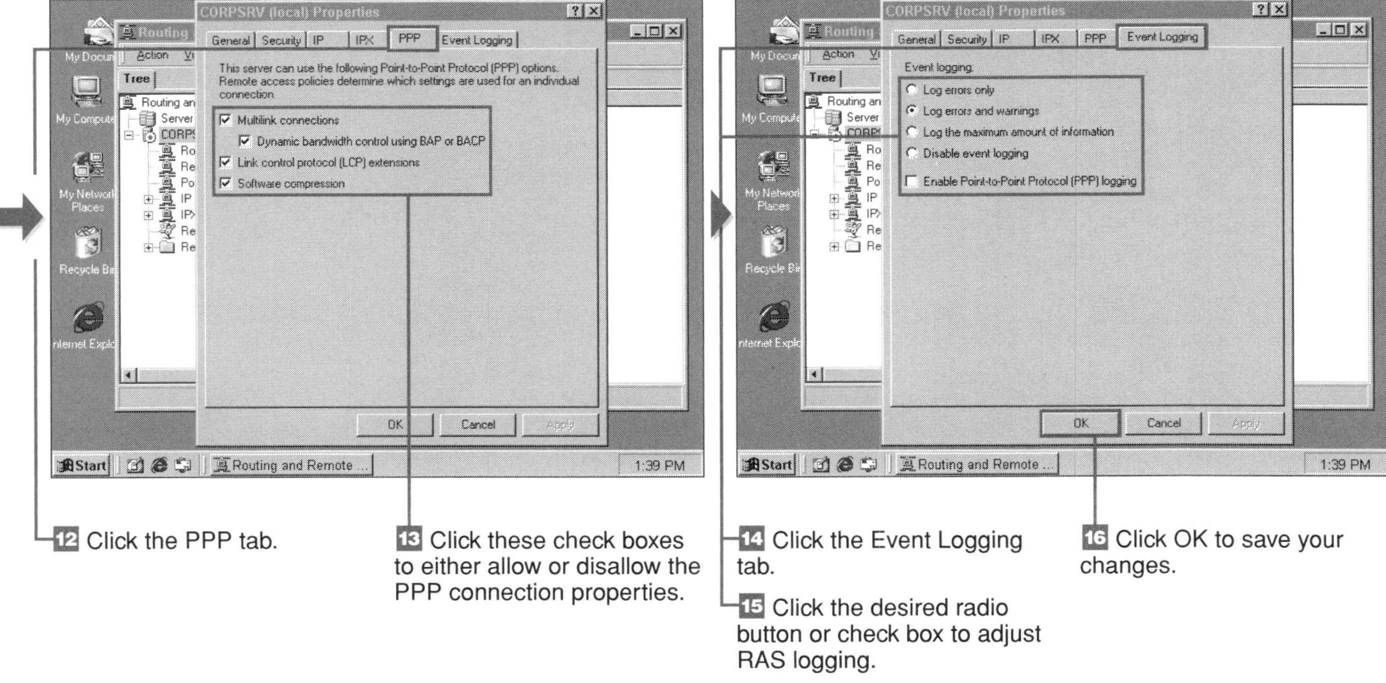

12 Click the PPP tab.

13 Click these check boxes to either allow or disallow the PPP connection properties.

14 Click the Event Logging tab.

15 Click the desired radio button or check box to adjust RAS logging.

16 Click OK to save your changes.

EXPLORING ROUTING INTERFACES

If you select Routing in the console pane under your RAS server, you can see the routing interfaces that are currently configured—if your server has been configured to be a router. You can select any of the current LAN and demand dial interfaces and use the Action menu to connect or disconnect, as well as set the interface credentials.

You can add a new demand dial interface by selecting Routing Interfaces in the console and clicking the Action menu. This option is only available if WAN routing is configured (see the General tab of the RAS server properties sheets). The demand dial connection establishes a connection to a remote site "on demand," or when data needs to be sent. The connection is established and maintained all the time, but only when it is needed.

If you want to establish a new demand dial interface, a wizard helps guide you through the process.

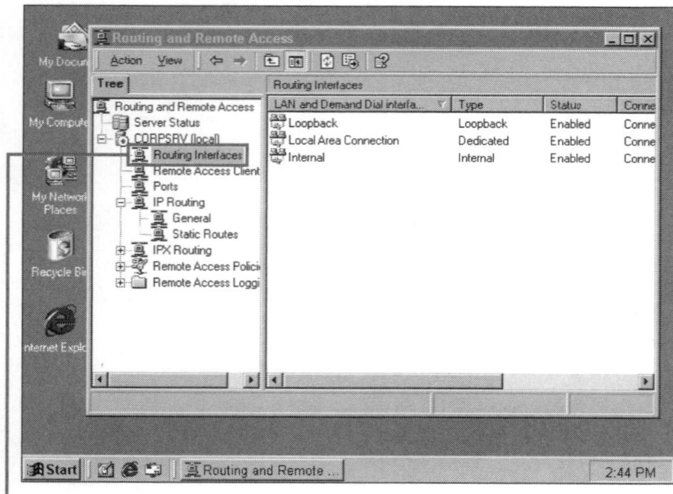

1 Expand the RAS server in the console and select Routing Interfaces.

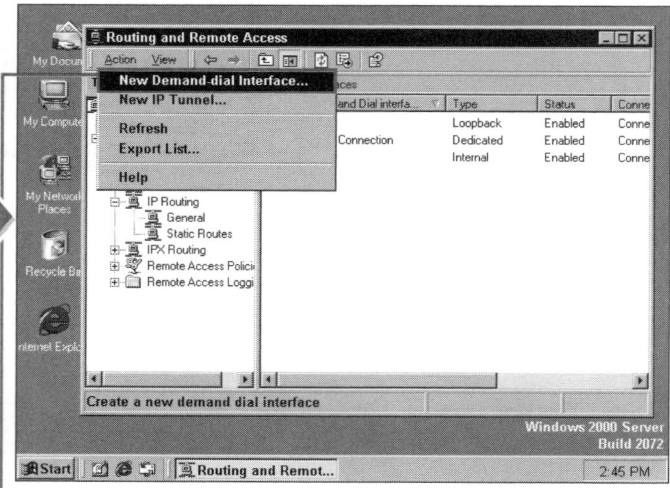

2 Choose Action⇨New Demand-dial Interface.

Why should I use demand-dial routing?

- Demand-dial interfaces use demand-dial routing, which allows the establishment of switched connections across Wide Area Networks (WAN). The connection is based on "demand," or a need for the connection. For example, an office in Portland and an office in New York, which are a part of a WAN, need to share information about three times a week. A modem or ISDN connection can connect with the router in the other office. With demand-dial, the modems or ISDN adapters dial up and connect on demand to the other router so that data transfer takes place. This is a cost-effective solution that provides connectivity when needed, but avoids the cost of having a dedicated WAN link.

Do I have to use demand-dial interfaces?

- Demand-dial is an optional component provided to help network administrators create inexpensive connectivity solutions. The use of demand-dial is based solely on the needs of your network.

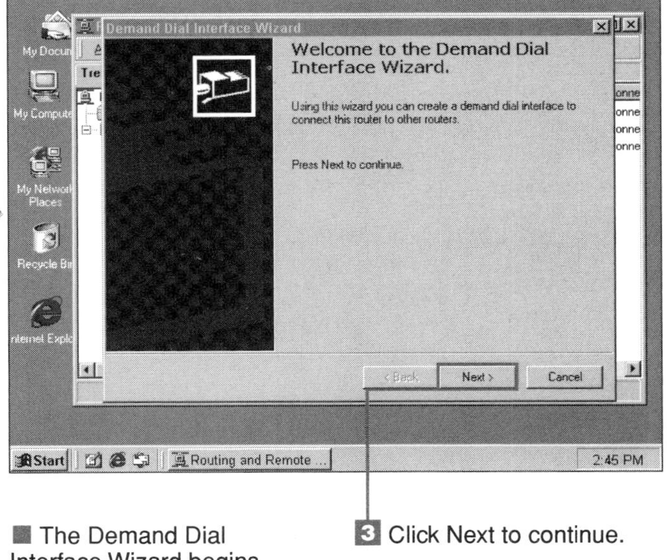

■ The Demand Dial Interface Wizard begins.

3 Click Next to continue.

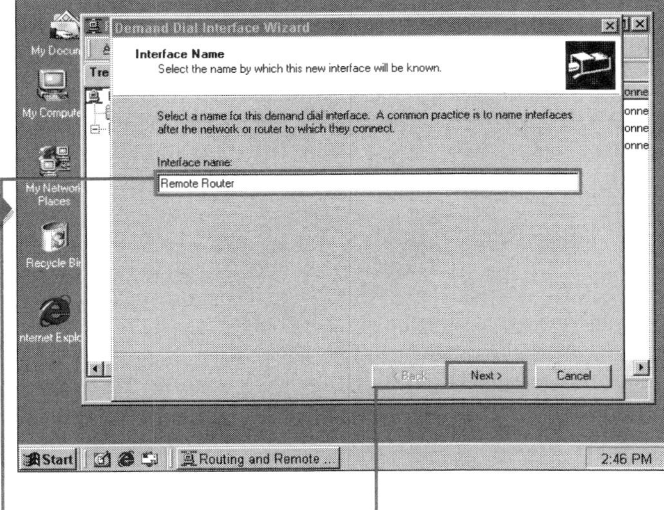

4 Type a name for the interface.

5 Click Next to continue.

CONTINUED

EXPLORING ROUTING INTERFACES
CONTINUED

When you run the wizard to configure a new demand-dial interface, you need to make some decisions about the router's use. First, you have to determine the kind of demand-dial interface you want to use. You can connect using a modem, ISDN adapter, or some other physical device connected to your computer, or you can connect using a *Virtual Private Network* (VPN). A VPN enables you to use the Internet as a private network by encapsulating network communication data into PPP frames so that they can be transmitted over the Internet.

Next, you need to determine the protocols and security features of the demand-dial interface. The available options are listed on the next page. Also, you need to determine an appropriate username, domain, and password so that the connection to the remote router can be made. The remote router must have an account configured for this purpose.

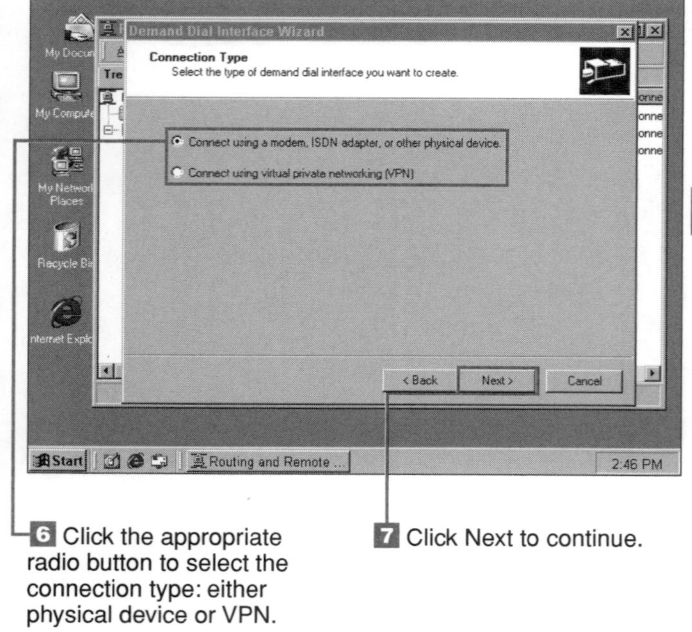

6 Click the appropriate radio button to select the connection type: either physical device or VPN.

7 Click Next to continue.

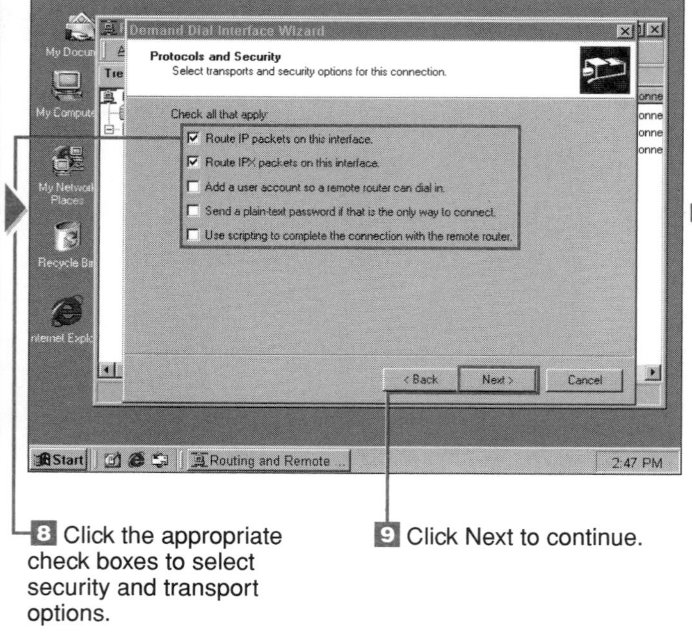

8 Click the appropriate check boxes to select security and transport options.

9 Click Next to continue.

What protocols and security features can I use?

✓ Demand-dial interfaces use the following protocols and security features:

- Route IP Packets on the interface—IP packets can be routed on this particular demand-dial interface.
- Route IPX packets on the interface—IPX packets can be routed on this particular demand-dial interface.
- Add a user account so a remote router can dial-in—Allows you to create a user account for the router so the router can connect and be authenticated.
- Send a plain-text password if that is the only way to connect—Allows plain text passwords to be used, which significantly lowers network security.
- Use scripting to complete the connection with the remote router—Allows you to create and implement connections scripts for demand-dialing.

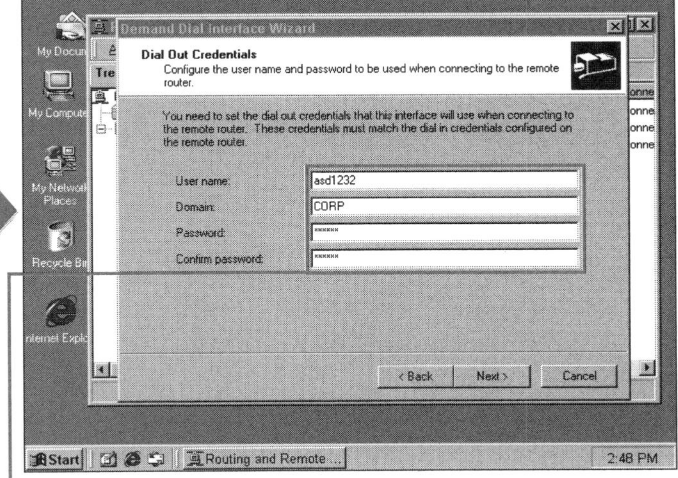

10 Type the dial-out credentials in these boxes.

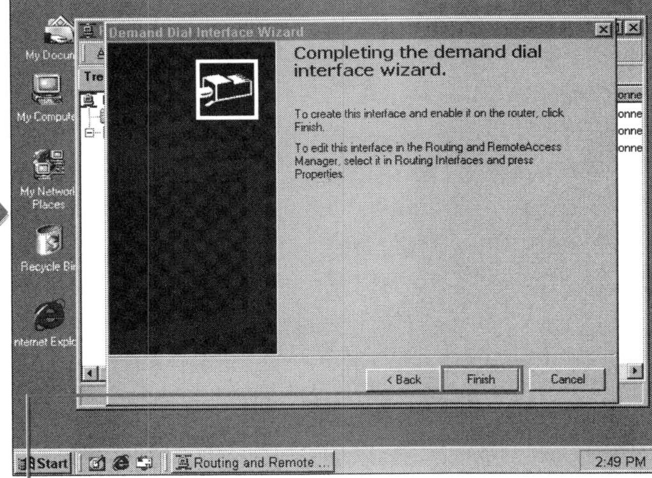

11 Click Finish to complete the wizard.

CREATING A NEW IP TUNNEL

Aside from the demand-dial interface, you can also create a new *IP tunnel* for your VPN connections. An IP tunnel is a logical interface, meaning that it's not created through a physical piece of hardware. The IP tunnel enables IP packets on your local network to be "tunneled" over the Internet or an intranet. This is accomplished by adding additional IP header information to the packet. The actual data is encapsulated in the new IP packet with additional header information. It can then be sent over the Internet or intranet and appears as normal IP Internet communication. The receiving computer can then decrypt the actual data in the packet. This feature enables you to use the Internet to transmit secure network data from one location to the next without the expense of a dedicated WAN link.

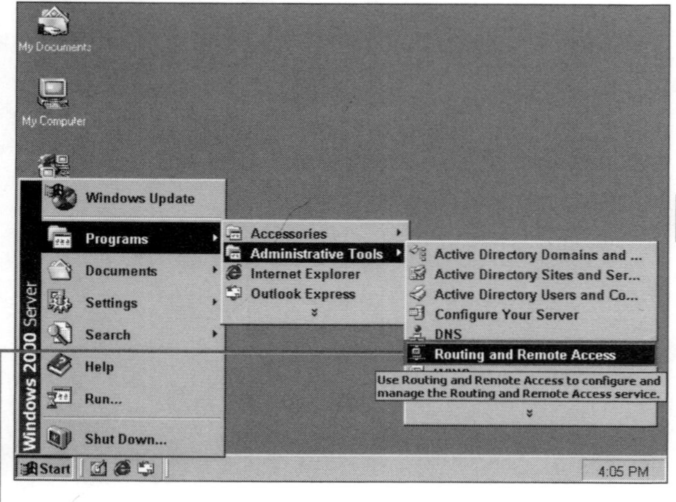

1 Click Start⇨Programs⇨Administrative Tools⇨Routing and Remote Access.

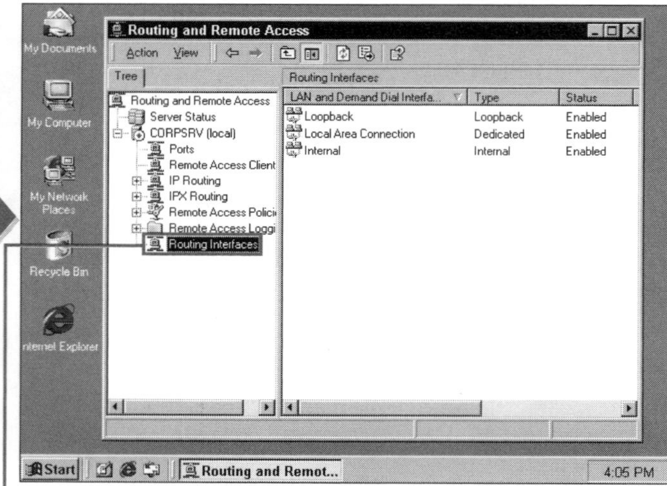

2 Expand the desired server and select Routing Interfaces.

Why would I want to use an IP tunnel?

- An IP tunnel allows you to securely send data over the Internet or an intranet. With this feature, you can make use of existing network topology to securely and inexpensively send data. The IP tunnel hides your data in a PPP frame so it appears as typical Internet or Intranet traffic. IP tunnels are an effective means to use the Internet to send data to remote locations without having to maintain an expensive WAN link.

What is the difference between an IP tunnel and a VPN?

- IP tunnels create "virtual private networks" (VPN), so the terms are basically interchangeable. The technology was originally referred to as VPNs, which use the Point-to-Point Tunneling Protocol (PPTP) to securely tunnel data over a public network, such as the Internet. This technology solution is commonly called IP tunnels.

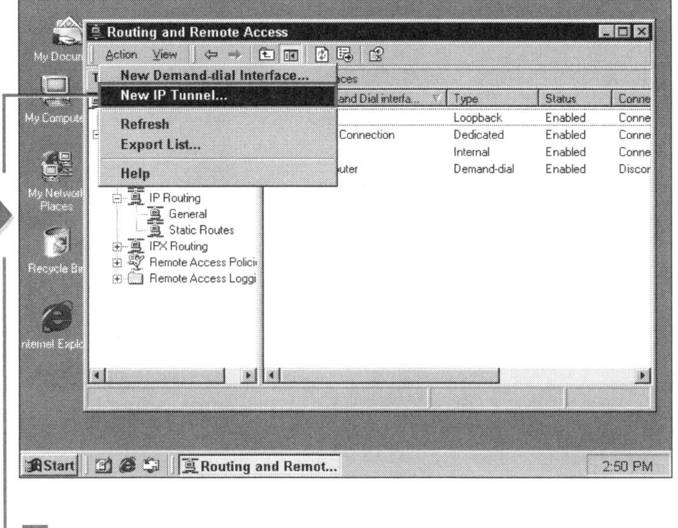

3 Choose Action⇨New IP Tunnel.

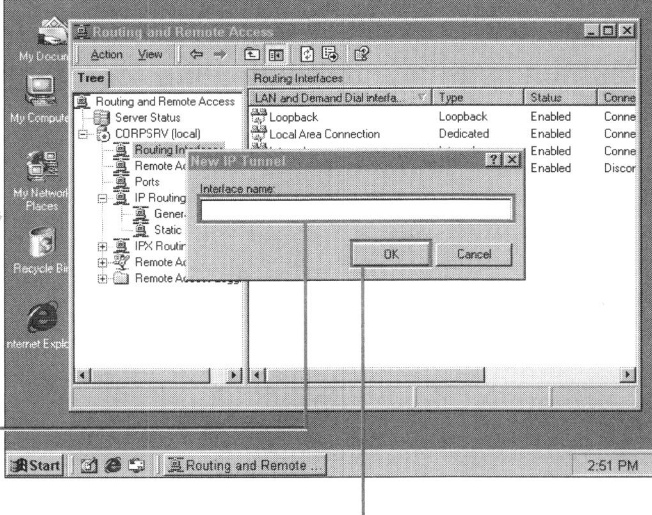

4 Type the name for the new IP tunnel.

5 Click OK.

ADDING RAS POLICIES

RAS Policies enable you to manage what users can do when dialing into a RAS server and what they can do after they are authenticated. You can also configure Group Policies that affect RAS (see Chapter 25).

By default, a RAS policy is created that enables you to define when RAS users can dial in to the RAS server and be authenticated. In other words, you can use this feature to restrict the dial-up time to business hours only, or any other combination that you choose. You can create additional RAS policies as desired by selecting Remote Access Policies in the console and choosing Action⇨New. All are configured the same, so the following sections show you how to configure the default policy.

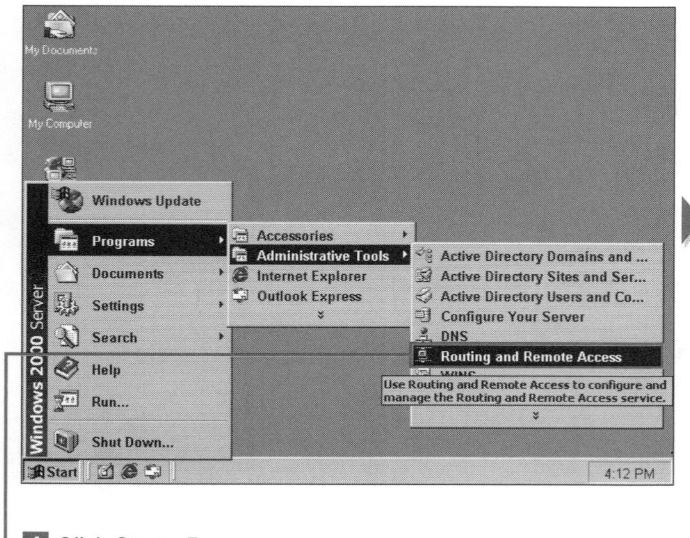

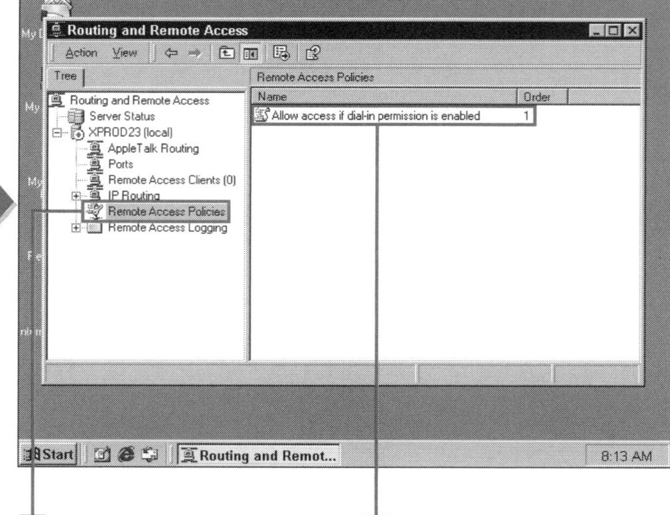

1 Click Start⇨Programs⇨ Administrative Tools⇨ Routing and Remote Access.

2 Click Remote Access Policies in the console tree.

■ A list of current policies appears in the details pane.

3 Double-click the desired policy in the details pane.

What types of attributes can I add to a policy?

- When you open the existing RAS policy, a window appears that tells you the parameters of the policy. You can add more parameters, or attributes, so that the policy affects more than one setting. For example, the dial-in constraints policy also allows you to add attributes, such as phone number restrictions, protocol restrictions, and so forth.

How do I edit an existing policy?

- You can configure this policy by clicking the Edit button and making changes to the dial-up hours as desired. After you set the configuration, you then determine whether remote access is granted or denied based on your settings. This allows you to create a policy that allows dial-in access Monday through Friday from 8:00 a.m. to 5:00 p.m., or you can select the appropriate grids for nighttime and weekend access using a deny button. This accomplishes the same thing, but the policy enables you to configure it either way for the same result. See the next section for more information.

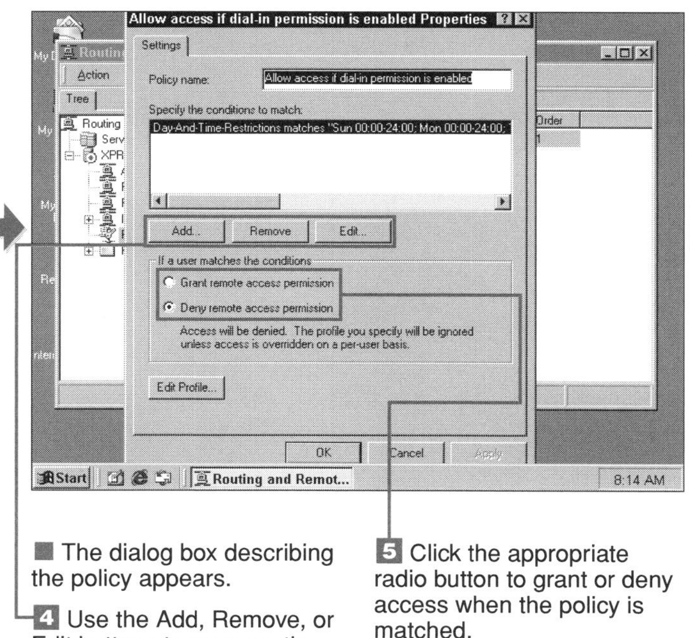

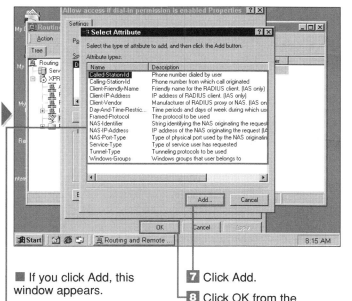

■ The dialog box describing the policy appears.

4 Use the Add, Remove, or Edit buttons to manage the policy.

5 Click the appropriate radio button to grant or deny access when the policy is matched.

■ If you click Add, this window appears.

6 Select an attribute you want to add to the policy.

7 Click Add.

8 Click OK from the Properties sheet to save the changes.

EDITING RAS POLICIES

If you click the Edit Profile button, you can make a number of additional changes for the RAS policy. First, you have a Dial-in Constraints tab, on which you can force a number of connectivity settings. You can have the server disconnect the call if it is idle for a configured period of time. Also, you can restrict the maximum session time so that the server automatically disconnects the session after a certain period of time. You can restrict access to certain days and times as desired. Additionally, you can restrict the dial-in connection to one specific phone number and one specific media, such as ISDN.

The IP tab enables you to determine how a client obtains an IP address, from either the server or client, or you can allow server settings to define the policy. You can also use this tab to configure different protocol filters, which prevents a user from using a certain IP protocol (such as UDP).

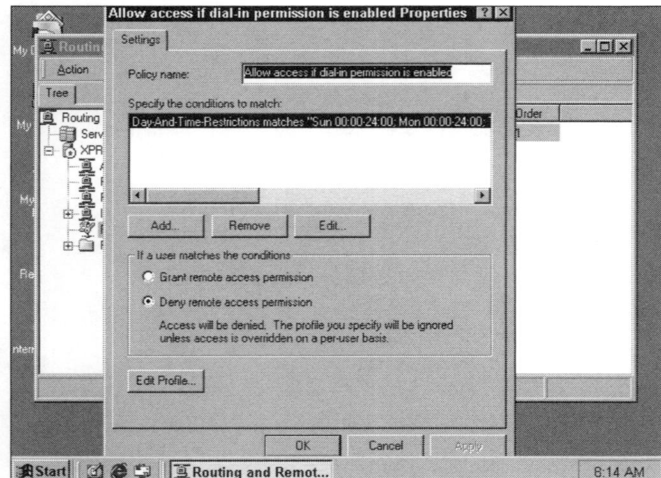

1 Double-click the policy you want to edit.

■ The policy's Properties sheet appears.

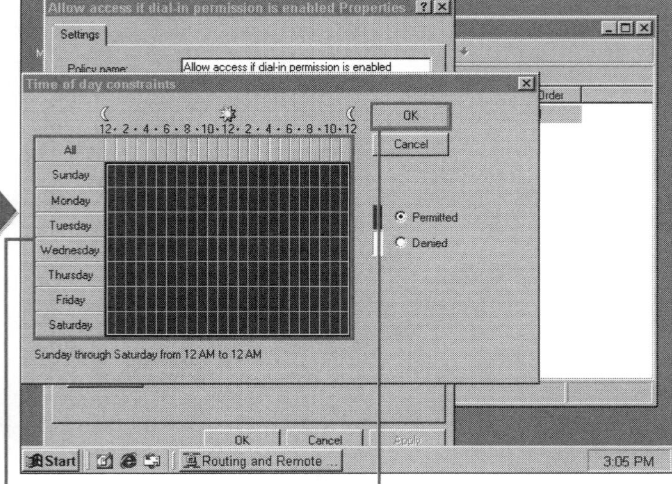

■ If you click the Edit button for a time restriction policy, this window appears.

2 Adjust the grid by clicking on the cells to create the desired logon availability times.

3 Click OK when you are done.

Why would I want to edit a policy?

- Windows 2000 creates predefined RAS policies, and you can also create custom policies as well. Often, the predefined policies will need some editing so they function in the manner necessary for your network. A common example is to allow remote access permission for certain times and days. In some environments, users can dial-in to the network 24 hours a day, 7 days a week, while other environments restrict users from dialing-in on the weekends.

Is there another way to edit RAS policies?

- Yes. RAS policies can also be created and edited using the Group Policy feature of Windows 2000, which is integrated with the Active Directory. You can learn all about Group Policy in Chapter 25.

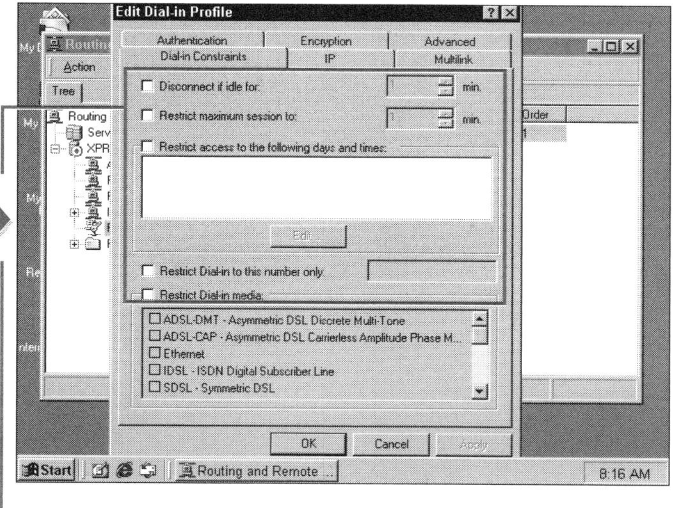

4 Click the Edit Profile button, then click the appropriate check boxes to adjust the dial-in constraints for the policy.

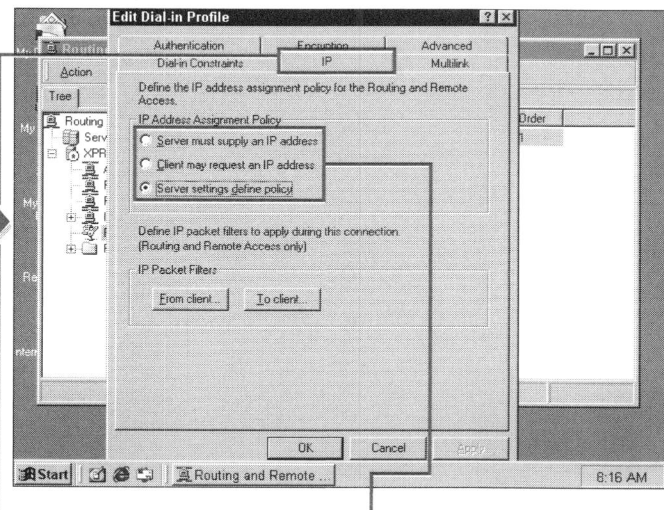

5 Click the IP tab.

6 Click the appropriate radio button to define the IP address assignment for the policy.

CONTINUED

EDITING RAS POLICIES CONTINUED

On the Multilink tab, you can allow multilink connections based on the default server settings, disable multilink, or allow multilink and set the maximum number of ports yourself. If you choose to allow multilink, you should also make a decision about BAP (Bandwidth Allocation Protocol). BAP manages the links within a multilink connection by dropping or adding links based on connection needs. For example, if a multilink connection falls below a certain bandwidth usage percentage, one of the links can be dropped because it is not needed, or vice versa. This feature helps conserve bandwidth so that it can be used for other connections. The default setting is a 50 percent reduction for two minutes. At that time, one of the links is dropped. You can adjust this setting so that the policy is more strict or lenient with bandwidth usage.

On the authentication tab, you can choose to enforce a certain protocol that is required for connection. Your choices are EAP, MS-CHAP v2, MS-CHAP, CHAP, SPAP, PAP, or unauthenticated access.

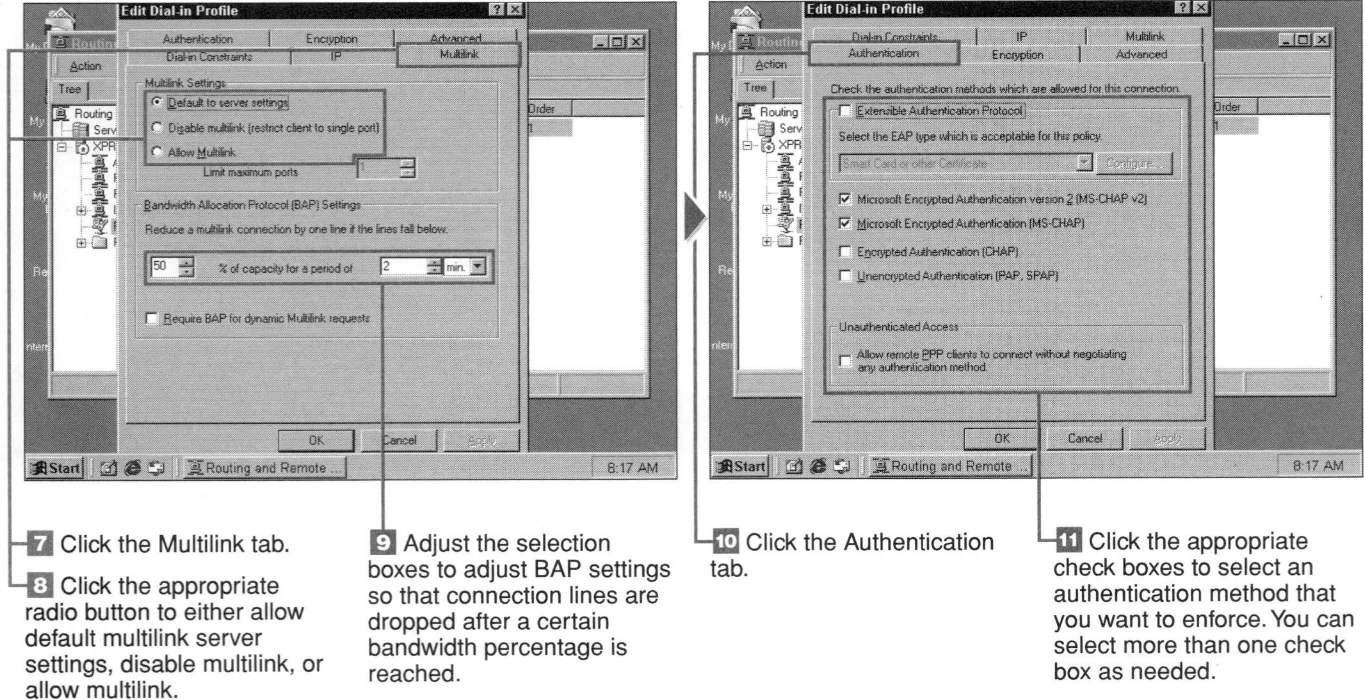

7 Click the Multilink tab.

8 Click the appropriate radio button to either allow default multilink server settings, disable multilink, or allow multilink.

9 Adjust the selection boxes to adjust BAP settings so that connection lines are dropped after a certain bandwidth percentage is reached.

10 Click the Authentication tab.

11 Click the appropriate check boxes to select an authentication method that you want to enforce. You can select more than one check box as needed.

What settings can I edit on the Encryption tab?

- You have the selection of no encryption, basic, or strong. You can use any combination of these, only one, or all of them. With one selection, users are restricted to that method. For example, if you select only strong encryption, then all connections require strong authentication. If all your RAS clients are capable of strong encryption, then this is the most secure choice. However, you may need to allow a combination of strong and basic (or even no encryption) to service all clients.

What settings can I edit on the Advanced tab?

- On the Advanced tab, you can specify additional attributes for policy. By clicking the Add button, you have an extensive list of attributes that you can use to meet the RAS needs of your organization. For example, if you are using a RADIUS server, you can add attributes for that server. If you are using AppleTalk or other networking methods, such as ATM, you can add attributes for those as well.

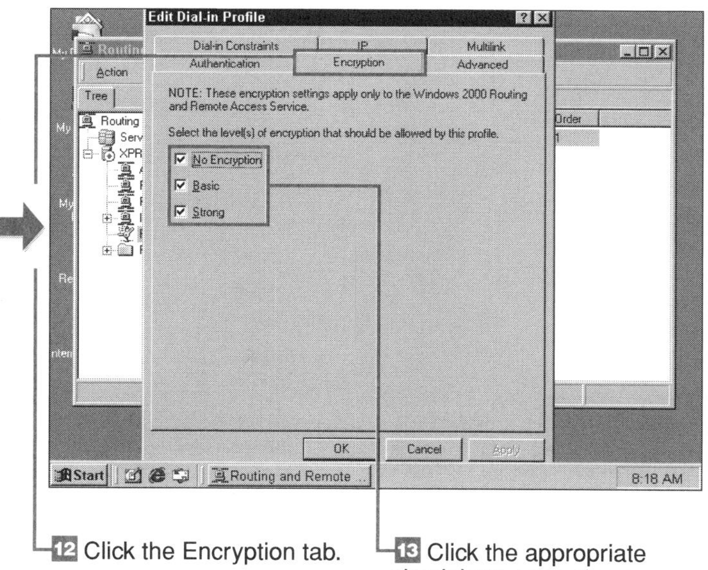

12 Click the Encryption tab.

13 Click the appropriate check boxes to enforce certain levels of encryption.

■ You can select all for the most leniency.

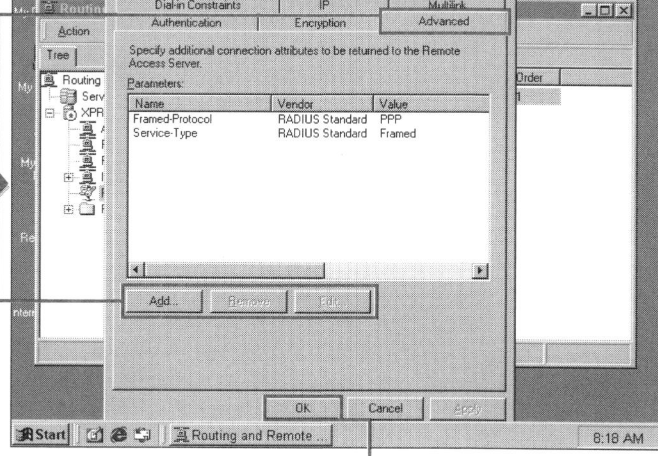

14 Click the Advanced tab.

15 Use the Add, Remove, or Edit buttons to manage additional connection attributes that you want to enforce for the policy.

16 Click OK to save the changes.

CONFIGURING RAS PORTS

Ports allow communication to flow in and out of a computer. Different devices can be connected to these ports that enable network communication. In the RAS snap-in, a Ports icon appears under the server name. The actual ports that are configured appear in the details pane. You may see a number of port types, such as various WAN Miniports for PPTP (VPN) connections and L2TP (Layer 2 Tunneling Protocol—also for VPN connections.) For each device, you can check the status (connected or not) and you can reset it.

Concerning port configuration, you can select Ports in the console and access the Properties sheet in the Action menu. From this view, you can select any device attached to your server that RAS uses and click the Configure button. Then you can make selections about how the device should be used, such as for inbound and outbound RAS and demand-dial connections.

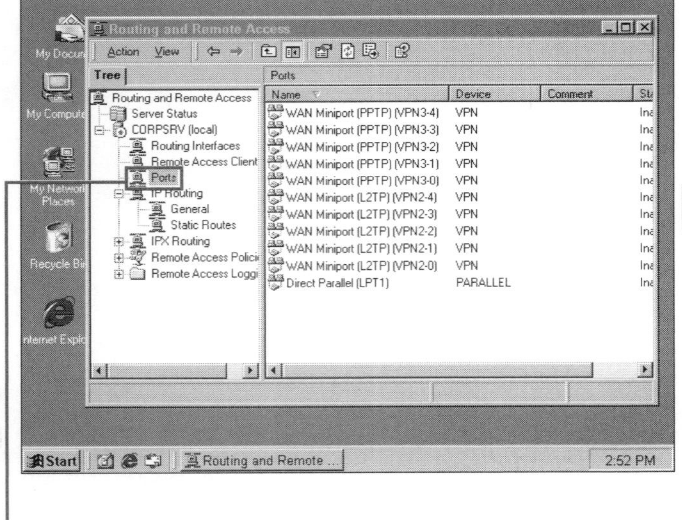

1 Select Ports in the console.

■ A list of ports appear in the details pane.

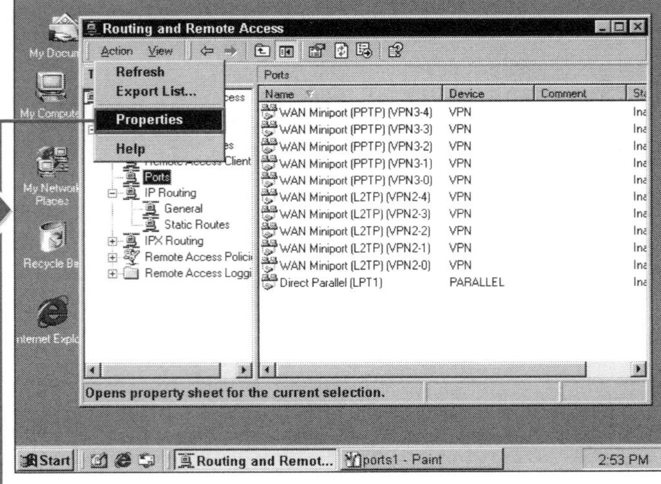

2 Choose Action⇨Properties.

What is the demand-dial routing option for?

✓ You can configure your devices to inbound (RAS) connections or for inbound and outbound (RAS and Routing) connections. The demand-dial feature is used by Routing to establish remote connections with other RAS servers in a WAN. Because the feature is demand-dial, a connected is established only when a "demand" exists to send data. This feature is particularly helpful to conserve bandwidth or connection time on slow or leased WAN links. Because there is not a persistent connection, the demand-dial component allows a connection to be establishing when there is a need for routing communication to occur.

What is the phone number box for?

✓ Each device, depending on your configuration, may have its own phone number that users dial to access your RAS server. Depending on the device, this dialog box appears for you to enter the phone number.

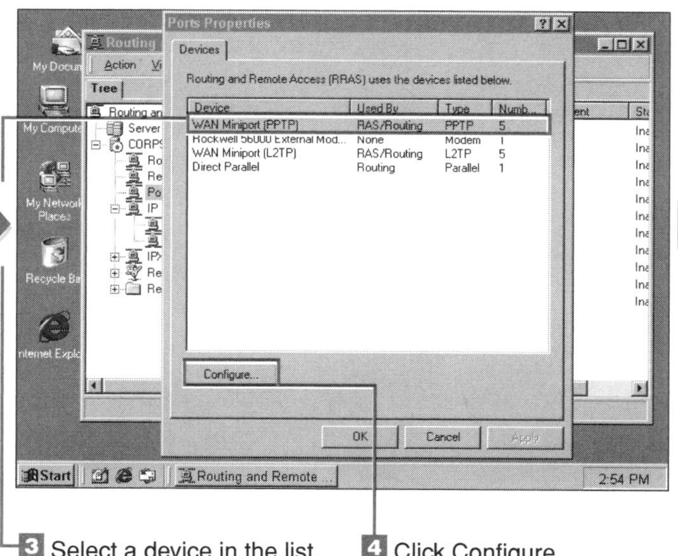

3 Select a device in the list.

4 Click Configure.

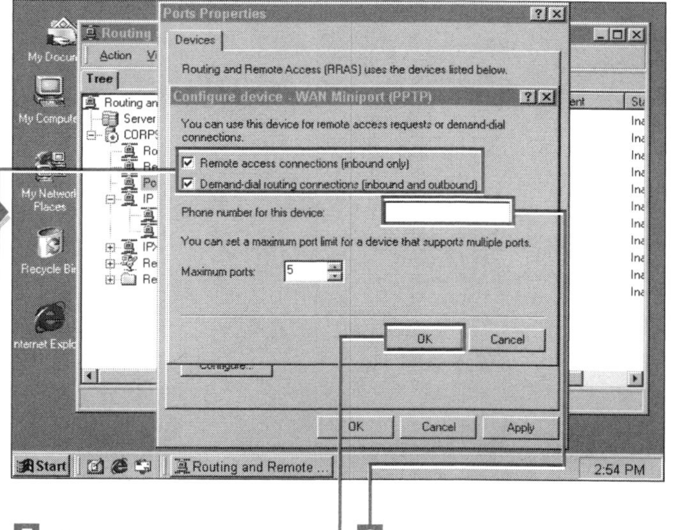

5 Click the appropriate check boxes for your configuration.

6 Type a phone number if necessary.

7 Click OK.

CONFIGURING IP ROUTING

Depending on your system configuration, you may have an IP Routing icon in the console and perhaps an IPX Routing icon. Both of these function in a similar fashion and are used for IP and IPX routing purposes. This section focuses on IP because it is the most common, and if you are using IPX, it is configured in a similar way.

For the most part, IP routing takes care of itself. You do have some configuration options through the properties sheets, and mostly, you can use the icon and the actual routing icons in the details pane to gain TCP/IP information, which is especially helpful for troubleshooting purposes.

On the properties sheets, you have four major tabs. First, the General tab allows you to enable IP router manager, which is automatically selected. You can also enable router discover advertisements. This feature allows your router to learn about routing table updates through discover advertisement packets. Windows 2000 sends these packets using multicast ICMP messages. Although helpful, they may produce a lot of excessive traffic on your network.

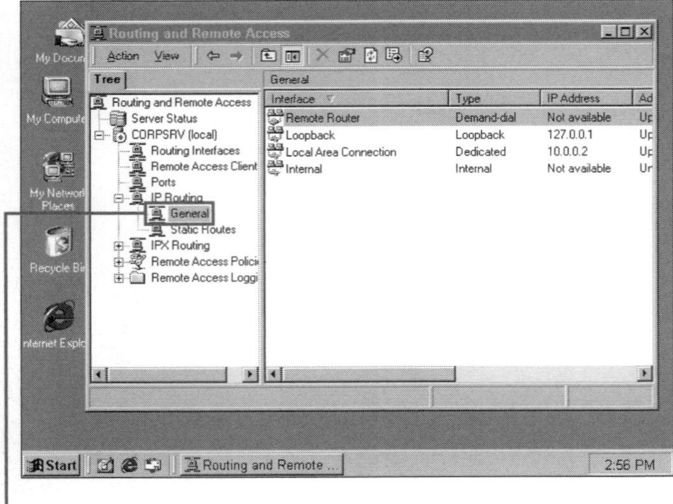

1 Expand IP Routing in the console and select General.

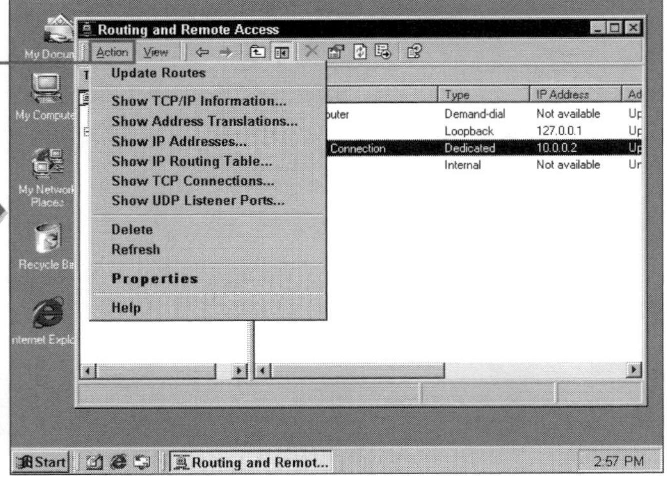

2 Select a desired IP connection in the details pane.

3 Click the Action menu.

■ From this menu, you can gain TCP/IP information by simply selecting the category to display the desired information.

What are the TCP/IP information options for the IP connections?

Find the following TCP/IP information by selecting the connection in the details pane and clicking the Action menu.

- Show TCP/IP Information shows basic TCP/IP configuration information.
- Show Address Translations—Shows the number of network addresses translations that have occurred.
- Show IP Addresses—Shows the IP address and Subnet masks of the connections.
- Show IP Routing Table—Shows the IP routing table including IP address, subnet mask, and default gateway.
- Show TCP Connections—Shows all network connections that occurred through TCP.
- Show UDP Listener Ports—Shows all UDP ports that are available.

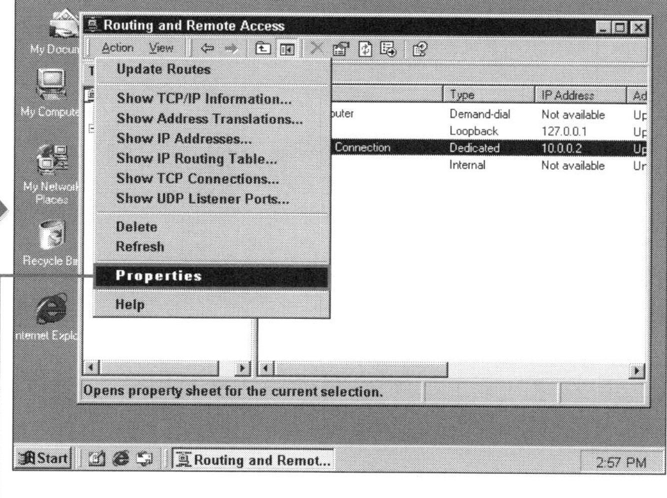

4 Choose Action⇨Properties.

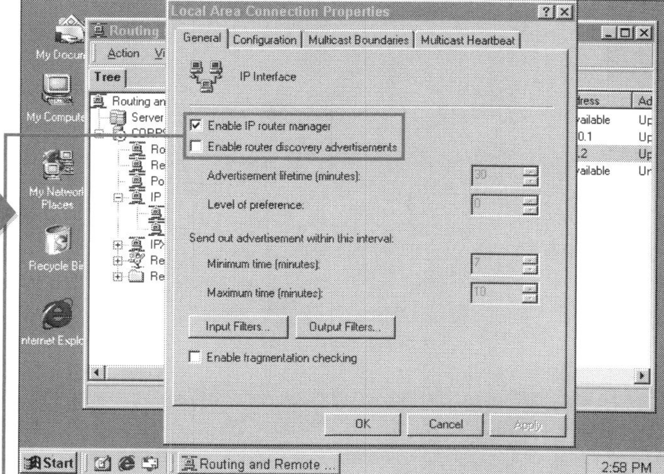

5 Select the appropriate check boxes to enable IP router management and router discovery advertisements.

CONTINUED

CONFIGURING IP ROUTING CONTINUED

On the Configuration tab, you can choose for the device to obtain an IP address from the DHCP server or you can specify a static IP address. Under many circumstances, you may prefer to use a static IP address for RAS IP Routing devices.

The Multicast Boundaries tab enables you to define a multicast scope for multicasting communication. *Multicasting* is the process of sending messages or communication to a group, much like you would send a group e-mail message. You must have multicasting scopes configured in the properties of the IP Routing General icon in the RAS console for this action to be available.

Finally, the Multicast Heartbeat tab enables you to enable multicast heartbeat detection. This feature listens for periodic multicast traffic to determine that multicasting is functioning properly on your network. The heartbeat detection determines this by an acceptable quiet time. If quiet time goes higher than the configured amount (default of ten minutes), an alert is sent to the administrator.

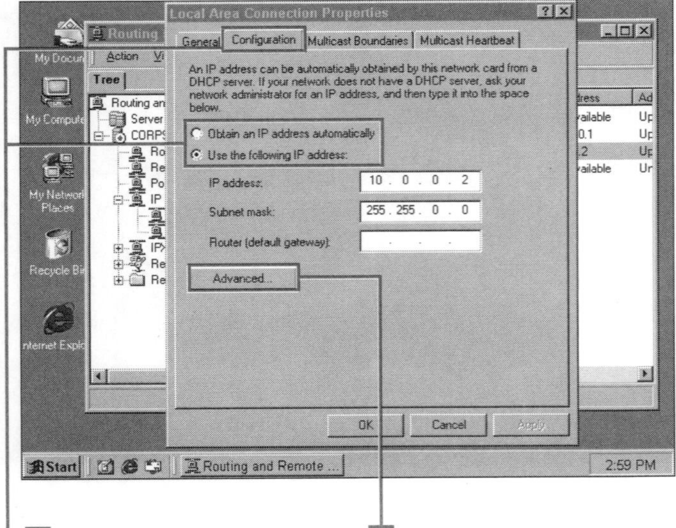

6 Click the Configuration tab.

7 Click the appropriate radio button for the device to obtain an IP address for DHCP or specify one manually.

8 Click the Advanced button.

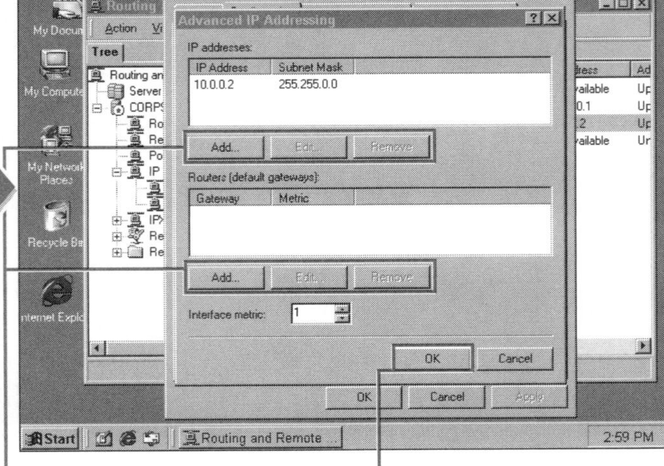

9 Use the Add, Edit, or Remove buttons to manage the IP address(es) and default gateway(s) for the device.

10 Click OK.

Should I allow my RAS devices to receive an IP address from DHCP?

Under normal circumstances, the best advice is to use a static IP address for all server hardware because dynamic IP addresses can cause communication problems, especially in the case of a router. You can choose DHCP, but you may experience some communication problems.

Why is it called a multicast heartbeat?

The heartbeat detection listens to multicast traffic on your network to determine if the traffic flow is normal. Much the same way that a doctor listens to a human heart for a pattern or rhythm, the multicast heartbeat listens to the traffic and sends an alert after an acceptable amount of quiet time has passed. A quiet time that is too long may indicate that multicast communication problems exist.

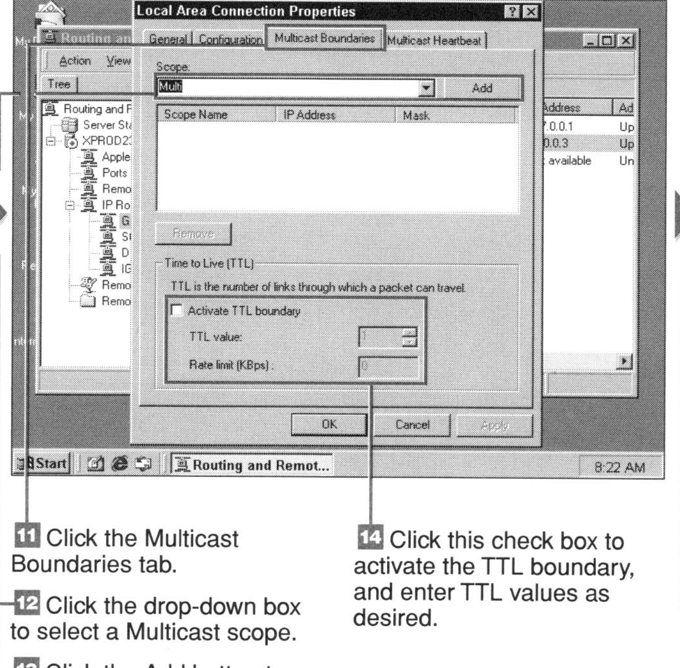

11 Click the Multicast Boundaries tab.

12 Click the drop-down box to select a Multicast scope.

13 Click the Add button to define a multicast boundary.

14 Click this check box to activate the TTL boundary, and enter TTL values as desired.

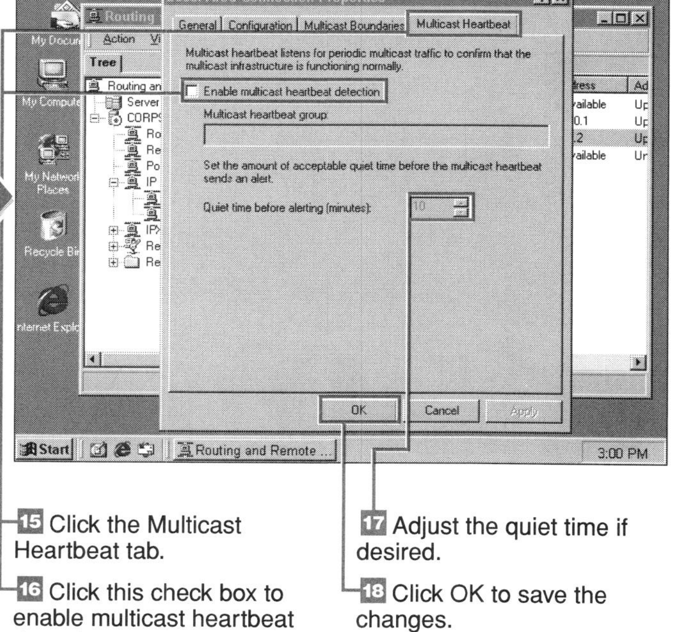

15 Click the Multicast Heartbeat tab.

16 Click this check box to enable multicast heartbeat detection.

17 Adjust the quiet time if desired.

18 Click OK to save the changes.

SECTION III

8) PLANNING THE ACTIVE DIRECTORY NAME

9) PLANNING THE ACTIVE DIRECTORY DOMAINS

10) PLANNING THE OU STRUCTURE

DNS
172.19.233.25
GATEWA
172.19.233.1

DNS NAMESPACE

To find out more about the DNS namespace before you begin your planning, refer to Chapters 1 and 6. Active Directory names are DNS names because the Active Directory naming scheme follows the DNS hierarchical naming format.

The overall purpose of the Active Directory is to enable users to easily find objects located on your network. This is accomplished by giving each object in the Active Directory a fully qualified domain name so that it cannot be confused with any other object. In order for this to occur in a manner that benefits your network, you must carefully plan your DNS namespace. This process begins by establishing your root domain.

WHY THE NAME IS SO IMPORTANT

DNS is a name resolution method—it maps IP addresses to hostnames so that clients and servers in a TCP/IP network can communicate with one another. This process occurs by resolving the fully qualified domain name to an IP address. Without this method of name resolution, network communication cannot take place.

On your network, DNS with the Active Directory is used to resolve computers to IP addresses. If you want to have a presence on the Internet, your domain name must be accepted and registered with Network Solutions. Because most companies host Internet sites, your DNS name will determine how customers contact and communicate with you and how users on your network see different domains. Commonly, the DNS name chosen for your network is based on the name of your company, but this is not always the case. As an IT professional, be aware that your DNS name affects your network and Internet presence and has as much to do with management and marketing decisions as it does IT decisions. Because of these issues, you should take care when determining your domain name and make certain that all necessary decision makers in your company participate in the planning process.

HOW SHOULD I DECIDE MY DOMAIN NAME?

The following sections point out several important issues you should consider when planning your domain name.

Choose a representative name

Your domain name should be a friendly, recognizable name for your business or organization. Common examples of recognizable domain names are microsoft.com, amazon.com, ucla.edu, and irs.gov. Each of these names represent the entire organization to which the namespace applies. You do not want your root domain to be a segment of a larger organization; the name you select should represent the entire organization or business. The Active Directory can only accommodate one root domain name for an organization—and that name should be static. In other words, companies merge and reorganize on a regular basis, but the company or organization name usually remains the same. In order to change the domain name of your organization, you have to completely reinstall the Active Directory, so plan your domain name carefully!

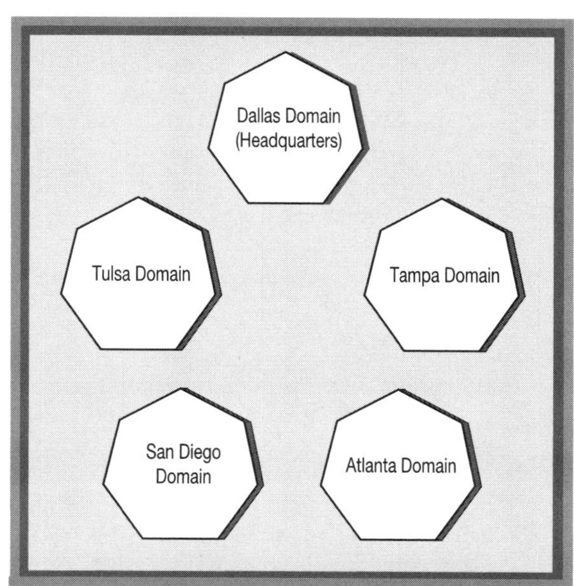

Consider this example: Wilson-Adams, Inc., is a large video game and entertainment software development company. Wilson-Adams is headquartered in Dallas, but they have offices and production plants in Tulsa, San Diego, Atlanta, and Tampa. Wilson-Adams does not currently have a presence on the Internet, but they plan to open an Internet site and sell their products online. To plan their DNS root, the network administrators at Wilson-Adams need to look at the entire organization as well as Internet access.

As Wilson-Adams plans the domain root, they need to make the name as all-encompassing as possible so that the name can cover everything in their organization. In other words, the domain root should not have to "grow and change" as the organization grows and changes.

Plan for Internet presence

Many companies and organizations host Internet sites. From these sites, the companies and organizations advertise their products and services and even sell those services over the Internet. When you plan your domain name, consider your organization's presence on the Internet. If you are planning or already have an Internet domain name, then your Active Directory DNS implementation can be the same as your Internet domain name.

For example, say that alphatoys.com has an Internet site and is implementing the Active Directory. Alpha Toys already has their domain name registered with Network Solutions, so they can simply use the alphatoys.com domain name as their Active Directory domain name.

If you do not have an Internet presence, but you intend to create one in the future, then you should register your name with Network Solutions before implementing the Active Directory domain name. By doing so, you can use the same name for your domain that you use on the Internet. You can register your domain name on the Internet through an ISP or directly at `www.networksolutions.com`.

What if you don't want an Internet presence? Before simply ruling out your organization's presence on the Internet, think about the future. Will your company want a presence in five years? What if you install the Active Directory using a certain domain name that represents your business and then you decide to build a Web site a few years down the road? What if another organization is already using your Active Directory domain name on the Internet at that time? Then, you either have to choose another domain name on the Internet (which may not be your business name) or reinstall the Active Directory to change the domain name.

The key is to plan carefully and into the future. For example, Wilson-Adams has decided that they want wilsonadams.com to be their domain name. Wilson-Adams wants a presence on the Web, but they do not want to implement this presence for several months. When they implement their Internet presence, they want the name to be the same as their Active Directory network, wilsonadams.com. So, they decide to register their name with Network Solutions now (and pay the annual fee—about $70) so that the name is reserved and they can implement their Web site when they are ready. Again, planning is of utmost importance.

Your first domain is the root domain

When you select a domain name, the first domain where the Active Directory is installed and named becomes the root domain for your organization. You should typically implement the root domain so that it is at the company headquarters or a major division. This domain becomes the root, and you build all the other domains in your organization from the root domain.

For example, Wilson-Adams is headquartered in Dallas, so they begin their Active Directory tree in the Dallas domain. In terms of DNS, the Dallas domain simply becomes wilsonadams.com.

Your other domains create the hierarchical tree

After you establish your root domain, your other domains fall into the hierarchical tree. For example, wilsonadams.com has domains in Tulsa, San Diego, Atlanta, and Tampa. You need to give these domains descriptive names that become child domains of the root domain, wilsonadams.com. You name your child domains using the same principles you did for the root domain — choose names that describe the domain and that are static. You may choose to name the domains by location, because the location usually doesn't change. For example, wilsonadams.com could name their child domains tulsa.wilsonadams.com, sandiego.wilsonadams.com, atlanta.wilsonadams.com, and tampa.wilsonadams.com.

This design creates a contiguous namespace where network users can find resources in any domain. You can learn more about planning your domain structure in Chapter 9.

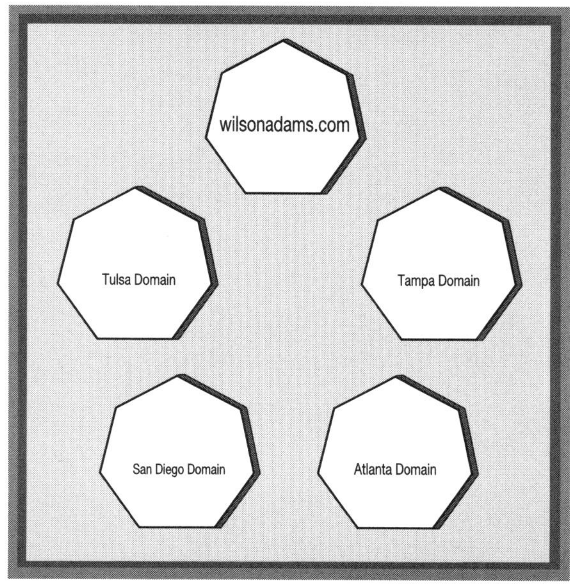

INTERNET PRESENCE AND NAMING OPTIONS

As mentioned in the previous section, you can use the same Active Directory DNS name you use on the Internet. However, some other options may serve your business or organization more effectively. Using the same Internet domain name as your local network domain name, as shown below, provides the easiest administration and makes your network naming scheme seamless with your Internet naming scheme. However, many businesses separate the two for greater Active Directory security against the Internet. If your external naming scheme is the same as your internal naming scheme, Internet intruders have a greater chance of gaining access to your internal network. The following sections point out some additional possibilities you may want to consider if you are hosting an Internet domain name that provide greater security features.

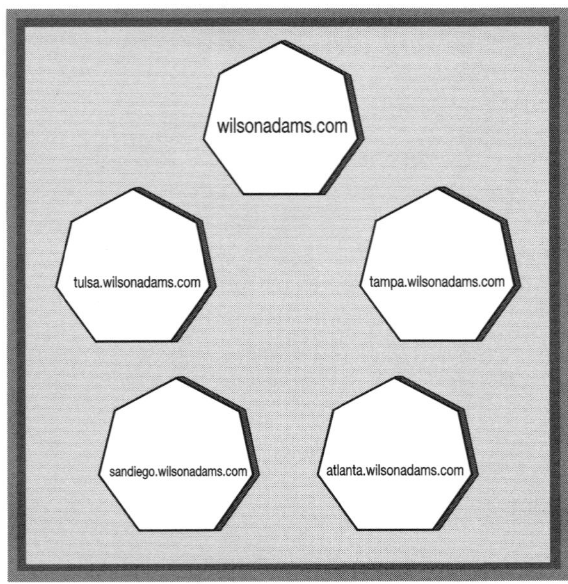

Use a subdomain for the Active Directory

You can use a subdomain of your Internet domain name for your Active Directory implementation. With this solution, the root domain is exposed to the Internet, but the subdomain naming scheme is not. In other words, Internet users can see alphatoys.com, but because alphatoys.com is not your internal root domain, your internal network is more "hidden" from Internet users.

For example, Wilson-Adams decides to use wilsonadams.com for its Internet presence, but use a subdomain for its Active Directory naming scheme. In this case, the root domain could become local.wilsonadams.com (or any subdomain name) and its child domains would be tulsa.local.wilsonadams.com, sandiego.local.wilsonadams.com, and so forth.

This solution requires you to create a new DNS zone to host the subdomain, and the subdomain requires its own DNS server. In the root domain, you need a delegation record to the other DNS server in the subdomain. DNS zones are network segments where particular DNS servers have authority and a delegation record allows the two zones to exchange DNS records. You can learn more about DNS in Chapter 6.

The advantage to this design is that your Active Directory domain tree is isolated from the root domain and more invisible to would-be intruders.

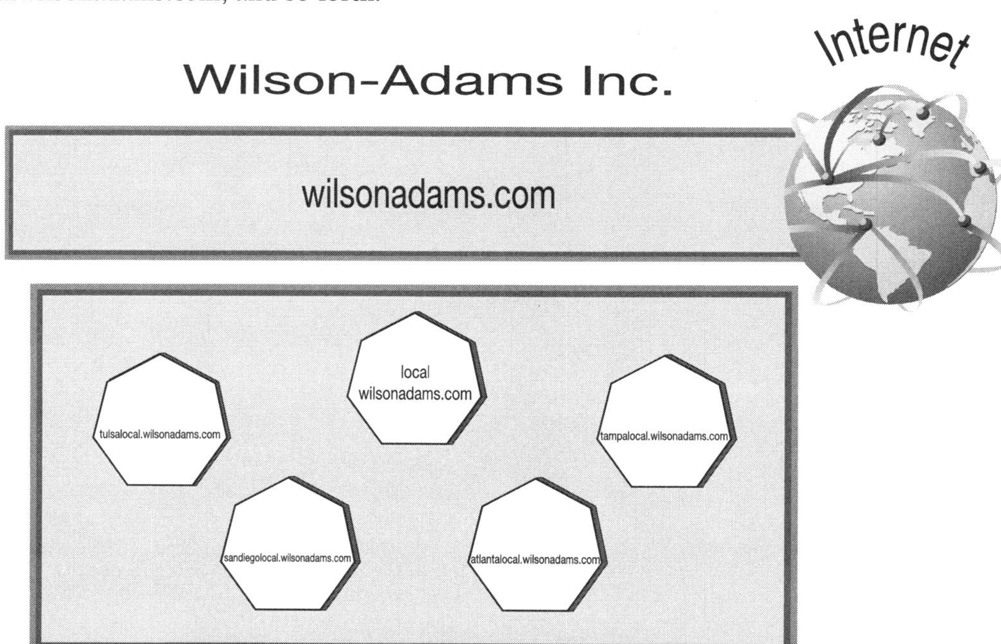

Use a firewall to separate the private network

You can also implement a firewall to protect your private network from the public network. This solution enables you to use the same root domain, such as wilsonadams.com for the private and public network, but a *firewall* (or *proxy server*) separates the two. In this case, two DNS zones are created, one on each side of the firewall. The external DNS server would maintain records for hosts that are accessed via the Internet. The internal DNS server would maintain records for the internal hosts and Active Directory objects. The firewall is used to manage the traffic between the two while keeping unauthorized persons out of the private network. This solution is effective, but can be challenging to implement and maintain if your internal clients need to have Internet access.

Using a private DNS domain name

A new draft exists for a first-level domain, the.local domain, which is reserved for private use. This reserved, private, first-level domain enables you to have a DNS naming scheme, such as wilsonadams.local, to effectively separate your Internet domain name from your local domain name. To accomplish this, you need to create a DNS zone where *yourname*.local is the root domain. The advantage is that your local network is separated from the Internet. The disadvantage is this private name cannot be registered for use on the Internet, and to change the DNS root later requires reinstallation of the Active Directory forest.

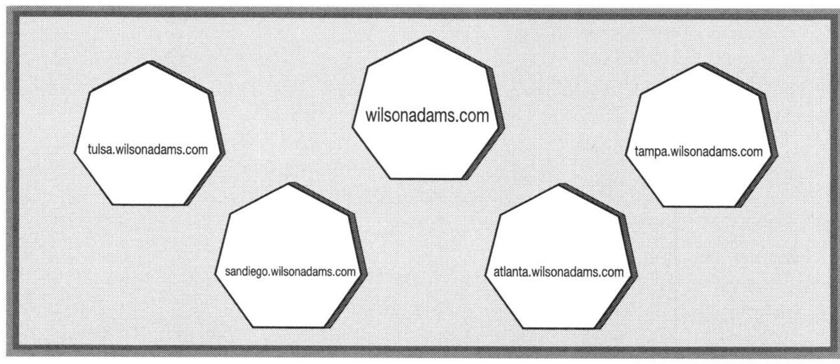
Internet
Wilson-Adams Inc.
wilsonadams.com
Firewall
wilsonadams.com
tulsa.wilsonadams.com
tampa.wilsonadams.com
sandiego.wilsonadams.com
atlanta.wilsonadams.com

WINDOWS 2000 DOMAINS

The word *domain* is used so often in Microsoft networking that IT professionals seldom give serious thought to the word. In Windows NT networks, multiple domains are very common and often quite necessary. In order to implement the Active Directory in the most effective manner, your thoughts and assumptions about domains need to change. One of Microsoft's major goals with Windows 2000 networking is to reduce the number of domains that organizations use, which reduces cost and administrative overhead.

A *domain*, by definition, is a logical grouping of computers and users that serves as a security boundary and administrative unit. The domain defines how resources are used within the domain and who can access those resources within the domain. Multiple domain organizations usually have different administrators in charge of each domain, and each domain usually has different security policies and rules.

To plan your domain structure for a Windows 2000 and Active Directory environment, you need to carefully consider the difference between domains and organizational units (OU) in the Active Directory.

Domains versus organizational units

Domains are logical groupings of computers and users for security and administrative purposes. *Organizational units* (OU) are administrative containers that follow your network or administrative model. By using OUs, you can develop a logical view of the groupings and resources within a domain. An OU is like a file folder in a filing cabinet. The folder itself does not have any functionality, but is designed to contain other objects. Active Directory OUs contain resources particular to that OU, or they can contain other OUs.

You can learn all about planning your OU structure in Chapter 10. OUs are mentioned here because you should carefully consider your domain and OU structure before installing and implementing the Active Directory. If you have an existing network with multiple domains, you may want to consolidate some of those domains so that they are absorbed as OUs.

Here is an example. Liner Toys has three domains: administration, sales, and marketing. The domains were established for administrative purposes, but after further consideration, there are no specific security requirements that need to segment each domain. After reviewing their network structure and needs, Liner Toys learned that they can consolidate all their domains into one domain with OUs for each division. Now, they have one domain that requires less cost and administration, but they can use the OUs to organize their business structure and Windows 2000 security to manage who can access what resources in each OU.

Before implementing the Active Directory, take a close look at your existing domain structure and look for ways to consolidate your existing domains into one domain, or least reduce the number of domains that currently exist.

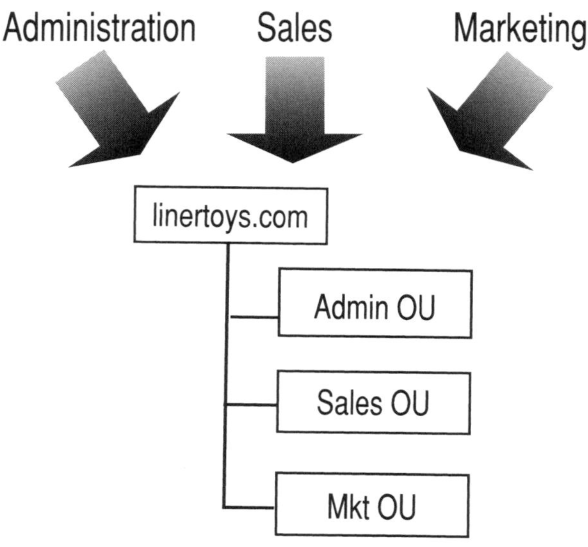

Should I use a single domain?

For many network environments, the single domain model provides the service and performance desired. You can use the Active Directory to segment the domain according to your administrative model through OUs. The advantage to this model is lower cost in hardware (fewer domain controllers) and a lower cost in administrative upkeep and configuration.

However, if you have network groups that can be logically assembled and have different security needs, then the multiple domain model may be best for your organization. If you have a large group of computers and users that need to be controlled by different administrators and who, in terms of security, need different configuration than the rest of the network, then that group may need to be a domain. For example, a company has offices in Houston and Portland. Although the two offices can function as a single domain, the Portland office needs to have very tight security to protect certain internal resources. In fact, the Portland office does not even provide Internet access to users. The Houston office has much looser security and users need the use the Internet to perform their jobs. With these two different groups, two domains would be best because you can implement very different security policies that meet the needs of each office.

USING MULTIPLE ACTIVE DIRECTORY DOMAINS

If you decide to use multiple Active Directory domains, then you need to understand the options you have and how the multiple domains interact with each other for resource access. You have three major options: the multiple-domain tree, multiple-tree forest, and multiple forests of trees.

Multiple-domain tree

The multiple-domain tree is established by installing the Active Directory in what becomes the Active Directory root domain. This domain is the top of the tree hierarchy. After you install the initial root domain, you then install the existing domains as child domains of the root or grandchild (which is a child of a child) domains of the root, and so forth. Only members of the Enterprise Admins Group can perform this process. With this structure, you create a hierarchy that contains a contiguous domain namespace.

For example, Acme Graphics has three domains: Atlanta, Toronto, and New York. Their Atlanta domain is the first Active Directory domain, so it becomes the root domain named acmegraphics.com. The existing domains become child domains.

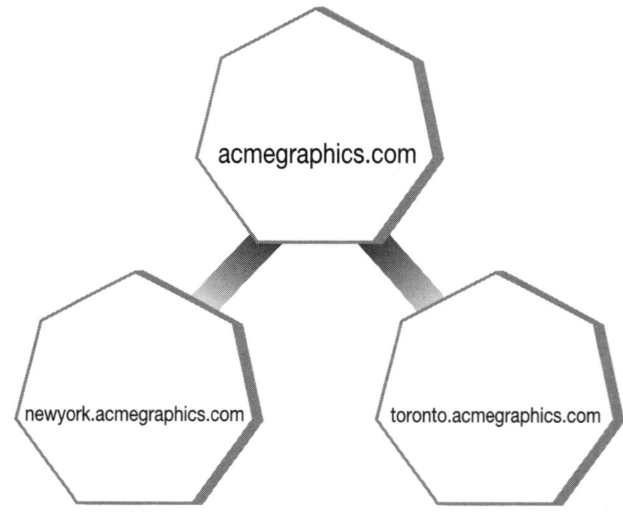

In the multiple-domain tree, all child domains get their names from the parent domain (root). Communication between the domains occurs through automatic transitive trusts. A trust relationship allows users to access resources in a different domain. The transitive trust feature allows each domain to trust the other domains so that users can access resources (for which they have permissions) in any domain. A transitive trust is a *two-way trust*, which means that if Domain 1 trusts Domain 2 and Domain 2 trusts Domain 3, then Domain 1 automatically trusts Domain 3. The trust relationships are established from the root domain so that all domains trust each other. For example, acmegraphics.com is the root domain and has transitive trust relationships with New York and Toronto. Even though New York and Toronto do not actually have a trust relationship established, they still indirectly trust each other through transitive trust.

The Active Directory multiple-domain model is an effective solution that provides decentralized administration, domain-level security, domain-level policies, and ease of management. Also, the multiple-domain model provides lower replication traffic because only changes to the global catalog server need be replicated. Because of the transitive trust relationships, users can find any resource in any domain using an LDAP search.

USING MULTIPLE ACTIVE DIRECTORY DOMAINS CONTINUED

Multiple-tree forests

A *forest* is a group of two or more Active Directory trees. The trees in the forest do not have contiguous namespaces, but are considered an overall hierarchy in which all names can be resolved. The trees in the forest are connected by two-way transitive trust relationships at the root domain of each tree. The trees share common configuration information, a global catalog, and a common schema. Connecting the two trees with a trust relationship creates the forest. Before they are connected, each tree is simply an individual Active Directory tree.

A forest configuration is useful in environments that are made up of several subcompanies or divisions that need to maintain their own DNS names. The forest configuration is also useful for two organizations that need to share resources on a partnership basis. This configuration allows for communication between the two trees while keeping each entity separated. The global catalog is used to maintain a resource list of what is available in each tree so that users can access information in each tree. Because the trust relationship between trees is transitive, if Tree1 trusts Tree2 and Tree2 trusts Tree3, then Tree1 automatically trusts Tree3, and so forth.

For example, Acme Graphics, Inc., has just acquired Bolton Graphics, Inc. Each company has implemented the Active Directory with the DNS names of acmegraphics.com and blgraphics.com, respectively. Rather than restructure Bolton Graphics, management would like to form a forest so that each company can maintain its own identity within the organization and on the Internet. To accomplish this, they establish a transitive trust relationship so that users in each tree can access resources in the other tree. Each company maintains its own identity and existing Active Directory Domain structure.

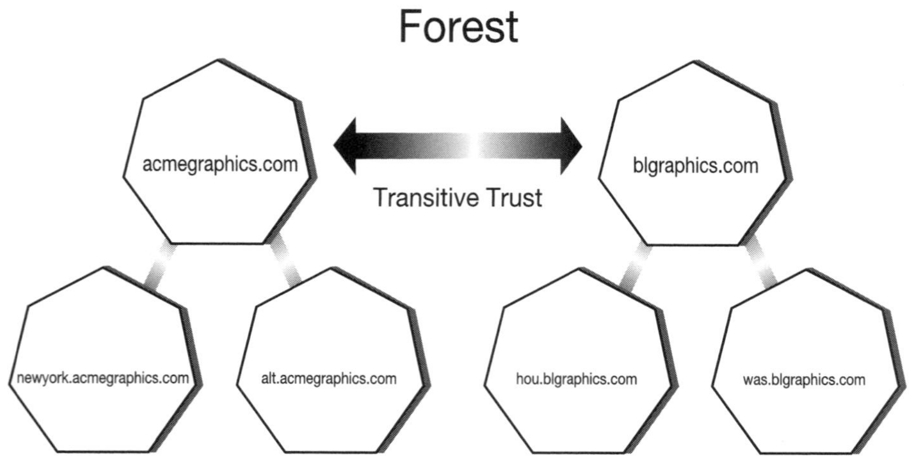

Multiple forests

You can also connect multiple forests together; however, this is not a configuration you should plan for. Microsoft Active Directory enables you to configure multiple forests for connectivity and sharing of resources, but this solution is designed for temporary circumstances in which two different organizations need to connect together. A multiple forest configuration is most often used in situations in which one company works directly with another company on a project or joint business opportunity. The configuration for multiple forests can be difficult and complex to create and manage. This solution requires you to create explicit one-way trusts between different domains to provide resource access. Although multiple forests can be an effective temporary solution, you should never plan and implement a multiple forest solution. A single forest always works instead and is much easier to manage.

UNDERSTANDING ORGANIZATIONAL UNITS (OU)

You can consolidate your existing Windows NT domains into one domain, or at least fewer domains, while maintaining your security standards and administrative control by using organizational units (OUs). In order to implement the Active Directory appropriately in your network, you must understand the importance of OUs and how you should use them in your implementation. An OU is like a file folder in a file cabinet and does not have any functionality on its own. Its purpose is to hold other OUs, users, groups, printers, applications, shared files—any Active Directory resource.

You can design your network administrative model by using OUs. The OU structure allows different administrators and differing security policies to exist in one domain because you can organize those divisions through the OU structure.

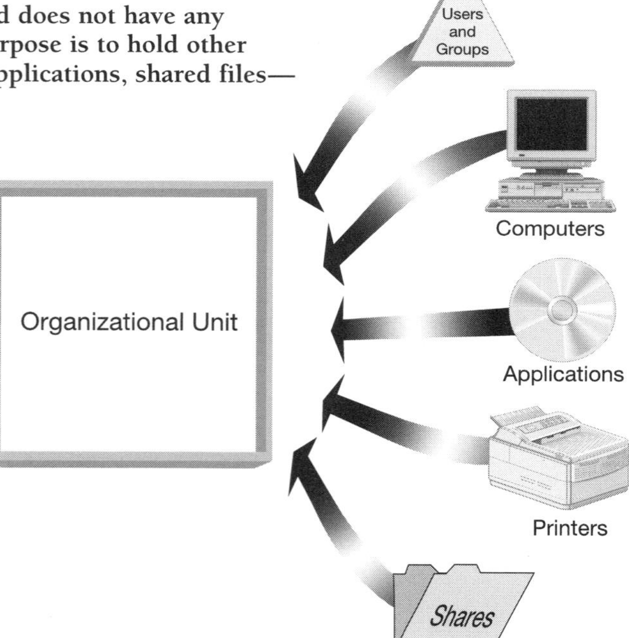

DEFINING AN OU STRUCTURE

Designing an OU structure for your network is relatively easy, and as with most major network issues, planning is the key to a long-lived OU structure and one that is free of problems.

Before planning your OU structure, you must learn one simple rule:

Plan your OU structure based on your network administration model.

The purpose of the OU structure is to organize and provide control to different network divisions or large groups. The OU structure allows your network administrators to effectively administer your network. A common mistake is to base the OU structure on the needs of users by planning the structure to make browsing easier. In other words, when a user browses the directory through My Network Places, they can see the OU structure in the domain(s).

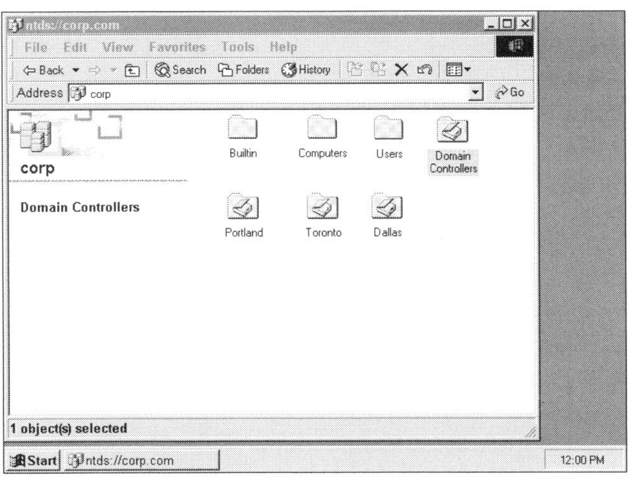

But, the OU structure itself is only useful to administrators. Although users can see the OU structure, you should not design it with the goal of helping them find resources. The Active Directory contains powerful query capabilities that users can access to find resources. Querying, not browsing, is the preferred method for finding resources on the network. Therefore, set up the structure of the OU to mirror your IT administrative model.

Before planning your OU structure, you should make certain you understand these points about OUs:

- OUs can contain only resources within the domain. An OU cannot contain a resource from a subdomain or any other domain.
- OUs are not a part of the DNS naming scheme.
- OUs are designed to follow your IT administrative model.
- OUs are not designed to make browsing easier for end users.
- OUs are visible to users, but are not returned as answers to an LDAP query.
- By default, members of the Domain Admins and Enterprise Admins groups have permissions to create and edit OUs.

PLANNING AN OU STRUCTURE

As with any planning process, the steps you should complete can sometimes be uncertain. However, planning an OU structure does not have to be a highly difficult task. When you complete your planning, your OU structure should accomplish the following goals:

- The design should follow your IT administrative model.
- The design should accommodate any upcoming IT changes.
- The design should allow for future growth.
- The design should be simple. Complex OU structures can become a headache and require more management time.
- The design should be as static as possible. You don't want to have to restructure your OU design every time a change comes along.
- If you have multiple domains, the OU structure in each domain does not have to follow the other domains. In other words, the OU structure is used for administrative purposes and you can set it up however you like for each domain. However, most organizations find it easier to at least adhere to some standard organizational OU structure for each domain.

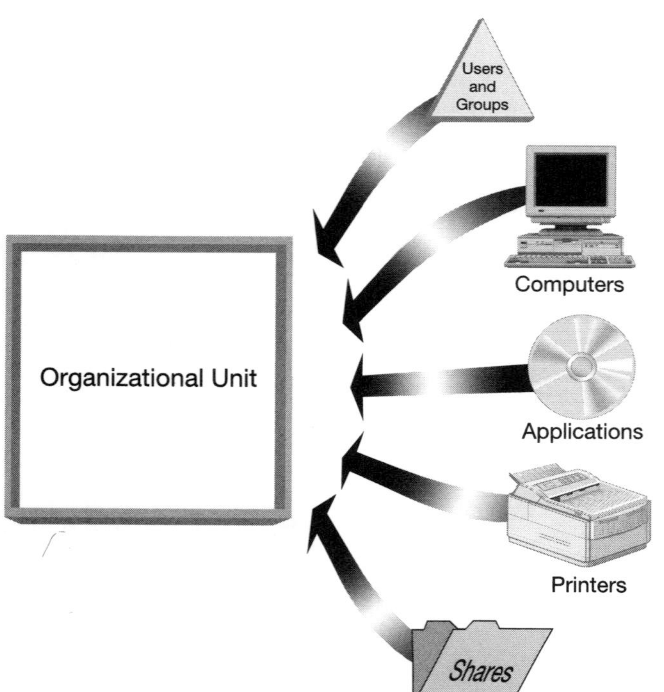

In order to reach these goals, consider the following planning steps:

1. Examine your current IT administration model. Explore possible changes that need to be made now due to organizational changes.
2. Start at the top of the IT model—you don't need a top-level OU for every single division or process on the model. (This issue is discussed in more detail later in the chapter.)
3. Examine the new features of Windows 2000, such as Group Policy, that you may want to implement. How do these features affect your IT model?
4. Create a test OU structure and examine it in a lab setting, if possible.

Understanding the OU hierarchy

As with the Active Directory itself, you can build OUs in a hierarchical fashion by having top-level OUs, second-level OUs, and third-level OUs. This structure enables you to have a few top-level OUs. Then you can create other OUs inside the top-level OUs. This process is called *nesting*.

Nesting is an important feature that allows you to further organize your network for administrative control.

However, do not lose sight of this simple point: OUs are designed to be useful to administrators. The time to create a new OU occurs when you need to group Active Directory resources for administrative control. As you can imagine, if you are not careful, nesting can quickly get out of hand. Too many nested OUs can be difficult to manage, especially if you implement Group Policy. The general rule with nesting is that you want to provide the needed administrative control without creating a confusing and difficult structure to manage.

Here are some other issues concerning nesting that you should keep in mind when planning your OU hierarchy:

- Each OU, including nested OUs, can be administered independently. However, by default, each nested OU inherits the properties of the parent OU.
- Group Policy (see Chapter 25) is applied from the domain root. A nested OU has at least two levels of logon policy that have to be applied, which can slow response time.
- Deeply nested OUs, or OUs that are several levels under the top-level OU, may have performance problems when users search for a resource residing in that deeply nested OU. With deeply nested OUs, the Active Directory query process has to wade through too many layers of OUs to find desired objects. Typically, three levels of nested OUs should be enough, and if you feel that you need more, re-examine your desired structure and look for ways you can consolidate some of the OUs.

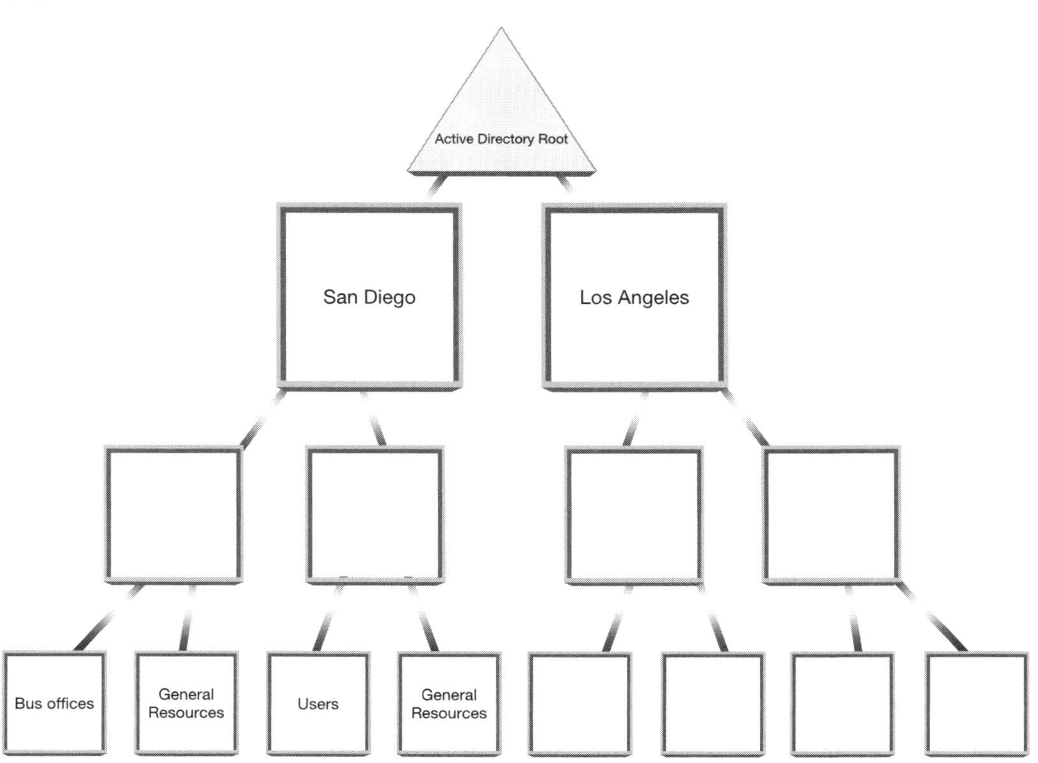

Planning the structure

There are no correct or incorrect ways to plan the OU structure per se. The purpose is to mirror your IT administrative model so that different administrators can control the contents of each OU. You can change the OU structure as needed, but doing so is a time-consuming task and one you should avoid if at all possible.

Begin your planning process with the top-level OU. Base your top-level OUs on something static, such as location or major division. Departments are often restructured and smaller groups change frequently, so begin at the top level with something unlikely to change. Many administrators use the names of sites or company offices in geographic locations for the top-level OUs.

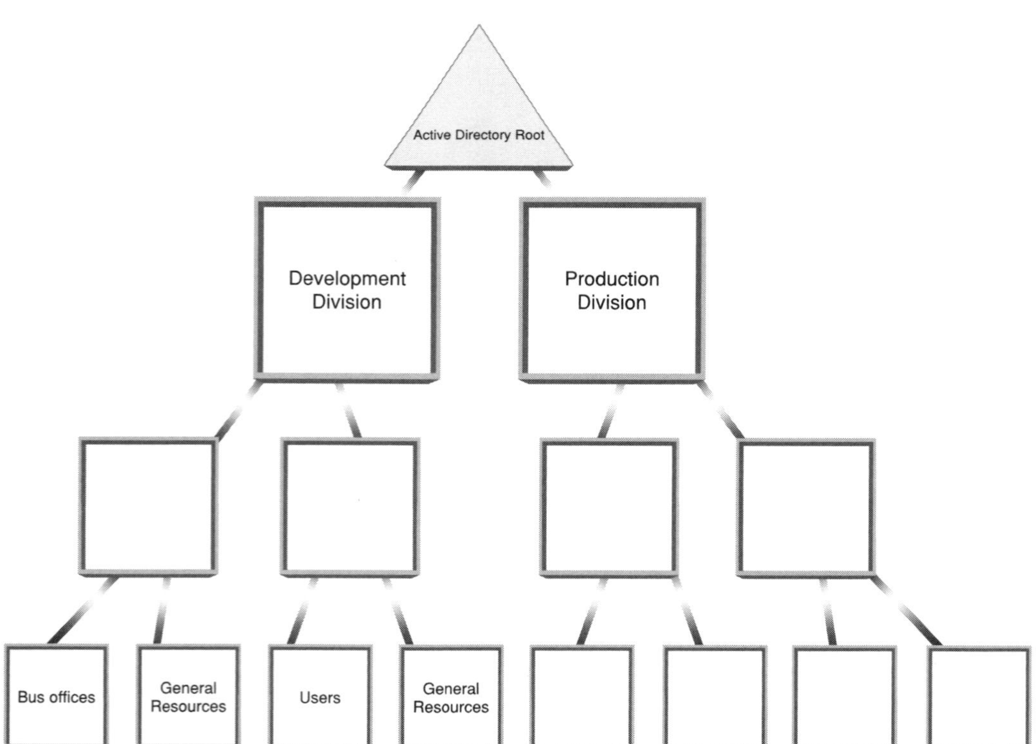

Or some administrators use major company divisions to create the top-level OUs. Again, closely examine your overall IT administrative model and ask what makes the most sense for your organization. This model is effective if you have infrequent changes in the company divisions, but can cause problems if a lot of restructuring takes place.

If your company has one domain and all offices or divisions are located in one geographic location, then you can base your top-level OUs on major company functions or divisions. This approach is also effective, but remember to base the top-level OUs on functions or divisions that are unlikely to change. A major restructuring can cause you to have to restructure all of your OUs. Remember, try to keep the top-level OUs as static as possible.

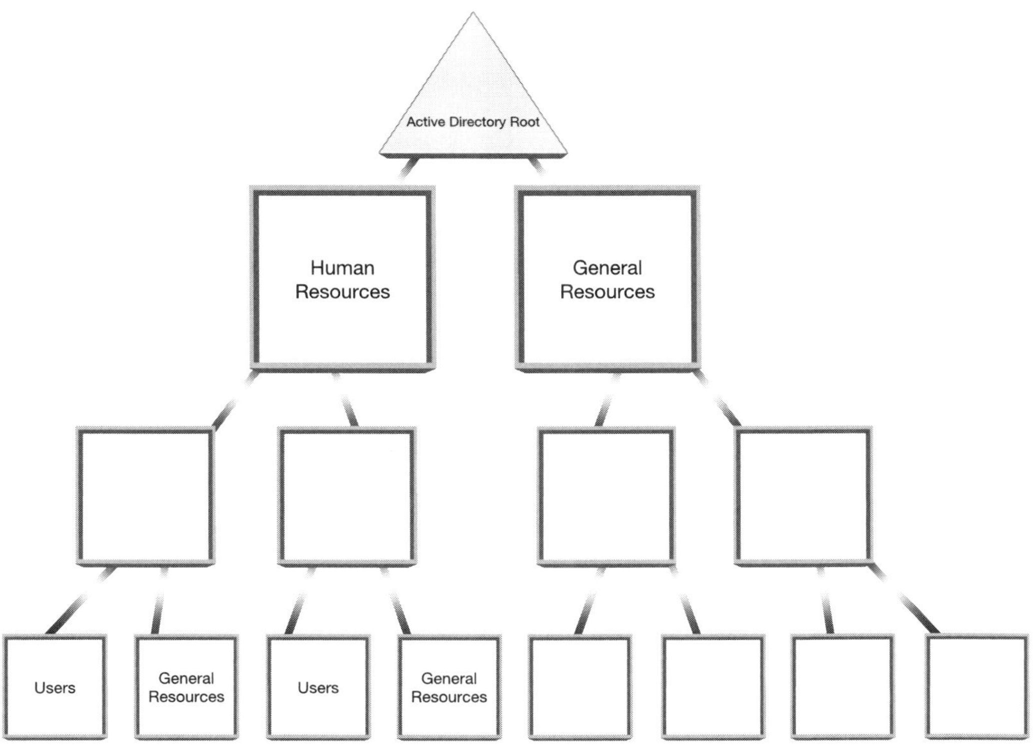

Next, when you are satisfied with your first level OUs, you should plan your nested OUs. Begin with second-level and work your way down as necessary. Remember, try to keep the OUs to a minimum and always ask the question "How does the OU benefit our administrative model" before creating it. Some models call for nested OUs to be created by office or divisions.

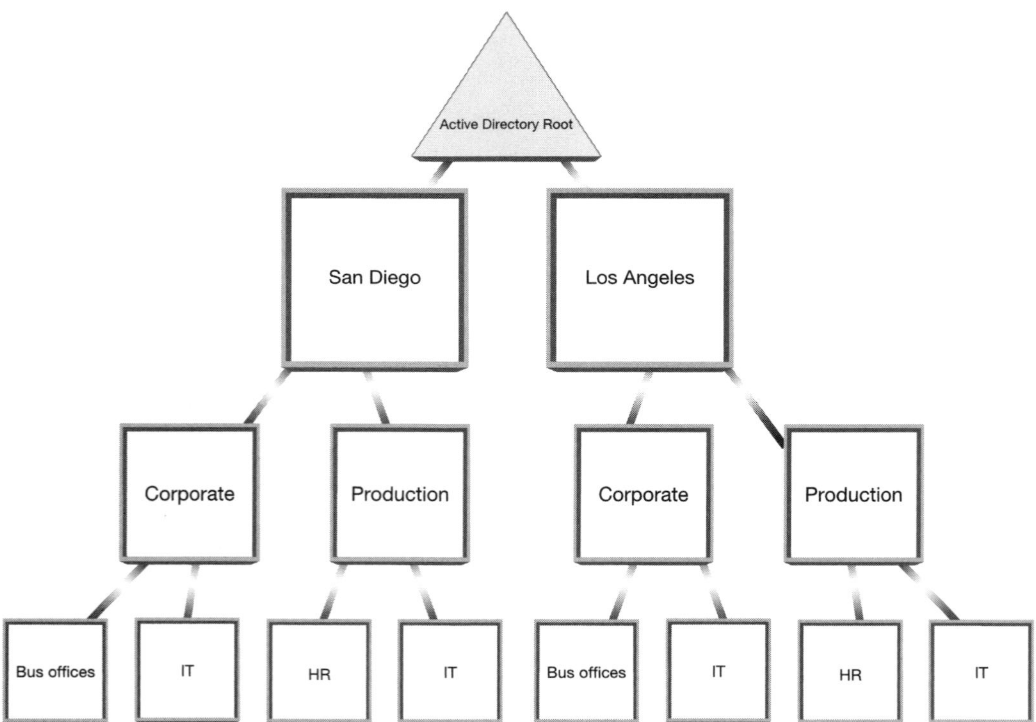

Some companies build the nested OUs based on administrators who have control over different resources. For example, one administrator may be in control of all users and groups for all OUs, or one administrator may be in control of a particular OU and all nested OUs in that OU.

After you install the Active Directory, you create your OU structure, determine the administrator who will control each OU, and then add resources to the OU structure. You can learn how to perform these operations in Chapter 17.

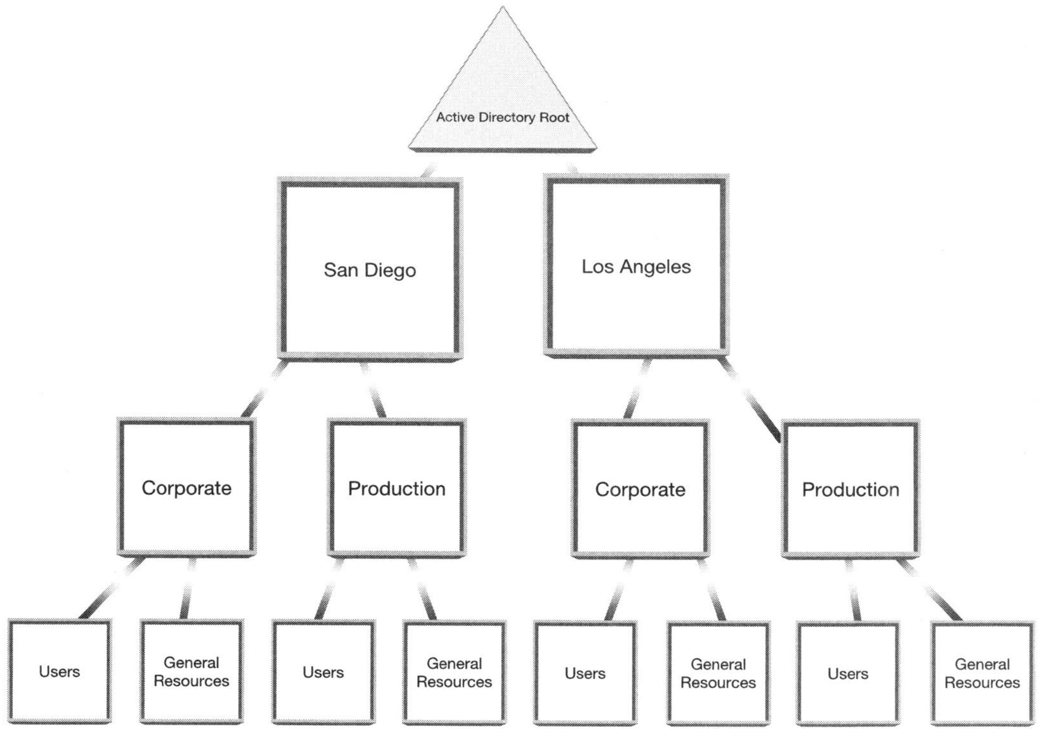

SECTION IV

11) INSTALLING ACTIVE DIRECTORY

12) USING THE MICROSOFT MANAGEMENT CONSOLE

13) SEARCHING THE ACTIVE DIRECTORY

Active
Directory

INSTALLING THE ACTIVE DIRECTORY

You install the Active Directory only on Windows 2000 domain controllers, and all domain controllers must have the Active Directory installed. In Windows 2000, every domain controller must run the Active Directory, and you cannot uninstall the Active Directory from a domain controller without demoting it to a member server. You need to remember that you can change the role of a server from a domain controller to a member server or a standalone server—and vice versa—without having to reinstall the Windows 2000 operating system.

Remember that Windows 2000 networks do not contain *primary domain controllers* or *backup domain controllers.* All domain controllers are simply *domain controllers.* Windows 2000 uses multimaster replication for the Active Directory, so all Windows 2000 domain controllers function as peers. In other words, no single domain controller is in charge of replication. Every domain controller has equal responsibility for maintaining the Active Directory replication.

If you upgrade a Windows NT 4.0 PDC to Windows 2000 Server, the installer prompts you to install the Active Directory during the operating system installation. This occurs because the upgrade must install the Active Directory in order to maintain the domain controller status. If you started with a clean installation, your server is installed as a member server. Installing the Active Directory upgrades it to domain controller status.

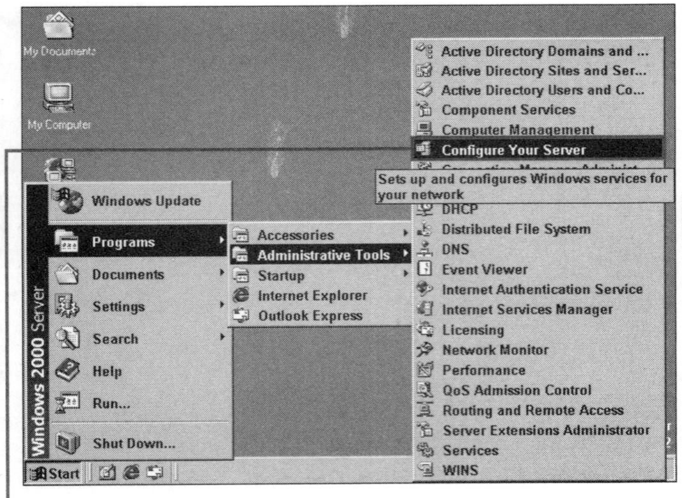

1 Choose Start⇨Programs⇨Administrative Tools⇨Configure Your Server.

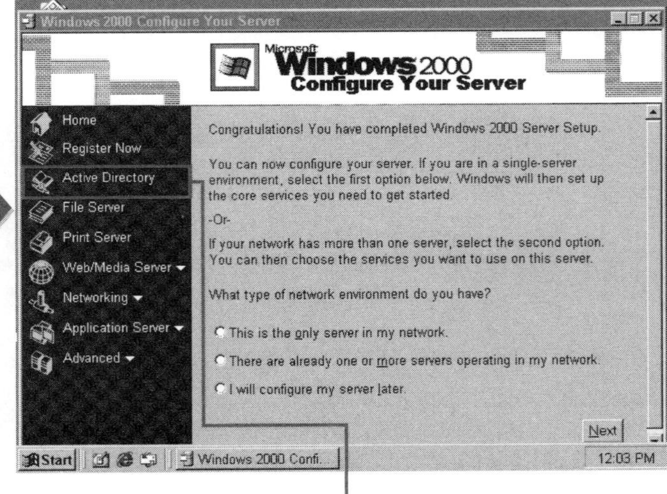

■ The Windows 2000 Configure Your Server window appears.

2 Click Active Directory in the left pane.

What happens to a member server when you install Active Directory?

- You can install the Active Directory only on domain controllers, so your member server is automatically upgraded to a domain controller. Likewise, if you later uninstall Active Directory, the server is demoted from a domain controller to a member server.

Is there another way to install Active Directory without using the Configure Your Server tool?

- Yes. You can also install Active Directory by choosing Start⇨Run and typing **dcpromo**. This action launches the Active Directory Installation Wizard. You can also use this command to uninstall the Active Directory.

What if I have a mix of Windows 2000 and Windows NT servers? Don't the NT servers look for a primary domain controller?

- Yes. Windows NT servers in mixed environments still look for a domain controller, so the upgraded PDC (which is now simply a Windows 2000 domain controller) acts as a PDC emulator for all downlevel servers and clients. The PDC emulator performs the PDC tasks that downlevel Windows operating systems expect it to perform.

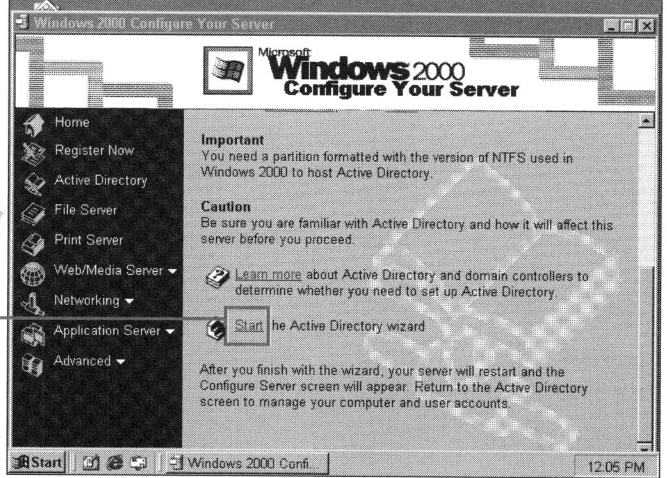

3 To start the installation wizard, scroll to the bottom of the screen and click the Start link.

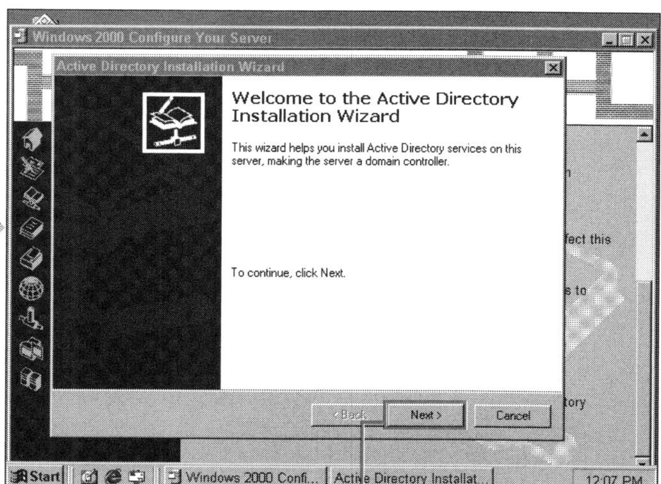

■ The Active Directory Installation Wizard begins.

4 Click Next to continue.

CONTINUED

INSTALLING THE ACTIVE DIRECTORY CONTINUED

Before proceeding with the installation, you need to make some decisions. First, you need to know if you're installing the Active Directory in a new domain or if you're joining an existing domain in your organization. If you're creating a new domain, you also need to know if the new domain is part of a new domain tree or part of an existing domain tree and forest. Your selection is determined by the structure of your Active Directory implementation (see Chapters 8 and 9). Finally, you need to enter the DNS name of your domain, such as `corp.com`. The Active Directory uses DNS as its primary naming system. To learn more about DNS, see Chapter 6.

Before proceeding with an Active Directory installation, you must carefully plan the implementation and know the Active Directory domain you will create or join. As with most implementations, planning is of utmost importance to create an effective Active Directory environment.

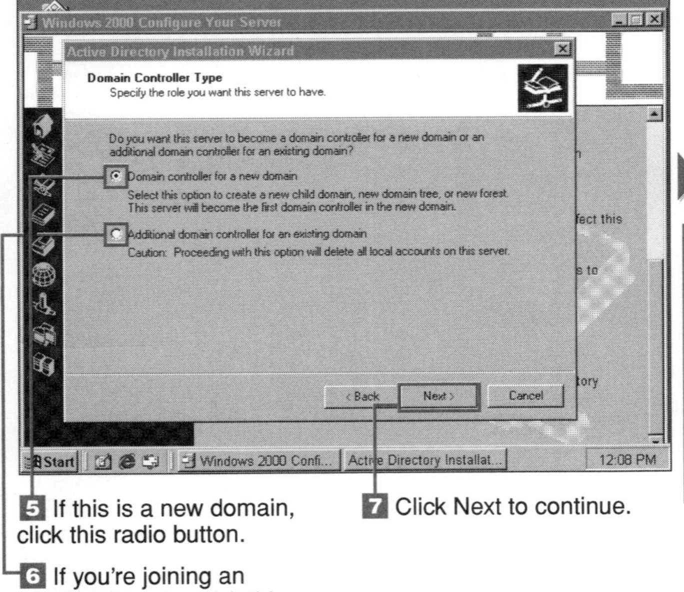

5 If this is a new domain, click this radio button.

6 If you're joining an existing domain, click this radio button.

7 Click Next to continue.

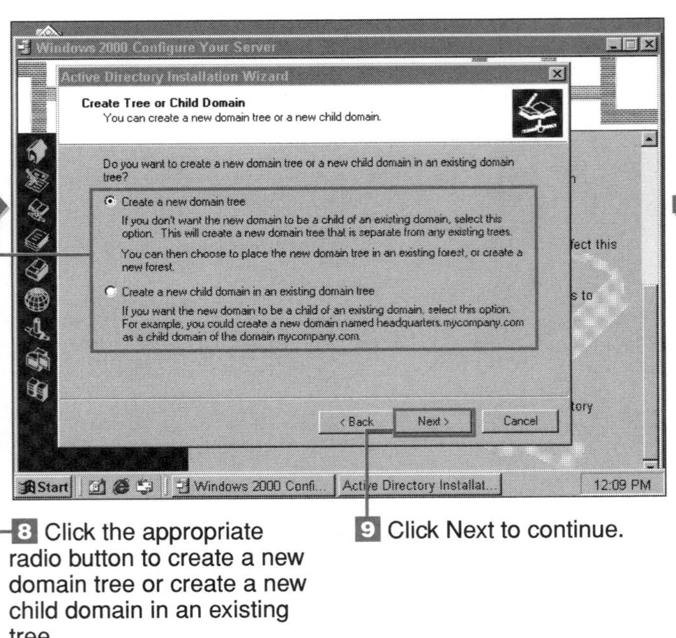

8 Click the appropriate radio button to create a new domain tree or create a new child domain in an existing tree.

9 Click Next to continue.

Why does installing the domain controller in an existing domain delete all local accounts on the server?

- Joining an existing domain deletes all local accounts on the server because all accounts must be configured through the Active Directory. This feature eliminates possible security problems or duplicate accounts. When you have a standalone server, you can configure user accounts so that users can log on to your local machine. After you upgrade the server to domain controller status with the Active Directory, users cannot log on locally to the domain controller, but must be authenticated through the Active Directory.

What is a child domain?

- A *child domain* exists beneath a parent domain. The parent domain is in control of the child domain. You can think of the parent domain as an umbrella, with the child domains existing beneath the umbrella. Child domains have a DNS extension of the parent domain. For example, if a domain is named `corp.com`, a child domain could be named `atlanta.corp.com`. See Chapter 9 to learn more.

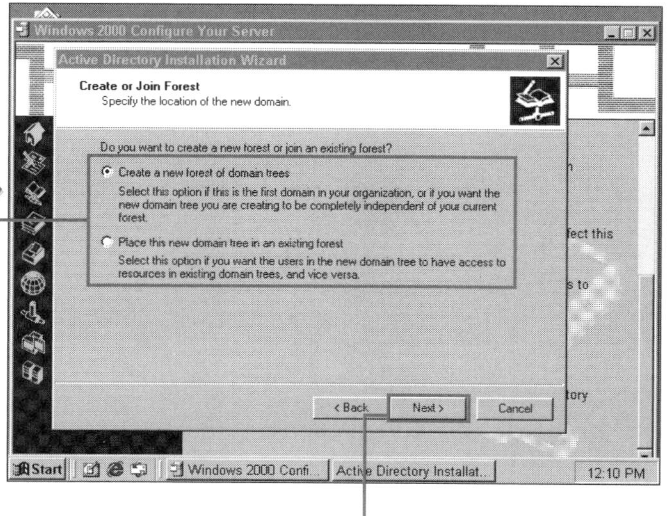

10 Click the appropriate radio button to create a new forest of domain trees or place the new domain tree in an existing forest.

■ Your selections may vary depending on the configuration you chose in Steps 5 and 6.

11 Click Next to continue.

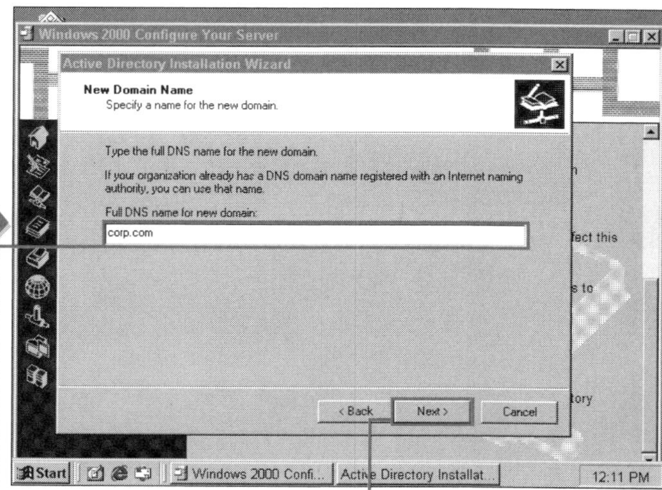

12 Type the DNS name for the domain.

13 Click Next to continue.

INSTALLING THE ACTIVE DIRECTORY
CONTINUED

After you establish the domain controller's place in the network and assign a DNS name, the downlevel NetBIOS name appears. This is the name of the domain that previous versions of Windows see. Keep in mind that Windows 2000 uses DNS for its naming scheme, but previous, or downlevel, versions of Windows use the NetBIOS naming scheme. The NetBIOS name is provided in Windows 2000 for backward compatibility.

The wizard shows the location of the log files, database, and System Volume folder. For best performance, you should store the log files on a separate disk if you have one available. The log files and database are stored by default in C:\WINNT\NTDS and the System Volume folder is stored by default in C:\WINNT\SYSVOL.

Also, if you have Windows NT 4.0 RAS users on your network, the wizard prompts you to weaken RAS permissions. This is a security feature of the Active Directory.

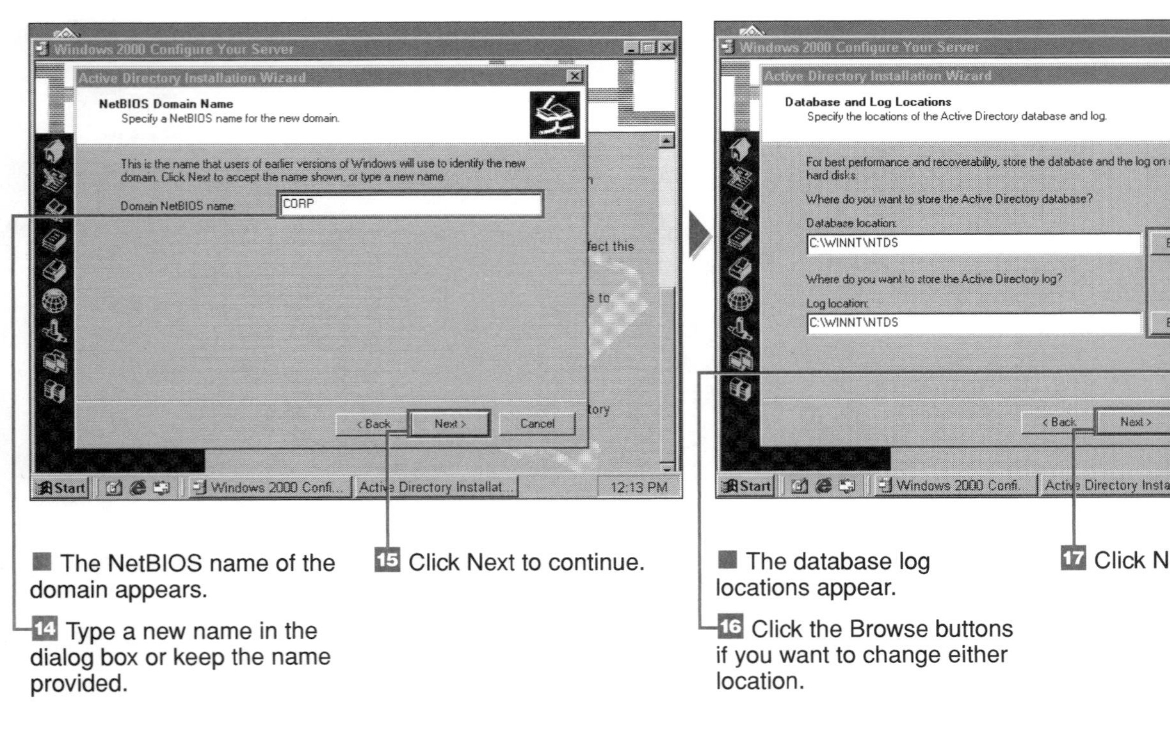

■ The NetBIOS name of the domain appears.

14 Type a new name in the dialog box or keep the name provided.

15 Click Next to continue.

■ The database log locations appear.

16 Click the Browse buttons if you want to change either location.

17 Click Next to continue.

Why should I store the log files on a different hard disk?

- For best domain controller performance, store the log files on a separate hard disk. This action speeds the server's performance because the log-write operations are moved to a different disk. Also, if you store the log files on a different disk, you can more easily recover Active Directory in the event of a failure.

Why should I weaken NT 4.0 RAS permissions?

- For installation, RAS permissions for Active Directory objects need to be weakened for security purposes. This limits RAS client access to Active Directory objects, like user objects. After all servers are running Windows 2000, you can strengthen permissions by using the Netsch.exe utility.

What is the SYSVOL folder?

- The SYSVOL folder is a shared directory that stores the server's copy of the domain's public files. SYSVOL is replicated among all domain controllers and is considered "System State" data in Windows 2000.

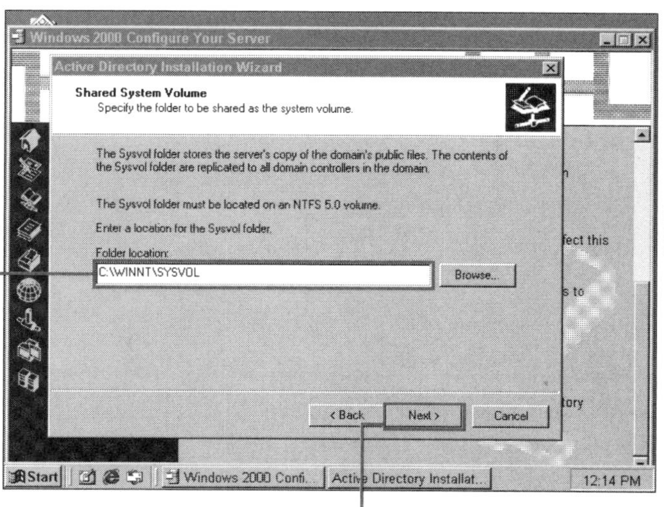

18 Enter a new location for the SYSVOL folder or keep the location provided.

Note: The SYSVOL folder must be stored on a Windows 2000 NTFS partition.

19 Click Next to continue.

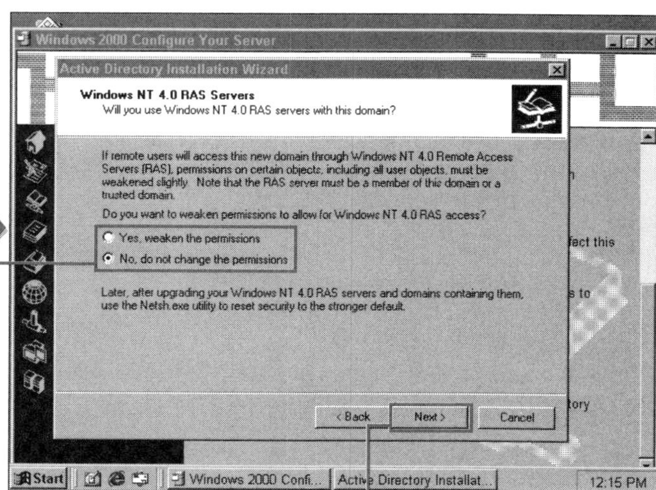

20 Click the appropriate radio button to either weaken NT 4.0 RAS permissions or leave them unchanged.

21 Click Next to continue.

CONTINUED

INSTALLING THE ACTIVE DIRECTORY
CONTINUED

The Active Directory Installation Wizard also prompts you for a password that you can use with Directory Services Restore mode. Directory Services Restore mode is a "safe" mode you can boot into by pressing the F8 key at startup. When in Directory Services Mode, you can troubleshoot problems with the Active Directory or you can run an Active Directory data restore if you have a failure. A number of Active Directory tools require you to run in Directory Services Restore Mode to fix and troubleshoot problems. You can learn more about these issues in Chapter 27.

After you reach the end of the wizard, you can either finish the installation, or use the Back button to make changes. Remember that after you finish the wizard, you cannot make major configuration changes, such as changing the DNS name of the domain, without reinstalling the Active Directory on your server, so make certain that you are satisfied with the installation before clicking Finish.

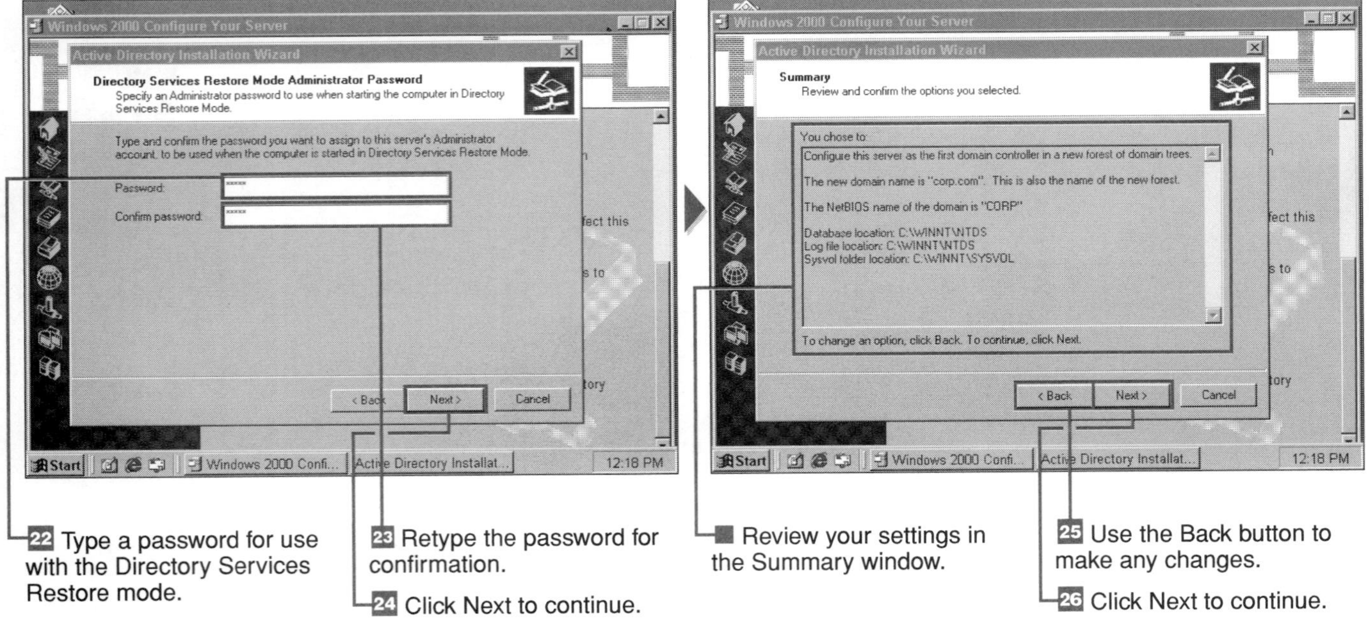

22 Type a password for use with the Directory Services Restore mode.

23 Retype the password for confirmation.

24 Click Next to continue.

■ Review your settings in the Summary window.

25 Use the Back button to make any changes.

26 Click Next to continue.

Can you make changes to the configuration after you reach the end of the wizard?

- You can make changes to your settings when you reach the review page by using the Back button. When you click the Back button, you simply move back through the wizard screens you have completed. After you click the Finish button, you cannot make major Active Directory changes, such as renaming the domain, without reinstalling the Active Directory.

Why do I have to enter a password to use the Active Directory Services Restore Mode?

- As a security feature, you must enter a valid password for using the Active Directory Services Restore Mode. This password prevents anyone else from booting into Directory Services Restore Mode. This is a security feature so that you can allow other administrators to manage the Active Directory on your domain controller without using the Directory Services Restore Mode.

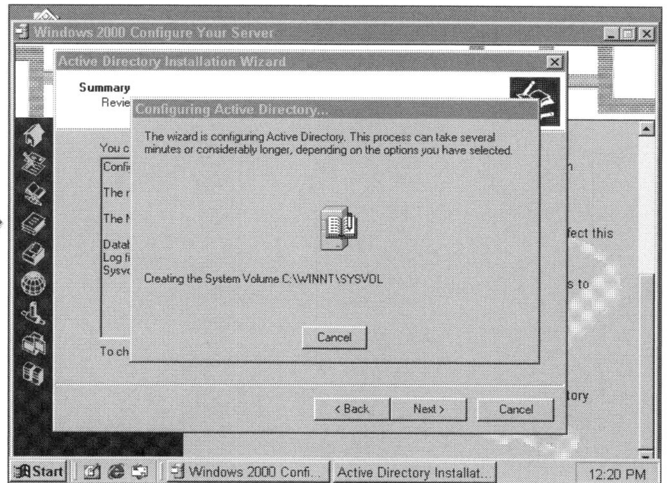

■ The system configures the Active Directory.

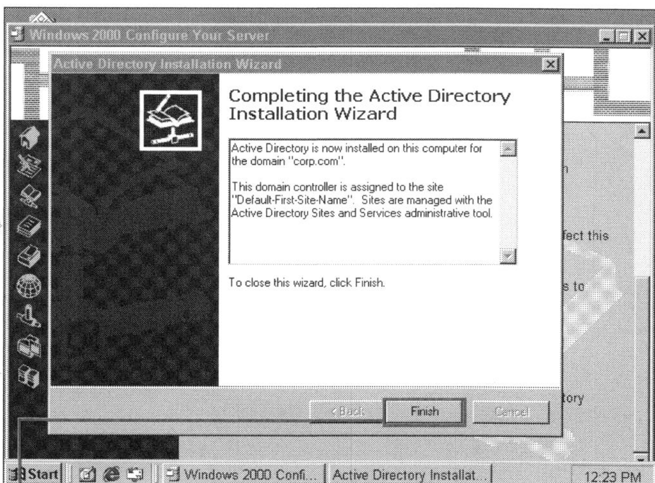

27 Click Finish to complete the installation.

UNINSTALLING THE ACTIVE DIRECTORY

You can choose to uninstall the Active Directory from a domain controller, but after you perform this action, the domain controller is demoted to a member server. Every domain controller must have the Active Directory installed.

From time to time, you may have reason to uninstall the Active Directory and demote your server. As hardware needs change and as your server becomes outdated, you can demote it and use it as a member server, a print server, or an application server. Older machines can perform these tasks effectively without having to run the intensive overhead of the Active Directory.

To uninstall the Active Directory, you use a command-line tool called dcpromo.exe. You can use dcpromo.exe to upgrade a server to the Active Directory or remove the Active Directory. The Configure Your Server tool does not provide you with a way to demote the domain controller, but it does give you the instructions for using dcpromo.exe.

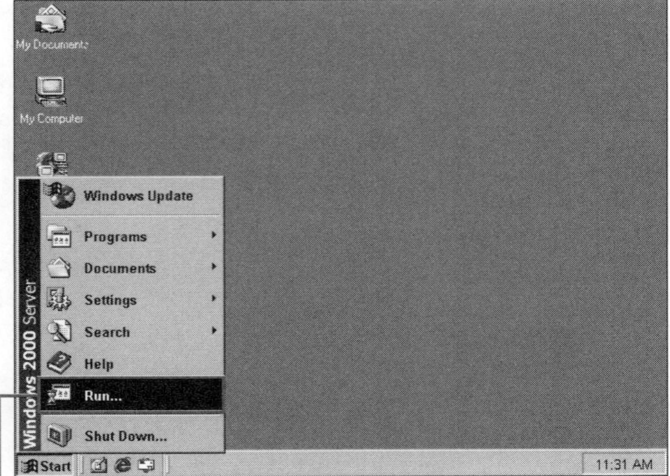

1 Choose Start⇨Run.

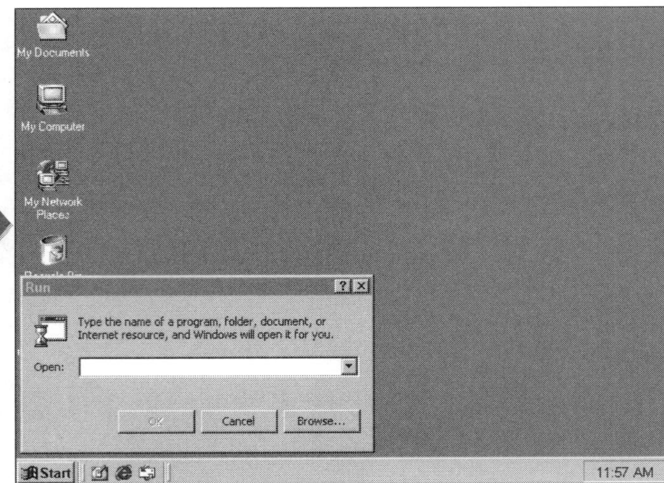

■ The Run window appears.

Does uninstalling the Active Directory on one server affect the Active Directory's functionality on the network?

- If you have more than one domain controller (DC), the Active Directory database functionality is not harmed. The Active Directory is replicated through multimaster replication so that all DCs have an exact copy of the database. Removing one DC does not affect the functionality of the other DCs or the Active Directory data. If your domain controller is the last domain controller in the forest, all data will be lost. This action, however, does not occur unless you are completely removing the Active Directory from your network.

Can I keep my machine a domain controller without the Active Directory?

- No. You can think of the Active Directory as being synonymous with a domain controller. Installation of the Active Directory automatically promotes a server to a DC, and uninstallation demotes the server to a member server. Likewise, you cannot promote a server to a DC without installing the Active Directory.

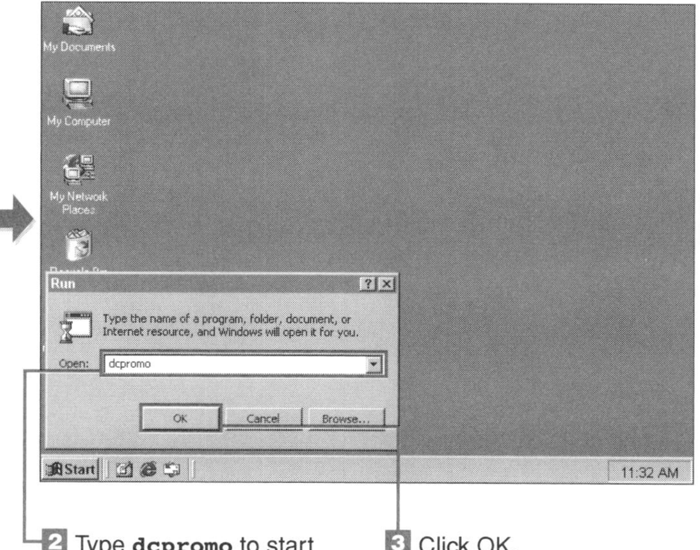

2 Type **dcpromo** to start the uninstall tool.

3 Click OK.

■ The Active Directory Installation Wizard begins.

4 Click Next to continue to uninstall.

CONTINUED

UNINSTALLING THE ACTIVE DIRECTORY CONTINUED

The Active Directory Installation Wizard prompts you for several pieces of information before it can perform the uninstall. First, the wizard wants to know if this is the last domain controller in the domain. If it is, the domain will no longer function after the uninstall is complete. If you are removing the Active Directory from your network, uninstallation of the last domain controller completely removes the Active Directory and all Active Directory data. Obviously, this is an option you should weigh carefully before proceeding because you will lose all objects, including all user accounts.

Next, the wizard prompts you for the Enterprise administrator account password for the domain controller; you also need to enter a new password for the computer because it will become a standalone server. The Enterprise admin password verifies that you have administrative rights to remove the Active Directory from the domain controller. After you remove the Active Directory, you log on to the standalone server with a typical admin account—not an Enterprise admin account.

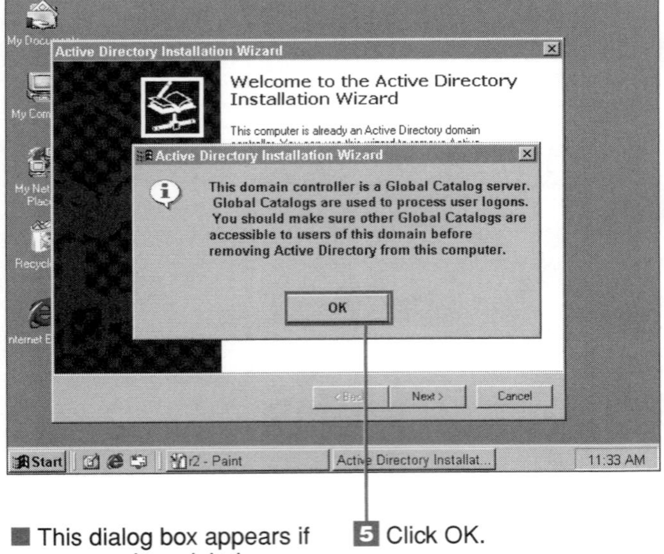

■ This dialog box appears if your server is a global catalog server.

5 Click OK.

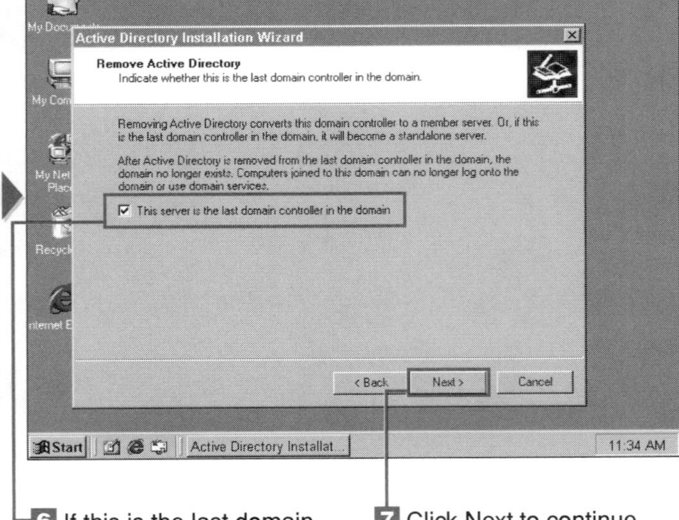

6 If this is the last domain controller in the domain, click the check box.

7 Click Next to continue.

What is the difference between the passwords?

Your current administrator account and password is for the Enterprise administrators group. You use this account on domain controllers. Because you are uninstalling the Active Directory, the administrator account is returned to a local standalone server account. The first password you are prompted for checks your account and permission to perform the uninstall. The second password box in the wizard asks you to assign a new password to the local standalone server administrator account.

If I reinstall the Active Directory after an initial uninstall, is the Active Directory data still current?

When you reinstall the Active Directory, or even install the Active Directory for the first time, the data, such as objects, are replicated from other domain controllers (assuming they exist). For example, all user accounts and other objects are replicated to the new domain controller automatically. You are not required to configure the data of each domain controller individually.

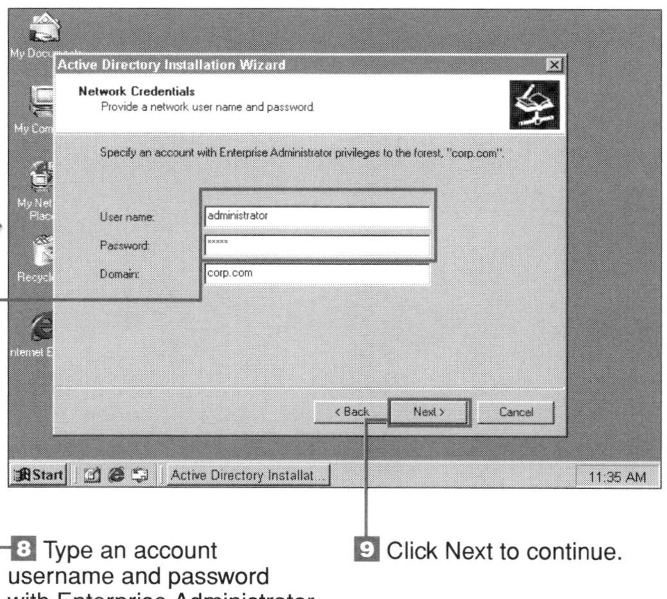

8 Type an account username and password with Enterprise Administrator privileges.

9 Click Next to continue.

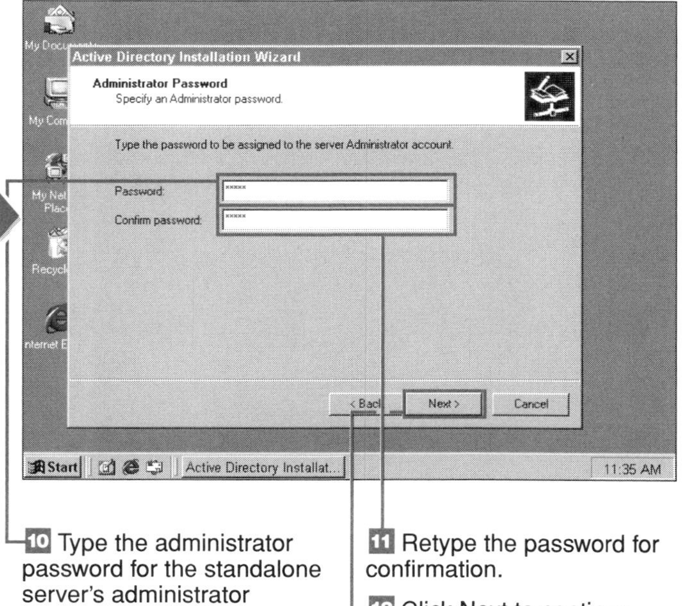

10 Type the administrator password for the standalone server's administrator account.

11 Retype the password for confirmation.

12 Click Next to continue.

CONTINUED

UNINSTALLING THE ACTIVE DIRECTORY CONTINUED

After you enter the information that the Active Directory needs to uninstall, you see a summary window in which you can review the configuration changes you made.

After you click Next, the Active Directory is removed from the system. A final window appears and prompts you to finish the uninstall. You then need to reboot your computer.

After you reboot your computer, you log on with your new local administrator password. The Enterprise admin password you previously used does not function because the server is now a member server and no longer a domain controller. After you reboot, you can begin to configure the new member server with services appropriate for the tasks you want the server to perform. If at any time you want to reinstall the Active Directory and upgrade the member server to a domain controller again, simply access the Configure Your Server tool or run dcpromo.exe at the Run prompt.

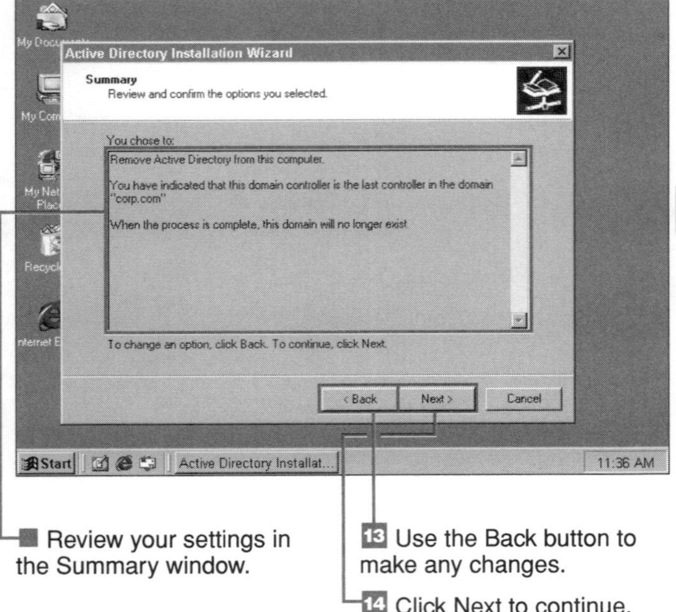

■ Review your settings in the Summary window.

13 Use the Back button to make any changes.

14 Click Next to continue.

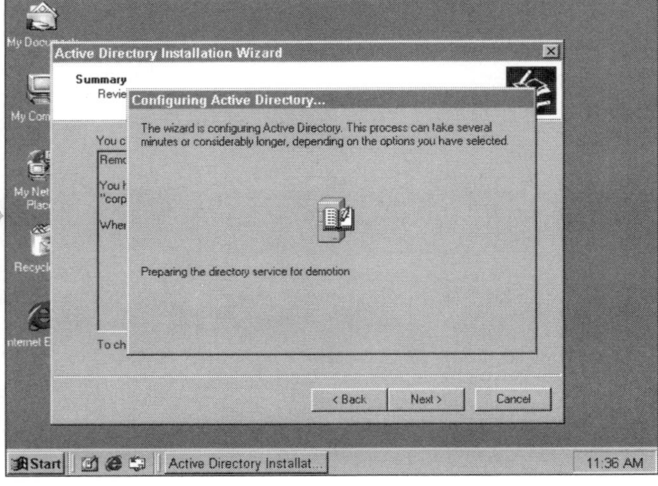

■ The system uninstalls the Active Directory.

TIPS

How can I quickly reinstall the Active Directory after an uninstall?

- After the uninstallation takes place, the only way to reconfigure your server and install the Active Directory is to run dcpromo.exe or use the Configure Your Server tool. This action opens the Active Directory Installation Wizard, at which time you must complete the entire installation process again. You cannot recover the Active Directory after you have uninstalled it.

Can member servers authenticate users?

- No. Only domain controllers, which run the Active Directory, can authenticate users. Keep in mind that all user accounts are stored in the Active Directory as objects. When a user logs on, a domain controller checks the Active Directory database for the validity of that user account. Member servers can use the Active Directory just like client computers, but they do not have the security privileges to authenticate users.

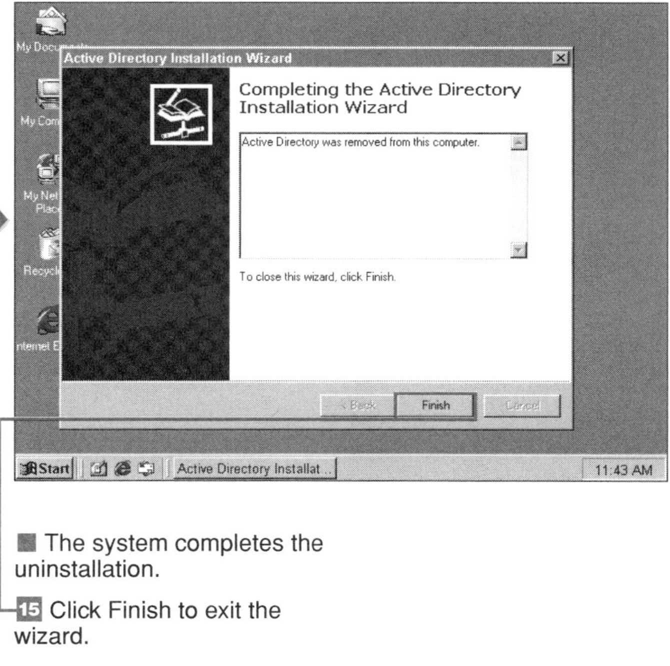

■ The system completes the uninstallation.

15 Click Finish to exit the wizard.

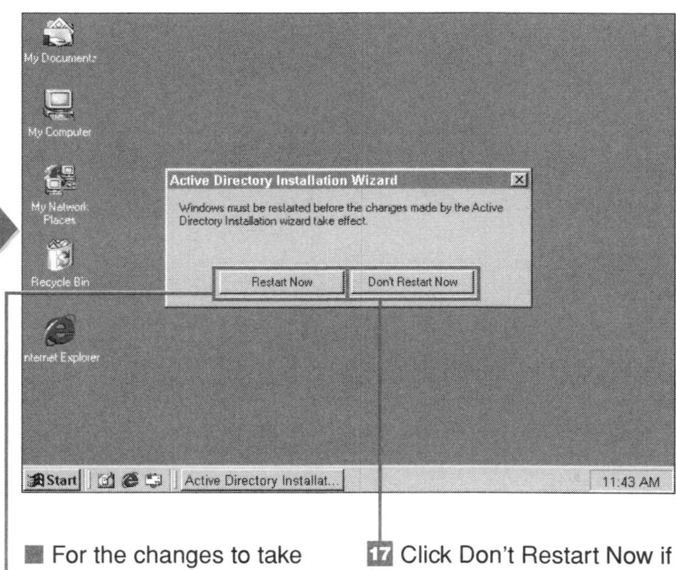

■ For the changes to take effect, you must restart Windows.

16 Click Restart Now to reboot your computer.

17 Click Don't Restart Now if you want to restart later.

ACCESSING THE MMC

The Microsoft Management Console (MMC) is a GUI interface, or shell, that you use often when working with Active Directory. The MMC houses the Active Directory tools and other tools in Windows 2000 Server.

The MMC is a basic interface that looks similar to Windows Explorer. The MMC alone does not provide any functionality, instead it allows you to load various tools, called *snap-ins*, into the MMC so you can complete various tasks. All Active Directory tools are MMC snap-ins.

If you have worked with any BackOffice products, such as Internet Information Server (IIS), Proxy Server, or Systems Management Server (SMS), you have used the MMC because these BackOffice products are snap-ins. If you have worked with these products, you are probably familiar with the MMC and its functionality.

The MMC is available at the Run prompt. When you launch the MMC, a standard interface appears.

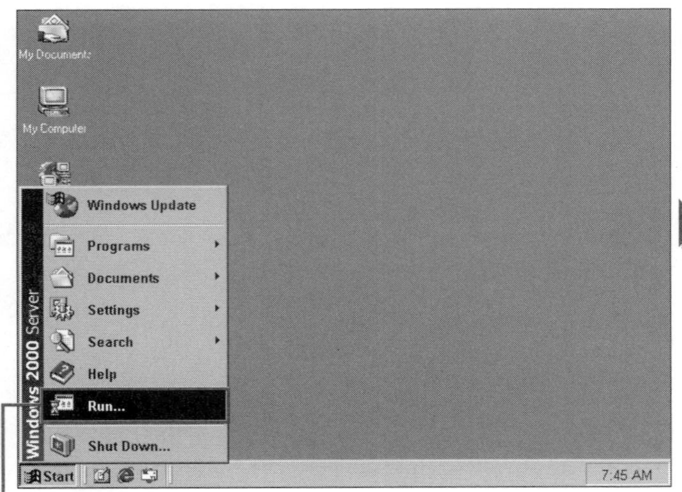

1 To access the MMC, choose Start⇨Run.

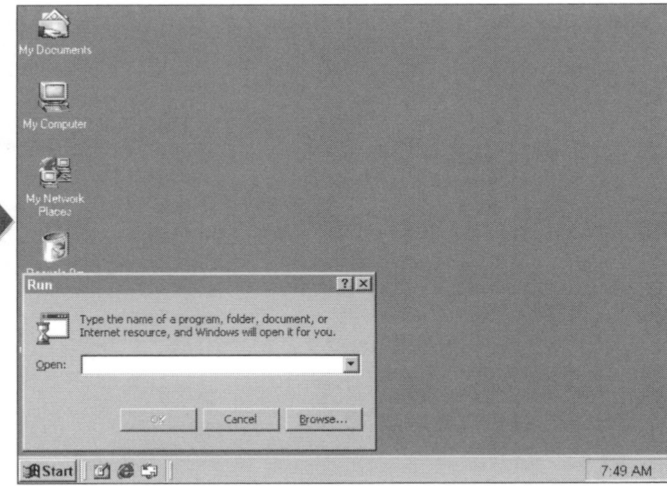

■ The Run dialog box appears.

Can I use a snap-in without the MMC?

- No. Snap-ins are created specifically to function within the MMC. The MMC provides the controls necessary to use the snap-in, and the snap-in does not function without the MMC. All Active Directory tools are MMC snap-ins, and these tools cannot be accessed and used without the MMC.

What does the MMC do without a snap-in?

- The MMC does not have any functionality without a snap-in. You can compare the MMC to a kitchen stove. Without something on the burners or in the oven, the stove does not have any real functionality. But if something is on the burners or in the oven, you use the stove to control it. For example, if a pot of water is on a burner, you can use the stove controls to heat the water, or cool it back down. The MMC is similar—you use the MMC controls to manage and use snap-ins.

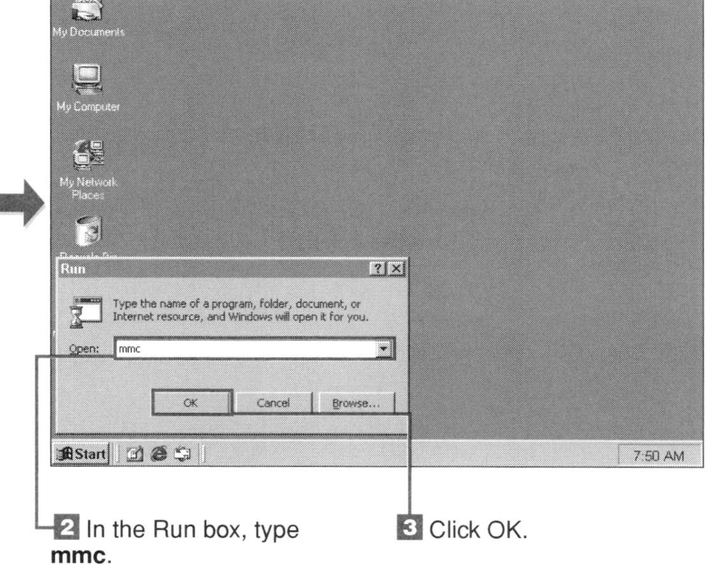

2 In the Run box, type **mmc**.

3 Click OK.

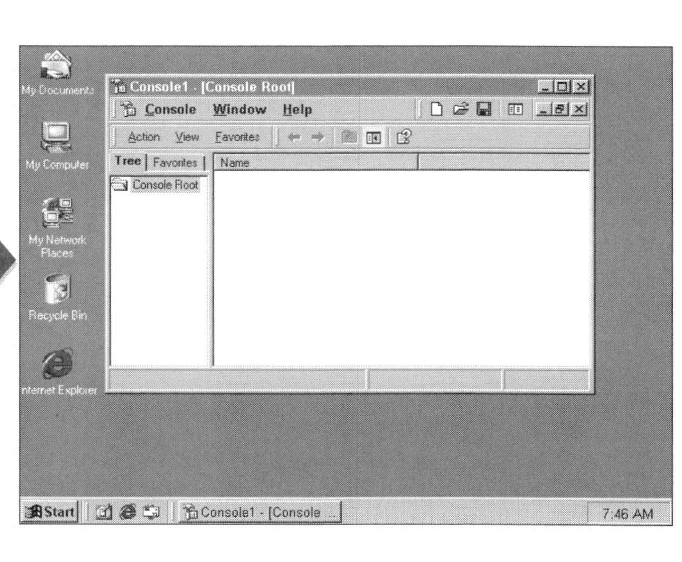

■ The MMC opens.

OPENING AND SAVING MMCS

At the top of the MMC, you see MMC menus, and immediately under those menus, you see root menus. The MMC menus enable you to control the overall appearance and behavior of the MMC. You also use the MMC Console menu to add or remove snap-ins.

If you click the Console menu, you can perform several actions. For example, you can create new MMCs or open existing ones on your system. This feature allows you to open several MMCs, and consequently several snap-ins, so you can work with many tools at one time. You can also save an MMC console, just as you would a document. This feature enables you to create custom MMC consoles that contain several snap-ins of your choice. Note that you do not need to manually create MMC consoles for the Active Directory tools—these are provided for you in the Programs folder.

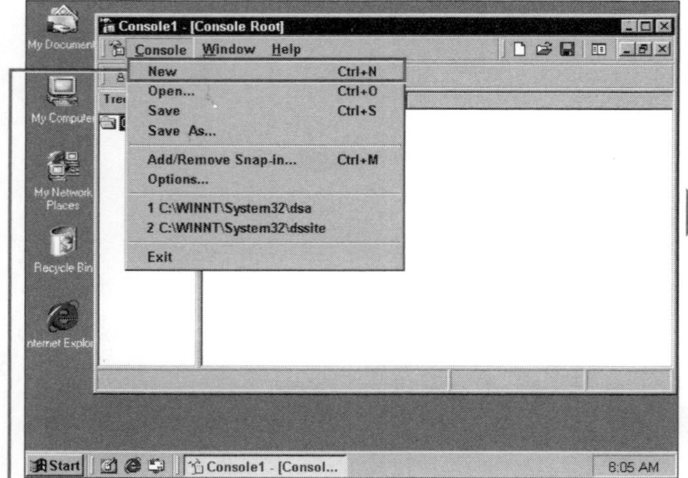

1 To open a new MMC, choose Console⇨New.

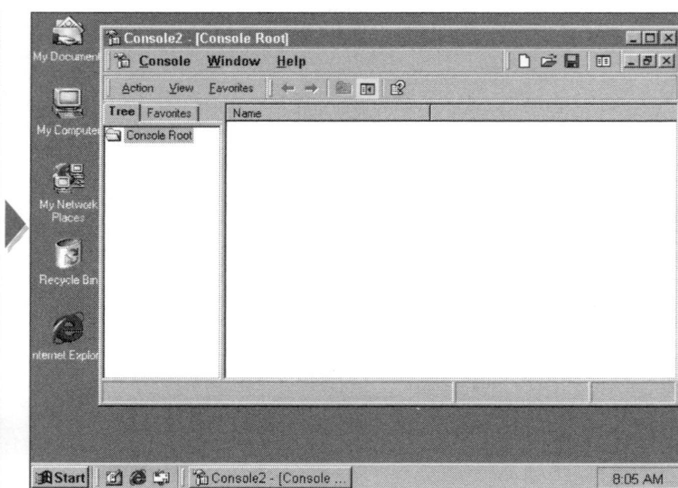

■ A new MMC opens.

Why would I want to open a new MMC when one is already open?

- You can load numerous snap-ins into one MMC if desired. But if you are working with several tools at once, you may want each snap-in to exist in its own MMC so that you can save them individually. In this case, the New command enables you to easily open several MMCs at one time. Some administrators prefer to create custom MMC consoles where they load several snap-ins and then save the console for future use. Other administrators find this approach confusing and prefer to use each snap-in in its own separate MMC.

Are saved MMCs text files?

- No. MMCs are saved as an .msc file, which is the Microsoft Management Console file type. You can then open and close saved MMCs as desired.

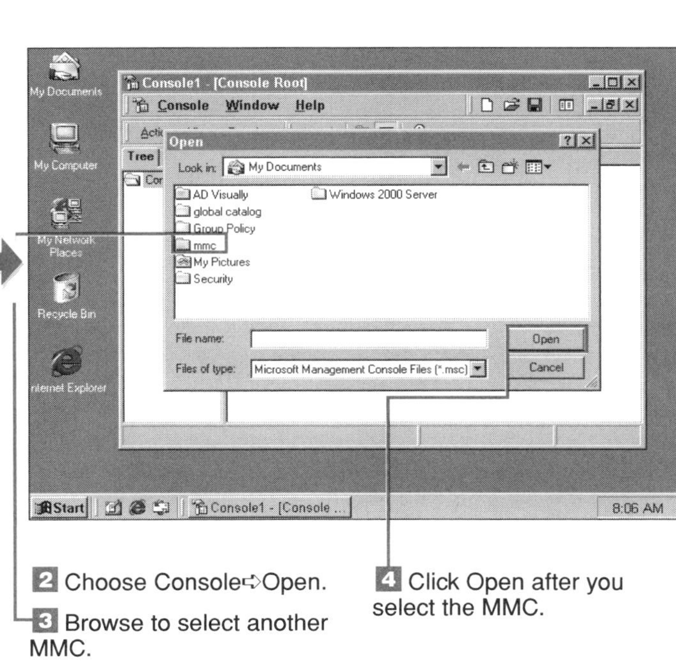

2 Choose Console⇨Open.

3 Browse to select another MMC.

4 Click Open after you select the MMC.

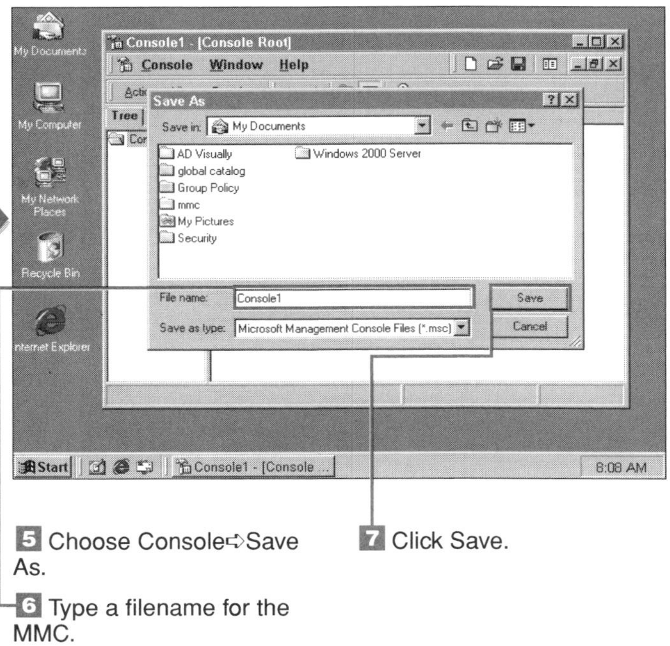

5 Choose Console⇨Save As.

6 Type a filename for the MMC.

7 Click Save.

ADDING AND REMOVING SNAP-INS

You'll use the Console menu mainly to add or remove snap-ins. You can add snap-ins to empty MMCs, or you can add them to existing MMCs so that you have more than one tool present within a given MMC. Keep in mind you can load snap-ins in several different ways. Some administrators prefer to use several snap-ins within one MMC, and other administrators prefer to use each snap-in within its own MMC.

When you choose to add or remove a snap-in, a Windows 2000 list of available snap-ins appears. You can then select the snap-in you want to use. After the snap-in loads, you can begin using the snap-in.

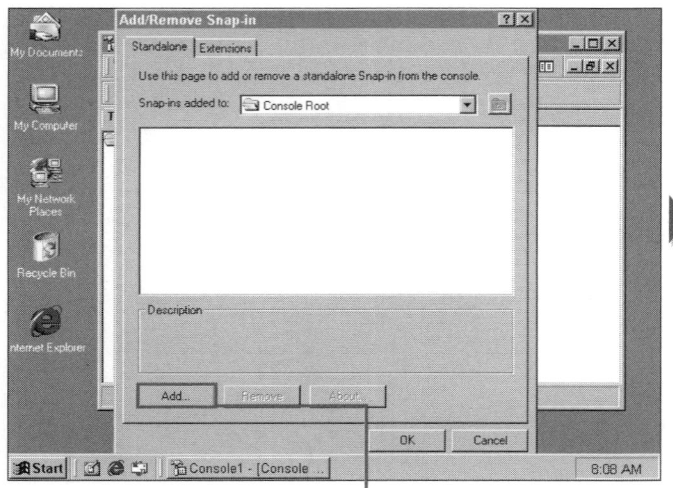

ADDING A SNAP-IN

1 Choose Console⇨Add/Remove Snap-in.

■ The Add/Remove Snap-in dialog box appears.

2 Click Add.

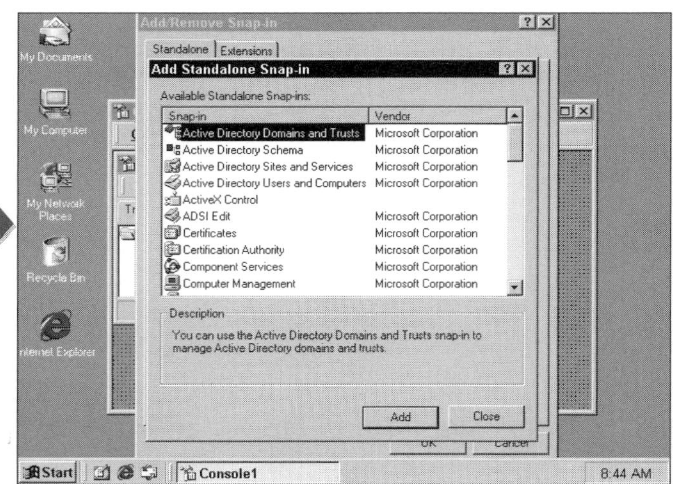

■ The Add Standalone Snap-in dialog box appears.

Why are so many tools in Windows 2000 snap-ins?

- The MMC is a major component of Windows 2000, and most major tools in Windows 2000 function as MMC snap-ins. This approach makes configuration and management easier. Instead of each tool having a different interface, the MMC brings a streamlined approach to management tools. Also, the snap-in structure easily enables Microsoft and other vendors to create new snap-ins that you can download from the Web.

Can I create custom consoles with the multiple snap-in so that I can use them over and over?

- Sure. Simply load the snap-ins you want, and then use the Console menu to save the console to the desired location on your system. Then you can use the MMC console over and over. For example, some administrators prefer all Active Directory snap-ins to appear in one console so they can configure the Active Directory from one console location. You could also load networking tools, such as DHCP, DNS, and WINS into one console so you can administer all of these services from one interface.

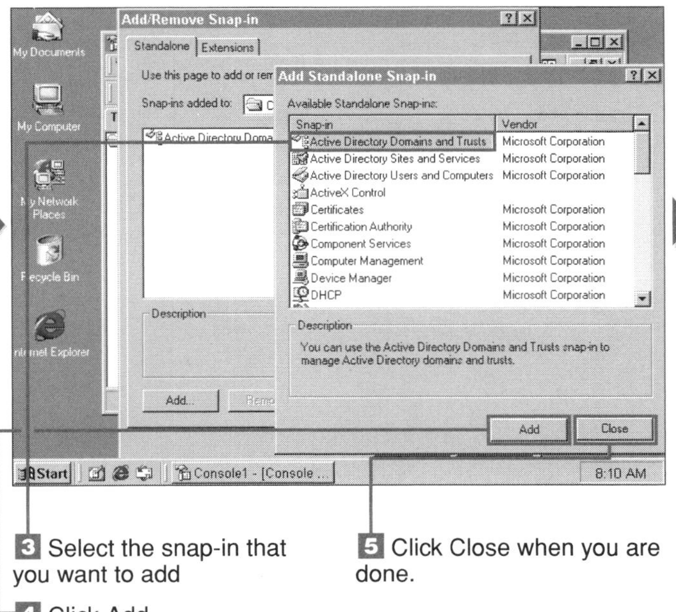

3 Select the snap-in that you want to add

4 Click Add.

Note: You can add additional snap-ins the same way.

5 Click Close when you are done.

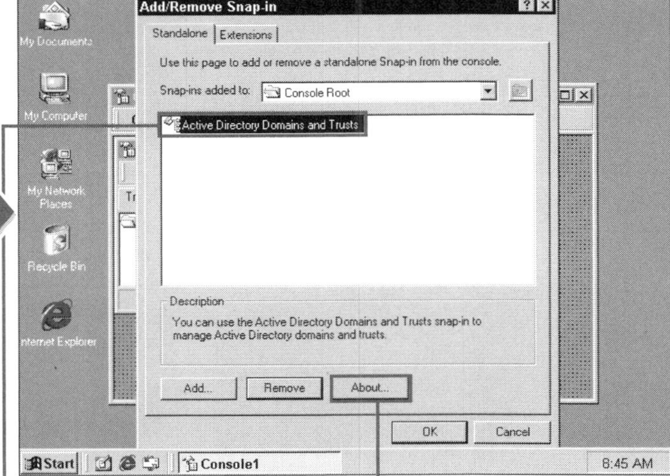

■ The Add/Remove Snap-in window now shows the snap-in loaded.

6 Select the snap-in.

7 Click About to learn more about the snap-in.

CONTINUED

ADDING AND REMOVING SNAP-INS CONTINUED

After you add the desired snap-ins, you can use the Add/Remove Snap-in Standalone and Extensions tab to manage the snap-ins before they are added to the MMC console. First, you can select any snap-in the Standalone window and click the About button to learn more about the snap-in. This feature provides you with a short paragraph describing the snap-in's functionality.

The Extensions tab enables you to manage each snap-in's extensions, if extensions are available for the particular snap-in. Extensions are other snap-ins which work with the snap-in you select. For example, the Active Directory Users and Computers snap-in contains several extensions to other snap-ins, such as Group Policy. By default, all extensions for each snap-in are loaded, so you do not need to specifically use the Extensions tab unless you only want to load particular extensions.

Finally, you can also use the Standalone tab to Remove snap-ins from the list before they are added to the console.

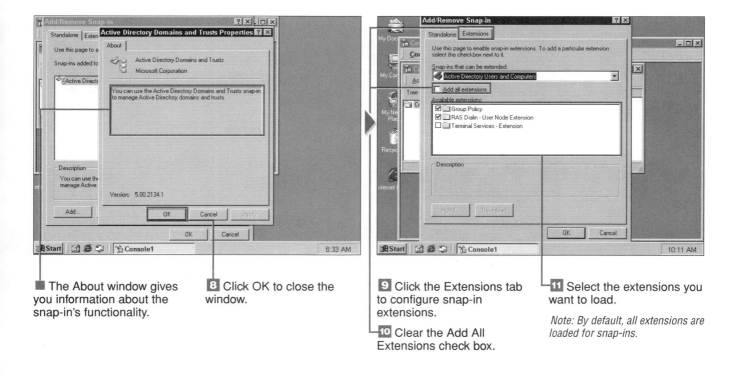

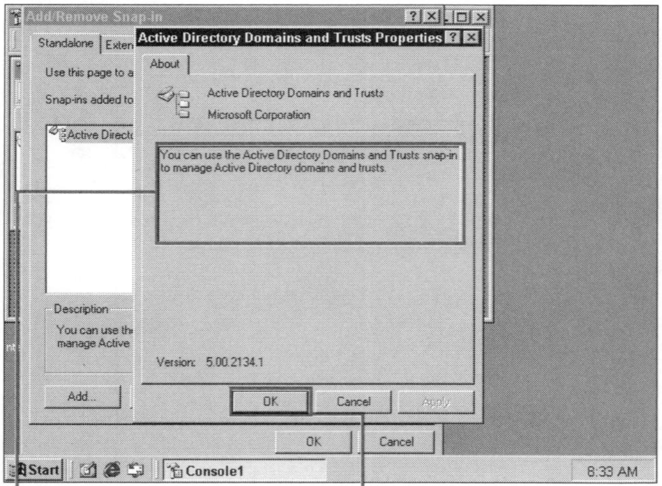

■ The About window gives you information about the snap-in's functionality.

8 Click OK to close the window.

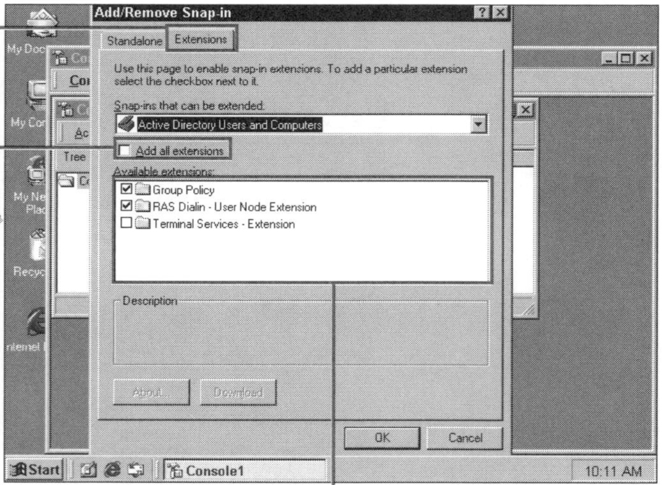

9 Click the Extensions tab to configure snap-in extensions.

10 Clear the Add All Extensions check box.

11 Select the extensions you want to load.

Note: By default, all extensions are loaded for snap-ins.

How are Extensions used?

- Some snap-ins contain extensions to other snap-ins. You can think of extensions as "links." Some snap-ins have configuration that requires the snap-in to open another snap-in. For example, in Active Directory Users and Computers, you can configure Group Policy for a domain. In order to configure Group Policy, the Group Policy snap-in has to be opened. The Users and Computers snap-in contains a link to the Group Policy snap-in so it can be automatically launched when you want to configure Group Policy. The extensions allow different, yet related, snap-ins to function together so you do not have to manually open related snap-ins.

When I remove a snap-in, is the snap-in deleted?

- No. When you remove a snap-in from the Standalone tab, you are simply telling the MMC not to load a previously selected snap-in. This action simply removes the snap-in from you list so it is not loaded.

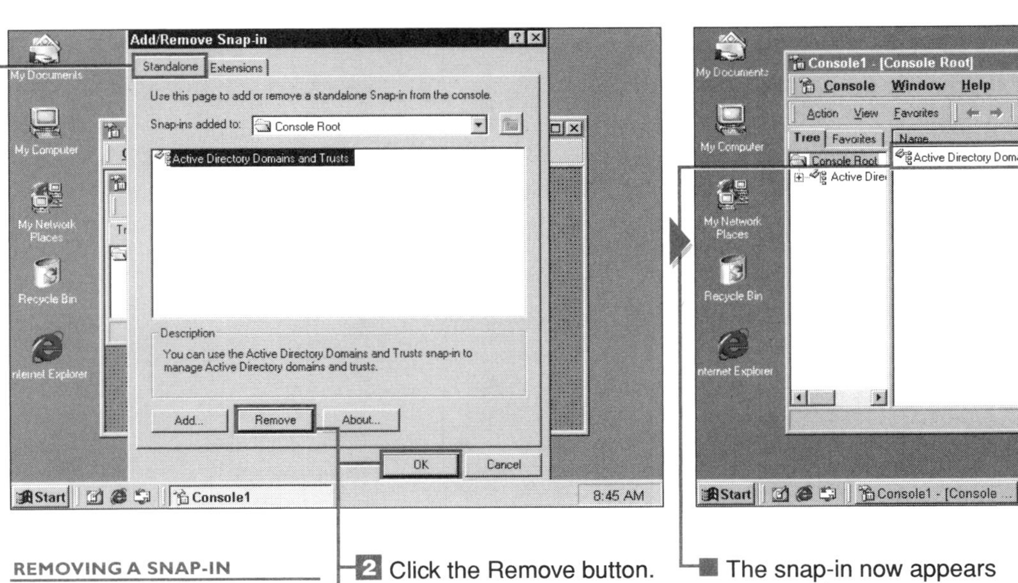

REMOVING A SNAP-IN

1 Select the Standalone tab, then select the snap-in you want to Remove.

2 Click the Remove button.

3 Click OK when you are done.

■ The snap-in now appears in the console.

CONFIGURING MMC OPTIONS

The Options command enables you to change the icon appearance of the MMC console and also change the mode. You have four mode options that you can implement. Each mode provides the user with different rights and permissions for using and configuring the MMC. The mode options are useful if several different people use the same MMC. One user may have "full control," while others can only make certain changes to the console.

Depending on which mode you choose, you can also use the check boxes at the bottom of the window to enable context menus, stop the user from saving changes to the console, or allow the user to customize views. You can customize the MMC views by using the Window menu on the console.

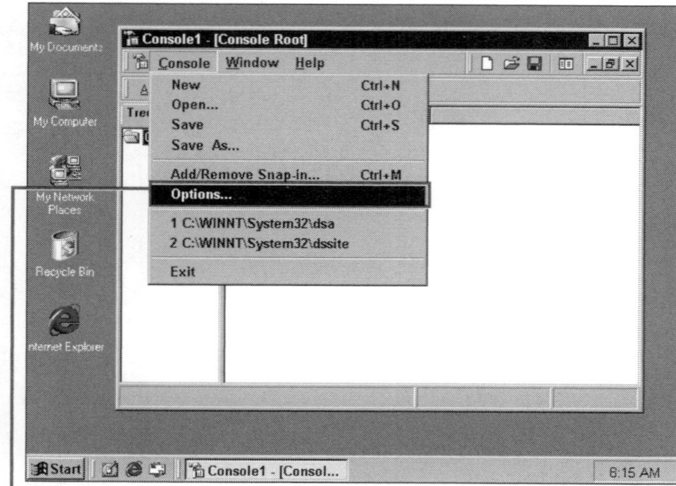

1 Choose Console⇨ Options to change the MMC console's functionality.

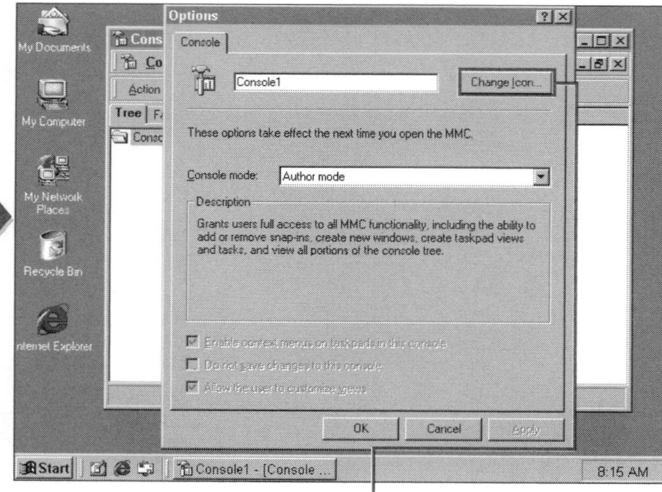

■ The Options dialog box appears.

2 You can change the MMC's icon by clicking Change Icon and selecting a new icon from the window that appears.

What are the different modes?

MMC modes allow the user different MMC permissions. The following list explains the MMC modes:

- **Author mode** provides full access to the MMC with the ability to add or remove snap-ins, create new windows, save or change any options, and view all parts of the console.
- **User mode – full access** gives users full access to all commands and the console, but the user cannot add or remove snap-ins or change the console properties.
- **User mode – limited access, multiple window** gives the user access only to areas that were visible in the console when the console was saved. Users can create new windows but cannot close existing windows.
- **User mode – limited access, single window** provides users access only to areas of the console that were visible when the console was saved.

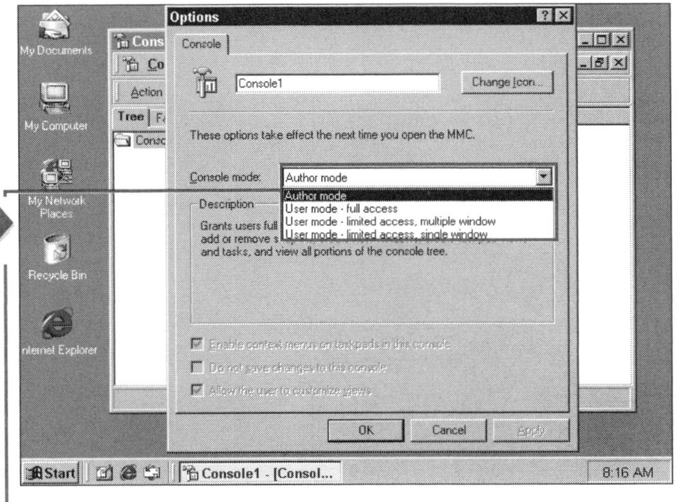

3 Click the Console Mode drop-down box and select the mode you want to use.

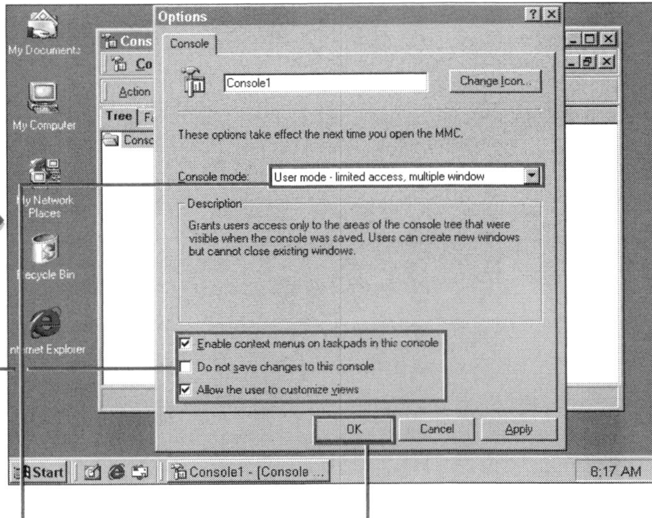

■ If you select one of the restrictive console modes, the check boxes become active.

4 Make any desired changes by clicking the appropriate check boxes.

5 Click OK when you are done.

USING THE MMC WINDOW MENU

The Window menu enables you to add new windows to the MMC and adjust the way you view the windows. This provides you an easy way to adjust the appearance of your MMC so that each snap-in loaded appears as desired.

You can open various windows in the MMCs and then arrange them in a manner you desire. For example, you can choose to either cascade or tile the open windows so that you can easily move from window to window in the MMC.

The Help Menu allows you to access MMC help by either accessing the Windows 2000 Help files or by accessing Microsoft on the Web. The "on the Web" option enables you to download new snap-ins, view product news, and even send feedback to Microsoft.

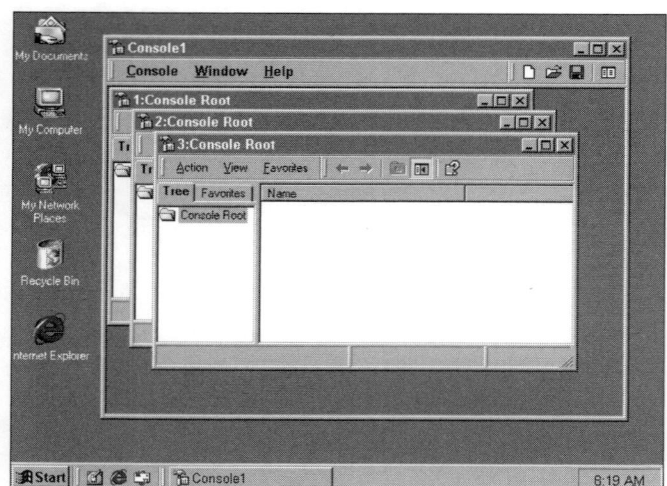

1 Choose Window⇨Cascade to cascade the open MMC windows.

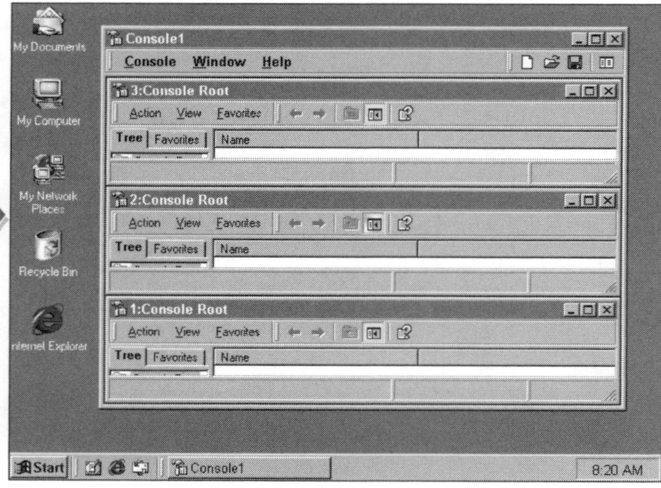

2 Choose Window⇨Tile to tile the open MMC windows.

Why would I want to use different windows within one MMC console?

- You can open various snap-ins in different windows instead of the same window. If you are working with several snap-ins, this feature is often helpful to keep the snap-ins organized. The functionality remains the same regardless of how you load the snap-ins —you can load various snap-ins in one window or several windows as desired.

What happens if I use the Microsoft On The Web help options?

- If you click one of the Microsoft On The Web options, your system opens a browser window and attempts to establish an Internet connection to access the particular Web page. When you use the Microsoft On The Web option, you can access the MMC snap-in gallery so you can download new snap-ins as they become available and read product news.

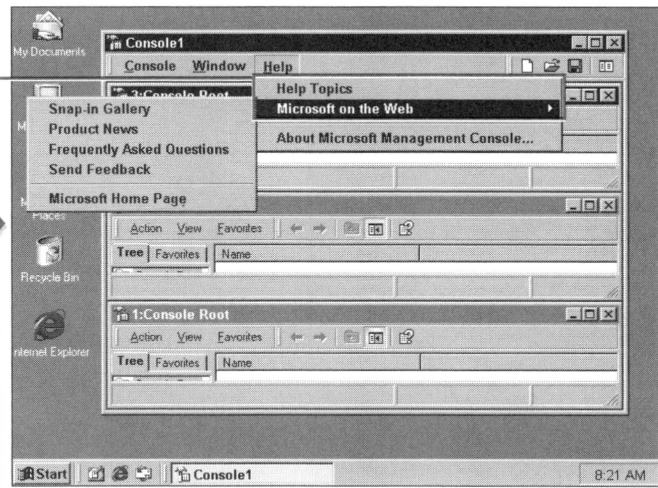

3 Click the Help menu, then select either Help Topics or Microsoft On The Web.

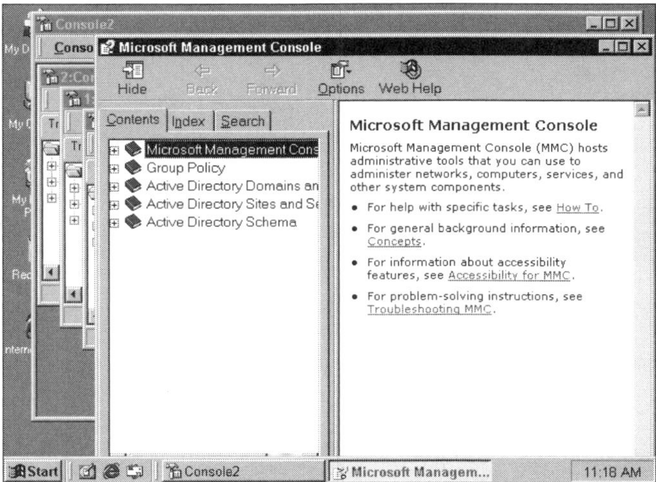

The Help menu gives you access to the Windows 2000 Help files or to help information on Microsoft's Web site, depending on the selection you made.

USING ROOT MENUS

Root menus enable you to adjust several options for the MMC root. The main MMC menus (Console, Window, and Help) affect the overall MMC. Root menus affect the snap-ins you have loaded into the MMC. The Action menu is the most common. If you select the root folder and choose the Action menu, a list of basic operations appears. After you begin using snap-ins, you can also use the Action menu to manage that particular snap-in. The options on the Action menu change depending on which snap-in you use.

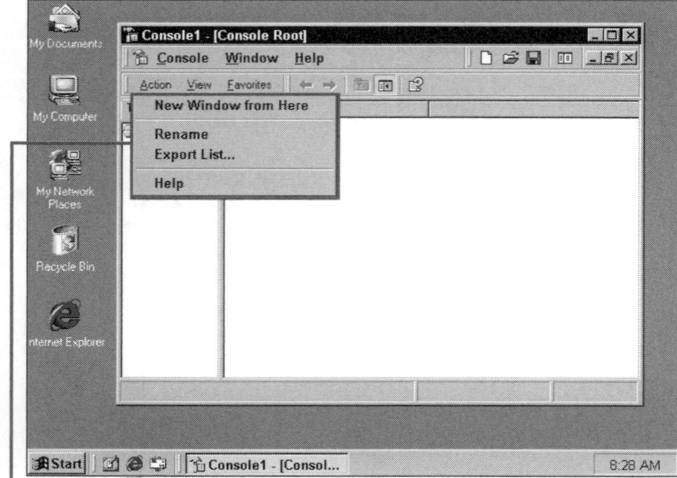

■ If you choose the Action menu, you see standard menu items that appear for every snap-in.

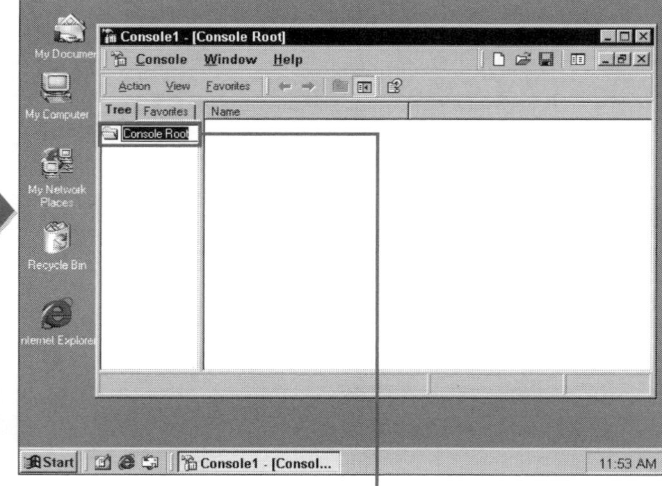

■ If you choose Action⇨Rename, you can rename the root folder in the console.

1 Type in the new name for the root folder.

What appears if I click the snap-in folder and click the Action menu?

- The Action menu contains a list of action operations that you can perform on a particular folder or snap-in. The actions that appear vary according to the snap-in that you have loaded, or the child folders of the snap-in. When you select different snap-ins or child folders and then choose the Action menu, the menu contains the actions that you can perform on that particular object.

Is there another way to configure items in the console without using the Action menu?

- Yes. You can select any item in the console and then right-click it to see a list of available actions. The right-click menu offers the same options that appear on the Action menu.

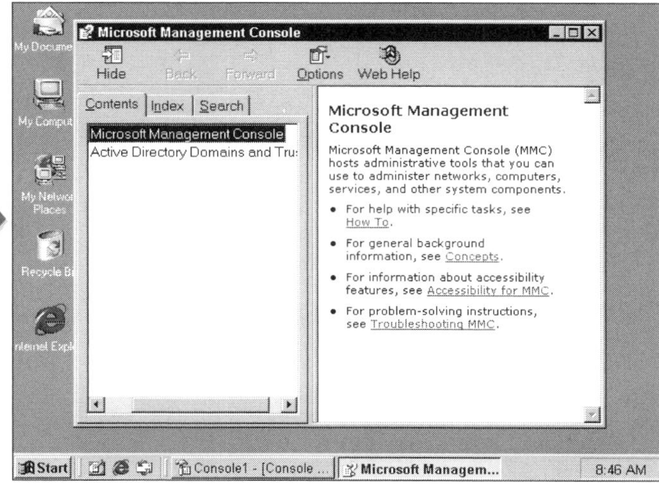

■ The Help option on the Action menu opens the Windows 2000 Help files.

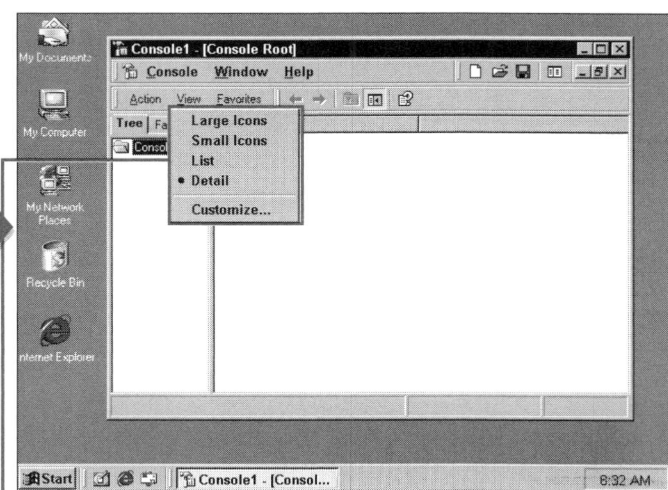

■ By choosing the View menu, you can choose large or small icons, a list, or details, or you can click Customize.

CONTINUED

USING ROOT MENUS CONTINUED

You can use the View menu to change the way the MMC root folder and snap-ins appear. You can choose to see the window with large icons or small icons, and you can use the Customize option to alter the appearance of the window. This option presents you with several check box selections, such as show or not show the console tree, standard menus, standard toolbar, status bar, description bar, and taskpad navigation tabs. You can also choose whether to show menus and toolbars for the snap-ins. By customizing your MMC, you can configure the interface so it easy for you to work with. You can also configure favorites in the MMC, just as you do for a Web browser. When you add favorites, you add console items so that they are easier to access by using the Favorites tab on the console.

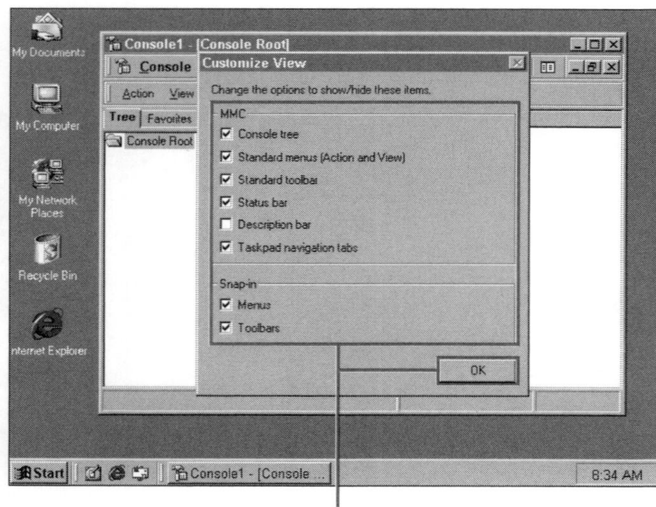

■ The Customize View dialog box appears when you choose View⇨Customize.

2 Click on the appropriate check boxes to adjust the views that are available and that appear for the root folder and snap-ins.

3 Click OK when you are done.

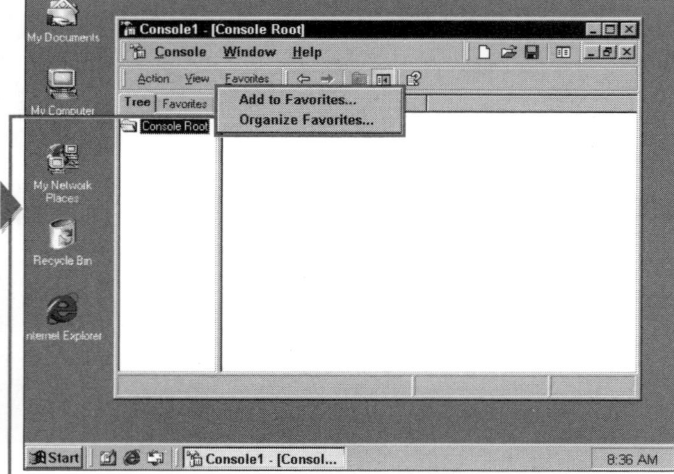

■ Choose the Favorites menu to either add an item to Favorites or organize your Favorites list.

What is a Description Bar?

- The Description Bar—a small tool bar that appears over the MMC details pane—is an option you can select from the View menu. When you select different items, a description of the item appears in the toolbar. The Description Bar may be a helpful feature to use as you are learning to work with the MMC.

What are favorites?

- *Favorites* are simply snap-in or child containers you select in the MMC windows and mark as a "favorite." A favorite is normally something you use often and want to access easily from the Favorites menu.

What can be a favorite?

- Any snap-in or child container of a snap-in (as well as the root container) can be a favorite. Basically, you can select anything you see in the console tree and add it to the favorites list.

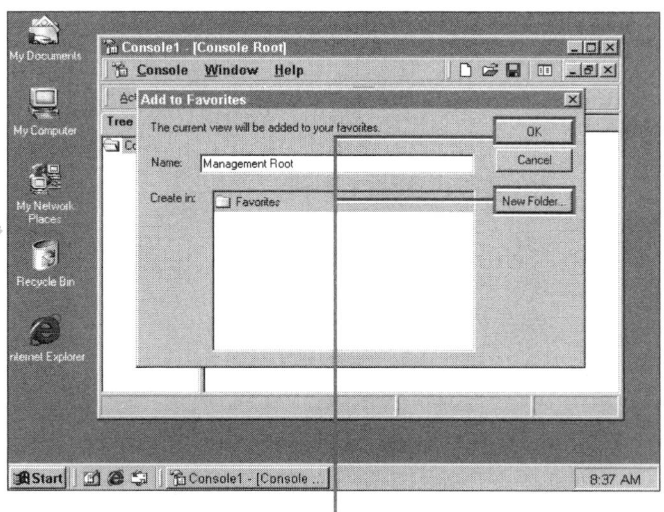

■ If you choose Add To Favorites, the selected folder or snap-in is added to your favorites list.

4 Click OK to add it.

5 Or, click the New Folder button to place your Favorites in a different folder.

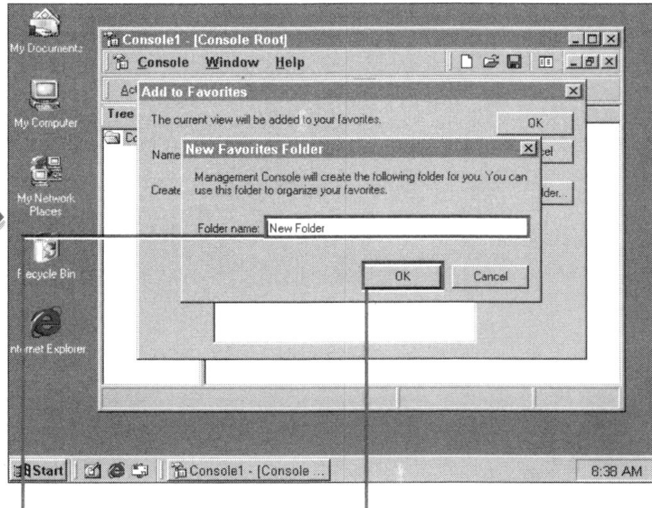

6 Type the name of the new folder.

7 Click OK.

ACCESSING THE SEARCH WINDOW

One of the most important components of any directory is finding the information you need. Whether you use a paper directory, such as a phone book, or an electronic directory, such as the Active Directory, success or failure depends on users being able to find the information they need.

The Active Directory stores all information in the global catalog, which contains pointers to the specific objects contained in the directory. You can use the search feature to search the global catalog to find any resource in the Active Directory. Search windows are available within the Administrative tools, but clients access the search function using My Network Places. Because the Active Directory is LDAP (Lightweight Directory Access Protocol) compliant, users can perform keyword searches so they can easily find the kind of information they need. For example, you can search for "printers" in the Active Directory and all available printer objects will be returned.

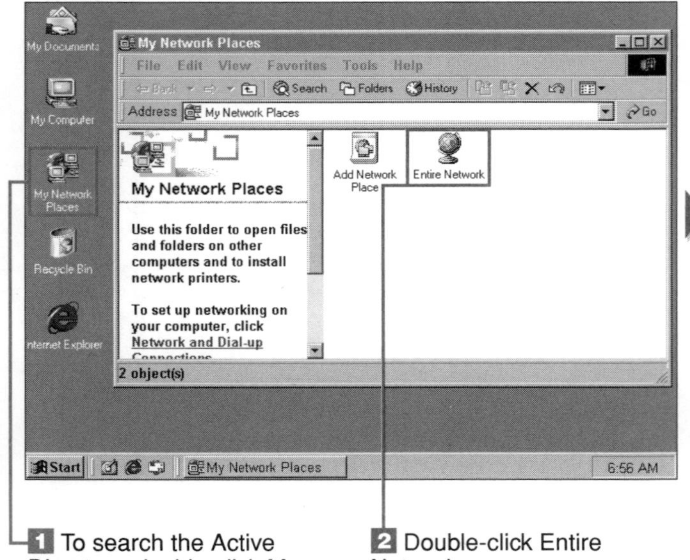

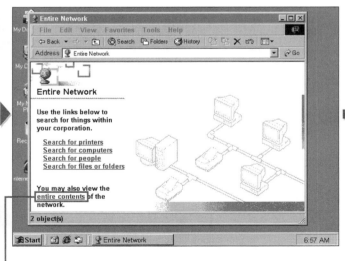

1 To search the Active Directory, double-click My Network Places.

2 Double-click Entire Network.

3 Click the Entire Contents link.

How does Windows search the Active Directory?

Active Directory searches are performed using the LDAP (Lightweight Directory Access Protocol), a communication protocol used for directory access on TCP/IP networks. LDAP is a more efficient protocol than DAP (Directory Access Protocol) and has been primarily associated with Internet functions. Access to domain controllers and global catalogs is performed using LDAP.

Can users browse for Active Directory objects?

Yes. Active Directory users can access My Network Places and browse the domain and OU structure to find resources they need. In small environments, this may work fine, but in Enterprise environments, users should find Active Directory resources using its powerful query capabilities. Users may need to be trained in Active Directory search operations so they can make the most of the Active Directory.

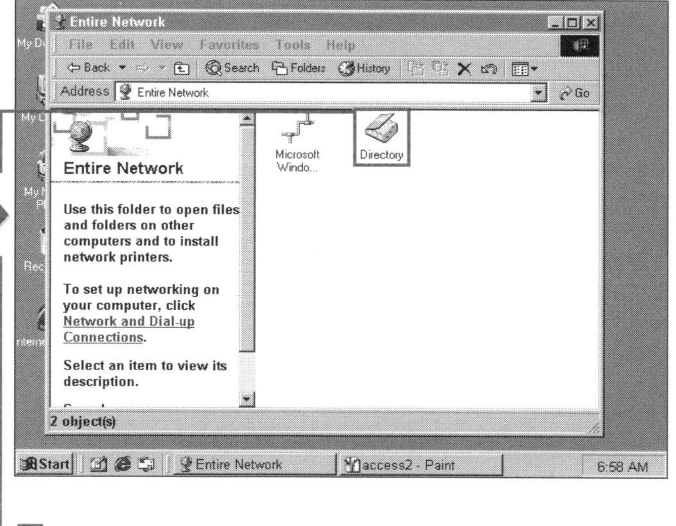

4 Double-click Directory.

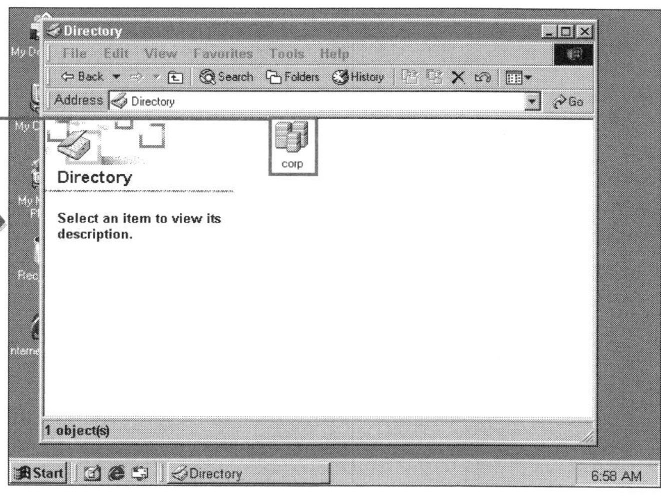

5 Double-click the domain icon.

CONTINUED

ACCESSING THE SEARCH WINDOW
CONTINUED

By accessing the search window, you can then find any object you would like to find within the Active Directory. Because the global catalog uses LDAP, you do not have to know the exact name of an Active Directory object to locate it. LDAP can perform full text searches to help you find certain kinds of objects or close matches to the requests that you need.

Because of the structure of the Active Directory and the attributes of Active Directory objects, you can perform a basic search, such as entering a user name or simply searching for "John." In either case, the Active Directory returns all possible matches. You can also perform a text search, which enables you to use a combination of words, such as "company documents and forms," and the Active Directory will use your word search to find possible matches.

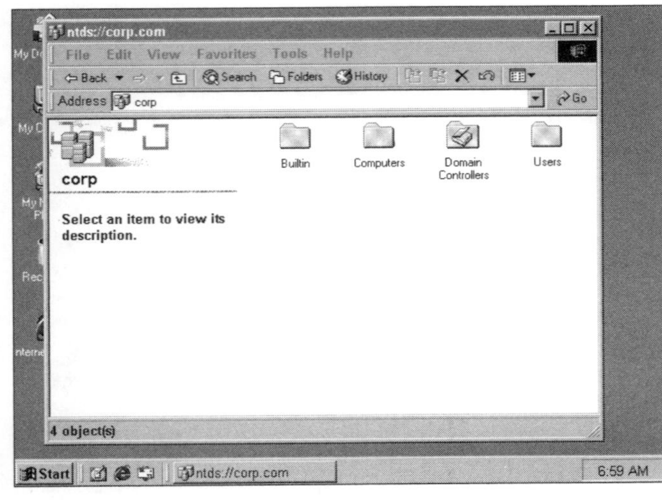

■ The Organizational Units (OUs) for the organization appear.

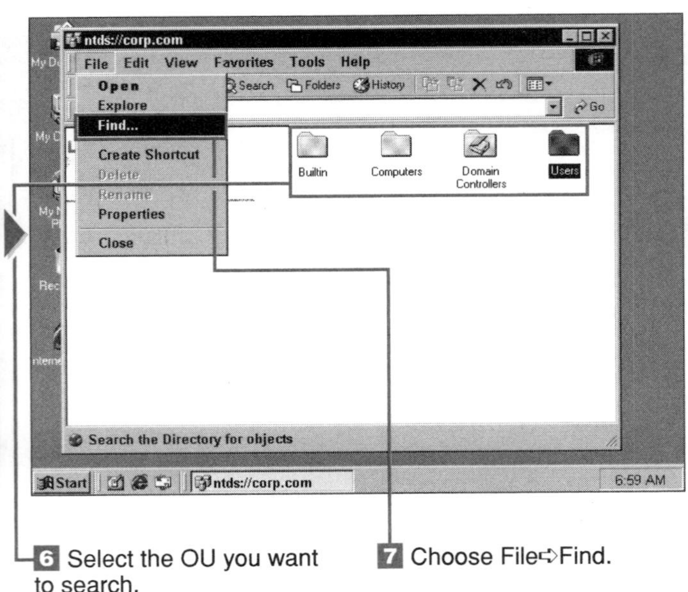

6 Select the OU you want to search.

7 Choose File⇨Find.

Do I have to find the OU in which an object is contained to search for it?

- No. This section of the book simply shows you an easy way to access the search window. After you access the search window, you can choose to search for any kind of object within the entire Active Directory as needed. The next section in this chapter shows you how.

I am in an Enterprise environment. Can I search the entire Enterprise or do I have to search each domain?

- You can search the entire Active Directory for your enterprise. Because the enterprise contains global catalog servers, which hold a "replica" of all Active Directory objects in the entire Active Directory, you can search the entire directory and the global catalog servers will find all objects that meet your search. Of course, in very large environments, narrow your search as much as possible so that you do not have too many match returns.

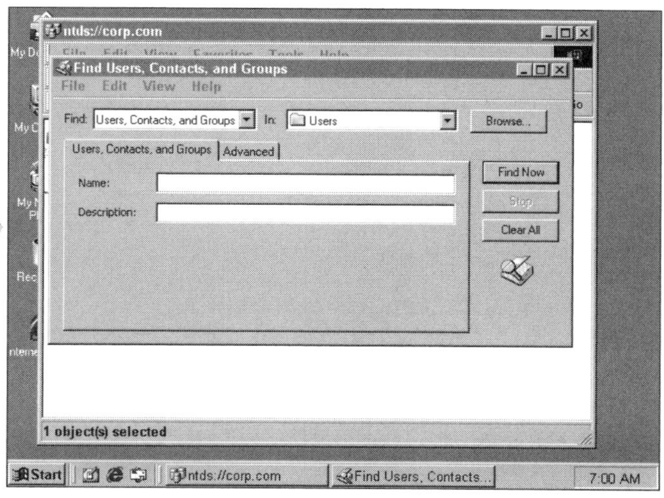

■ The search window appears.

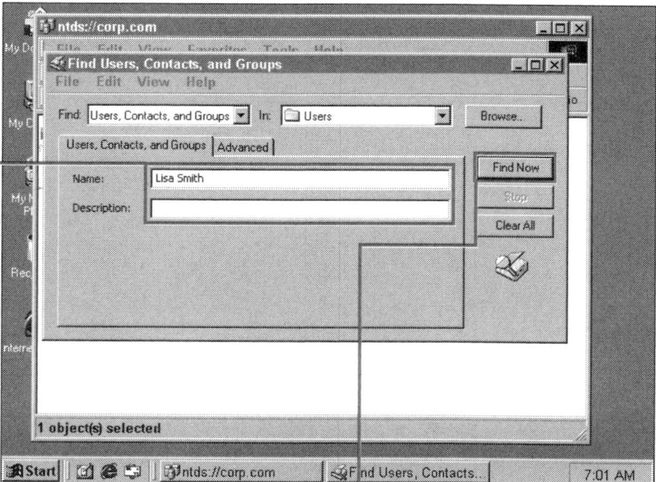

8 To search for the selected category, type a name or description

9 Click Find Now to begin the search.

UNDERSTANDING SEARCH WINDOW BASICS

From the search window, you can specify what Active Directory objects you want to search for and in what location. The In drop-down menu enables you to search for an Active Directory object within a particular container or domain, or you can choose to search the entire directory for the object.

The Find drop-down menu enables you to select the kind of object you want to search for, whether it's a user, folder, OU, printer, or any other Active Directory object. You can also choose to perform a custom search, which allows you to specify what you want to find by using LDAP keywords.

Essentially, the search window allows you to determine what you want to search for and where you want to search for it. You can search for objects at the entire Active Directory level, domain level, or OU level. This feature enables you to have a very broad or very narrow search as desired.

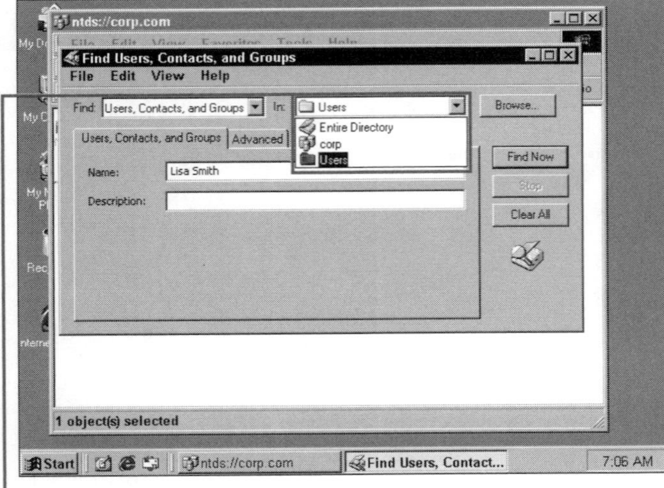

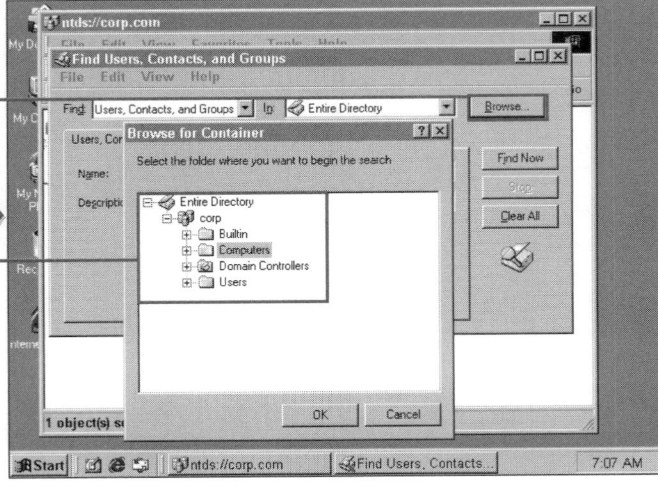

1 Open the Search window (see the previous task for instruction).

2 Click the In drop-down menu to select the location of your search.

■ You can search particular OUs, domains, or the entire directory.

3 If the desired location is not available, click Browse to browse for the specific OU or container you want to search.

Why do I have the option to search within a particular domain or container? Can't I just search the entire directory?

- Depending on the size of your organization, simply searching the entire directory for the resource you need may be easier. However, in large environments that contain multiple domains and even multiple sites, you can restrict your search to a particular area.

Why would I perform a search within an OU?

- An OU search is particularly useful if you know that a resource exists in a certain OU, but you do not know the name of the resource. For example, you may know that a certain printer exists in a particular OU, but you do not know the printer's name. You can use an OU search and simply look for "printers' to find the printer in the OU you want. If you searched the entire directory for the printer, you would have a much lengthier search return list you would have to sort through.

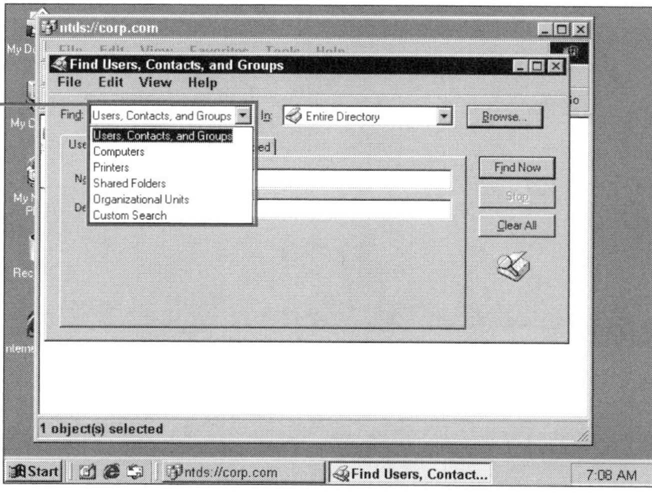

4 Click the Find drop-down menu to specify the kind of Active Directory object that you want to find.

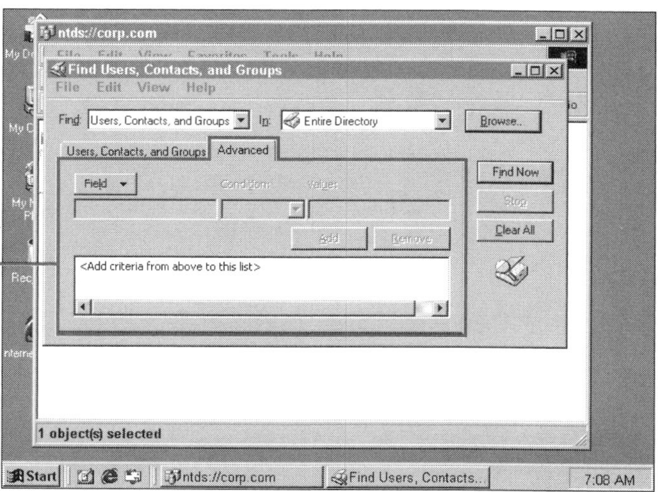

5 Optionally, use the Advanced tab to specify search criteria.

FINDING USERS, CONTACTS, AND GROUPS

The Active Directory contains powerful search capabilities to help you find users, contacts, and groups. To find a user, contact, or group, you use the Find drop-down menu and select Users, Contacts, and Groups.

You can also use the Advanced tab on the search window to set specific criteria for the search. This feature is useful when you do not know the specific name of an object, but you know some information about it. For example, if you are trying to find a user in the marketing department named John—but his first name is all you know—you can use the advanced search function to refine the search to look for all instances of "John" in the marketing department. This action is accomplished using fields, conditions for the fields, and a value for the search.

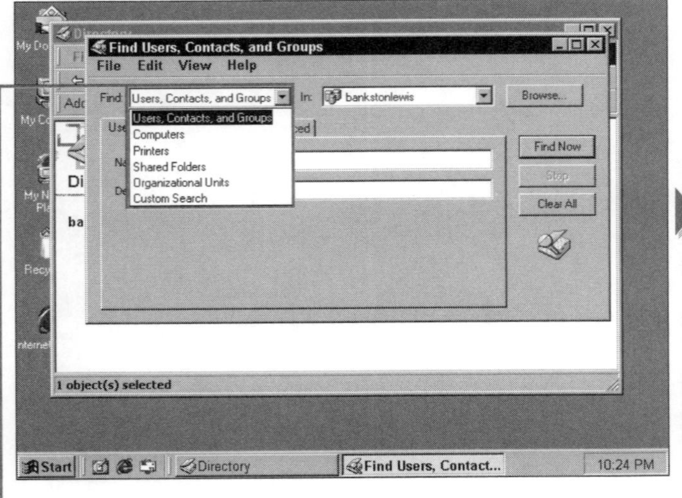

1 Click the Find drop-down menu and select Users, Contacts, and Groups.

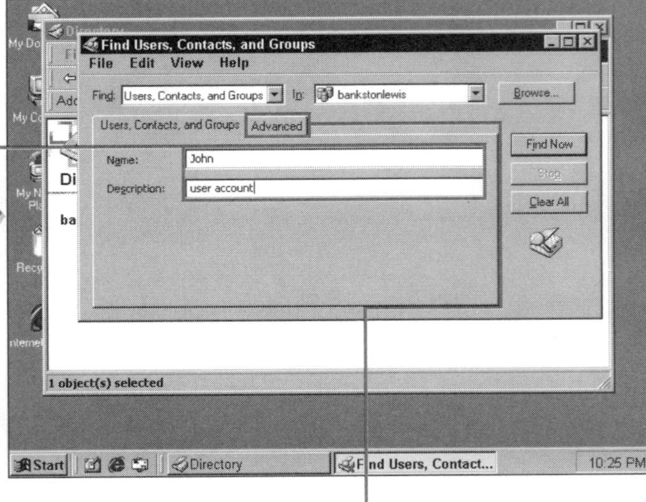

2 Type the name and a description for the search.

3 Click the Advanced tab.

Can I find a user in the Active Directory if I know only the user's e-mail address?

- Yes, by using the Advanced tab. Click the Field button, select User, and then select E-mail Address. If the e-mail address is exact and correct, select the Is (Exactly) condition, and then type the e-mail address in the value box. Click Add, and then click Find Now to find the user.

Can I find a group without knowing the exact name of the group or its location?

- Yes, by using the Field button. Select Group, and then select Description. In the Condition drop-down menu, select Starts With and then type a description in the Value box.

Can I find a user based on his or her initials?

- Yes. Click the Advanced tab, then in the Field value, select User, then select Initials. Use the Condition drop-down menu as needed, then enter the value, which is the person's initials. This search will return all user name initials that match your request.

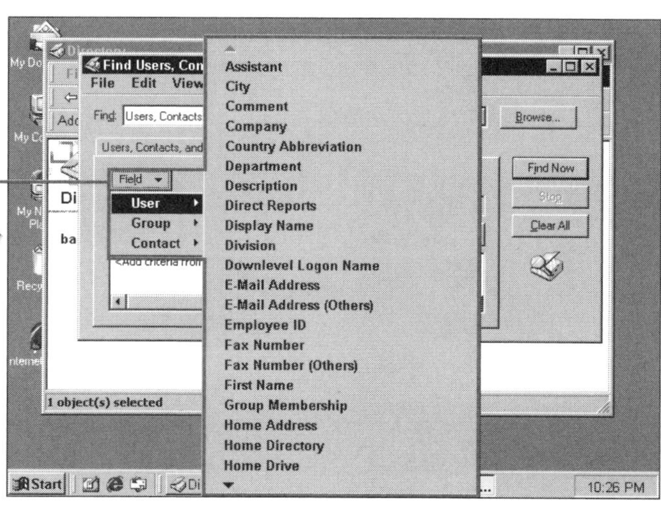

4 Click the Field button and select a desired field for the user, contact, or group search.

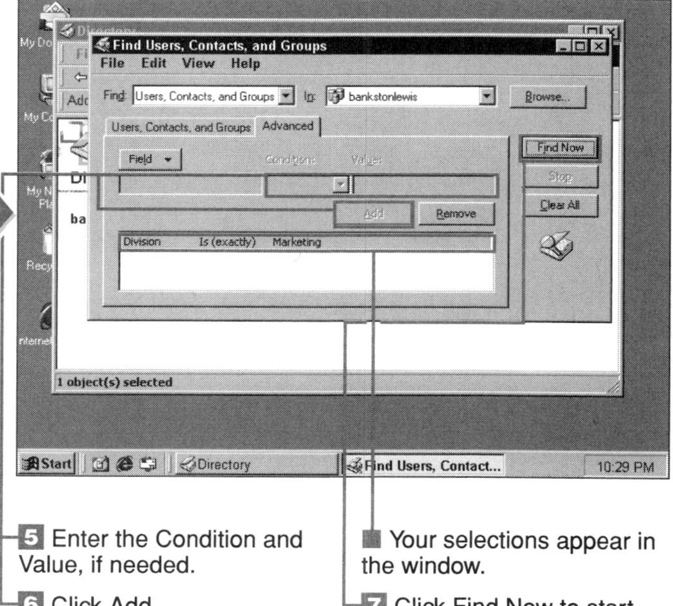

5 Enter the Condition and Value, if needed.

6 Click Add.

■ Your selections appear in the window.

7 Click Find Now to start the search.

FINDING COMPUTERS

You can use the Active Directory to find computers on your network. To find a computer, you use the Find drop-down menu and select Computers. You can use the Role drop-down menu to select the role (such as workstation, server, or domain controller) the computer plays on the network.

You can also use the Advanced tab on the search window to set specific criteria for the search. This feature is useful when you do not know the specific name or information about the computer, but you know some information that you can use for the search. For example, if you know of a computer managed by a particular person, but don't know the computer's name, you can use the advanced search function to refine the search so that it looks for all instances of computers managed by that person. This action is accomplished using fields, conditions for the fields, and a value for the search.

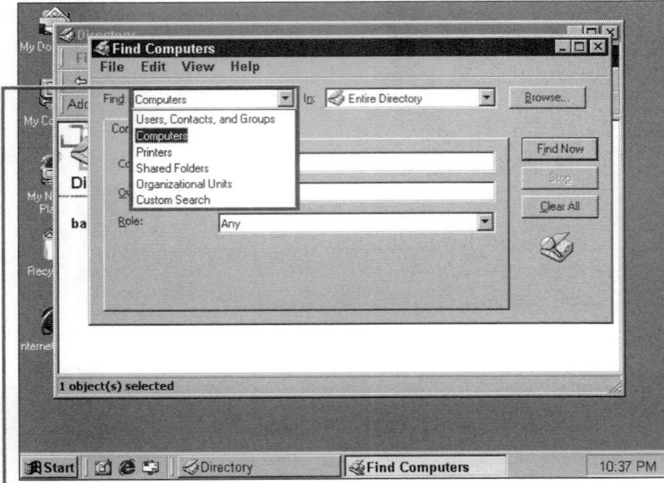

1 Click the Find drop-down menu and select Computers.

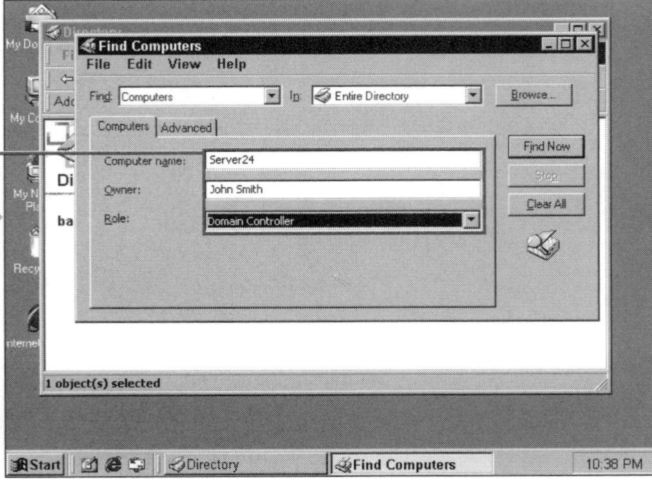

2 Enter the Computer name, Owner, and Role (if some of the information is unknown, you can leave the fields blank.

TIPS

How can I find a list of computers that are managed by a particular user?

- Select Computers from the Find drop-down menu, and then click the Advanced tab. In the Field drop-down menu, choose Managed By. In the Condition drop-down menu, choose Is (Exactly), and then in the Value dialog box, type the user's name. Click the Add button, and then click Find Now. The search function finds all the computers managed by that user.

I need to find all computers that run a certain operating system. Can I do this?

- Yes. Use the Advanced tab and select the Operating System field, then use the "is exactly" condition and enter the operating system in the Value dialog box. Click the Add button, then click Find Now. This action will find all computers running the specified operating system in either the entire directory or the domain or OU you select.

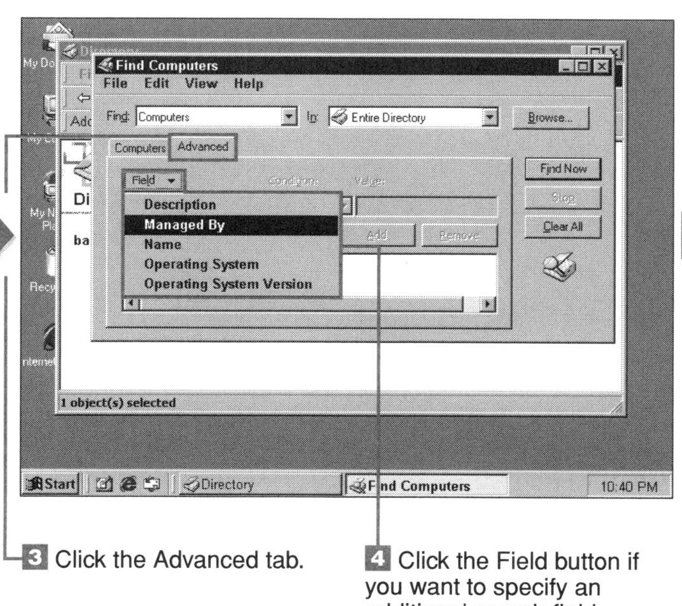

3 Click the Advanced tab.

4 Click the Field button if you want to specify an additional search field.

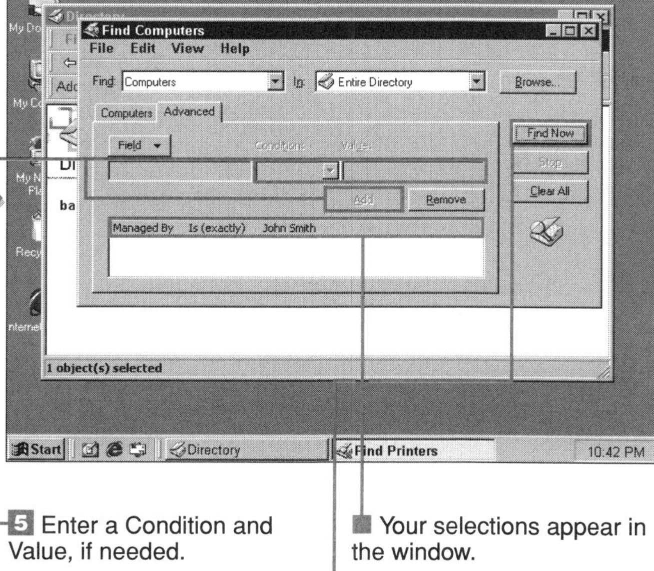

5 Enter a Condition and Value, if needed.

6 Click Add.

■ Your selections appear in the window.

7 Click Find Now to start the search.

FINDING PRINTERS

You can use the Active Directory to find printers on your network. To find a printer, you use the Find drop-down menu and select Printers.

On the Features tab, you can search for a printer by features. For example, you can look for color printers or printers that can staple, and so forth.

You can also use the Advanced tab on the search window to set specific criteria for the search. This feature is useful when you do not know the specific name or information about the printer, but you know some information that can be used for the search. For example, if you know of a printer that prints at a certain speed, you can use the advanced search function to refine the search to look for all instances of printers that print at that speed. This action is accomplished using fields, conditions for the fields, and a value for the search.

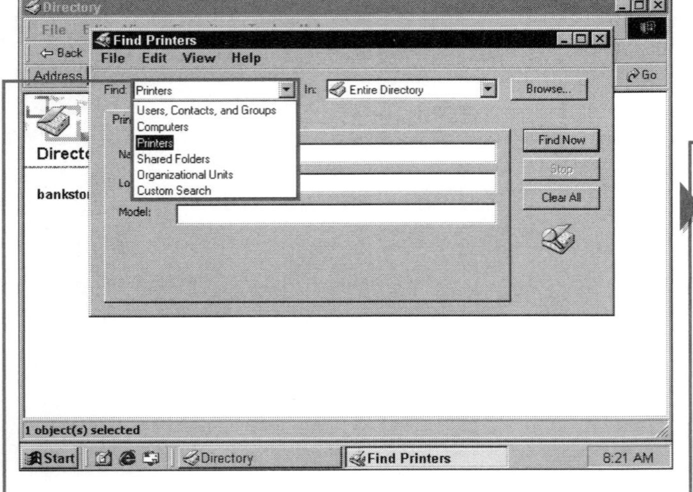

1 Click the Find drop-down menu and click Printers.

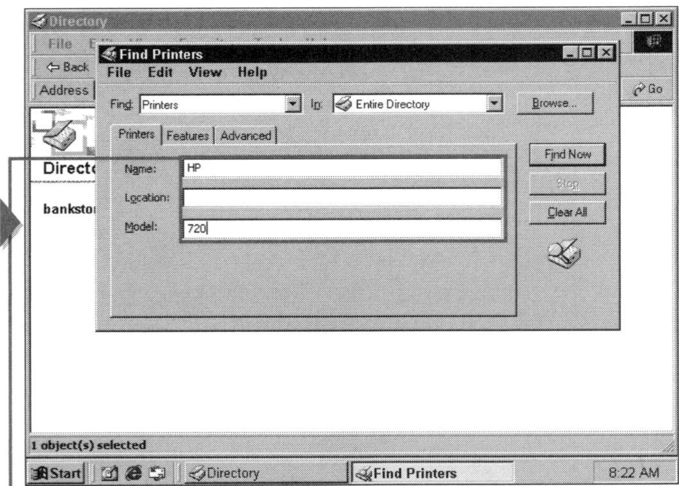

2 Enter a name, location, and model (if known) on the Printers tab.

I need to find a printer on my network that can print 12" x 11" size paper. How can I do this?

- Select Printers in the Find drop-down menu, and then click the Features tab. Click the Has Paper Size drop-down menu, and then select 12x11. Click Find Now. The search function finds all the Printers in the Active Directory that meet this requirement.

Can I search for printers that support double-sided printing?

- Yes. You can use the Features tab to select the Can Print Double-Sided check box and begin the search, or you can use the Advanced tab. On the Advanced tab, select the Supports Double-Sided Printing field, then select the Is TRUE condition, then click Add. You don't need a value for this search because the field is actually the value you are looking for. Click the Find Now button to begin the search.

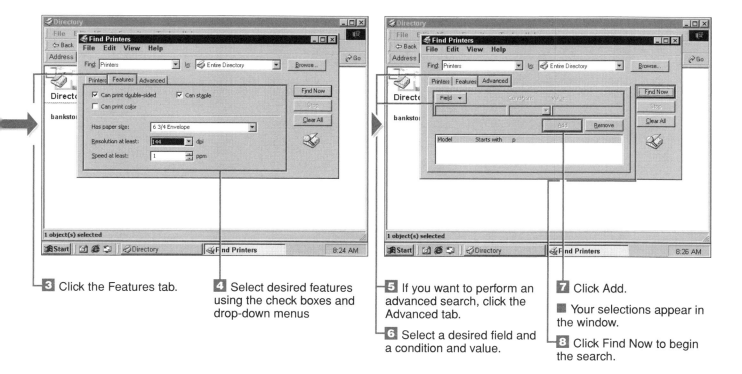

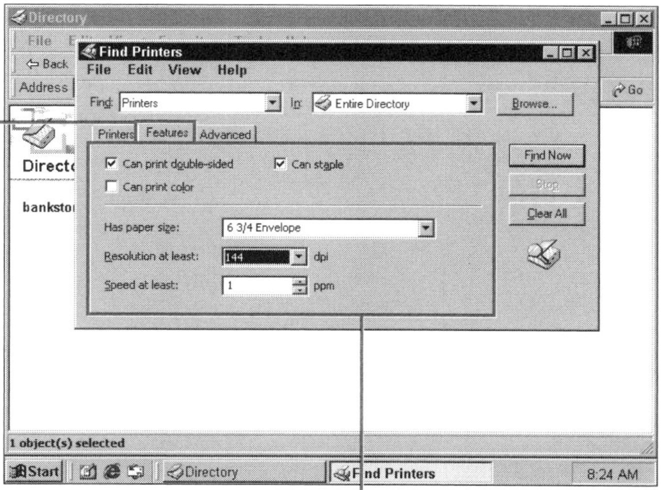

3 Click the Features tab.

4 Select desired features using the check boxes and drop-down menus

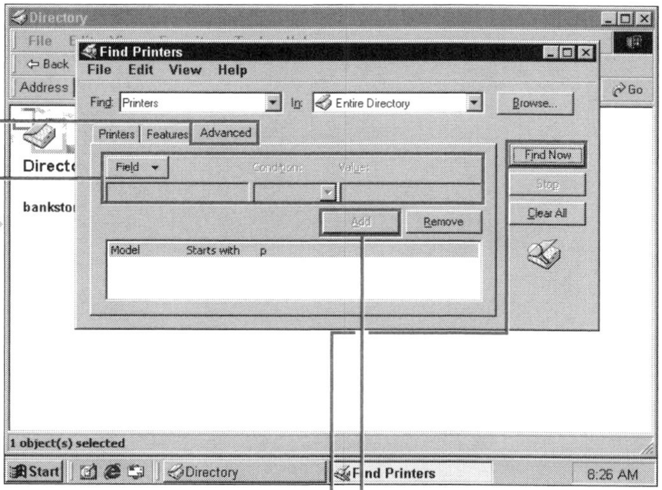

5 If you want to perform an advanced search, click the Advanced tab.

6 Select a desired field and a condition and value.

7 Click Add.

■ Your selections appear in the window.

8 Click Find Now to begin the search.

FINDING SHARED FOLDERS

You can use the Active Directory to find shared folders on your network. To find a shared folder, you use the Find drop-down menu and select Shared Folders.

You can also use the Advanced tab on the search window to set specific criteria for the search. This feature is useful when you do not know the specific name or information about the shared folder, but you know some information that you can use for the search. For example, if you know of a shared folder that contains company documents, you can use the advanced search function to refine the search to look for all instances of the keywords "company documents." This action is accomplished using fields, conditions for the fields, and a value for the search.

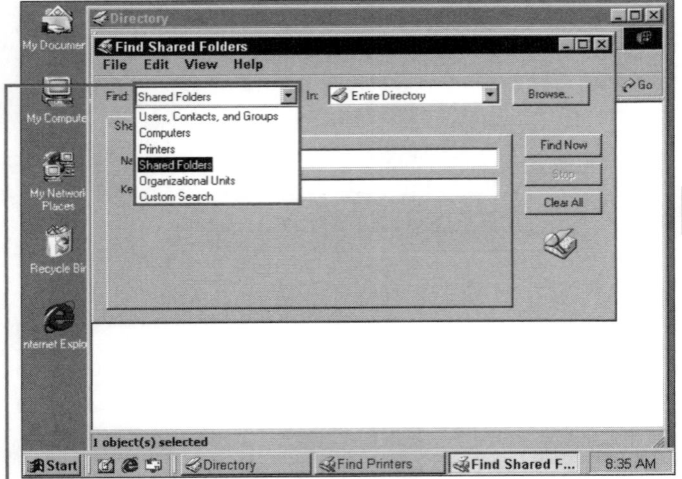

1 Click the Find drop-down menu and click Shared Folders.

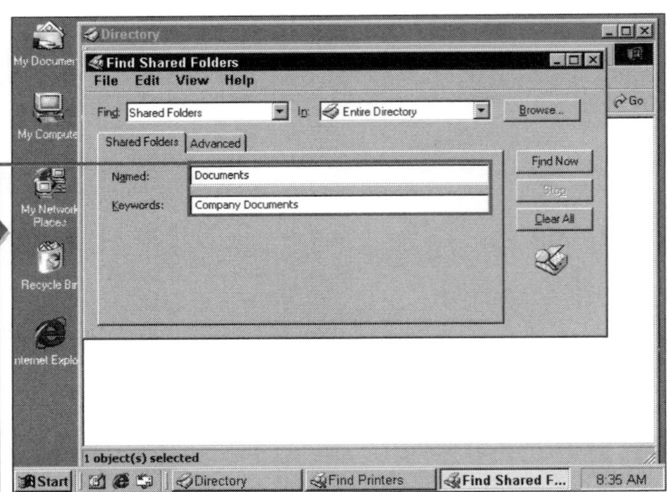

2 Enter a name and keywords for the folder search.

How can I use keywords to search for a shared folder?

- When a shared folder is added to the Active Directory, the administrator can enter keywords to help Active Directory users find the shared folder. For example, if a shared folder resides in the marketing department and contains marketing guidelines and related documents, the keywords for the folder could be *marketing*, *guidelines*, and *documents*. When a user searches for the folder using keywords, the matches for those keywords are retrieved so that the user can select which folder he or she wants to use.

Can I find a folder in the Active Directory using the Network Path?

- Yes. If you know the network path to a shared folder, such as \\server1\documents, you can use the Advanced tab and click Network Path from the Field drop-down menu. If you are certain that the network path is correct, use the Is (Exactly) condition, and then enter the network path in the Value box. Click the Add button and then click Find Now.

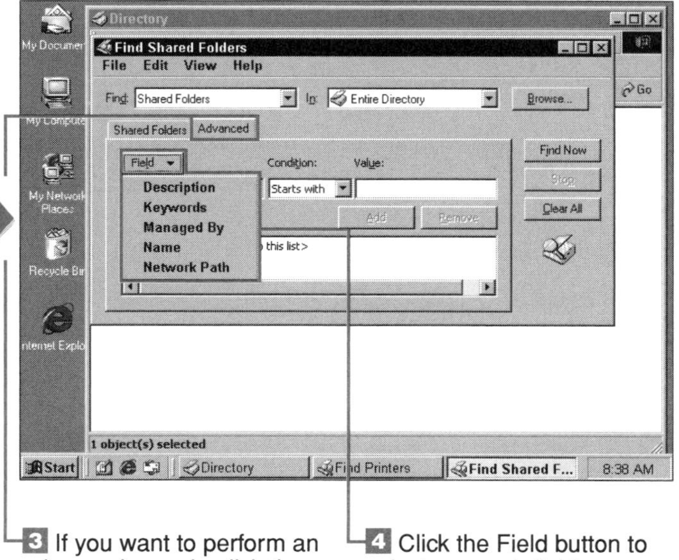

3 If you want to perform an advanced search, click the Advanced tab.

4 Click the Field button to select a search field.

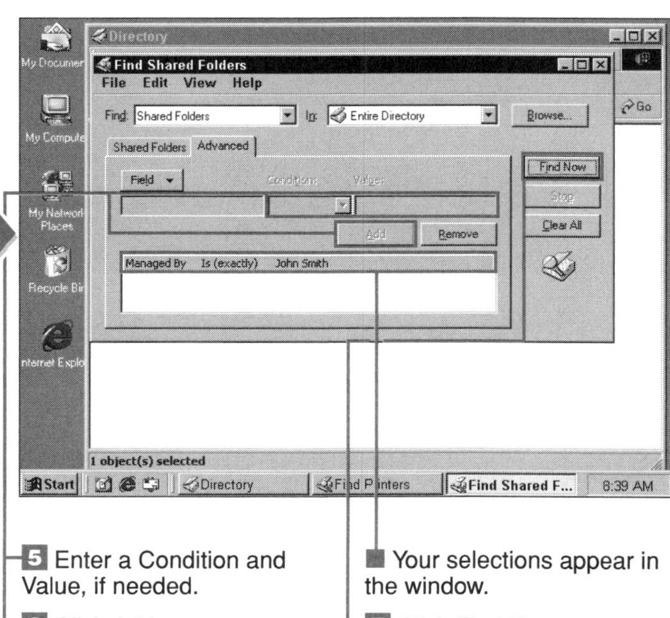

5 Enter a Condition and Value, if needed.

6 Click Add.

■ Your selections appear in the window.

7 Click Find Now to start the search.

FINDING ORGANIZATIONAL UNITS

You can use the Active Directory to find organizational units (OUs) by either using the browse button, or by using the Find menu and searching for them as you would any other object. Click the Find menu and select Organizational Units, then you can search for the OU by name on the Organizational Units tab.

You can also use the Advanced tab on the search window to set specific criteria for the search. This feature is useful when you do not know the specific name or information about an OU, but you know some information that you can use for the search. For example, if you know of an OU managed by John Smith, but you do not know the name of the OU, you can use the advanced search function to refine the search so that the it looks for all instances of OUs managed by John Smith. This action is accomplished using fields, conditions for the fields, and a value for the search.

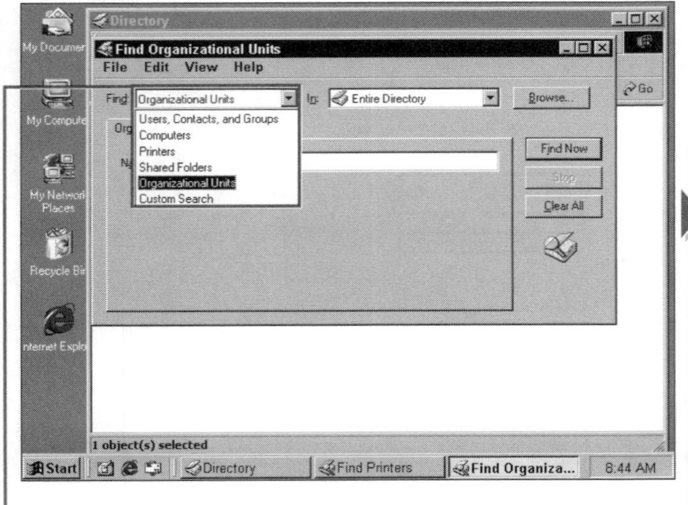

1 Click the Find drop-down menu and click Organizational Units.

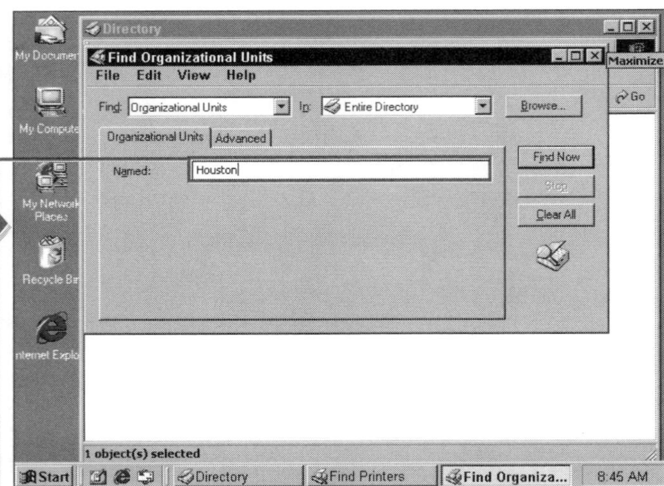

2 Enter a name for the OU search.

Why would I want to find an Organizational Unit?

You can use the Browse button to browse the domain structure and find an OU, or you can locate an OU by using the Active Directory search function. In complex environments, this feature may be useful to locate a particular OU for which you only know the manager or some details. If you do not know the name of the OU, you cannot find it by browsing, so the search function is included to allow you to find the OU.

Can I find an OU if all I know is a description?

Yes. Use the Advanced tab and select the Description field. Then, use either the Starts With condition or the Is Exactly condition, then enter a description in the Value box. Be as specific as possible. Click the Add button, then click Find Now to begin the Active Directory search.

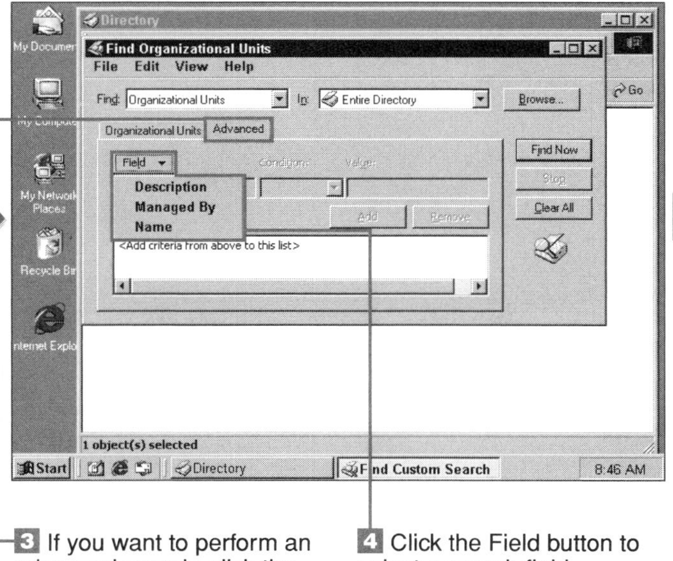

3 If you want to perform an advanced search, click the Advanced tab.

4 Click the Field button to select a search field.

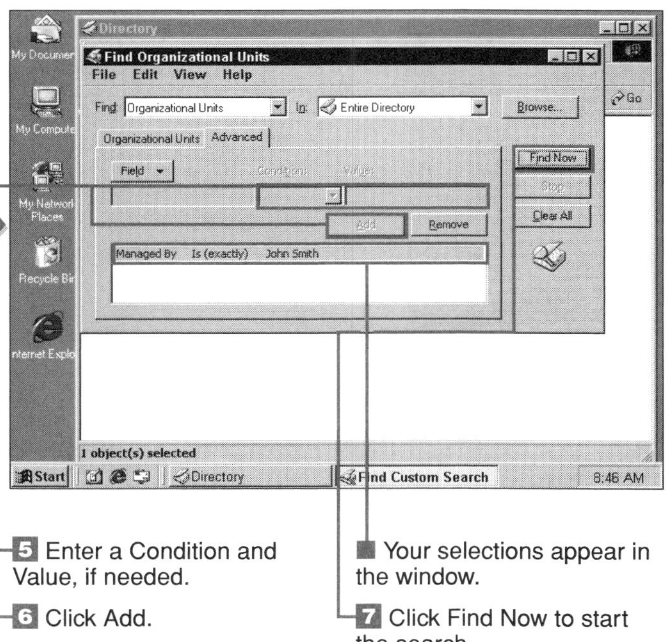

5 Enter a Condition and Value, if needed.

6 Click Add.

■ Your selections appear in the window.

7 Click Find Now to start the search.

CREATING A CUSTOM SEARCH

The Active Directory allows you to create a custom search. To perform a custom search, you select Custom Search from the Find menu, which provides you with a Custom Search tab and an Advanced tab.

The Custom Search tab allows you to set specific criteria for the search. This feature is useful when you do not know the specific name or information about an object, but you know some information that you can use for the search. The fields available in the Custom Search basically give you every Active Directory object you may want to find and detailed fields about each.

On the Advanced tab, you can run an LDAP query where you simply type the search string. This can be any combination of words and the Active Directory will look for a match using your query.

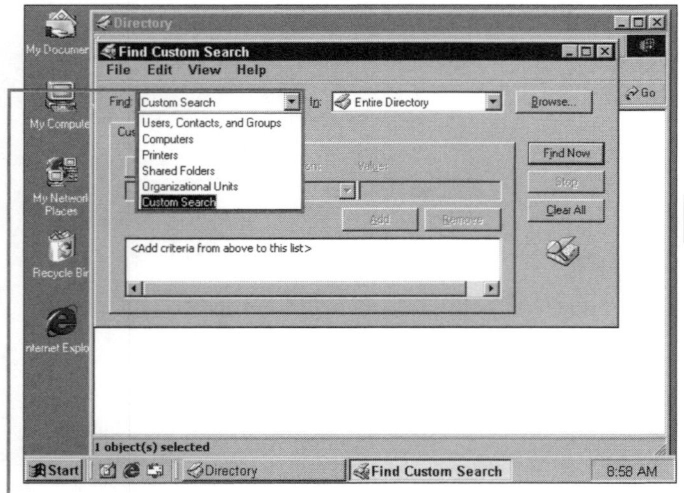

1 Click the Find drop-down menu and click Custom Search.

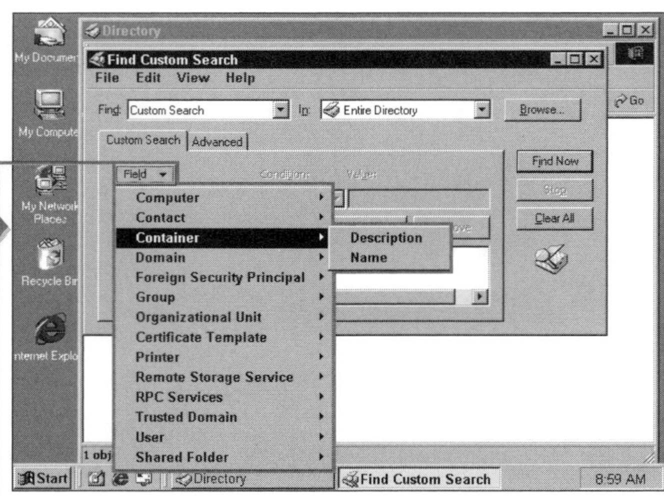

2 Click the Field button to select a search field.

What is the purpose of a custom search?

- The custom search option enables you to select from a greater list of Active Directory objects, some of which are not available in the other Find categories. This feature allows you to search for an Active Directory object that is closest to what you actually need. By using the Custom Search option, you can search for domains, Certificate Templates, RPC Services, and so forth.

What is an LDAP search?

- An LDAP search, which is available on the Advanced tab of the Custom Search, enables you to perform a simple text search for the object you want to find. The search function uses the words you type in and attempts to locate Active Directory objects that contain the same words or keywords.

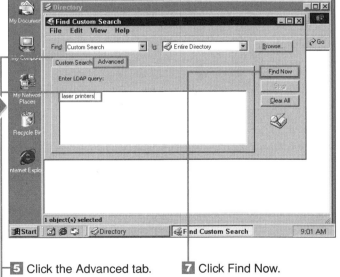

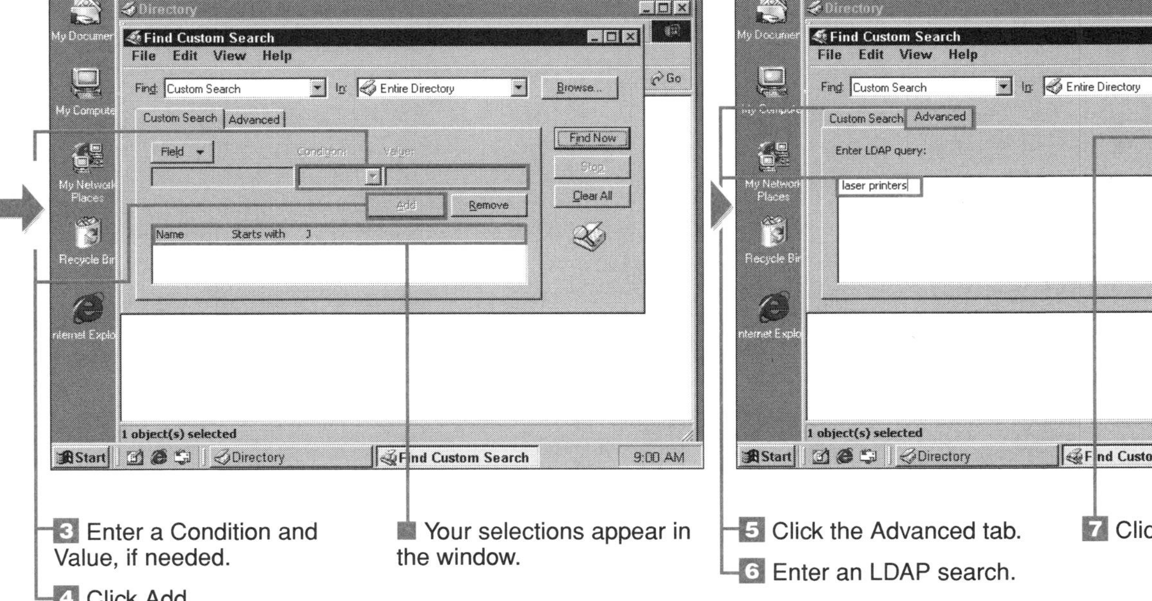

3 Enter a Condition and Value, if needed.

4 Click Add.

■ Your selections appear in the window.

5 Click the Advanced tab.

6 Enter an LDAP search.

7 Click Find Now.

SECTION V

14) CREATING AND MANAGING USER ACCOUNTS

15) CREATING AND MANAGING GROUP ACCOUNTS

16) CREATING AND MANAGING COMPUTER ACCOUNTS

USERS, GROUPS, COMPUTERS

17) CREATING AND MANAGING OUS AND OBJECTS

18) MANAGING ACTIVE DIRECTORY DOMAIN CONTROLLERS

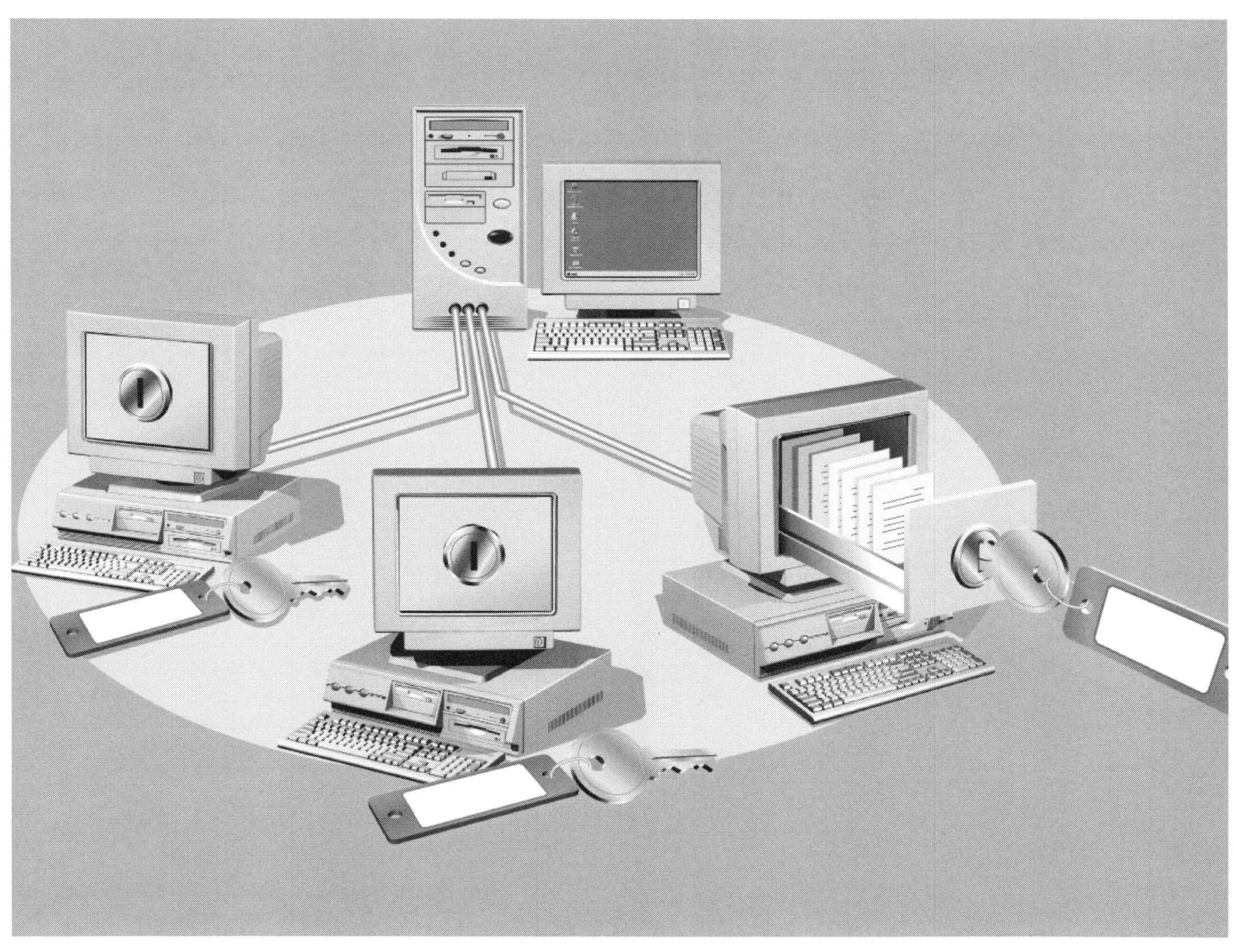

ACCESSING THE USERS AND COMPUTERS SNAP-IN

All Active Directory configuration concerning users and computers is performed in the Active Directory Users and Computers MMC snap-in.

This snap-in is one of the three main Active Directory MMC snap-ins that you use to configure and manage the Active Directory. From this interface, you can manage user, group, and computer accounts, and you can also manage some aspects of domain controllers that appear in the directory. All objects and OUs are configured with this snap-in.

Within the Active Directory Users and Computers snap-in, the Action menu gives you a list of tasks you can accomplish for each object, OU, container, computer, and domain.

Most of your everyday Active Directory tasks are performed with this snap-in, including the creation of your OU structure (see Chapter 10).

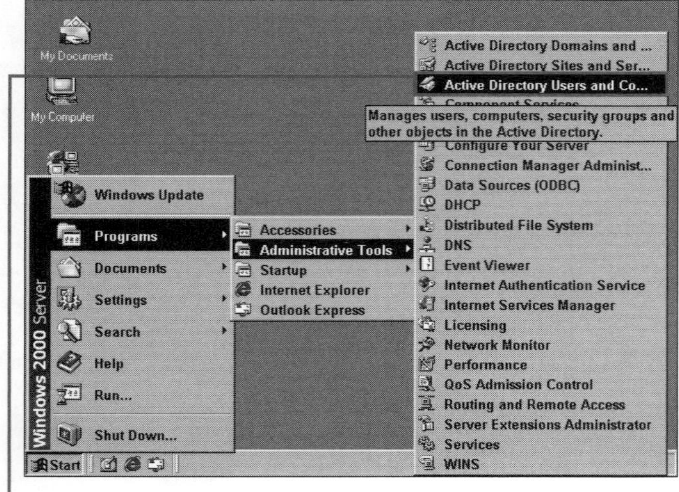

1 Choose Start⇨ Programs⇨Administrative Tools⇨ Active Directory Users and Computers.

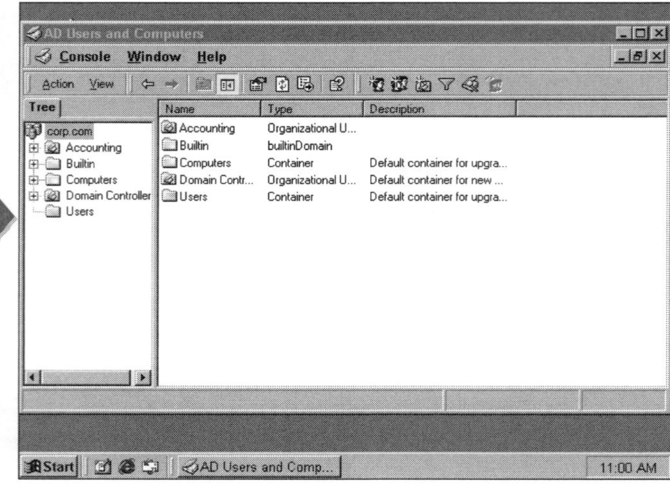

■ The console appears listing your domain and OUs.

Is there another way to access the Active Directory Users and Computers snap-in?

- The Active Directory snap-ins appear in Administrative Tools, which you can access using the Start menu. You can also open Control Panel and open the Administrative Tools folder to access the snap-in. Finally, you can click Start⇨Run and then type **MMC** in the dialog box. An empty MMC opens. Click the Console menu, and then click Add/Remove Snap-in. Click Add on the screen that appears, and then select the Users and Computers snap-in from the list that appears.

I need to create OUs for this domain. How can I do that?

- You can create OUs for your domain by using this snap-in. For specific instructions, see Chapter 17 and also review Chapter 10 to learn about developing an OU structure.

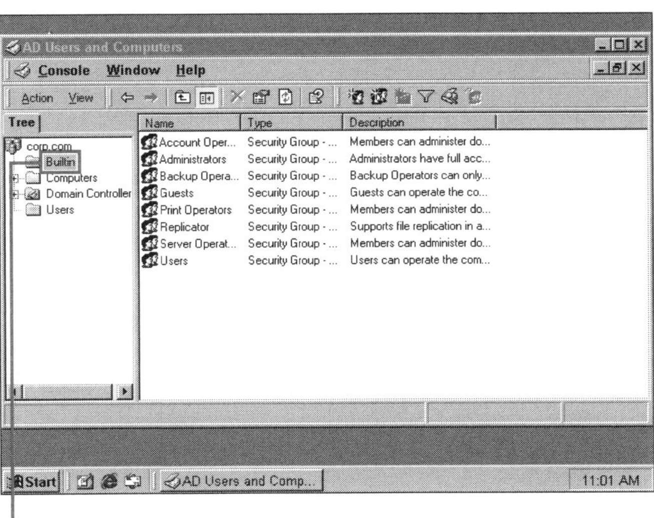

■ If you click one of the OUs in the left pane, the contents of the OU appear in the right pane.

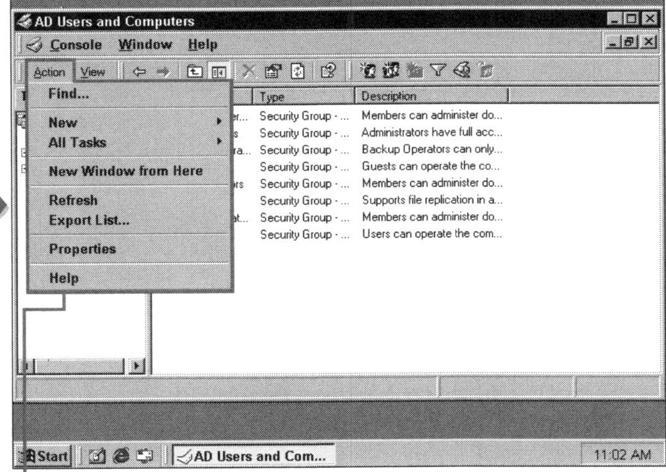

■ The Action menu presents you with configuration actions that you can take for each domain, OU, and object.

CREATING A NEW USER ACCOUNT

Domain users are created in the Active Directory from an Active Directory domain controller. Domain users are both created and managed by using the Active Directory Users and Computers MMC snap-in, which provides one simplified interface for managing users. If you are used to working with Windows NT, you have probably searched for User Manager for Domains, which is no longer a part of Windows 2000. All user accounts are configured for your Active Directory domains using this snap-in.

Creating a user account is really no different in Windows 2000 than it has been in previous versions of Windows. You provide a username for a specified user and a default password. The New User window displays both the Active Directory username, such as **`Jwilliams@alpharun.com`** and the down-level name, or NetBIOS, name for earlier versions of Windows, such as Jwilliams.

After you determine a default password, you can choose whether the user must change the password at the next logon, whether the password expires, and so forth.

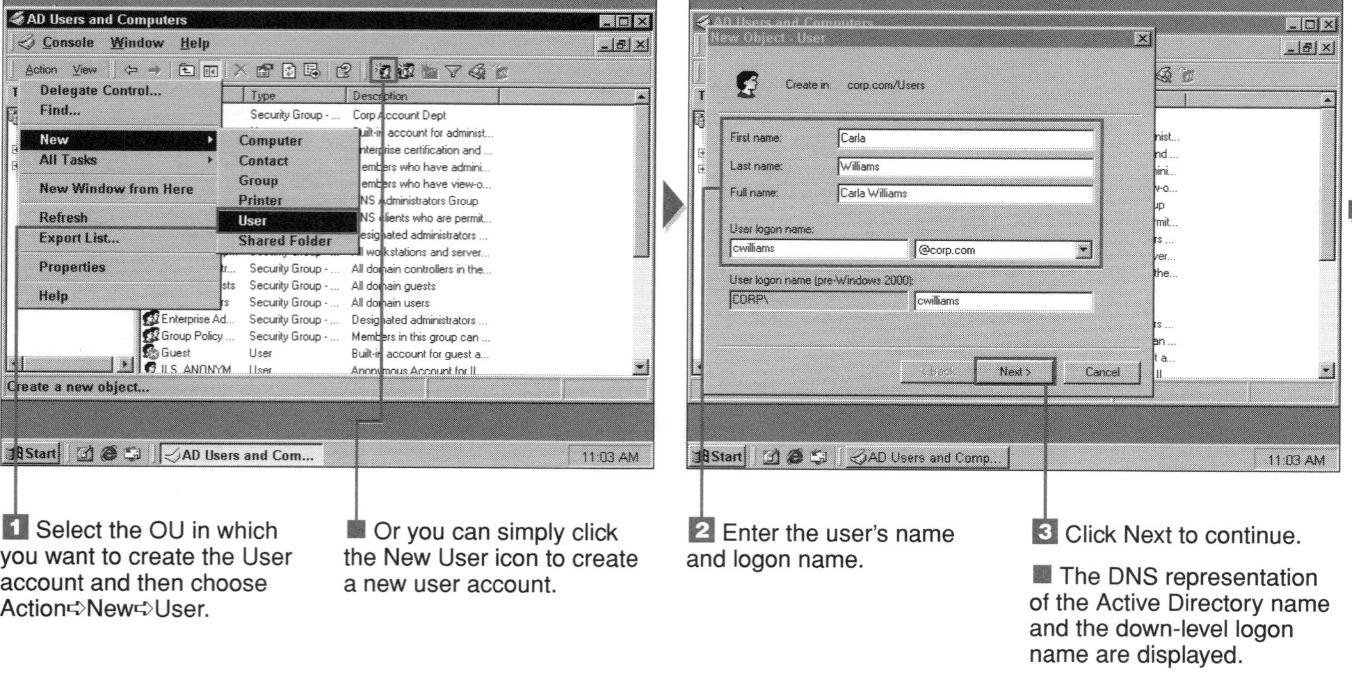

1 Select the OU in which you want to create the User account and then choose Action⇨New⇨User.

■ Or you can simply click the New User icon to create a new user account.

2 Enter the user's name and logon name.

3 Click Next to continue.

■ The DNS representation of the Active Directory name and the down-level logon name are displayed.

What logon convention should I use?

- Most network environments implement a standard logon naming convention, such as a first initial and last name (`ksmith`) or first name and last initial (`karens`). This is done for administrative purposes.

What password should I enter and what requirements should I use for the password?

- Normally, the administrator enters a standard password, such as the user's logon name, and then requires the user to change the password at the next logon by checking the appropriate box. However, in certain cases, the administrator may want to assign a password and select the "User cannot change password" and "Password never expires" check box options.

What password parameters should be required?

- Users should be required to create passwords of minimum lengths—five or six characters provides higher security than shorter passwords. Also, users should not use the names of family members or common words for passwords. Finally, a password combination of letters and numbers is the most secure approach.

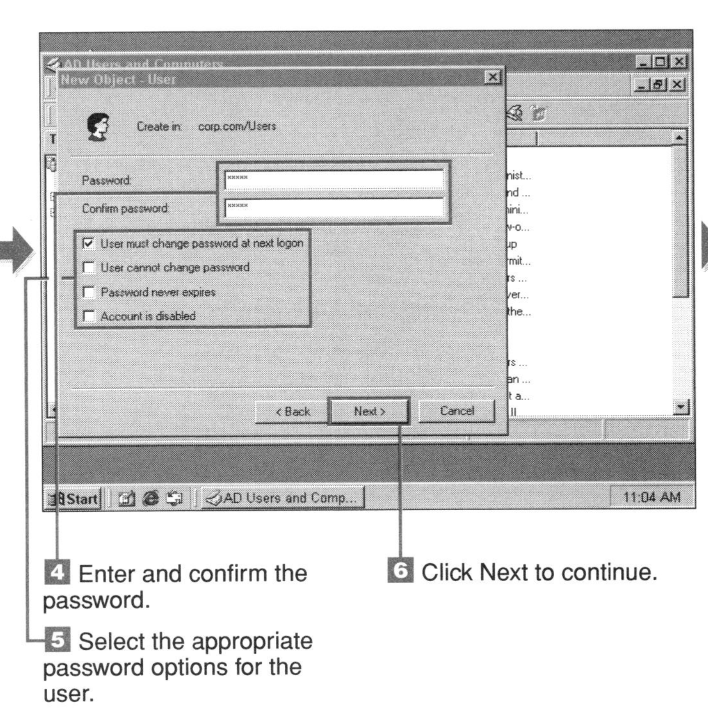

4 Enter and confirm the password.

5 Select the appropriate password options for the user.

6 Click Next to continue.

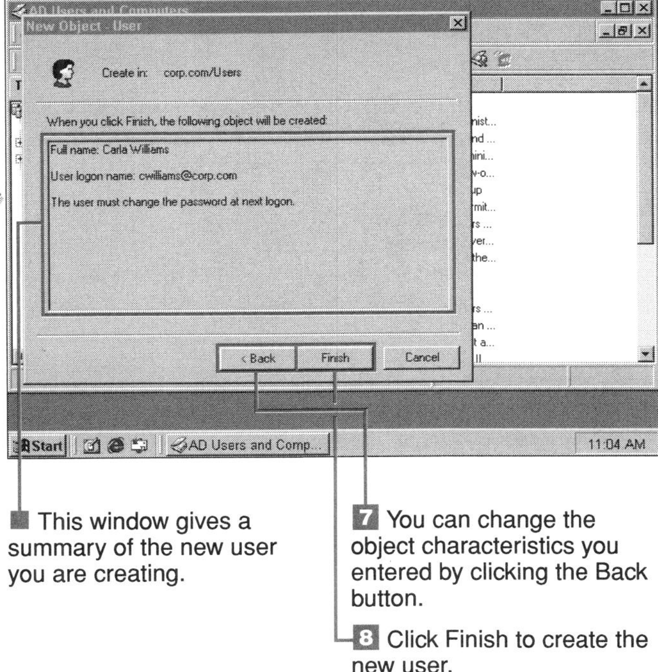

■ This window gives a summary of the new user you are creating.

7 You can change the object characteristics you entered by clicking the Back button.

8 Click Finish to create the new user.

CONFIGURING USER ACCOUNT PROPERTIES

After you create a new user account, you can further define the user's properties. As you create and configure user accounts, you will notice you have a lot of options available. Remember that the configuration options presented in the Properties pages are not specifically required for the user account to become active. In other words, all you have to do is create the account and assign a default password for the user to be able to log on.

The General and Address tabs enable you to configure contact information for the user, such as the user's phone numbers and address information. This information helps users locate and contact other users in the Active Directory. Some environments choose to provide complete information on these tabs and others only provide phone numbers. This is an administrative decision and not one that affects the functionality of the user's account in the Active Directory.

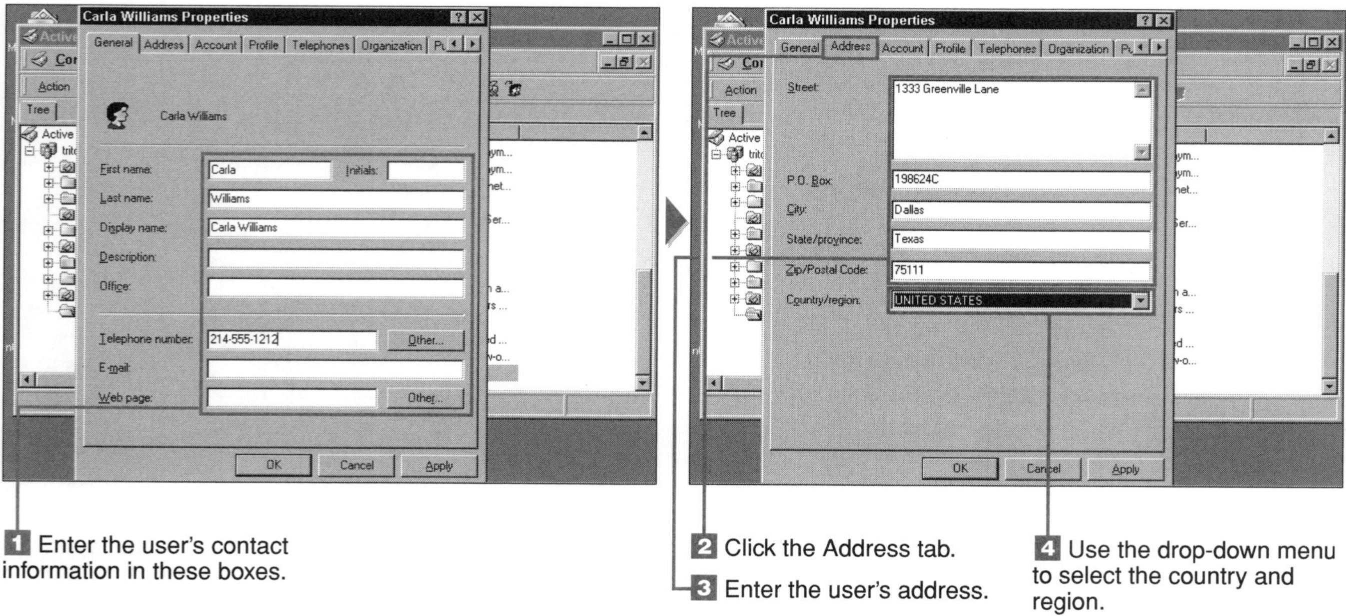

1 Enter the user's contact information in these boxes.

2 Click the Address tab.

3 Enter the user's address.

4 Use the drop-down menu to select the country and region.

Some of your most important configuration options for user accounts appears on the Account tab. The account tab allows you to determine when the user can logon and to which computer the user can logon. Depending on the security structure of your environment, you may wish to restrict users' logon hours. This action prevents users from gaining access to the network during certain times of the day (such as at night). This is a security feature for both your users and for persons who may try to gain access to the network with a valid user name and password.

In a similar manner, you can restrict users to only certain computers. This action stops a user from gaining access to the network from any computer available. As with logon hours, this too is an effective security feature.

With both of these options, it is important, however, that you are not so restrictive that you prevent users from accomplishing their jobs effectively.

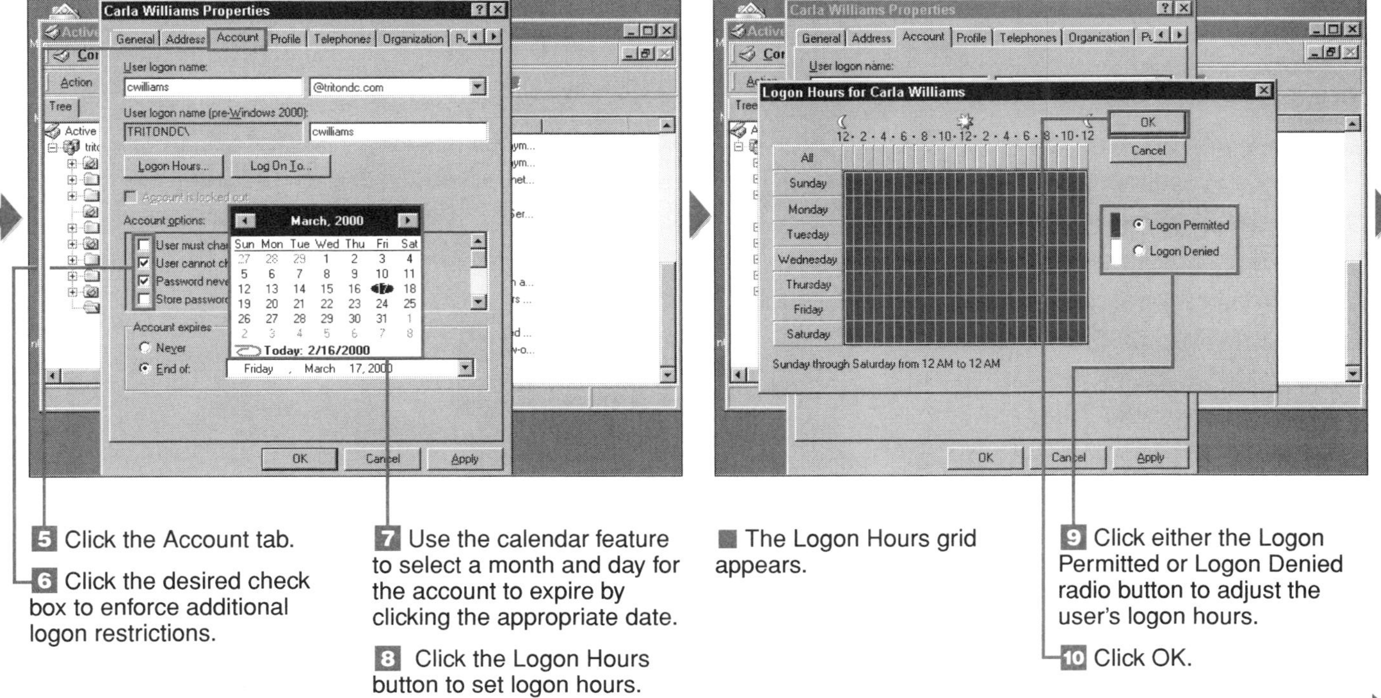

5 Click the Account tab.

6 Click the desired check box to enforce additional logon restrictions.

7 Use the calendar feature to select a month and day for the account to expire by clicking the appropriate date.

8 Click the Logon Hours button to set logon hours.

■ The Logon Hours grid appears.

9 Click either the Logon Permitted or Logon Denied radio button to adjust the user's logon hours.

10 Click OK.

CONTINUED

CONFIGURING USER ACCOUNT PROPERTIES CONTINUED

Aside from the importance of the Account tab configuration, you also have the Profile tab where you can enter a profile or home folder path if profiles are in effect for your environment. Profiles are useful to control user accounts and grant or restrict privileges. You can also control user accounts using the powerful features of Group Policy, which you can learn about in Chapter 24.

The Telephones and Organization tabs may seem somewhat repetitive to other tabs, but they simply enable you to list more information about the user. In environments where users have multiple phone numbers, as in the case of a mobile user or one who works from home, the Telephones tab gives you another way to give this information to Active Directory users. Likewise, you can also list very specific information about the user's employment position on the Organization tab.

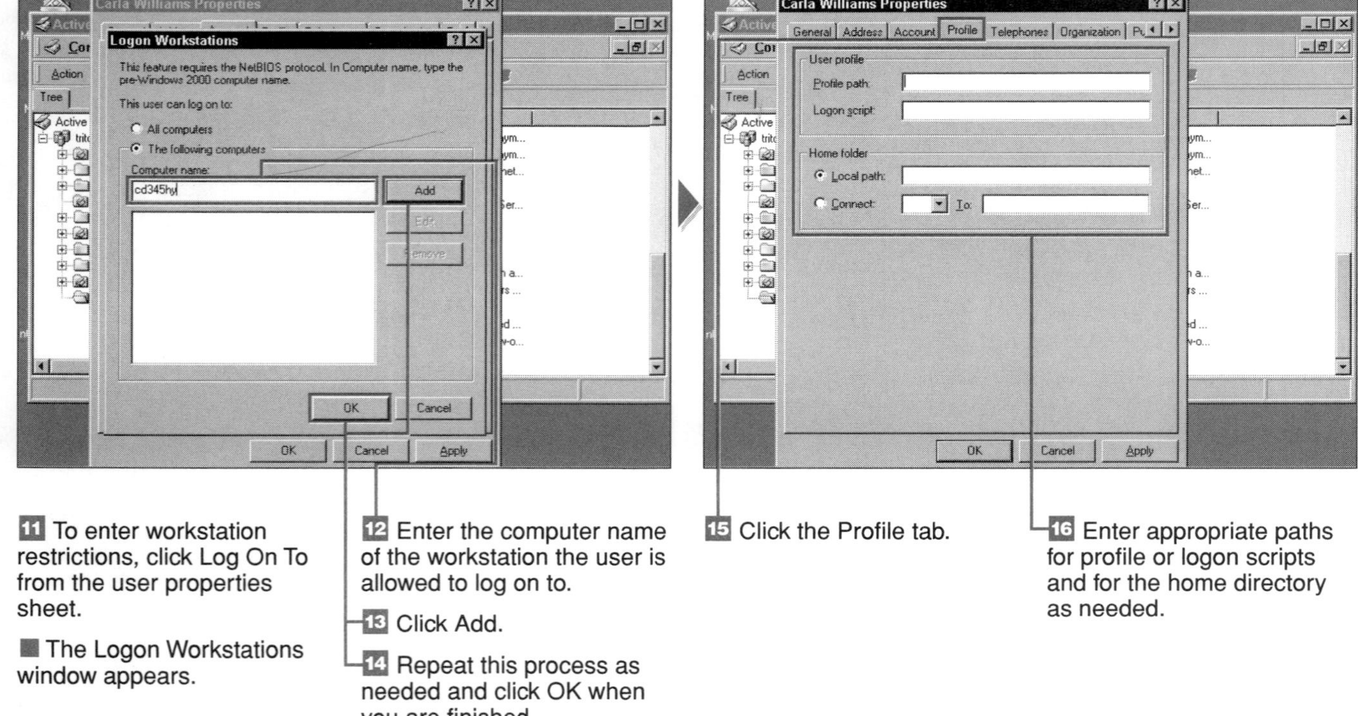

11 To enter workstation restrictions, click Log On To from the user properties sheet.

■ The Logon Workstations window appears.

12 Enter the computer name of the workstation the user is allowed to log on to.

13 Click Add.

14 Repeat this process as needed and click OK when you are finished.

15 Click the Profile tab.

16 Enter appropriate paths for profile or logon scripts and for the home directory as needed.

Should users be restricted to certain workstations?

- Depending on the design and security needs of your organization, you may want to restrict certain users so that they can log on only to certain workstations. This is a security feature that may or may not be needed in your environment. For example, you may need to restrict certain users to certain computers within a certain part of building. The workstation restriction feature prevents users from logging onto the network anywhere in the office.

How can I use the Comments box on the Telephone/Notes tab

- You can use the Comments box to point out useful contact information about the user. For example, if Sally works from home every Tuesday and Thursday, you can place a note in the Comments box instructing users to contact Sally at her home number on those days.

How can I enter the name of the user's manager?

- The user's manager has to have a user account in the Active Directory to be listed on the Organization page. Click the Change button, which opens the Active Directory, and select the manager's user account.

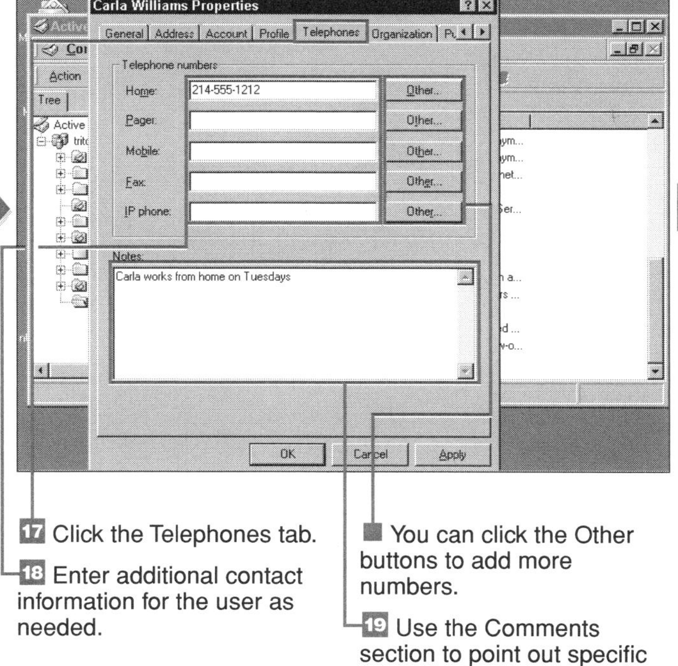

17 Click the Telephones tab.

18 Enter additional contact information for the user as needed.

■ You can click the Other buttons to add more numbers.

19 Use the Comments section to point out specific contact information concerning the user.

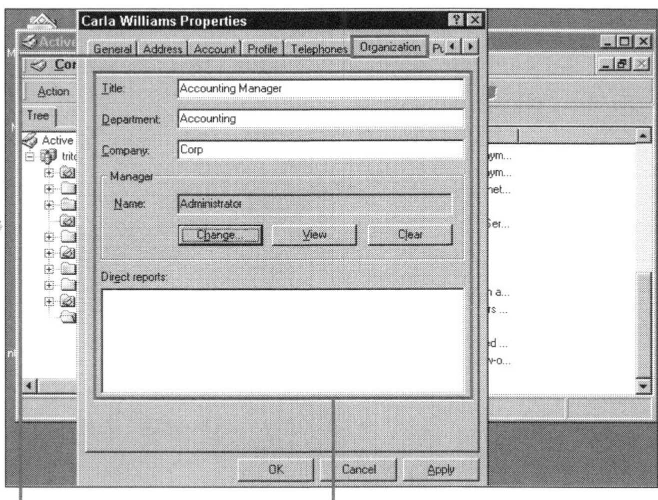

20 Click the Organization tab.

21 Enter organizational information about the user as well as the user's manager and other individuals who report to the user.

CONTINUED

CONFIGURING USER ACCOUNT PROPERTIES CONTINUED

Finally, you also see a Member Of tab and a Dial-in tab. The Member Of tab allows you to add or remove groups to which the user account belongs. This tab enables you to easily configure group membership for user accounts.

The Dial-in tab allows you to grant or deny dial-in access to network clients. For clients using Remote Access to gain access to the network from a remote computer, you can either allow or deny access and configure callback options. As in Windows NT, each user must be allowed to gain dial-in access on this tab. In other words, no user has automatic rights for dial-in.

Depending on your server configuration and the services available on your network, other tabs (such as those for Terminal Services) may appear as well. Although these services are not a part of the Active Directory, they still appear as a configuration option on the user's account properties pages.

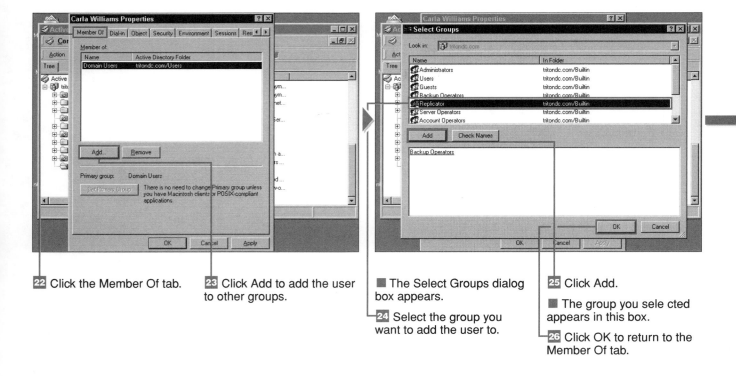

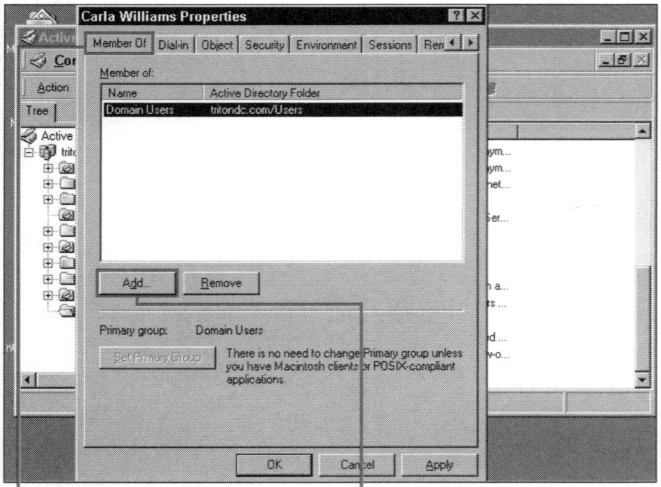

22 Click the Member Of tab.

23 Click Add to add the user to other groups.

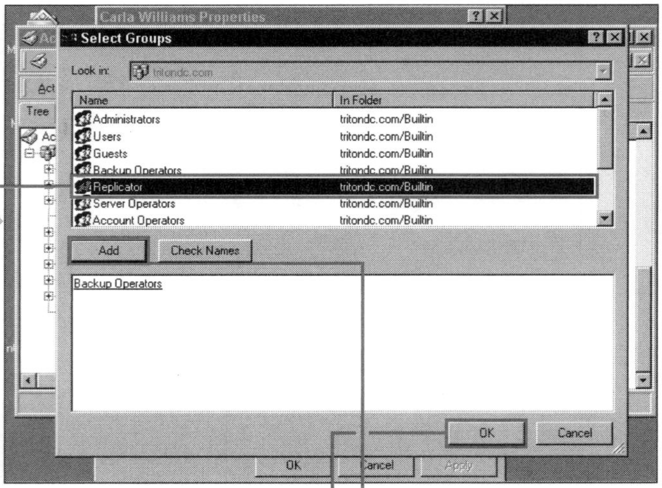

■ The Select Groups dialog box appears.

24 Select the group you want to add the user to.

25 Click Add.

■ The group you sele cted appears in this box.

26 Click OK to return to the Member Of tab.

Should I add every user to groups?

- Groups are designed to organize users and reduce administrative overhead. You can use groups to configure permissions that give the group members access rights to certain resources. This design enables you to configure the permissions one time for the group instead of on an individual basis.

What is the difference between dial-in and Virtual Private Network (VPN)?

- Dial-in allows a client to dial in to a RAS server and gain access to network resources from a remote location. VPN also allows clients to dial in, but with a VPN, packets are encapsulated and routed over a public network, such as the Internet. Depending on the security configuration of Windows 2000 Server, the VPN can also provide encryption of data.

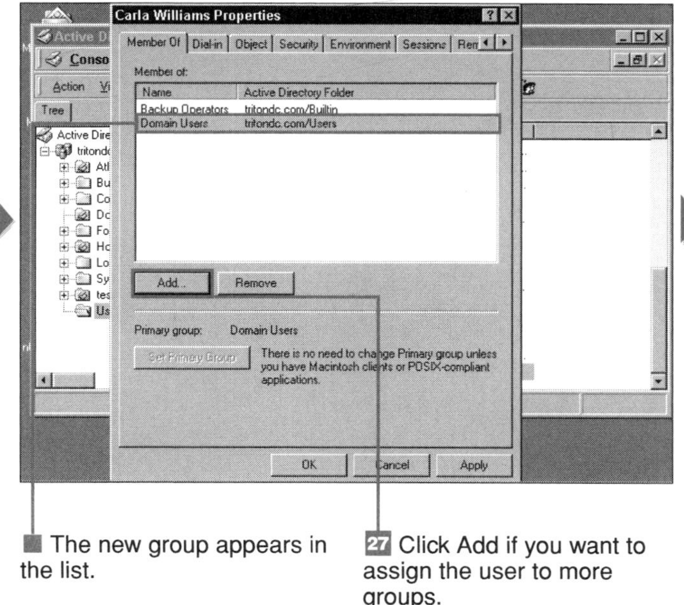

■ The new group appears in the list.

27 Click Add if you want to assign the user to more groups.

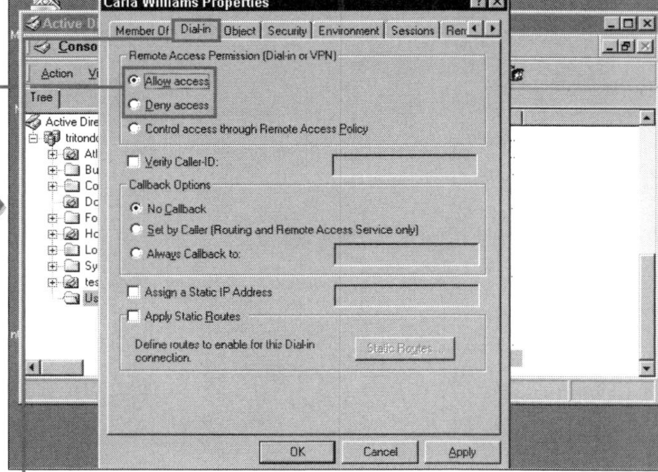

28 Click the Dial-in tab.

29 Click the appropriate radio button to allow or deny dial-in access.

■ Depending on your routing and remote access configuration, you can assign a callback feature and provide a static IP address and route for the user when dialing in.

MANAGING A USER'S ACCOUNT

Aside from configuring an account's properties, you can also manage each account by using the Action menu.

First, you can easily disable the account by selecting Disable Account. When you perform this action, a red X appears over the account's icon. In the same manner, you can enable an account that has been disabled. You can also reset the password, move the account, open the home page, or send an e-mail message to the user if these options are configured in the user's properties.

If you click All Tasks, you see a repeat of the same tasks that appear at the top of the window. You have the options to delete, rename, or refresh the account as well. Windows 2000 provides the All Tasks option, which you can also see by right-clicking the User Accounts icon, so you can configure these options either through the Action menu or by using a simple right-click.

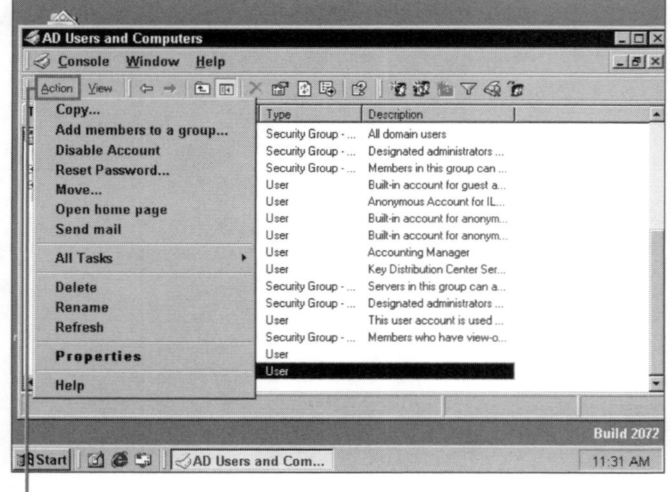

1 Select the user account in the console and click the Action menu.

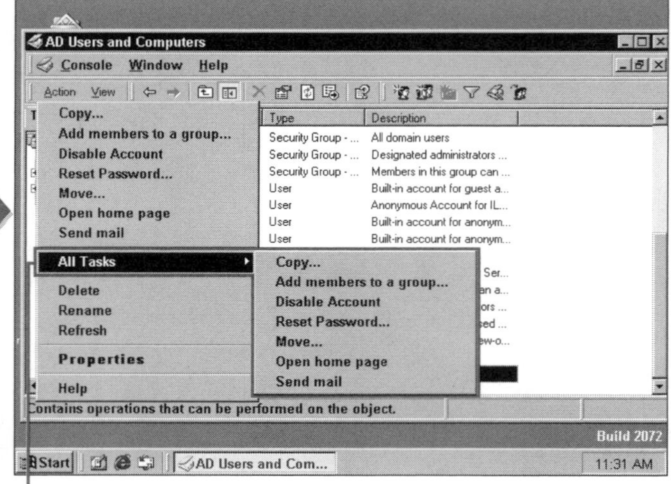

■ The All Tasks option contains the same actions you can perform from the Action menu or by right-clicking the User Accounts icon.

Why would I need to disable an account?

- You can easily disable an account by choosing Disable Account from the Action menu. You may need to perform this action for a variety of reasons. For example, if a company employee takes a leave of absence, you may want to disable the employee's account until he or she returns. This action increases network security.

What happens if I click Send Mail?

- You can send a user an e-mail by clicking Send Mail. When you do this, the user's e-mail account is read from the user's properties and your default mail client opens with a new mail message directed to the user. You can then type your message and send it to the user.

If I rename an account, is the logon name changed as well?

- No. If you rename an account, you are simply renaming the object in the Active Directory. This action does not alter the user's logon name or other information in the user's properties.

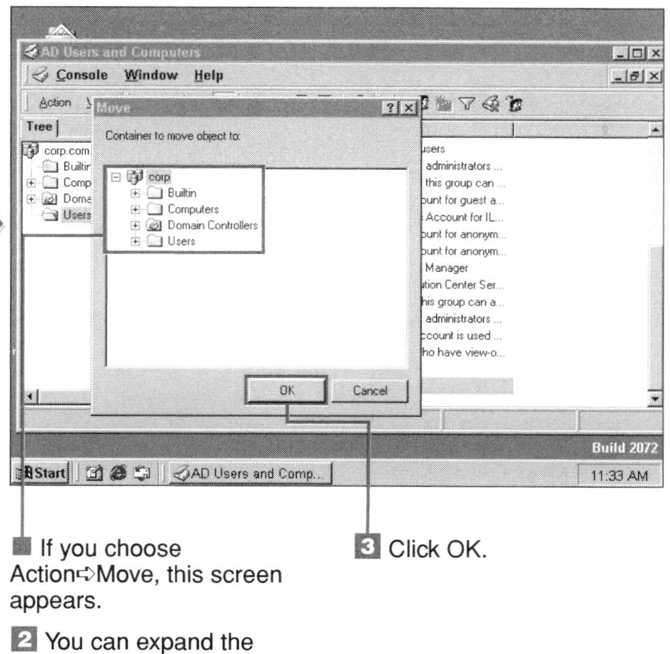

■ If you choose Action⇨Move, this screen appears.

2 You can expand the directory folders to select where you want to move the account

3 Click OK.

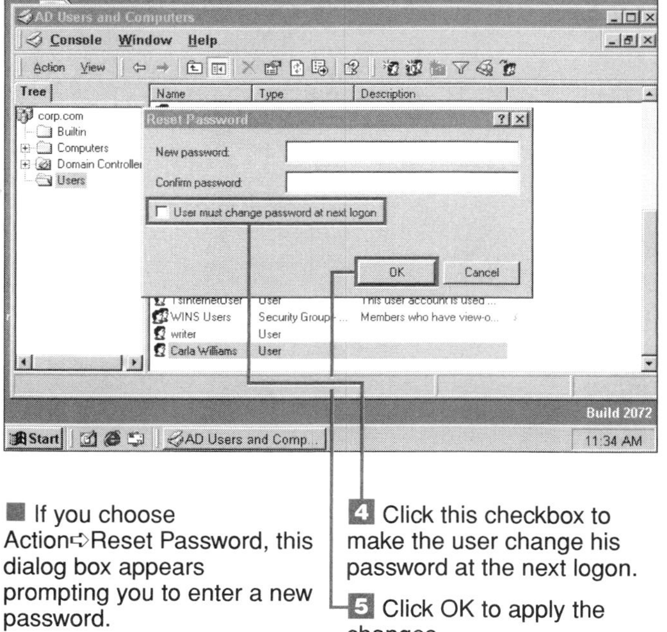

■ If you choose Action⇨Reset Password, this dialog box appears prompting you to enter a new password.

4 Click this checkbox to make the user change his password at the next logon.

5 Click OK to apply the changes.

DELEGATING CONTROL OF A USER ACCOUNT OU

You can easily delegate control of user accounts or groups by selecting the OU that holds the user accounts. You cannot delegate control of an individual user account or group account, and when you delegate control of an OU, the delegate is given administrative rights to manage the accounts in that OU.

When you perform this action, you allow another user or a group of users to control certain user accounts or other groups. Depending on the design of your organization, this may be an effective solution to reducing overhead for senior administrators.

Delegation is a powerful tool that allows you to assign certain administrative tasks to other users you select. For example, you can allow a certain employee to create user accounts, but not configure or delete them. Using this tool, you can tailor your administrative needs to reduce administrative overhead while still maintaining the security of your network and your administrative control.

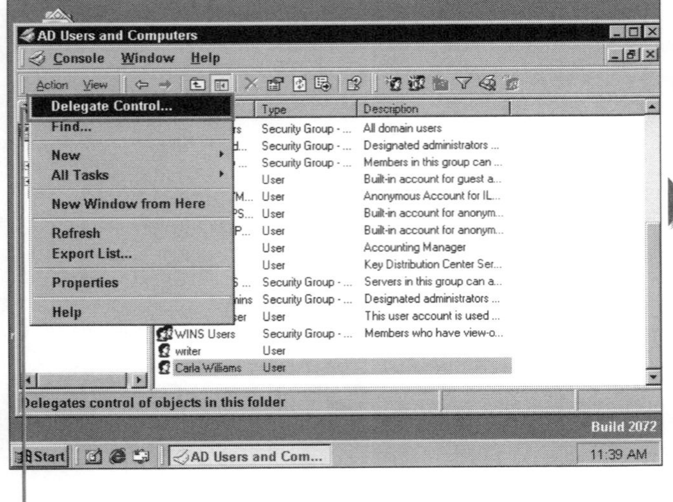

1 Select the OU you want to delegate and choose Action⇨Delegate Control.

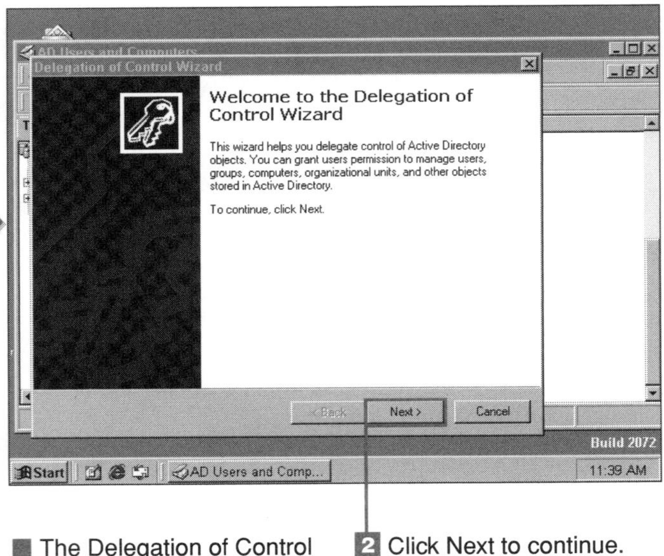

■ The Delegation of Control Wizard begins.

2 Click Next to continue.

Should I delegate control to several groups or users?

- This is normally not a good idea. Only a select few should have delegation control so that only those few can make administrative changes to the delegated folder.

When I delegate control, do I have to give the delegate full control over the OU?

- No. Delegation is a powerful tool in Windows 2000 because you can give other users or groups administrative permissions, but you do not have to "turn over" all the rights and permissions. As a network administrator, you can delegate some permissions while denying others. For example, you could allow a delegate to create user accounts, but not reset passwords. By using the delegation wizard, you can finely control what your delegates can do.

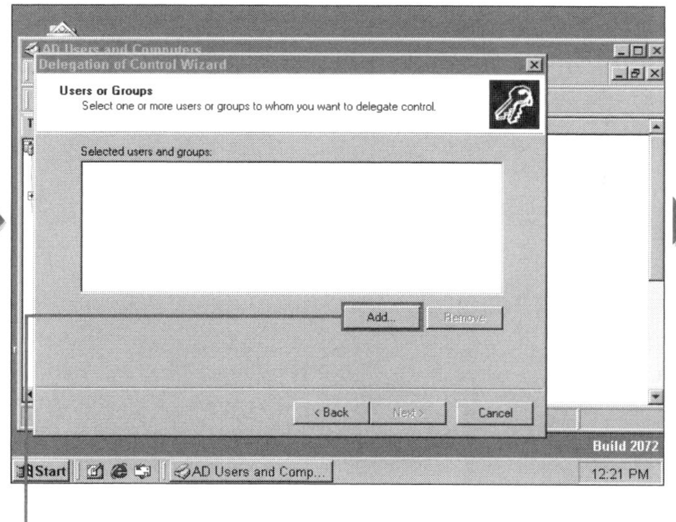

3 Click Add to select the users or groups you want to delegate to.

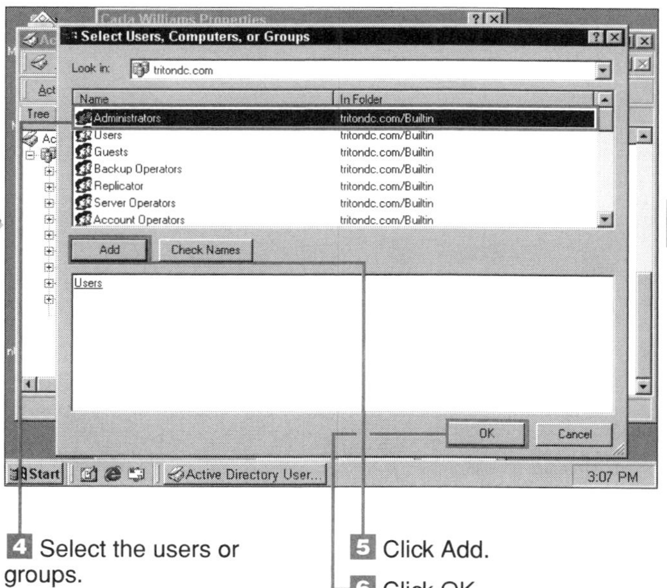

4 Select the users or groups.

5 Click Add.

6 Click OK.

CONTINUED

DELEGATING CONTROL OF A USER ACCOUNT OU CONTINUED

When you delegate control, you can choose to delegate either predefined tasks or a custom task. From the predefined tasks, you can select the check boxes you want to delegate control. The predefined options include typical tasks, such as creating, deleting, and managing user accounts.

Make selections that give the delegate the power he or she needs to perform the task you assign. However, do not give a delegate more power than needed. For example, if you do not want the delegate to manage group membership, do not assign that permission.

You can define standard permissions, such as full control, read, write, and so on. But, you can also finely control what the delegate can do, such as manage child objects, delete child objects, and so on. Delegation is another example of how the Active Directory enables you to fine-tune your configuration to meet the needs of your network.

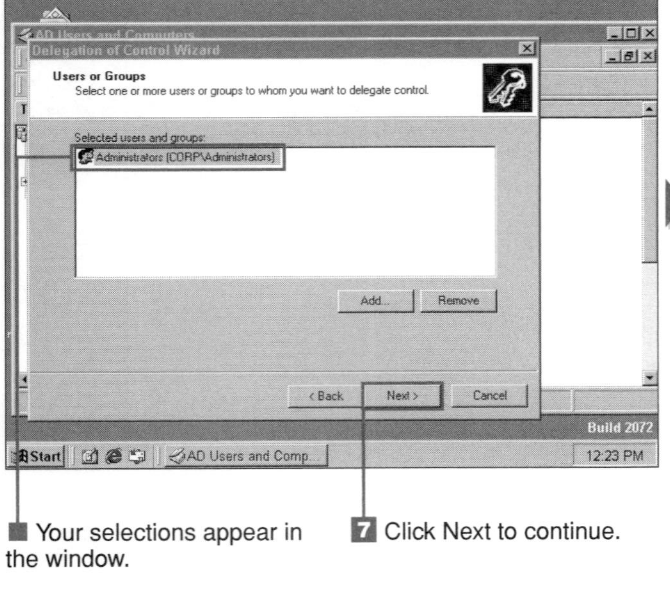

■ Your selections appear in the window.

7 Click Next to continue.

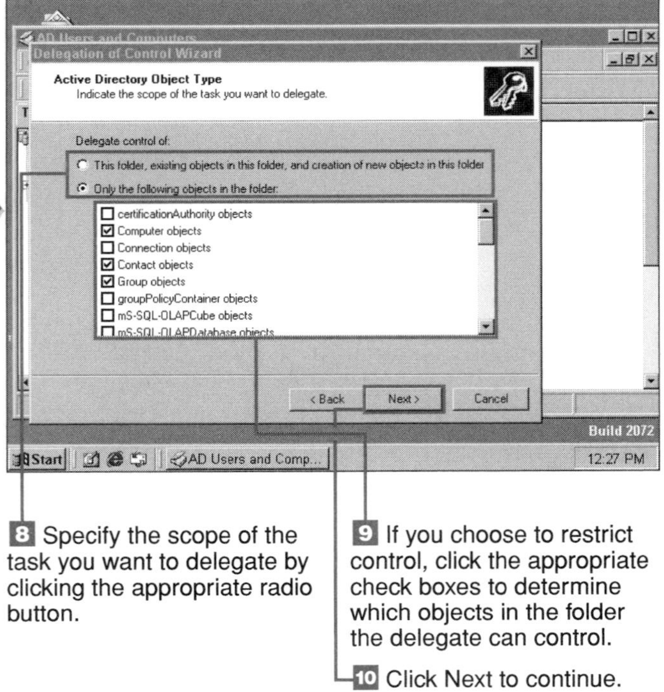

8 Specify the scope of the task you want to delegate by clicking the appropriate radio button.

9 If you choose to restrict control, click the appropriate check boxes to determine which objects in the folder the delegate can control.

10 Click Next to continue.

Which predefined delegations should I use?

✔ Generally, you want to be somewhat restrictive. In other words, do not give the delegation user or group the right to reset a user's password unless you explicitly want this done. Allow enough control to accomplish the tasks, but do not give more control than necessary.

What if I want to delegate control only on certain objects in the Active Directory?

✔ You can click the Custom button and then select Objects in Folder to delegate control of certain objects. This feature enables you to finely control what tasks a delegate can perform.

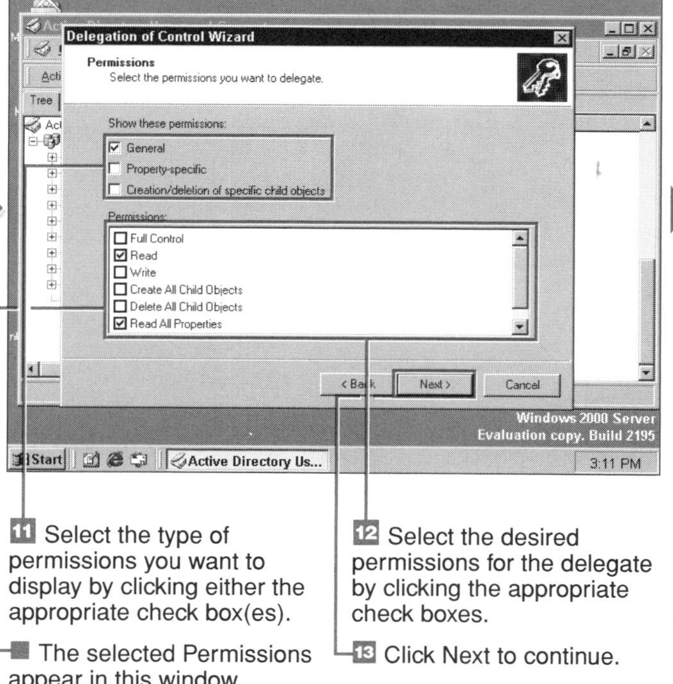

11 Select the type of permissions you want to display by clicking either the appropriate check box(es).

■ The selected Permissions appear in this window.

12 Select the desired permissions for the delegate by clicking the appropriate check boxes.

13 Click Next to continue.

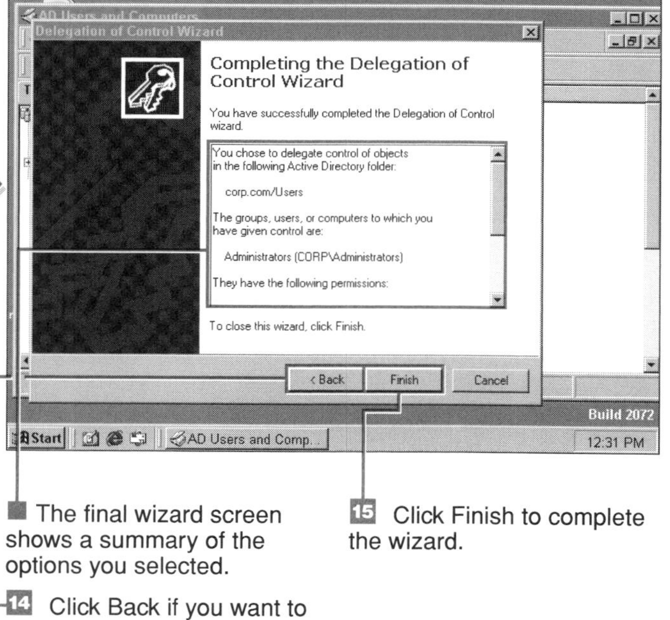

■ The final wizard screen shows a summary of the options you selected.

14 Click Back if you want to return to a previous step and change your answers.

15 Click Finish to complete the wizard.

WHAT NETWORK USERS CAN VIEW

Because user account information is stored in the Active Directory, you may wonder what information network users can view in Active Directory. After all, you do not want network users to be able to see confidential information about other users.

Network users can use the Active Directory to view basic contact information about other users. This information includes the user's name, phone numbers, e-mail address, and postal addresses. The Active Directory users can also find another user's manager or the names of people who report to that user. This feature allows a user to search for a particular person and find that person's contact information and general information about his or her job. This information allows a user to search for another user by e-mail address or first or last name.

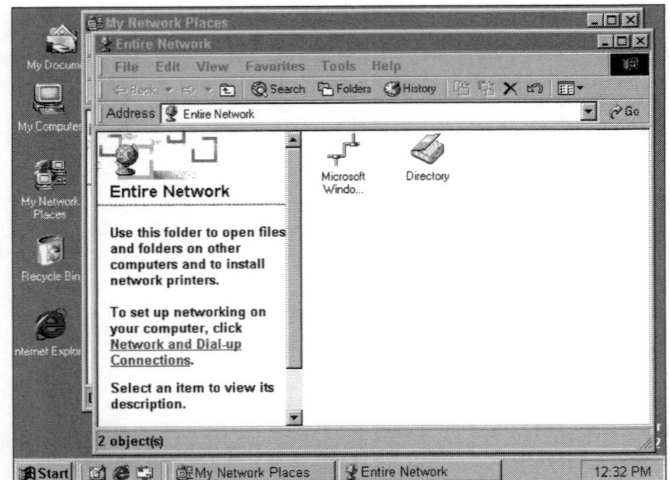

1 Active Directory users can access the directory by first opening My Network Places and then double-clicking Entire Network.

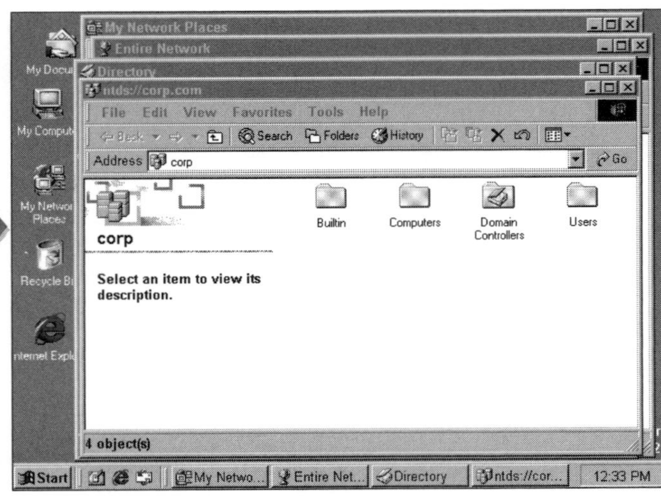

2 Double-click Directory and double-click the domain name.

What if I do not want certain user information to appear in the directory?

- If you do not want user certain information about the user to appear in the directory, such as a user's telephone number, simply do not include that information in the user's account properties. Remember that aside from management, the purpose of the Active Directory is to provide network users a way to find the resources they need. If you do not want some information to appear, simply leave those fields blank when you configure the account.

What is the best way to find an Active Directory user? I only know the first name.

- The easiest way to find an Active Directory user is to perform an LDAP search using the Windows search feature. Simply type the first name of the user and the search function returns all users from the Active Directory with that first name. You can then find the user you desire to contact. The LDAP search feature is a great improvement in Windows 2000 compared to previous versions of Windows that required browsing the network to find what you need.

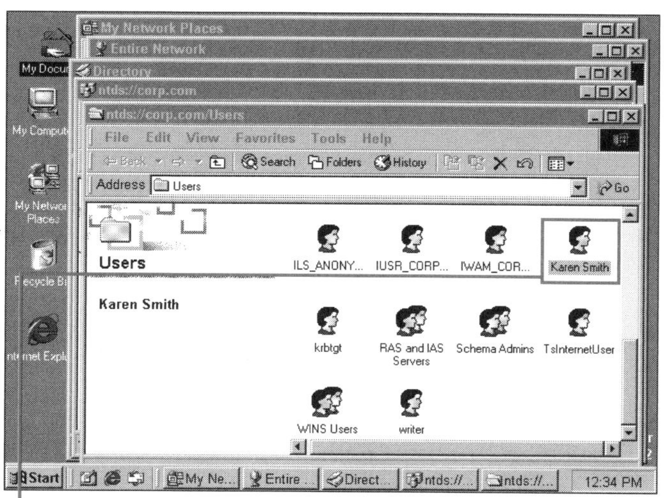

3 Double-click the Users folder and then double-click the name of the user you want to view.

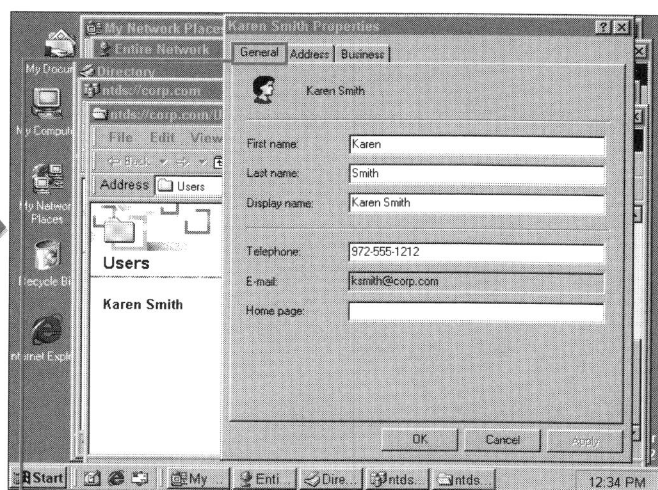

■ The user's name, phone number, and e-mail address appear on the General tab.

■ The Address and Business tabs contain the user's address and business title.

VIEWING AND CREATING WINDOWS 2000 GROUP ACCOUNTS

Group accounts are used to organize users so that permissions can be assigned with less administrative overhead. By adding users to groups, you can configure group settings instead of managing user permissions on an individual basis. In Windows 2000, you create and manage groups in the Active Directory Users and Computers MMC snap-in.

Windows 2000 includes a number of built-in groups, and you can create your own as well. If you click the built-in container in the left console pane, the built-in groups appear in the right console pane. Built-in groups include Account Operators, Administrators, Backup Operators, Guests, Print Operators, Replicator, Server Operators, and Users. You can also click the Users container in the left console pane to see additional domain local and global groups that are built in. Beside each group in the details pane, you can see a description of the group and which users should belong to each group.

You can also create your own groups, in addition to the built-in groups, to meet the needs of your organization. Table 15-1 describes some of the most important groups in Windows 2000.

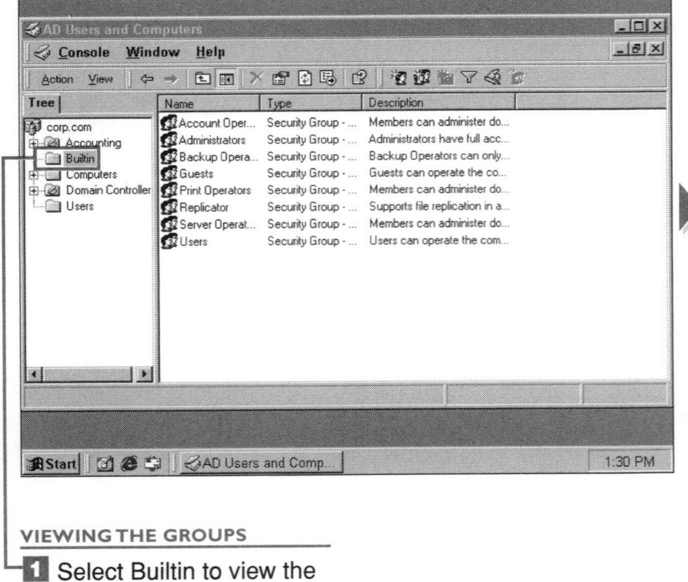

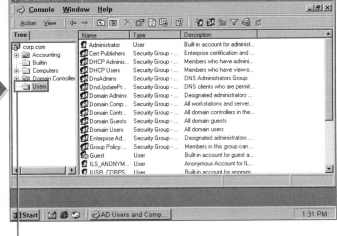

VIEWING THE GROUPS

1 Select Builtin to view the built-in groups and descriptions.

2 Select Users to view the domain s local and global groups.

Table 15-1: Group Scopes in Windows 2000

Scope	Description
Global Groups	Global groups are organizational units that allow users to access resources. Global group members come from one domain, but can access resources in any domain.
Local Groups	Local groups are used to assign permissions for a local resource. Group members can come from any domain, but members can access only resources in the local domain. Global groups are assigned to local groups.
Universal Groups	Universal groups can come from any domain and access resources in any domain. Universal groups are only available in domain native mode, not mixed mode.

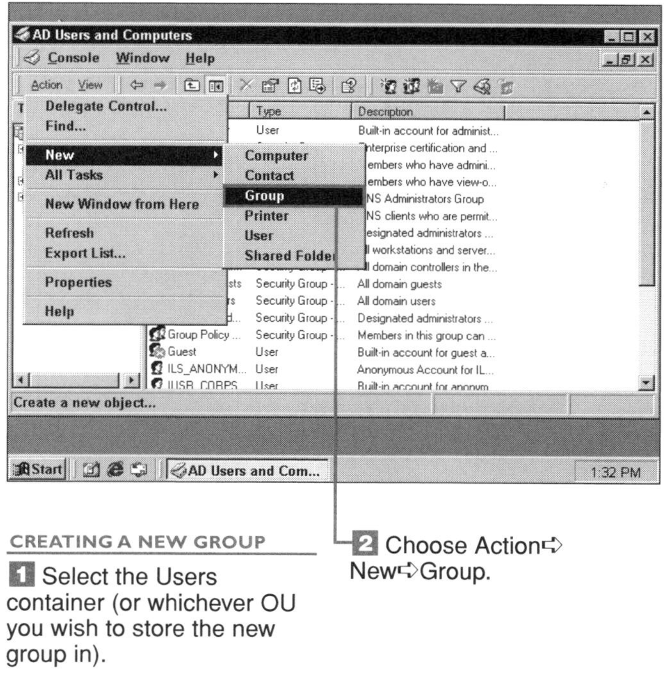

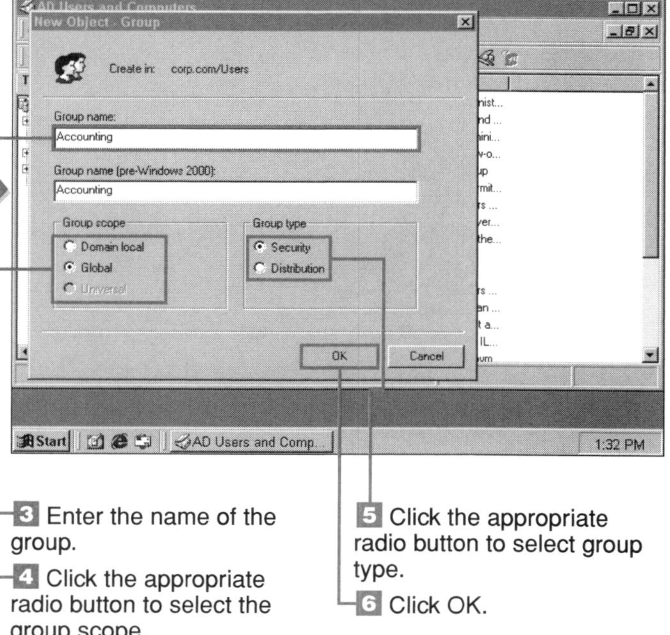

CREATING A NEW GROUP

1 Select the Users container (or whichever OU you wish to store the new group in).

2 Choose Action⇨New⇨Group.

3 Enter the name of the group.

4 Click the appropriate radio button to select the group scope.

5 Click the appropriate radio button to select group type.

6 Click OK.

CONFIGURING GROUP PROPERTIES

You can change the configuration for any group (including built-in groups) by accessing the group object's properties.

The General tab contains the name and description of the group, as well as the e-mail address for the group. You can use the group's e-mail address to send an e-mail message to every member of the group. The group type and group scope you selected when creating the group also appears. You can change the group type or scope if needed.

The Members tab lists the users that are members of that particular group. You can add or remove members from the group as needed. Because group membership can change frequently, this tab offers you an easy way to manage group membership.

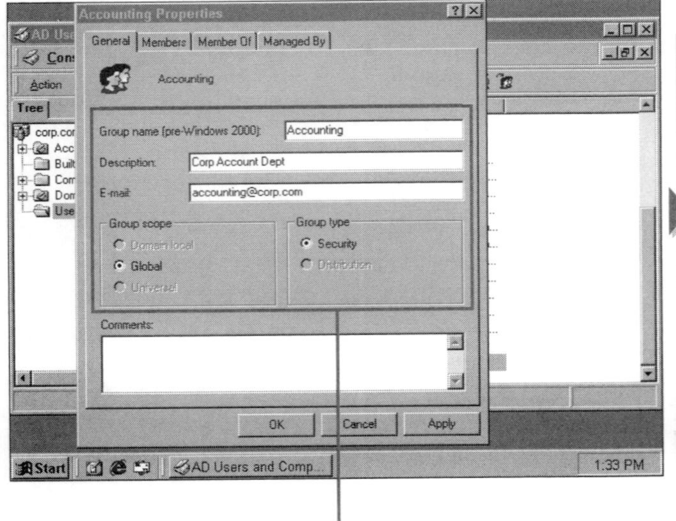

1 From the console, select the group you want to administer.

2 Choose Action⇨Properties.

3 You can alter the group's description, e-mail address, group name, group type, or scope as needed.

4 Click the Members tab.

■ You can use the Members tab to add or remove users, groups, or computers to or from the group.

5 To add users, groups, or computers, click Add.

Should I give a group membership to another group?

- You can add groups to a group just as you can add computers or users. This process, called *nesting*, essentially gives the members of one group an additional group membership by including that group within a group. For example, you could have a group called Marketing and another group called Publicity. You could give the Marketing group membership in the Publicity group, which basically gives all the Marketing group members permission rights that exist in the Publicity group. Nesting is a quick management tool, but you should be careful—multiple groups within multiple grops often create permission conflicts and problems, and those problems are usually difficult to troubleshoot.

Can I put a local group inside a global group?

- No. Just as in Windows NT, local groups define access to resources—global groups go into local groups so that global groups can access those local resources.

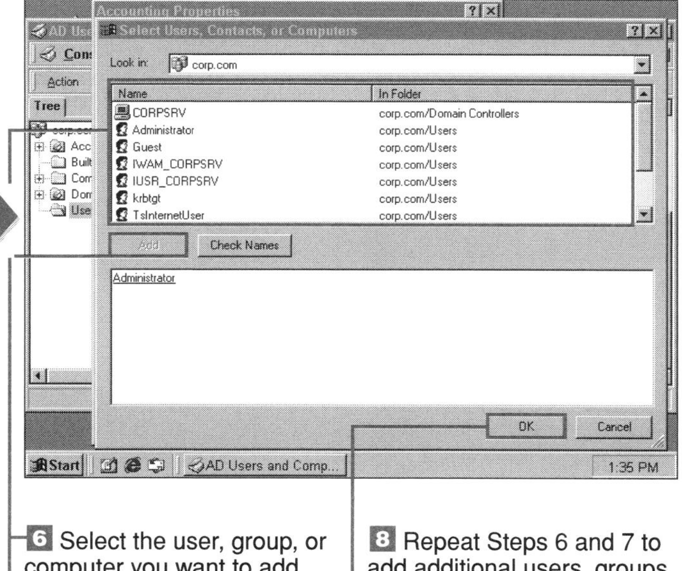

6 Select the user, group, or computer you want to add.

7 Click Add.

8 Repeat Steps 6 and 7 to add additional users, groups, or computers as needed.

9 Click OK when you are done.

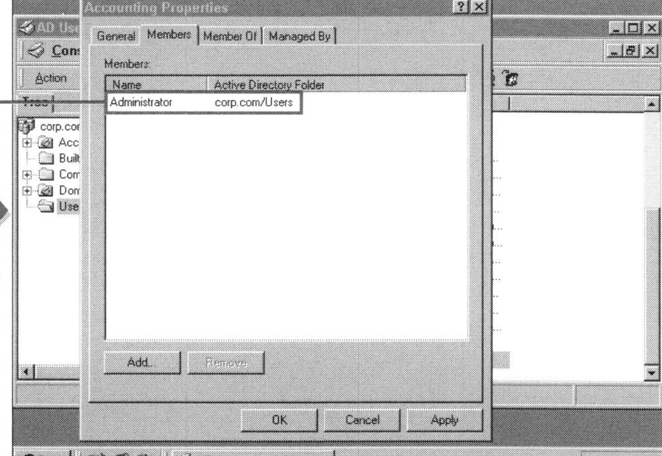

■ The object(s) you added to the group now appear in the Members list.

CONTINUED

CONFIGURING GROUP PROPERTIES
CONTINUED

The Member Of tab enables you to add a group to other existing groups. For example, you could add the Accounting group to the Administrators group. As you can imagine, this feature takes careful thought and planning so that excessive permissions are not given to users who do not need them. One of your best actions as an Active Directory administrator is to first organize your group structure on paper before every implementing that structure in the Active Directory.

The Managed By tab lists the name and contact information for the person that manages the group. You can change this information by clicking the Change button and selecting a new manager from the Active Directory. The address and phone information are automatically filled in according to the user's properties. You can also click the View button to find more information about the manager (such as additional phone numbers) contained in the Active Directory.

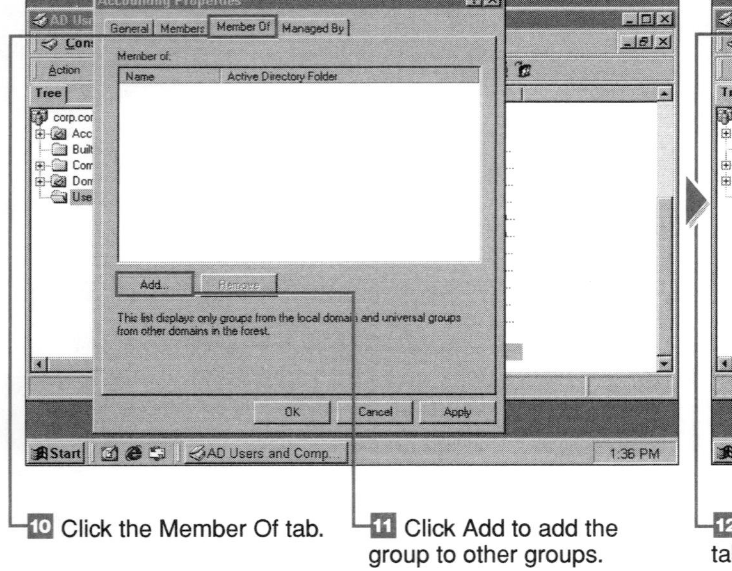

10 Click the Member Of tab.

11 Click Add to add the group to other groups.

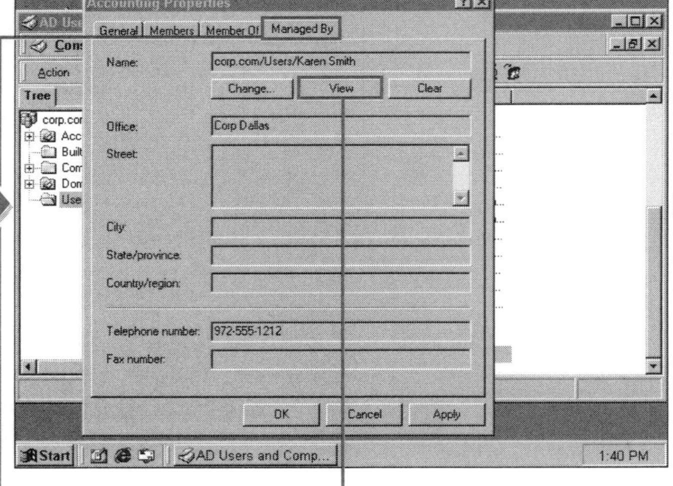

12 Click the Managed By tab.

■ Here you can view information about the group manager or change information if necessary.

13 Click View to see additional information about the manager that is contained in the Active Directory.

TIPS

Who should be given group management?

✓ Depending on the design of your organization, you can assign "regular" users to manage a group. Obviously, that user has to be trustworthy and contain strong computer and management skills. A good idea is to allow someone within the group to manage the group. This way, the manager is also a user and can understand any problems or concerns that may arise with members of the group.

Can someone that does not have a user account in the Active Directory manage a group?

✓ No. Windows 2000 security requires that a group manager have a valid user account in the Active Directory. If a manager could be a person who gains access to the network without a valid username and password, this would obviously be a serious security breach.

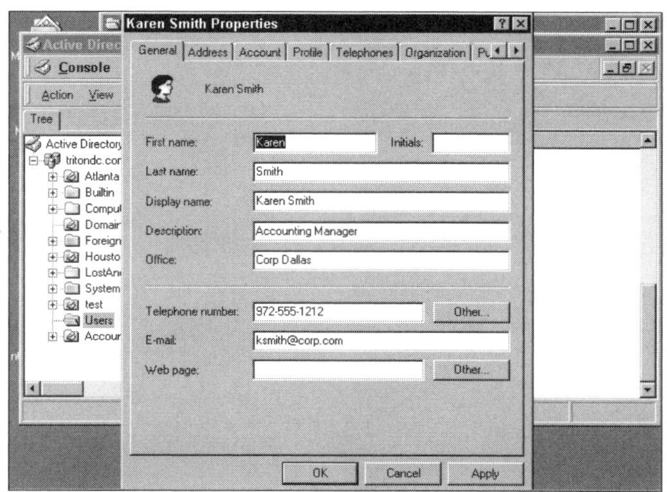

■ The manager's properties appear. You can use this sheet to edit the manager's properties.

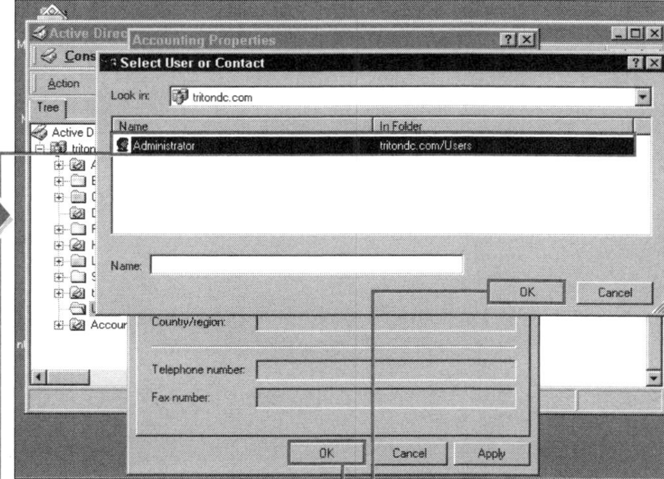

■ If you click Change on the Account Properties' Managed By tab, you can select a new manager from the Active Directory.

14 Click the person or group you want to manage the group.

15 Click OK.

16 Click OK to exit the Accounting Properties sheet.

MOVING GROUPS OR SENDING GROUP E-MAIL

The Active Directory enables you to move a group object to another location within the Active Directory. This feature is useful because the organization of a business or company does not remain static. As the organization changes and the structure changes, your groups can be moved to different OUs so that the Active Directory maintains the same organizational structure of your business. When you choose to move a group to a different OU, the group membership is not affected by the move.

You can also use group accounts to send group e-mail. This feature is particularly useful for departments that need to receive blanket notices or instructions. For example, if you need to send an e-mail to each employee in the Accounting group, you can send a single group e-mail instead of individually e-mailing each employee.

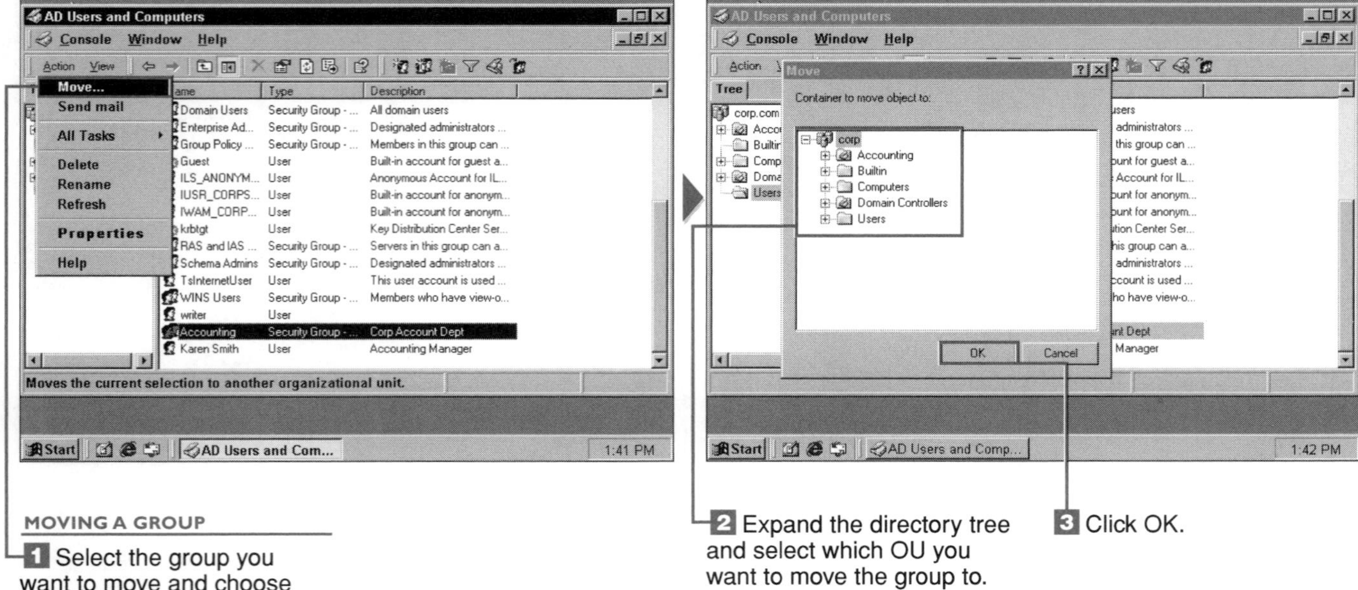

MOVING A GROUP

1 Select the group you want to move and choose Action⇨Move.

2 Expand the directory tree and select which OU you want to move the group to.

3 Click OK.

Must each group have an e-mail address?

- As with each user account, you can decide what information you want to configure for the Active Directory. If you do not want the group to have an e-mail address, simply do not enter one on the group's properties sheets. Then, users cannot send e-mail to the group as a whole. The advantage, of course, in using a group e-mail address is the ease of sending mail to the group.

How often can I move groups?

- You can move a group as often as necessary. In order to avoid this management task, however, be careful to create an OU structure that remains as static as possible. Highly defined OU structures introduce more management tasks, which can be avoided by creating a more static OU structure. Some organizations even choose to have a users and groups OU so that all user and group accounts are always contained in one location.

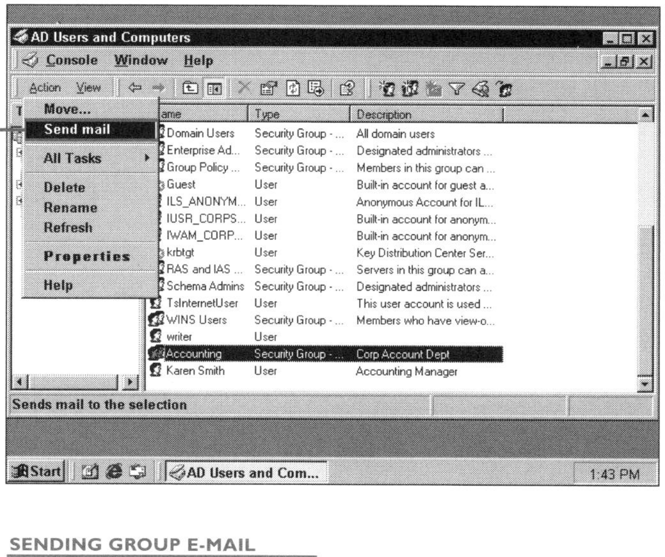

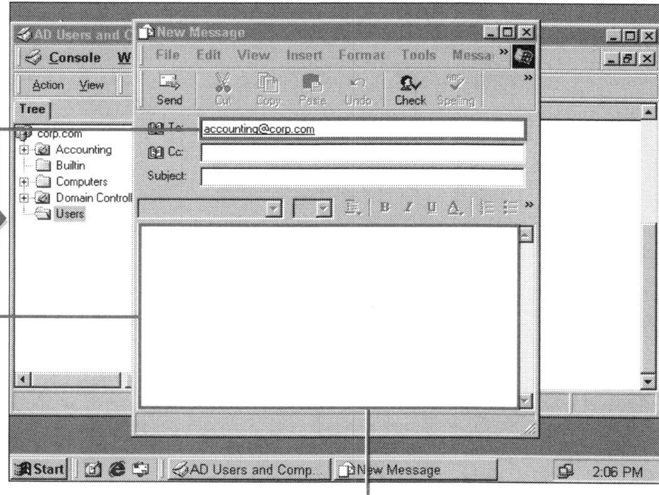

SENDING GROUP E-MAIL

1 Select the group you want to send e-mail to and choose Action➪Send Mail.

■ The e-mail address for the group is taken from the Active Directory and used to address an e-mail message from your default e-mail client.

2 Type a message and send it to the group.

WHAT CAN NETWORK USERS VIEW?

As with other Active Directory objects, Active Directory users can view information about groups by browsing for the desired group or performing an LDAP search to locate the group object.

A first question is usually, "Can users see who belongs to each group?" The answer is yes. The names of the members of that group are available for Active Directory users to see, and the names can be very helpful if an Active Directory user needs to contact a member of a group. For example, an Active Directory user needs to contact a manager in the Marketing department. The user knows that the management group exists but does not have any information about the manager's name or e-mail address. The user can find the management group and browse the users that belong to the group so that he or she can find the information needed to contact a manager.

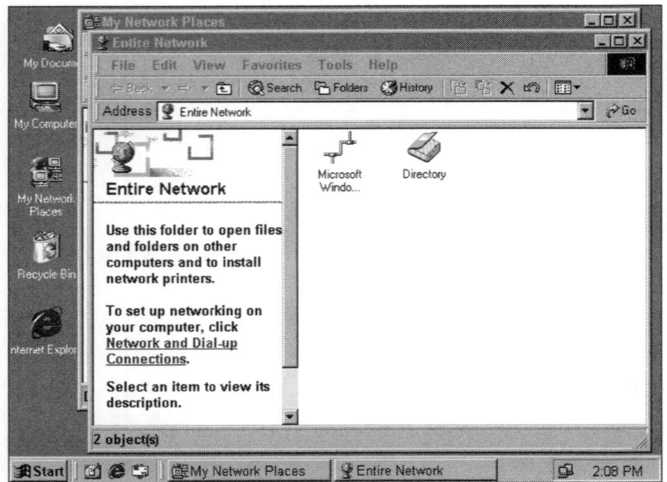

■ A user can view group information by double-clicking My Network Places and then double-clicking Entire Network.

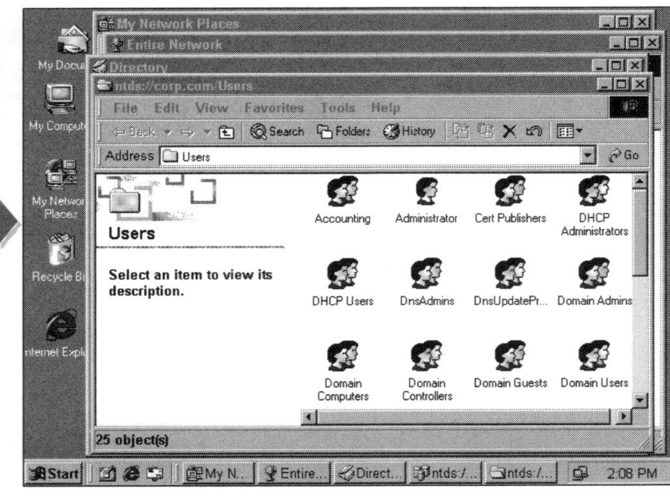

1 Double-click Directory, double-click the domain icon, and then double-click Users (or the OU in which the groups are stored).

TIPS

Can Active Directory users make changes to group membership?

No. You must have appropriate permissions to be able to change group membership. The interface provided for users allows them only to view the group members—they cannot access properties sheets for the group object or use the Add button without appropriate permissions.

Besides browsing the directory, is there another way to find a group?

Yes. As with any Active Directory object, you can perform an LDAP search. For example, if you wanted to find the Management group, you can access a search window and run a search for Management. The Active Directory returns the matches, and then you can access the members list of the Management group.

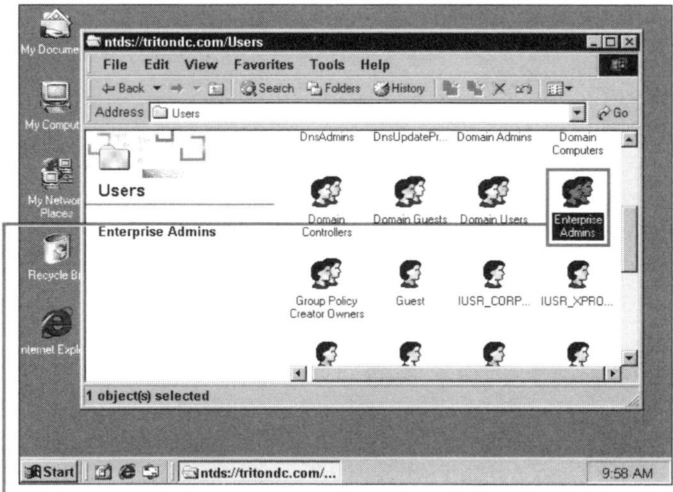

2 Double-click the group icon that you want to view.

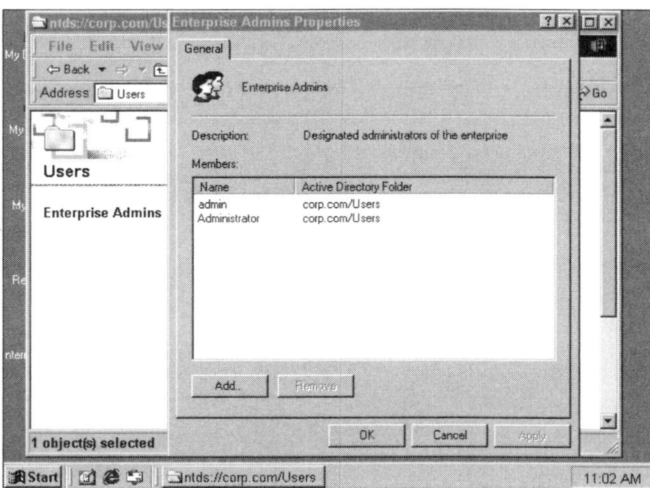

The group members and a description of the group appear.

CREATING A NEW COMPUTER ACCOUNT

Just as a domain user has a user account that represents that person, a computer account represents an actual computer on the network. Each Windows 2000 and Windows NT computer in a Windows 2000 network has a computer account in the Active Directory. Windows 9*x* computers do not have the security features of Windows 2000 and Windows NT, and therefore do not have computer accounts, but they can still log on to the domain and access resources.

You can also manually add a computer account to the Active Directory, and the process for adding a computer account is very similar to adding a user or group. By adding computer accounts to the Active Directory, you can identify computers on the network that do not automatically have a computer account configured for them (Windows 2000 and Windows NT). Windows 2000 and Windows NT computers must have computer accounts in the Active Directory in order for them to actively participate in the domain.

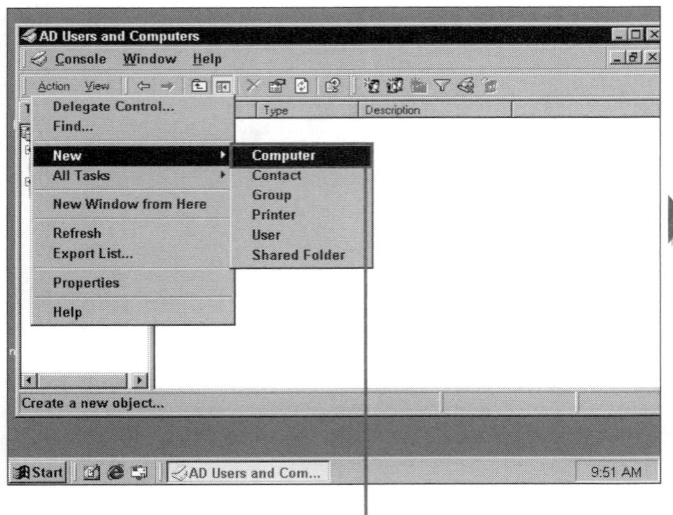

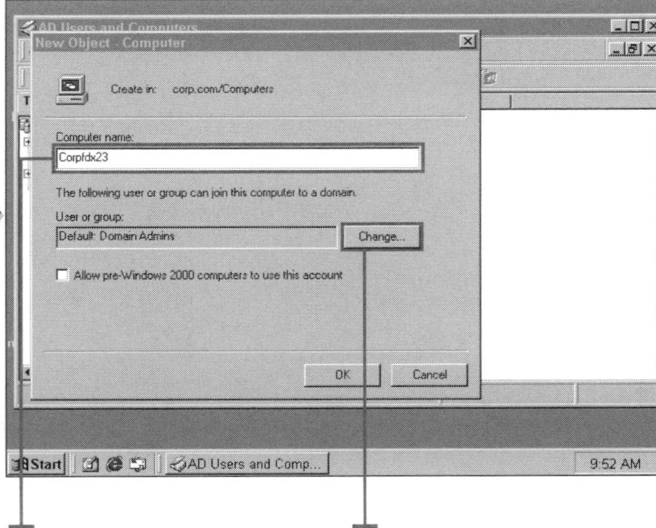

1 Select the Computers OU (or another OU in which you want to store the computer account).

2 Choose Action⇨New⇨Computer.

3 Type the name of the computer.

4 Click Change if you want to change the group that can join the computer to the domain.

How can I use computer accounts?

- Just as you can organize users into a group to assign permissions, you can organize physical computers into groups to assign permissions. For example, if you want only a particular set of computers to use a certain printer, you can assign permissions for that group of computers. This way, no matter what user is logged on to the computer, that user can access the printer for that group.

How can I create a computer account for a Windows 98 computer?

- Only Windows 2000 and Windows NT computers can have accounts in the Active Directory. This is due to the lack of advanced security features in the Windows 9*x* generation. Windows 9*x* computers can, however, log on to a Windows 2000 server and participate on the network.

Can previous versions of Windows use a computer account I create?

- Yes. When you create the computer account, click the Allow Pre-Windows 2000 Computers To Use This Account check box to enable this feature.

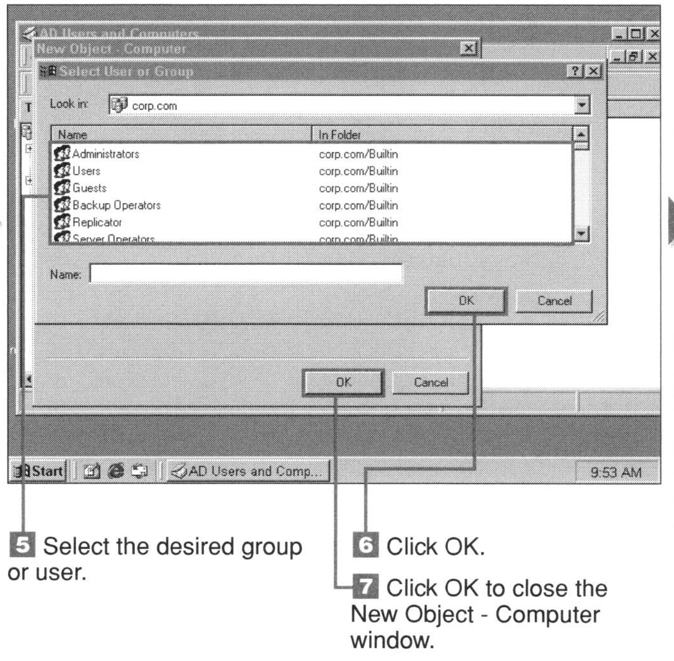

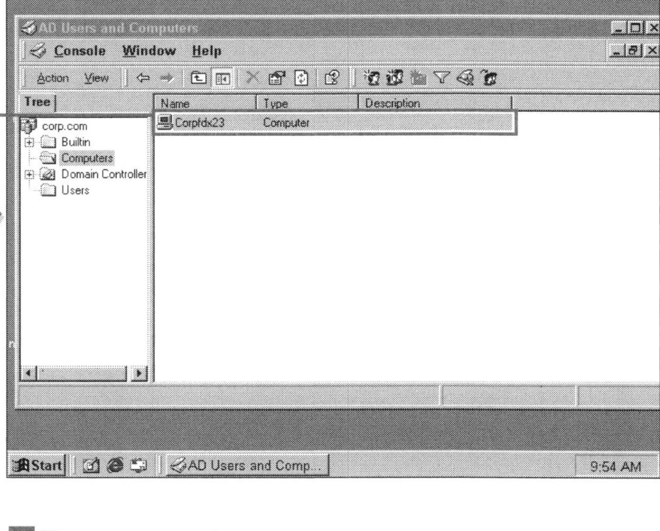

5 Select the desired group or user.

6 Click OK.

7 Click OK to close the New Object - Computer window.

8 The new computer account appears in the details pane.

CONFIGURING COMPUTER ACCOUNT PROPERTIES

Just like users and groups, computer accounts have Properties sheets. You can configure computer accounts by accessing the properties sheet. To access the properties sheet, select the computer account, access the Action menu, and click Properties.

Configuring computer accounts is rather easy. Of particular interest on the General tab, you can choose to click the Trust Computer For Delegation check box. Just as you can delegate duties to user accounts, you can also delegate duties to computer accounts. This feature does require careful consideration so that you do not create security breaches with computers operated by nonadministrative personnel.

The Operating System tab simply displays OS version and service pack information about the computer, and as with other properties sheets, the Member Of tab allows you to configure the computer account's group memberships.

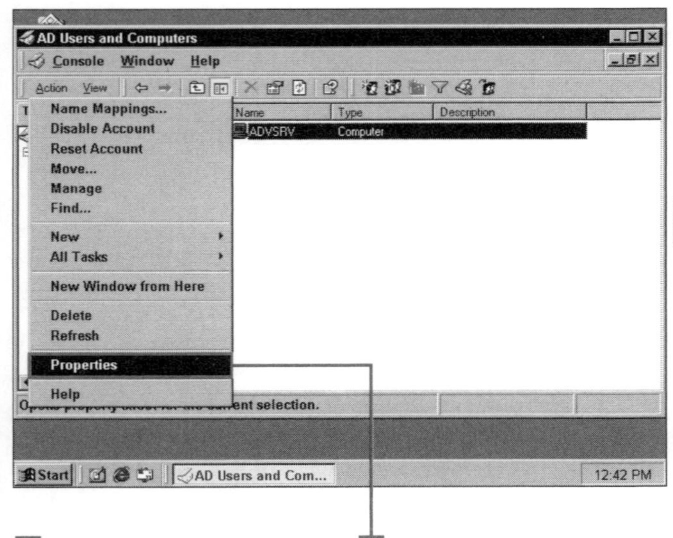

1 To access the properties sheet, select the computer you want to administer.

2 Choose Action⇨Properties.

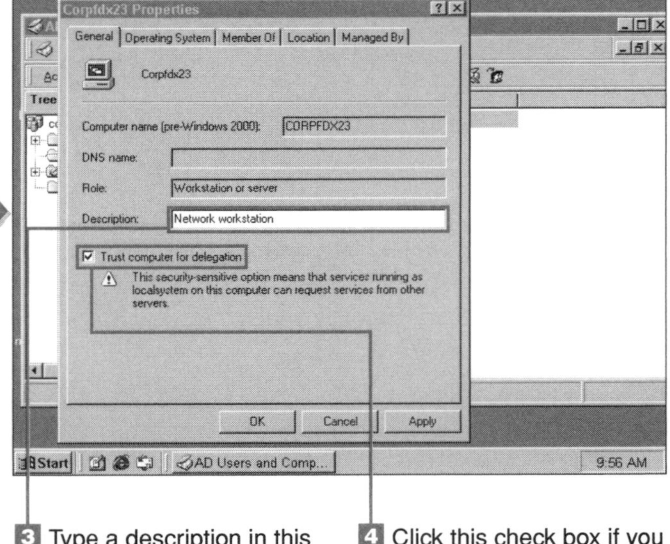

3 Type a description in this box if desired.

4 Click this check box if you want the computer to be trusted for delegation.

TIPS

To how many groups should a computer belong?

- In order to manage access permissions and keep your network organization from becoming confusing, assign computers only to groups that they absolutely need to belong. Also, remember that after a user logs on to that computer, the user effectively has membership to the groups that the computer is assigned. As with group accounts for users, planning is of utmost importance.

What is the down-level name?

- In Windows 2000, all earlier versions of Windows, such as NT and 9*x*, are called *down-level computers*. Down-level computers used NetBIOS to establish a friendly name, such as Server12. In Windows 2000, DNS is used for name resolution, so in mixed environments, both the DNS and the NetBIOS name are often displayed for objects.

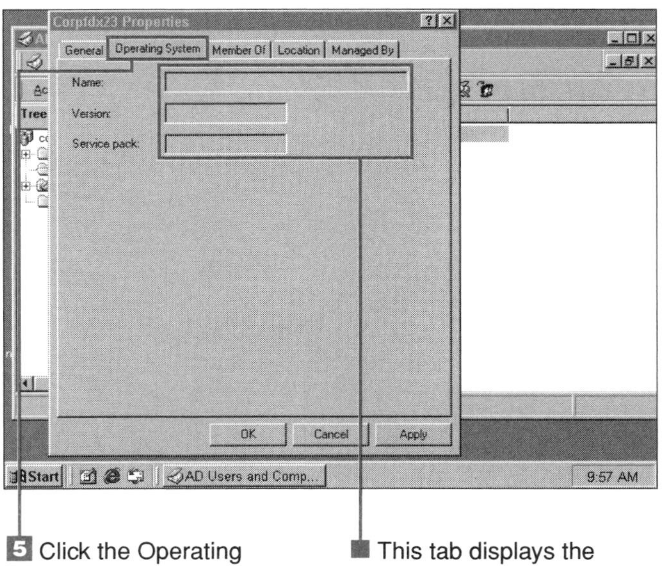

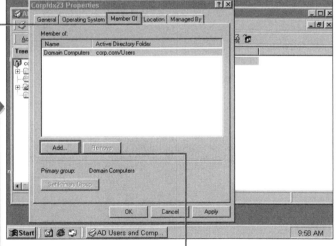

5 Click the Operating System tab.

■ This tab displays the computer's operating system, version number, and the service pack that is applied (if any).

6 Click the Member Of tab.

■ This tab tells you what groups the computer currently belongs to.

7 Click Add to add the computer to more groups.

CONTINUED

CONFIGURING COMPUTER ACCOUNT PROPERTIES CONTINUED

The Location and Managed By tabs provide the same configuration options as other properties sheets. The Location tab tells which locations are served by the site in the directory setup. You can use the Browse button to change site locations if necessary.

The Managed By tab allows you to enter a manager for the computer account. When you enter a manager, the manager's contact information (such as telephone, address, and so on) is extracted from the manager's user account and placed on this tab, if the information is available in the user account. You do not have to assign a manager to a computer account, but the Active Directory provides you this option so you can decentralize administrative duties in your network. Like delegation, you can assign managers to various Active Directory objects to remove the management burden from senior IT administrators.

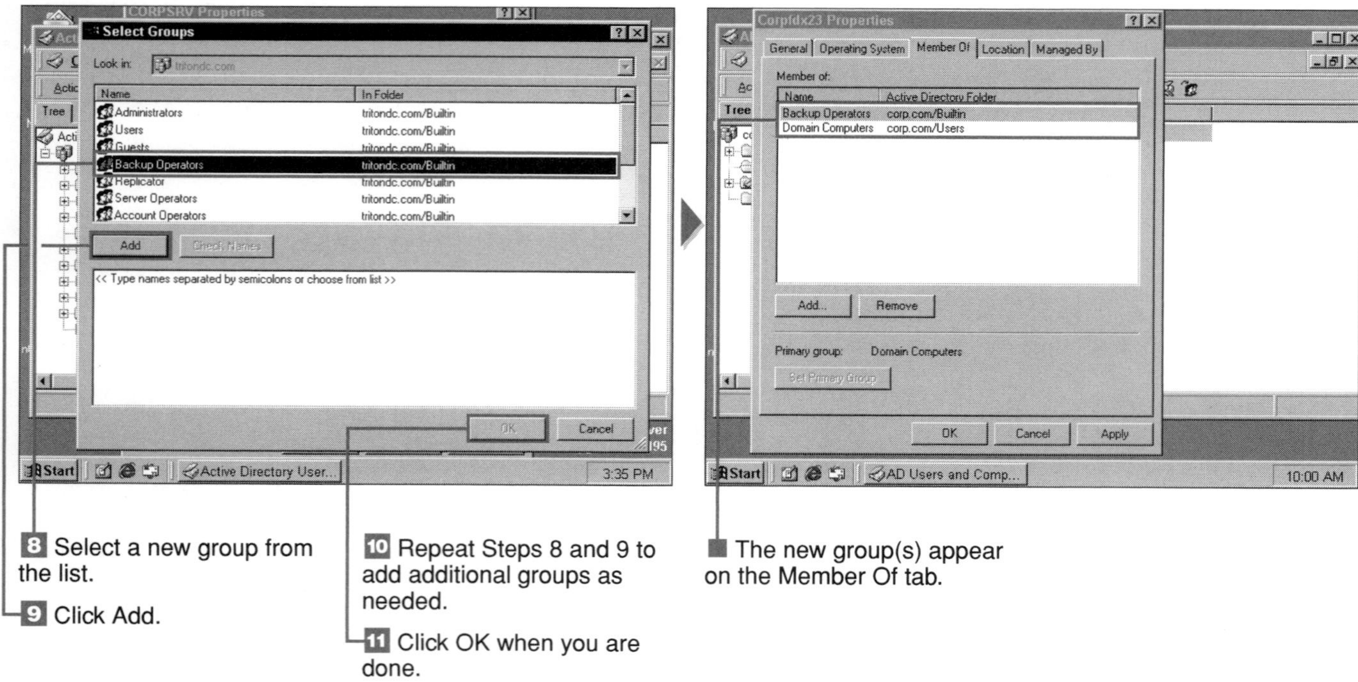

8 Select a new group from the list.

9 Click Add.

10 Repeat Steps 8 and 9 to add additional groups as needed.

11 Click OK when you are done.

■ The new group(s) appear on the Member Of tab.

Who should manage a computer account?

- Any number of domain users can be the manager of a computer account. You should select someone who works primarily with the physical computer or manages a group of computers and employees. Remember that group memberships should be carefully configured, so the manager needs to understand the dynamics of group membership and group management. Also, you should minimize the number of people who manage Active Directory objects, for security purposes as well as administrative control.

Should a computer account belong to different groups?

- You can give a computer account membership in any group, just as you can a user account. The group memberships define what actions that particular computer can perform and how that computer can be used on the network. The rule of thumb is to give group memberships that are necessary, but do not assign excessive memberships to either users or computers.

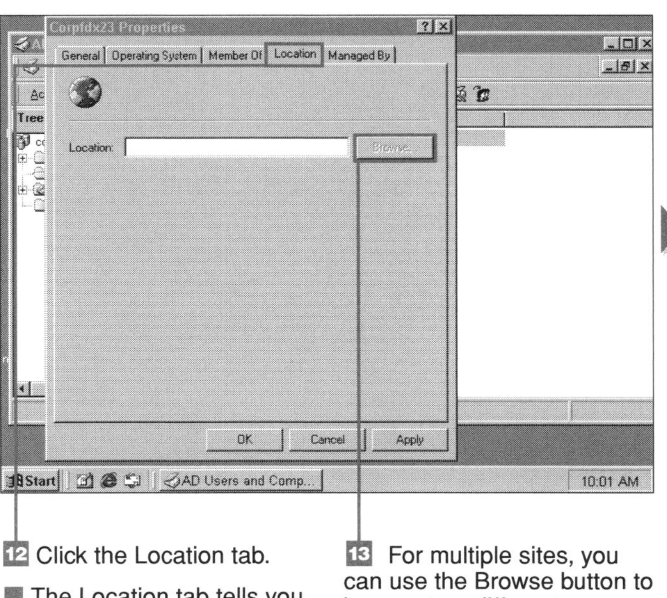

12 Click the Location tab.

■ The Location tab tells you which locations are served by the site.

13 For multiple sites, you can use the Browse button to browse to a different location.

14 Click the Managed By tab.

■ The Managed By tab gives you the name and contact information for the account manager.

15 Use Change to change the computer account manager.

16 Click OK to close the Properties sheet.

MANAGING COMPUTER ACCOUNTS

You can easily manage computer accounts by performing the typical tasks of disabling and resetting accounts, deleting accounts, and refreshing accounts.

Two very helpful actions are the Move and Manage features. The Move action enables you to move the object to a different OU in the Active Directory. Although you should try to keep the Active Directory as static as possible, restructuring may occur from time to time, and you may have to move objects to different locations. With the Move feature, you can easily perform this action without having to delete and recreate the object in the desired location.

The Manage feature is particularly helpful because it allows you to open the Computer Management snap-in for the computer account. With appropriate administrative rights, you can configure remote computers, install and remove devices, and even configure hard disks—all while sitting at your own server.

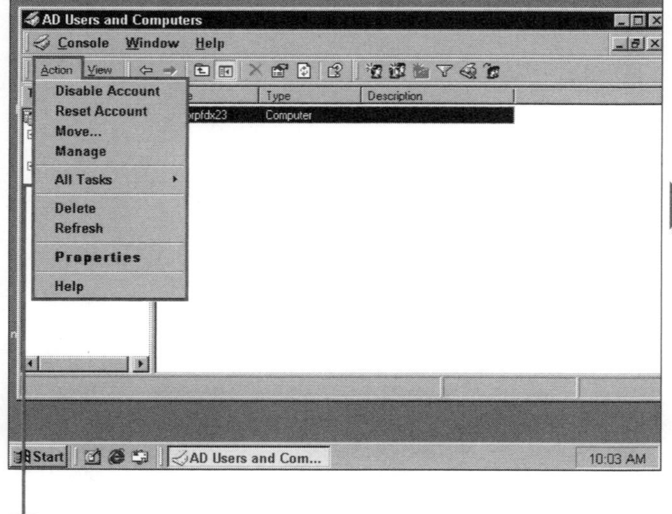

1 Click the Action menu to see account management options.

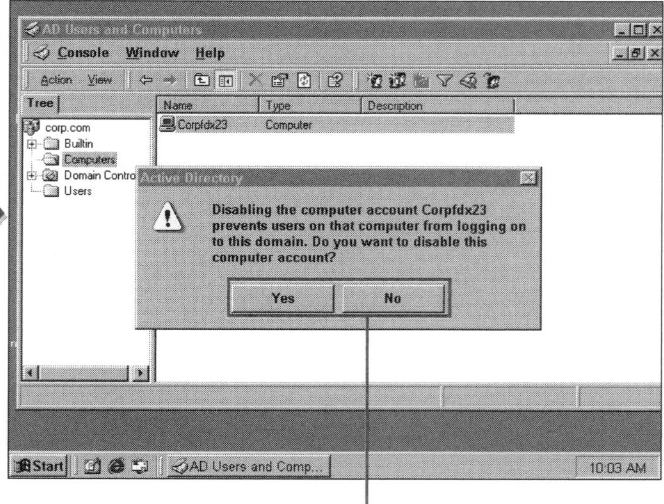

■ If you click Disable Account, a warning message tells you that users will not be able to log on to the domain from that computer.

2 Click Yes to disable the account; click No to cancel.

Does disabling the account delete it?

- No. If you disable the computer account, users cannot log on to the domain from that computer. The computer account object in the directory appears with a red X over it. You can re-enable the account by right-clicking the account object and choosing Enable Account.

When should a computer account be deleted?

- You should always use the Disable Account option unless the computer has been physically removed from the network and is no longer in service. In that case, you can delete the account from the directory.

If I choose to manage another computer, what can I do?

- The Manage option opens the Computer Management console on other Windows 2000 computers. You can perform any task within the console, such as using system tools, configuring shared folders, managing storage, and even managing services and applications.

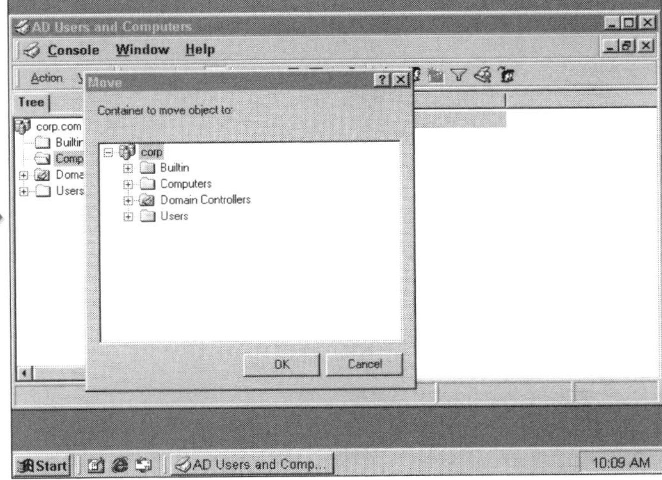

■ If you choose Action⇨Move, the Move window appears, which allows you to select the folder to which you want to move the account.

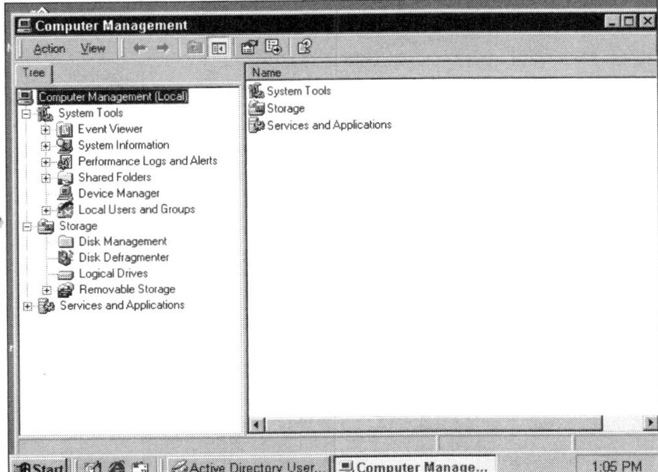

■ If you choose Action⇨Manage, the Computer Management snap-in opens (if you have administrative privileges). You can configure the computer from this window.

CREATING ORGANIZATIONAL UNITS

Organizational units (OU) are provided in the Active Directory to help you organize resources in a logical manner so that your Active Directory structure models your administrative structure. You can think of an OU as a file folder—a container into which you can put other files or documents. In the Active Directory, an OU is simply a container where you can place and organize similar OUs and Active Directory objects.

As with all aspects of the Active Directory, you should carefully plan what OUs you will create and what other OUs and resources will reside in those OUs. You can learn about planning your Active Directory OU structure in Chapter 10. You can easily create OUs in the Active Directory Users and Computers snap-in.

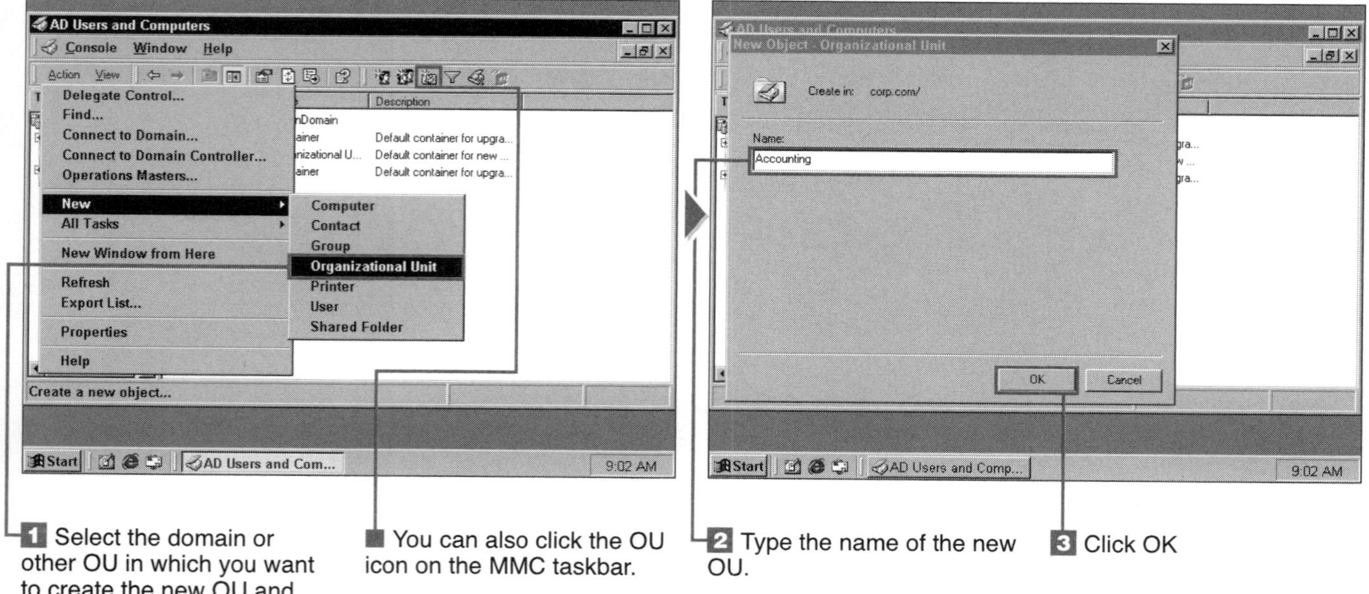

1 Select the domain or other OU in which you want to create the new OU and choose Action⇨New⇨Organizational Unit.

■ You can also click the OU icon on the MMC taskbar.

2 Type the name of the new OU.

3 Click OK

Should I create additional OUs within an OU?

✓ Think of an OU as a folder on your hard disk. You can create additional folders within that folder to further organize information. Additional OUs within an OU help you organize the resources that are available within the OU. This process is called *nesting*. Depending on the purpose of the OU, you may not need additional OUs, but the overall goal is to make the OU's resources organized, logical, and easy for users to find and access. However, you should also be aware that deeply nested OUs may cause problems or slow response time for Active Directory object discovery—in other words, nested OUs can slow down resource search times.

How many OUs can I create?

✓ You can create as many first-level OUs and nested OUs as needed for your network. However, you should have a firm understanding of OU planning and carefully plan the structure before implementation, or OUs can quickly get out of control.

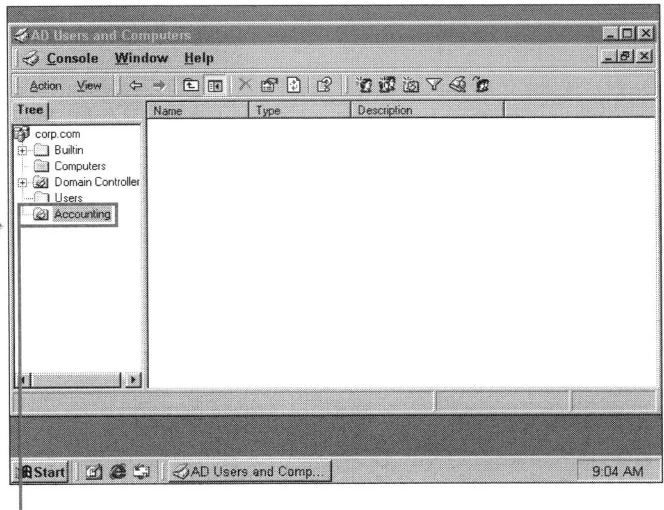

■ The new OU appears in the console tree. If you want to create additional OUs within the OU, repeat Steps 1 through 3.

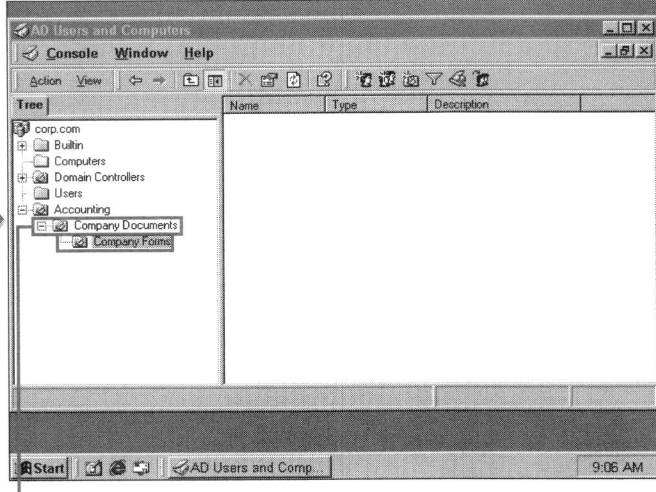

■ These are examples of nested OUs.

CREATING ORGANIZATIONAL UNITS CONTINUED

Like most Active Directory components, you can use the Action menu and select Properties to further configure the OU. The OU properties sheet contains three tabs.

On the General tab, you can enter a description and address information for the OU if desired. This information is useful in large environments in which different OUs are based on a physical location. For example, an Atlanta OU can contain the network segment at an Atlanta site. The address information can identify the physical location of the resources within the OU. On the Managed By tab, you can click the Change button to assign a manager from the Active Directory to the OU. Also, you can click the Group Policy tab to implement additional group policies for the OU if necessary, depending on the policies you have configured in Windows 2000 Server.

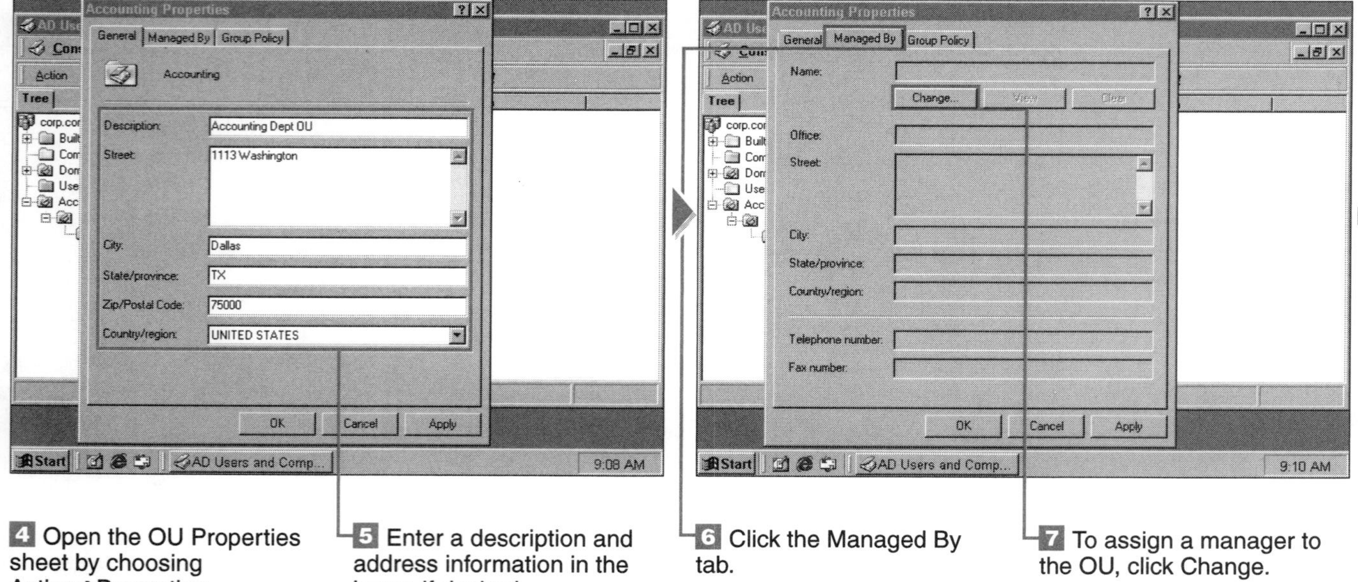

4 Open the OU Properties sheet by choosing Action⇨Properties.

5 Enter a description and address information in the boxes if desired.

6 Click the Managed By tab.

7 To assign a manager to the OU, click Change.

Must I provide a description and address for an OU?

No. The description and address feature allows you to enter organizational information about the OU, but it is not required. Depending on the structure of your Active Directory environment and the particular OU you are working with, a description and address may not be desired or needed.

What about group policies?

Group policies are a powerful new feature of Windows 2000 that enables you to implement highly detailed policies applying to groups, OUs, or even domains. You can learn all about group policies in Chapter 24.

Is it necessary to assign a manager to an OU?

Depending on the needs of your organization, you may wish to assign a manager to certain top-level OUs. The manager can then create additional OUs within the OU and manage how resources are organized.

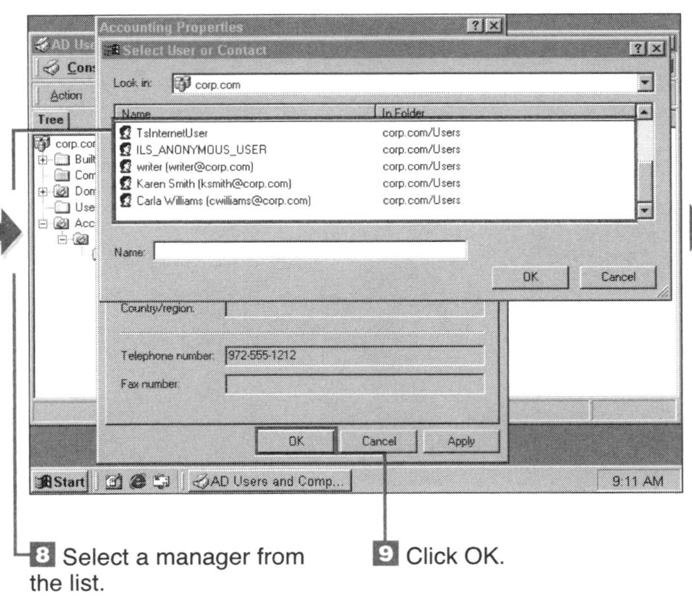

8 Select a manager from the list.

9 Click OK.

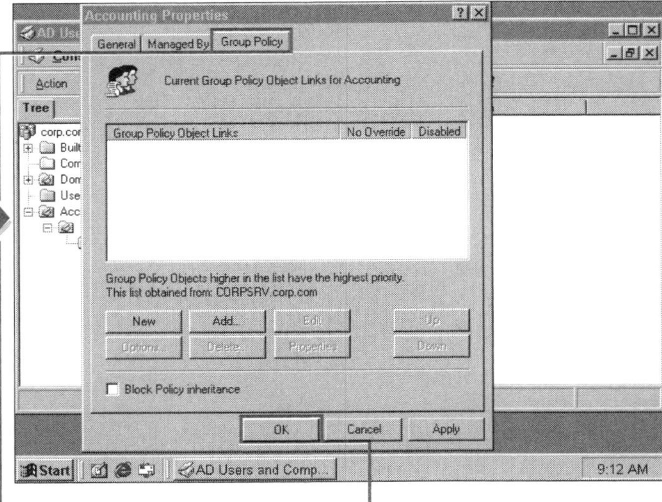

10 Click the Group Policy tab.

■ Use this tab to add policies you have created in Windows 2000 Server that affect the OU. See Chapter 25 for more information.

11 Click OK to close the Properties sheet and save your changes.

CREATING AND CONFIGURING A CONTACT

The Active Directory provides a way to keep track of people that may or may not be employed with your company through the use of contacts. A *contact* is similar to a personal address book entry in an e-mail application. You can use contacts for a variety of purposes, but they are particularly useful for keeping track of temporary or contract employees and others who provide services to users. The contact information is stored in the Active Directory so that other users can view the contact's information.

After you create a contact, the contact appears in the OU you selected. You can then configure the properties for the contact by using the Action menu.

On the General tab, you can enter additional contact information about the person, such as a telephone number, description, e-mail address, and Web site location. This is optional configuration data, and this does not affect your network communication process.

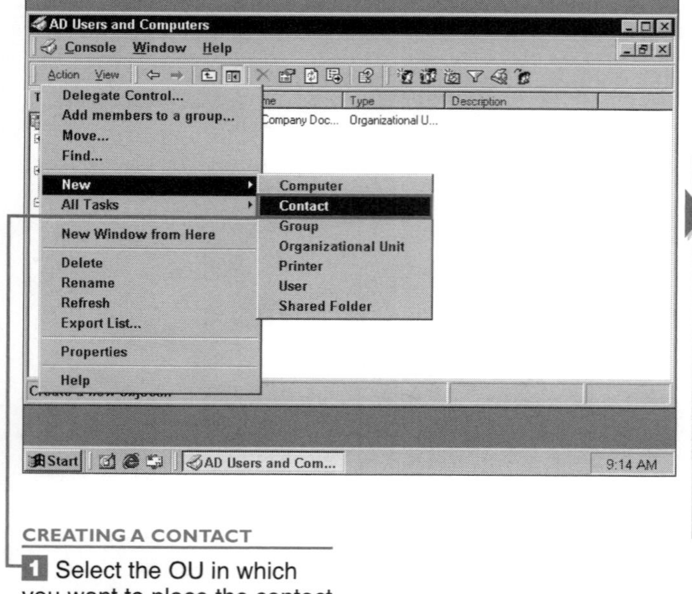

CREATING A CONTACT

1 Select the OU in which you want to place the contact object and choose Action⇨New⇨Contact.

2 Type the name of the contact and the display name.

3 Click OK.

TIPS

Who should be a contact?

Because network user information is stored in the Active Directory, you do not need to create contacts for network users. You can, however, use the contact feature to store information about temporary employees who do not have a network account, consultants, or other business associates who you frequently contact.

How should contacts be organized?

No hard and fast rules for organizing your contacts exist, but if you want your Active Directory users to easily find the contacts, consider creating an OU that identifies itself as a contact OU, and then storing the contact objects in the OU. Of course, the contact OU can also reside in another OU, depending on your Active Directory structure.

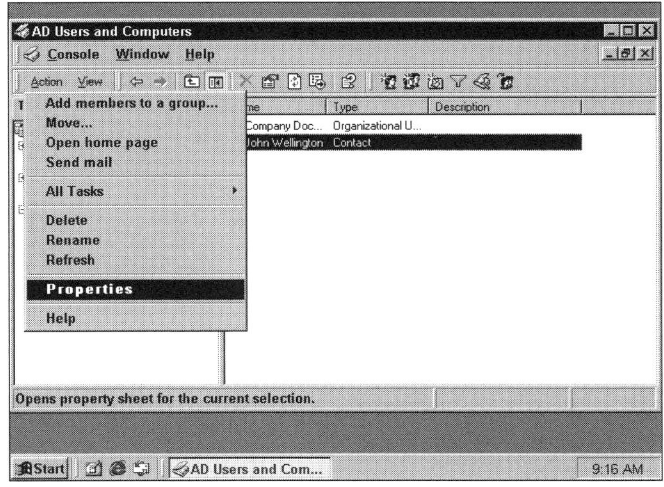

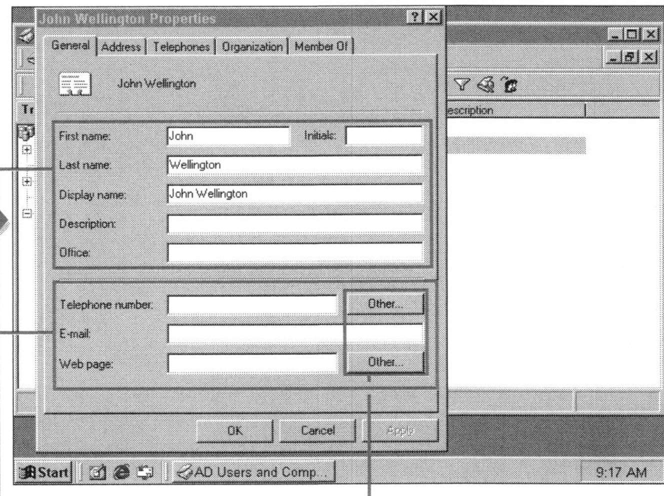

CONFIGURING A CONTACT

1 After you create a contact, choose Action⇨Properties.

2 Use these boxes to enter contact information.

3 Use these boxes to enter phone, e-mail, and Web information.

4 Use the Other buttons to list additional phone or Web information.

CONTINUED

CREATING AND CONFIGURING A CONTACT CONTINUED

On the Address tab, enter information in the boxes about the contact's address.

The Telephones tab provides a number of boxes for the contact's phone and pager information. You can enter additional information about contacting the user in the comments section.

On the Organization tab, you can enter information about the contact's organization. If the contact is a member of your organization, you can click the Change button to enter the manager's name from the Active Directory. The Direct Reports box lists the people within your organization who directly report to the contact.

The Member Of tab enables you to add the contact to groups within the Active Directory. Use the Add button to add the selected group(s).

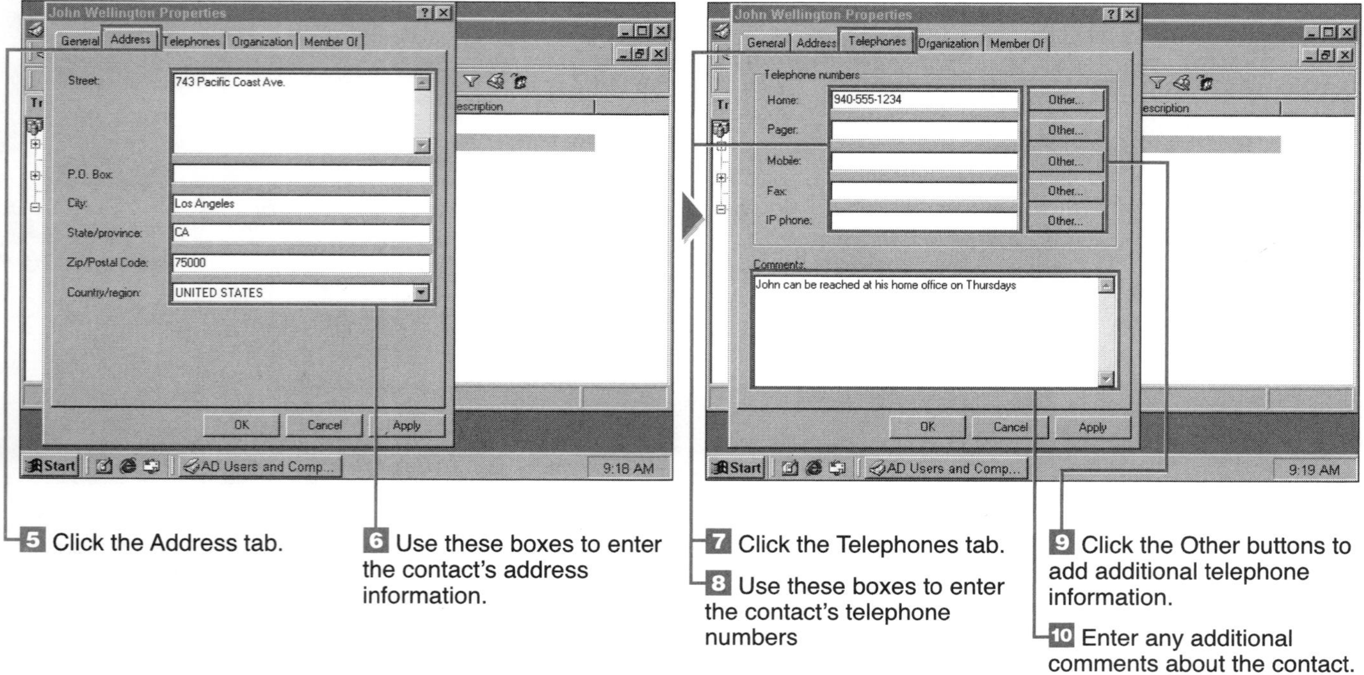

5 Click the Address tab.

6 Use these boxes to enter the contact's address information.

7 Click the Telephones tab.

8 Use these boxes to enter the contact's telephone numbers

9 Click the Other buttons to add additional telephone information.

10 Enter any additional comments about the contact.

TIPS

Why would a contact have a manager?

- Remember that contacts in the Active Directory are loosely defined and can be used in an appropriate manner for your organization. Many organizations hire contractors who directly report to management at the company. These managers are a part of the Active Directory, even though the contractor may not be.

Should contacts have group access?

- Contacts may be considered part of groups as necessary. Without a valid logon and password, however, they cannot use the network or directory resources. Again, the contact can be used in a number of ways, depending on the needs of your organization.

What is the purpose of the Telephone tab when you can enter the contact's phone number on the General tab?

- The Telephone tab is simply another place to enter additional phone information—such as home phone, pager, cellular phone, and so on—about the contact.

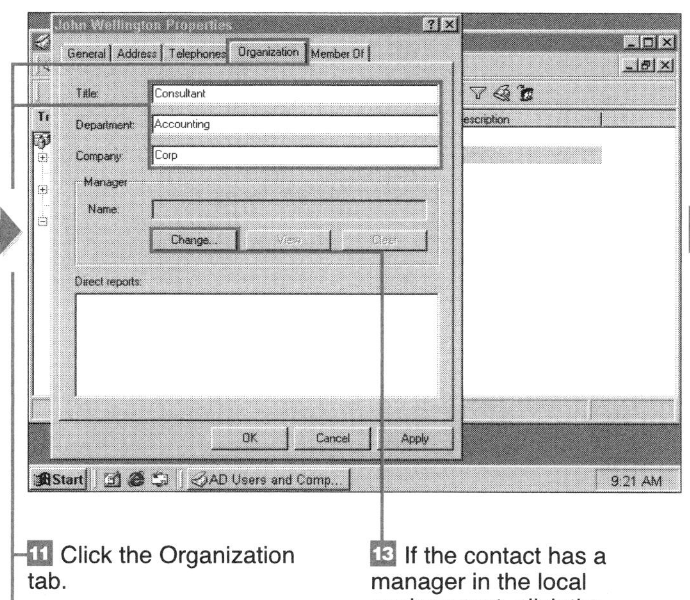

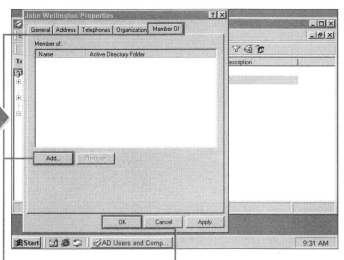

11 Click the Organization tab.

12 Enter the contact's position and company information.

13 If the contact has a manager in the local environment, click the Change button to select the manager from the Active Directory.

14 Click the Member Of tab.

15 If you want the contact to be a member of a group, click Add and select the group.

16 Click OK to save your changes.

USING SHARED FOLDERS

You can publish shared folders in the Active Directory so that users can more easily find information. In the past, a user had to know which server or workstation stored a shared folder. Now, you can store that information in the Active Directory so that users can more easily find shared folders and even search for them. The shared folders and the information they contain still reside on the hosting computer's hard drive, but the directory keeps track of the folder's location so that users don't have to.

With the powerful search features of the Active Directory, a user can perform a search for shared folders, find the folder he or she needs, and simply open the folder from the Active Directory. Knowing the network path to the shared folder is not necessary.

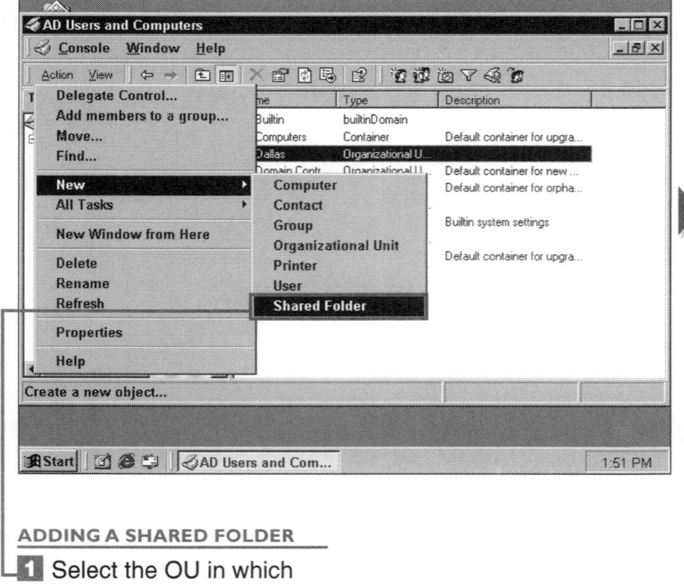

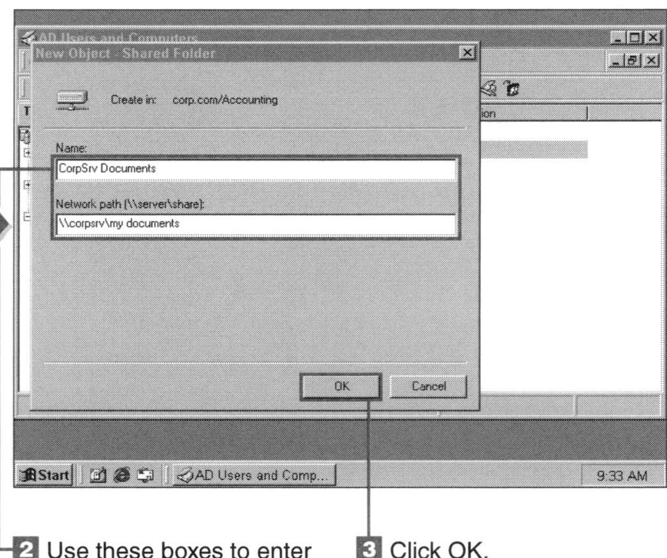

ADDING A SHARED FOLDER

1 Select the OU in which you want the object to reside and choose Action⇨New⇨Shared Folder.

2 Use these boxes to enter the shared folder's name and the UNC path.

3 Click OK.

What information can reside in a shared folder?

- Virtually any information can reside in a shared folder. Common examples include documents, applications, databases, or other shared folders. Shared folders function the same as they did in Windows NT and contain any shared information. The Active Directory simply provides a directory object for the folder and keeps track of where it is located on the network.

Where is the information in the shared folder?

- The shared folder object in the Active Directory is simply a pointer to a computer that contains the shared folder and the information in the shared folder. The method allows a user to contact a computer, such as CORP64737, and use the shared folder on that computer without having to know that the folder actually resides on CORP64737.

Does the Active Directory keep track of a shared folder's contents?

- No. A shared folder object only provides the pointer to the shared folder and a description of the contents in the shared folder, which an administrator enters.

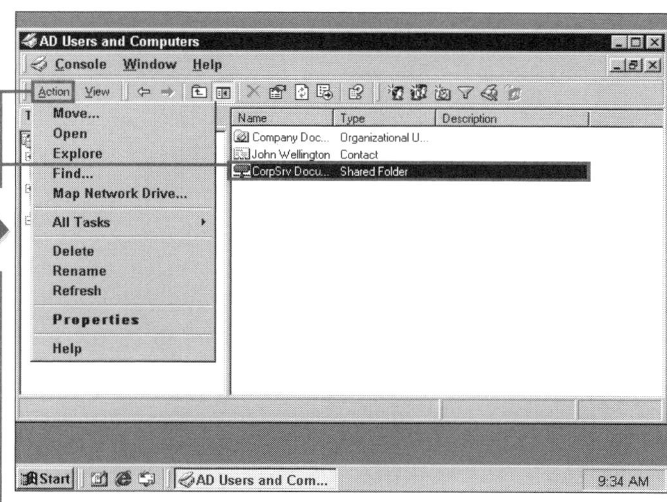

4 To perform additional configuration, select the shared folder.

5 Choose the Action menu.

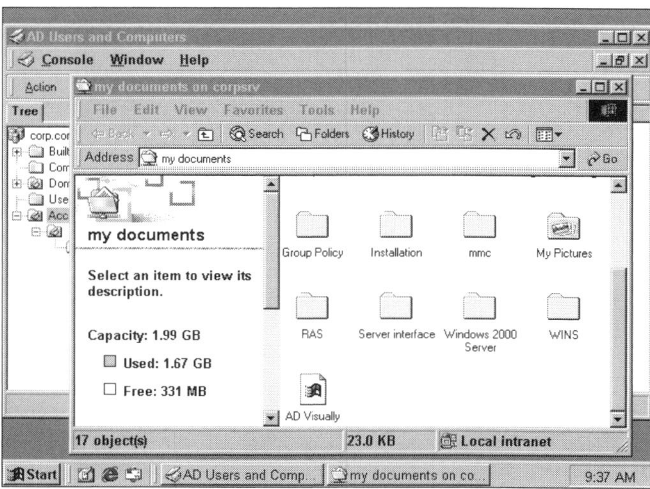

OPENING A SHARED FOLDER

■ Choosing Action⇨Open displays the shared folder and its contents.

CONTINUED

USING SHARED FOLDERS CONTINUED

You can also click Explore in the selection list so that you can see the network directory structure in an Explorer window.

If you click Map Network Drive in the selection list, you can map a network drive to the shared folder that will connect each time you log on. This feature enables you to use My Computer to connect to the share and is a useful feature for shares that you access regularly. The Map Network Drive window enables you to specify a drive letter and shared folder You can also connect using a different username. This feature is provided for anonymous access and allows administrators to connect to shares as other users. You can also connect to Web folder or FTP site by clicking the link. This opens the Add Network Place Wizard, which allows you to create the a connection object on your system. With the ever-growing use of intranet sites, this feature is particularly helpful if you need to connect to a shared folder on the intranet or even the Internet.

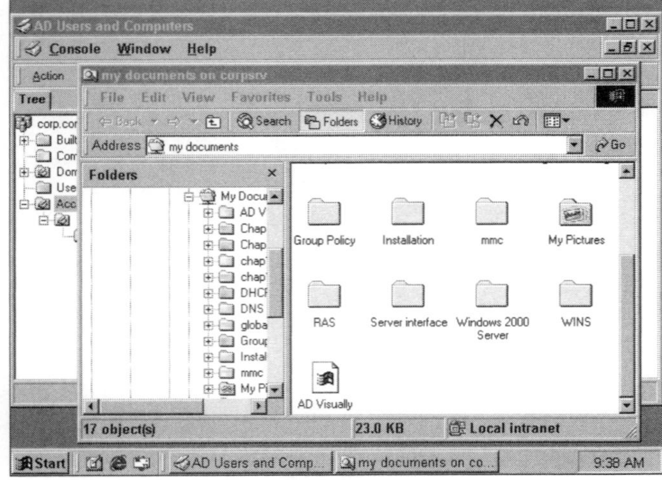

EXPLORING A SHARED FOLDER

■ Choosing Action⇨Explore brings up an Explorer window presenting the directory location of the shared folder.

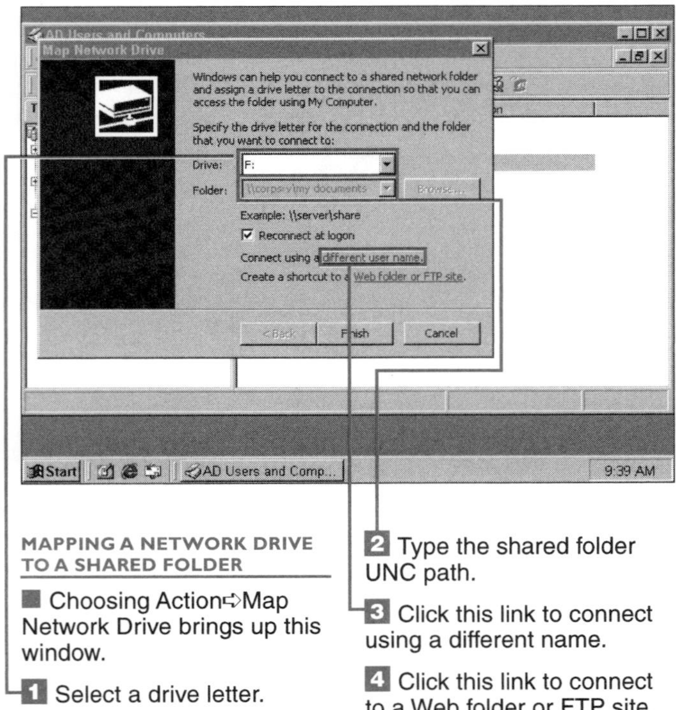

MAPPING A NETWORK DRIVE TO A SHARED FOLDER

■ Choosing Action⇨Map Network Drive brings up this window.

1 Select a drive letter.

2 Type the shared folder UNC path.

3 Click this link to connect using a different name.

4 Click this link to connect to a Web folder or FTP site.

Why is mapping a drive to a Web folder or FTP site an option?

- One of the goals of Windows 2000 is to provide seamless integration with the Internet. You can map a network drive to a Web folder or FTP site on the Internet or intranet just as though the folder was available on your LAN. This feature enables you to access any resource you may need, whether local or not. An important feature of Web folders is user contact over the Internet. A company in several geographic locations can set up a Web site with shared folders available so that network users in other geographical locations can access the information via the Internet. This possibility can reduce site bandwidth by using the Internet.

Do I need to connect to a shared folder using a different username?

- In most cases, no. This option is provided for anonymous access and for users who want to connect using a very secure account (such as an administrator's account).

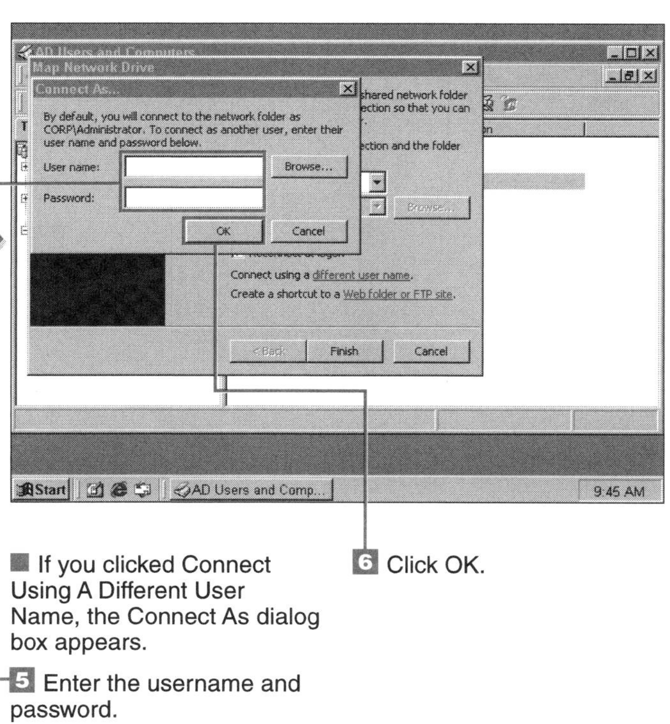

■ If you clicked Connect Using A Different User Name, the Connect As dialog box appears.

5 Enter the username and password.

6 Click OK.

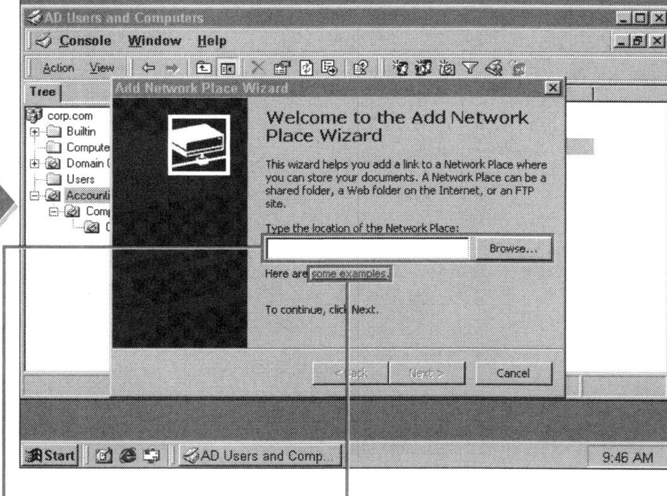

■ If you clicked to connect to a Web folder or FTP site, the Add Network Place Wizard appears.

7 Type the location information or click Browse.

8 Click here to see some examples of shared folder, Web folder, and FTP site syntax.

9 Click Next to continue, and then click Finish.

CONTINUED

USING SHARED FOLDERS CONTINUED

You can also access the properties sheet for the shared folder using the Action menu.

The properties sheet has two tabs: General and Managed By. On the General tab, you can enter a description of the shared folder. The UNC path also appears. The UNC path is the network location of the shared folder. When users access the shared folder object in the Active Directory, they are redirected to the computer that holds the shared folder by the UNC path. If a shared folder ever changes locations on the network, you (as the administrator), will need to change the UNC path so it is correct, or users will not be able to access the shared folder from the directory.

If you click the Keywords button, you can enter keywords for the shared folder, which help users find the folder when they search the Active Directory. You can enter any keywords desired, but they should carefully and accurately describe the contents of the shared folder so that users can find the resources they are searching for.

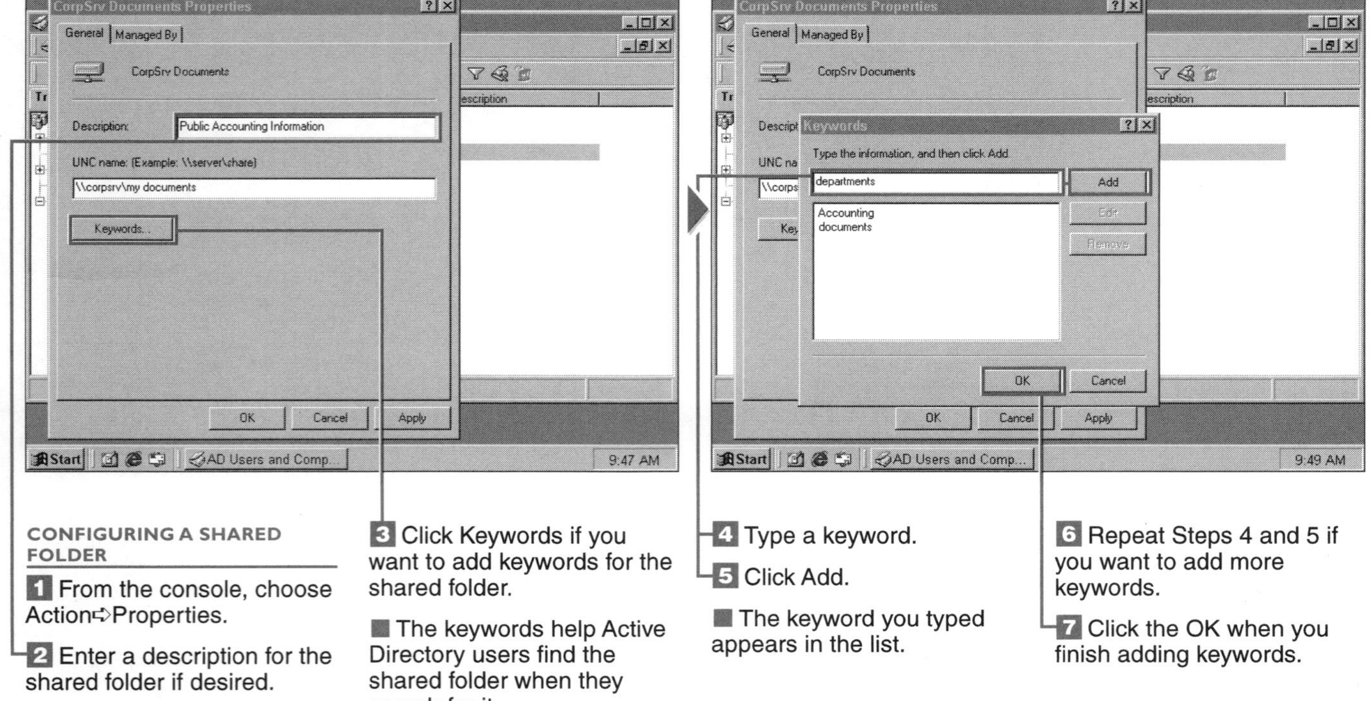

CONFIGURING A SHARED FOLDER

1 From the console, choose Action⇨Properties.

2 Enter a description for the shared folder if desired.

3 Click Keywords if you want to add keywords for the shared folder.

■ The keywords help Active Directory users find the shared folder when they search for it.

4 Type a keyword.

5 Click Add.

■ The keyword you typed appears in the list.

6 Repeat Steps 4 and 5 if you want to add more keywords.

7 Click the OK when you finish adding keywords.

What keywords should I use?

You can use any combination of keywords to help identify a shared folder. The purpose of the keywords is to allow Active Directory users to perform searches. For example, if users know that a folder resides on a marketing server that contains the marketing department's policies, but they do not know the name of the folder, users can search for "marketing shares documents." If the keywords for this share, such as "marketing, folders, documents, shared folders, marketing policies," and so on, have been entered, users can find the folder they need using the search operation.

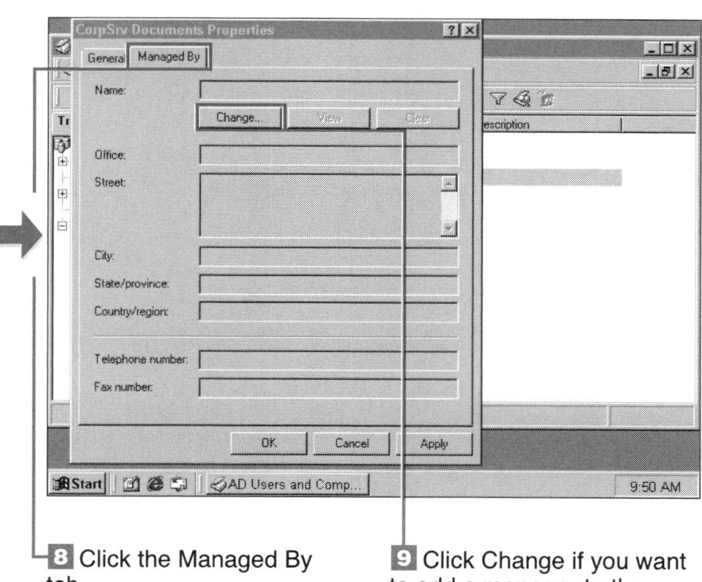

8 Click the Managed By tab.

9 Click Change if you want to add a manager to the shared folder from the Active Directory.

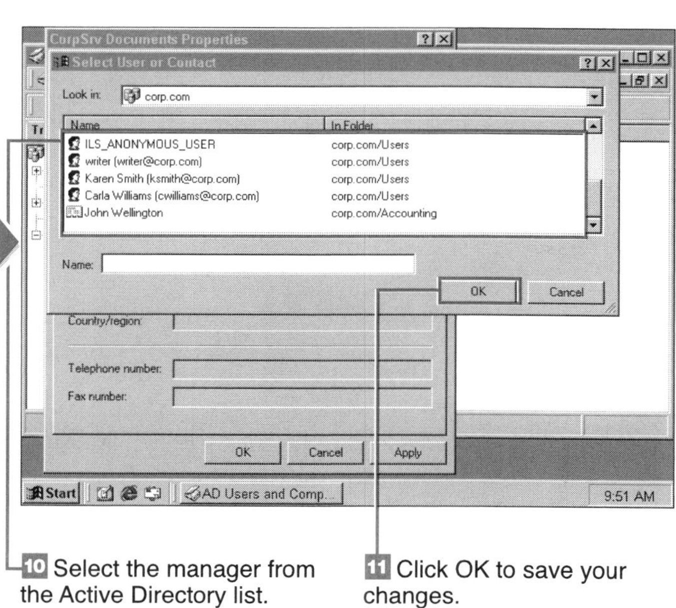

10 Select the manager from the Active Directory list.

11 Click OK to save your changes.

USING NETWORK PRINTERS

You can add network printers to the Active Directory so that users can more easily find them. Typically, various printers are attached to print servers or even users' computers. The Active Directory makes it easy for users to find printers because users do not have to know the UNC path to the printer. Printers connected to Windows 2000 computers can be automatically published in the Active Directory without administrator intervention.

You can use the Active Directory Printer object to connect to the printer, and you can open it to see what is in the print queue. You can also select Properties using the Action menu.

The printer properties sheet has two tabs: General and Managed By. On the General tab, you can add information about the printer's location, model, and additional comments if desired. On the Managed By tab, you can click the Change button to assign the printer object to an Active Directory user.

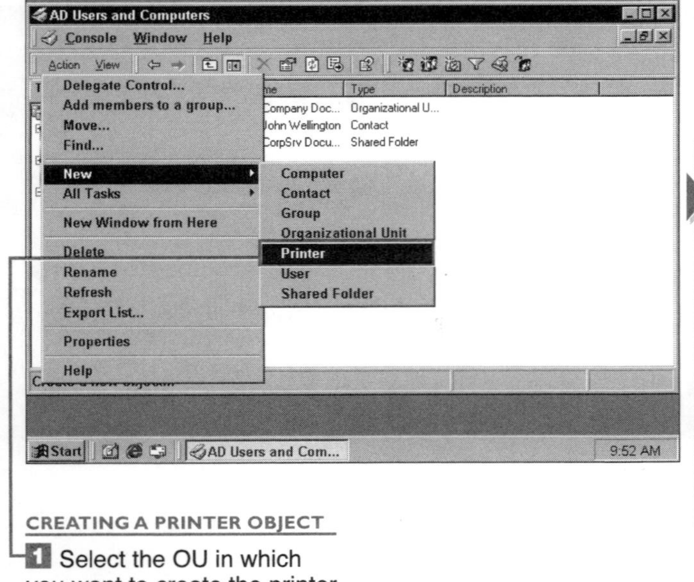

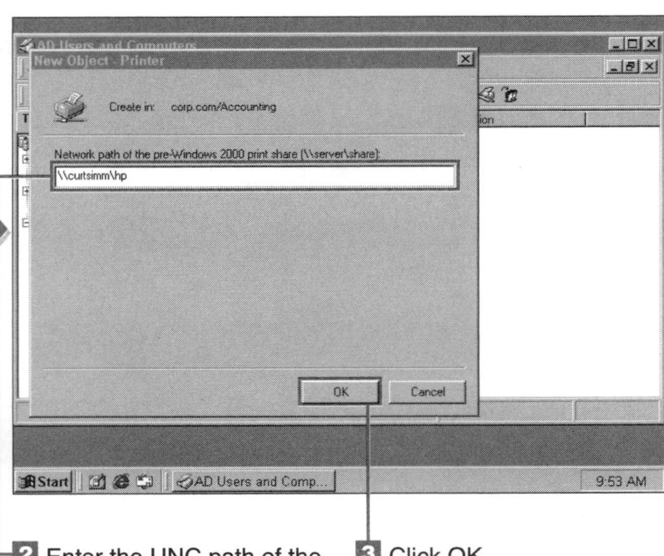

CREATING A PRINTER OBJECT

1 Select the OU in which you want to create the printer and choose Action⇨New⇨Printer.

2 Enter the UNC path of the printer location.

3 Click OK.

Can users access various printers directly through the Active Directory or will they still need the UNC path?

- Users, provided they have appropriate permissions, can access the printers directly from the Active Directory. The object stores the UNC path information to the printer so that users do not have to know this information to reach the printer.

How can I keep certain groups from using a printer in the Active Directory?

- Just because an object, such as a printer, resides in the Active Directory does not mean that any user or group can use the resource. Permissions are configured on the actual shared object on the machine that houses the printer. You can set permissions there and deny whatever groups or users you so choose. Even though users can access the printer object in the directory, they must have appropriate permissions to use the object.

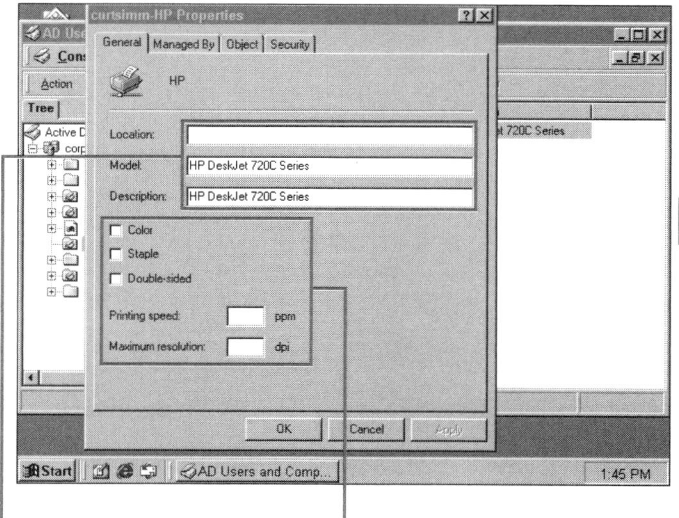

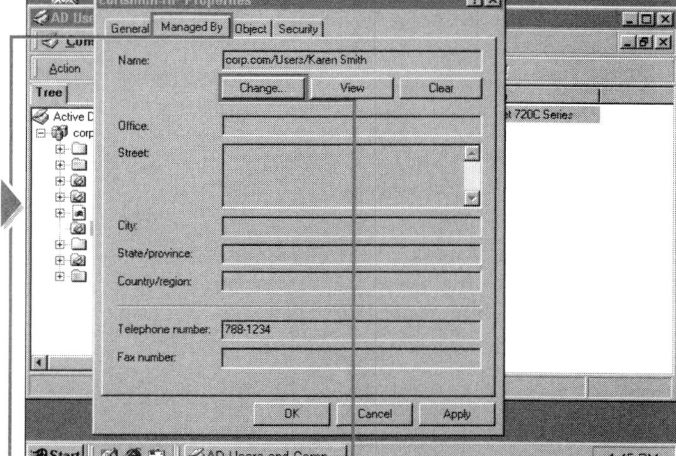

CONFIGURING A PRINTER OBJECT

1 Select the printer object and choose Action⇨Properties.

2 Enter the location, model, and description.

3 Enter additional information about the printer's properties.

4 Click the Managed By tab.

5 Click Change to assign a manager to the printer object. Select an Active Directory user from the list that appears and click OK.

MANAGING DOMAIN CONTROLLERS

You can use the Active Directory Users and Computers snap-in to manage domain controllers and their properties that apply to the Active Directory within this snap-in. With proper permissions, you can even manage the actual machine itself from within the Active Directory. Certain functions, such as trust relationships, replication, and others that affect the entire Active Directory, are managed from other snap-ins that are discussed later in the book.

If you click the Domain Controllers OU, you see a list of domain controllers for your particular domain appears in the right details pane of the console. If you select a domain controller and use the Action menu, you can see the actions you can perform.

You can perform a number of configuration tasks, such as move domain controllers, manage domain controllers, and even access the domain controller's properties sheets for further configuration options.

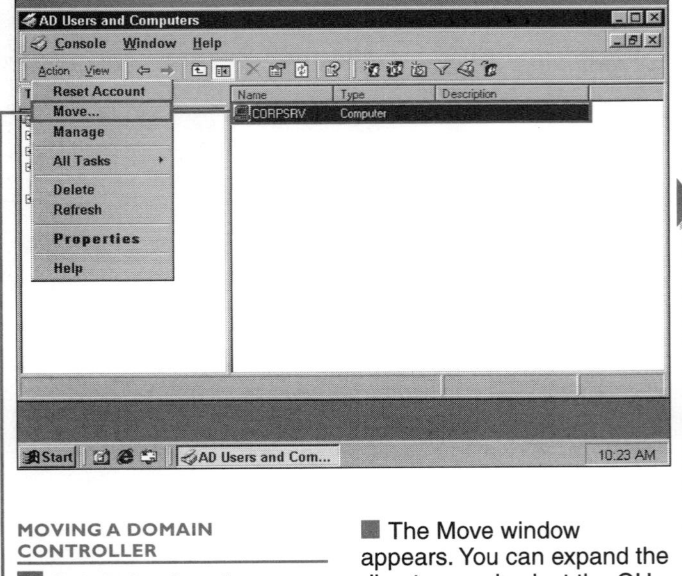

MOVING A DOMAIN CONTROLLER

1 Select the domain controller you want to administer, and then click Action⇨Move.

■ The Move window appears. You can expand the directory and select the OU you want to move the domain controller to.

2 Make your selection and click OK.

What does *delegation* mean?

- You can assign both computers and users the right to be ***delegates***. This means that other resources can be assigned to the user or computer so that those resources can be managed by that person or computer. Delegation is a powerful feature of Windows 2000 that is designed to reduce administrative overhead b allowing other people to manage certain aspects of the Active Directory. Delegation, however, still allows you to maintain control over what you delegate and how the delegate manage the object.

Do I need to enter a description for the server on the General tab?

- A description is not required; however, the description appears in the details pane in the Active Directory for the object. Generally, entering a description for all Active Directory objects is a good idea so that you can easily find needed objects.

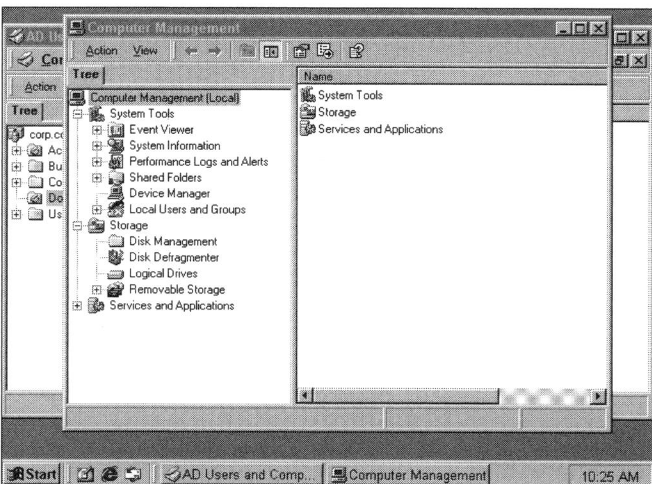

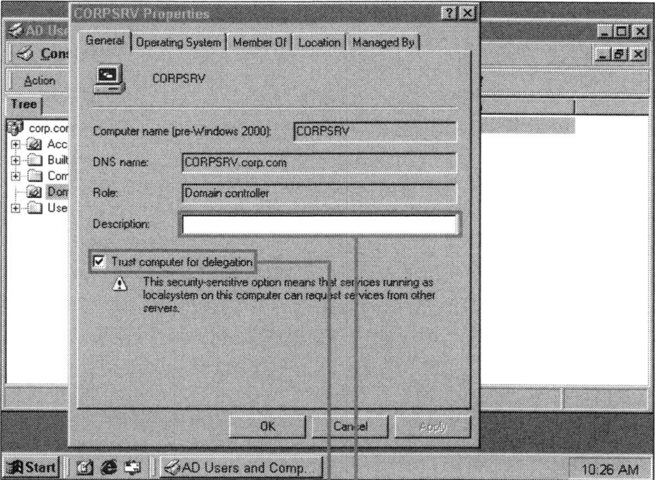

SELECTING MANAGE OPTIONS

1 Choose Action⇨Manage.

■ The Computer Management snap-in opens. You can then perform a number of configuration options (provided you have appropriate permissions).

CONFIGURING A DOMAIN CONTROLLER

■ Return to the Active Directory Users and Computers snap-in, select the desired domain controller, then choose Action⇨Properties.

1 You can enter a description in this box on the General tab.

2 Click this check box if you want the server to be trusted for delegation.

CONTINUED

MANAGING DOMAIN CONTROLLERS CONTINUED

The Operating System tab tells you the operating system, version number, and the service pack that has been applied (if any). As service packs are released for Windows 2000 and applied to the domain controller, the service pack version number appears in this tab. This is any easy way to track your domain controllers and make certain that they all have the most current service pack applied.

The Member Of tab tells you which groups the server belongs to. As with users, a computer account can belong to different groups. Use the Member Of tab to manage the groups to which the domain controller belongs. By using the Add and Remove buttons, you can easily manage the group membership of the domain controller and change them when necessary.

The Location tab tells you which locations are served by the site in the directory. If you have multiple sites, you can click the Browse button to choose additional locations.

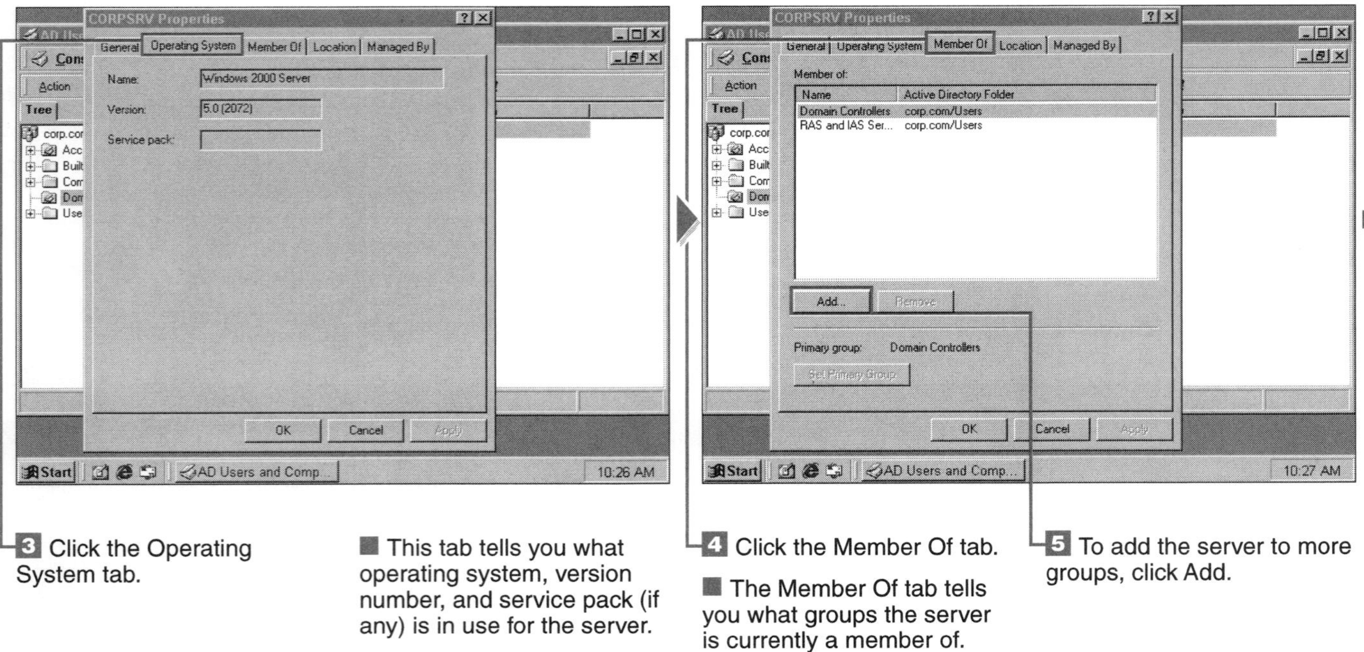

3 Click the Operating System tab.

■ This tab tells you what operating system, version number, and service pack (if any) is in use for the server.

4 Click the Member Of tab.

■ The Member Of tab tells you what groups the server is currently a member of.

5 To add the server to more groups, click Add.

To how many groups should a domain controller belong?

- You can allow the domain controller to be a member of any group you choose. However, for administrative purposes, you should limit group membership to those that are necessary. Excessive group memberships may cause permission problems. See Chapter 14 for more information about group accounts.

If I use the Remove button to take a group membership away from a server, will this affect the other groups?

- No. Each group functions on its own, so you can add and remove group membership for the server without affecting other groups. The server should, however, remain in any default groups configured by Windows 2000 (such as the Domain Controllers group). Keep in mind that computer group membership functions in much the same way as user group membership. The purpose is to organize computer accounts so they can access desired resources and have rights applied for the desired groups.

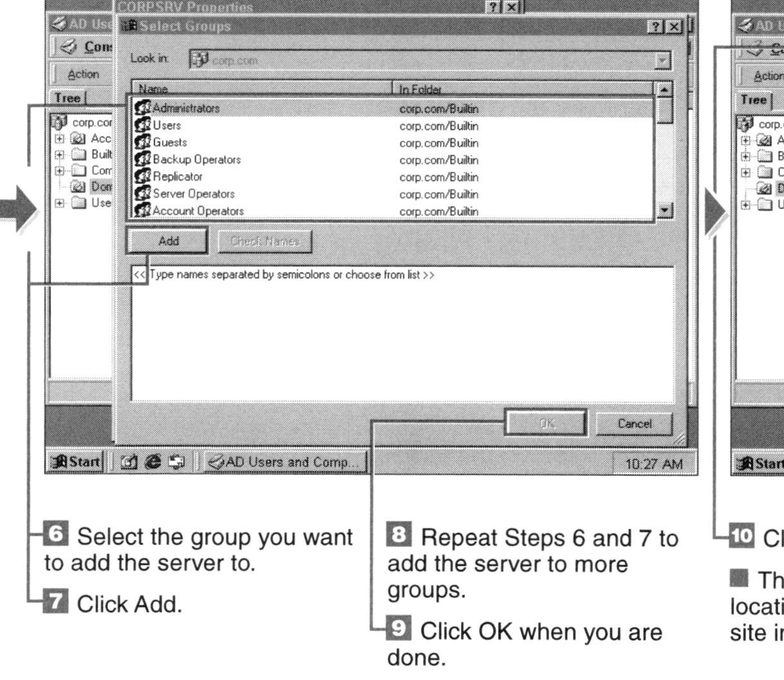

6 Select the group you want to add the server to.

7 Click Add.

8 Repeat Steps 6 and 7 to add the server to more groups.

9 Click OK when you are done.

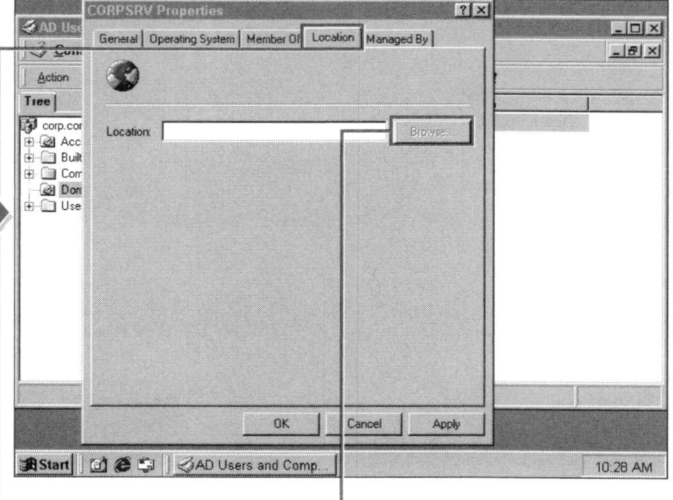

10 Click the Location tab.

■ This tab tells you which locations are served by the site in the directory.

11 Click Browse to choose a different location.

CONTINUED

MANAGING DOMAIN CONTROLLERS

CONTINUED

On the Managed By tab, you can assign a manager for the domain controller. After you configure a manager for the domain controller, the manager's name and contact information is taken from the Active Directory and automatically entered on the Managed By tab. This feature enables you to easily see who manages various domain controllers and how to contact the manager. Of course, this information is not required on this tab and does not appear if the contact information is not configured in the manager's Active Directory user account.

You can also see more information about the manager by clicking the View button. This action opens the properties sheet for the user or group from the Active Directory who manages the domain controller. If no additional information is configured in the manager's user account, then it will be not be viewable.

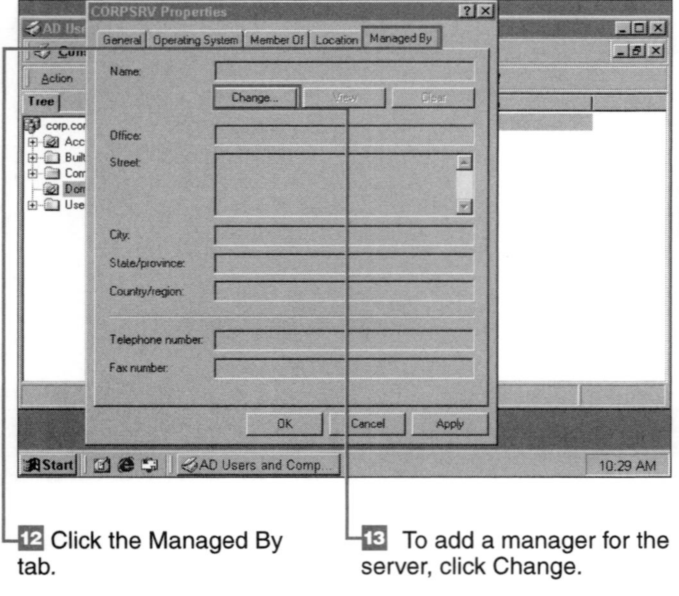

12 Click the Managed By tab.

13 To add a manager for the server, click Change.

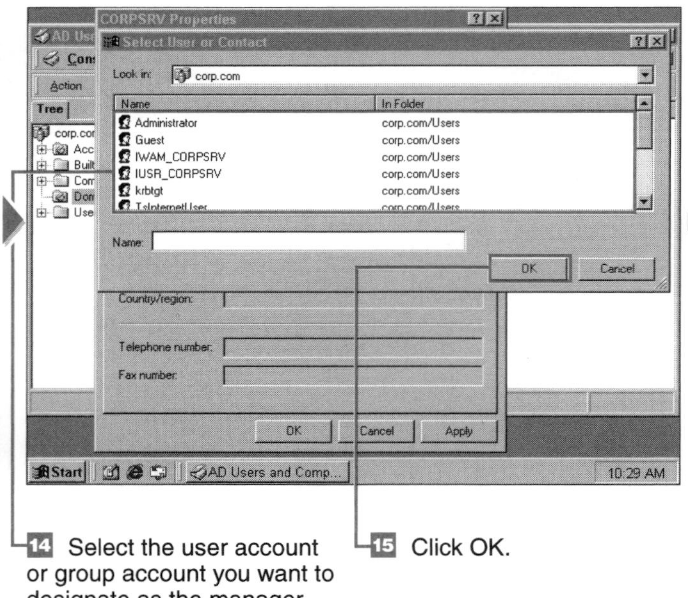

14 Select the user account or group account you want to designate as the manager.

15 Click OK.

How can I keep a manager's contact information private?

A manager's contact information is taken from the information configured in the manager's Active Directory user account. In order to keep the contact information (such as the manager's phone number) private, you have to delete this information from the manager's user account in the Active Directory. By doing so, no Active Directory users can read the information because it does not appear in the manager's account.

Do I have to assign a manager?

No. You are not required to assign a manager on this tab. In some cases, a single person or group manages all domain controllers, in which case, you do not need to assign a manager using the Managed By tab. This is strictly an administrative issue and not a required configuration component of the Active Directory.

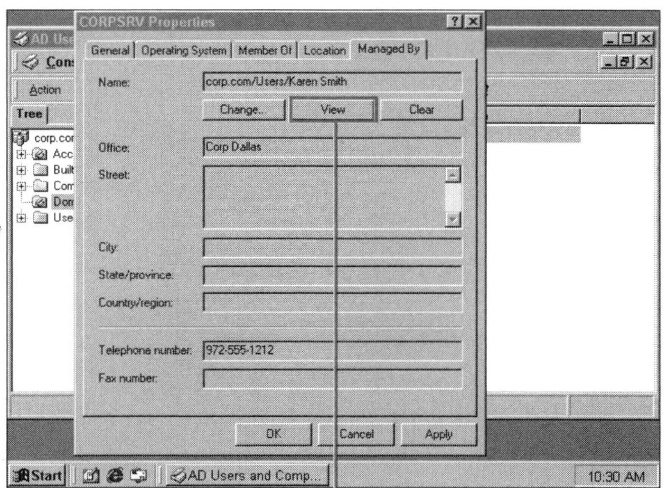

■ The new manager's name and contact information — taken from the Active Directory — now appears.

16 To view additional Active Directory information about the manager, click View.

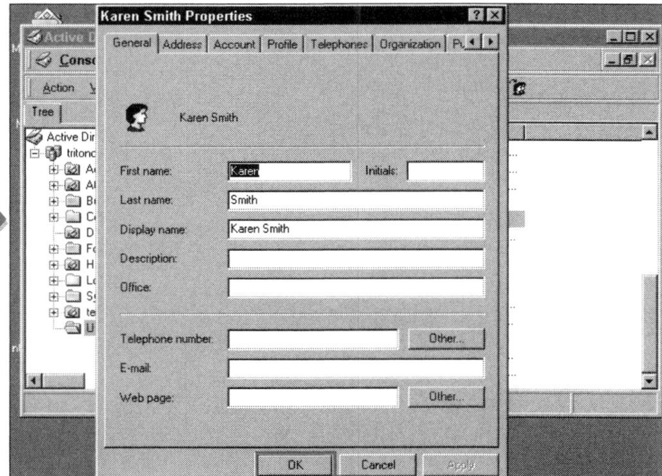

■ The Properties sheet for the manager appears.

17 Click OK when you are done.

SECTION VI

19) ACTIVE DIRECTORY REPLICATION CONCEPTS

20) USING THE ACTIVE DIRECTORY DOMAINS AND TRUSTS CONSOLE

21) MANAGING DOMAINS AND TRUSTS

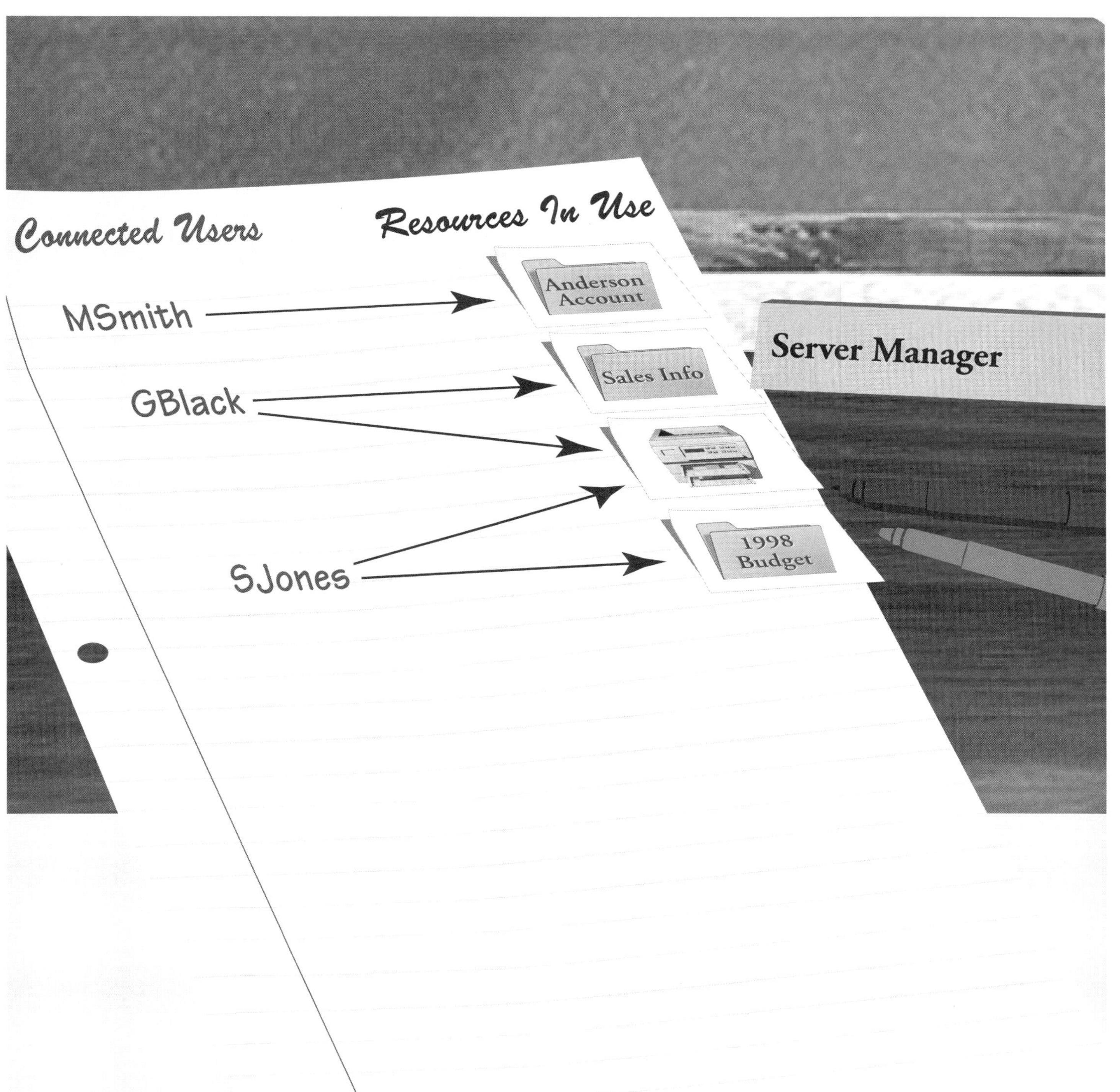
Connected Users
Resources In Use
MSmith
GBlack
SJones
Anderson Account
Sales Info
1998 Budget
Server Manager

WHAT IS REPLICATION?

Replication is the process of sending update notifications to other Active Directory domain controllers when changes or updates occur in the Active Directory. Imagine you have two documents that are exactly alike. If you change a sentence in one document, you must also change the same sentence in the second document to keep them exactly the same.

The purpose of replication is the same—to *replicate*, or copy, changes to other Active Directory databases so that all Active Directory data on all domain controllers is exactly the same. Through Active Directory replication, all domain controllers are assured of having correct database information that accurately reflects the resources available in the Active Directory environment.

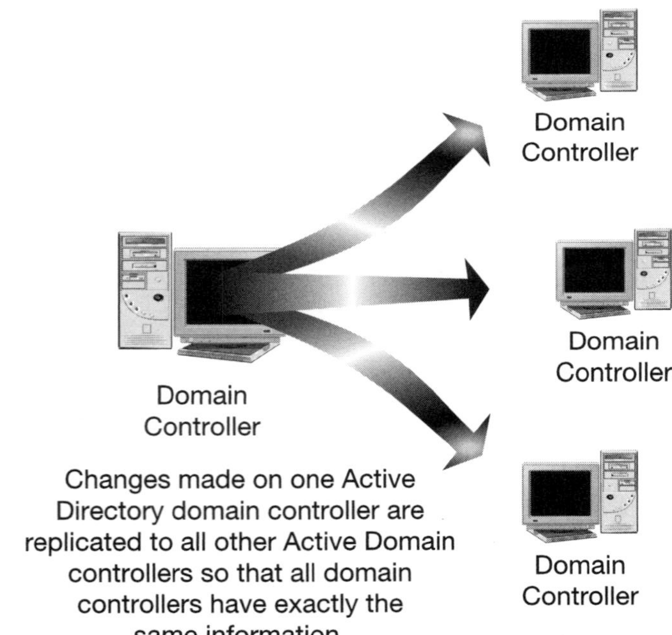
Domain Controller
Domain Controller
Domain Controller
Domain Controller
Changes made on one Active Directory domain controller are replicated to all other Active Domain controllers so that all domain controllers have exactly the same information.

UNDERSTANDING REPLICATION TOPOLOGY

Active Directory replication occurs between two topologies—intrasite and intersite. *Intrasite replication* occurs within a site, which is a grouping of computers or domains connected by high-speed bandwidth. (You can learn more about sites in Chapters 22 and 23.) Within a site, or intrasite, the Active Directory automatically generates a replication topology; it determines how the domain controllers replicate data to one another. This feature is a great administrative benefit because it removes the burden of manually configuring replication between domain controllers.

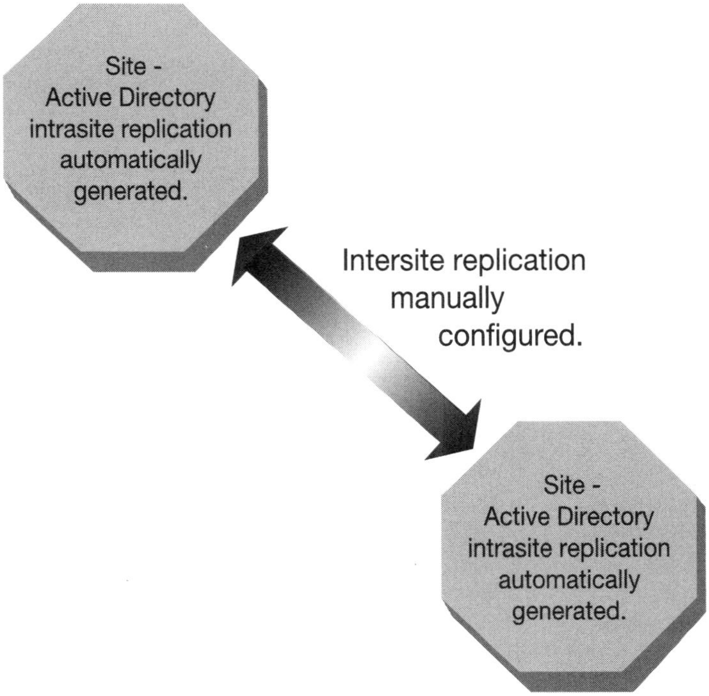

For *intersite replication*, you manually establish the site link used to replicate data (see Chapter 23). Sites are generally connected by slower or less reliable links, and a replication topology is not automatically generated between sites.

In order to fully understand the replication process, you should understand how the Active Directory automatically generates the intrasite replication topology. *Replication topology* defines the pathways between domain controllers through connection objects and the Knowledge Consistency Checker (KCC).

Replication occurs through domain controller partners. The Active Directory determines whether a domain controller is a direct partner with another domain controller or if it receives replication indirectly from a domain controller through transitive replication. This simply means that if Server1 is a direct partner with Server2, and Server2 is a direct partner with Server3, then Server3 receives replication data indirectly (transitively) from Server1. The KCC determines how domain controllers are partnered so that all domain controllers receive replication data. Direct connections are called *connection objects* and are unidirectional between the two domain controllers. In other words, a potential direct partner domain controller is seen as a connection object in terms of the replication topology. The Active Directory automatically generates connection objects based on information about the sites, subnets within the sites, and cost of connections. The KCC uses this information to generate a replication topology in a bi-directional ring (by default). When a change is made to the Active Directory that needs to be replicated, the replication engine on the domain controller begins the replication process at a defined interval when replication can occur (every five minutes by default). Then, it notifies its first replication partner, which notifies its partner, and so forth. By this design of direct and indirect replication, replication within a site generally takes about 15 minutes to replicate to all domain controllers.

Site -
Active Directory
intrasite replication
automatically
generated.
Intersite replication
manually
configured.
Site -
Active Directory
intrasite replication
automatically
generated.

HOW REPLICATION WORKS IN THE ACTIVE DIRECTORY

Windows 2000 functions using *multimaster replication*, which means that no single master replicator domain controller exists; all domain controllers function as peers and are equally responsible for replication. Through the use of multimaster replication, changes to the Active Directory can be made at any domain controller in the Active Directory environment, and those changes are replicated to all other domain controllers in the environment. Without effective, timely replication, domain controllers would lose the accurate view of Active Directory resources because each domain controller would not be aware of changes made at other domain controllers. So, you can see that replication is a highly important part of the Active Directory's functionality and without it, the Active Directory would be full of errors in a short period of time.

Windows 2000 uses multimaster replication. All domain controllers are responsible for sending and accepting replication data.

Replication begins with a *change notification*, which is a message that a domain controller sends to other domain controllers to inform them of a change in the Active Directory. For example, if you add a new object, such as a user account, to the Active Directory, the domain controller on which you added the object sends a change notification to all other domain controllers telling them that a new object has been added.

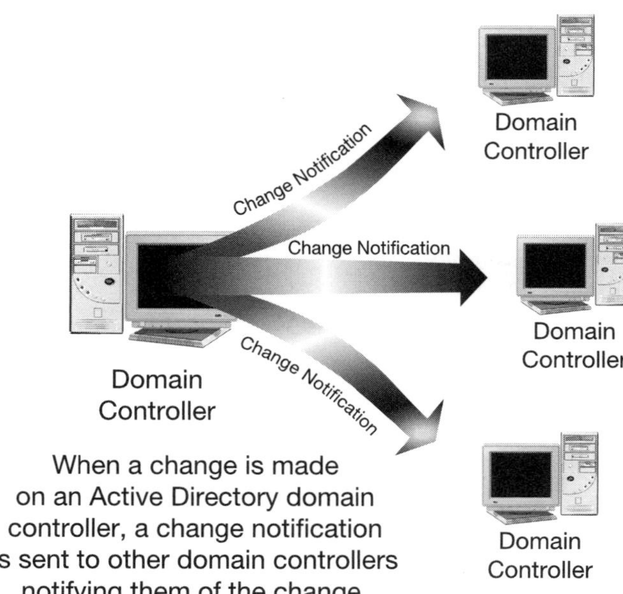

When a change is made on an Active Directory domain controller, a change notification is sent to other domain controllers notifying them of the change.

After a change notification is sent, the process continues with an *update request*. When a domain controller needs to replicate data to other domain controllers, an *originating update* is created. An originating update determines what kind of change needs to be made to the Active Directory data. There are four kinds of originating updates: Add, Modify, ModifyDN, and Delete. The Add originating update adds something to the Active Directory—for example, if you add a new user account. If you modify something in the Active Directory, such as user account's password, the Modify originating" update is used. The exception to the Modify originating update is the ModifyDN originating update. The ModifyDN originating update is used if you change the name of an object or an object's parent. Because changing the name of an object or an object's parent is different than changing an attribute (such as a user account password), the ModifyDN is used to modify the name. Keep in mind that Active Directory objects have a number of LDAP names that are hidden from users. The DN portion of the name is the "distinguished name" of the object—or what you normally call the object. Finally, if you delete something, such as a user account, the Delete originating update is used.

Originating updates occur on the domain controller where the change was made and are replicated to other domain controllers. When other domain controllers receive the originating update, the update becomes a replicated update in their databases.

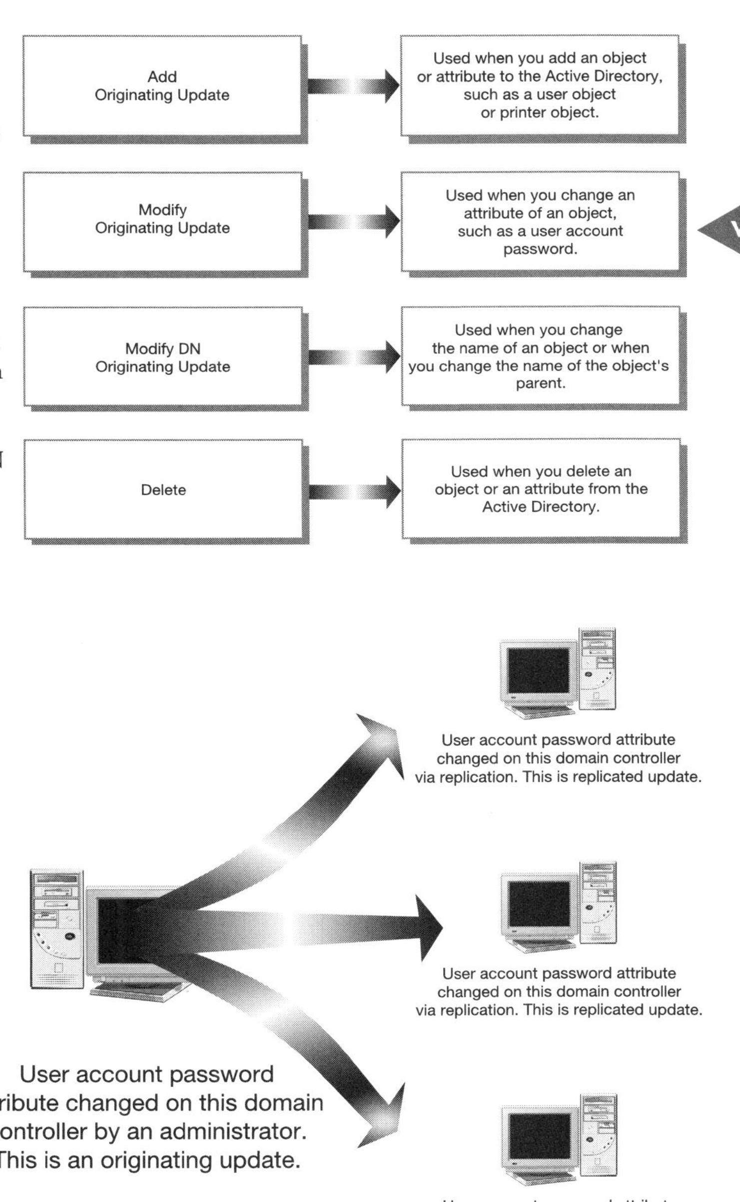
Add
Originating Update
Used when you add an object or attribute to the Active Directory, such as a user object or printer object.
Modify
Originating Update
Used when you change an attribute of an object, such as a user account password.
Modify DN
Originating Update
Used when you change the name of an object or when you change the name of the object's parent.
Delete
Used when you delete an object or an attribute from the Active Directory.
User account password attribute changed on this domain controller via replication. This is replicated update.
User account password attribute changed on this domain controller via replication. This is replicated update.
User account password attribute changed on this domain controller via replication. This is replicated update.
User account password attribute changed on this domain controller by an administrator. This is an originating update.

HOW REPLICATION WORKS IN THE ACTIVE DIRECTORY

Update Sequence Numbers

The replication process works, in part, due to the use of *Update Sequence Numbers (USN)*. USNs are assigned numbers that are stored on a USN table on each domain controller. USNs determine the updates that need to occur between domain controllers. When a domain controller needs to change, delete, or update an object, the USN number for the updated attribute changes. For example, if you change a user account's password, the password attribute USN number is updated on the domain controller so that all other domain controllers have an outdated USN for that user account's password. This way, other domain controllers know they have an outdated USN that needs to be updated. The other domain controllers accept the replication change and update their USN table so that each domain controller maintains the highest USN numbers for each object and for the attributes of that object.

Because of USNs, timestamps are not used in the normal replication process, but they are still maintained for special circumstances, such as tie-breaking. For example, if an administrator on one domain controller changes a user account's password, and at the same time on a different domain controller, an administrator makes the same change, the timestamp is used to break the tie. The highest timestamp wins.

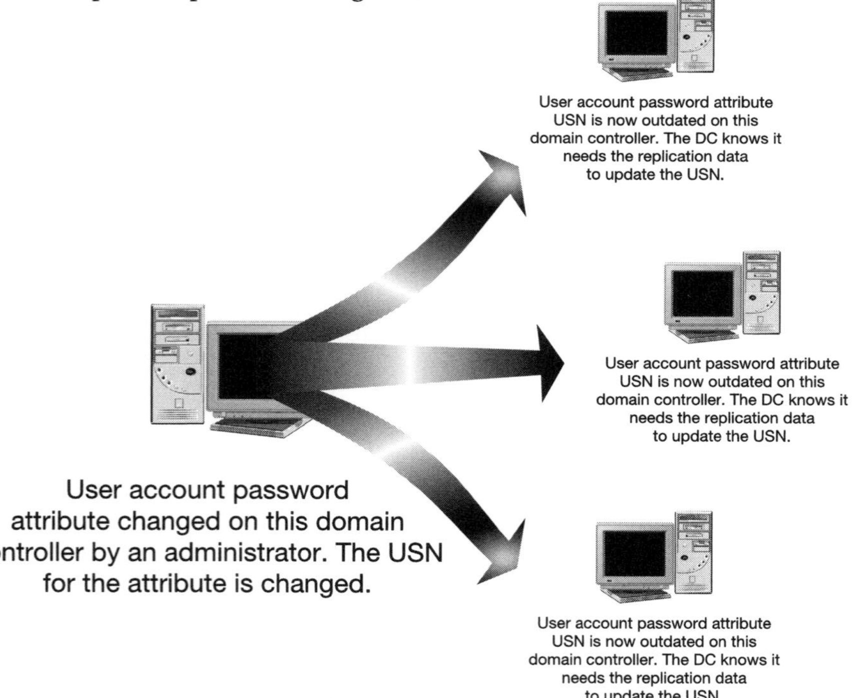
User account password attribute USN is now outdated on this domain controller. The DC knows it needs the replication data to update the USN.
User account password attribute USN is now outdated on this domain controller. The DC knows it needs the replication data to update the USN.
User account password attribute changed on this domain controller by an administrator. The USN for the attribute is changed.
User account password attribute USN is now outdated on this domain controller. The DC knows it needs the replication data to update the USN.

HOW REPLICATION WORKS IN THE ACTIVE DIRECTORY

Propagation Dampening

The Active Directory maintains a *loop* of traffic so that replication reaches all domain controllers. However, this loop can potentially allow unnecessary replication traffic. To avoid this, propagation dampening is used. Basically, *propagation dampening* prevents the same replication traffic from visiting the same domain controller twice. Domain controllers detect when data has already been replicated to another domain controller, and when this detection occurs, the domain controller "kills" the replication so that it is not sent to the same domain controller twice.

This process occurs through the use of two *vectors*, which are made up of pairs of data containing the USN and the Globally Unique Identifier (GUID). The two vectors are called the *Up-to-date vector* and the *High Watermark vector*. The Up-to-date vector contains the server USN pairs containing the highest originating update. The High Watermark vector holds the USN numbers for attributes that have been changed or modified in the Active Directory and are stored in the replication metadata (which is data about data) for that attribute. Through the use of both vectors, domain controllers can detect when another domain controller has already received the replication data so that propagation dampening can occur. This is a system process and one that is not configurable and is invisible to administrators.

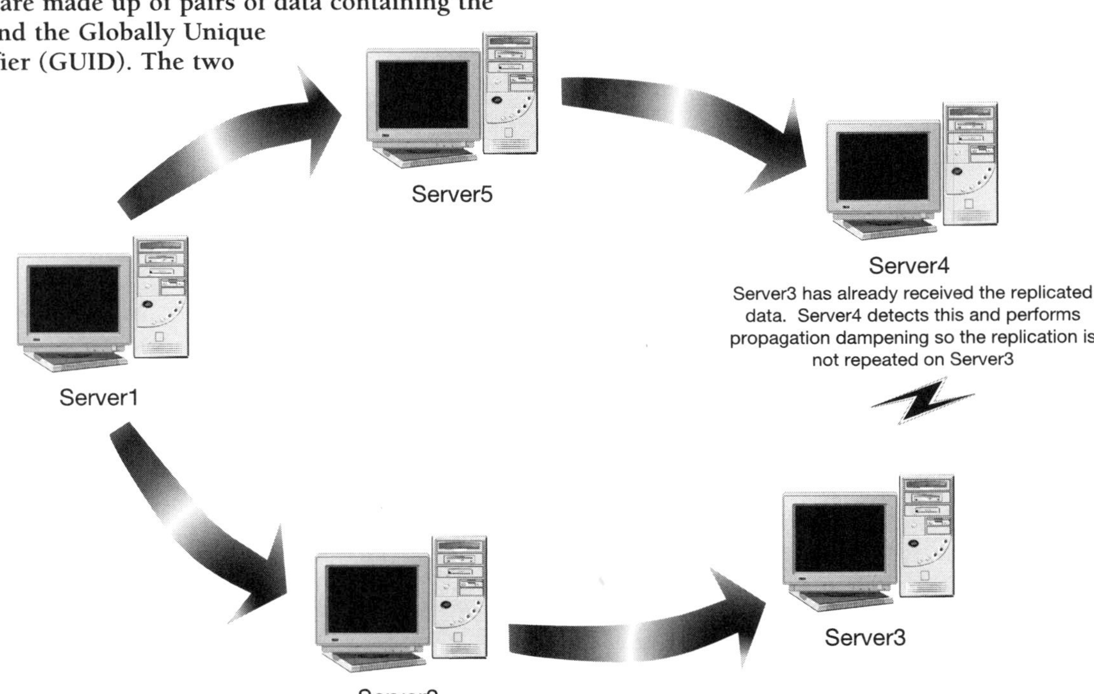
Server5
Server4
Server3 has already received the replicated data. Server4 detects this and performs propagation dampening so the replication is not repeated on Server3
Server1
Server2
Server3

HOW REPLICATION WORKS IN THE ACTIVE DIRECTORY

Solving replication collisions

Because Active Directory replication occurs through multimaster replication, replication conflicts can occur. One of the Active Directory's internal tasks is to solve replication conflicts. A conflict occurs when the same attribute is changed at the same time on two different domain controllers. The Active Directory avoids collisions by using *attribute replication* rather than *object replication*. For example, when you change a user account's password, only the password attribute is replicated instead of the entire user object. If another administrator on another domain controller is changing the user object's group membership at the same time, a conflict does not occur because each administrator is changing a different attribute.

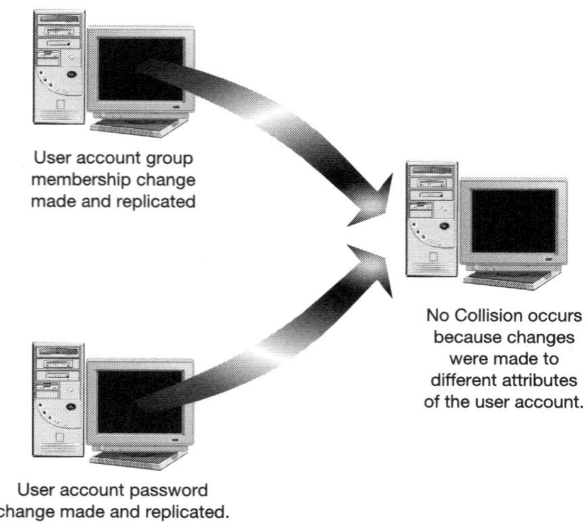
User account group membership change made and replicated
No Collision occurs because changes were made to different attributes of the user account.
User account password change made and replicated.

However, even though data is replicated at the attribute level, conflicts can still occur. If an administrator on one domain controller changes a user's password and another administrator on another domain controller changes the same user's password, and if replication occurs at the same time, then a replication collision occurs.

In this case, *replication resolution* occurs to correct the collision. Resolution is accomplished by using the USN numbers and timestamps recorded in the attribute's metadata. The domain controller on which the collision occurs looks for the highest USN or timestamp to resolve the collision and determine which change should be replicated. In extreme cases in which the USN and timestamp are the same, then the GUID is used to break the tie. The collision resolution process makes certain that the latest change to the attribute is the one that is replicated.

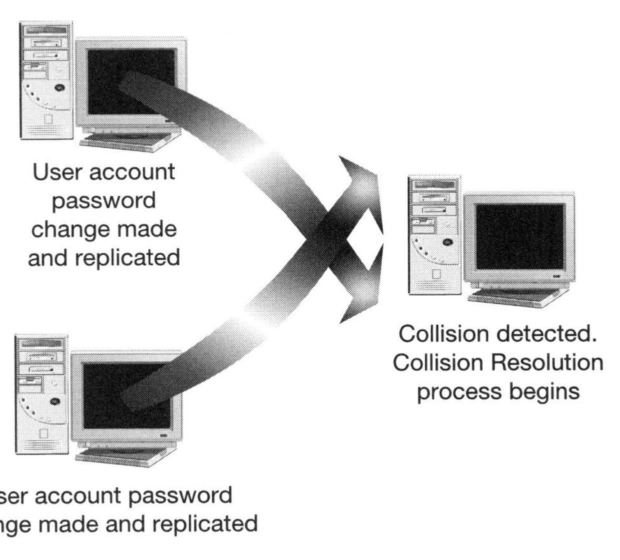
User account password change made and replicated
User account password change made and replicated
Collision detected. Collision Resolution process begins

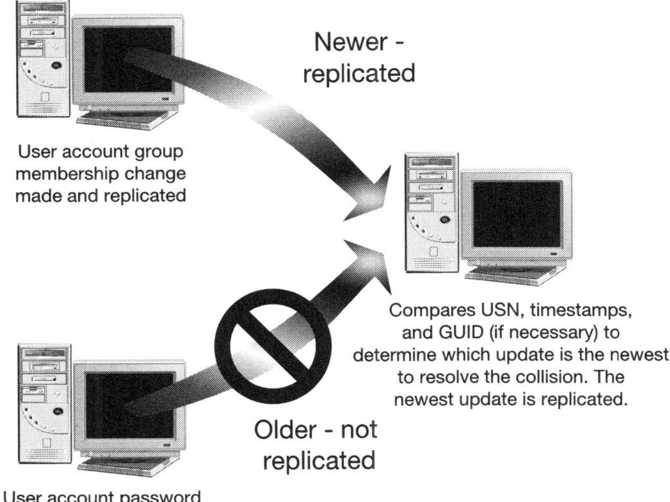
Newer - replicated
User account group membership change made and replicated
Compares USN, timestamps, and GUID (if necessary) to determine which update is the newest to resolve the collision. The newest update is replicated.
Older - not replicated
User account password :hange made and replicated.

UNDERSTANDING REPLICATION PARTITIONS

Active Directory replication occurs at three major levels of the Active Directory. Understanding how replication occurs at these levels is important because replication can have an impact on designing an Active Directory environment. The following sections examine each of the replication partitions.

Schema partition

The Schema partition contains definitions for objects, classes of objects, and the attributes for each object. In other words, the Schema (which you can learn more about in Chapter 27) contains metadata that determines what can be stored in the Active Directory and how the metadata is defined. The Active Directory Schema applies to the entire enterprise. In other words, schema changes are replicated to the fullest extent of your Active Directory environment, whether that be a tree or forest. An enterprise contains only schema that is exactly the same in all domains, trees, and forests in the environment.

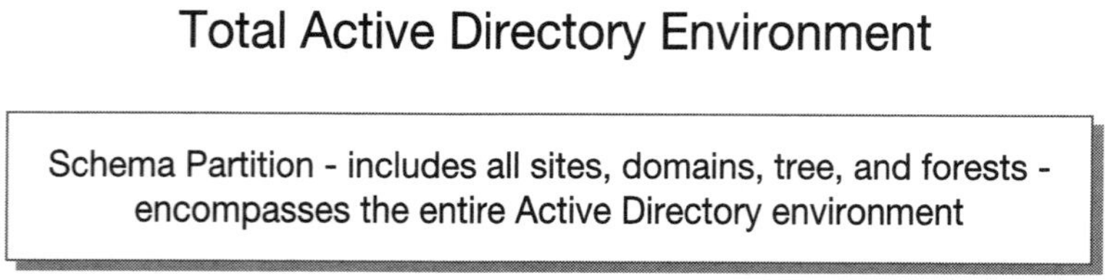

Total Active Directory Environment

Schema Partition - includes all sites, domains, tree, and forests - encompasses the entire Active Directory environment

Configuration partition

The Configuration partition contains information about the physical design of the Active Directory. This includes your sites and domains and where domain controllers physically reside on the network. Configuration replication applies to the entire enterprise and is sent to all domain controllers in every domain, tree, and forest.

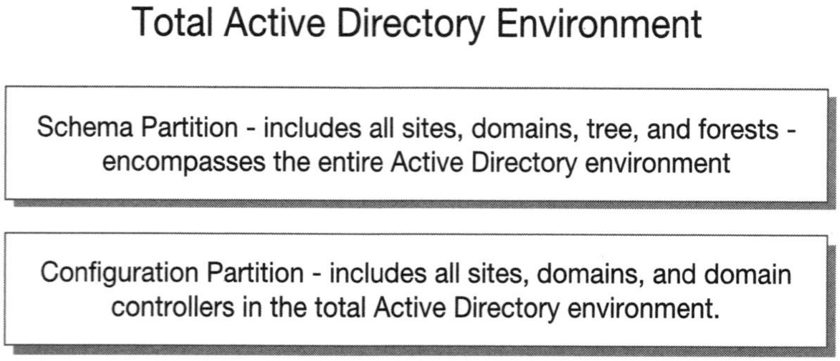

Total Active Directory Environment

Schema Partition - includes all sites, domains, tree, and forests - encompasses the entire Active Directory environment

Configuration Partition - includes all sites, domains, and domain controllers in the total Active Directory environment.

Domain partition

The Domain partition contains information about all Active Directory objects in a domain (such as users, groups, printers, shared folders, and so on). Domain partition information is completely replicated to all domain controllers within the domain. A read-only replica of the domain partition is also replicated to all global catalog servers in other domains. This allows all domain controllers to know what resources reside in other domains, but changes to the domain partition can only occur within the domain for which it applies. This feature maintains domain security, but still allows users in other domains to see what resources are available.

Total Active Directory Environment
Schema Partition - includes all sites, domains, tree, and forests - encompasses the entire Active Directory environment
Configuration Partition - includes all sites, domains, and domain controllers in the total Active Directory environment.
Domain Partition - includes Active Directory objects for the domain only. Replicas are sent to global catalog servers in other domains within the Active Directory environment.

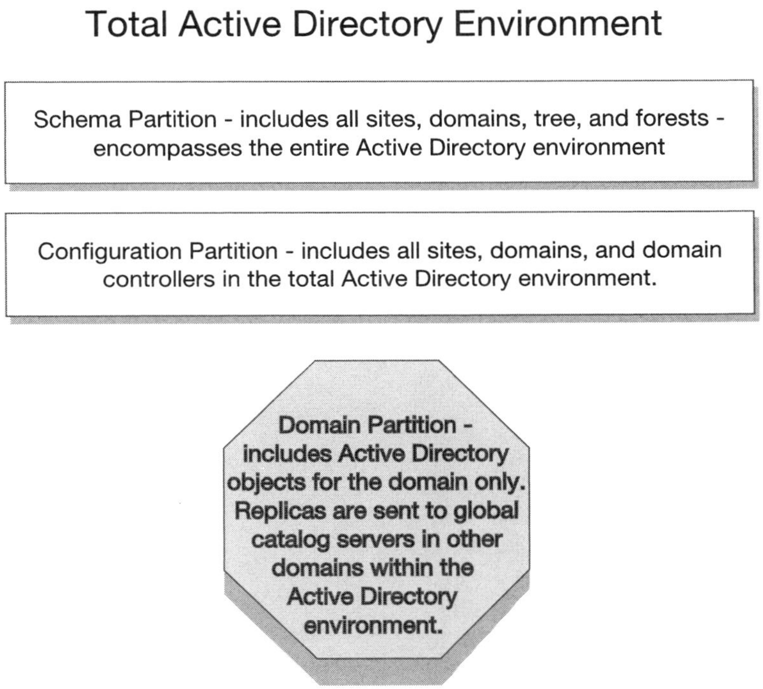

CONNECTING TO A DOMAIN CONTROLLER

The Active Directory Domains and Trusts MMC snap-in is one of the three Active Directory tools. You can use this snap-in to manage Active Directory domains and trust relationships between domains.

From this snap-in, you can connect to different domain controllers, both within the domain and in other domains that are part of the Active Directory tree or forest. By connecting to other domain controllers within the domain, you can make changes to the domain, such as changing the operations master. This task is explained later in this chapter. By connecting to domain controllers in other domains, you can manage trust relationships between the domains as necessary.

This console does not enable you to perform a lot of different tasks, but it does give you an easy way to manage the domains in your network and their relationships to one another.

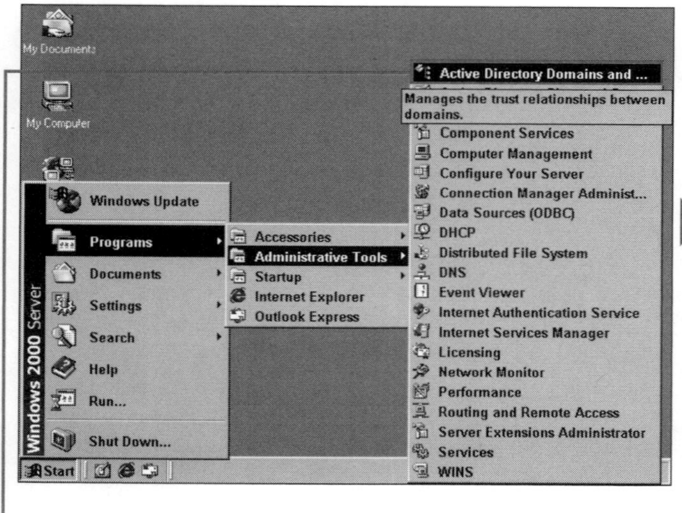

1 Choose Start⇨Programs⇨Administrative Tools⇨Active Directory Domains and Trusts.

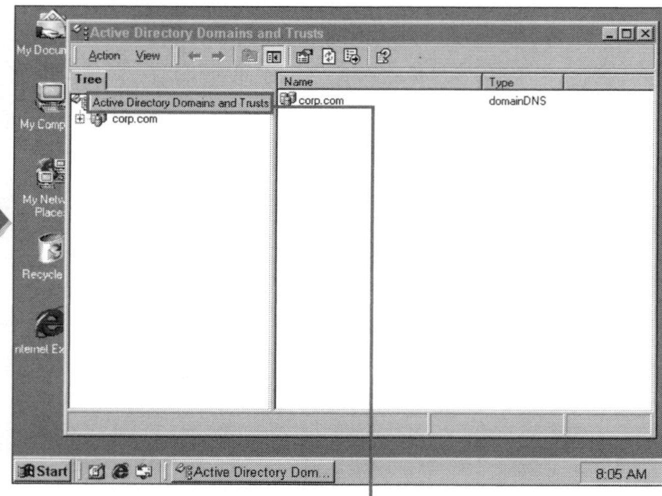

■ The console opens.

2 Select Active Directory Domains and Trusts.

What permissions do I need to connect to other domain controllers?

- Permissions may vary depending on your network configuration, but generally you need to be a member of the Enterprise Admins group. For most Active Directory operations, your user account should be a member of this group so that you can have proper permissions to handle Enterprise tasks and issues.

Why would I want to connect to other domain controllers in different domains?

- You may need to connect to other domain controllers in different domains to manage communication issues between the domains. For example, you can connect to domain controllers in other domains to establish proper trust relationships. You can learn more about establishing trust relationships in Chapter 21. Remember that Windows 2000 allows you to use one interface to manage different domain controllers and even different domains. This design saves administrators time and promotes streamlined management.

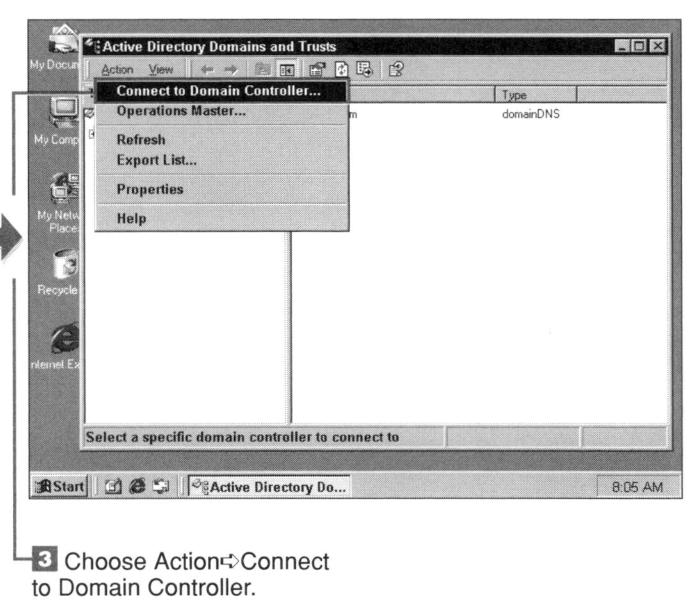

3 Choose Action⇨Connect to Domain Controller.

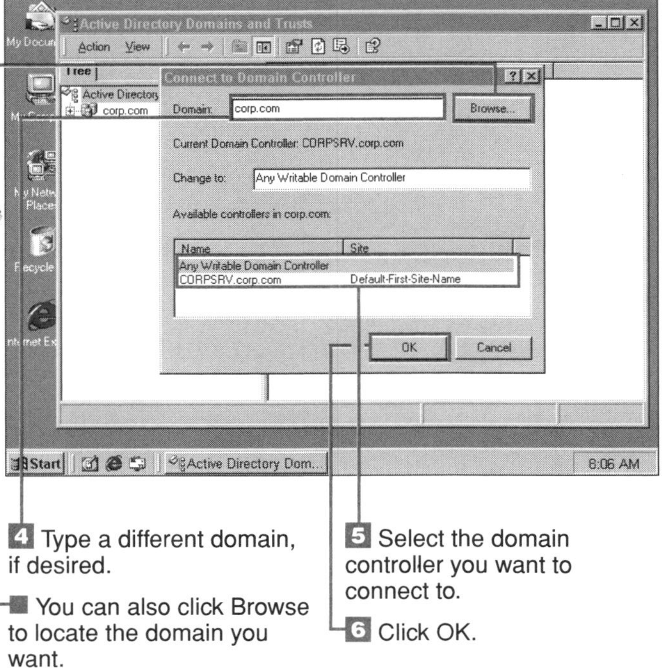

4 Type a different domain, if desired.

■ You can also click Browse to locate the domain you want.

5 Select the domain controller you want to connect to.

6 Click OK.

CHANGING THE OPERATIONS MASTER

You can change the operations master for the domain by connecting to a different domain controller in the domain and transferring the role to that domain controller.

An *operations master* is a domain controller that is assigned one or more special roles within an Active Directory domain. Domain controllers that are assigned the role of operations master perform tasks that are called *single-master*. In other words, these tasks must be performed by the operations master domain controller and are not permitted to occur at different places on the network at the same time. The operations master can handle such tasks as resource identifier allocation, schema modification, PDC elections, and so forth. A major role of the operations master is to perform domain-naming operations. The operations master makes certain that all domain names are unique.

Typically, only one domain controller in the Enterprise performs the role of operations master. By default, the first domain controller where the Active Directory is installed in the root domain becomes the operations master. You can, however, change this role to another domain controller by using the Active Directory Domains and Trusts snap-in.

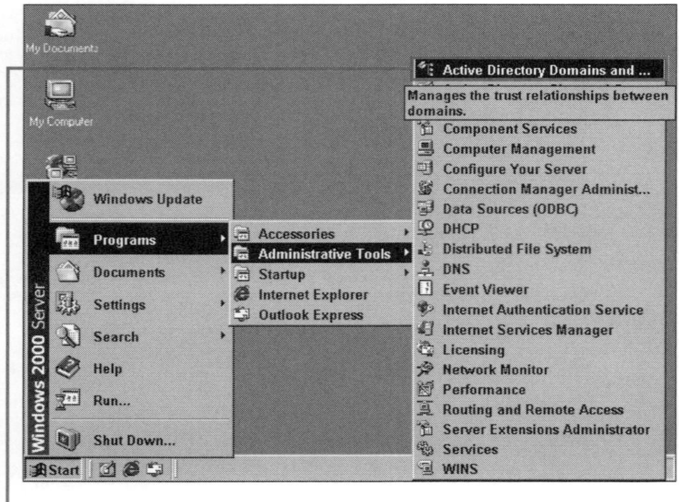

1 Choose Start⇨Programs⇨Administrative Tools⇨Active Directory Domains and Trusts.

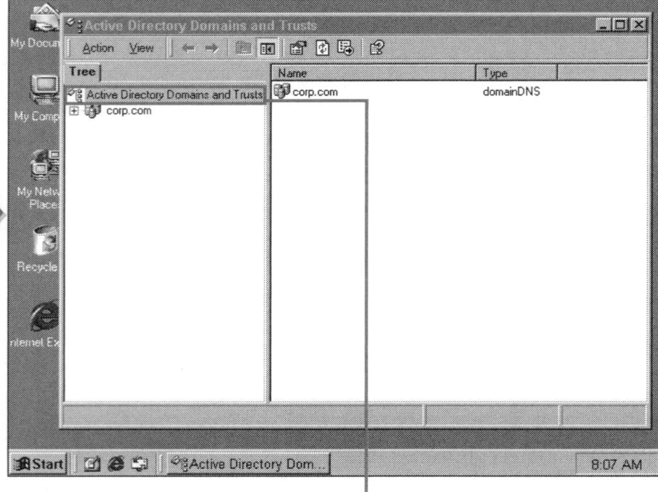

■ The console opens.

2 Select Active Directory Domains and Trusts.

TIPS

What permissions do I need to change the operations master?

- Permissions may vary depending on your network configuration, but generally, you need to be a member of the Enterprise Admins group. For most Active Directory operations, your user account should be a member of this group so that you can have proper permissions to handle Enterprise tasks and issues, such as transferring the operations master role.

Is there more than one operations master role?

- Yes. By using the transfer option, you are transferring the operations master that handles domain naming, which is called the *domain-naming master*. Other operations master roles exist, depending on your Enterprise configuration, including Schema Master, Relative ID Master, PDC Emulator, and Infrastructure Master. These master roles are automatically configured by the Active Directory. For example, if you upgrade a PDC from Windows NT 4.0 in a mixed environment, that server will automatically be a PDC Emulator.

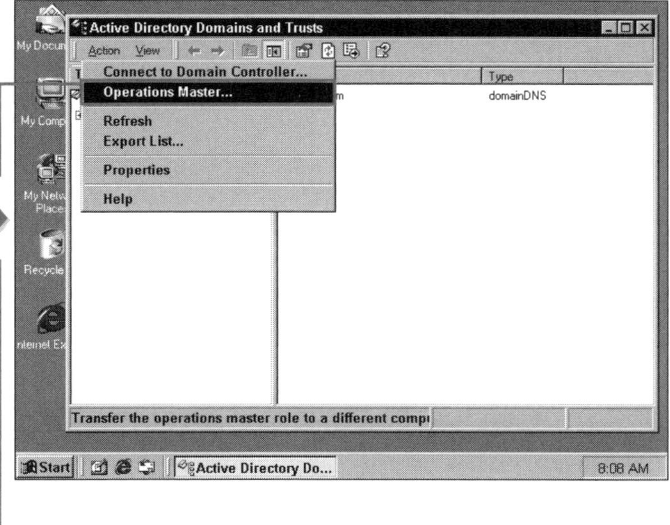

3 Choose Action⇨Operations Master.

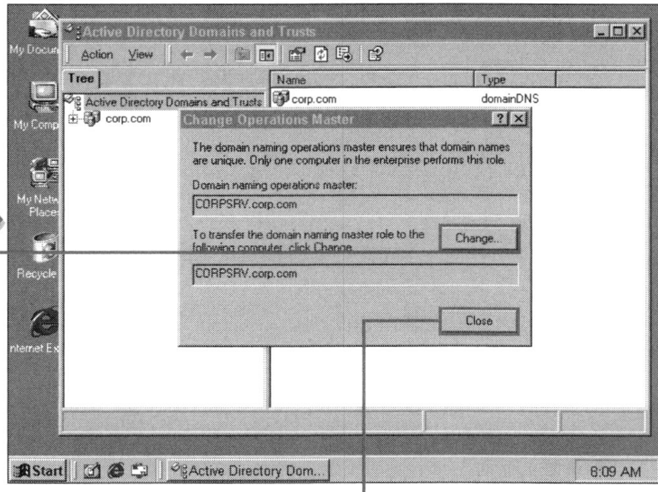

4 Click Change to transfer the operations master role to the other domain controller you have connected to.

5 Click Close.

CREATING UPN SUFFIXES

Every user account is given a User Principal Name (UPN). The UPN is made up of a prefix and a suffix. The prefix is the user's logon name, such as jwilliams. The prefix is the domain name, such as corp.com. The prefix and suffix are combined with the @ symbol to create the UPN, such as `jwilliams@corp.com`. The UPN functions as both a username in a Windows 2000 network and an e-mail address.

Typically, the UPN suffix is the domain name; however, you can assign additional UPN suffixes to provide additional security and to simplify the logon process in a Windows 2000 domain tree or forest.

You use the Active Directory Domains and Trusts to assign additional UPN suffixes for the domain. For example, in a domain tree that has several subdomains, a user's logon name could be `jwilliams@production.tx.namerica.corp.com`. You can simplify this by assigning an alternative UPN for this particular domain. For example, you could substitute the long domain name (production.tx.anamerica.corp.com) with prodtx. Now, the user can logon with the optional suffix as `jwilliams@prodtx.com`. This option can be particularly effective in large enterprise environments.

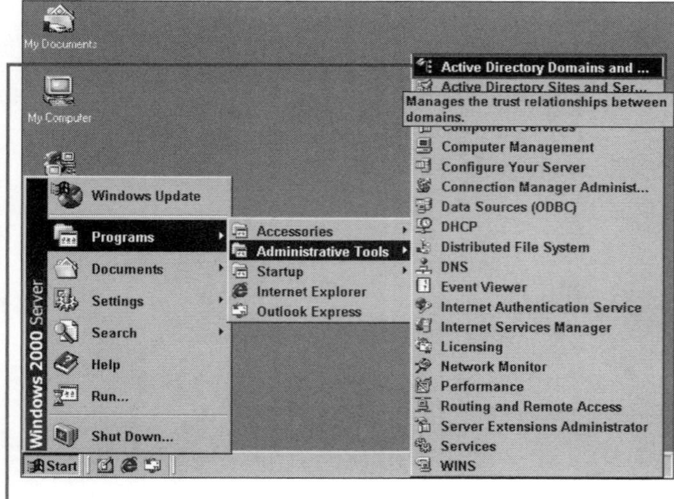

1 Choose Start⇨Programs⇨Administrative Tools⇨Active Directory Domains and Trusts.

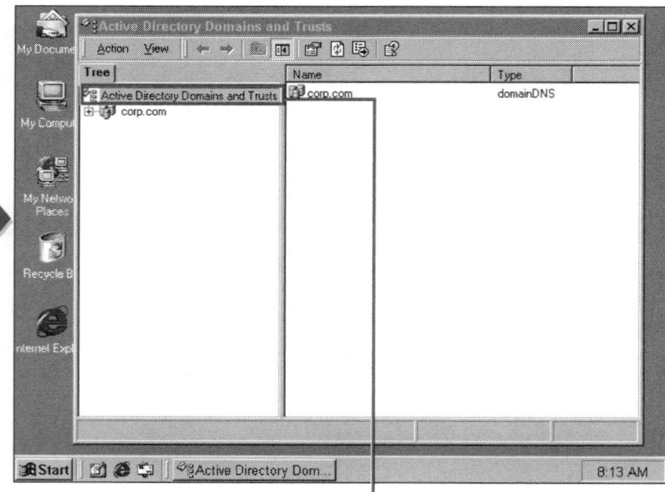

■ The console opens.

2 Select Active Directory Domains and Trusts.

Wouldn't the domain name have to be changed to use a new UPN?

No. The purpose of additional UPN suffixes is to substitute the real domain name for another one. In other words, the new UPN suffix acts as an alias. This can provide greater security because users can logon without revealing the actual Active Directory structure (production.tx.namerica.corp.com) during the logon process. This feature also simplifies user logon by making the domain name shorter.

Can I have more than one UPN suffix?

Yes, but under normal circumstances, just one is enough. If you wanted some users in the domain to logon using different UPN suffixes, then you could create additional suffixes. However, you should carefully consider creating more than one UPN suffix and whether it can actually benefit your domain. You do not want to make the logon process confusing for users either.

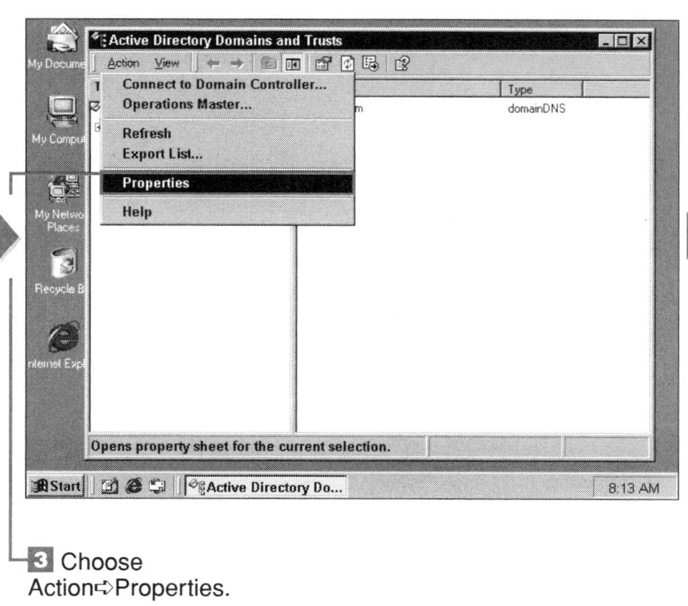

3 Choose Action⇨Properties.

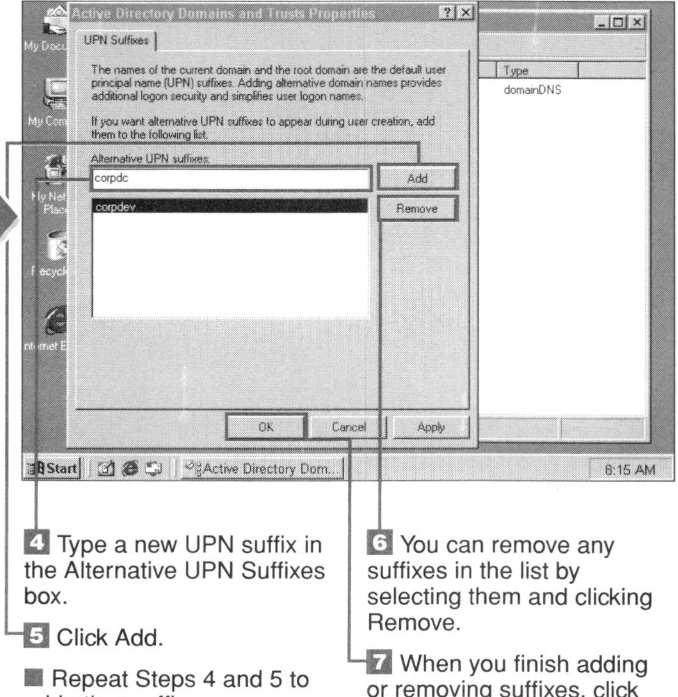

4 Type a new UPN suffix in the Alternative UPN Suffixes box.

5 Click Add.

■ Repeat Steps 4 and 5 to add other suffixes.

6 You can remove any suffixes in the list by selecting them and clicking Remove.

7 When you finish adding or removing suffixes, click OK.

MANAGING DOMAIN CONTROLLERS

The Active Directory Domains and Trusts MMC snap-in is one of the three Active Directory tools. You can use this snap-in to manage Active Directory domains and trust relationships between domains.

You can use the snap-in to manage other domain controllers, even those in different domains. When you choose to manage an Active Directory domain controller, the Active Directory Users and Computers snap-in opens for that domain. From your server, you can then manage that domain through the Users and Computers snap-in. This feature enables an administrator to make Enterprise-wide changes by accessing different domain controllers in different domains without having to physically visit each computer and each domain controller. After you access a domain controller, you can perform any management functions available within the Active Directory, including operation master roles and security.

In order to manage another domain controller, you must first add the domain controller to your snap-in so that you can access it. See Chapter 19 for specific instructions on how to connect to another domain controller.

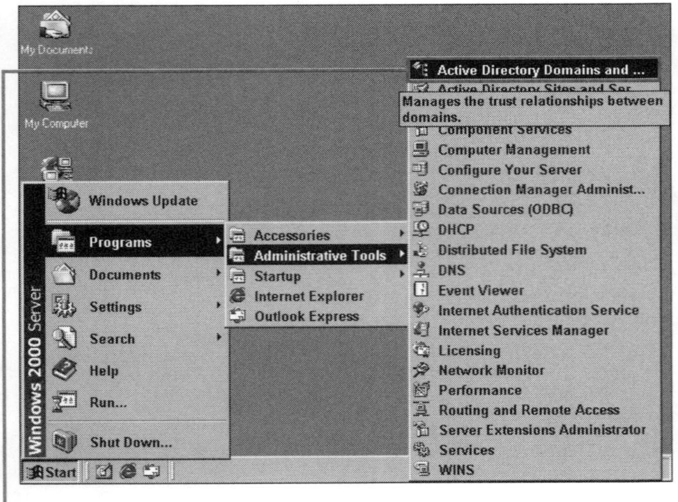

1 Choose Start⇨ Programs⇨Administrative Tools⇨Active Directory Domains and Trusts.

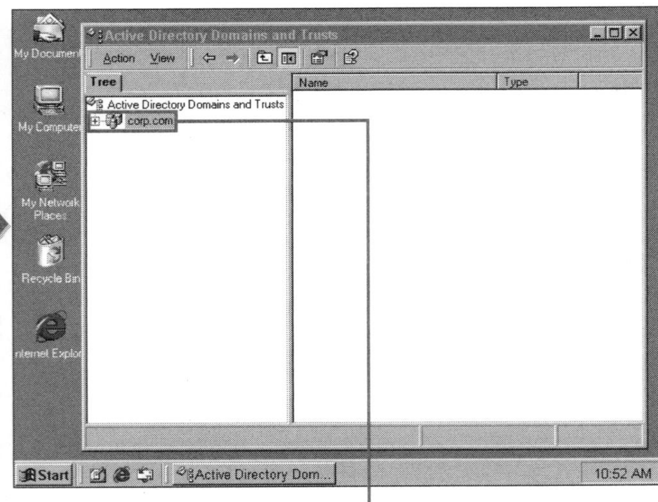

■ The console opens.

2 Select the domain you want to manage.

Why would I want to manage another domain controller?

- In Enterprise environments, several Active Directory domains may exist in domain trees and domain forests. The management feature from within the Active Directory Users and Computers console enables you to connect and manage other domain controllers from one location. This feature allows certain administrators to be in control of the entire Enterprise and manage the domain controllers from one central location.

What permissions do I need to manage another domain controller?

- The permissions you need to manage another domain controller may vary according to the security design of your Enterprise. In most cases, your administrator account needs to be a member of the Enterprise Admins group. This group is designed for global domain management of the Active Directory in Enterprise environments. Under normal circumstances, only Active Directory administrators have enterprise admin permissions.

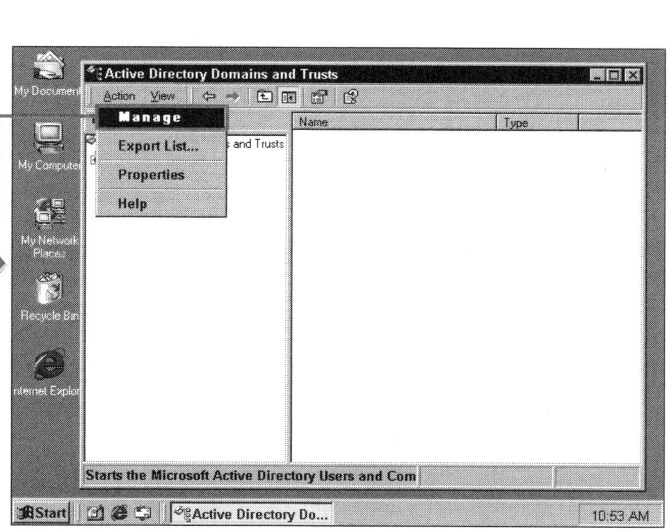

3 Choose Action⇨Manage.

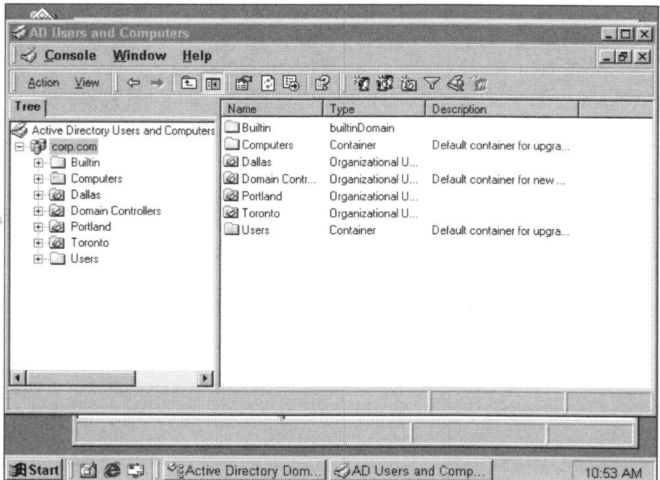

■ The Active Directory Users and Computers snap-in opens where you can manage the domain.

ACCESSING DOMAIN PROPERTIES

The domain properties sheets enable you to configure your domain operation as desired. When you access the properties sheets for a domain, you select the domain desired in the console and use the Action menu to access the properties sheets.

The properties sheets for each domain contain three tabs: General, Trusts, and Managed By. By using these properties sheets, you can determine the operation mode and trust relationships for the domain.

The domain properties sheets should not be configured with domain controller properties sheets that are available in the Active Directory Users and Computers snap-in. Those properties sheets enable you to manage the actual domain controller while the domain properties sheets in the Active Directory Domains and Trusts snap-in allows you to configure settings for the entire domain. Although you mainly have the options of changing the domain mode from mixed mode to native mode and configuring trust relationships, both of those are very important and are explained in the following sections.

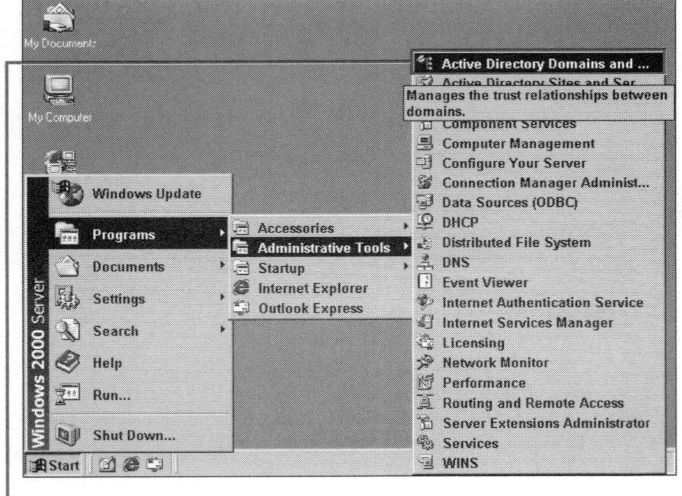

1 Choose Start⇨Programs⇨Administrative Tools⇨Active Directory Domains and Trusts.

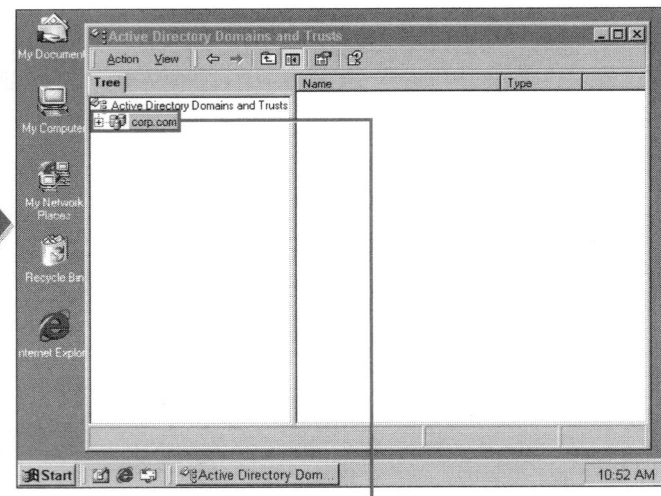

■ The console opens.

2 Select the domain you want to configure.

What permissions do I need to change the properties of a domain?

- Permissions may vary depending on your network configuration, but generally, you need to be a member of the Enterprise Admins group. For most Active Directory operations, your user account should be a member of this group so that you can have proper permissions to handle enterprise tasks and issues.

Is there another way to access the properties sheets for a domain?

- Yes. As with most MMC snap-ins, you can right-click any object to see a list of available actions. In most cases, the choices that appear when you right-click are the same choices you see in the Action menu. So, you can access the properties sheets for a domain in the Active Directory Domains and Trusts snap-in by right-clicking the domain icon in the left pane and then choosing Properties from the menu that appears.

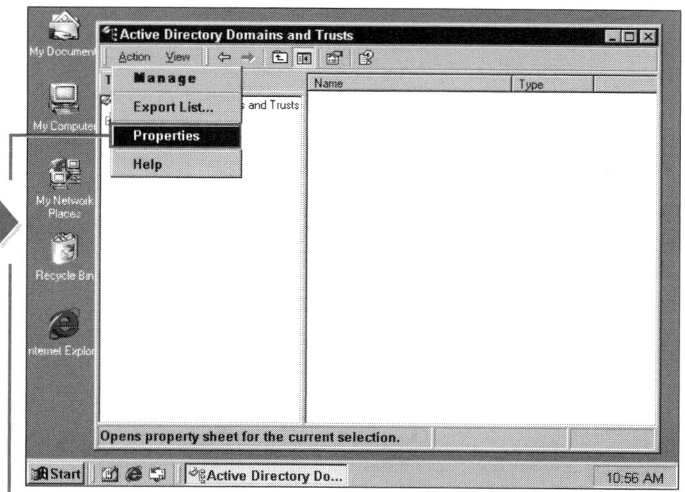

3 Choose Action⇨Properties.

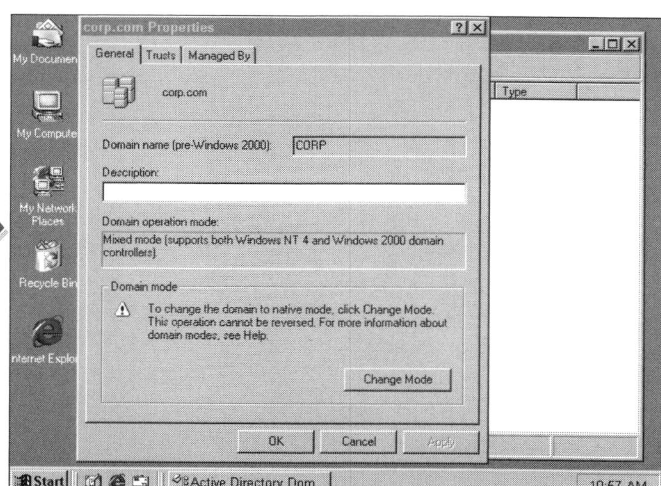

■ The properties sheets for the domain opens.

CHANGING THE DOMAIN MODE

Windows 2000 domains can function in two modes: mixed mode and native mode. *Mixed mode* allows Windows NT and Windows 2000 domain controllers to coexist in the domain. However, when mixed mode is in effect, you cannot use some of the Windows 2000 enhancements, such as universal groups and nested groups. When you install the first Active Directory domain controller for a domain, mixed mode is selected by default. With mixed mode, you can slowly implement Windows 2000 domain controllers instead of having to upgrade all your domain controllers at one time.

Native mode allows only Windows 2000 domain controllers. After you change a domain to native mode, Windows NT domain controllers cannot be used in the domain. Although you should change to native mode as soon as you are ready, make certain that you do not intend to use any Windows NT domain controllers in the future. After you change to native mode, you cannot move back to mixed mode.

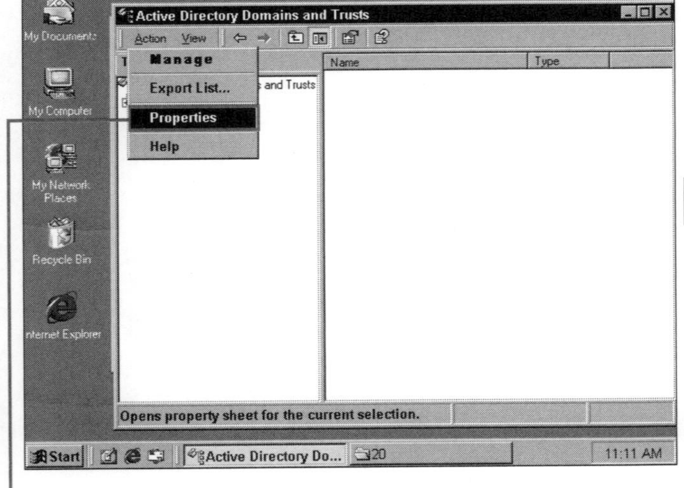

1 Select the domain you want to administer, and then choose Action⇨Properties.

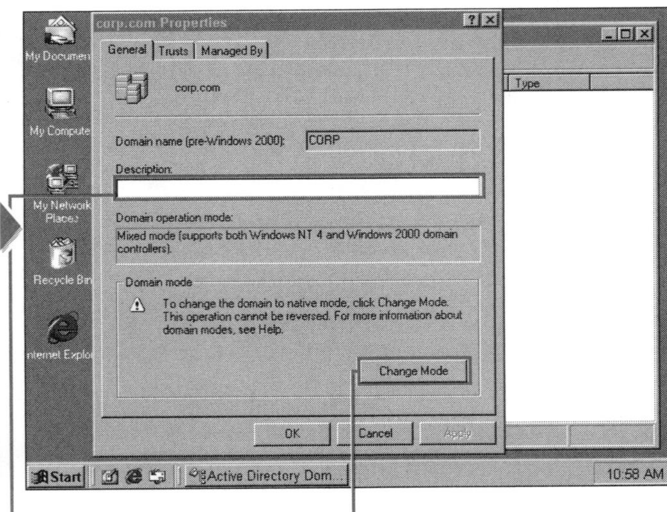

■ The Properties sheet appears.

2 Enter a description for the domain if desired.

3 To change the domain mode, click Change Mode.

■ ***Warning:*** *After you change to native mode, you cannot return to mixed mode!*

Can I still use Windows NT Workstation or Windows 9*x* client computers in the domain after a change to native mode?

Yes. The change to native mode affects only domain controllers. After you make the change, only Windows 2000 domain controllers can be used. However, client computers are not affected by the change to native mode, and you can still use a mix of Windows 2000, Windows NT, or Windows 9*x* client computers.

Can't I still use a Windows NT BDC after the change to native mode?

No. Native mode allows only Windows 2000 servers. You cannot use Windows NT servers in the domain, regardless of the role they once played in a Windows NT network. Keep in mind that native mode ceases any functionality with downlevel NT servers, so if your environment still uses NT servers, you should not change to native mode until they have all been upgraded.

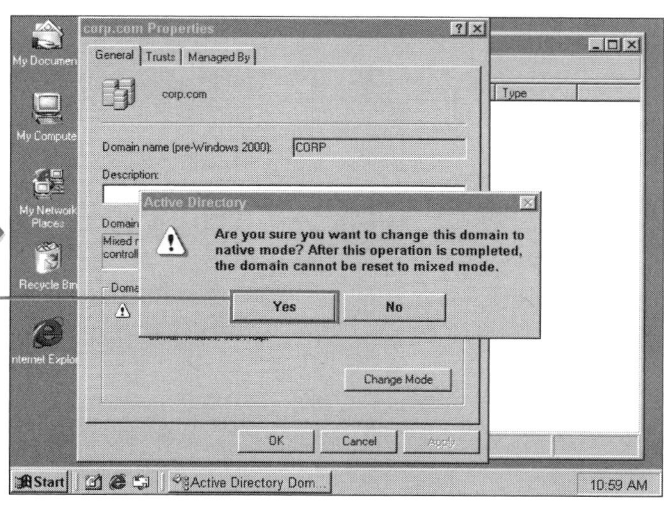

4 Click Yes to continue with the mode change.

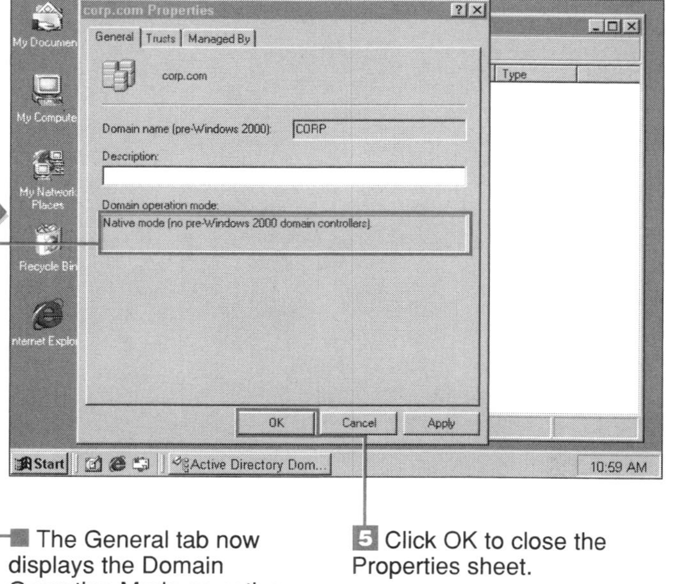

■ The General tab now displays the Domain Operation Mode as native mode.

5 Click OK to close the Properties sheet.

CONFIGURING TRUSTS

Trust relationships allow two domains to share information. Windows 2000 makes trust relationships easier by implementing transitive trusts through the Kerberos security protocol. Windows 2000 domain controllers in the same domain, domain tree, or domain forest automatically trust each other through transitive trusts that are configured automatically.

You can also establish trust relationships with other domains that are not Windows 2000 Active Directory domains. This is performed by manually establishing the nontransitive trust on the Trusts tab of the domain properties. You must also manually establish a trust relationship for two Active Directory forests that want to communicate with each other.

After you configure trust relationships, you can access the trust's properties sheets. You can use the properties sheets to specify service principal name (SPN) suffixes, if desired. Servers identify themselves by using an SPN. Normally, this is the full DNS name of the server, but you can create different SPN suffixes for externally trusted domains so that the server does not have to reveal its full DNS name. This is a security feature of Windows 2000.

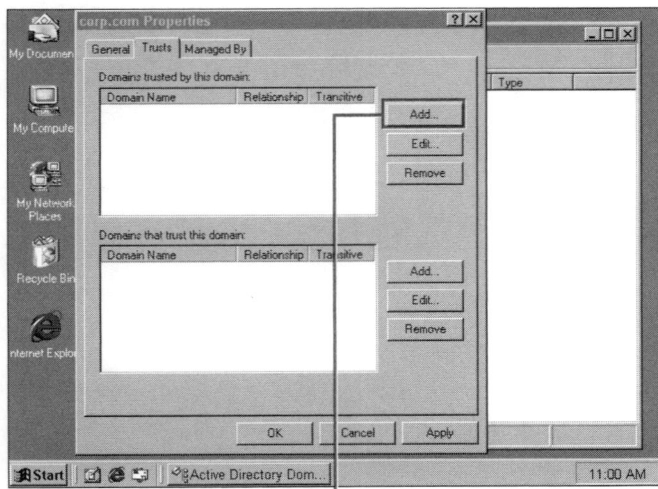

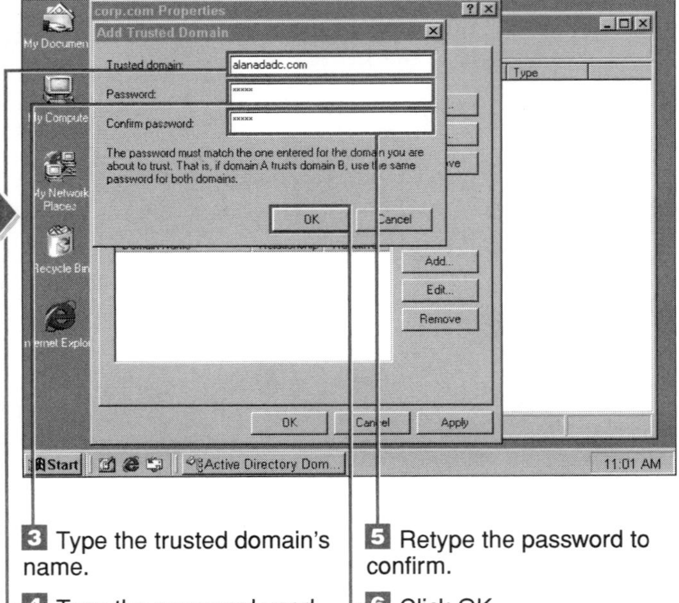

1 Select the domain you want to administer, and then choose Action⇨Properties.

2 To create a trust relationship, click Add to enter domains that trust and are trusted by your domain.

■ The Add Trusted Domain dialog box appears.

3 Type the trusted domain's name.

4 Type the password used to establish the trust relationship.

5 Retype the password to confirm.

6 Click OK

What is a *transitive trust?*

- A transitive trust is a feature of the Kerberos security protocol built into Windows 2000. A transitive trust is two-way between two domains. Also, Kerberos trusts are transitive —this means that a domain can automatically trust another domain without a direct trust relationship. For example, if Domain1 trusts Domain2 and Domain2 trusts Domain3, then Domain1 automatically trusts Domain3. Transitive trusts are automatically created for Active Directory domain controllers in a tree or forest. This is a new way of establishing trust relationships in Windows 2000; Windows NT did not allow any type of transitive trusts.

What is a *nontransitive trust?*

- Nontransitive trusts are trust relationships that do not support the Kerberos security protocol. Administrators on each side of the trust relationship must configure a nontransitive trust. If DomainA trusts DomainB, this doesn't mean that DomainB trusts DomainA as it does in a transitive trust relationship. Nontransitive trusts are also static. In other words, if DomainA trusts Domain B and DomainB trusts DomainC, DomainA does not automatically trust DomainC.

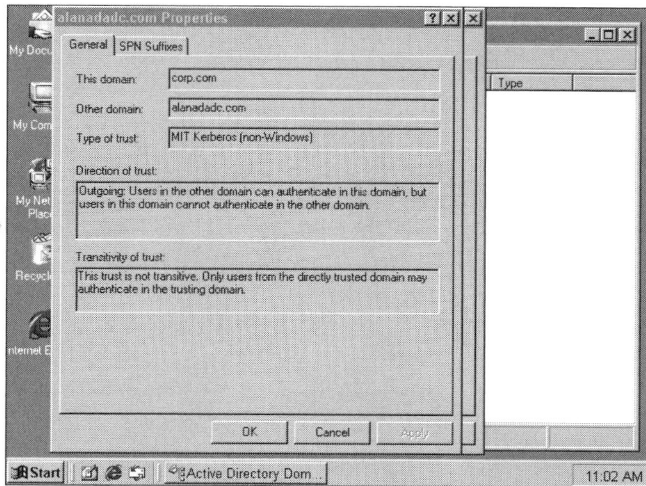

7 On the Trusts tab, select a trust relationship and click Edit to see the properties page.

■ The properties sheet appears. The General tab gives you information about the trust relationship.

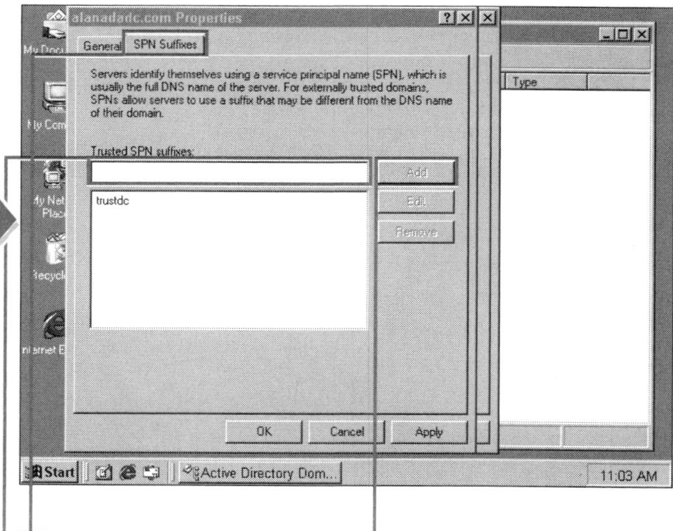

8 Click the SPN Suffixes tab.

9 Enter trusted SPN suffixes as desired.

10 Click Add.

ASSIGNING A DOMAIN MANAGER

As with other Active Directory components and services, you can assign a manager to the domain. A *manager* is the person who can "manage" the domain properties. This feature enables you to distribute the administrative duties and roles to other Active Directory users as necessary.

As with any Active Directory administration, you should be careful who you choose to be manager of the domain. That person should have the skills necessary to administer the domain, and that person must act responsibly with any configuration changes. Remember that a manager can change the domain mode and configure trust relationships. Both of these actions can cause severe problems in your domain without proper planning, and you only want highly skilled administrators making these kinds of changes. So, the key advice is to use a manager if needed, but wisely assign the role.

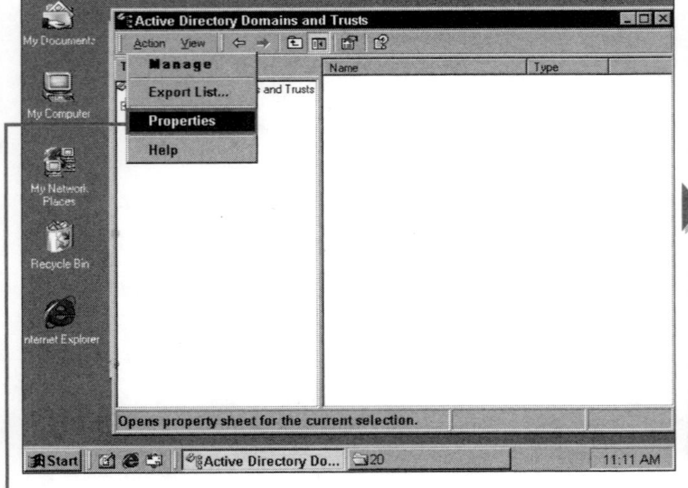

1 Select the domain where you want to assign a manager, and then choose Action⇨Properties.

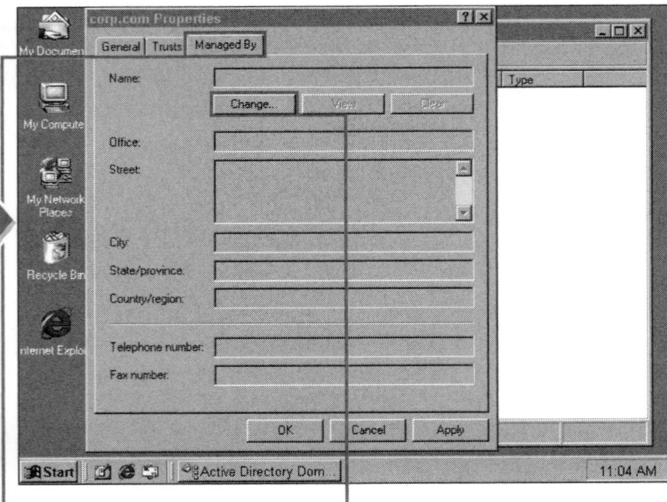

2 Click the Managed By tab.

3 Click Change.

What qualifications should I look for in a potential manager?

Anyone that is assigned a managerial role in the Active Directory should meet these qualifications:

- The manager should have solid technical skills concerning the Active Directory.
- The manager should be aware of domain problems, issues, and upcoming changes.
- The manager should have a direct reporting line so that he or she can gain correct information before undertaking any configuration changes.
- The manager should be reliable and responsible.

Can I change the domain manager?

You can change the manager of the domain, or the manager of any Active Directory object at any time by accessing the Managed By tab and clicking the Change button. You can then select a new manager from the Active Directory. Of course, changes in managers should always be carefully planned to ensure that you are assigning managerial roles to acceptable users or system administrators.

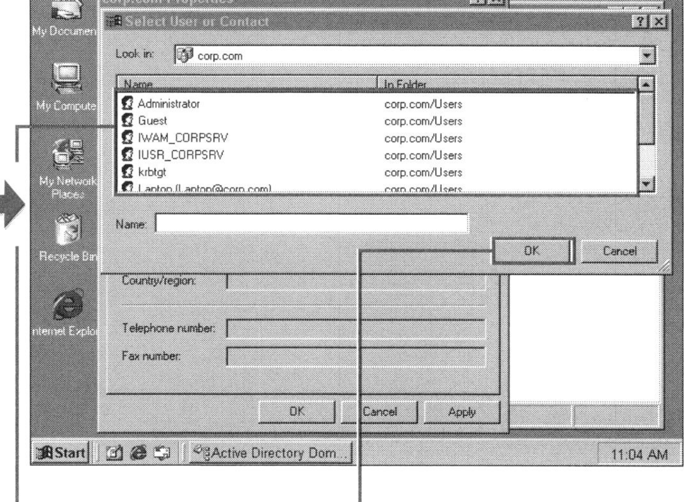

4 Select the user that you want to become the domain manager.

■ The selected name appears in the Name dialog box.

5 Click OK.

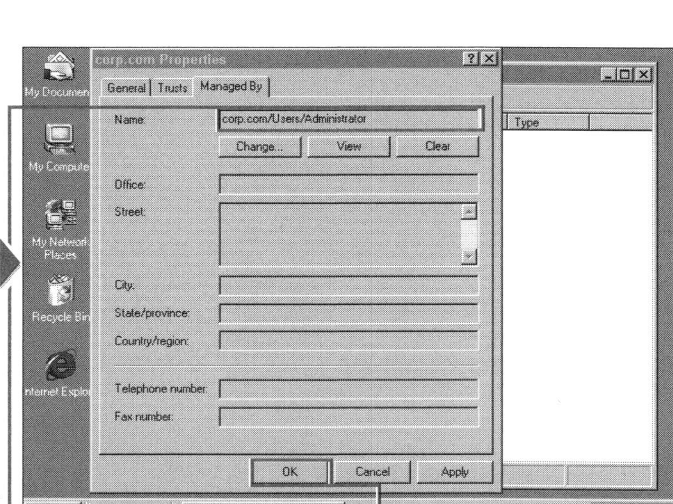

■ The new manager now appears on the Managed By tab.

6 Click OK to close the Properties sheets.

SECTION VII

22) MANAGING ACTIVE DIRECTORY SITES

23) CONFIGURING ACTIVE DIRECTORY SITE COMMUNICATIONS

Manager

INTRODUCTION TO ACTIVE DIRECTORY SITES

The Active Directory Sites and Services MMC snap-in is used to manage both Active Directory sites as well as services pertaining to sites. Before you take a look at the configuration of sites in this chapter, this section examines the function of sites and related technologies.

What is a site?

A Windows 2000 site is a physical grouping of computers and/or domains. A site organizes computers, domain controllers, and even domains in a particular location. Typically, sites are used in WAN environments in which a company has offices in several geographic locations. For example, if Wellington Consultants has offices in New York, Dallas, and Phoenix, each city location can be a site within the WAN.

What is the difference between a site and a domain?

The terms *site* and *domain* are often confused. A domain is a logical grouping of computers; a site is a physical grouping of computers. You can have multiple domains within a single site. Domains organize users and computers within a site; a site is the physical location of those users, computers, and domains. For example, within the New York site of Wellington Consultants, you could have two domains: one for Accounting and one for Marketing.

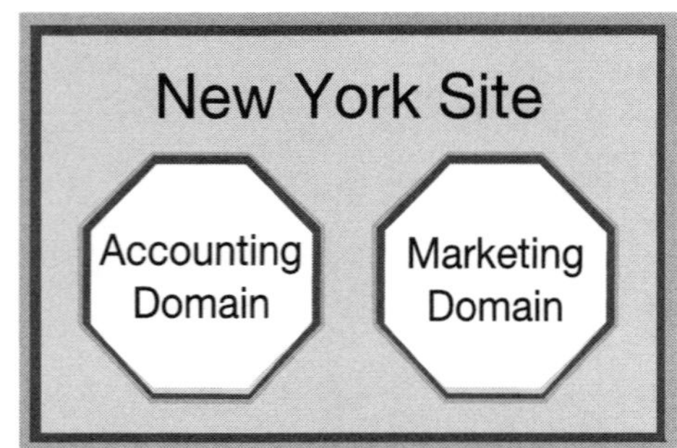

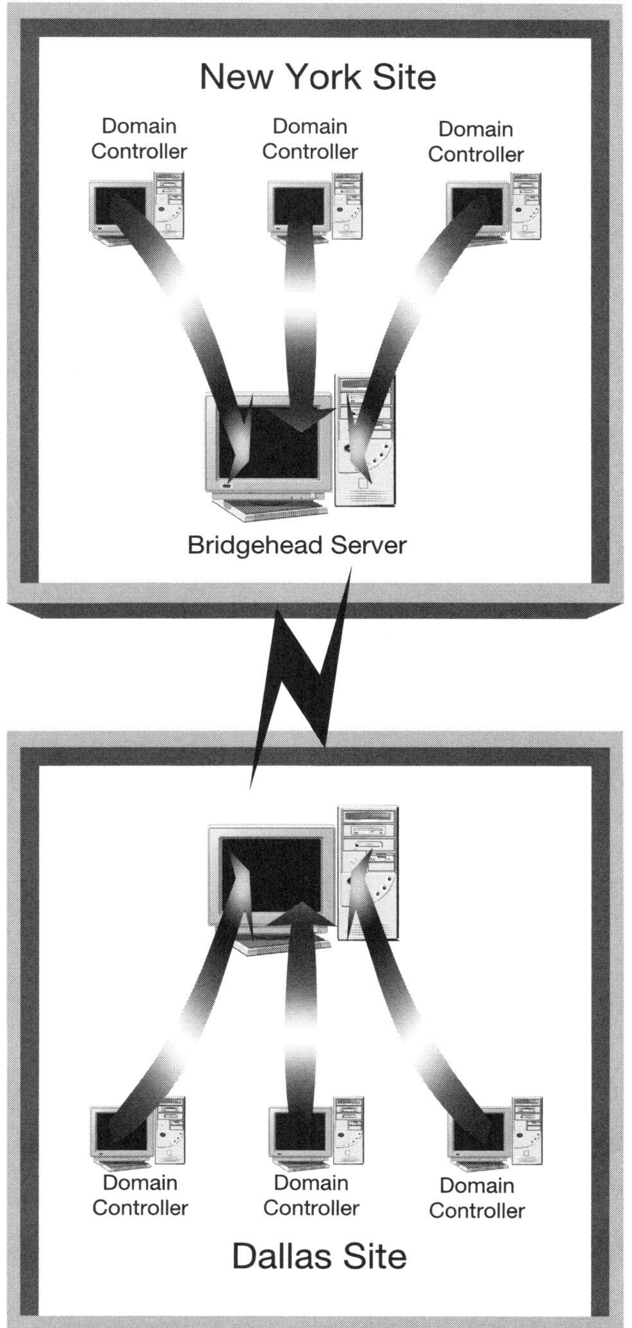

Why use sites?

Because sites are typically used to segment physical locations of the WAN, sites help control how users access services and how bandwidth is conserved. A site can keep user access within its own subnet, unless a particular service becomes unavailable.

First, a subnet helps user authentication. Because the Active Directory uses multimaster replication, any Windows 2000 domain controller on the network can authenticate any user. This can present a problem with WAN bandwidth. The site keeps user authentication within the subnet so that the domain controllers in that subnet can first authenticate the user before the request is sent to other sites. This keeps the traffic localized on the subnet.

Next, you can use site links to control how the Active Directory replicates information among domain controllers at different sites. This feature helps you control bandwidth usage and fault tolerance among the sites. Along with the site links, you can also specify a bridgehead server. A *bridgehead server* is a server that is specified to send and receive intersite replication data. By default, all domain controllers replicate information to each other. The bridgehead server takes care of this process because it is dedicated to intersite replication.

Aside from authentication and replication, the sites also control user service requests to domain controllers. As with authentication, the service requests are directed to the domain controllers within the site instead of domain controllers in other sites.

USING THE ACTIVE DIRECTORY SITES AND SERVICES SNAP-IN

You can manage all aspects of site configuration by using the Active Directory Sites and Services MMC-snap-in. By accessing this snap-in, you can perform a number of site-related functions.

You can use the snap-in to administer sites, and you can also use this interface to connect to other domain controllers and Active Directory forests. This feature enables you to administer all your network's sites from one location and through one interface.

As with all components of the Active Directory, site configuration is replicated across all sites and enforced through the Active Directory configuration.

Why would I want to connect to another forest?

- In WAN environments, different sites may have their own Active Directory forests. By using the connect to forest feature, you can connect to another site's root forest and administer the site in that manner. This feature enables an administrator to have control over all Active Directory forests within the network.

Can I use the Sites and Services snap-in and the Users and Computers snap-in together?

- Keep in mind that the Active Directory tools are all MMC snap-ins. You can open an MMC console and manually load the two snap-ins so that they appear in one console window. Using this feature, you can create custom consoles that contain any combination of snap-in tools you desire. Choose Start⇨Run and type **MMC**, then use the Console menu and select Add/Remove Snapin. You can then load the snap-ins and save the console.

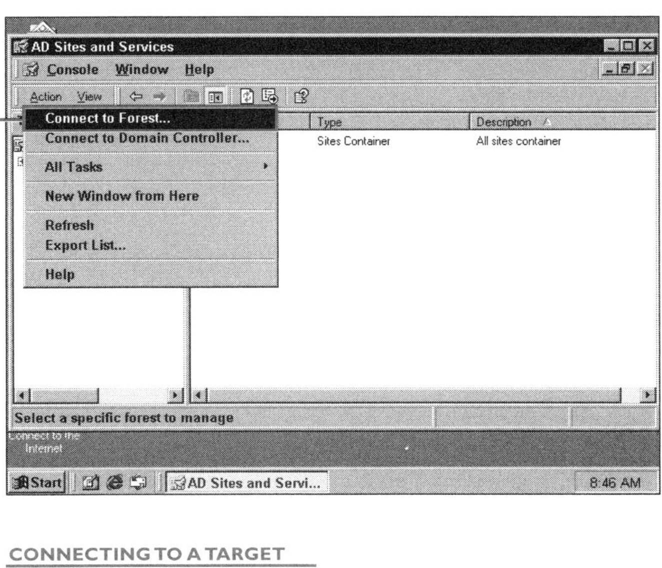

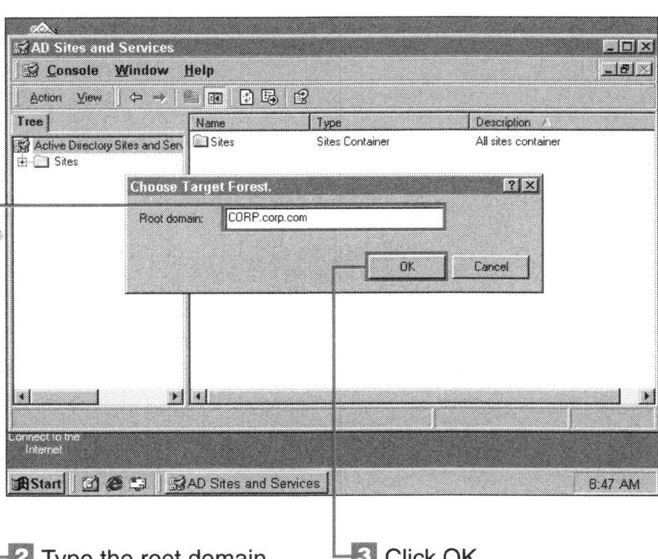

CONNECTING TO A TARGET

1. Select the Active Directory Sites and Service object in the console tree and Choose Action⇨Connect to Forest.
2. Type the root domain.
3. Click OK.

CONTINUED

USING THE ACTIVE DIRECTORY SITES AND SERVICES SNAP-IN CONTINUED

Aside from connecting to a different Active Directory forest, you can also use the Active Directory Sites and Services tool to connect to another domain controller. This feature enables you to administer other sites by connecting to a domain controller within that site. Senior administrators in large WAN environments find this feature particularly useful because they can manage all aspects of the site configuration from one location and through one interface. This feature is particularly useful in environments that have multiple domains or sites, but want administrators to be able to configure and manage the entire WAN environment. By using one console, you can connect to different sites, domains, and domain controllers from your desk.

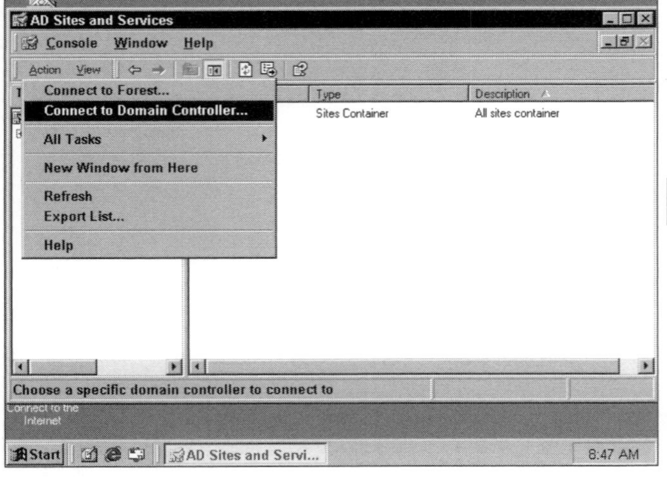

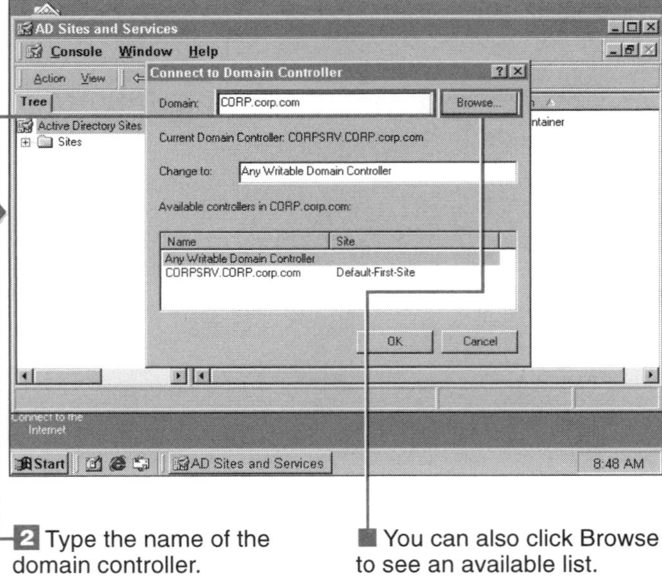

CONNECTING TO A DOMAIN CONTROLLER

1 Select Active Directory Sites and Services and choose Action⇨Connect to Domain Controller.

2 Type the name of the domain controller.

■ You can also click Browse to see an available list.

Why would I need to connect to another domain controller?

Depending on the role your domain controllers play within the domain, you may need to connect to a different domain controller for administrative purposes. For example, if one of your domain controllers is designated as a bridgehead server, you can use the connect to domain controller feature to administer replication and connectivity for the bridgehead server from this interface.

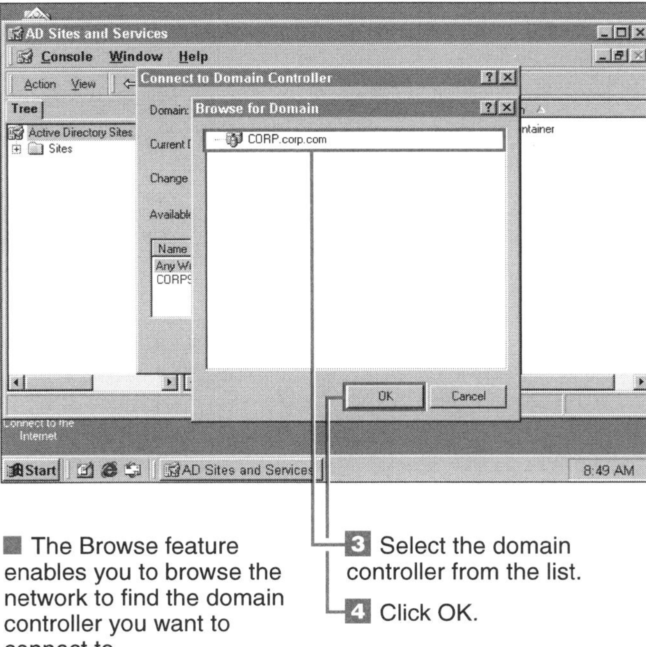

■ The Browse feature enables you to browse the network to find the domain controller you want to connect to.

3 Select the domain controller from the list.

4 Click OK.

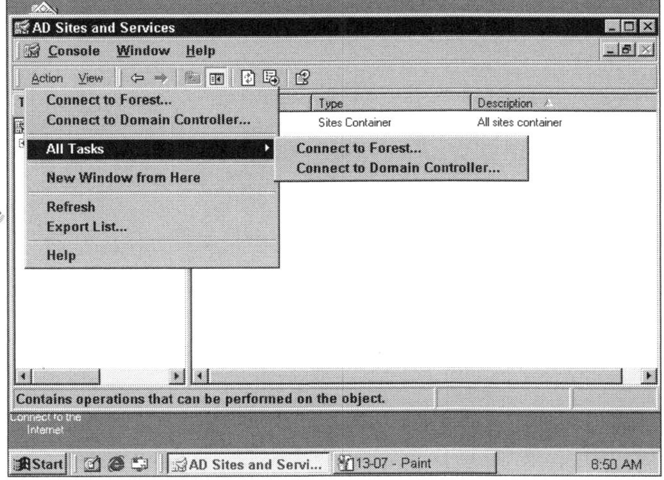

■ If you select the Active Directory Sites and Services object and then choose Action⇨All Tasks, you have the same options of connecting to a forest or connecting to a domain controller.

ADMINISTERING THE SITES CONTAINER

The first OU under the Active Directory Sites and Services object is the sites container. The sites container contains configured sites, intersite links, and subnets.

You can perform several actions to configure the site container as desired. Like most Active Directory objects, you can access the container's properties sheets to configure information about the container and security for the container.

Of particular interest is the Security tab. You can use the Security tab, like all Security tabs in the Active Directory, to control who can access the Sites container and what permissions they have for the container.

The General and Object tabs give you information about the Sites container. On the Object tab, you can view the original and current Update Sequence Number (USN), which tells you the last time the object has been updated in any way.

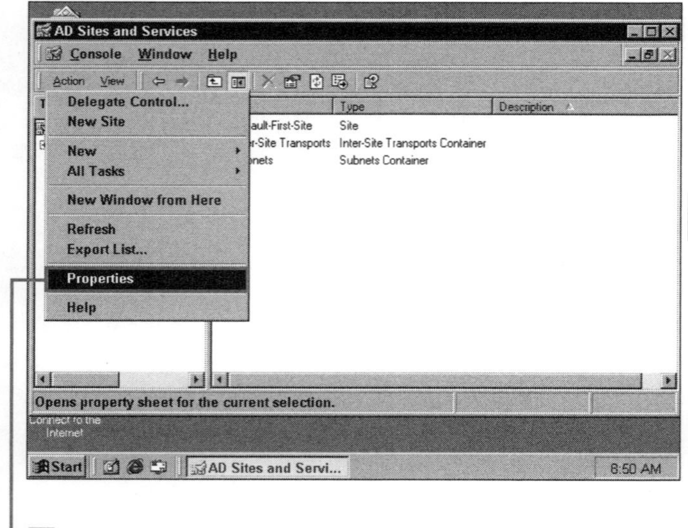

1 Select the Sites container, and then choose Action⇨Properties.

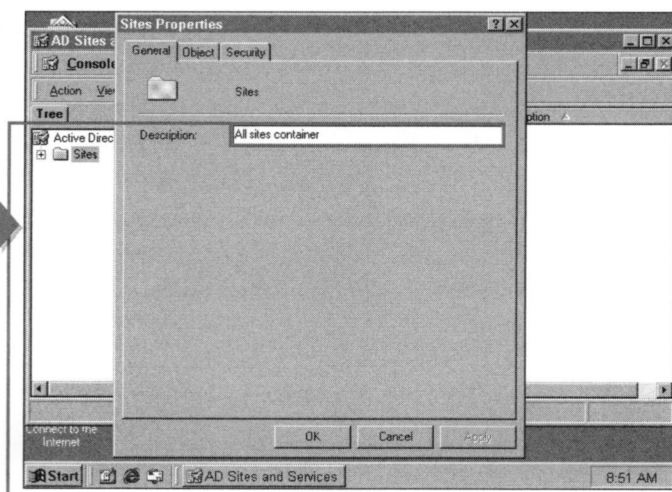

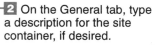

2 On the General tab, type a description for the site container, if desired.

How is a description helpful?

- In large environments that have many OUs and containers, the description, which you can type in on the General properties tab, is helpful to keep track of containers and OUs. You can use the description to help point to the contents of the OU and better organize data.

What is a *fully qualified name*?

- The fully qualified name is used with DNS naming schemes. The fully qualified name shows the complete DNS path to the object, starting at the root, such as corp.com.

What is a *USN*?

- You can see on the Object tab the original and current USN numbers. USN (Update Sequence Numbers) are numbers that the Active Directory uses to track changes to particular objects. The USNs are used by sites to make certain that replication has taken place and is current.

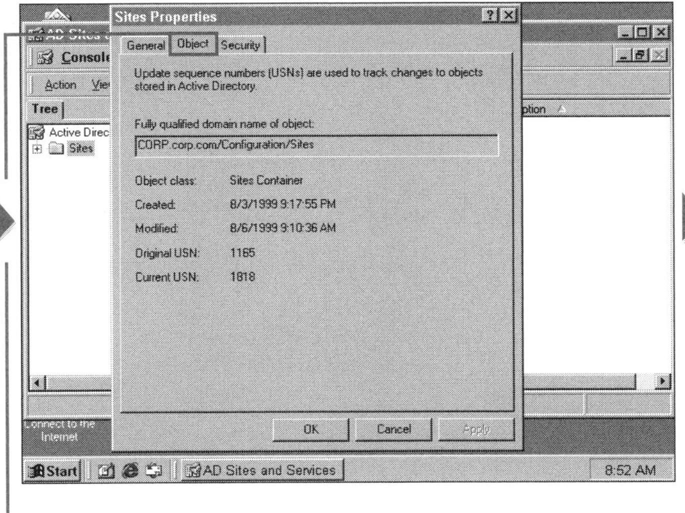

3 Click the Object tab.

■ This tab shows the fully qualified name of the site object.

■ This tab also gives you information about the date of installation and the last time the object was modified, as well as USN numbers.

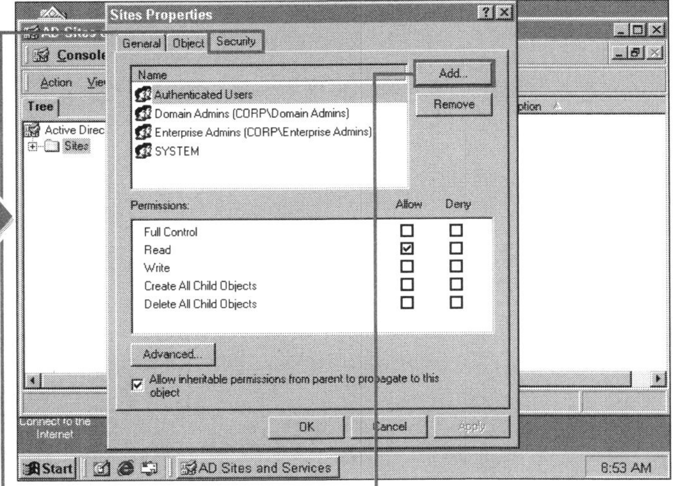

4 Click the Security tab to configure security access options.

5 Click Add.

CONTINUED

ADMINISTERING THE SITES CONTAINER
CONTINUED

The major configuration option you have with the site container properties sheets is security. This tab enables you to determine who can access this container within the Active Directory and what tasks they can perform. The standard permissions for the sites container are Full Control, Read, Write, Create All Child Objects, and Delete All Child Objects. By default the following groups have these rights:

- **Authenticated users**: Read
- **Domain admins:** Read, Write, and Create All Child Objects
- **Enterprise admins**: Full Control (which includes all other permissions)
- **System:** Full Control (which includes all other permissions)

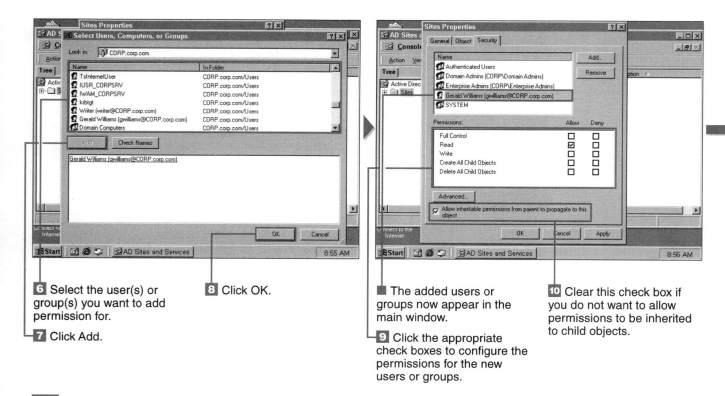

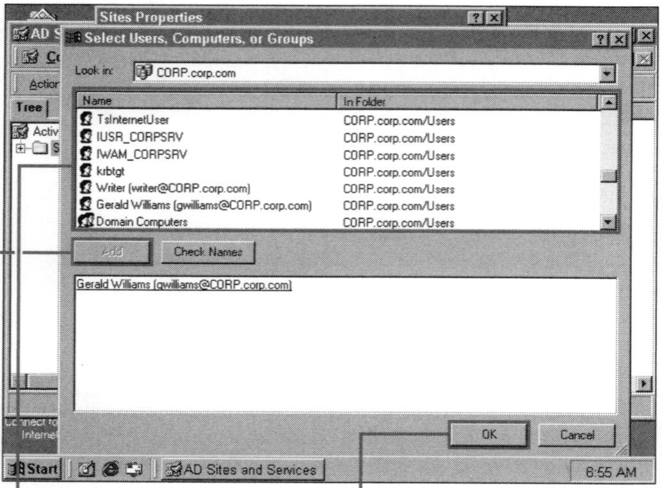

6 Select the user(s) or group(s) you want to add permission for.

7 Click Add.

8 Click OK.

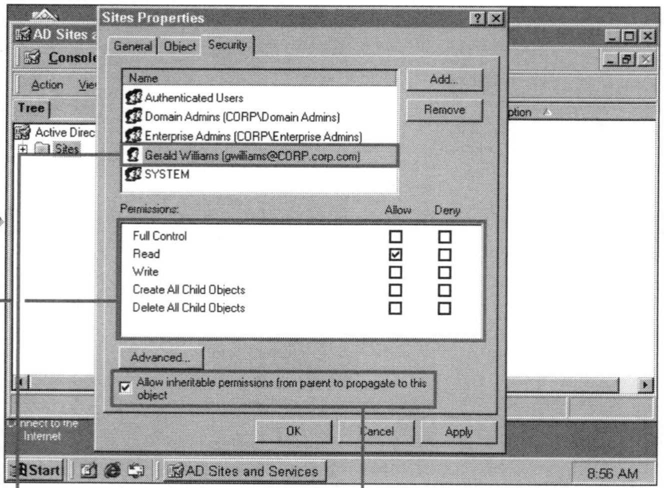

■ The added users or groups now appear in the main window.

9 Click the appropriate check boxes to configure the permissions for the new users or groups.

10 Clear this check box if you do not want to allow permissions to be inherited to child objects.

Who should have access to the sites container?

- By default, all users can read the information in the sites container. However, only administrators should have any further rights for configuration. Because site configuration is a senior administrative duty, you should take care when giving access rights to anyone else.

What is the purpose of the Advanced permission entries?

- In most cases, the general permissions you can assign are all you need. However, Windows 2000 provides detailed and advanced security options so that you can further refine what permissions you assign on what objects. This feature allows Windows 2000 to work within the security needs of your network.

What is the inheritable permissions check box on the Security tab?

- The inheritable permissions check box allows the permissions you configure for the Site container to "flow down" to child containers. For example, if a user, Gerald Williams, has Read permission for the Sites container and you check the Allow Inheritable Permissions check box, then Gerald will have Read permissions for all child containers in the Sites container as well.

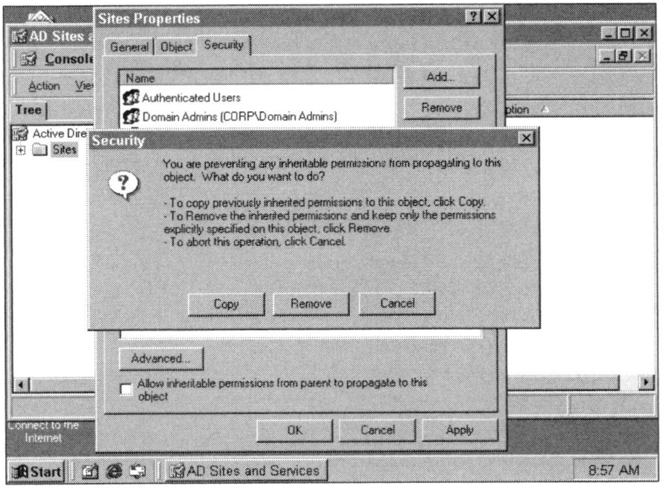

■ If you choose to clear the Allow Inheritable Permissions check box, a security window appears that enables you to either copy or remove the inheritable permissions from the child objects.

11 Click the desired button.

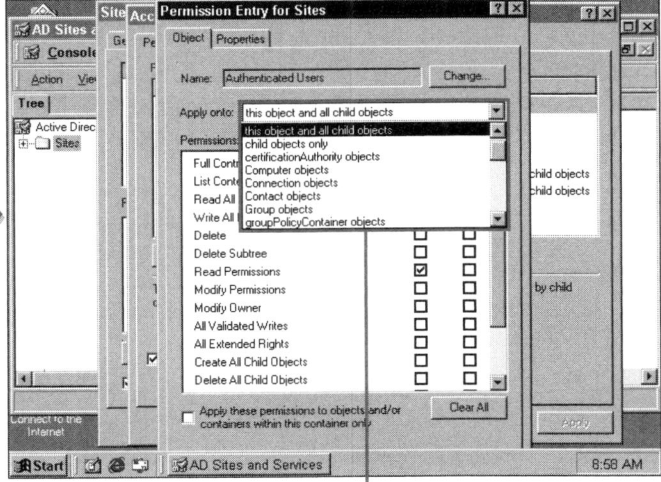

■ To access the advanced security features, click Advanced on the Security tab, select the user or group, then click View/Edit to display the Permission Entries window.

12 Click the Apply Onto drop-down menu to select how you want the permissions applied.

CONTINUED

ADMINISTERING THE SITES CONTAINER
CONTINUED

The Advanced Security features for Active Directory objects in Windows 2000 gives you greater control over the permissions you give to users and groups. This feature is particularly helpful if you want to define certain security permissions to either allow or deny access to those options.

The advanced options also enable you to configure auditing for the object as well. Auditing is configured in Windows 2000 Server, but after you configure auditing, you can choose to audit any object with the Active Directory using the advanced security options.

In most cases, you do not need to assign advanced security options to users or administrators. Under normal circumstances, the default options are all you need to give administrators the access permissions they need while not allowing Full Control permissions to unauthorized users. However, in specific cases where you need to further define a user's security permissions, the advanced features can be used and are appropriate.

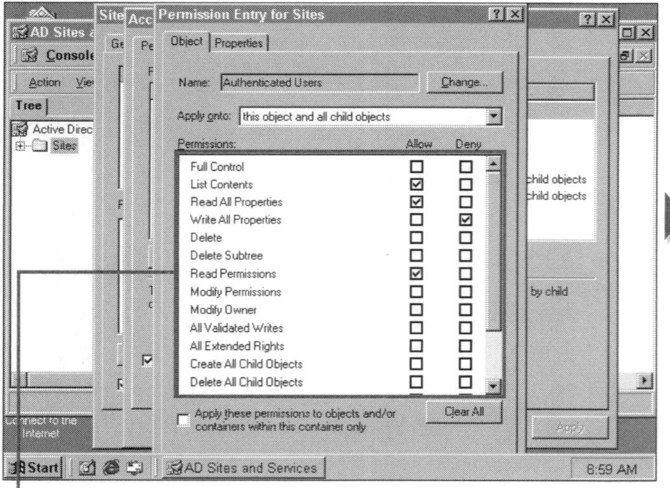

13 Click the appropriate check boxes to apply or clear permissions.

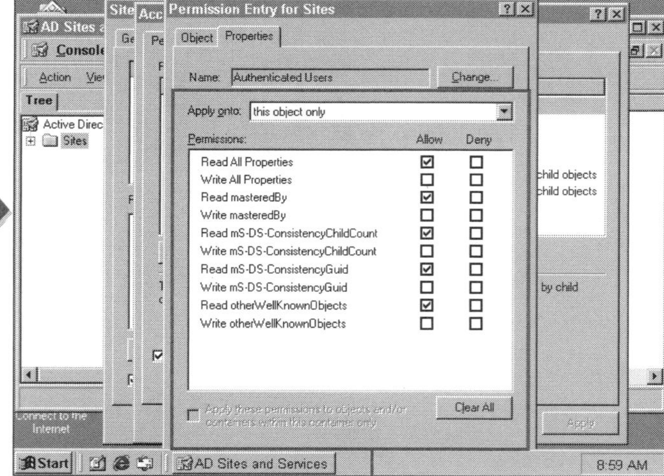

■ If you click the Properties tab, you can also adjust the permissions for the user or group concerning the object s properties.

14 Use the Apply Onto drop-down list and Allow or Deny check boxes to assign permissions for the object s properties and that user or group.

How does the Full Control permission apply to advanced permissions?

- Remember that normal permissions, such as Read, Write, Full Control, and so on, are still in effect. The advanced permissions are simply subsets of the normal permissions. When you give a user Full Control permissions, all the advanced permissions are allowed. Likewise, if you give a user no access permission, the user is not given access in any way. The advanced permissions simply enable you to further refine any permissions you may have already given the user. In this manner, you can specify specific tasks to either permit or deny.

Do I need to configure advanced permissions for each group?

- No. Advanced permissions give you a way to finely control the permissions you give to users or groups. However, the use of advanced permissions should be incidental and not a normal part of your security plan. Under most conditions, the normal permissions you assign are all you need.

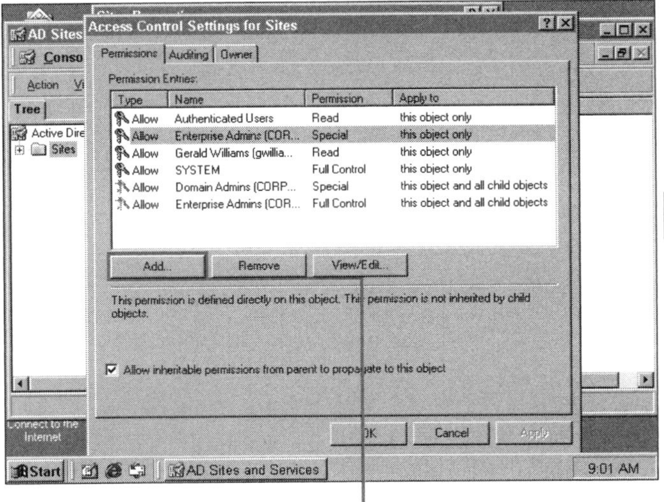

■ You can add or remove users and groups and assign them access permissions from the Access Control Settings window as well.

15 Click Add to add users or groups and define access permissions.

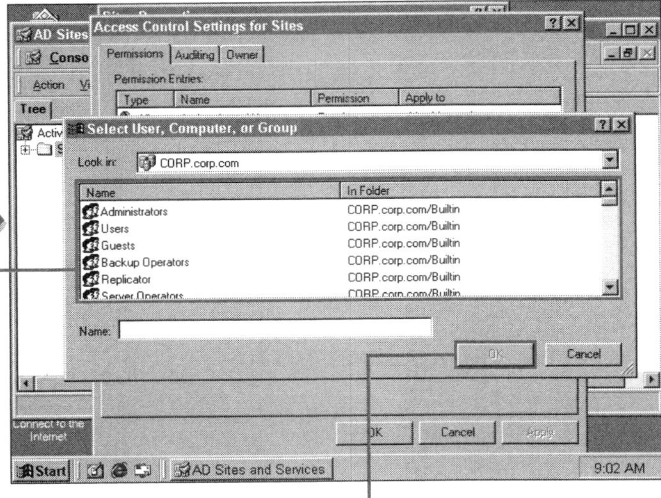

16 Select the user or group account from this list.

17 Click OK.

CREATING A NEW SITE

You create new sites by using the Active Directory Sites and Services snap-in. A *site* is a physical grouping of computers, normally contained within a geographic location and network subnet. A site can contain a domain or multiple domains.

When you install the Active Directory, a first site is installed by default. You can then add new sites as needed for your environment.

Each site that you create within the console should naturally reflect a physical segment of your network that has been set up to be a site. Keep in mind that each site is then connected with other sites through some kind of WAN link. You use the Sites and Services snap-in to create these sites, then you will create links between them for replication purposes.

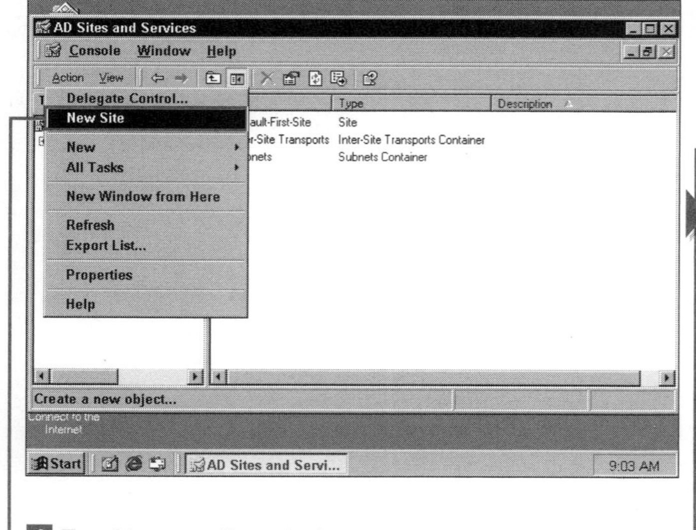

1 To add a new site, select the Sites container and choose Action⇨New Site.

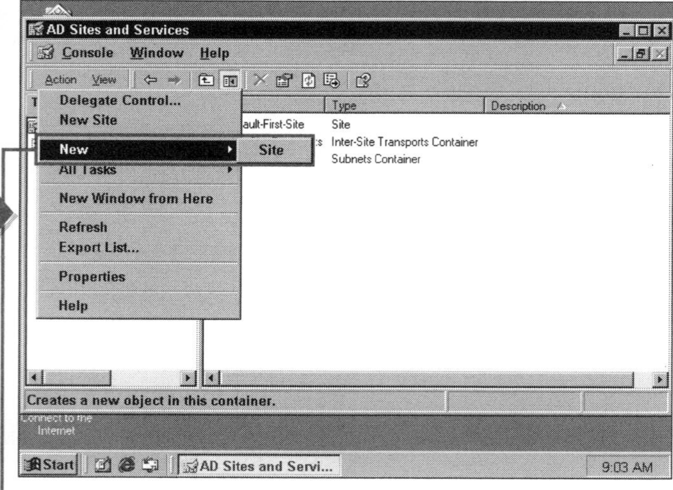

■ Or select the Sites container and choose Action⇨New⇨Site.

How should I name sites?

- You can choose any naming configuration for your sites that fits your needs. The only Active Directory restriction is that site names are limited to 63 characters and cannot contain a period (.). Frequently, sites are named by their geographic location. For example, if a company has sites in Dallas, New York, and Los Angeles, the site names would reflect the cities in which those WAN sites are located.

What is a *site link*?

- A site link is a communication mechanism that allows one site to communicate with another. Links are typically some kind of WAN communication technology and are more expensive than a LAN connection. Active Directory site links can use Internet Protocol or Simple Mail Transport Protocol for communication.

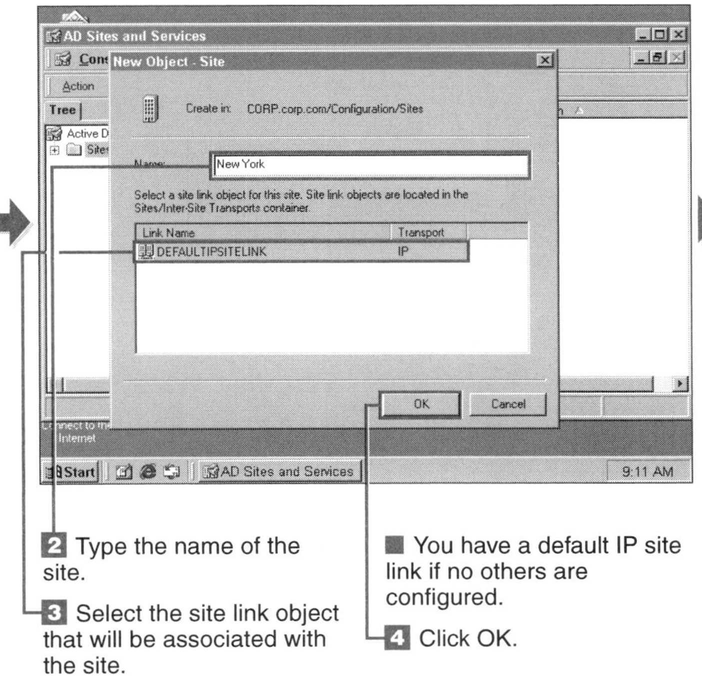

2 Type the name of the site.

3 Select the site link object that will be associated with the site.

■ You have a default IP site link if no others are configured.

4 Click OK.

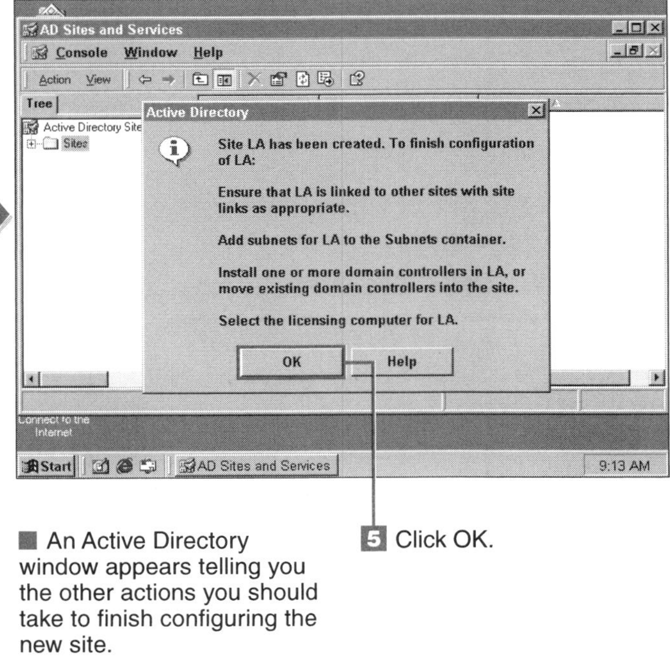

■ An Active Directory window appears telling you the other actions you should take to finish configuring the new site.

5 Click OK.

DELEGATING CONTROL OF THE SITES CONTAINER

You can delegate control of most Active Directory OUs or containers. When you delegate control, you allow another user or group to have control of that Active Directory object. The user or group then "owns" the object in that he or she can administer it and configure the object as needed.

As you can imagine, you should exercise great care before delegating control of Active Directory objects, especially the Sites container.

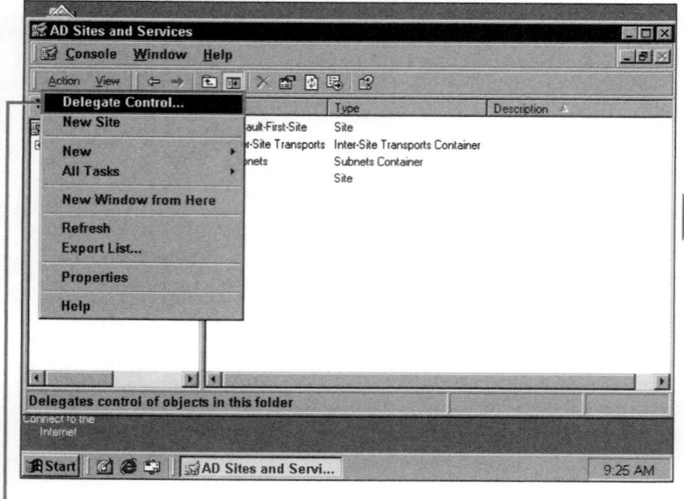

1 Select the Sites container and choose Action⇨Delegate Control.

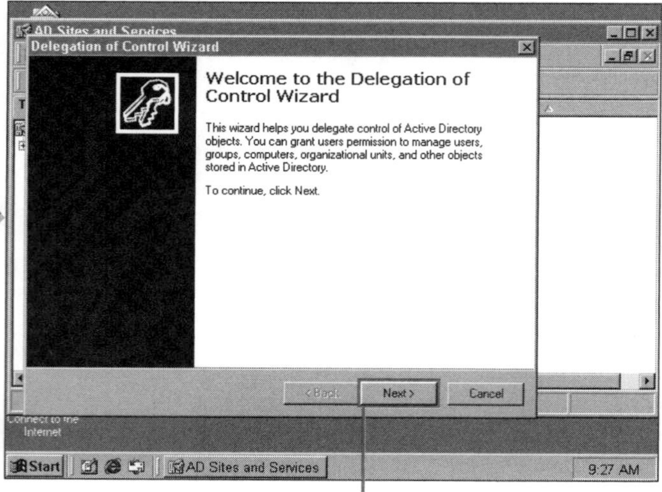

■ The Delegation of Control Wizard appears.

2 Click Next to continue.

Should I delegate control of the Sites container to a group?

- Who you delegate control to depends a lot on the organizational structure of your company. Generally, one or two people should be in control of the Sites container rather than a group of people. Because configuration of the sites and site links is crucial for Active Directory communication and replication, you should be careful who is delegated control of the container, and those who do have control should be properly trained.

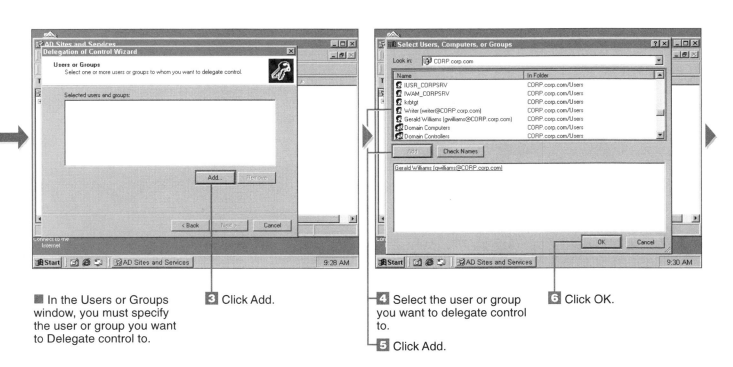

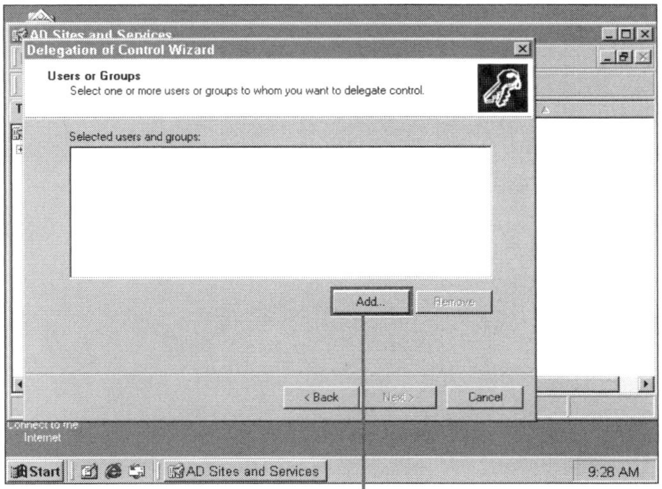

■ In the Users or Groups window, you must specify the user or group you want to Delegate control to.

3 Click Add.

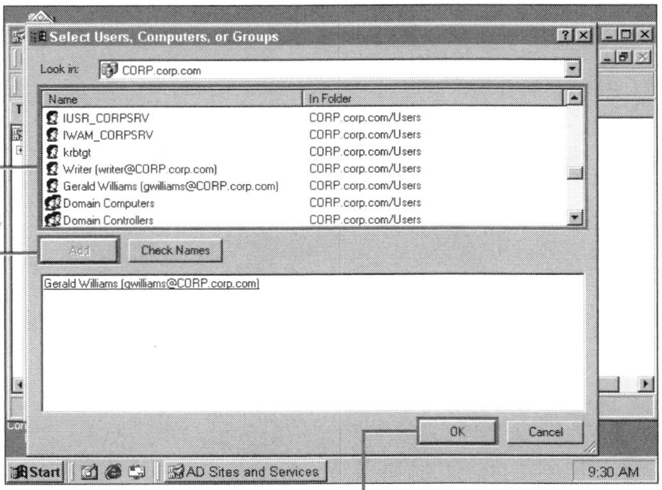

4 Select the user or group you want to delegate control to.

5 Click Add.

6 Click OK.

CONTINUED

DELEGATING CONTROL OF THE SITES CONTAINER CONTINUED

After you determine who you will delegate control to, you can further refine the actions that person or group can take. The delegation wizard enables you to specify what permissions that person or group has for the Sites container. This feature is useful because you can delegate certain responsibilities to a group or a user and not others. In other words, this feature enables you to delegate control but also maintain your own level of control over the Sites container as needed.

Keep in mind that when you delegate an OU for a container, such as the Sites container, you are not simply turning over control to another administrator or group of administrators. Delegation is a powerful tool that enables you to assign tasks to different individuals. In this manner, you can allow one person to add objects to the Sites container, but not delete them.

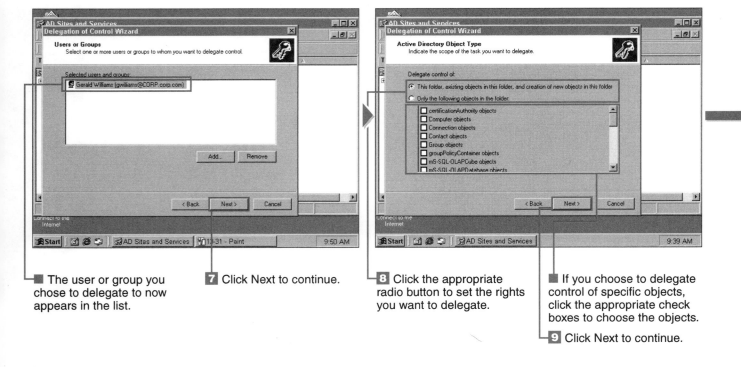

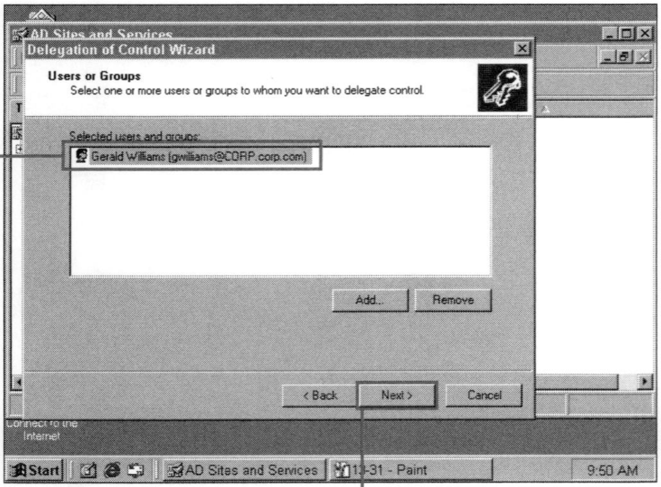

■ The user or group you chose to delegate to now appears in the list.

7 Click Next to continue.

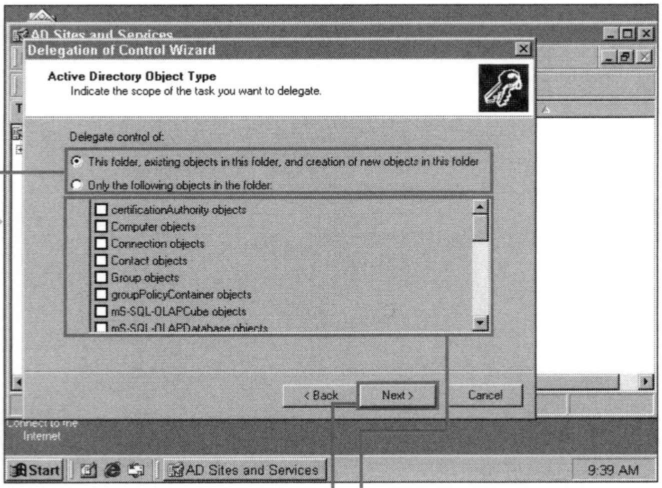

8 Click the appropriate radio button to set the rights you want to delegate.

■ If you choose to delegate control of specific objects, click the appropriate check boxes to choose the objects.

9 Click Next to continue.

What permissions should be assigned?

- If you want the delegate to be able to perform any action with the Sites container, then the delegate should be given full control permission. With full control, however, the delegate can make any change he or she desires. If you choose to limit the permissions, you should carefully consider what permissions you assign. Remember that these permissions restrict what the delegate can do, so you do not want to be so restrictive that the delegation has no purpose, yet you do want to be restrictive enough to protect any actions you do not want the delegate to perform.

Do I have to use delegation?

- No. Delegation is provided in Windows 2000 as a tool you can use to reduce administrative overhead. With the often overwhelming amount of work administrators must perform on a daily basis, delegation enables you to assign tasks to other individuals.

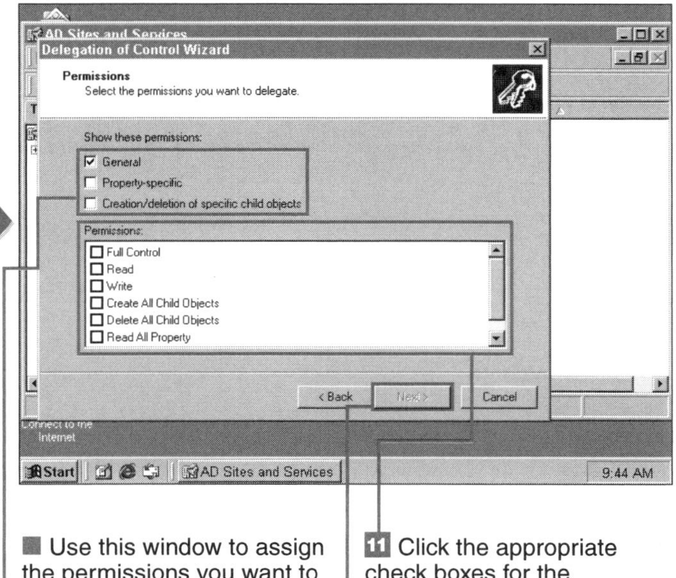

- Use this window to assign the permissions you want to delegate.

10 Click the appropriate check boxes for the permissions you want to show.

11 Click the appropriate check boxes for the permissions you want to assign for the delegate.

12 Click Next to continue.

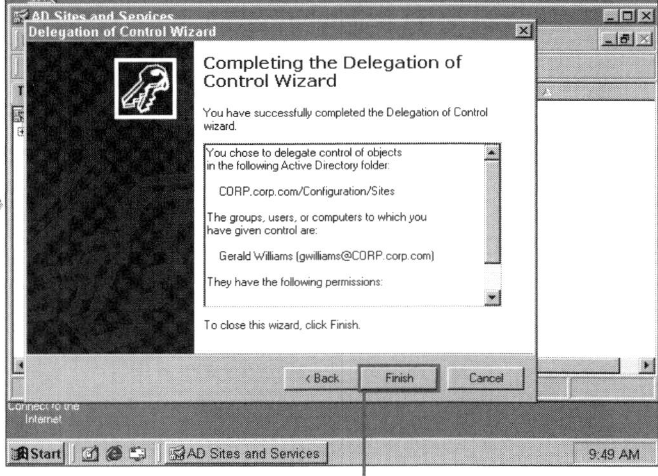

- A summary window appears.

13 Review your settings and click Finish.

EXAMINING SITE PROPERTIES

You use the Active Directory Sites and Services snap-in to add new sites to the Active Directory. Remember that a *site* is a physical representation of a grouping of computers usually contained within a geographic area. A site can contain any number of domains.

After you create the site, you can configure the site, the server for the site, and inter-site transports for directory replication. To begin configuring a site, you should access the site's properties pages.

The most configurable aspects of the site's properties pages concern security for the site and group policy. Concerning security, the site object in the Active Directory works like all other objects. You can set security so you can manage who can access the site object and what they can do with it. By default, only Enterprise Admins have full control over the site object. Additionally, you use the Group Policy tab to apply a desired group policy to the site. Group policies can be applied at the site, domain, or OU level.

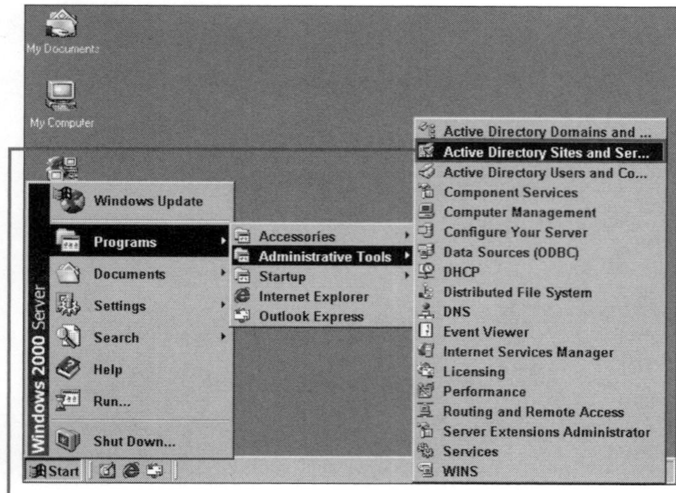

1 To access the Active Directory Sites and Services snap-in, choose Start➪Programs➪Administrative Tools➪Active Directory Sites and Services.

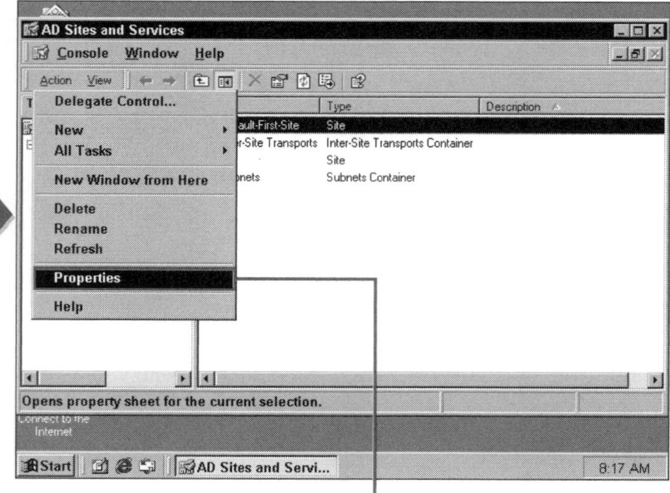

■ The AD Sites and Services window appears.

2 Expand Sites, and then select the site you want to administer in the details pane.

3 Choose Action➪Properties.

Can a domain contain more than one site?

✔ Yes. A site can contain several domains or a domain can contain several sites. Remember that a domain is simply a logical grouping while the site refers to a physical location, usually one or more particular subnets.

Are sites a part of the Active Directory namespace?

✔ No. Computers and users grouped into domains and OUs can be browsed in the Active Directory, but sites are not a part of the Active Directory namespace. Sites contain computer objects and connection objects for replication within the Active Directory.

What happens if I apply group policy at a site and not the domains within the site?

✔ Group policy, by default, filters down from the highest level, which is the site. If no policies are applied at the domain or OU level, then the policy applied at the site level is inherited by the domains and OUs within the site. If a policy is applied at the domain or OU level, then that policy overrides the site policy.

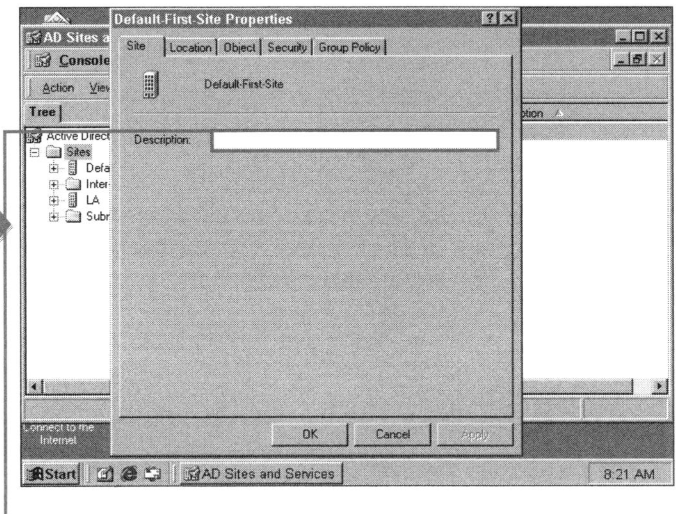

4 On the Site tab, type a description of the site, if desired.

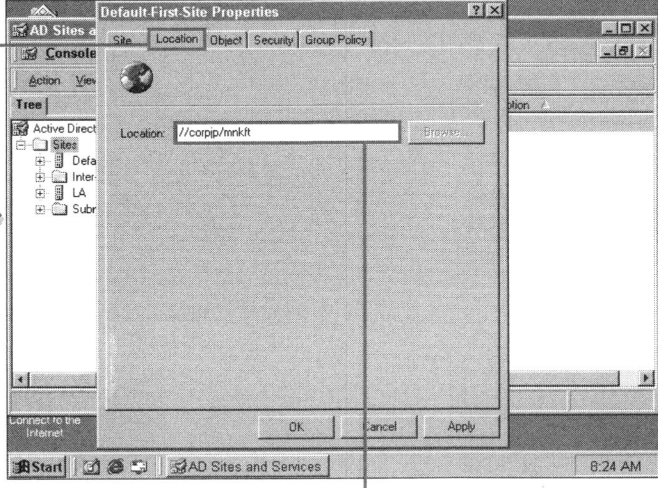

5 Click the Location tab.

6 Type a path location for the physical site or subnet, if desired.

CONTINUED

EXAMINING SITE PROPERTIES CONTINUED

You may notice the USN numbers on the Object tab. The *USN (Update Sequence Numbers)* are used by domain controllers to replicate Active Directory information. Each object contains an original USN number and a current USN number. The Active Directory uses the current USN number to make certain replication for that object is current at all sites. When a change occurs on the object, for example, if you changed a security setting for the site object, then the USN is updated so that all other USNs on other domain controllers are now outdated. When the replication process occurs, the updated USN and changes made to the object are sent to all other domain controllers so they will have the most current information.

You can configure Security settings for the site object just as you would any other Active Directory component. Also, group policies can apply to the site object if you would like a group policy to be in effect at the site level.

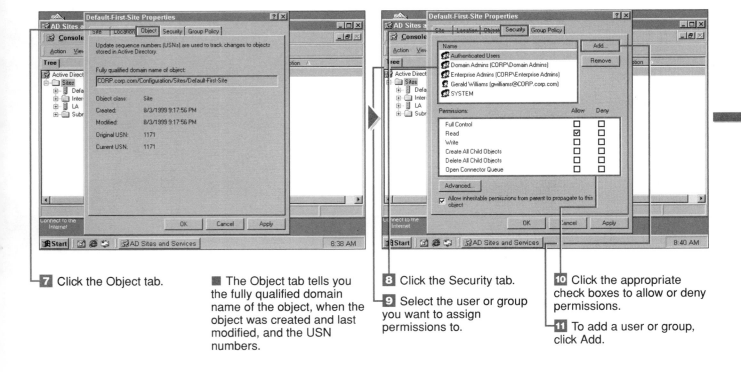

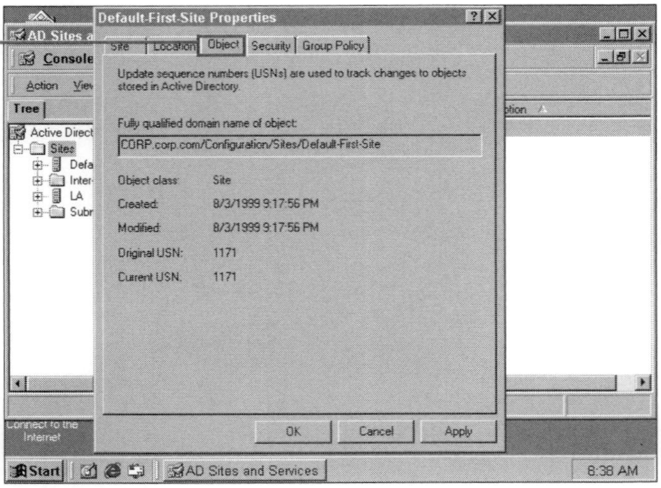

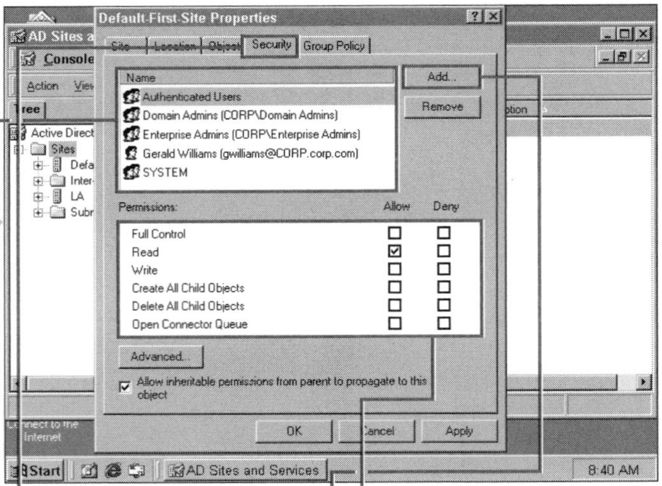

7 Click the Object tab.

■ The Object tab tells you the fully qualified domain name of the object, when the object was created and last modified, and the USN numbers.

8 Click the Security tab.

9 Select the user or group you want to assign permissions to.

10 Click the appropriate check boxes to allow or deny permissions.

11 To add a user or group, click Add.

How do group policies affect the site object?

Group policies are applied in the Active Directory and can contain a wide variety of settings that are imposed on users and groups belonging to that group policy. If you use a group policy setting for the site object, the users and groups that access the object have certain permissions either granted or denied, depending on the configuration of the group policy. If no other policies exist for domains and OUs within the site, then the site group policy will by inherited by the domains and OUs.

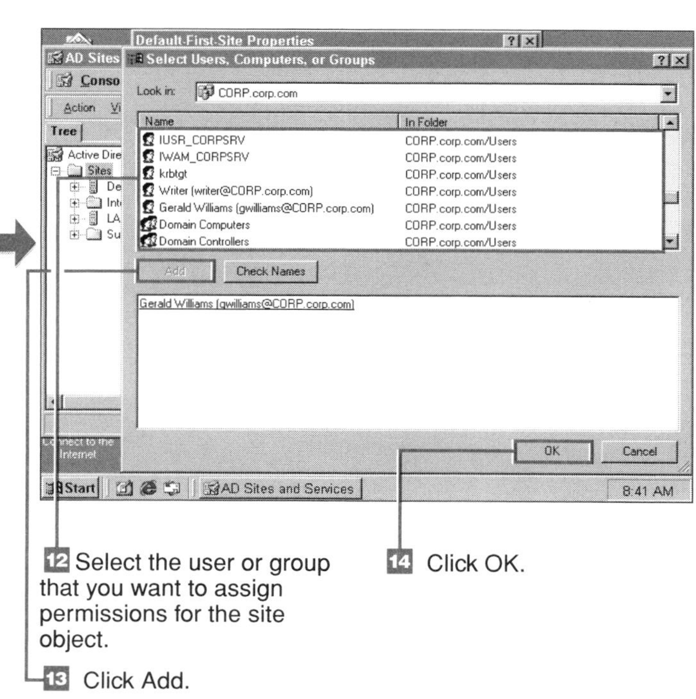

12 Select the user or group that you want to assign permissions for the site object.

13 Click Add.

14 Click OK.

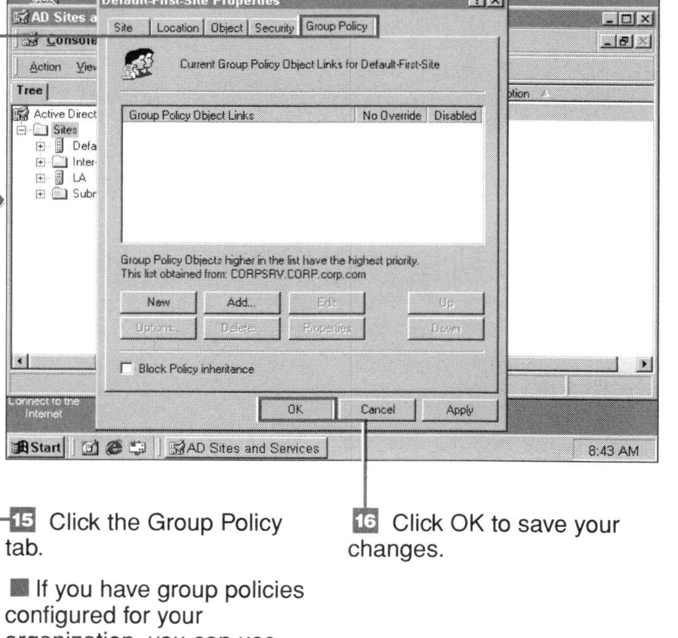

15 Click the Group Policy tab.

■ If you have group policies configured for your organization, you can use the Add or New buttons to add a group policy for this object.

16 Click OK to save your changes.

CONFIGURING SITE SETTINGS

Aside from basic properties sheets, you can expand the site you want to administer to configure the site. After you expand the site, you have a Servers container, Licensing Site settings object, and an NTDS Site Settings object. You can configure each of these as needed.

First, each site must have at least one domain controller. The domain controllers for the site appear in the Servers container, and you can access the domain controller's properties sheets to determine the domain controllers function in reference to the site. With the domain controller's properties sheets, you can configure how the domain controller behaves in terms of site configuration and replication.

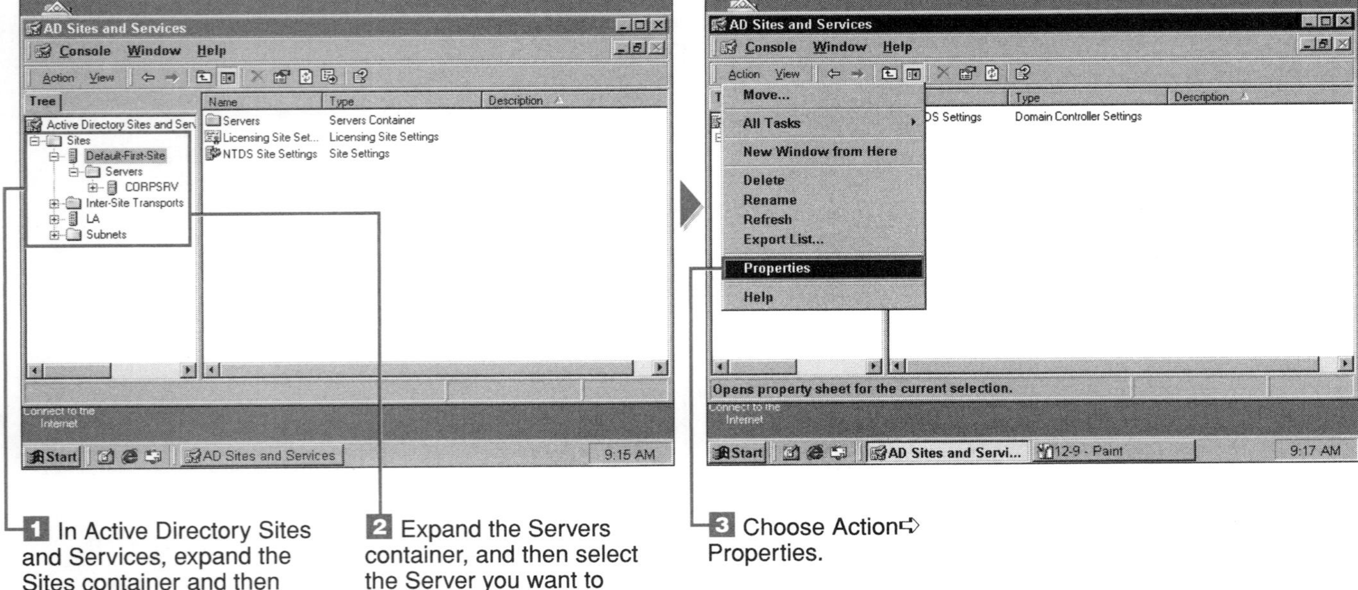

1 In Active Directory Sites and Services, expand the Sites container and then expand the site you want to administer.

2 Expand the Servers container, and then select the Server you want to administer.

3 Choose Action⇨ Properties.

What is a preferred bridgehead server?

- A *preferred bridgehead server* is the server that exchanges Active Directory replication data with other sites. The preferred bridgehead server must have an appropriate amount of bandwidth available to exchange replication data for your organization, and if you protect your site using a proxy server or firewall, a preferred bridgehead server is required. The preferred bridgehead server sends and receives replication data, and then shares that data with other domain controllers within the site.

I want to know when the last modifications were made on the domain controller that required replication. Where can I examine this?

- You can use the Object tab on the domain controllers properties pages and examine the date and time the object was created and the last date and time the object was modified. The USNs also give you some clues about changes made to the domain controller object that required replication.

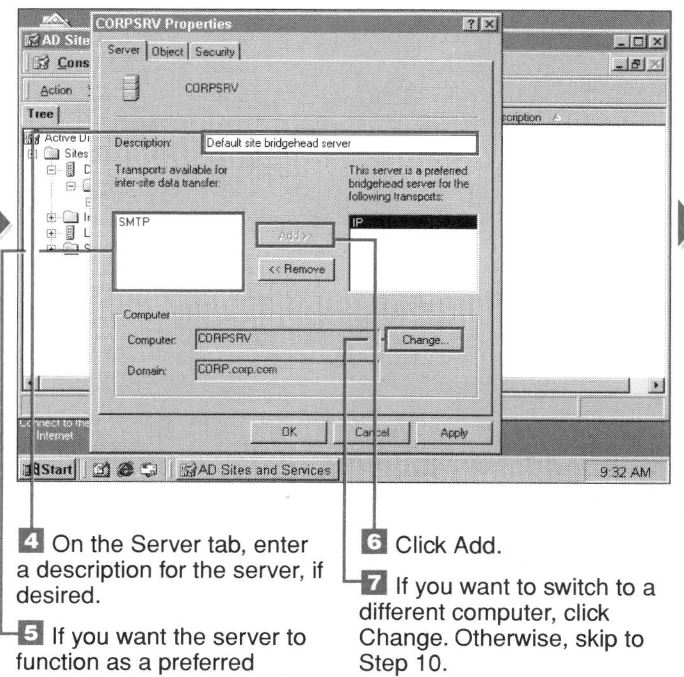

4 On the Server tab, enter a description for the server, if desired.

5 If you want the server to function as a preferred bridgehead server, click the transport you want to use.

6 Click Add.

7 If you want to switch to a different computer, click Change. Otherwise, skip to Step 10.

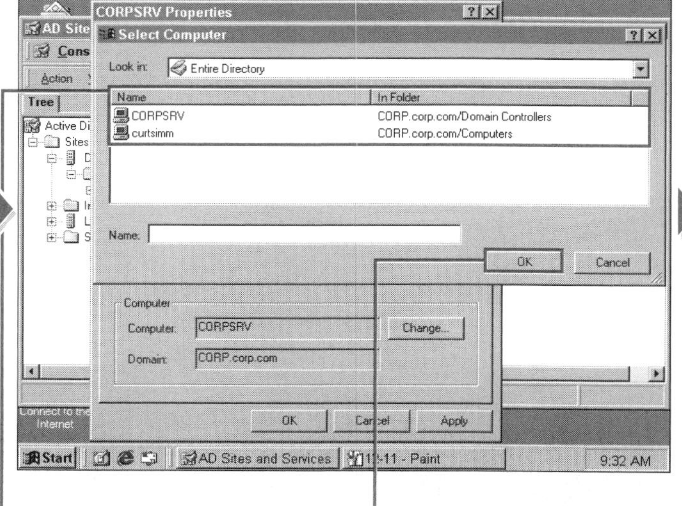

8 Select the computer you want to switch to.

9 Click OK.

CONTINUED

CONFIGURING SITE SETTINGS
CONTINUED

After you configure the Server tab, you can also examine the Object tab and configure any security settings you may wish to use on the Security tab.

The Object tab gives you the fully qualified domain name of the server, the Active Directory creation and modification date, and the USN numbers. Keep in mind that you can use the Object tab to see the last day and time that changes were made to the object that required replication.

The Security tab functions like all other Security tabs you have seen in the Active Directory. By default, only Enterprise Admins have full control permission for the object. You can change this as necessary, but you should give careful consideration before assigning any person or group permissions to the domain controller object. You want certain individuals only to have permission to make changes for this object.

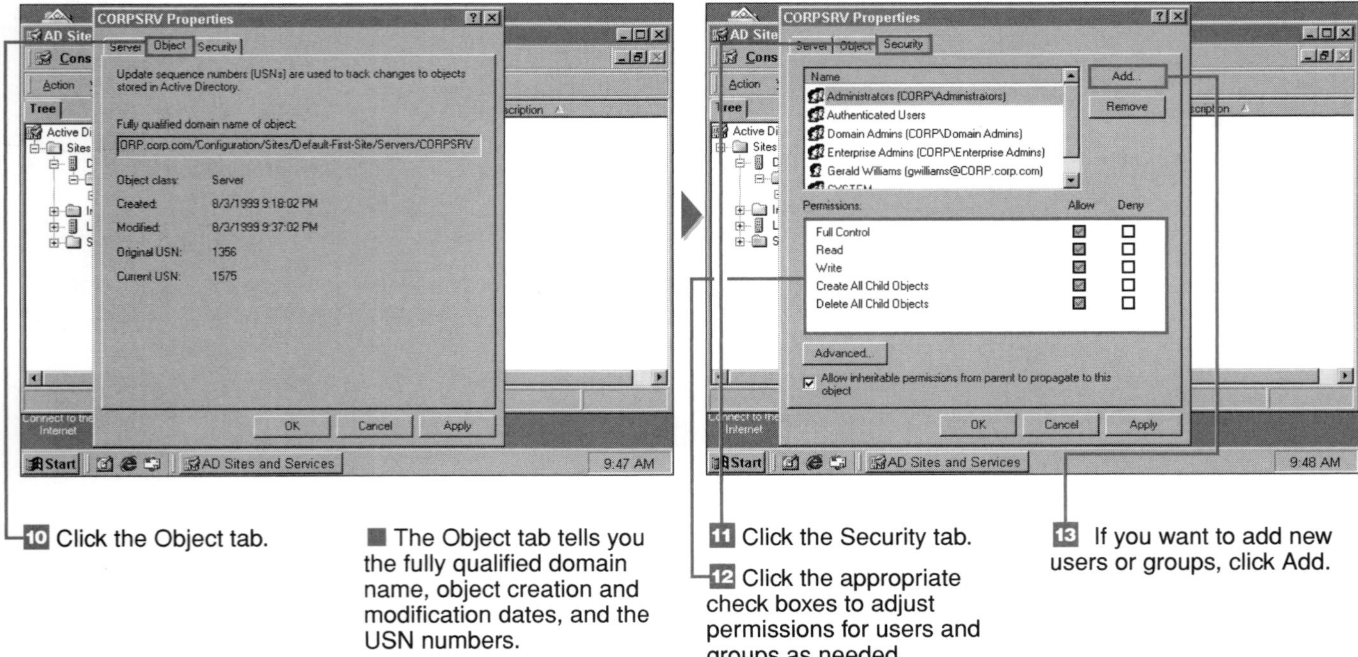

10 Click the Object tab.

■ The Object tab tells you the fully qualified domain name, object creation and modification dates, and the USN numbers.

11 Click the Security tab.

12 Click the appropriate check boxes to adjust permissions for users and groups as needed.

13 If you want to add new users or groups, click Add.

Can I give a user access to the server but not to the other containers, such as the Servers and Sites container?

- Yes. You can use the Security tab to give a user or a group access privileges to the server object in the Active Directory, but not to parent or child objects. Add the user or group, and then assign the desired permissions. Clear the Allow Inheritable Permissions From Parent To Propagate To This Object check box at the bottom of the window.

How can I stop inheritable permissions?

- By default, any object inherits the permissions of its parent. For example, the domain controller object permissions are inherited from the container in which they reside. You can use the Security tab to block inheritable permissions by clearing the check box at the bottom of the window. However, inheritable permissions are effective and save you a lot of configuration time, so try to avoid blocking permissions as much as possible.

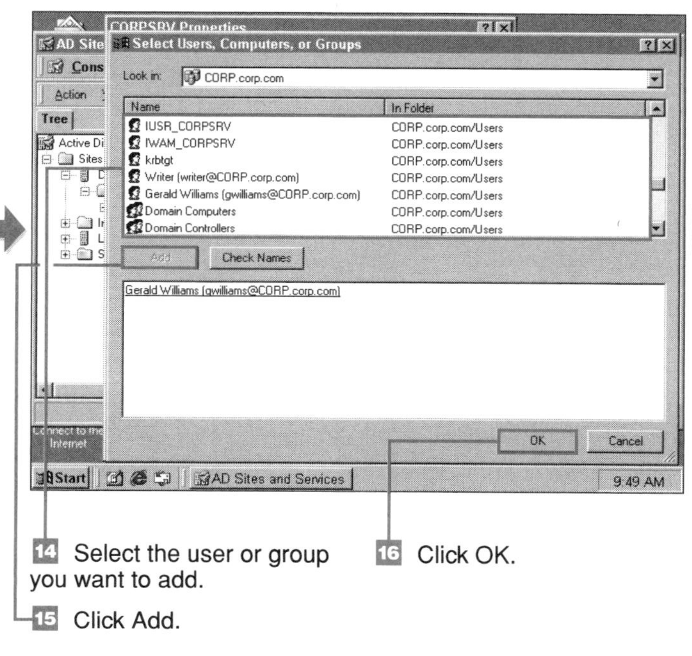

14 Select the user or group you want to add.

15 Click Add.

16 Click OK.

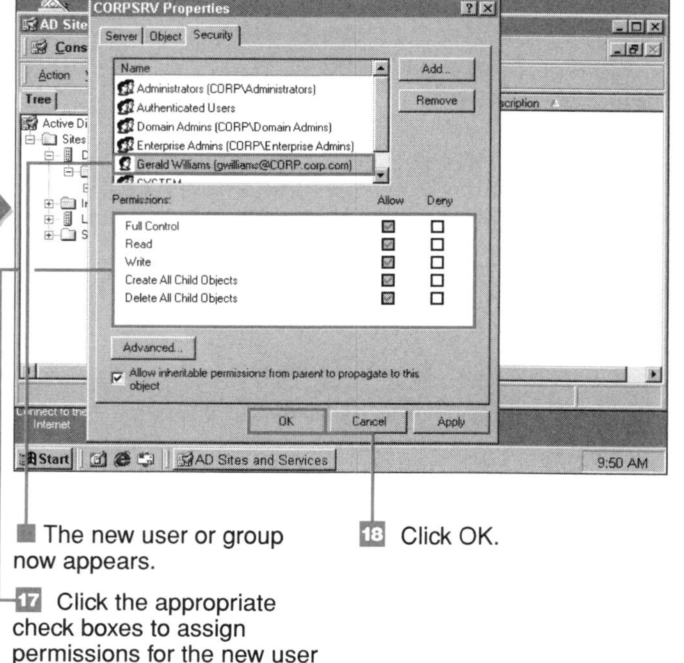

■ The new user or group now appears.

17 Click the appropriate check boxes to assign permissions for the new user or group.

18 Click OK.

CONFIGURING SITE SETTINGS
CONTINUED

You can also use the Action menu to move a domain controller to a different site. This feature allows a domain controller to function within a particular site so that it can serve as the bridgehead server for that site. You do have to keep in mind, however, the physical design of your network and how the move will affect replication traffic.

You can designate the licensing computer for a site, which does not have to be a domain controller or the bridgehead server. For the best performance, the site's licensing computer should be within the site. The Active Directory automatically designates a licensing computer for the site, but you can easily change this.

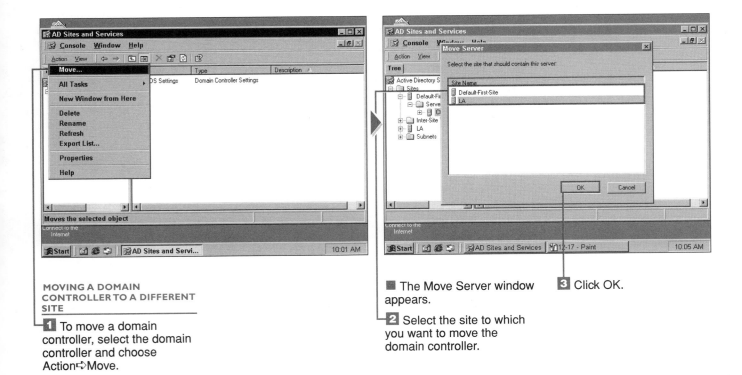

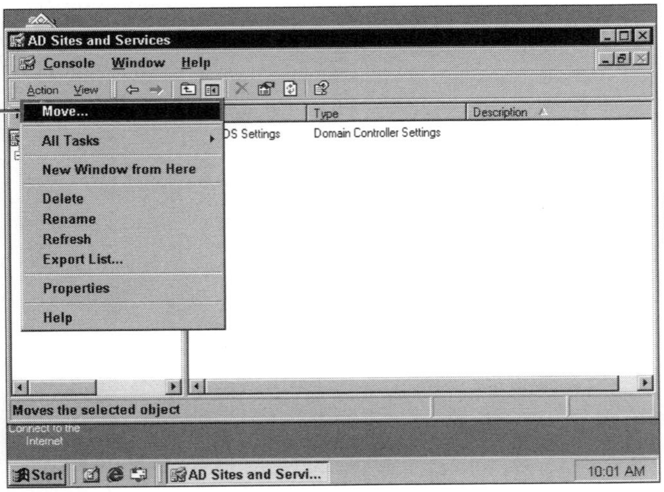

MOVING A DOMAIN CONTROLLER TO A DIFFERENT SITE

1 To move a domain controller, select the domain controller and choose Action⇨Move.

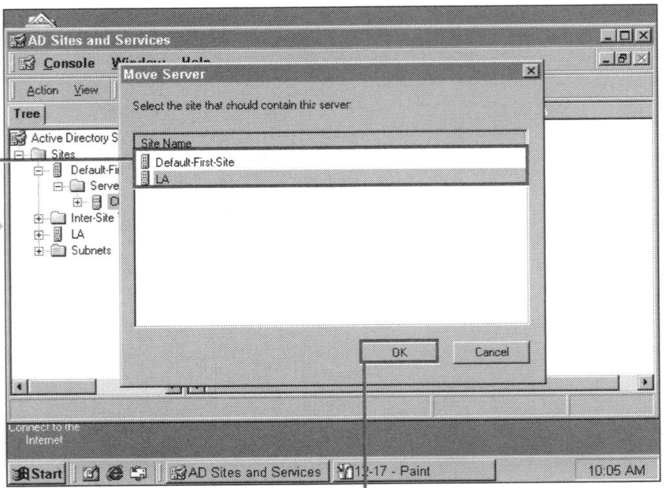

■ The Move Server window appears.

2 Select the site to which you want to move the domain controller.

3 Click OK.

Why would I want to move a domain controller?

- You can use the Active Directory Sites and Services tool to move domain controllers between sites. Keep in mind that the configuration changes you make within this tool should accurately reflect the physical layout of your network. When you move a domain controller to a site, the domain controller then functions within that site for replication purposes.

What is a licensing computer?

- Each Active Directory site must have a licensing computer, which does not have to be a domain controller. When a site is configured, a licensing computer is selected by default, but you can change this. The role of the licensing computer is to track licenses for that particular site.

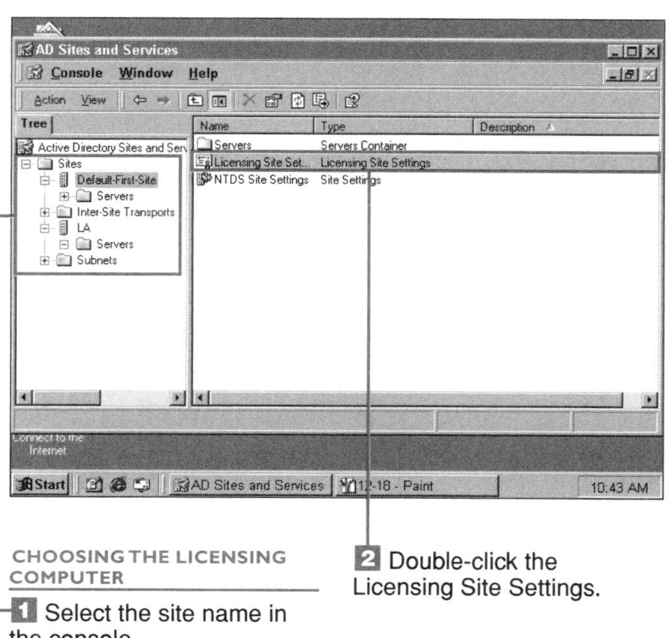

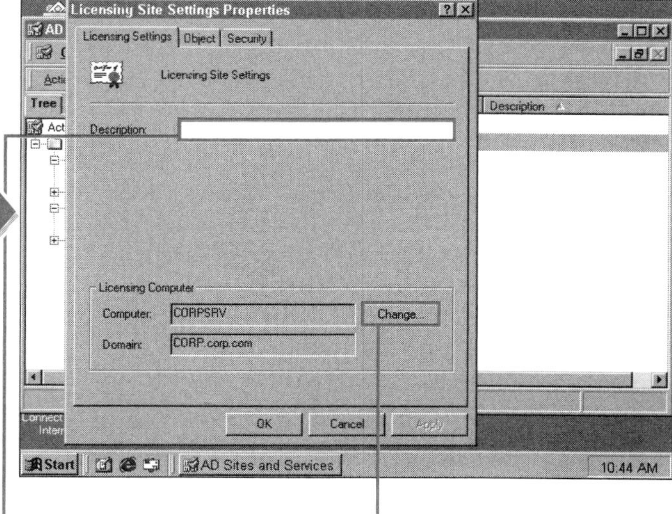

CHOOSING THE LICENSING COMPUTER

1 Select the site name in the console.

2 Double-click the Licensing Site Settings.

3 Type a description if desired.

4 If you want a different computer to serve as the licensing computer, click Change and select the new computer from the list that appears.

CONTINUED

CONFIGURING SITE SETTINGS
CONTINUED

Finally, you use the site to adjust the NTDS site settings. This feature enables you to configure the replication time for this site. You can learn more about setting up replication in the next section. The NTDS site settings allow you to determine how often replication should occur for the site.

The Active Directory configures a default schedule for the site, typically one replication process per hour. You can use the NTDS site settings to make changes to this schedule as necessary.

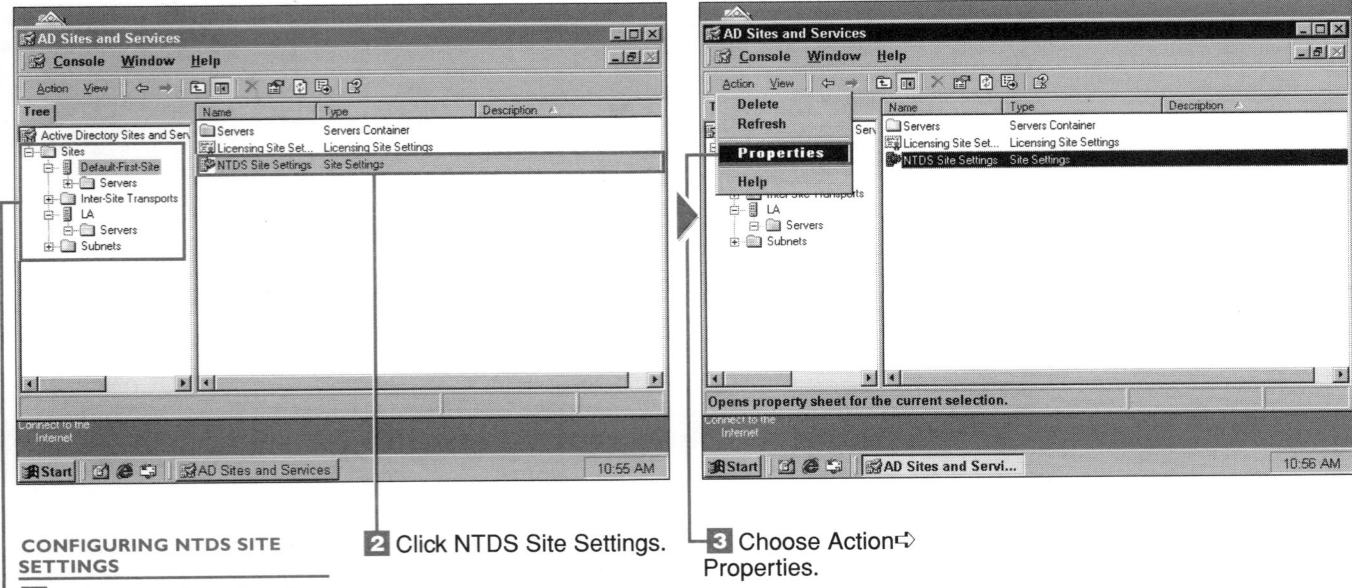

CONFIGURING NTDS SITE SETTINGS

1 In the console, select the site you want to administer.

2 Click NTDS Site Settings.

3 Choose Action⇨Properties.

How often should replication occur?

- The default replication setting is once every hour of every day. This setting typically is enough for most networks. However, if you expect many changes or if you expect only a few, you can change the replication schedule to meet the needs of your organization. Under normal circumstances, however, the default setting is the best choice. Keep in mind that replication is always a trade-off. If you have high-speed connectivity between your WAN sites, then you can lower the replication time so that replication occurs more frequently. This reduces the amount of time that domain controllers do not have consistent data, which is called *latency*. However, due to the expense of bandwidth, you must find a balance between what is best and what you can afford.

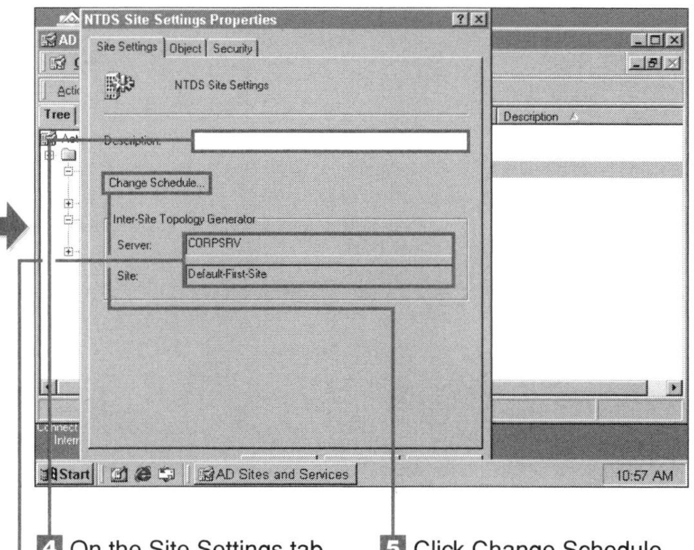

4 On the Site Settings tab, type a description of the site settings, if desired.

■ The server name and site name are listed here.

5 Click Change Schedule to change the replication schedule.

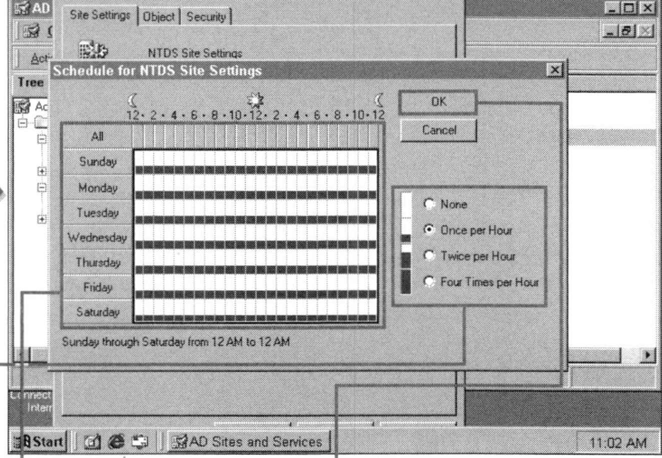

6 Adjust the schedule by clicking the grids for each day and time.

7 Click the desired radio button for either none, once per hour, twice per hour, or four times per hour.

■ Remember that excessive replication consumes network bandwidth resources.

8 Click OK.

CREATING SITE LINKS

After you create and configure the sites you need for your network, the next step is to establish site links for the sites. This action may take some planning depending on the number of sites you have in your organization. For replication, you must consider how you want to link your sites together so that each site can replicate with the other sites. This action is performed by first determining how you want the sites to communicate with each other, how often they should replicate data, and the cost of the site link.

You can use the default site link for either IP or SMTP traffic, depending on the needs of your organization. If you select either the IP or SMTP container, you can configure the existing default site link or you can create new ones.

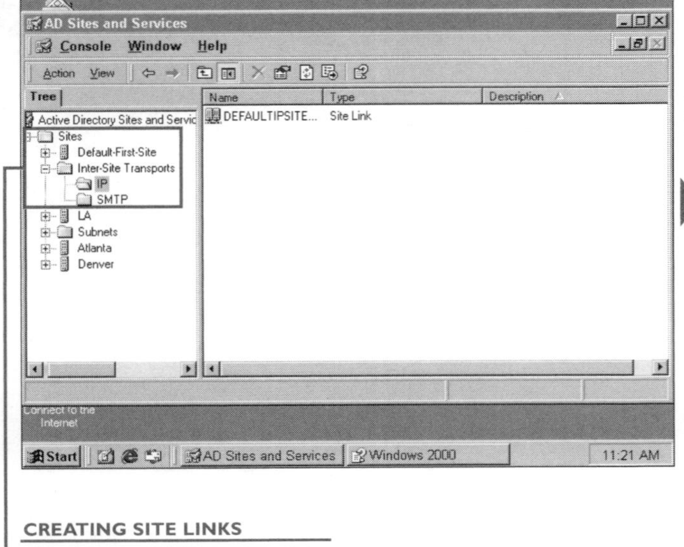

CREATING SITE LINKS

1 Expand the Inter-Site Transports container and select either the IP or SMTP container.

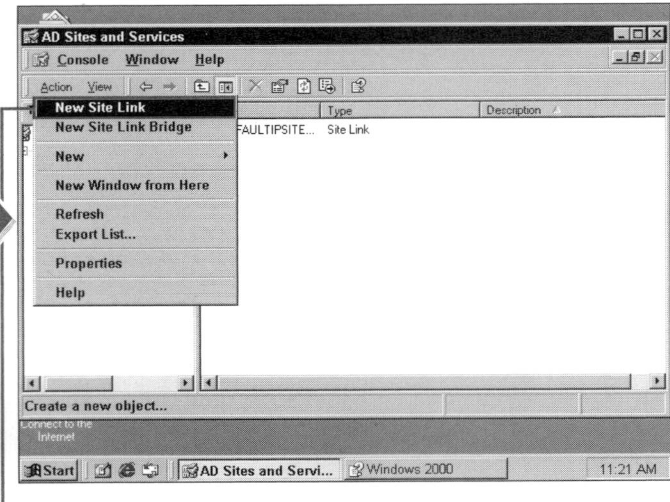

2 Choose Action⇨New Site Link.

How should sites be linked together?

- Remember that the purpose of site links is to connect Active Directory sites so that directory replication can occur. This process ensures that all directory information for the network is current, regardless of the physical location. Sites should be linked so that replication can occur between all sites. If you have multiple sites, you can also use site link bridges, which are discussed in the next section.

What transports are available?

- A transport is the protocol used to transport replication data between sites. The Active Directory supports both Internet Protocol (IP) and Simple Mail Transport Protocol (SMTP) for inter-site replication. Under most circumstances, you will use IP because the Active Directory is built on your TCP/IP network.

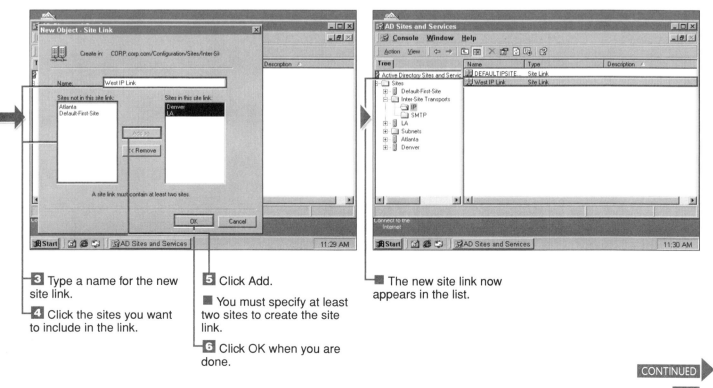

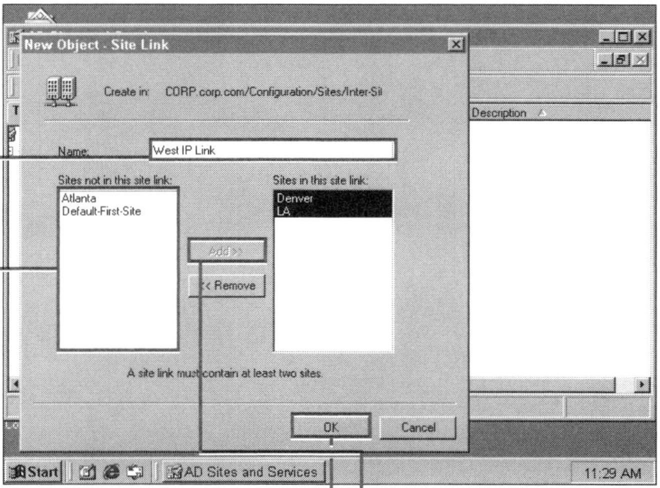

3 Type a name for the new site link.

4 Click the sites you want to include in the link.

5 Click Add.

■ You must specify at least two sites to create the site link.

6 Click OK when you are done.

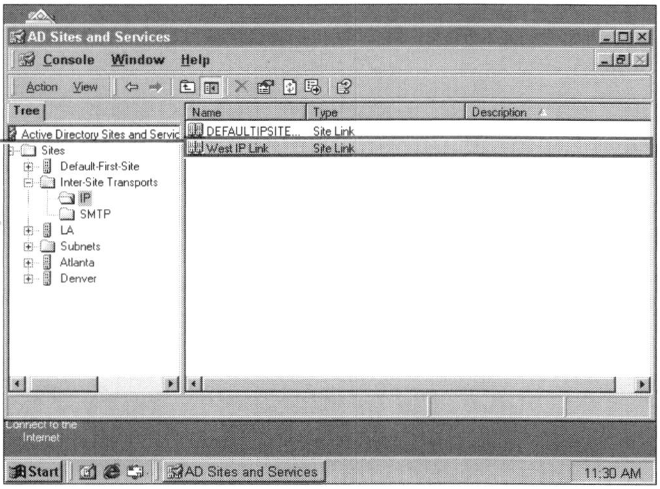

■ The new site link now appears in the list.

CONTINUED

CREATING SITE LINKS CONTINUED

After you create site links, you may need to also add one or more site link bridges. Just as a site link connects two or more sites, a site link bridge connects one or more site links. For example, if you have site links configured between Houston and Dallas and one configured between San Diego and Los Angeles, you can link those two site links together for replication purposes. In order to create a site link bridge, you must have at least two site links.

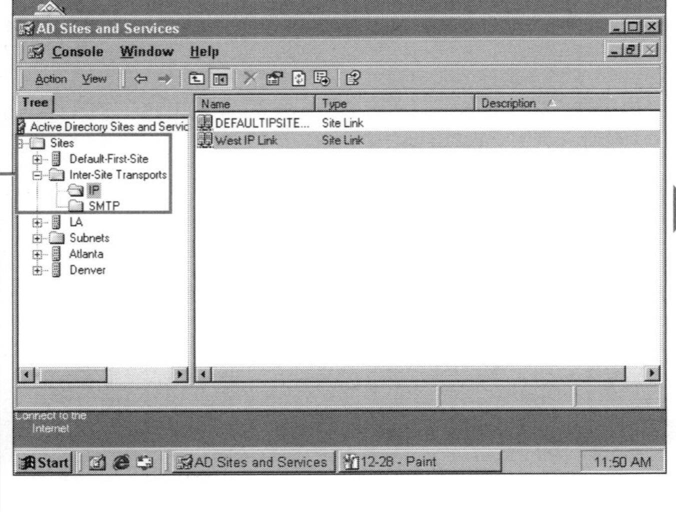

CREATING A SITE LINK BRIDGE

1 Expand the Inter-Site Transports container and click either the IP or SMTP container for the type of site link bridge you want to create.

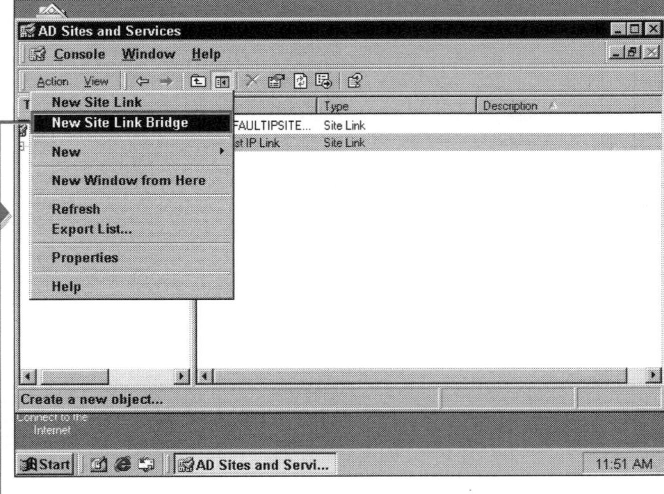

2 Choose Action⇨New Site Link Bridge.

Can you link all site links with one bridge?

Yes. If you have several site links configured, you can use one site link bridge to link all the site links together. To perform this action, simply select all your site links in the left window and use the Add button to move them to the right window. This causes the new site link bridge to link all site links.

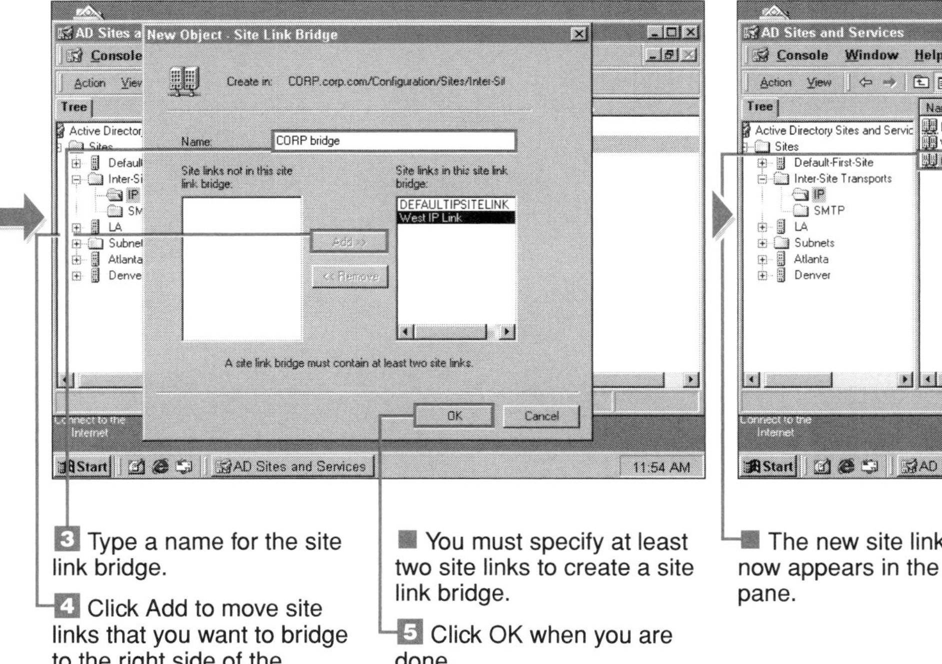

3 Type a name for the site link bridge.

4 Click Add to move site links that you want to bridge to the right side of the window.

■ You must specify at least two site links to create a site link bridge.

5 Click OK when you are done.

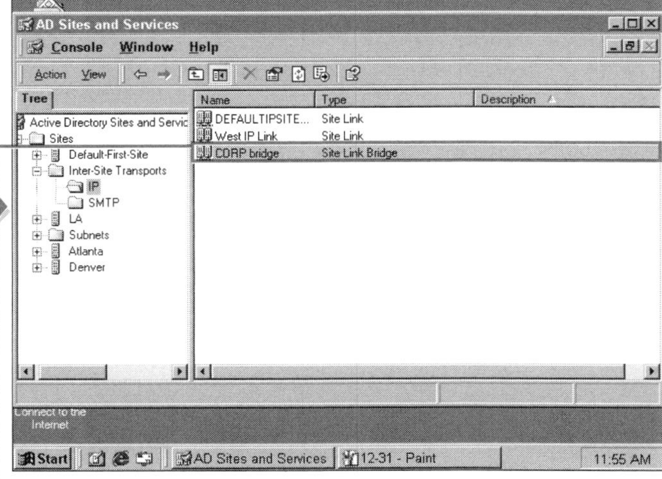

■ The new site link bridge now appears in the details pane.

CONFIGURING SITE LINKS CONTINUED

After you create the site links and bridges that you need, you can configure them to replicate in the manner that is appropriate for your environment. This is accomplished by configuring each site link to replicate at a certain time and a certain cost. *Cost* is the priority at which site links are used. For example, if you have a T1 link that should be used for replication under normal circumstances, and you have a dial-up connection as a backup solution, you would want to configure the T1 link with a lower cost than the dial-up connection. The Active Directory always attempts to replicate over lower-cost links as opposed to higher-cost links.

If you are using an SMTP link, you don't need to worry about scheduling the replication, because SMTP is asynchronous—it ignores schedules. SMTP traffic is exchanged from one server directly to the next and not over intermediary links.

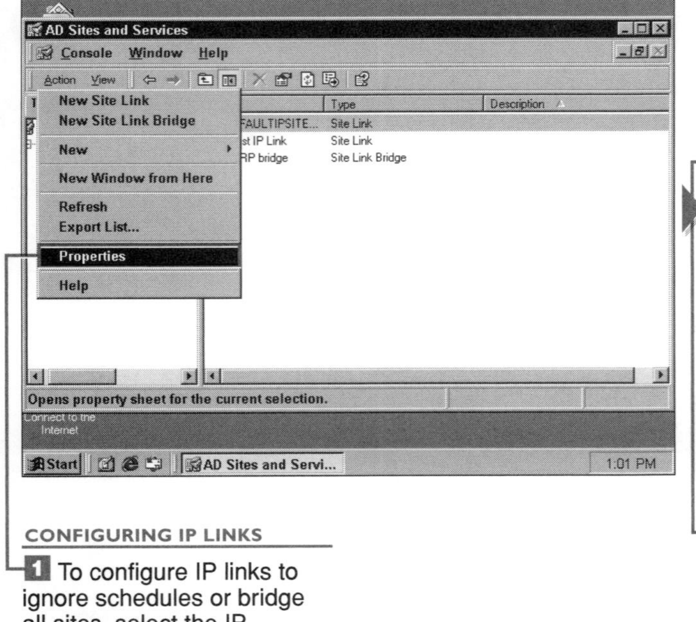

CONFIGURING IP LINKS

1 To configure IP links to ignore schedules or bridge all sites, select the IP container and choose Action⇨Properties.

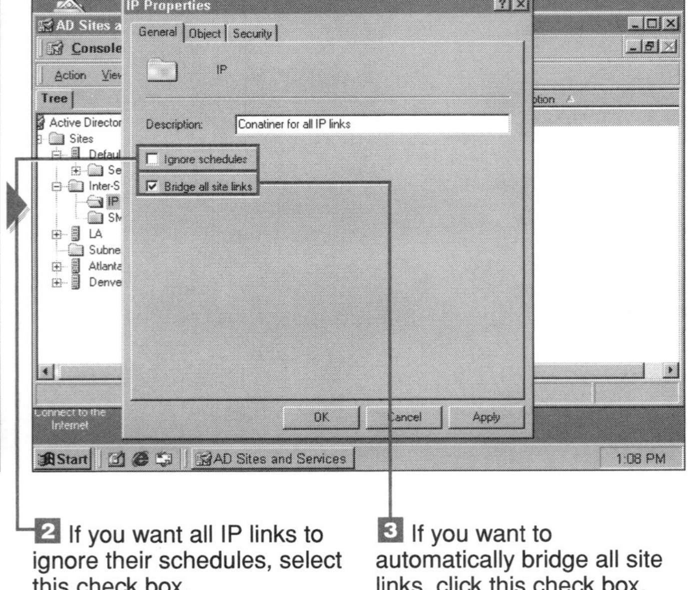

2 If you want all IP links to ignore their schedules, select this check box.

3 If you want to automatically bridge all site links, click this check box.

How should I configure the site link cost?

- The site link is configured depending on the *cost* of the site link. The Active Directory always attempts to use the site link with the lowest cost. For example, if T1 link is your main link, you could configure the cost as 1. If you have a dial-up connection to use to backup purposes, you could configure the dial-up connection as 100. With this configuration, the Active Directory always tries to use the T1 link first because it has the lowest cost.

What schedule option is available for site links?

- You can change the site link schedule so that replication is either available or unavailable. This allows you to determine the days of the week that replication is available. By default, all days are available, but you could configure the link so that replication is only available on certain days. As with any configuration, you should make certain you have firm reasons for restricting the days that replication is available.

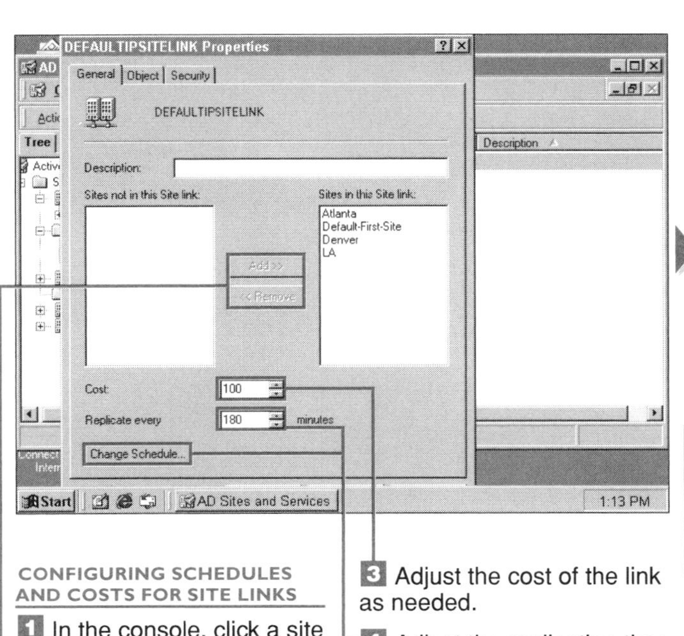

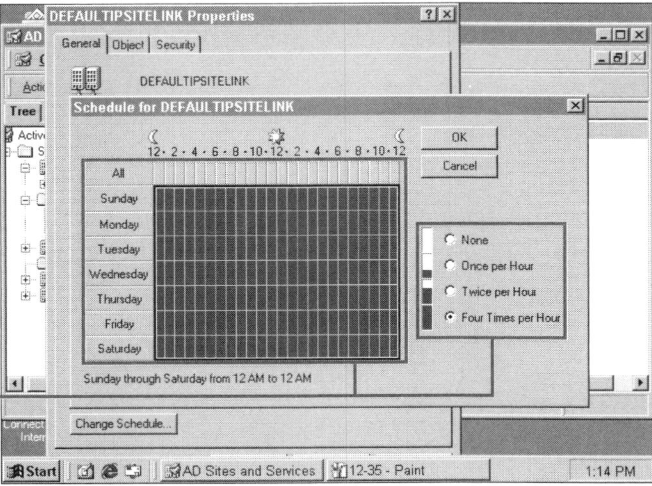

CONFIGURING SCHEDULES AND COSTS FOR SITE LINKS

1 In the console, click a site link and choose Action⇨Properties.

2 Use the Add or Remove buttons to add or remove sites from the site link.

3 Adjust the cost of the link as needed.

4 Adjust the replication time as needed.

5 If you want to adjust the replication schedule, click Change Schedule.

6 Click the schedule grid and click the appropriate radio button to configure replication for each hour of each day.

CREATING AND CONFIGURING SUBNETS

Subnets are divisions within a TCP/IP network. Subnets are used to segment network traffic and make the network more manageable. In the Active Directory, you can configure subnets that represent the subnets within your network, and then associate a site with a subnet.

Each site must have a subnet associated with it. The subnet you use depends on your network's TCP/IP configuration.

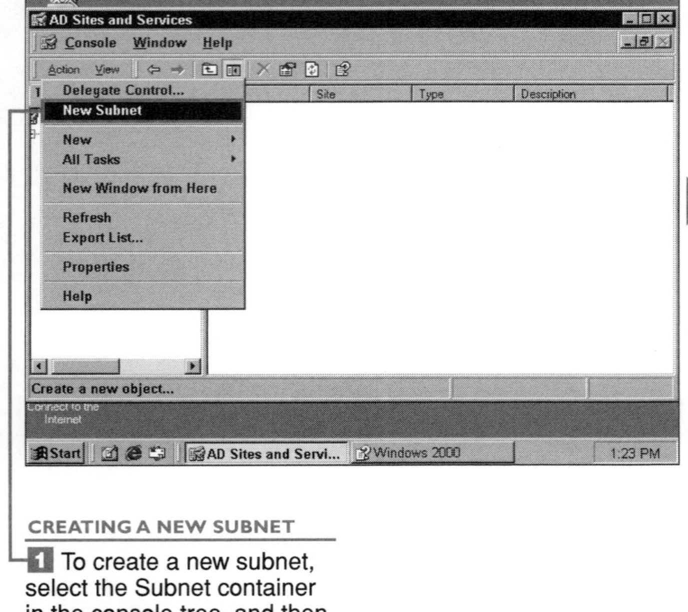

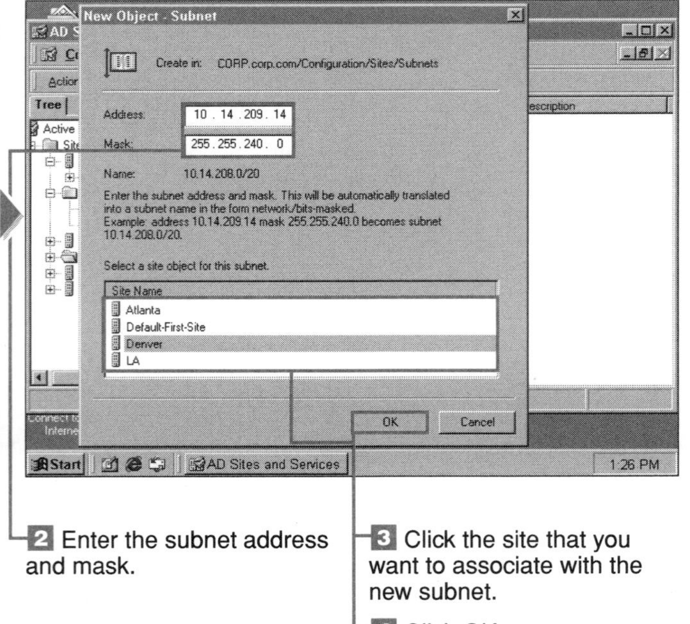

CREATING A NEW SUBNET

1 To create a new subnet, select the Subnet container in the console tree, and then choose Action⇨New Subnet.

2 Enter the subnet address and mask.

3 Click the site that you want to associate with the new subnet.

4 Click OK.

Must each site be associated with a subnet?

Each site must be associated with a physical subnet. This action ensures Active Directory communication with the site and replication.

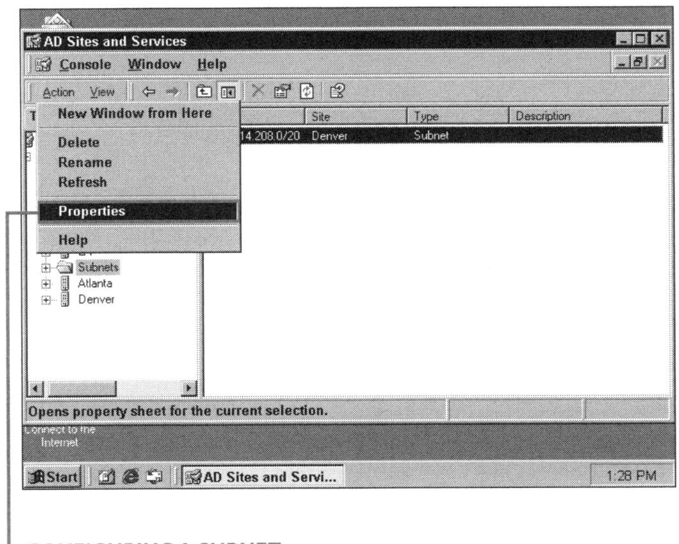

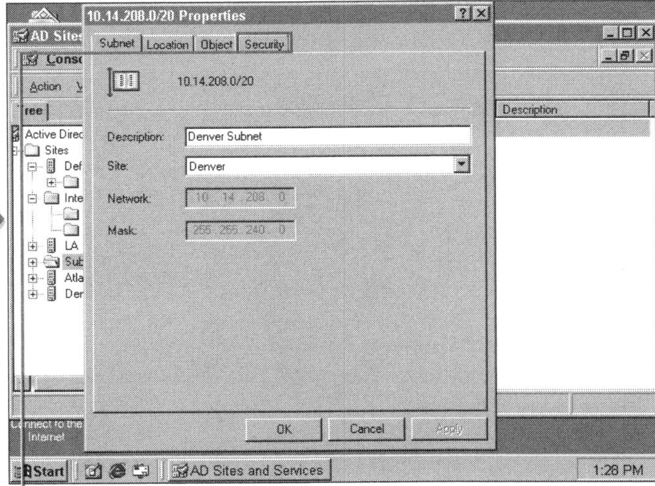

CONFIGURING A SUBNET

1 To access a subnet's properties, select the subnet in the Subnet container and choose Action⇨Properties.

■ The Properties sheets appear. The Properties Sheets provide information about the subnet. You can configure permissions for the subnet by using the Security tab.

SECTION VIII

24) ACTIVE DIRECTORY SECURITY MANAGEMENT

25) GROUP POLICY

26) PUBLISHING ACTIVE DIRECTORY RESOURCES

27) ACTIVE DIRECTORY SCHEMA

28) MAINTAINING THE ACTIVE DIRECTORY

IMPLEMENTATION

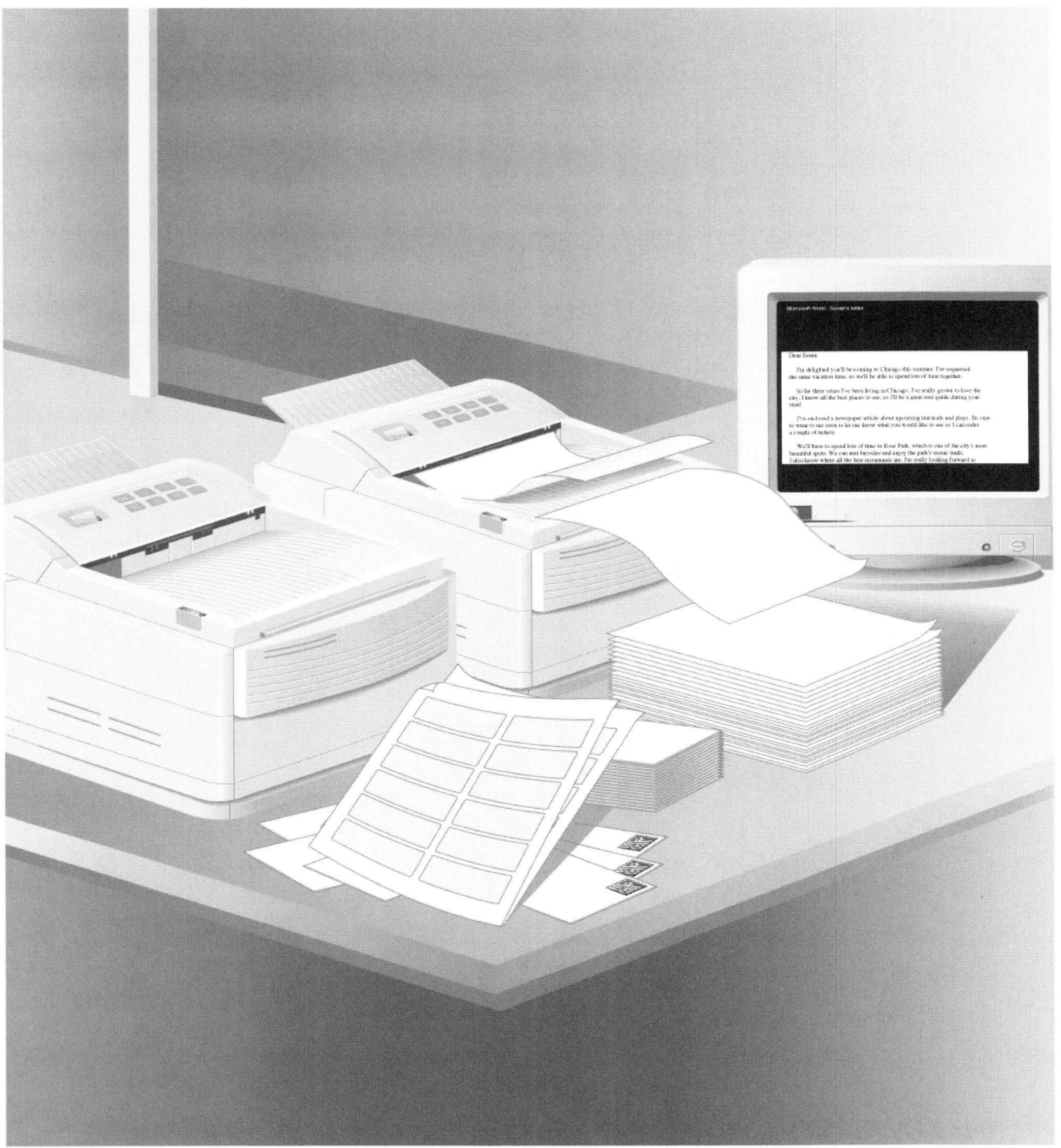

ACTIVE DIRECTORY SECURITY FEATURES

Security is a complex topic in Windows 2000. If you have explored your server's security options or read any information about security, you realize that Microsoft includes many technologies so that organizations can develop security solutions based on need. Kerberos, encrypting file system, IP Security, and Certificate services are only a few of the security features available to enable a network to lock out intruders.

All these security features are often confused with the Active Directory. But remember that the Active Directory is an integrated component of a Windows 2000 network—not a process that stands on its own. All security features in Windows 2000 affect the Active Directory in some way, but for the most part, you can implement four major secuirty options to secure the Active Directory's resources.

Domain, OU, and object security

You can secure your Active Directory domains, organizational units, and individual objects in the Active Directory. Through the properties sheets for domains, OUs, and objects, you can control who can access them and what those users can do.

An important feature concerning security is inheritance. For example, the resources (objects) residing in an OU can inherit the security settings of the actual OU. Or you can set the security permissions for each object individually. The point is you have a fine level of control over the resources in the Active Directory, from the domain level down to a simple user account.

This chapter shows you the basic process of setting up security on domains, OUs, and objects, but you can also learn about this task in Chapters 14, 15, 16, and 17 on an individual basis.

Delegation

Delegation is a tool that allows an administrator to delegate administrative authority of domains, OUs, and containers to other users or groups. This feature enables you to implement distributed security and administrative control so that a single group of administrators is not faced with the task of managing all aspects of a Microsoft Enterprise environment. Delegation of different domains, OUs, and objects is performed through the Delegation Wizard. You can learn about delegation in this chapter as well, or you can see examples of delegation in Chapters 14, 15, 16, and 17.

Group policy

Group policy is a powerful security feature of Windows 2000 that enables you to apply a variety of policies to a particular group of users. You can assign group policy at the domain and OU level. In other words, the users in a particular OU can have a group policy while users in another OU may have another group policy. Group policy enables you to manage security settings, desktop settings, system settings, applications, and a host of other features. Group policy is integrated with the Active Directory and is the method of choice for managing Enterprise users. You can learn all about group policy in Chapter 25.

Class and attribute security

As mentioned earlier, you can apply security measures to every object in the Active Directory on an individual basis. You can also set security on classes of objects and even attributes of objects.

Active Directory objects are divided into *classes*, such as the User class. For each class of objects, you can determine which users or groups should access that class of objects and what permissions they have for the class. At an even lower level, you can set security on object attributes. Attributes are *qualities* of an object that define the object. For example, a user account has the attributes of a username, e-mail address, and group membership. You can finely control the security of attributes so that users can see a user account's e-mail address but not the group membership, or any other combination. This level of security enables you to completely control your Active Directory environment. To set security on classes and attributes, you use the Active Directory Schema Manager, which you can learn about in Chapter 27.

SETTING UP OBJECT SECURITY

An Active Directory object is basically any resource within the Active Directory. Objects include users, groups, shared folders, printers, shared applications, contacts, and so on. The Active Directory enables you to set security for each object in the Active Directory. By design, you can control which groups or users can access particular objects and what they can do with those objects after they access them.

Security for Active Directory objects is configured on the Security tab that appears on each object's properties sheets. Each Security tab has the same basic options. For example, a user's Security tab allows you to configure who can access the user's account and what they can do with the account; a printer's Security tab lets you control who can access the printer and what they can do with the printer. This level of administration enables you to finely control your Active Directory resources and what groups and users can do with those resources.

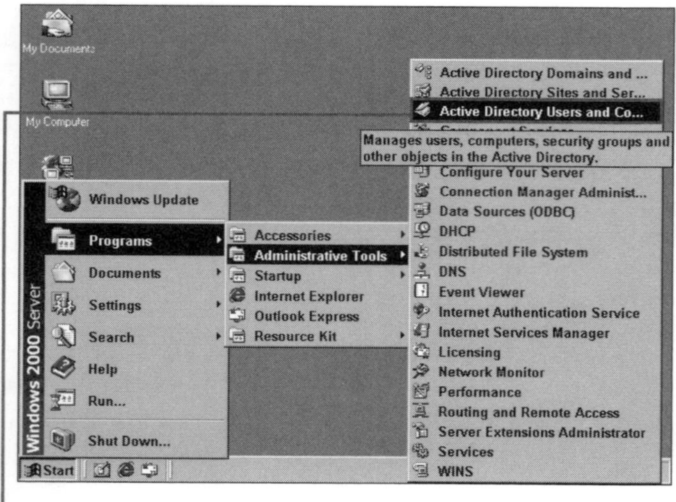

1 Choose Start➪Programs➪Administrative Tools➪Active Directory Users and Computers.

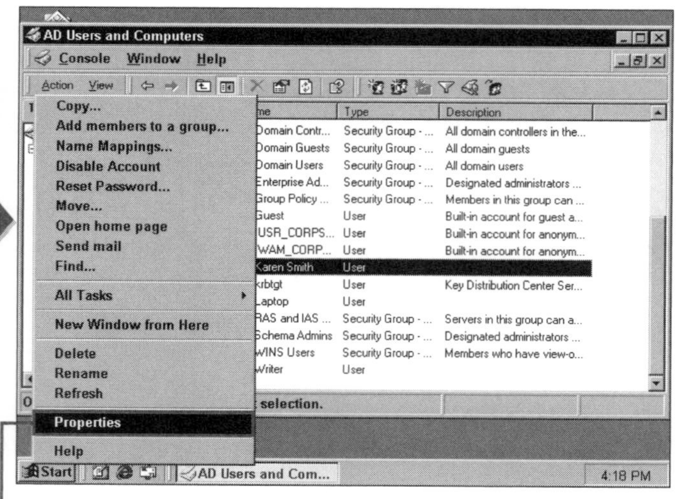

2 Select the desired object and choose Action➪Properties.

Can I give a user full control for one object and not for another?

- Each object in the Active Directory is managed separately in terms of security. You can assign any permission you want to any group or user for each object. For example, you can give Full Control to user on one printer and no access on another printer for the same user.

Should I apply security to individual users or groups?

- The preferred method for managing users in any manner is to organize them into groups. Then, you can assign resource access permissions based on groups instead of on an individual basis. In large environments, individual security permission would be a daunting task. Groups alleviate this problem, and you can even further manage group access through group policies, which you can learn about in Chapter 25.

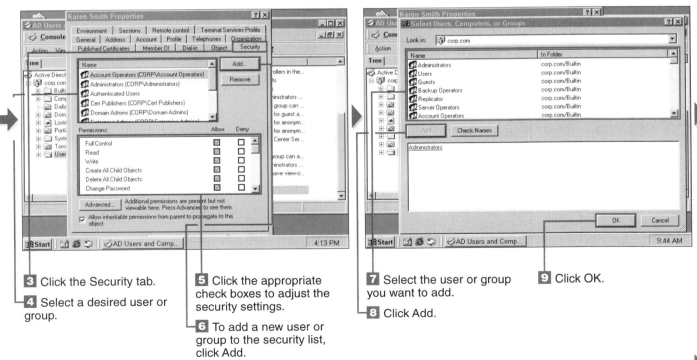

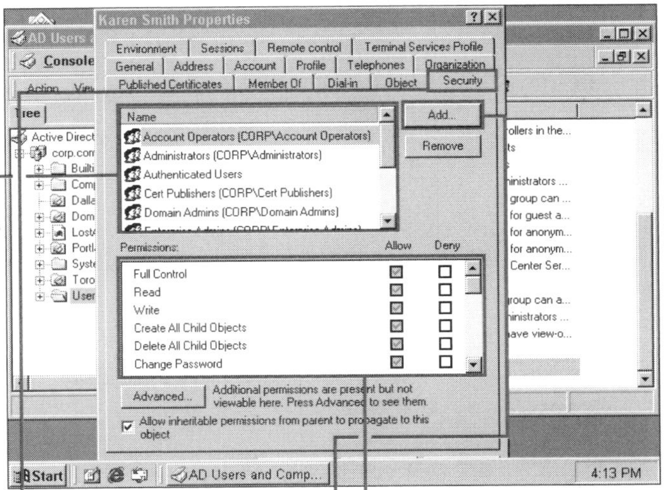

3 Click the Security tab.

4 Select a desired user or group.

5 Click the appropriate check boxes to adjust the security settings.

6 To add a new user or group to the security list, click Add.

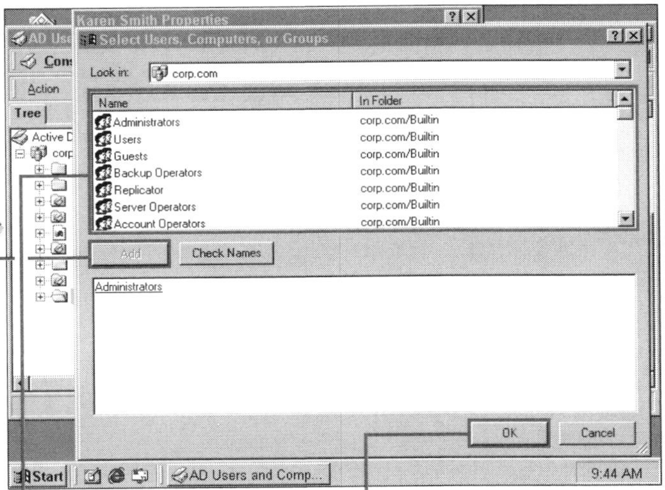

7 Select the user or group you want to add.

8 Click Add.

9 Click OK.

CONTINUED

SETTING UP OBJECT SECURITY
CONTINUED

For each Active Directory object, you can also assign advanced permissions. You can access the advanced permissions by clicking the Advanced button on the Security tab of the object's properties.

The Advanced options enable you to define the permissions that a user or group has for a particular object and that object's properties. The options presented are more detailed than the general security options and allow you finer control over the object.

Generally, you do not need to define advanced security permissions for all objects. The standard set of permissions available on the Security tab is usually enough to define all the security needs you may have. However, with certain objects, you may wish to define advanced features so that even if a group has "full control" permission, you can still deny some permissions through advanced features. The overall purpose of the advanced features is to enable you to configure security in a manner that best benefits your environment.

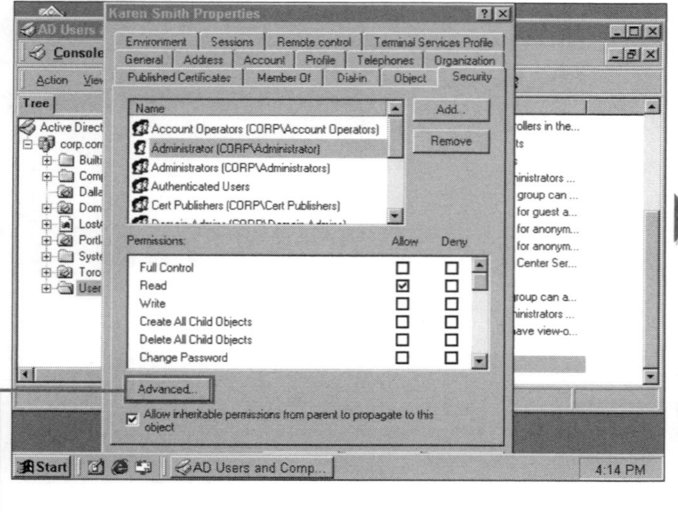

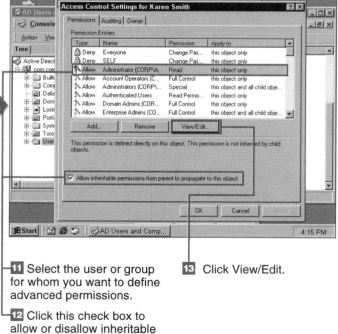

10 To access advanced security options, click Advanced.

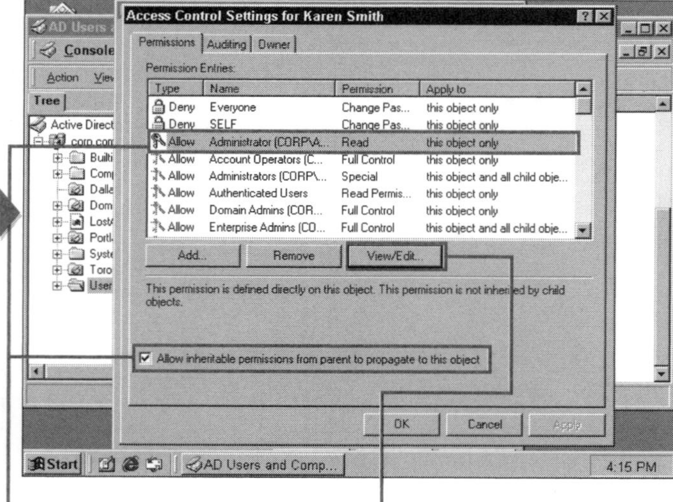

11 Select the user or group for whom you want to define advanced permissions.

12 Click this check box to allow or disallow inheritable permissions from the parent object to a child object.

13 Click View/Edit.

Should I give advanced property settings to most users or groups?

- In general, the standard settings, such as full control, read, write, and so forth, are all you need to implement an effective security policy. Use the advanced rights for situations in which you need finer control of what a user or group can do with permissions.

When would I want to use advanced permissions?

- You don't need to use advanced permissions on a regular basis, but they are useful for custom security situations. For example, let's say that you want to assign a user full control over an object, but you do not want the user to be able to delete the object or take ownership of it. You can assign full control, then use the Advanced permissions entries to override the Full Control permission for delete and take ownership. Using the Advanced feature, you can customize permissions as necessary for your environment.

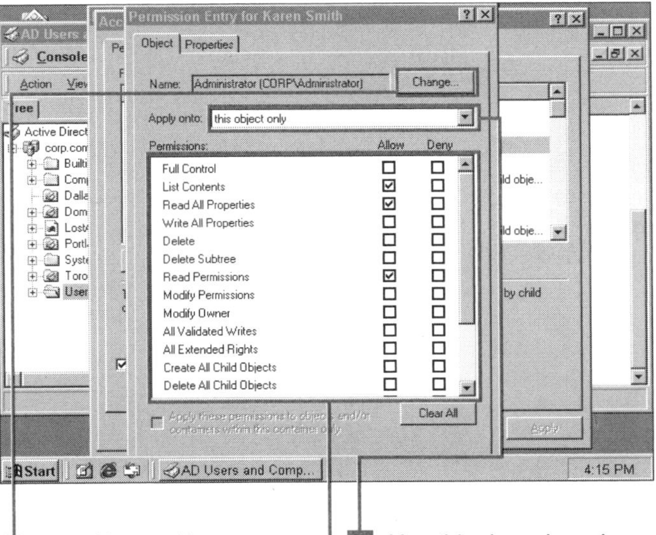

■ Click Change if you want to move from one user/group to another to set permissions for another object.

14 Use this drop-down box to choose whether to apply permissions to only this object or to all child objects.

15 Click the appropriate Allow or Deny check boxes to configure the desired security features.

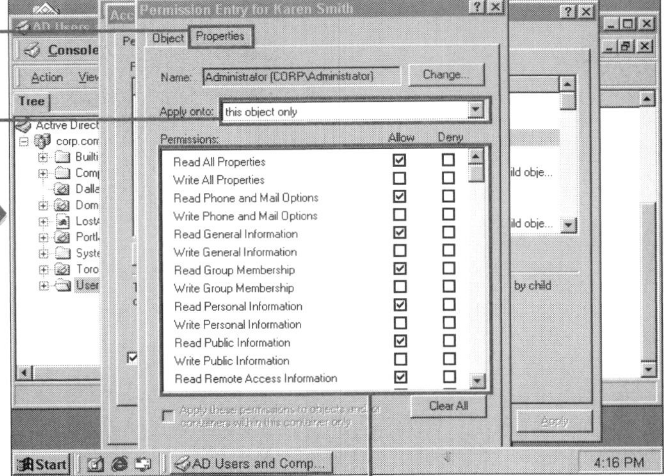

16 Click the Properties tab.

17 Use this drop-down box to choose whether to apply permissions to only this object or to all child objects.

18 Click the appropriate Allow or Deny check boxes to configure the desired security features. Click OK.

SETTING UP OU SECURITY

An *organizational unit* (OU) is a container that is designed to hold resources and other OUs. OUs are built on a hierarchy structure in which OUs can hold other OUs. This process is called *nesting*, and you should take great care when designing your organization's OU structure. The Active Directory enables you to set security for each OU in the Active Directory. By design, you can control which groups or users can access the OU and what they do with the resources inside the OU.

Security for Active Directory OUs is configured on the Security tab on each OU's properties sheets. The Security tabs for each OU appear the same and have the same basic options. This level of administration enables you to finely control your Active Directory OU and how users and groups can access an OU.

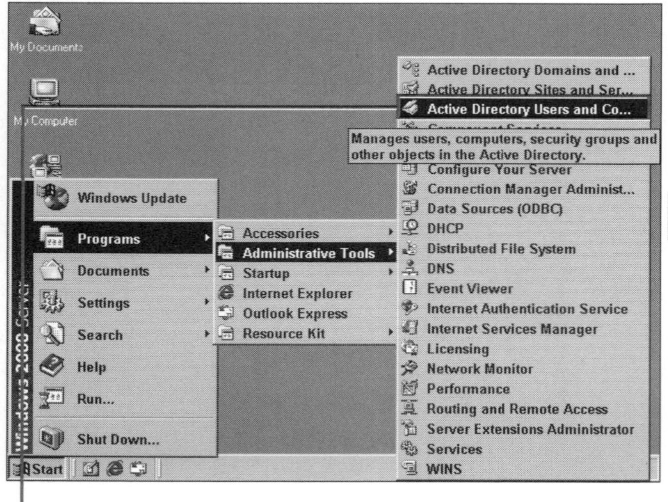

1 Choose Start⇨Programs⇨Administrative Tools⇨Active Directory Users and Computers.

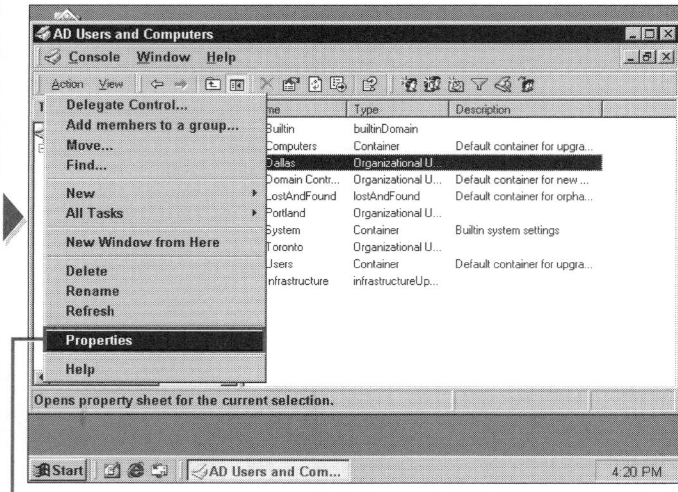

2 Select the desired OU and choose Action⇨Properties.

What default settings do most users have for the OU?

- Most users have a default setting of Read. In other words, they can read the OU and what it contains. Access to resources within the OU or to other nested OUs can be individually controlled.

Does a user's permissions for an OU apply to all resources within the OU?

- Permissions can "filter" down through an OU to other nested OUs and resources within those OUs. This is called *inheritance*. You can allow inheritance to occur or you can set permissions for each nested OU and resource. If you choose to block inheritance, then you can allow a user to access some resources and not others. The decision is based on your security needs and corporate security policies.

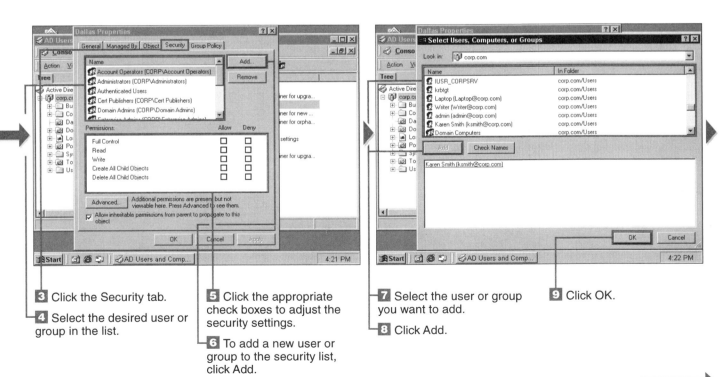

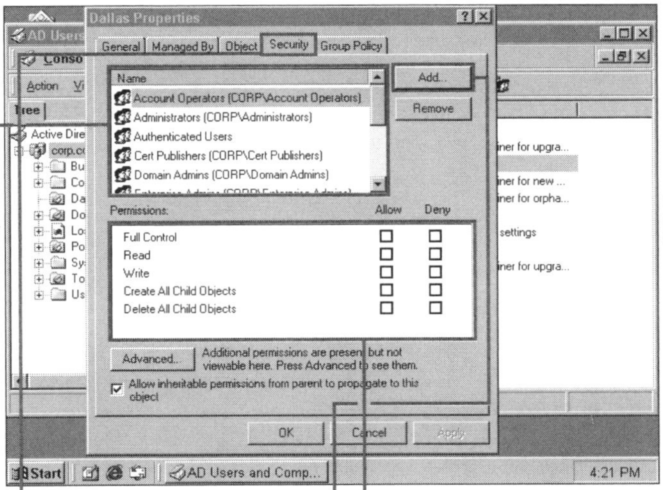

3 Click the Security tab.

4 Select the desired user or group in the list.

5 Click the appropriate check boxes to adjust the security settings.

6 To add a new user or group to the security list, click Add.

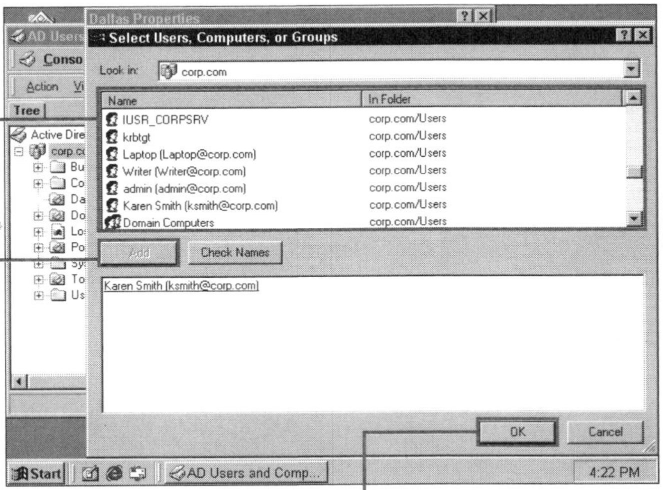

7 Select the user or group you want to add.

8 Click Add.

9 Click OK.

CONTINUED

SETTING UP OU SECURITY CONTINUED

For each Active Directory OU, you can also assign advanced permissions. You can access the advanced permissions by clicking the Advanced button on the Security tab of the object's properties sheets.

The Advanced options enable you to define the permissions that a user or group has for a particular object and that object's properties. The options presented are more detailed than the general security options and allow you finer control over the OU.

Generally, you do not need to define advanced security permissions for all OUs. The standard set of permissions available on the Security tab is usually enough to define all the security needs you may have. However, with certain OUs, you may wish to define advanced features so that even if a group has Full Control permission, you can still deny some permissions through advanced features.

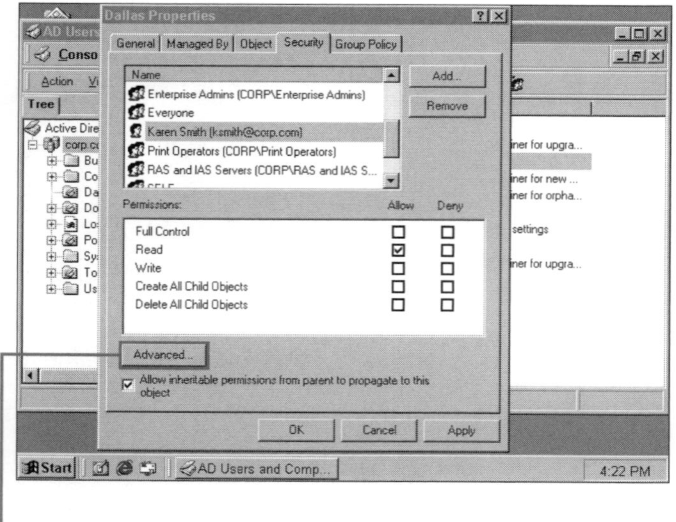

10 To access advanced security options, click Advanced.

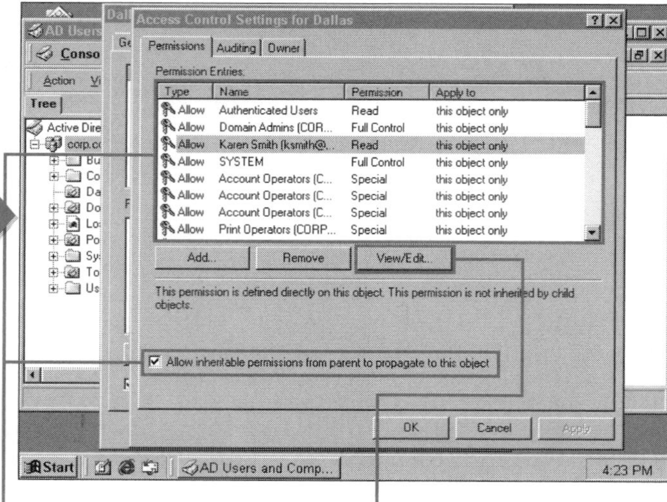

11 Select the user or group in this window for whom you want to define advanced permissions.

12 Click this check box to allow or disallow inheritable permissions from the parent object to a child object.

13 Click View/Edit.

What permissions should generally be allowed for OUs?

- In most environments, the typical permissions are assigned by default. This gives enterprise admins Full Control while allowing users Read access. You want your users to be able to read the OUs and their contents, but you do not want them to be able to make any configuration changes. In the same manner, you typically want enterprise admins, who administer the Active Directory, to have Full Control over all objects, including OUs.

What is the easiest way to configure OU security?

- The easiest way to configure OU security is to simply leave the default settings and use them. The default settings for all Active Directory objects are typically all that are needed in most Active Directory environments. You can make changes to the security settings as desired, but do take a look at your security plan and your real-world security needs before making excessive changes to default settings.

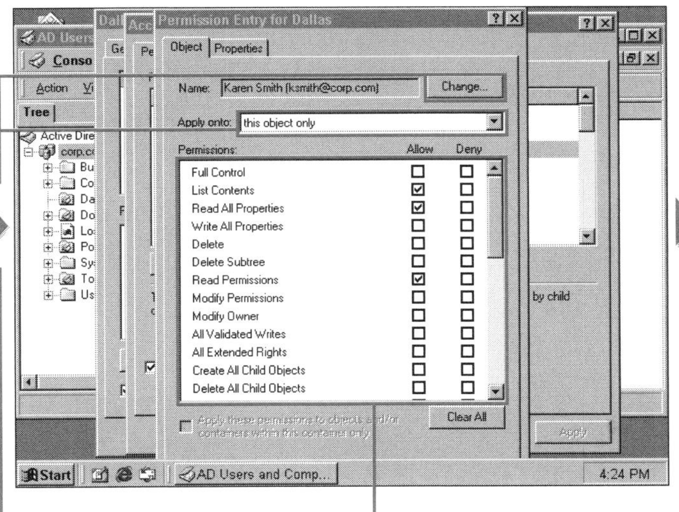

■ Click Change if you want to move from one user/group to another to set permissions for another object.

14 Use this drop-down box to choose whether to apply permissions to only this object or to all child objects.

15 Click the appropriate Allow or Deny check boxes to configure the desired security features.

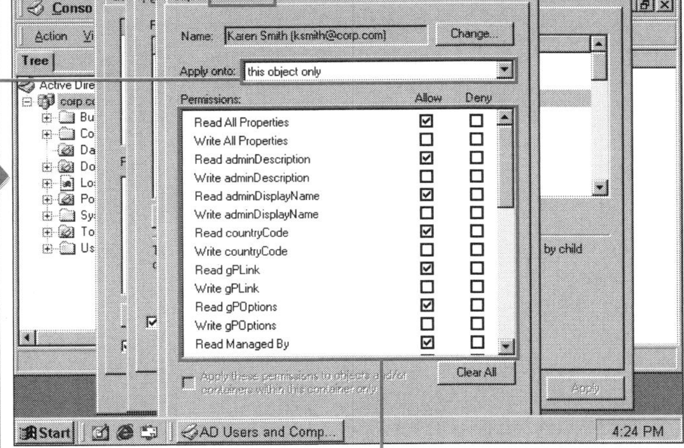

16 Click the Properties tab.

17 Use this drop-down box to choose whether to apply permissions to only this object or to all child objects.

18 Click the appropriate Allow or Deny check boxes to configure the desired security features. Click OK.

SETTING UP DOMAIN SECURITY

Domain security, in terms of the Active Directory, affects how users access the domain for resources. Obviously, you can implement additional security features, such as encryption and certificates, for domain logon. After users are authenticated and become Active Directory users, the security you set on the domains for the Active Directory determines how users access resources in those domains. The Active Directory enables you to set security for each domain in the Active Directory. By design, you can control which groups or users can access the domain and what they do with the resources inside the domain.

Security for Active Directory domains is configured on the Security tab on each domain's properties sheets. The Security tabs for each domain appear the same and have the same basic options. This level of administration enables you to finely control your Active Directory domain and how users and groups can access a domain.

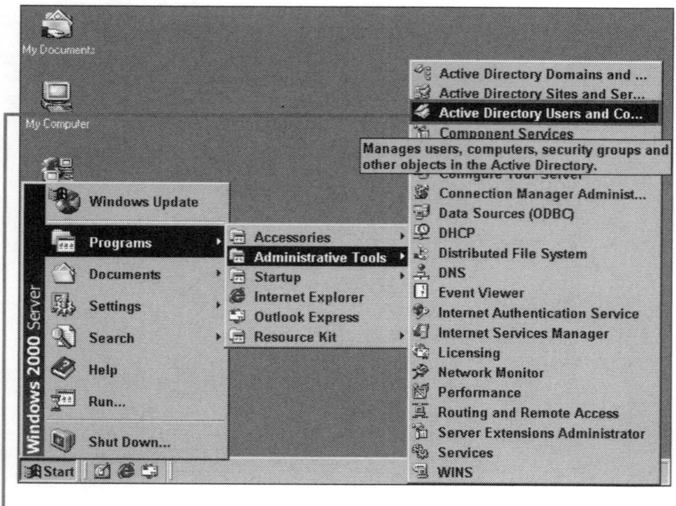

1 Choose Start⇨Programs⇨Administrative Tools⇨Active Directory Users and Computers.

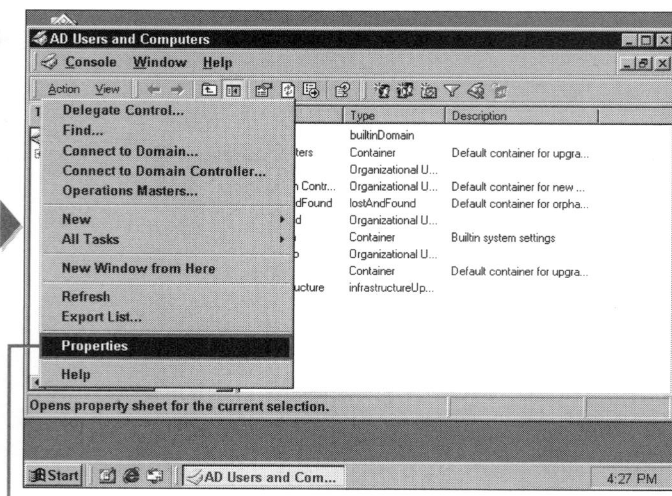

2 Select the desired domain and choose Action⇨Properties.

What default settings do most users have for the domain?

- Most authenticated users have a default setting of Read. In other words, they can read the domain and what it contains. Access to resources within domain, such as OU and resource access, can be individually controlled.

Does a user's permissions for a domain apply to all resources within domain?

- Permissions can "filter" down through the domain to OUs, nested OUs, and resources within those OUs. This is called *inheritance*. You can allow inheritance to occur or you can set permissions for each OU and resource. This would allow a user to access some resources and not others. The decision is based on your security needs and corporate security policies.

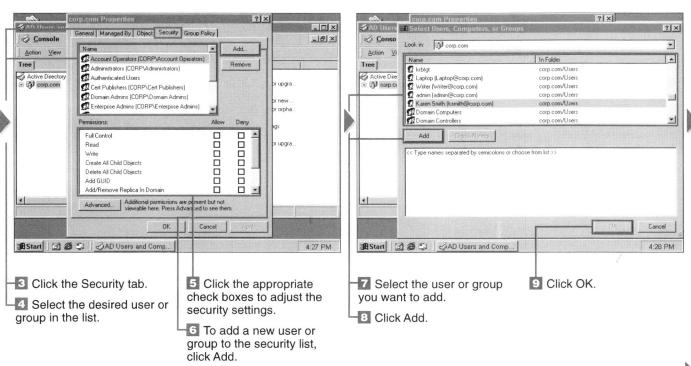

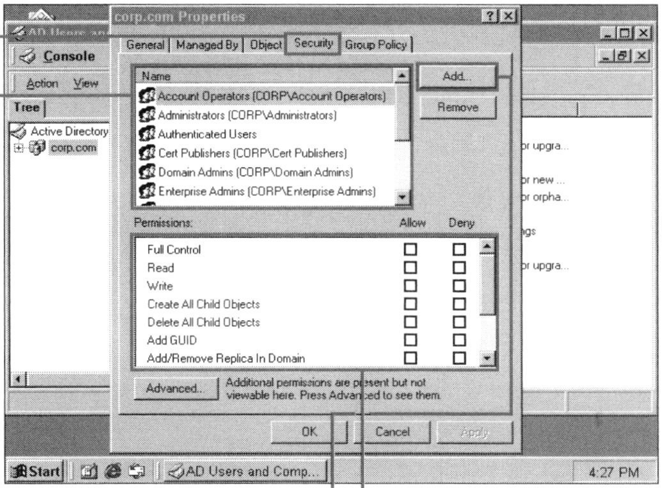

3 Click the Security tab.

4 Select the desired user or group in the list.

5 Click the appropriate check boxes to adjust the security settings.

6 To add a new user or group to the security list, click Add.

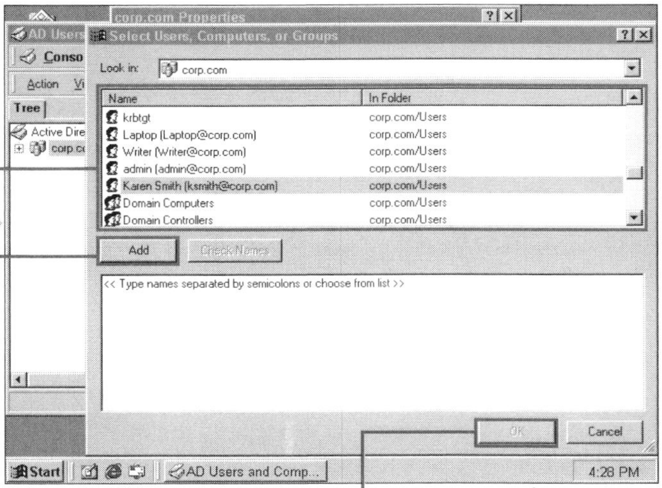

7 Select the user or group you want to add.

8 Click Add.

9 Click OK.

CONTINUED

SETTING UP DOMAIN SECURITY
CONTINUED

For each Active Directory domain, you can also assign advanced permissions. You can access the advanced permissions by clicking the Advanced button on the Security tab of the domain's properties.

The Advanced options enable you to define the permissions that a user or group has for a particular domain and that domain's properties. The options presented are more detailed than the general security options and allow you fine control over domain permissions.

Generally, you do not need to define advanced security permissions for all domains. The standard set of permissions available on the Security tab is usually enough to define all the security needs you may have. However, with certain groups, you may wish to define advanced features so that even if a group has Full Control permission, you can still deny some permissions through advanced features. The overall purpose of the advanced features is to enable you to configure security in a manner that best benefits your environment.

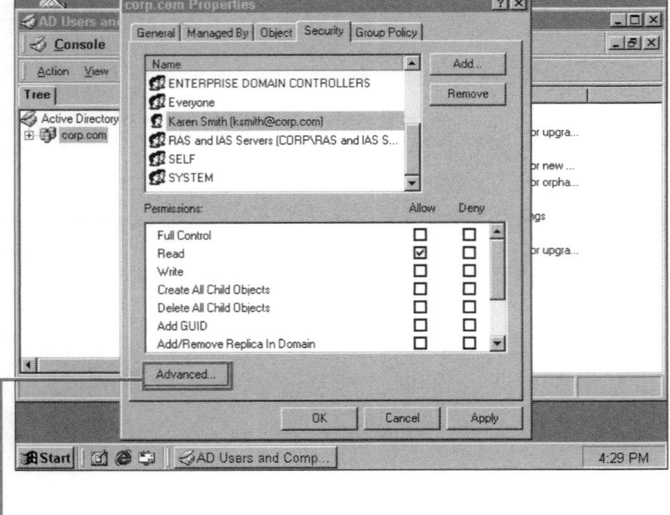

10 To access advanced security options, click Advanced.

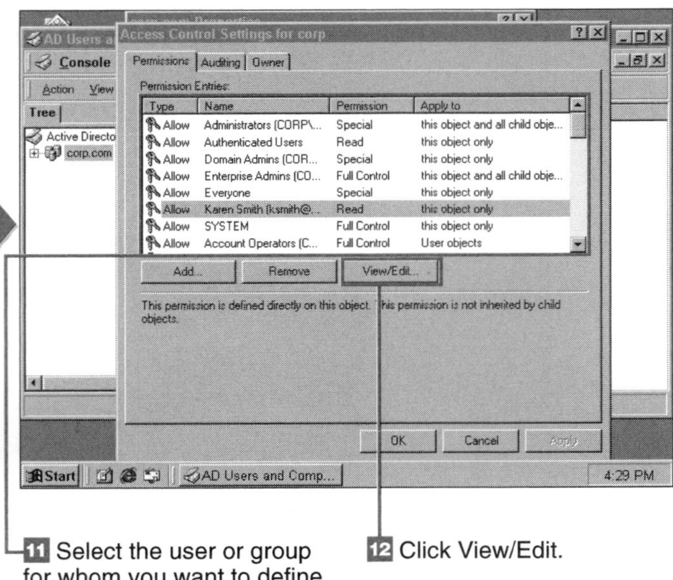

11 Select the user or group for whom you want to define advanced permissions.

12 Click View/Edit.

Should most users or groups be given advanced property settings?

- In general, the standard settings, such as Full Control, Read, Write, and so forth, are all you need to implement an effective security policy. You should use the advanced rights for situations in which you need finer control of what a user or group can do with permissions.

What group should have Full Control permission over a domain?

- The enterprise admins group in Windows 2000 is established for an Active Directory implementation. Enterprise admins are those administrators that configure and administer the Active Directory. In most circumstances, only the enterprise admins group should have Full Control. Before assigning Full Control to another group or user, you should carefully examine your security plan.

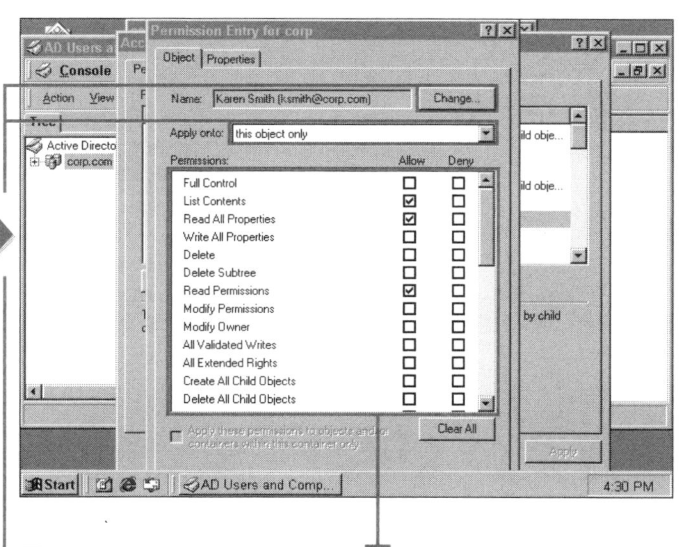

■ Click Change if you want to move from one user/group to another to set permissions for another object.

13 Use this drop-down box choose whether to apply permissions to only this object or to all child objects.

14 Click the appropriate Allow or Deny check boxes to configure the desired security features.

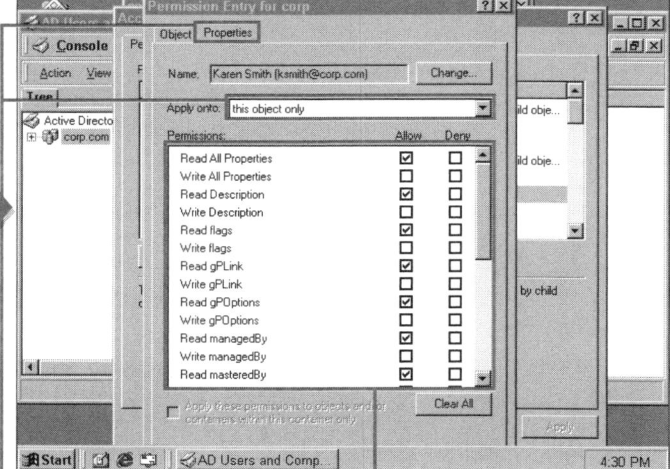

15 Click the Properties tab.

16 Use this drop-down box to choose whether to apply permissions to only this object or to all child objects.

17 Click the appropriate Allow or Deny check boxes to configure the desired security features.

SETTING UP DELEGATION

Delegation is both a powerful tool and a powerful concept in Windows 2000. Delegation enables you to create *delegates* who control certain aspects of the Active Directory. This feature allows you to delegate administrative control of certain Active Directory domains, OUs, and containers to others within your organization. The delegate can then administer the domain, OU, container, and the objects residing in them. Delegation lets you easily set up decentralized administration while still maintaining control of your overall Enterprise network.

Delegation is accomplished through a wizard that walks you through the necessary steps to set up delegation.

For each domain, OU, and container in the Active Directory, you can use the Action menu to access the Delegation Wizard. Delegation is easy to configure, but you should carefully establish your delegation plan before implementing it.

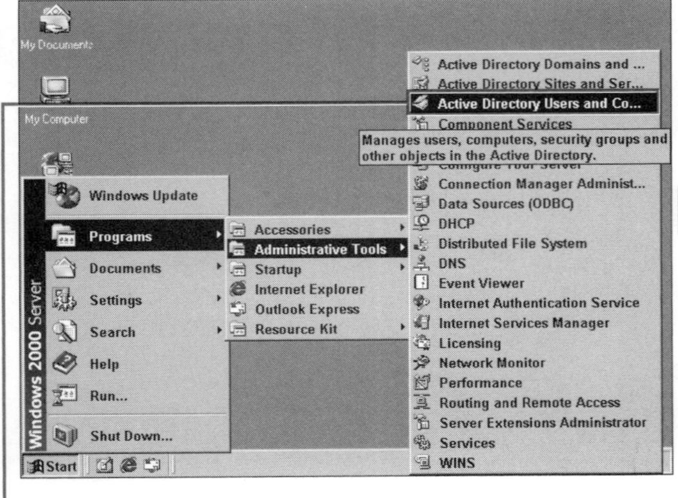

1 Choose Start➪Programs➪Administrative Tools➪Active Directory Users and Computers.

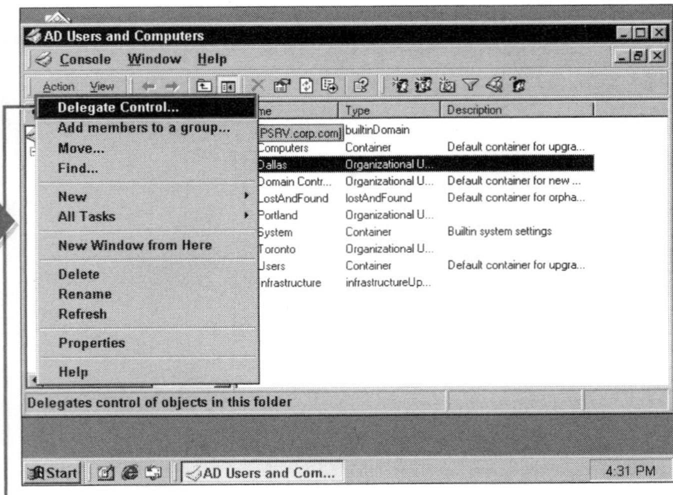

2 Select the desired domain, OU, or container and choose Action➪Delegate Control.

Can I delegate control to anyone?

- An authenticated user can be a delegate. Your decision, of course, must be made on that individual's qualifications and responsibilities. You should delegate control only to users who are skilled and can be trusted with administrative control.

Why would I delegate control to a group?

- You can delegate control to a user or group. Group delegations are usually given to some kind of administrative group that can effectively manage the domain, OU, or container. You should remember that when you delegate control to a group, every member of the group becomes a delegate and can administer the delegation. As with any administration delegation, you should practice care and consideration.

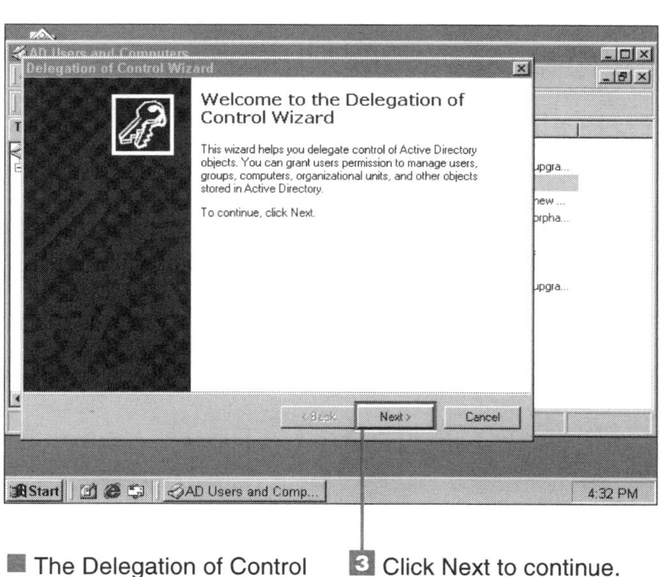

■ The Delegation of Control Wizard appears.

3 Click Next to continue.

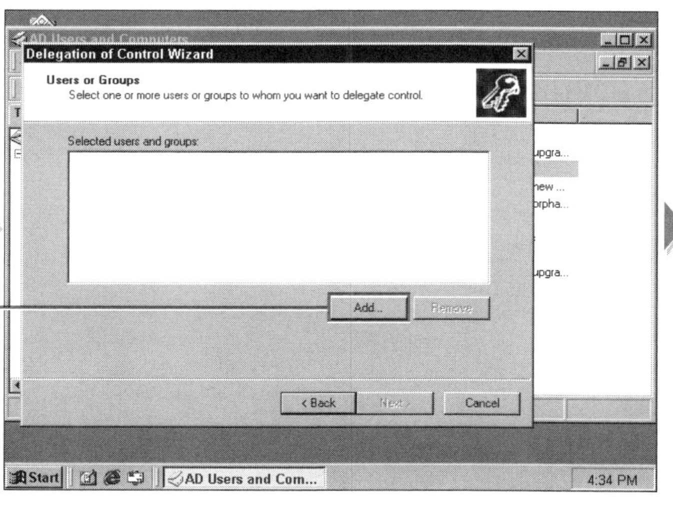

4 Click Add to locate the person or group you want to delegate to.

CONTINUED

SETTING UP DELEGATION CONTINUED

When you delegate control to a user or group, you have the option to control the delegation. This feature enables you to delegate some responsibilities but not necessarily all of them. This is a powerful way to allow other users or groups to handle certain administrative tasks while you continue to keep firm control.

For example, you could delegate an OU that contained users so that the delegate could create new user accounts or reset passwords. You could allow the delegate to complete these tasks while denying the delegate the right to delete a user account or view sensitive user account information.

With this design, you can delegate simple administrative tasks to other users so that they do not consume too much senior administrative time.

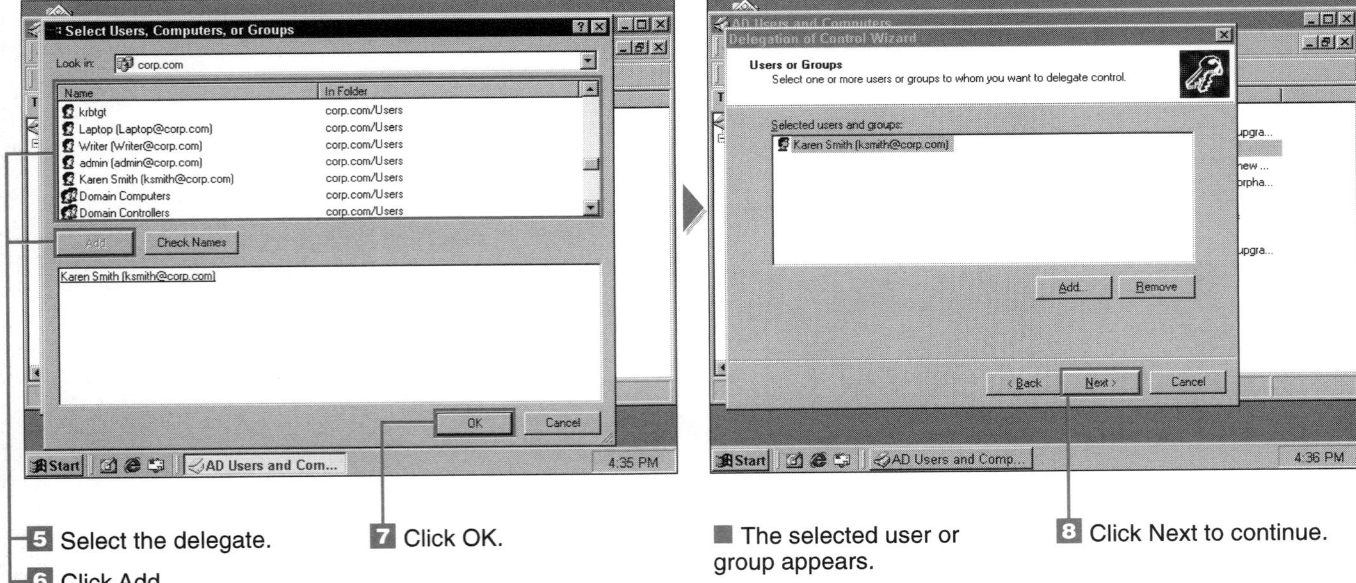

5 Select the delegate.

6 Click Add.

7 Click OK.

■ The selected user or group appears.

8 Click Next to continue.

How much control should I give to a delegate?

- The amount of control, or administrative power, you give to a delegate is entirely your decision, or you can base your decision on the security policies in effect for your organization. A good rule of thumb is to delegate only the administrative responsibilities the delegate needs. In other words, allow the delegate the power to complete the tasks necessary, but no more.

Is the Delegation Wizard exactly the same for every domain, OU, or container?

- The Delegation Wizard varies somewhat depending on what you are delegating. The basic tasks you perform with the wizard are determining the delegate and assigning that delegate administrative rights over certain aspects of the domain, OU, or container. Depending on what you are delegating, you may have additional administrative rights to assign with the wizard.

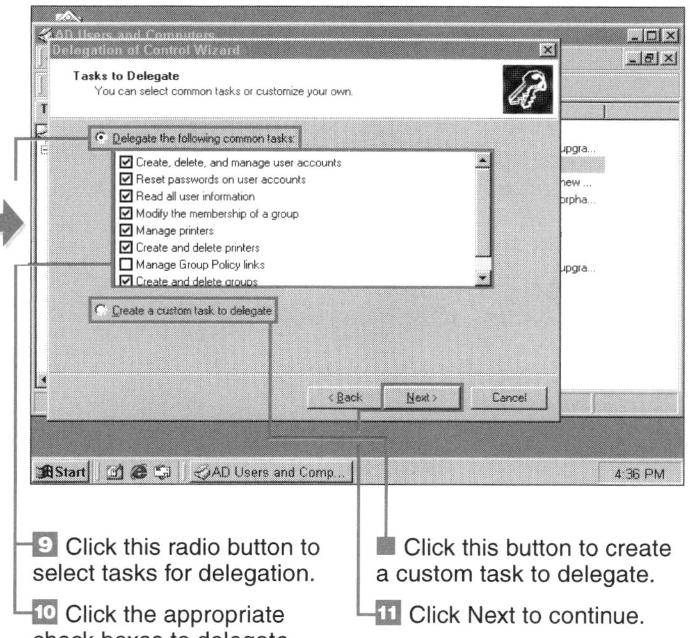

9 Click this radio button to select tasks for delegation.

10 Click the appropriate check boxes to delegate tasks.

■ Click this button to create a custom task to delegate.

11 Click Next to continue.

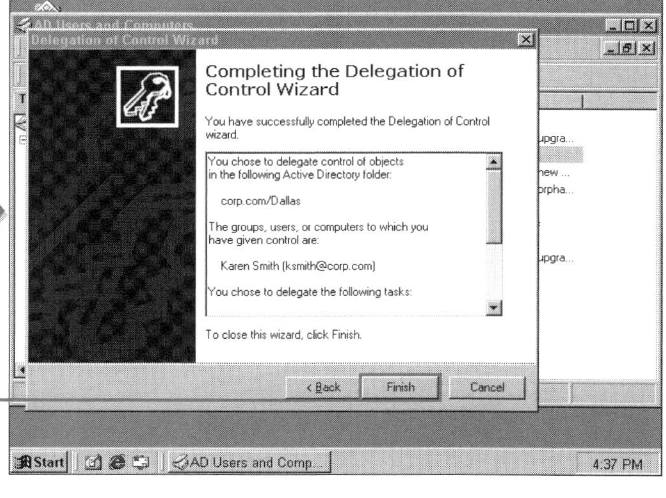

12 Click Finish to complete the delegation.

INTRODUCTION TO GROUP POLICY

Windows 2000 introduces a powerful new tool called *Group Policy* that is integrated with the Active Directory. Group policies are an effective way to implement corporate policies so that a user's desktop, documents, programs, access rights, and virtually any other computer component complies with corporate dictates and operating procedures. A Group Policy enables you to impose a set a rights and rules on a particular Active Directory domain or even site.

What is Group Policy?

Microsoft designed Group Policy to give administrators more user control over the Active Directory. Group Policy can also reduce an organization's *total cost of ownership* (TCO) by reducing user downtime due to misconfiguration. In other words, a Group Policy enables a group of users to do the work they need to do while maintaining a standard corporate system configuration.

What you can do with Group Policy

Group Policy enables you to impose a set of standards for every user's computer in the group. This can include custom Start menu items, software configuration, access to Active Directory objects, document and file availability, security settings, and even the automation of common tasks (such as network connections). Generally, group policies are applied at either the site or domain level and can give you a "one policy" control of the users and groups within that domain or site.

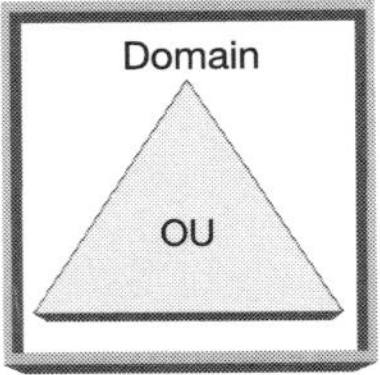

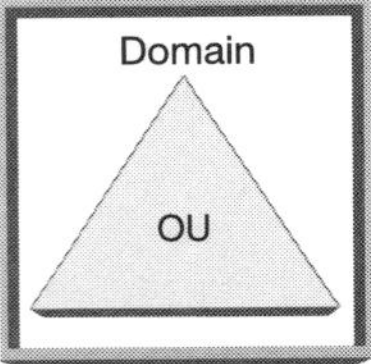

What are the Group Policy components?

Three major components make up a Group Policy. First, *Group Policy Objects* (GPOs) contain the configuration settings for particular Active Directory objects. The GPO is then applied to a particular site, domain, or even OU. You can use multiple GPOs, and a GPO can be applied to multiple sites, domains, or OUs. GPOs store information in two locations: Group Policy Containers (GPC) and Group Policy Templates (GPT).

Group Policy Containers (GPC) are Active Directory objects that contain property information and even subcontainers for GPOs. The property information includes version information so that GPOs are synchronized with GPCs. GPCs contain information that does not change frequently, and they also contain class store information for GPO application deployment.

Group Policy Templates (GPT) reside in the System Volume folder (Sysvol) of domain controllers and contains the folder structure for GPOs. The GPT contains the security information, software policies, scripts, files, and additional system setting information.

What about inheritance?

The term *inheritance* refers to the way multiple group policies affect each other. For example, if you have a site policy and also a domain policy, which one goes into effect? The inheritance order for group policies are site, domain, and OU. In other words, site group policies are applied first, then domain policies, then OU policies. If the OU policies contradicts a setting in the site or domain policy, the site or domain setting is overwritten. The policy closest to the user is the effective policy for that user. You can change this inheritance behavior if desired, and this chapter shows you how.

ACCESSING THE GROUP POLICY MMC SNAP-IN

The Group Policy MMC snap-in is not considered one of the Active Directory tools per se, and it does not appear in your Administrative Tools folder. Like many MMC snap-ins in Windows 2000, you have to manually add the snap-in to the MMC. You can then save the MMC after the snap-in loads so that you may access it more easily.

You can also access the Group Policy from either the Active Directory Users and Computer snap-in or the Active Directory Sites and Services snap-in by accessing the properties sheets for the site, domain, or OU. You use this interface to manage the Group Policy for the site, domain, or OU. You can also use this interface to create or edit a new Group Policy.

It does not matter whether you manually add the MMC snap-in or access it from within a Group Policy properties sheet within the Active Directory. The configuration is the same and can be applied at whatever level is desired. You learn how to access the Group Policy from within the Active Directory later in the chapter.

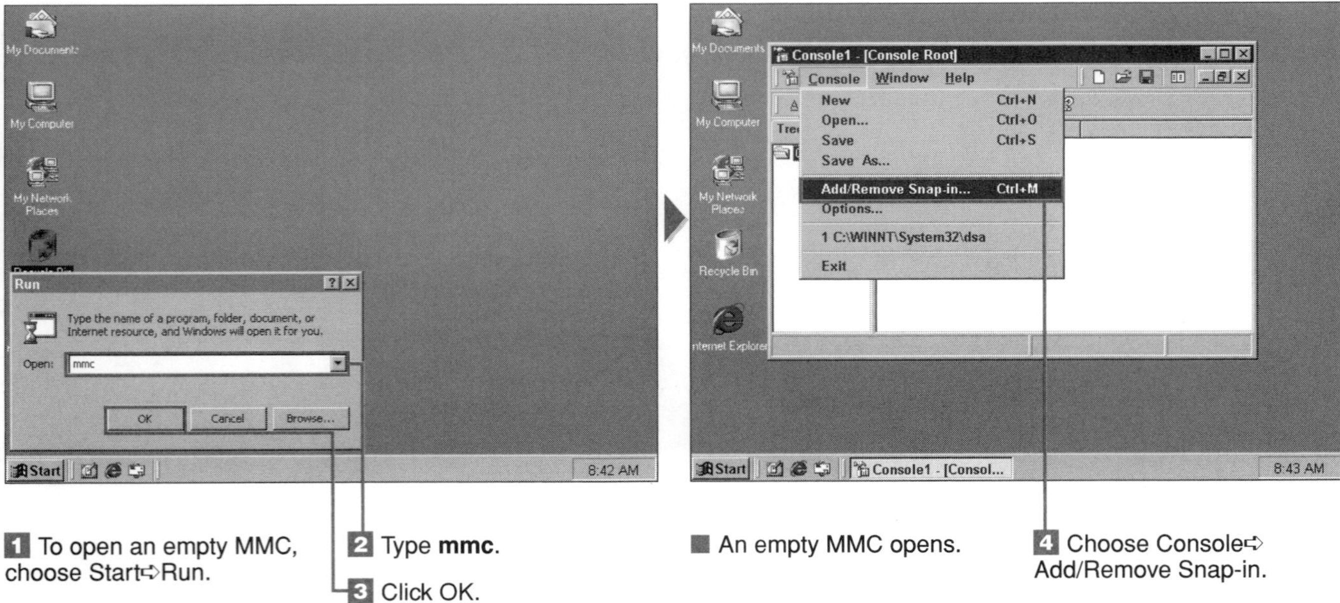

1 To open an empty MMC, choose Start⇨Run.

2 Type **mmc**.

3 Click OK.

■ An empty MMC opens.

4 Choose Console⇨Add/Remove Snap-in.

Why is the Group Policy snap-in not a part of the Active Directory administrative tools?

- Remember that the Active Directory does not stand alone. It is the service that drives all directory functions in a Windows 2000 network. You use the administrative tools to manage actual components of the Active Directory. However, many other tools, such as the Group Policy snap-in, function within the Active Directory and configure it for various organization needs. Remember that even from within the Active Directory tools, you can still access the Group Policy snap-in as well as other snap-ins.

Can I create a new Group Policy from within the Active Directory?

- Yes. You can create a new Group Policy by accessing the Group Policy properties sheet for the site, domain, or OU to which the policy will be applied. From this location, you can create a new policy just as you would using the manual snap-in.

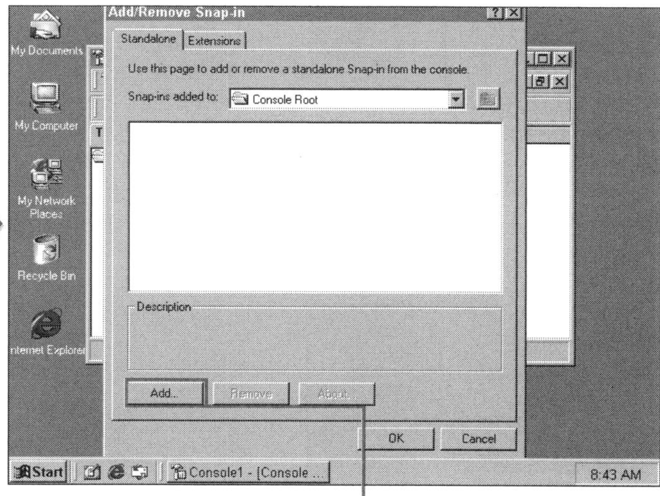

■ The Add/Remove Snap-in window appears.

5 Click Add.

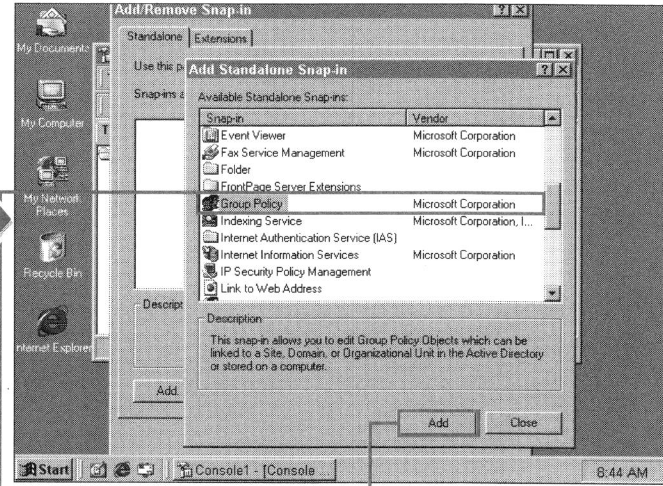

■ A list of available standalone snap-ins appears.

6 Scroll down and select Group Policy.

7 Click Add.

CONTINUED

ACCESSING THE GROUP POLICY MMC SNAP-IN CONTINUED

When you access the Group Policy snap-in, you need to determine whether you want the Group Policy to be stored on the local computer or in the Active Directory. A Group Policy can apply to a local computer so that the settings you specify apply only to that local machine. However, if you want the Group Policy settings to apply to groups on a site, domain, or OU basis, you must configure the policy for use in the Active Directory.

Because you want the Group Policy to be stored in the Active Directory, you can browse to select the domain controller on which you initially want to save the Group Policy. The Group Policy is then saved in the Active Directory and then replicated to the other domain controllers within the organization.

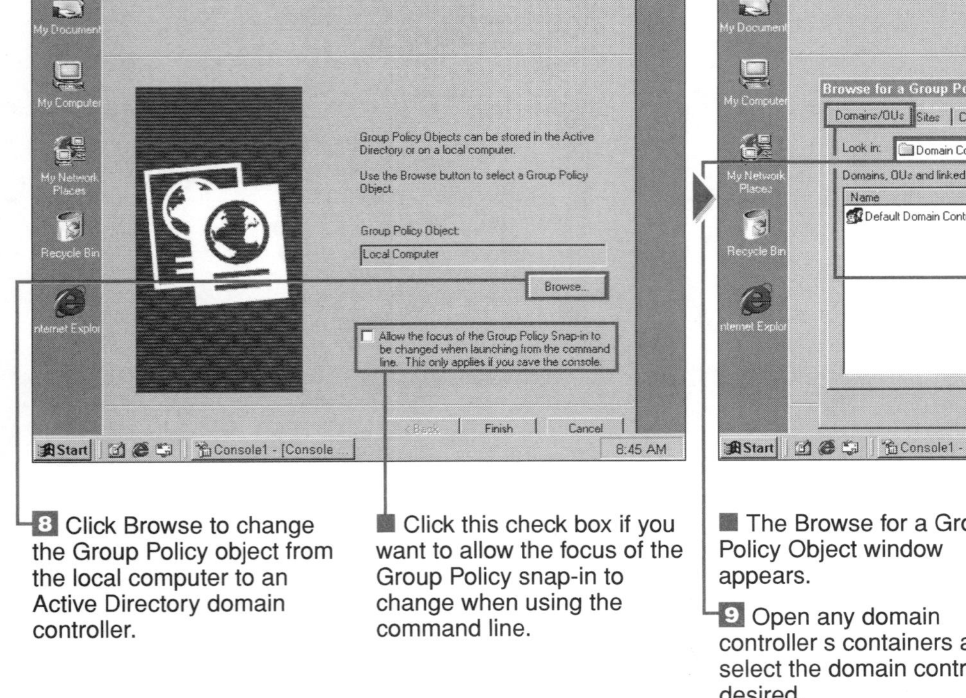

8 Click Browse to change the Group Policy object from the local computer to an Active Directory domain controller.

■ Click this check box if you want to allow the focus of the Group Policy snap-in to change when using the command line.

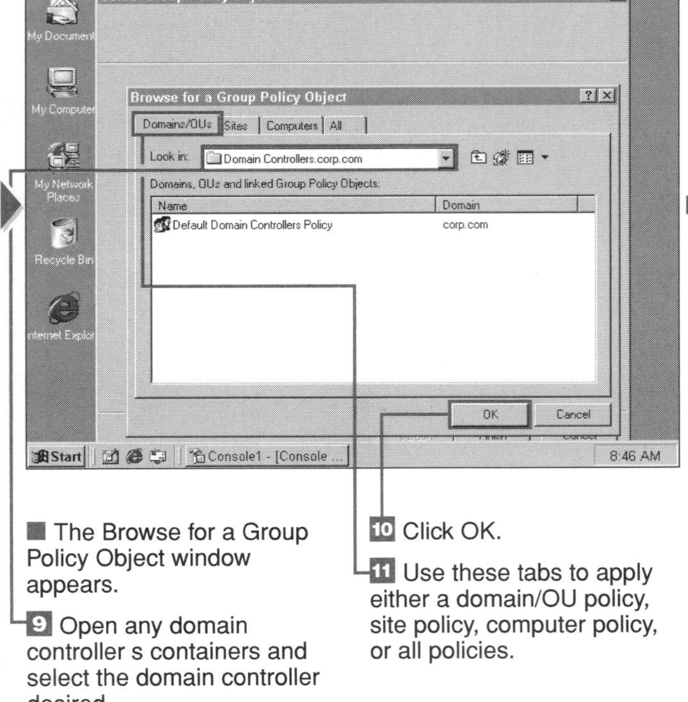

■ The Browse for a Group Policy Object window appears.

9 Open any domain controller s containers and select the domain controller desired.

10 Click OK.

11 Use these tabs to apply either a domain/OU policy, site policy, computer policy, or all policies.

What is the difference between a local policy and an Active Directory policy?

✓ An Active Directory policy, also called a nonlocal policy, is stored on domain controllers and applies to users and computers within the site, domain, or OU with which the GPO is associated. The local policy is stored on a computer running Windows 2000 and applies to that computer only. Both Active Directory and local policies can be applied to the same computer, but the Active Directory policy overwrites the local policy.

Can I create both a local policy and a nonlocal policy?

✓ You can create as many group policies as needed for your organization. Depending on your needs, you may have a combination of local policies and nonlocal policies that are applied to computers and Active Directory groups, respectively.

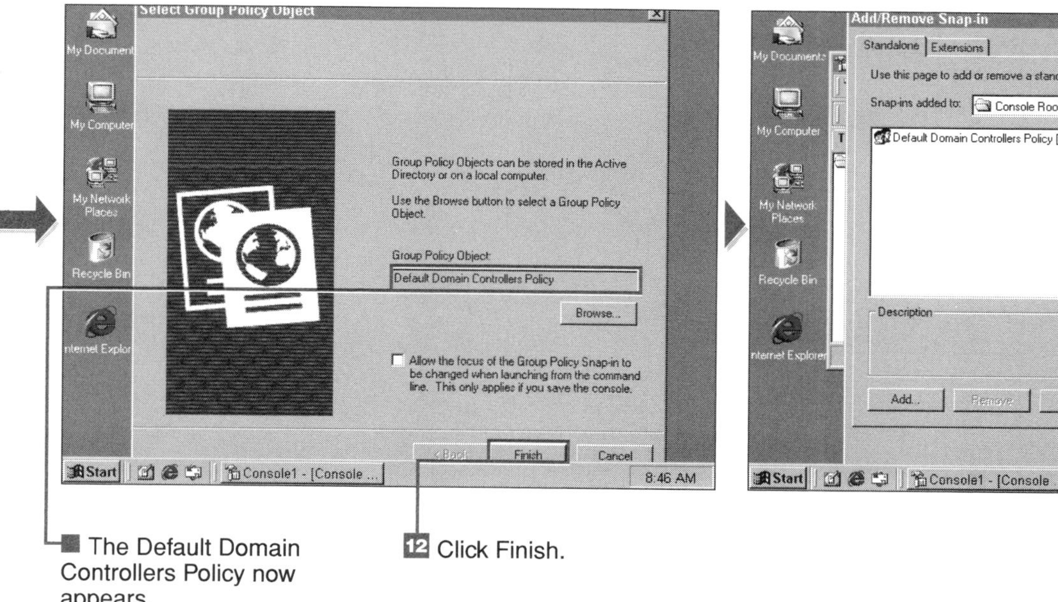

■ The Default Domain Controllers Policy now appears.

12 Click Finish.

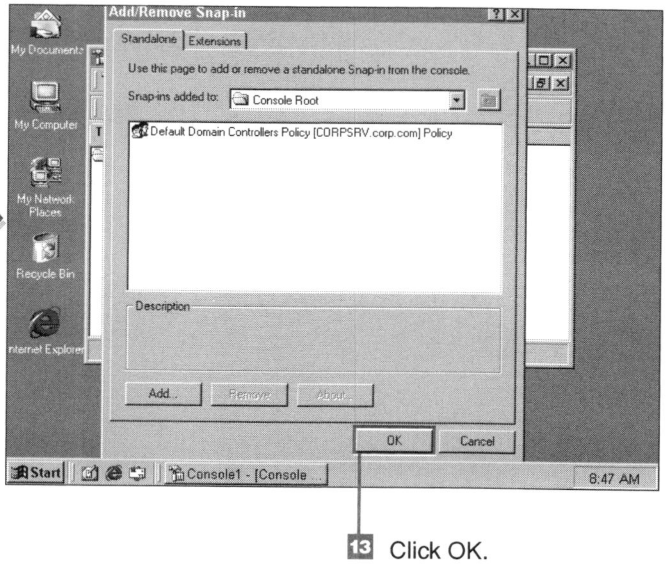

13 Click OK.

CONFIGURING GENERAL POLICY PROPERTIES

You can configure general properties for the overall Group Policy by accessing the policy's properties pages.

In the Properties dialog box, you are given General, Links, and Security tabs. The General tab gives you information about the policy, but you can use the Disable Computer Configuration settings and Disable User Configuration settings check boxes if desired. This action disables either the user or computer portion from the policy and would be used if you wanted to apply only computer settings. Doing this helps system performance because the nonused configuration does not have to be parsed each time a user logs on.

On the Links tab, you can run a global catalog search for other sites, domains, and OUs that use this policy. The Security tab enables you to configure what users and groups have access to the policy settings and what rights they have.

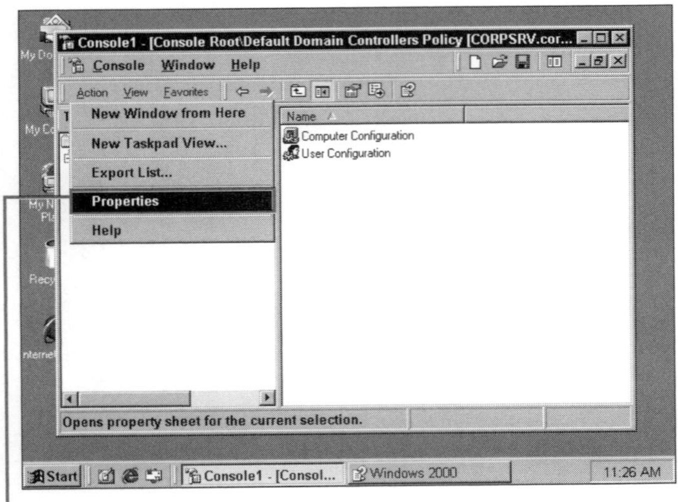

1 Select the Policy object and choose Action⇨Properties.

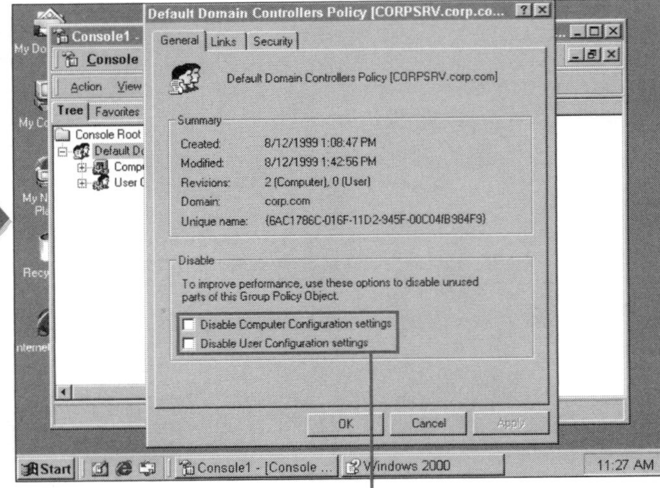

■ The General tab gives you information about the policy and its creation date.

2 Click either of these two check boxes to disable computer configuration or user configuration.

When should I disable user or computer configuration?

- You do not want to disable either option if they are in use. However, under some circumstances, you may have a Group Policy that applies only to computer settings and all the user settings are not configured. Even though you did not configure the user settings, the system still has to parse the policy to check the configuration. If you disable it, the logon process speeds up because the configuration does not have to be parsed.

How can I find out which domains use a particular Group Policy?

- The easiest way to determine which domains use a particular Group Policy is to access the properties sheets for that policy. As an administrator in a large distributed network, it may be helpful to know which domains use a particular Group Policy. The properties sheet is the easiest way to access this information.

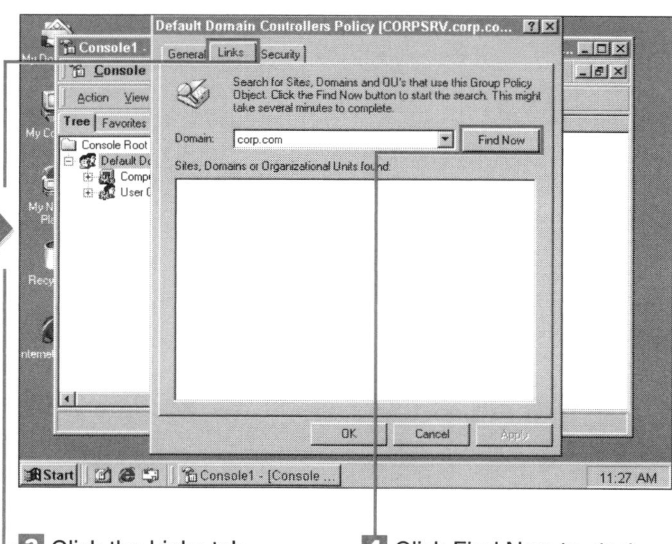

3 Click the Links tab.

■ The Links tab enables you to run a search in the Active Directory for all sites, domains, or OUs that use this particular Group Policy.

4 Click Find Now to start the search.

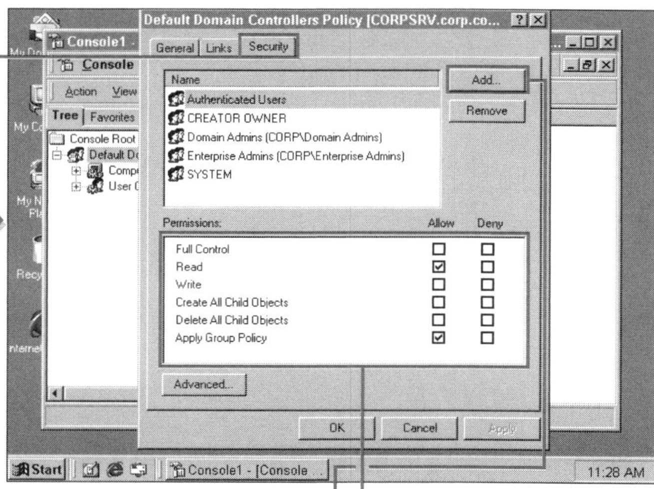

5 Click the Security tab.

■ The Security tab lists the default groups that have access to the policy.

6 Click the appropriate check boxes to adjust each group s permissions.

7 Click Add to add new groups or users for policy access.

CONTINUED

CONFIGURING GENERAL POLICY PROPERTIES CONTINUED

As with other objects in the Active Directory, you can use the Security tab to determine who can access the Group Policy and what permissions they have for that policy. This feature enables you to assign certain permission rights to particular groups or individual users. Depending on the needs of your organization, you may want certain groups or users to be able to read the policy but not change it, while you may want other groups or users to have full control to the policy and be able to make policy changes. Obviously, you should carefully consider the permissions you assign for the policy.

You can also use the Advanced button to refine permissions for users or groups to suit the needs of your organization. This feature allows you finer control over policy so that you can define exactly what groups or users can do with the policy.

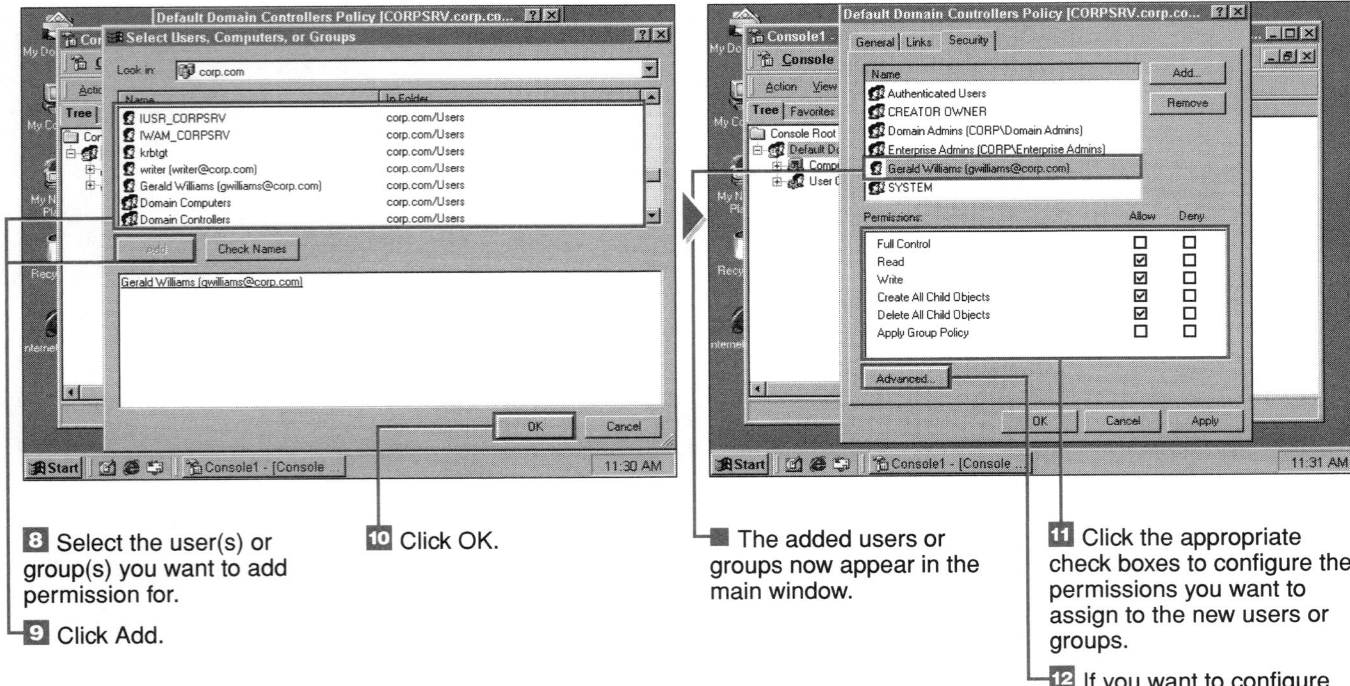

8 Select the user(s) or group(s) you want to add permission for.

9 Click Add.

10 Click OK.

■ The added users or groups now appear in the main window.

11 Click the appropriate check boxes to configure the permissions you want to assign to the new users or groups.

12 If you want to configure advanced security options, click Advanced.

Who should have access to the Group Policy object?

Because the Group Policy object affects the configuration of computer and user accounts in the Active Directory, you should be very careful who is assigned permissions to the policy object. You would not want a user or group member changing the policy without specific and authorized reasons to do so.

What is the purpose of the advanced permission entries?

In most cases, the general permissions are all you need. However, Windows 2000 provides detailed and advanced security options so that you can further refine what permissions you assign on what objects. This feature allows Windows 2000 to work within the security needs of your network.

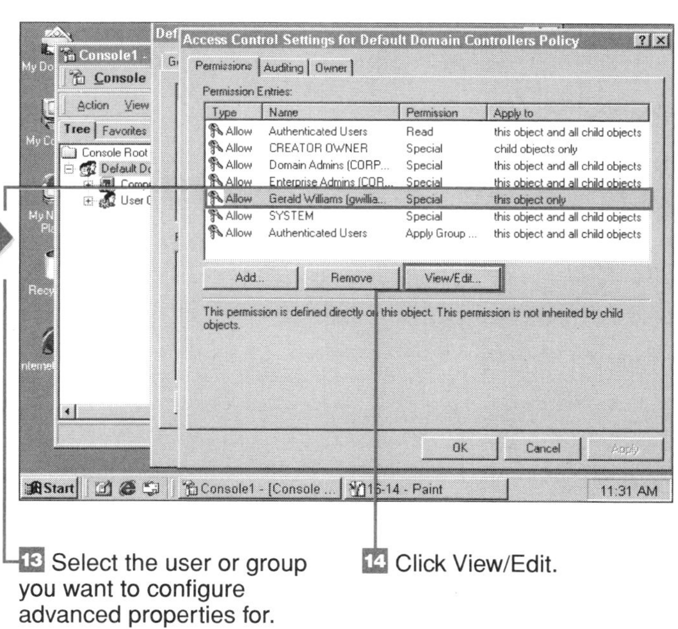

13 Select the user or group you want to configure advanced properties for.

14 Click View/Edit.

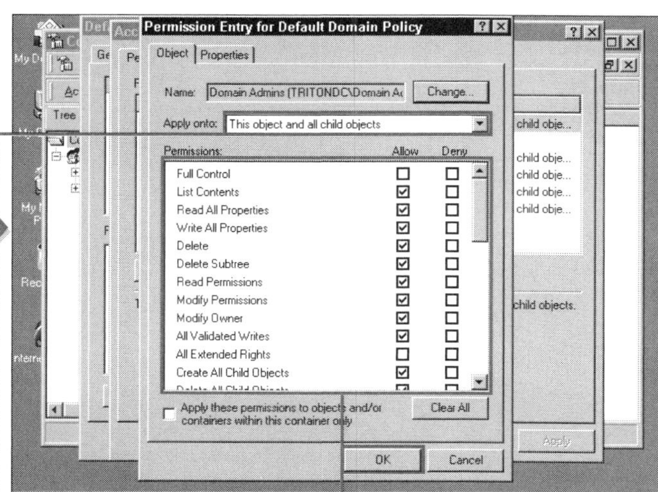

■ A list of additional permission options appears.

15 Use this drop-down box to choose whether to apply permissions to only this object or to all child objects.

16 Click the appropriate Allow or Deny check boxes to configure the desired security features.

17 Click OK.

GROUP POLICY COMPUTER CONFIGURATION

You have a number of possibilities when configuring client computers using Group Policy. The computer configuration portion of the Group Policy is divided into three major categories: software settings, Windows settings, and administrative templates. Each of these containers have different policy files that you can configure for your policy. (See Appendix A for more information on configuring Group Policies.)

The software settings container has an icon for software installation. You can use the Group Policy to automatically install applications onto a user's computer using the Windows installer. This feature enables you to create custom application packages that are *pushed* to the user's computer and automatically installed. This feature allows each user in the group to have a particular set of applications automatically installed.

Explaining how to configure custom packages for your Group Policy is beyond the scope of this book, but you can refer to the Windows Help files or the Windows 2000 Server Resource Kit to learn more about software package development.

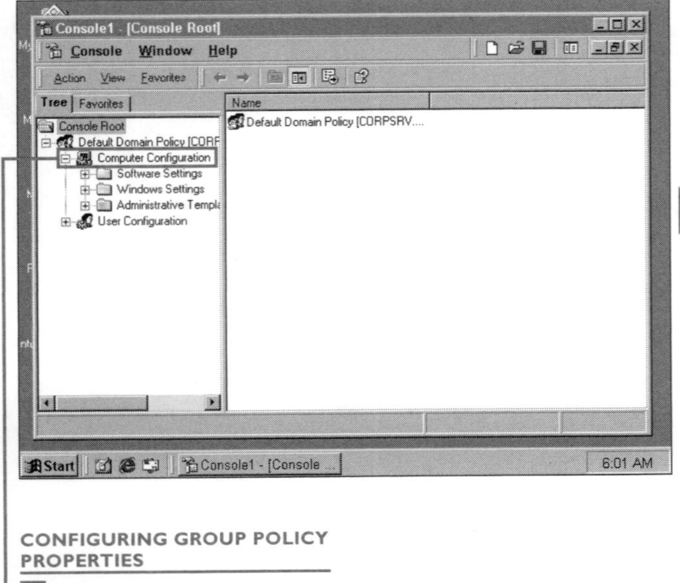

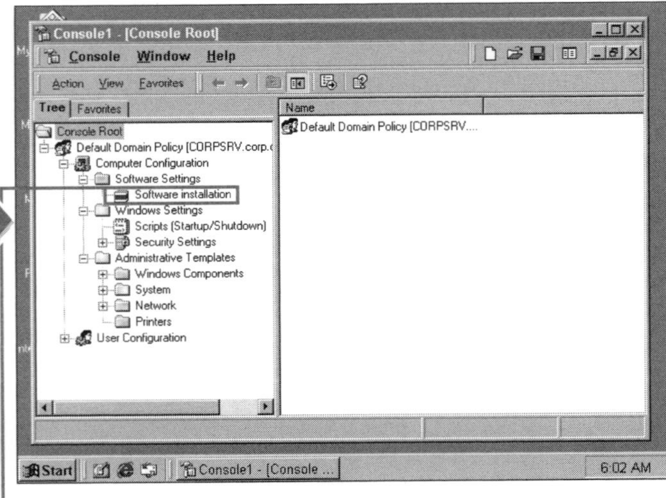

CONFIGURING GROUP POLICY PROPERTIES

1 Expand the policy you want to configure and click Computer Configuration.

2 Expand the Software Settings, Windows Settings, and Administrative Templates containers to see the contents.

3 Select Software Installation.

How does the software installer work?

- Just as a policy can download system and user settings, the Group Policy can be configured to push the installer application and installation files to a user's desktop. This feature allows the user to obtain a software installation without having to perform any of the installation manually. This feature ensures that all users have the same software applications installed and configured appropriately.

Can a user manually change the software configuration as he would do during a normal setup routine?

- The installation settings are defined by the Group Policy administrator when a software package is created. The entire package is then run on the client system. Depending on configuration, the user may be able to make some configuration choices, but this depends on the configuration of the package. This feature prevents users from making configuration changes during setup that are not desirable and ensures that all users in the group have the same software setup configuration.

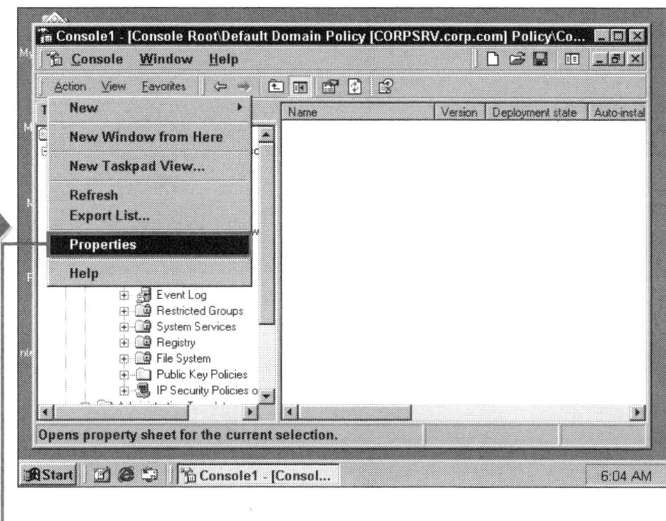

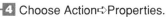

4 Choose Action⇨Properties.

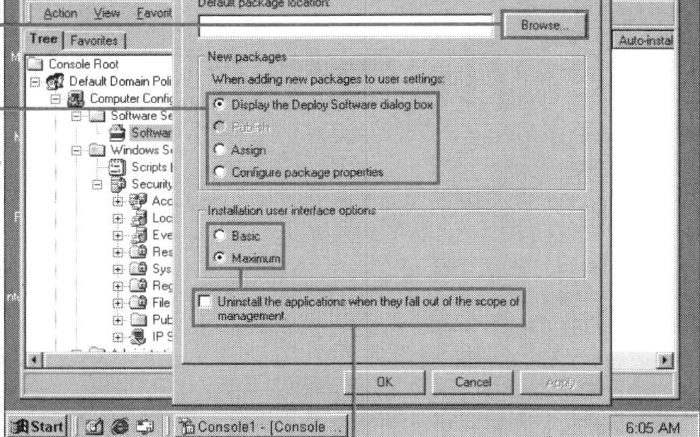

5 Click Browse to establish a default software installation package.

6 Use these buttons to configure options for user settings when a new package is added to a client computer.

7 Use these buttons to specify a basic or minimum user interface during the installation.

8 Click to uninstall the applications.

CONTINUED

GROUP POLICY COMPUTER CONFIGURATION CONTINUED

By accessing the properties sheets for the package installation object, you can configure general options for the package installer. On the General tab, you can load a default package, and you can use the radio buttons to establish the way the packages appear to users. Under the New Packages category, you can choose the options:

- **Display the Deployment Software dialog box:** This dialog box appears when you deploy a new package so that you choose whether to assign, publish, or configure the package properties.
- **Publish:** This option specifies that you want the new package to be published when it is added. Publishing occurs to users only, not computers.
- **Assign:** This option specifies that you want the new package to be assigned with the standard package properties. Assignment can occur to either users or computers.
- **Configure Package Properties:** This option specifies that the configure package properties form should appear when a new package is added. You can use this if you expect to stray from the standard package properties.

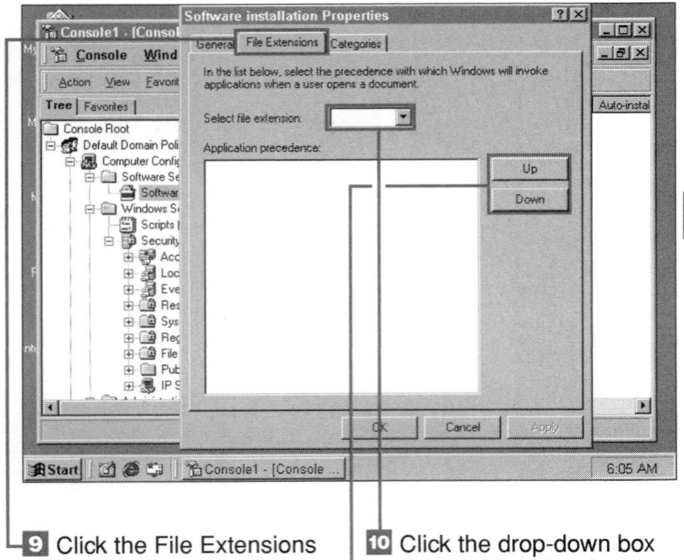

9 Click the File Extensions tab.

■ Use the File Extensions tab to generate a list of file extensions that will invoke the application to open on the user's desktop.

10 Click the drop-down box to select a file extension.

11 Click Up or Down to rearrange the precedence.

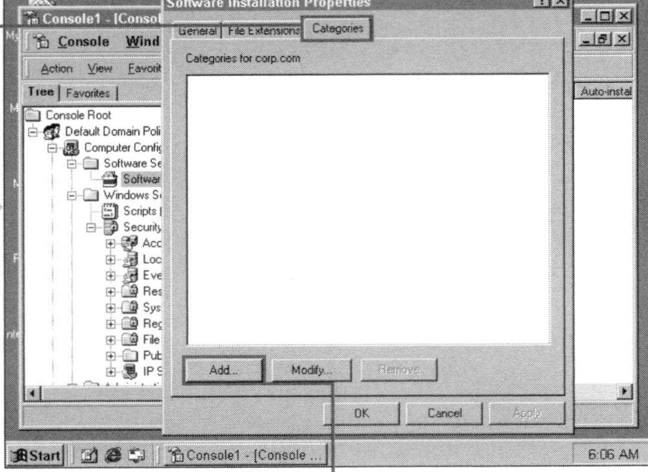

12 Click the Categories tab.

■ Use the Categories tab to configure categories under which the applications appear in Add/Remove programs in Control Panel.

13 Click Add.

Can I change the file extensions that are associated with a software package?

- Yes. The File Extensions tab enables you to list the file extensions that are to be associated with the package. For example, if you installed Microsoft Office, you can specify that the application should open automatically when a user attempts to open a Word (.doc) file. This feature is useful for programs that can handle a number of different file types and ensures that users use a certain program to work on a certain kind of file.

Can I modify the way that programs appear under Add/Remove Programs in the Control Panel?

- Yes. The Categories tab enables you to add categories in Add/Remove Programs in Control Panel where the software program will exist. This feature allows you to add custom categories so that all corporate software programs appear in one place. For example, the ABC Engineering has some custom programs. You can add a category labeled ABC Apps that appears in Add/Remove Programs in Control Panel so that the custom programs are stored in one location.

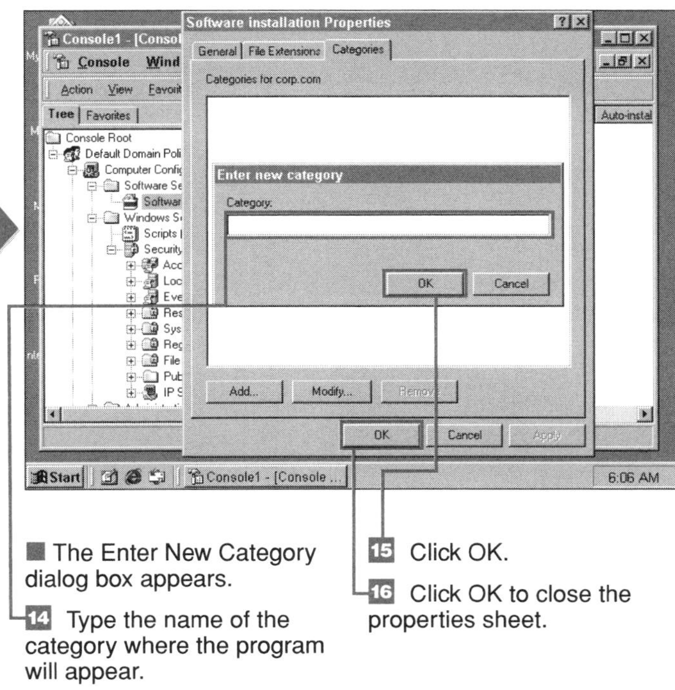

- The Enter New Category dialog box appears.

14 Type the name of the category where the program will appear.

15 Click OK.

16 Click OK to close the properties sheet.

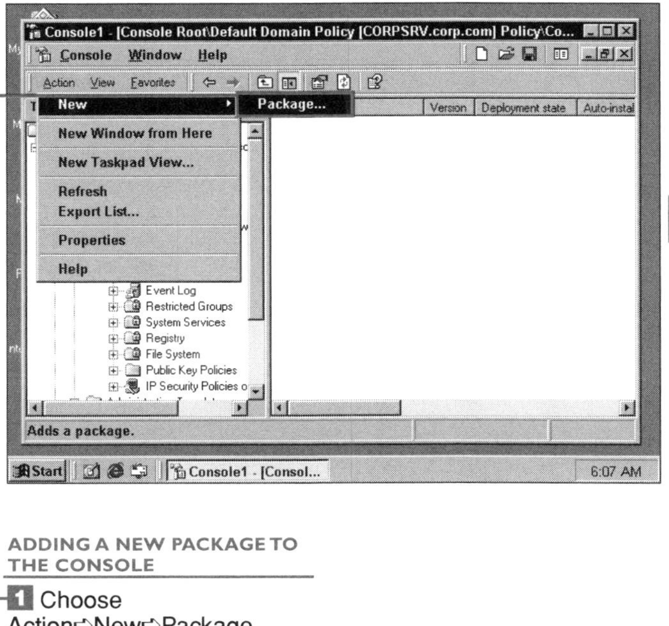

ADDING A NEW PACKAGE TO THE CONSOLE

1 Choose Action⇨New⇨Package.

CONTINUED

GROUP POLICY COMPUTER CONFIGURATION CONTINUED

You can easily add different installer packages to the console by using the Action menu. You may have existing installer packages (.msi files) that have been previously created, and this option allows you to use those packages.

Next, you can configure the Windows settings so that they apply to the members of the Group Policy. You can expand the Windows Settings container, which enables you to configure both script and security settings. The Script icon in the console tree allows you to add startup and shutdown scripts that run automatically when a Group Policy member starts up and shuts down his or her computer. Scripts can be written and customized to meet the needs of your environment; then you can add them to the Group Policy from this location.

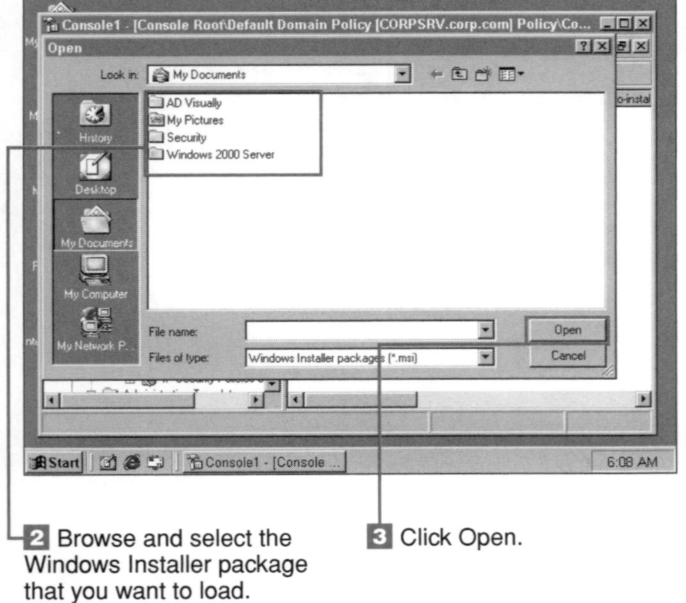

2 Browse and select the Windows Installer package that you want to load.

3 Click Open.

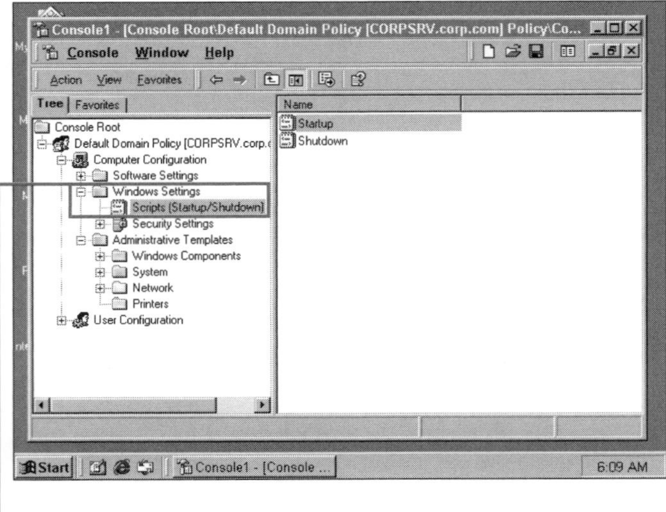

WINDOWS SETTINGS

1 Expand the Windows Settings Container and click the Scripts icon to configure the Startup and Shutdown scripts.

How many software packages can I add to the Group Policy?

✓ You can add as many software packages to the Group Policy as needed for your organization. This is an issue that you should plan carefully so that the software installation feature of the Group Policy is used in an effective manner. Too many software packages can create management and traffic problems. The key rule is to use them as they are needed and to avoid unnecessary or trivial packages.

What are startup and shutdown scripts?

✓ Startup or shutdown scripts are custom scripts that run on the client computer when the computer is either started or shutdown. The script may perform system checks or file checks—basically anything that you want to run at either startup or shutdown. Scripts are often created fro specific network or company needs.

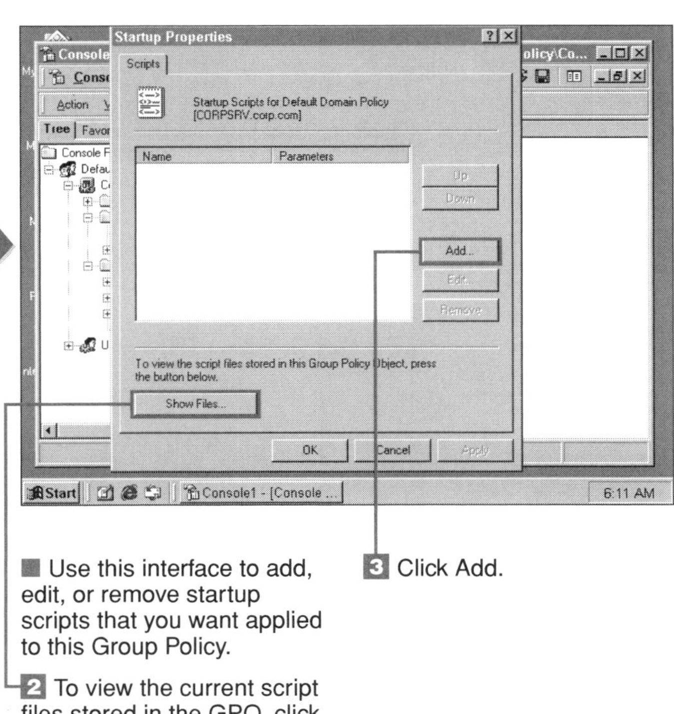

■ Use this interface to add, edit, or remove startup scripts that you want applied to this Group Policy.

2 To view the current script files stored in the GPO, click Show Files.

3 Click Add.

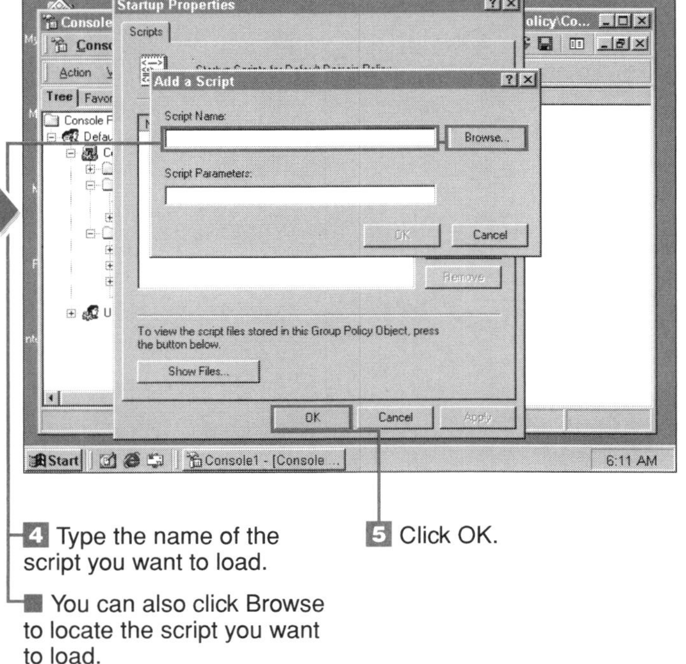

4 Type the name of the script you want to load.

■ You can also click Browse to locate the script you want to load.

5 Click OK.

CONTINUED

GROUP POLICY COMPUTER CONFIGURATION CONTINUED

The second component of Windows Settings is the Security Settings. If you click the Security Settings icon in the console, the available policies appear. You see a number of possible security configuration policies, such as account policies, local policies, event log, restricted groups, and so forth. If you click a policy, the policy settings appear in the details pane. By double-clicking each setting, you can configure the setting options as you desire.

For example, the Account Policy object contains policy settings for passwords, account lockout, and Kerberos. If you double-click the policy setting in the details pane, a window appears in which you can enable or disable the policy and configure any settings for the policy. Fortunately, all the windows look the same or very similar so that you can configure Group Policy quickly and without having to learn a lot of different interfaces.

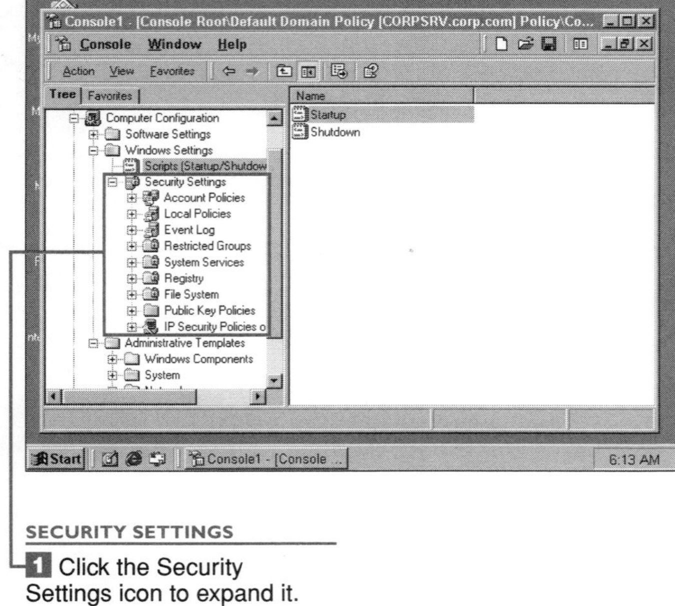

SECURITY SETTINGS

1 Click the Security Settings icon to expand it.

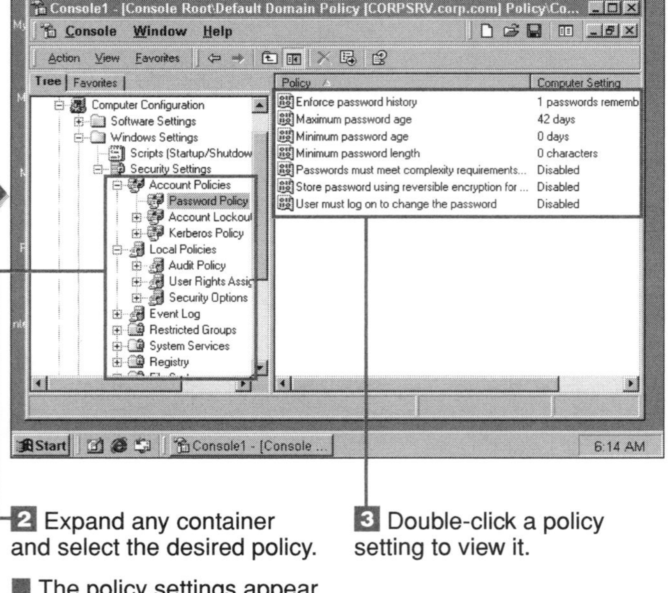

2 Expand any container and select the desired policy.

■ The policy settings appear in the details pane.

3 Double-click a policy setting to view it.

How can I disable a policy setting?

- You can disable a policy setting by double-clicking it in the details pane and then clearing the check box that enables the policy. For example, on Account Lockout, the check box enables you to define the policy setting and enter the number of times a user may attempt to logon before the account is locked. If you clear the check box, the policy is not enabled and no limit is in place for the number of times a user can attempt to logon. Obviously, this choice reduces network security.

Do all policy configuration windows appear the same?

- Most of the policy configuration windows look the same or very similar. All of them allow you to either enable or disable the policy and configure it as appropriate or if necessary. Although the configuration windows may vary slightly depending on the policy, they have the same "feel" that lets you easily and quickly configure the policy.

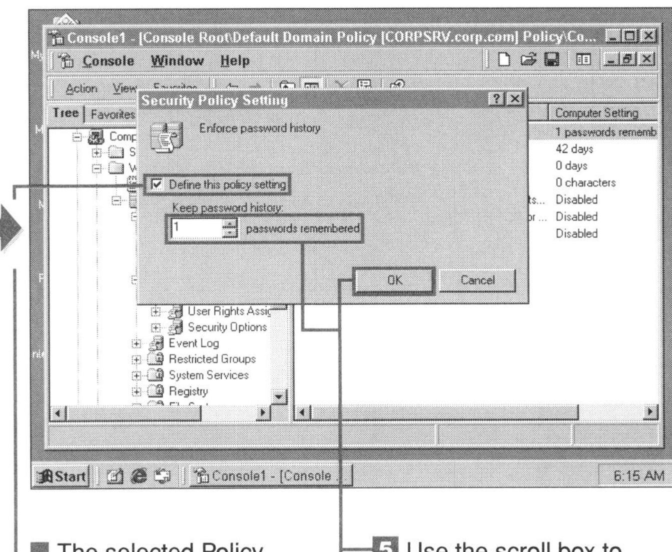

■ The selected Policy Setting window appears.

4 Click the check box to either enable or disable the policy setting.

5 Use the scroll box to configure the setting as desired.

6 Click OK.

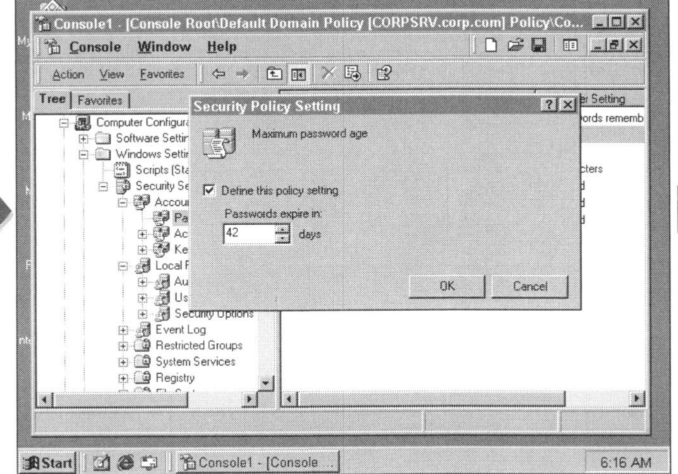

■ This is another example of a policy setting. Notice that the policy settings have the same interface, which is provided for ease of administration.

CONTINUED

GROUP POLICY COMPUTER CONFIGURATION CONTINUED

To configure the security policy for the Group Policy, simply work your way through the various categories and policies. For each policy, you can enable or disable the specific policy and configure it as desired.

As you move into additional security categories, such as system services, the registry, file services, and so forth, you notice that most of the options are not configured by default. This feature allows you to enable the security features you want to enable without having to wade through the entire list. For example, in the System Services container, every service listed in the details pane is not defined in the policy. Say that you want each member of the group to be a DHCP client. Simply double-click the DHCP client icon in the details pane, enable the policy, and then configure it as desired.

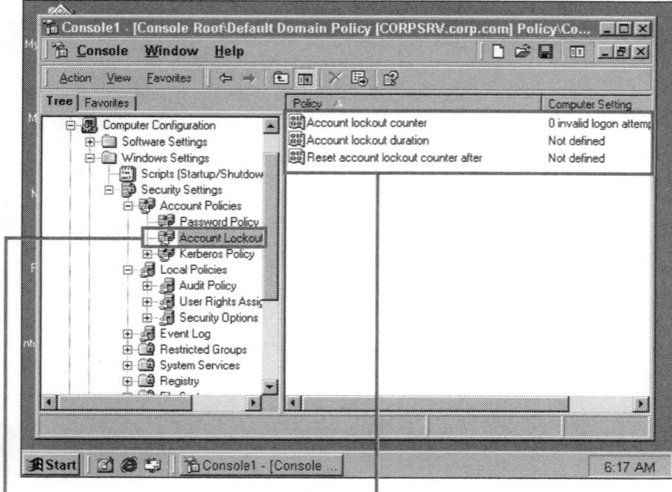

7 Select another policy and the settings for that policy appear in the details pane.

8 Double-click a policy setting to configure it.

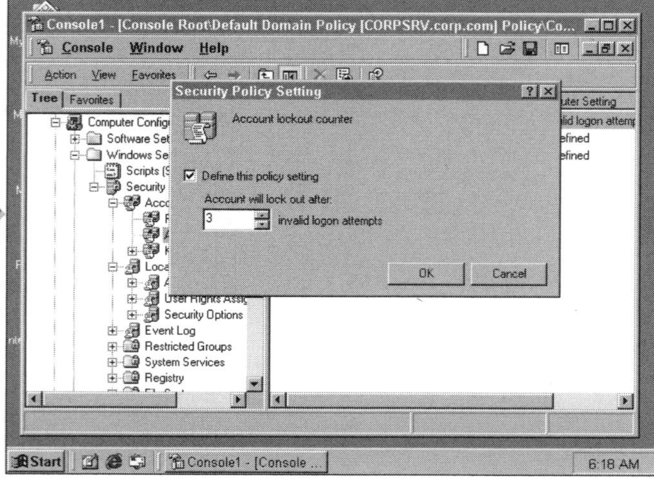

■ The policy window appears.

■ Note that the setting window is similar to the previous example.

TIPS

I want all the clients in a certain Group Policy to share their Internet connections. Can I define this for my Windows 2000 Professional computers?

✓ Yes. Select System Services in the console and then double-click Internet connection sharing. You can then enable this policy and configure it as automatic, manual, or disabled. You can also click Edit Security to edit the security page for this policy. When users log on, their systems are automatically configured for Internet Connection Sharing.

If I don't want to define any System Services for my clients, do I need to do anything in the console?

✓ No. System Services are not defined for the Group Policy by default, so if you do not want them enabled, simply do nothing. If you want to enable some of them, simply double-click the appropriate icon in the details pane.

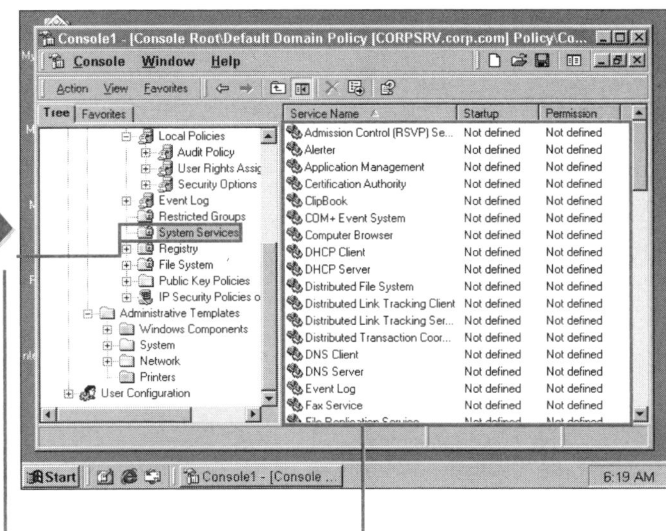

9 For each other security category, you can click the container and the policy settings available appear in the details pane.

10 Double-click any policy in the details pane to configure it.

■ The policy window appears.

11 For this particular policy, click Edit Security to make the security changes for the policy object.

CONTINUED

GROUP POLICY COMPUTER CONFIGURATION CONTINUED

For some security settings, especially those in the System Services container, you see an Edit Security button on the policy configuration window. If you click this button, you see a standard security settings window in which you can configure security permissions for various users or groups. This security setting defines who has permission for the particular policy object, so you should be cautious before assigning lenient permissions for the object.

The final portion of the Group Policy computer configuration is the administrative templates container. This container provides a number of templates that define additional computer settings and either allow or deny users to perform a variety of tasks. You can use the templates to give users control over certain networking components or printers. You can also use the Action menu to add additional templates to the console or remove existing ones.

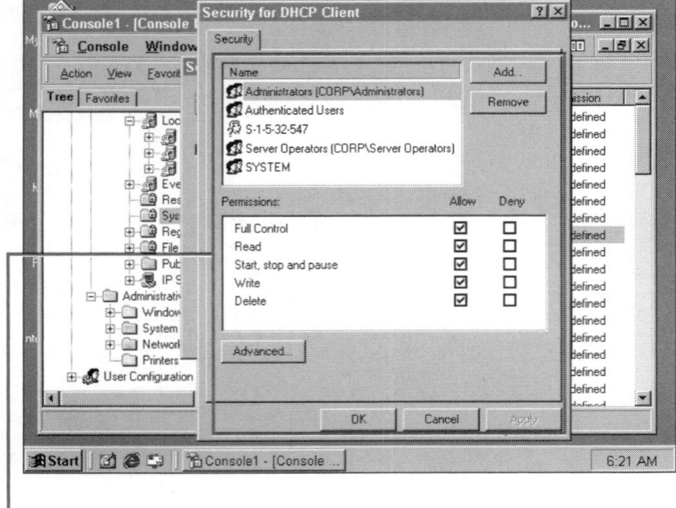

12 Make the security changes for the policy object as desired and click OK.

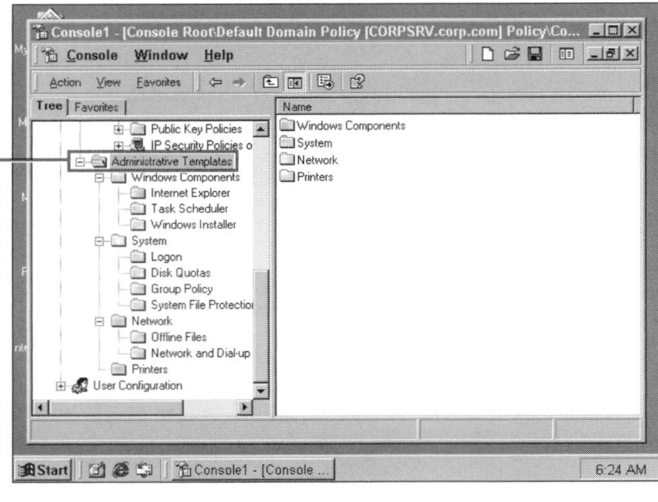

ADMINISTRATIVE TEMPLATES

1 Click the Administrative Templates container to expand it.

What all can I do with administrative templates for the computer configuration?

- The templates are divided into major categories, such as Windows Components, System, Network, and Printers. Within each container, you can configure a variety of policies that relate to the category. For example, in the Window Components container, you can configure settings for Internet Explorer, Task Scheduler, and Windows Installer. In the System container, you can configure settings for Logon, Disk Quotas, Group Policy, and System File Protection.

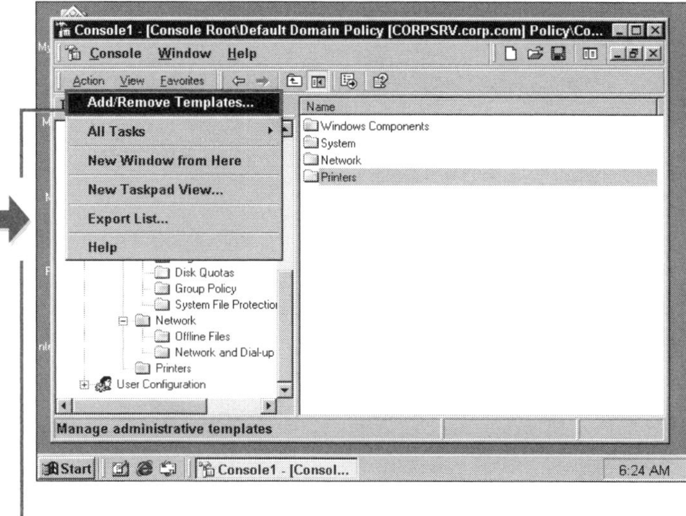

2 To add or remove an administrative template, choose Action⇨Add/Remove Templates.

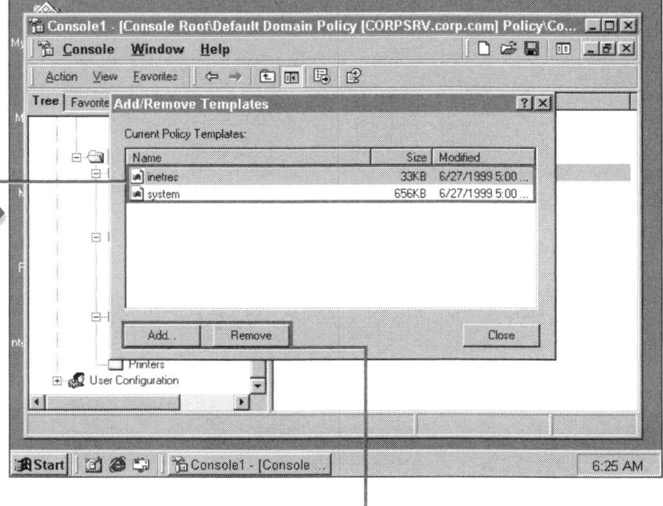

3 Select the policy template you want to use.

4 Click Add to add the administrative template or Remove to remove it.

CONTINUED

GROUP POLICY COMPUTER CONFIGURATION CONTINUED

When you double-click a policy in the templates section, a window appears that enables you to either enable, disable, or not configure the policy. Either enabling or disabling a policy causes the registry to be written accordingly. If you click Not Configured, then the policy is not written to the registry.

You can also click the Explain tab to read an explanation of what the policy enforces if enabled. This feature is useful to make certain that the policy will benefit your Group Policy members.

Some policies contain additional information that must be configured. For example, on the Disk Quota limit and warning level, you input the value for the Disk Quota limit and the type of warning that is returned to the user if the limit is exceeded.

Finally, you can use the Previous Policy and Next Policy buttons to easily navigate from policy to policy.

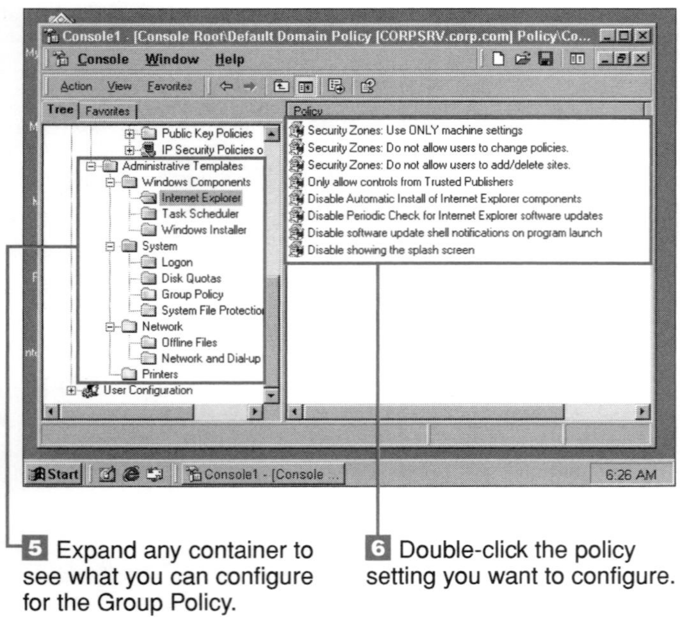

5 Expand any container to see what you can configure for the Group Policy.

6 Double-click the policy setting you want to configure.

7 Click the appropriate radio button to enable, disable, or not configure the policy.

8 Use the Next and Previous Policy buttons to navigate through the policy list for that category.

What is the default setting for the security templates?

- By default, the security template settings are not configured, which means that the value is not written to the registry. You should leave the setting as "not configured" for policy settings that you do not want to use to lower the overhead of your Group Policy. Enabled policies and disabled policies are written to the registry on client computers.

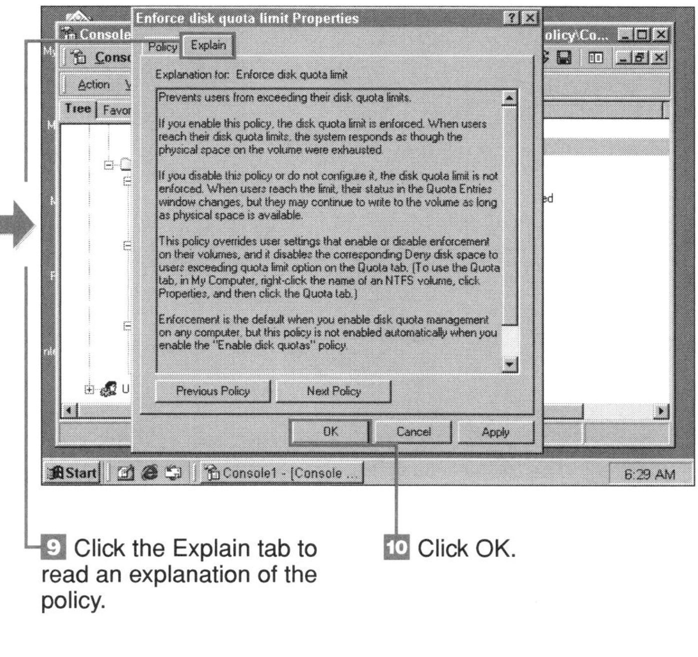

9 Click the Explain tab to read an explanation of the policy.

10 Click OK.

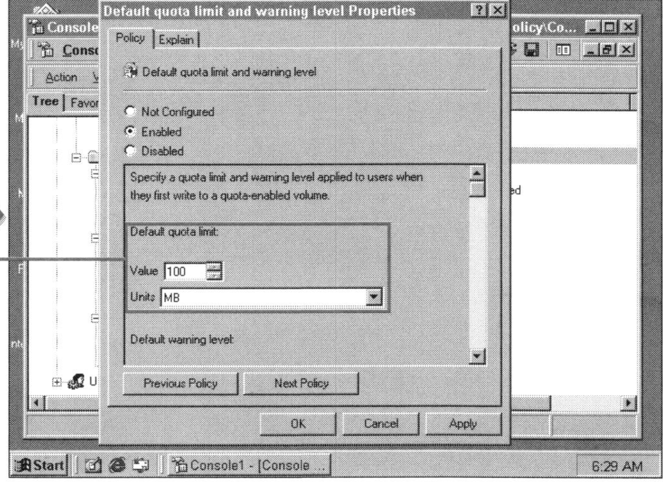

■ Some policy windows, such as this one, allow you to configure additional options that appear in the dialog box.

GROUP POLICY USER CONFIGURATION

Configuration of user policies is very similar to configuring the computer policy. If you expand User Configuration in the console, you have Software Settings, Windows Settings, Security, and Administrative Templates. Most of the settings for the user are the same as for the computer. This feature enables you to define the same kind of settings for computers as well as user accounts. You have some additional options, such as Internet Explorer Maintenance, Remote Installation Service, and Folder Redirection.

The Internet Explorer Maintenance feature enables you to configure Internet Explorer for the Group Policy users. With this feature, you can configure the browser's user interface, connection, URLs, security, and the programs that IE uses. This allows you to customize IE for your environment so that it meets corporate policies while meeting the needs of your users.

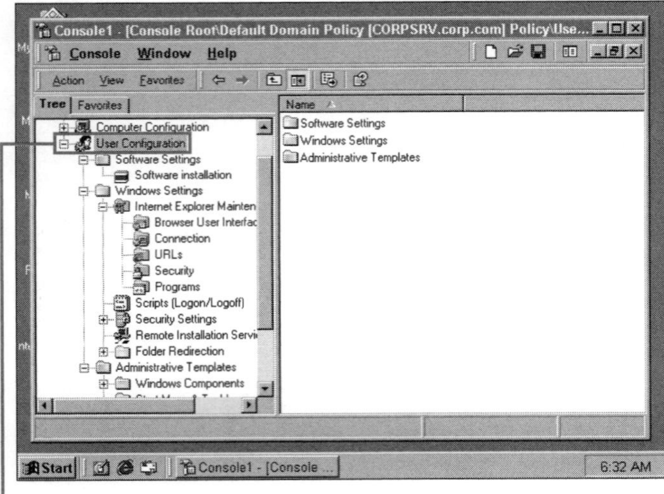

1 Click User Configuration in the console to expand it.

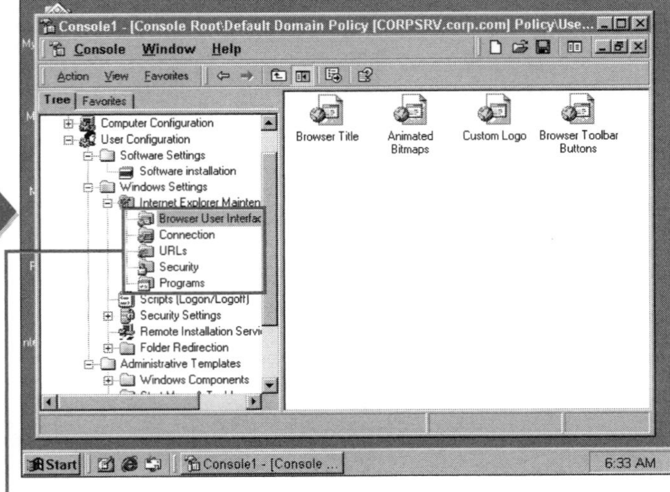

2 Select a category in Internet Explorer Maintenance to see the policy options in the details pane.

TIPS

I want to customize Internet Explorer for the Group Policy members so that IE opens a particular home page each time it launches. Can I do this?

Yes. Select Internet Explorer Maintenance in the console and then double-click URLs in the details pane. Next, double-click Important URLs in the details pane. In the window that opens, click the Customize Home page URL check box and then enter in the dialog box the URL you want to load. When a user launches IE, this home page opens each time.

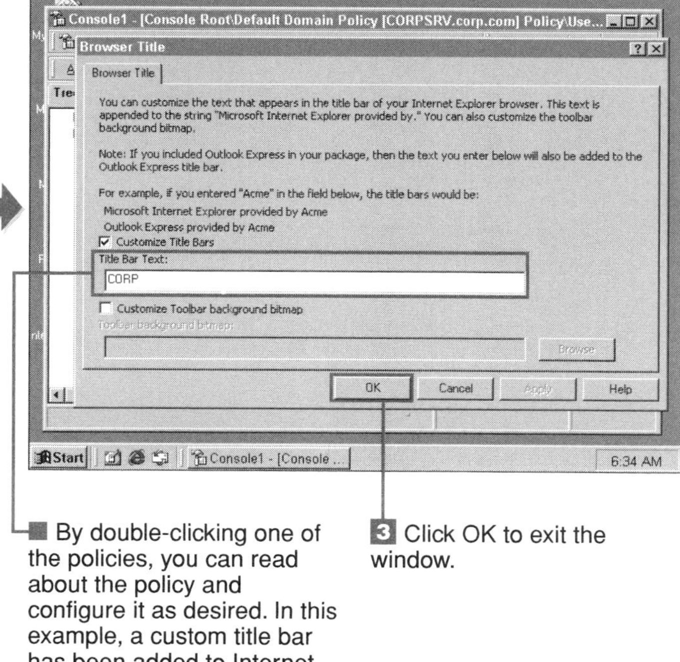

■ By double-clicking one of the policies, you can read about the policy and configure it as desired. In this example, a custom title bar has been added to Internet Explorer for the Group Policy members.

3 Click OK to exit the window.

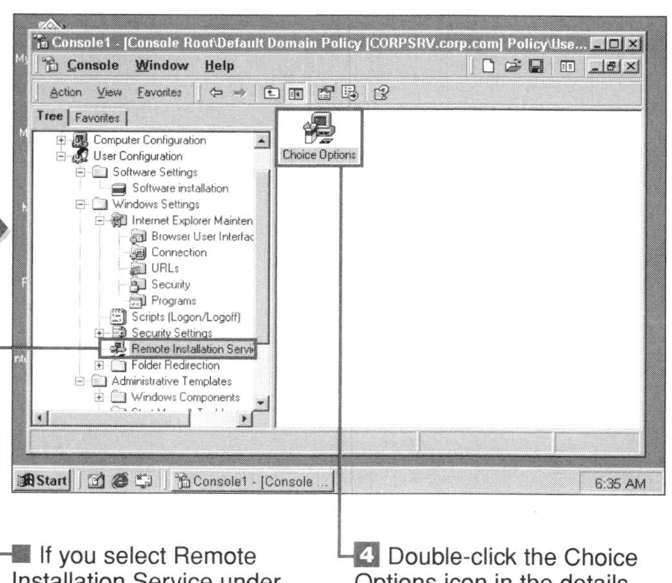

■ If you select Remote Installation Service under Security in the console, a Choice Options program appears in the details pane.

4 Double-click the Choice Options icon in the details pane.

CONTINUED

GROUP POLICY USER CONFIGURATION CONTINUED

Windows 2000 includes Remote Installation Services, which enable administrators to remotely install Windows 2000 Professional on client computers that are booted with a boot floppy or have a boot-enabled BIOS. Remote Installation is also included in the Group Policy so that the Windows 2000 operating system can be set up remotely and then all the Group Policy features applied. Within the Group Policy, you have the option of setting installation choices that are made available to the user by accessing the Choice Options icon in the details pane. This feature presents you with a simple window of radio buttons so that you can choose allow, deny, or "don't care" options for automatic setup, custom setup, restart setup, and tools.

The rest of the policy options for user configuration work the same as with computer configuration.

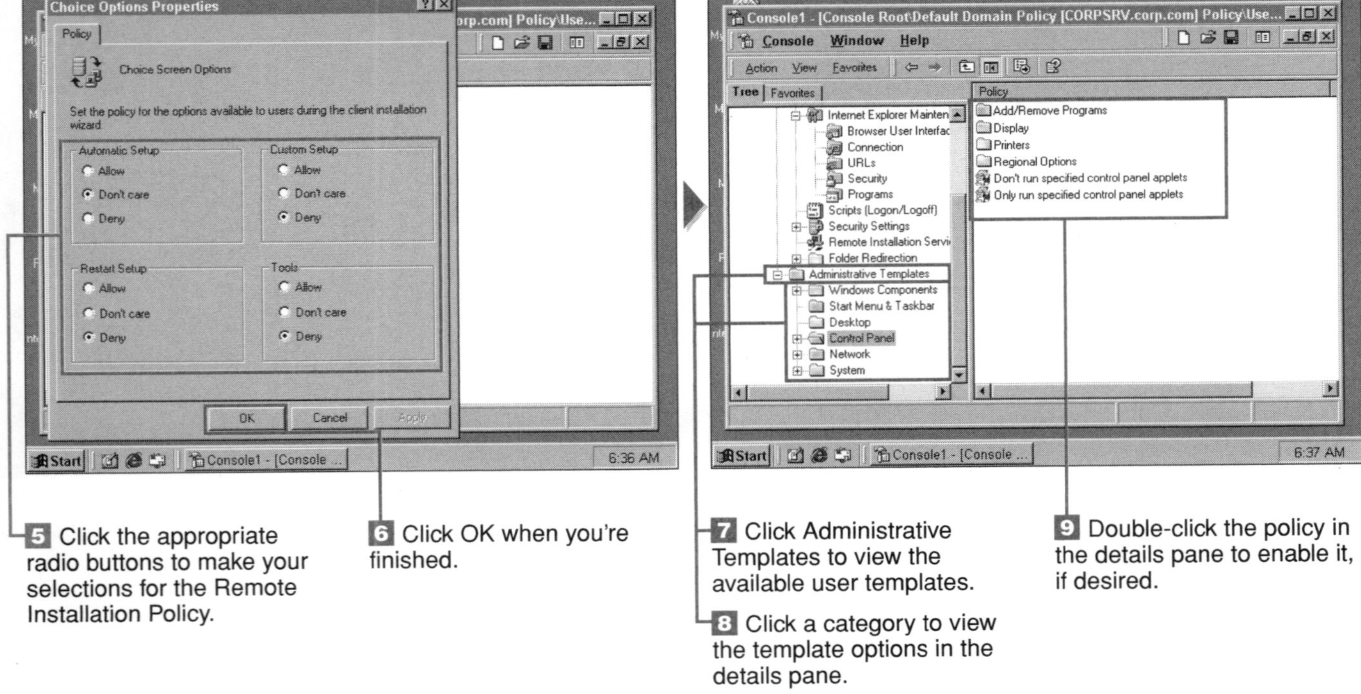

5 Click the appropriate radio buttons to make your selections for the Remote Installation Policy.

6 Click OK when you're finished.

7 Click Administrative Templates to view the available user templates.

8 Click a category to view the template options in the details pane.

9 Double-click the policy in the details pane to enable it, if desired.

What else do I have to do to use the Remote Installation Service?

✔ The Remote Installation Service Choice Options in the Group Policy allow you to simply configure the options presented to the user. To actually use the Remote Installation Service, you have to add it to your server using Add/Remove Programs in Control Panel. Then you must configure the service so that a Windows 2000 Professional package is ready for installation to remote computers. Consult the Windows 2000 Server documentation for more information.

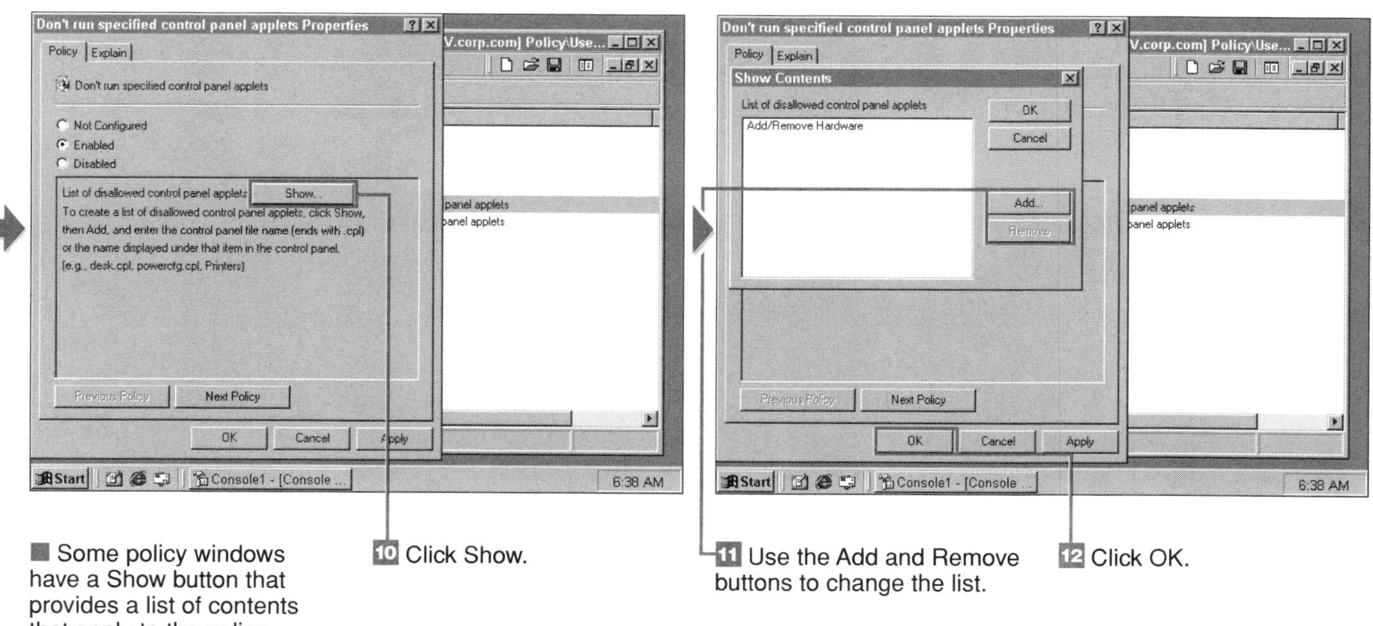

■ Some policy windows have a Show button that provides a list of contents that apply to the policy.

10 Click Show.

11 Use the Add and Remove buttons to change the list.

12 Click OK.

APPLYING GROUP POLICIES TO THE ACTIVE DIRECTORY

You use either the Active Directory Users and Computers snap-in or the Active Directory Sites and Services snap-in to apply group policies to Active Directory sites, domains, or OUs. You can do this by accessing the properties sheets and clicking Group Policy. From this location, you can apply the desired Group Policy to the site, domain, or OU.

If you click Edit, you can also make changes to the policy, and those changes apply to that particular site, domain, or OU. This feature is useful if you want to use the same Group Policy for two domains, but alter them slightly. You can simply make the changes from this location and the changes apply to only that site, domain, or OU.

As far as policy configuration is concerned, all the options work the same as when you use the manual snap-in.

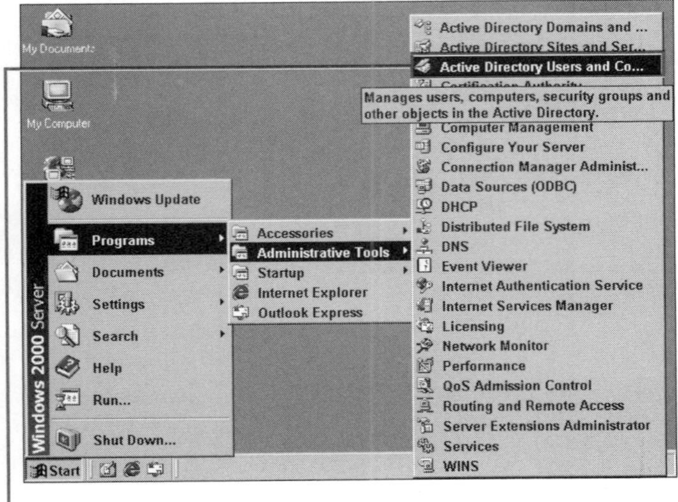

1 Choose Start⇨Programs⇨Administrative Tools⇨Active Directory Users and Computers.

■ Or, choose Start⇨Programs⇨Administrative Tools⇨Active Directory Sites and Services if you want to apply a Group Policy to a site.

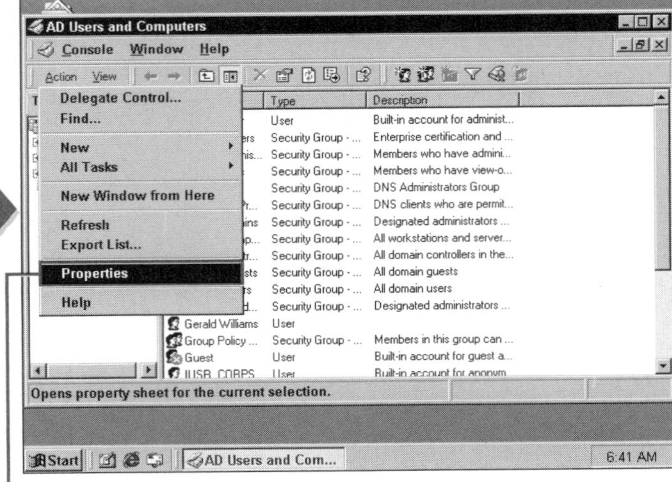

2 Select the domain or OU to which you want to apply the Group Policy and then choose Action⇨Properties.

Can I create a new Group Policy from this location?

✔ Yes. If you want to create a new Group Policy from the Group Policy properties sheet, simply click New and a new policy object appears in the window. You can enter a name for the policy, select it, and then click Edit to begin configuring the policy for that site, domain, or OU. The configuration options are the same as when you use the manual snap-in.

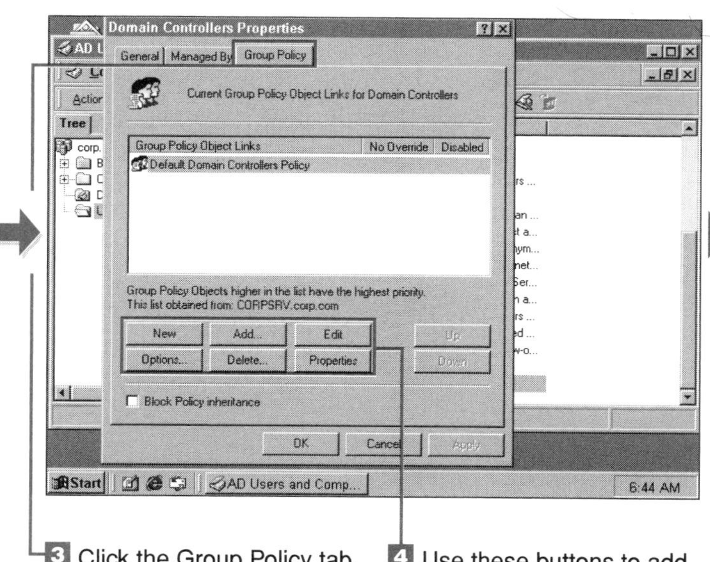

3 Click the Group Policy tab.

4 Use these buttons to add, remove, edit, delete, select options, or view properties for a Group Policy you want to apply.

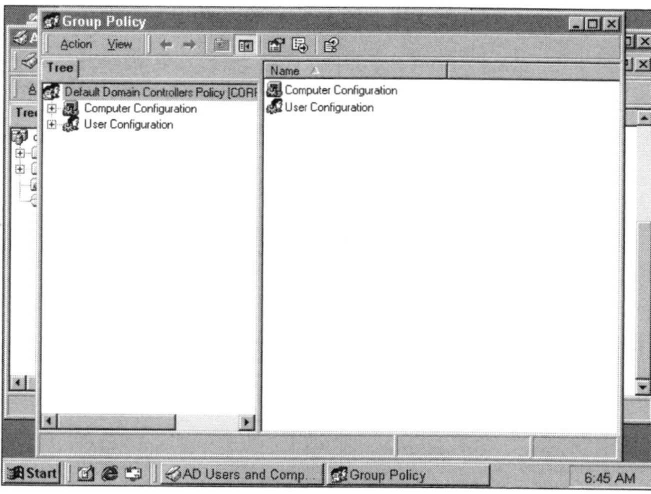

■ If you click Edit, the snap-in window appears. You can make direct changes from this location that apply to this site, domain, or OU.

SHARING FOLDERS

Some Active Directory resources, such as users and groups, are automatically published when they are created in the Active Directory. However, other resources, such as files, folders, applications, and down-level printers, must first be shared on the computer where they reside. Then they must be placed in the Active Directory so that other users can access these resources.

You can share folders so that they are placed in the Active Directory. Typically, a group of files or applications are placed in an appropriate folder and the folder is shared. The network administrator(s) determine in what OU the shared folder should reside, and then it can be published so that Active Directory users can find the folder that contains the files or applications they need.

In order to publish a folder to the Active Directory, you must first share it on that computer.

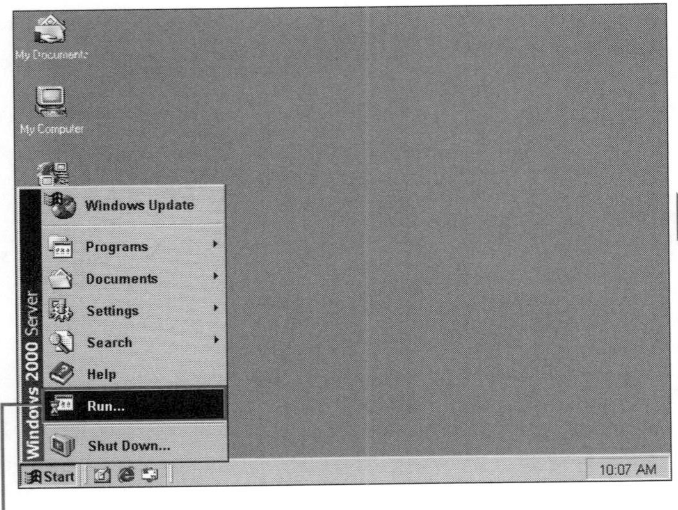

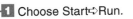

1 Choose Start⇨Run.

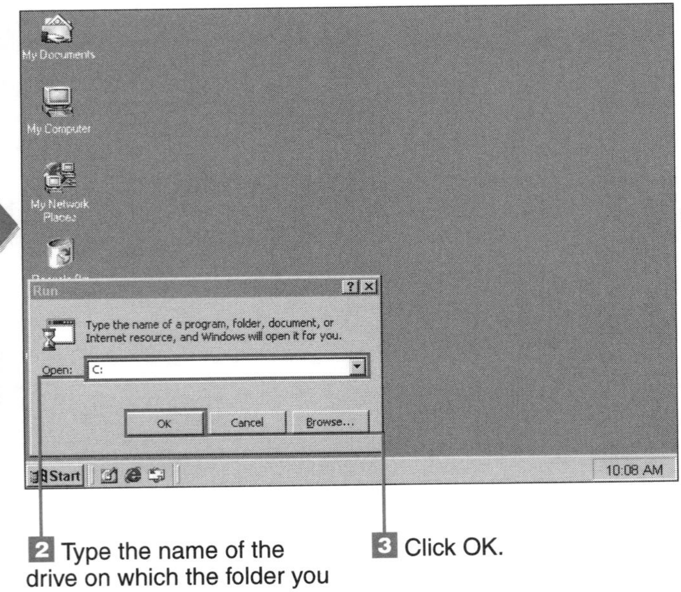

2 Type the name of the drive on which the folder you want to share is located.

3 Click OK.

Can I share an individual file without sharing a folder?

- You can share individual files under the NTFS file system, but under most circumstances those shared files should be placed in a folder. Placing files in a folder allows ease of administration, and you can group similar documents in one folder.

Where is Windows Explorer? I would rather use Explorer to view my drives and folders.

- Windows Explorer, which you used extensively in Windows 9*x* and Windows NT, is provided in Windows 2000 for backwards compatibility and user ease. You can now access Windows Explorer by clicking Start⇨Programs⇨Accessories⇨Windows Explorer.

If I share an application folder, is the application downloaded to the client when the client runs it?

- No. Shared applications reside on a server or computer. When a user accesses the shared application and runs the application, the server or computer actually runs the application, performs all processing, and sends the information to the client.

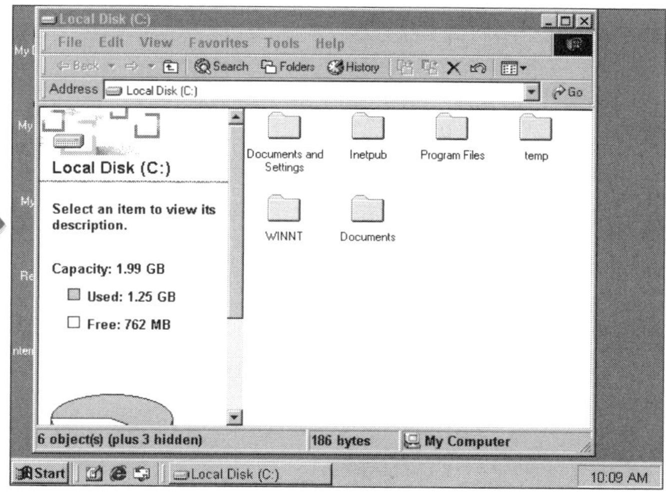

■ The drive window appears.

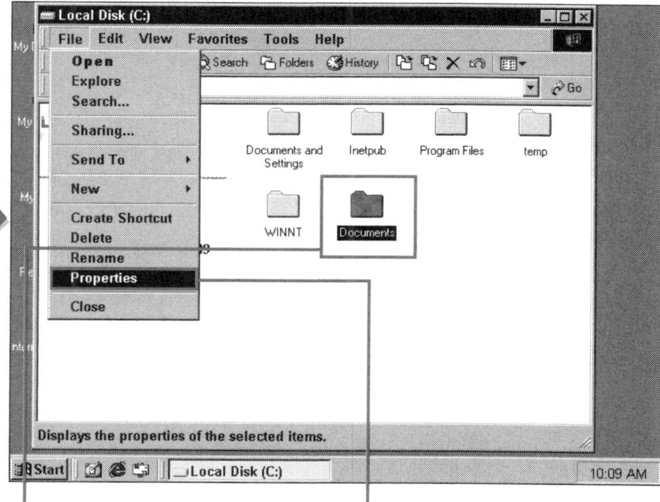

4 Select the folder you want to share.

5 Choose File⇨Properties.

CONTINUED

SHARING FOLDERS CONTINUED

You can share folders on any Windows 2000 computer or down-level Windows computer, such as 9*x* or NT. After an administrator or user shares a folder, he or she can set permissions for the folder. This determines who can access the folder and the contents in the folder.

By default in Windows 2000, the Everyone group has Full Control permissions for a shared folder. If no overriding permissions for the contents in the folder exist, the Everyone group has full control of the documents as well. In most cases, you want to change this to Read only or at least a more restrictive permission. For private documents, you can simply remove the Everyone group and select users for whom you want to provide permissions.

When assigning permissions, you want to determine who you want to access the folder and its contents and then determine what level of permissions those different groups or individuals should be assigned. Normally, you only want to allow a few trusted users to have full control of a shared folder.

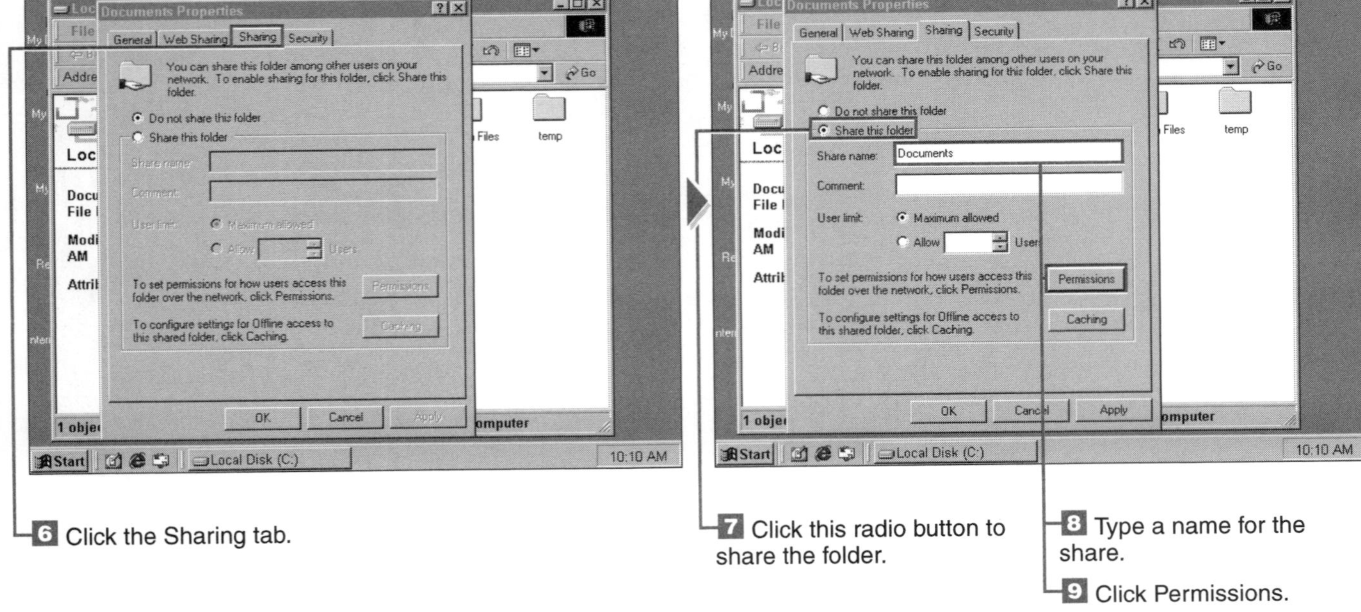

6 Click the Sharing tab.

7 Click this radio button to share the folder.

8 Type a name for the share.

9 Click Permissions.

TIPS

Can I give access permissions to only a few people?

Yes. You can assign the desired permissions to only a few users and deny all permissions for all others. However, if this is the case, you should question whether you should actually store the folder in the Active Directory. Because only a few people are allowed access, you may wish to consider other means of sharing the folder rather than placing an object in the Active Directory.

Can I give Read access to the folder and individual access rights to the documents in the folder?

Yes, and this is very common. You can give read access to the folder, and then you can set the desired permissions for each document in the folder by accessing the Security tab of that document's properties sheets. This feature allows users to have access to some documents and not to others, or differing permissions for different documents.

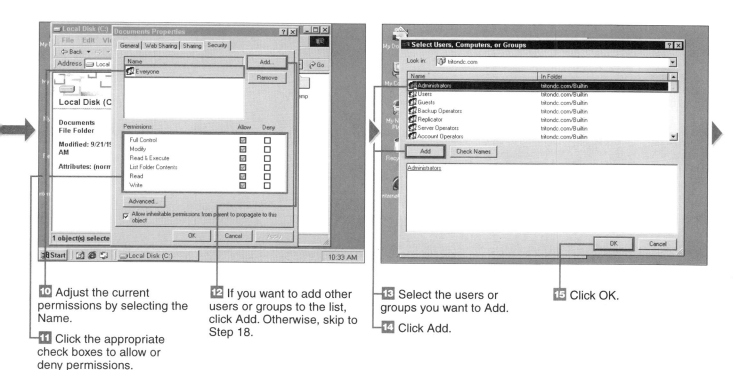

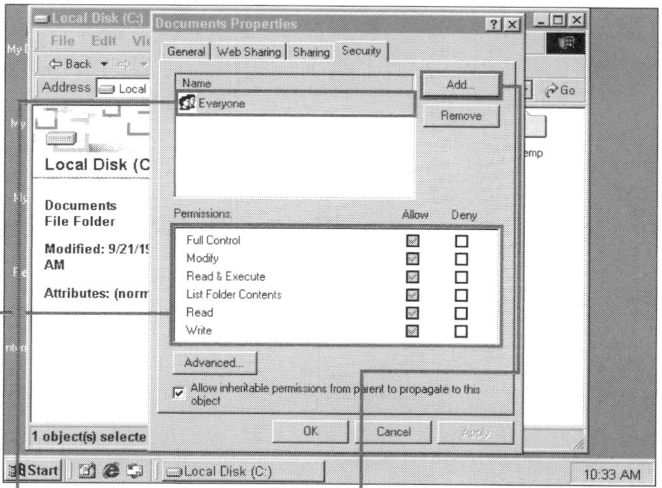

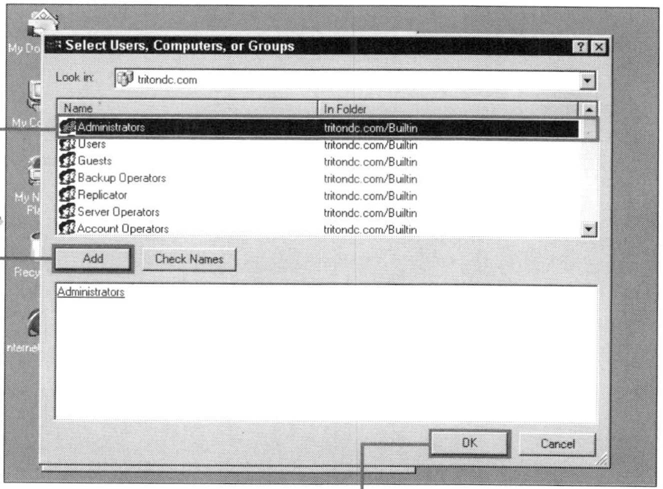

10 Adjust the current permissions by selecting the Name.

11 Click the appropriate check boxes to allow or deny permissions.

12 If you want to add other users or groups to the list, click Add. Otherwise, skip to Step 18.

13 Select the users or groups you want to Add.

14 Click Add.

15 Click OK.

CONTINUED

SHARING FOLDERS CONTINUED

After you have the security permissions configured for the shared folder, you can place your documents or even applications in the shared folder. Then, you can access the properties sheets for those shared documents or applications. This way, you can set different permissions for each item that exists in the shared folder.

All shared folders on your computer are displayed with a hand under the folder icon. You can stop sharing a folder at any time by accessing the properties sheet for the folder and clicking the button on the Sharing tab to stop sharing the folder. When you perform this action, all the documents or applications in the shared folder stop being shared as well.

With shared folders, documents, and applications published in the Active Directory, you can allow users in an Enterprise network to access the information in the shared folder. The next sections shows you, as the administrator, how to publish a shared folder in the Active Directory.

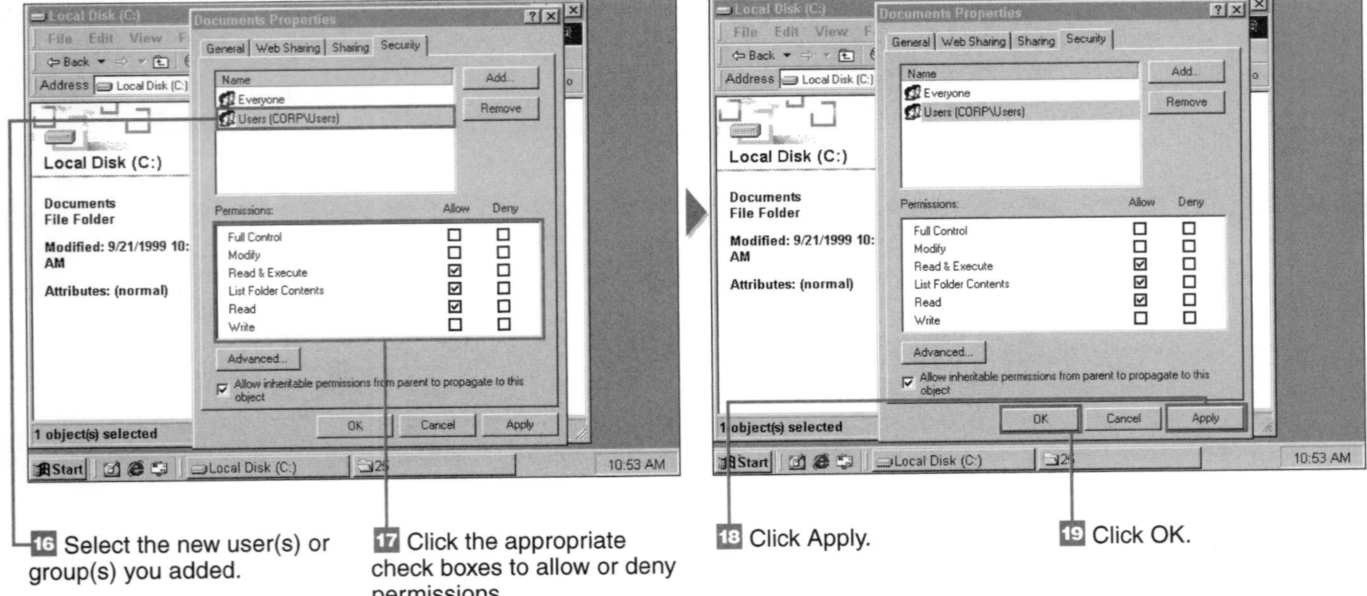

16 Select the new user(s) or group(s) you added.

17 Click the appropriate check boxes to allow or deny permissions.

18 Click Apply.

19 Click OK.

Can I add or remove documents from a shared folder as necessary?

- Yes. You can add documents to a shared folder as needed. When you add a document, you should make certain that you set the desired permissions for the file.

Can I store a document in a shared folder without sharing the document?

- Yes. You can store a document in a shared folder and simply deny all access to the Everyone group on the document's Security tab on the properties sheet. Users can see the file but cannot access it. Generally, this is not a good practice. If you have documents that should not be shared, then you should store those documents in folder that is not shared. This avoids confusion and removes unnecessary clutter from the shared folder.

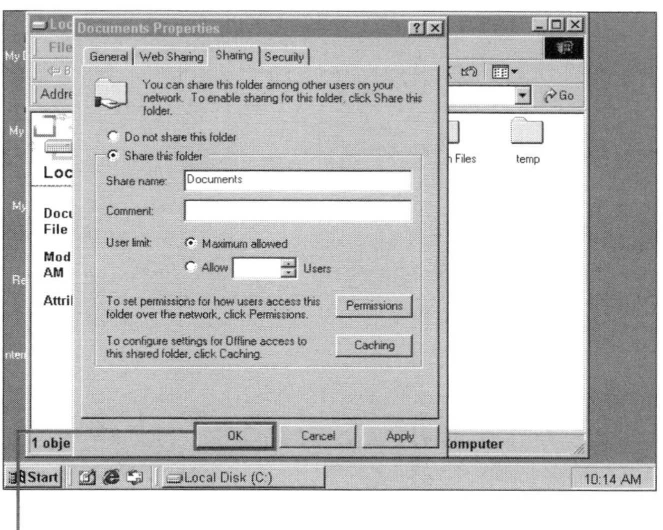

20 Click OK to complete the sharing task.

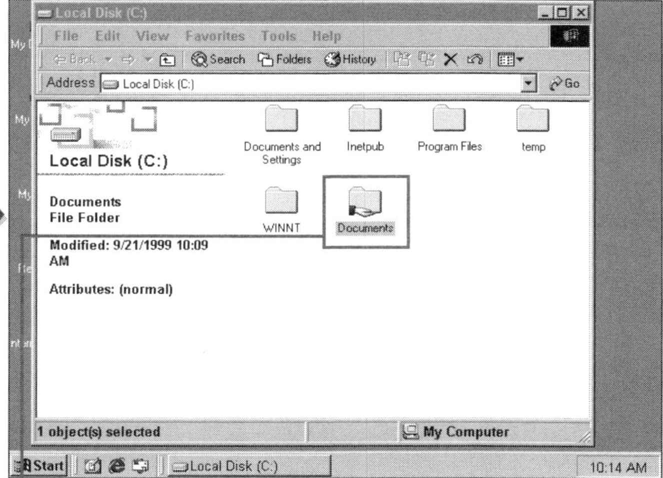

■ The folder is now shared, as indicated by the hand that appears under the folder.

PUBLISHING A SHARED FOLDER

After an administrator or user shares a folder, that folder can then be published to the Active Directory. Publication allows users to find the shared folder through an Active Directory LDAP search.

Only administrators with appropriate permissions can add a shared folder to the directory. Typically, a shared folder resides in some OU, and the administrator that manages that particular OU adds the shared folder.

This is an easy and quick process. All you need to do to publish a shared folder is enter a name for the shared folder that Active Directory users can see and the network path to the shared folder, such as \\server15\documents.

After you share the folder, users can find the folder through the search function, or they can find it by browsing the directory using My Network Places.

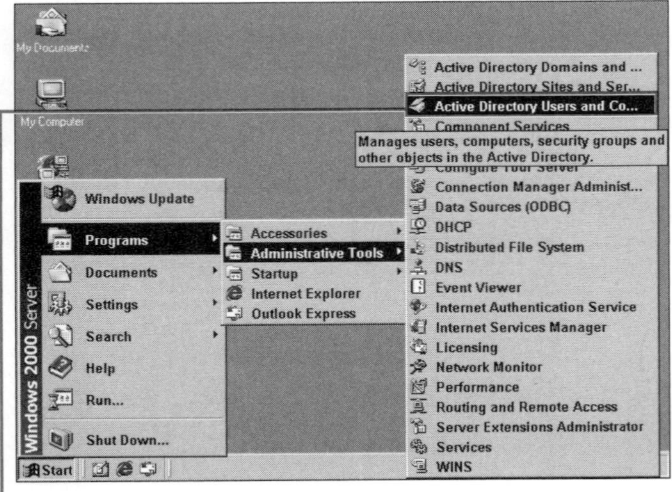

1 Choose Start⇨Programs ⇨Active Directory Users and Computers.

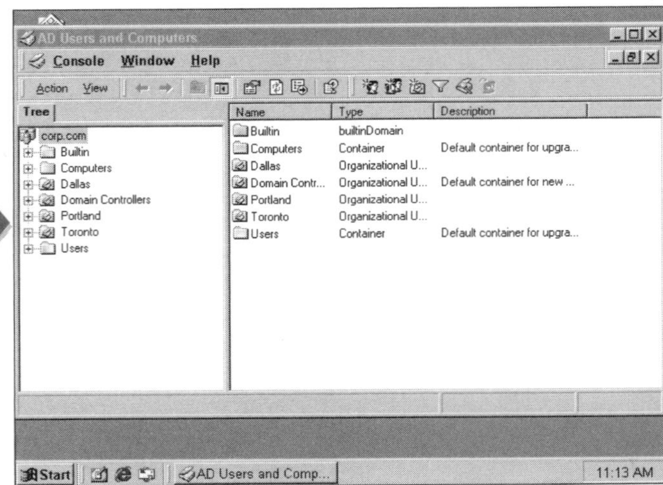

■ The console opens.

Does the Active Directory upload and store the shared folder and documents in the folder on a domain controller?

No. The Active Directory simply stores information about the shared folder so that users can locate it. When a user finds the shared folder in the Active Directory and wants to access it, the request is redirected to the computer that physically houses the shared folder. Active Directory uses the LDAP functionality to locate the shared folders on the network. At that computer, permissions are checked and access is either granted or denied.

Is the network path to the shared folder revealed to Active Directory users?

No. The users are not aware of the shared folder's physical location on the network. This is by design so that users do not have to remember which servers or computers hold which resources. They simply access the shared folder in the Active Directory, and the redirection process to the computer that physically houses the shared folder is invisible to user.

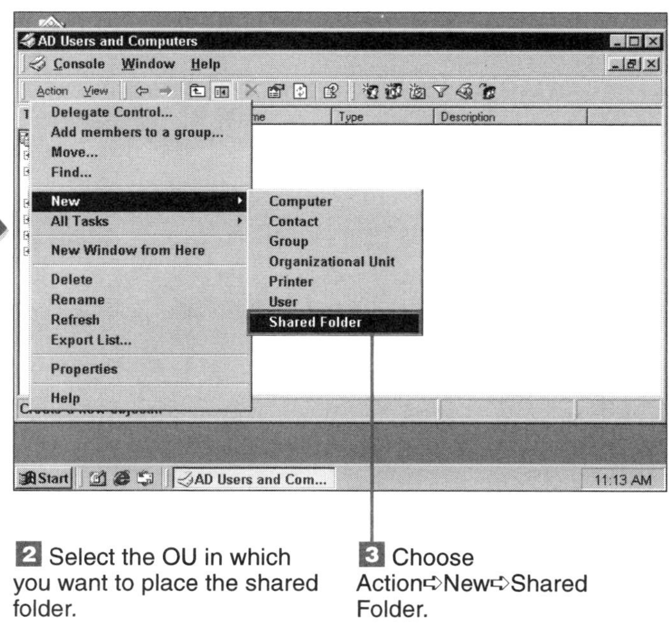

2 Select the OU in which you want to place the shared folder.

3 Choose Action⇨New⇨Shared Folder.

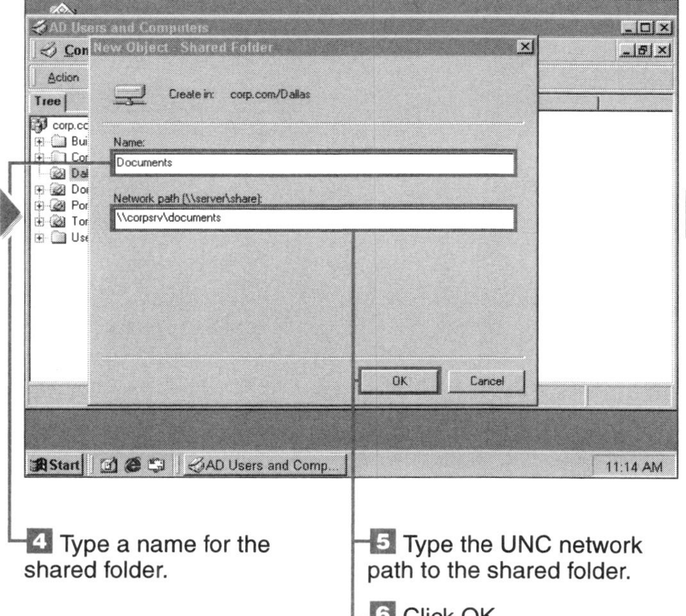

4 Type a name for the shared folder.

5 Type the UNC network path to the shared folder.

6 Click OK.

CONTINUED

PUBLISHING A SHARED FOLDER
CONTINUED

After you publish a folder, it appears in the details pane within the OU selected. You can access the shared folder's properties by using the Action menu.

You see two tabs on the shared folder's properties sheet. First, the General tab enables you to enter a description of the shared folder that Active Directory users can view. This description helps the users determine the contents of the shared folder. Also, you can use the Keywords button to enter keywords for the share. The keywords help Active Directory users find the shared folder by performing a keyword search. For example, if you shared a documents folder that contained general corporate documents, you may use such keywords as *share*, *documents*, *corporate*, and so forth, so that a user searching for *corporate documents* would find the folder in the directory.

You also see a Managed By tab, which allows the administrator to assign a manager for the shared folder, if necessary.

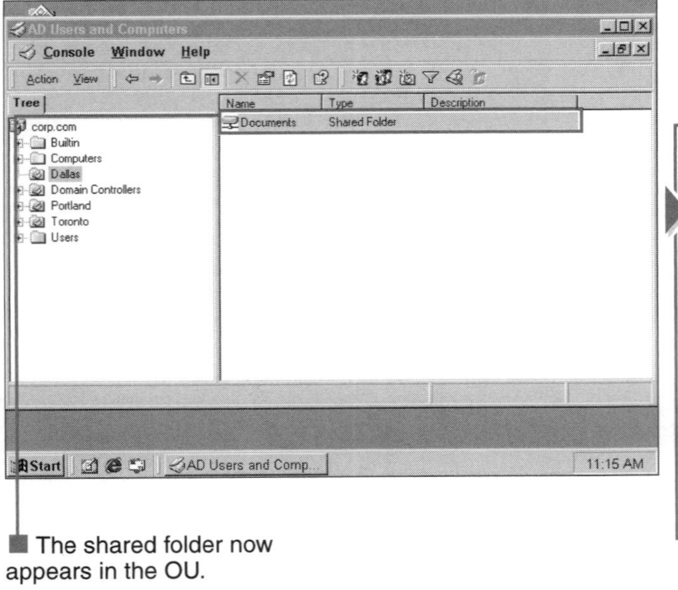

■ The shared folder now appears in the OU.

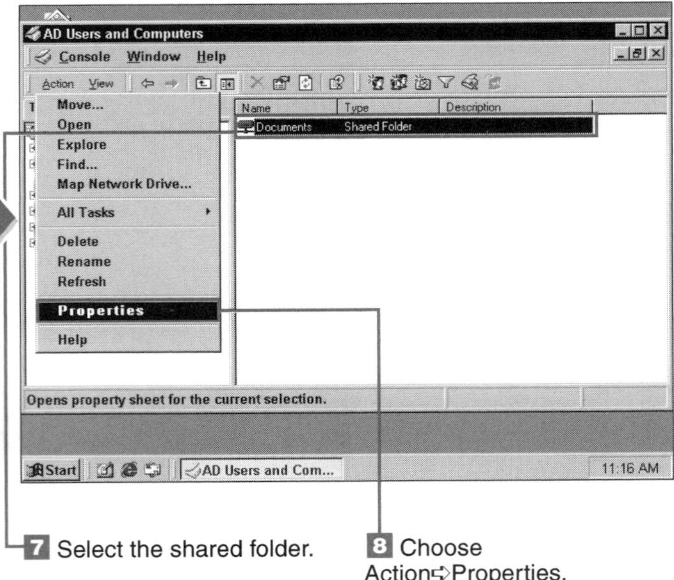

7 Select the shared folder.

8 Choose Action⇨Properties.

TIPS

Can users find the folder if I don't enter keywords?

- Yes. All objects contain built-in ***attributes*** that define the object. If a user searches for ***shared folders***, he or she will find the folder. However, in large environments, such a search could return many results. The keywords help you define the folder's contents so that those users can perform a more detailed search for the kind of shared folder or documents they are searching for.

A shared folder on my network has been moved to a different computer. Do I have to remove the shared folder from the Active Directory and recreate it?

- No. If a shared folder is physically moved to a different computer, simply access the shared folder's properties sheets in the Active Directory and change the UNC path on the General tab so that it points to the correct location. Remember that the Active Directory shared folder is really just a pointer that redirects the users to the appropriate server or computer on which the folder physically resides.

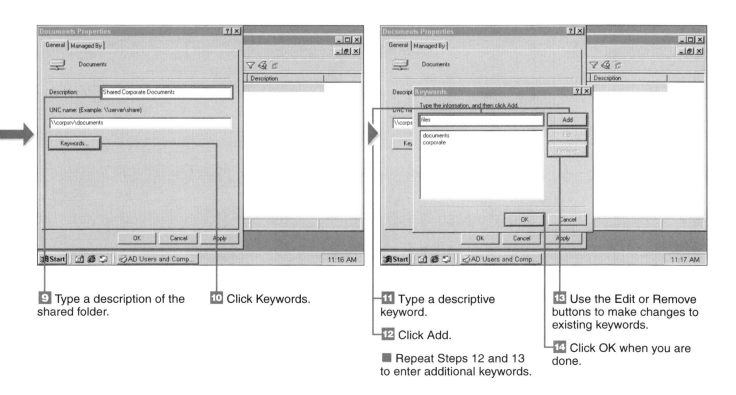

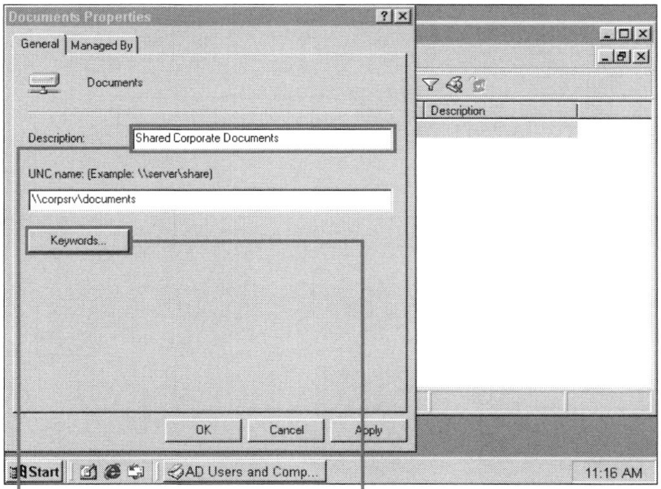

9 Type a description of the shared folder.

10 Click Keywords.

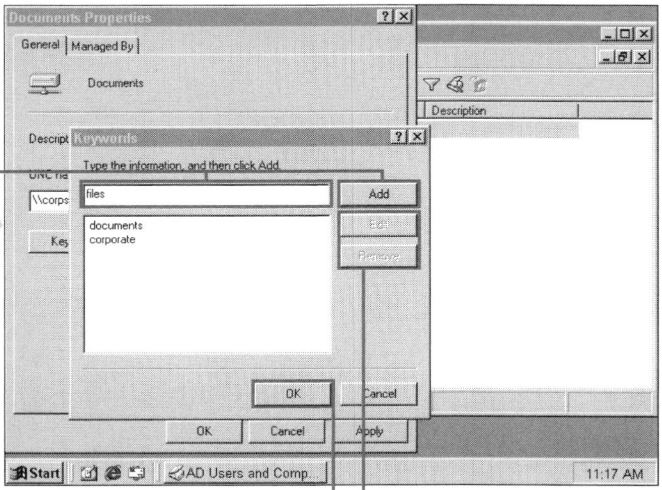

11 Type a descriptive keyword.

12 Click Add.

■ Repeat Steps 12 and 13 to enter additional keywords.

13 Use the Edit or Remove buttons to make changes to existing keywords.

14 Click OK when you are done.

SHARING PRINTERS

The Active Directory can also store information about shared printers so that users can perform a search, locate a shared printer they want to use, and then use the shared printer.

As with a shared folder, the Active Directory stores pointer information for the printer that redirects the user to the actual computer to which the print device is physically connected. This process allows users to find the shared printer they want to use and then print to that printer.

Printers that are connected to Windows 2000 computers function in a different manner with the Active Directory than printers connected to down-level computers. Windows 2000 computers can share a printer and automatically publish the shared printer to the Active Directory. Also, Windows 2000 printers can hold drivers for down-level computers and then send those drivers to those computers when they want to use the printer. All this is done in the background without user intervention.

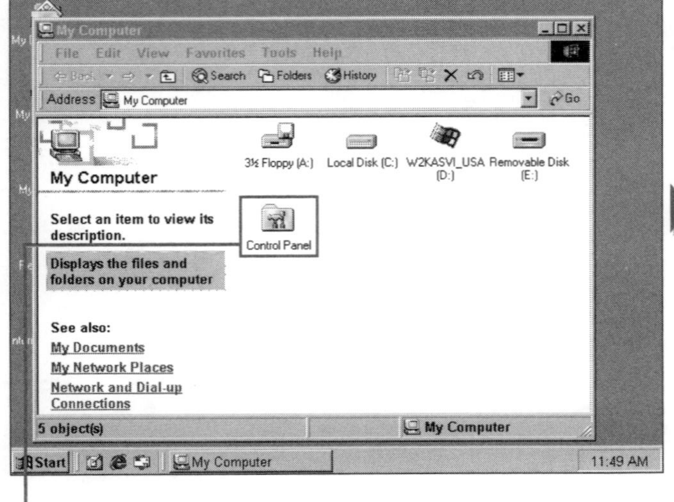

1 Double-click My Computer and then double-click Control Panel.

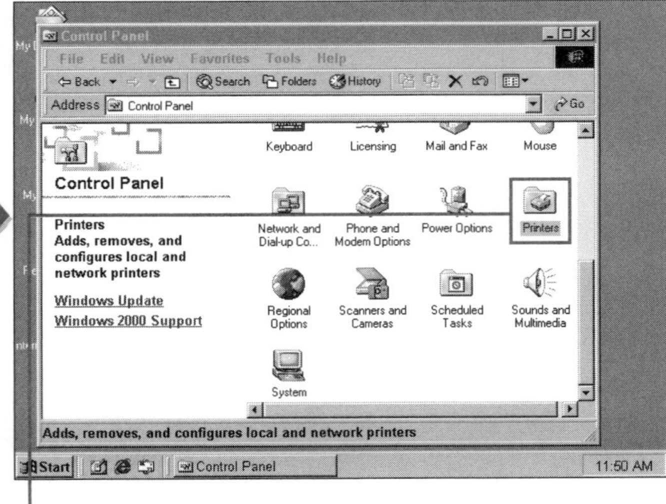

2 Double-click the Printers folder.

Can a computer other than a Windows 2000 computer publish a printer to the Active Directory?

- Any printer on any computer can be published to the Active Directory, but only Windows 2000 computers can perform this process automatically. In the case where a printer is connected to a down-level computer, the administrator must manually add the printer to the Active Directory.

Can only certain types of printers be published in the Active Directory?

- No. If a printer is connected to a computer and the printer is shared, it can be published in the Active Directory. Remember that the Active Directory simply stores pointer information that redirects the user's request to the computer to which the printer is physically attached.

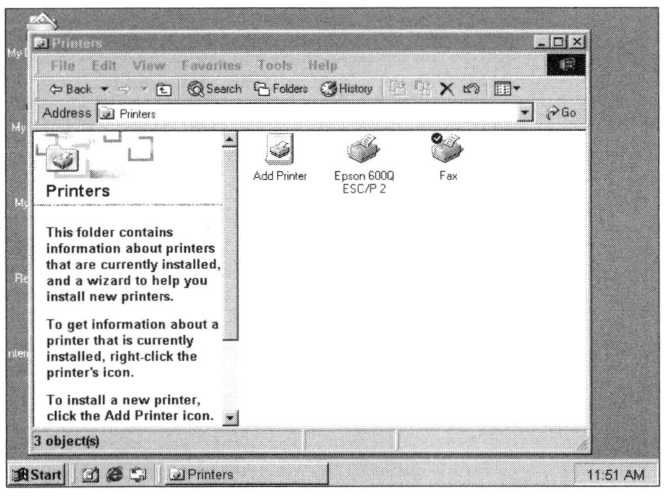

■ The Printers folder opens.

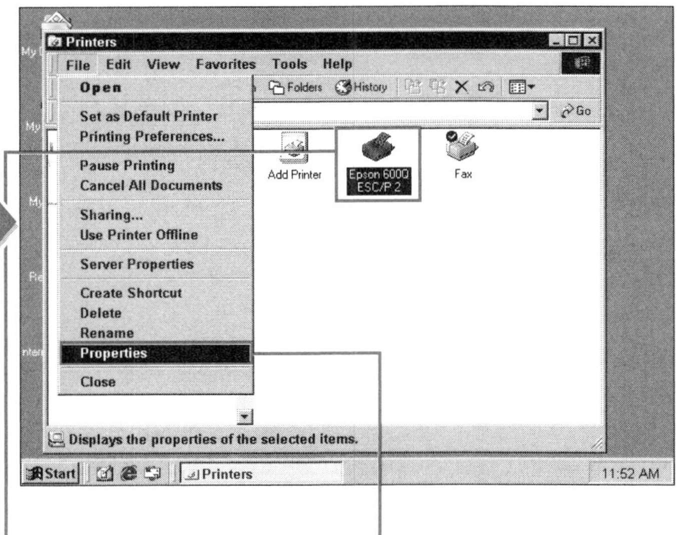

3 Select the printer you want to share.

4 Choose File⇨Properties.

CONTINUED

SHARING PRINTERS CONTINUED

When you share a printer connected to a Windows 2000 computer, you have the option of selecting a List in the Directory check box. This action automatically lists the printer in the Active Directory. Of course, this option is not available on down-level computers and the printer must be manually added to the directory.

You also have the option to provide drivers to down-level Windows computers. This option gives you a list of operating systems to select, and then the driver files are copied from the installation CD-ROM. When a down-level client connects to a printer on a Windows 2000 computer, the driver for that operating system can be automatically downloaded. This process is invisible to the user.

As with a shared folder, you can access the Security tab and configure permissions for the printer as desired. The main permissions for printing are print, manage printers, and manage documents. By default, the Everyone group can print to the printer.

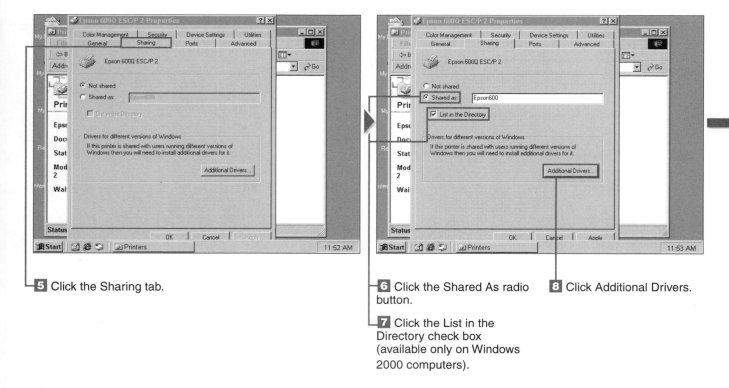

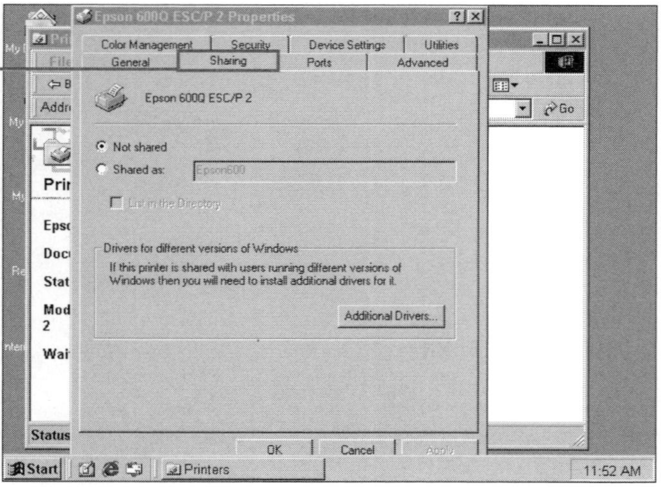

5 Click the Sharing tab.

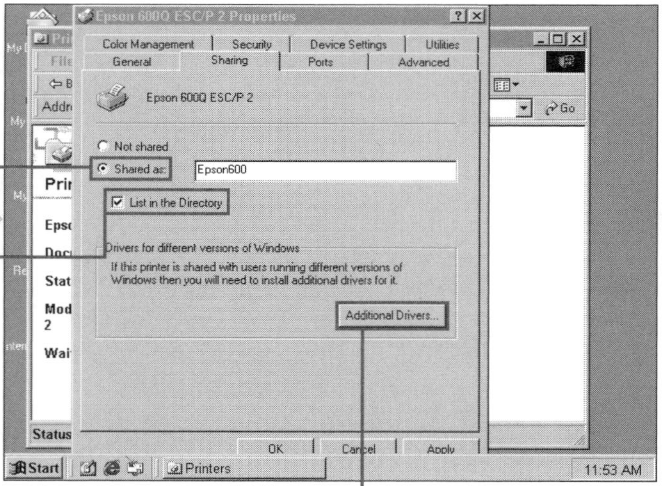

6 Click the Shared As radio button.

7 Click the List in the Directory check box (available only on Windows 2000 computers).

8 Click Additional Drivers.

Can I force a down-level computer to automatically store the shared printer in the directory?

✔ No. Only Windows 2000 computers have this capability. An administrator must manually enter down-level computers with shared printers into the directory.

What advanced permissions are available?

✔ If you click the Advanced button on the Security tab and then select a user/group and click View/Edit, you can see that the advanced printer settings also contain permission to Read, Change, and Take Ownership of the print device.

Who has default permissions for print, manage printers, and manage documents?

✔ By default, members of the Administrators group, Print Operators group, and Server Operators group have the rights to print, manage printers, and manage documents.

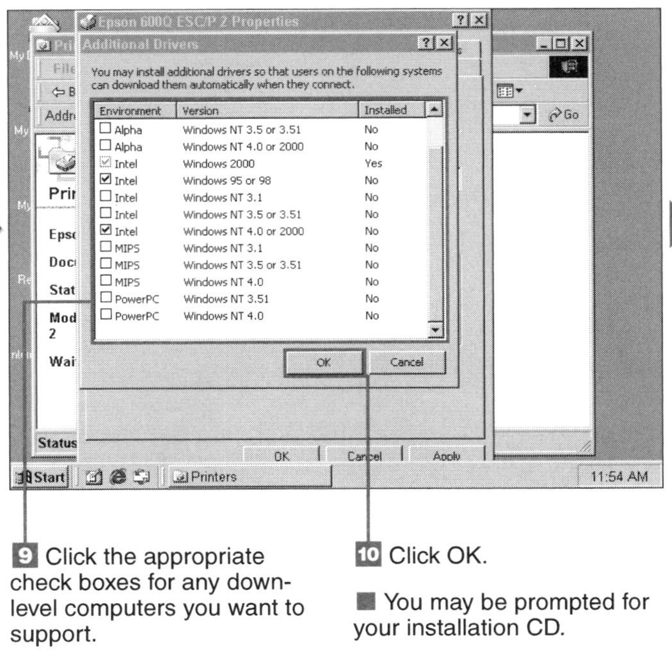

9 Click the appropriate check boxes for any down-level computers you want to support.

10 Click OK.

■ You may be prompted for your installation CD.

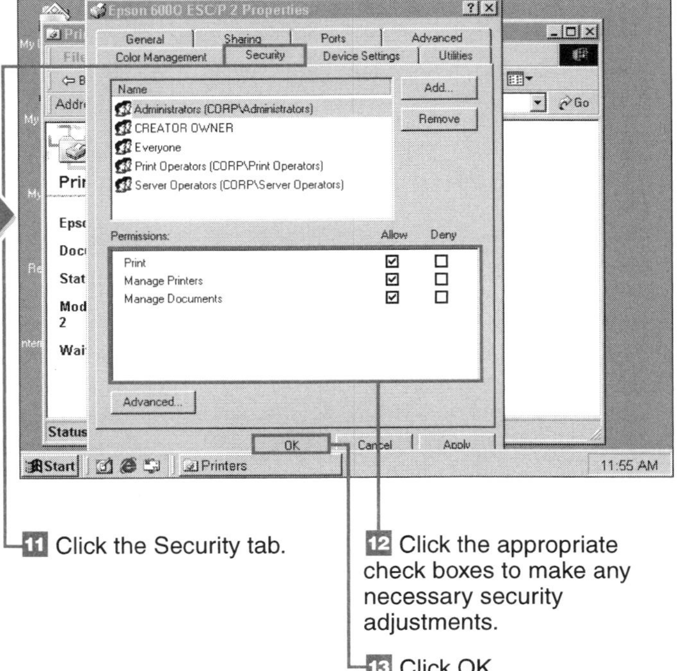

11 Click the Security tab.

12 Click the appropriate check boxes to make any necessary security adjustments.

13 Click OK.

PUBLISHING PRINTERS NOT CONNECTED TO WINDOWS 2000 COMPUTERS

Printers that are shared and are attached to Windows 2000 computers are automatically shared in the Active Directory. If the printer is later not shared, then it is automatically removed. Users who run a search query for printers automatically find the printers connected to Windows 2000 computers, and no additional configuration is required on the part of the administrator.

However, down-level computers, such as those running Windows 9*x* or NT, cannot automatically publish their shared printers to the Active Directory. This must be manually done by an administrator.

The process is an easy one. Simply choose which OU you want the printer to reside in and add the printer using the Action menu. All you have to do is enter the network path, and if the printer is actually shared, it is published. You can also access the properties sheets for the down-level shared printer to make slight adjustments to its printing options as well as assign a manager.

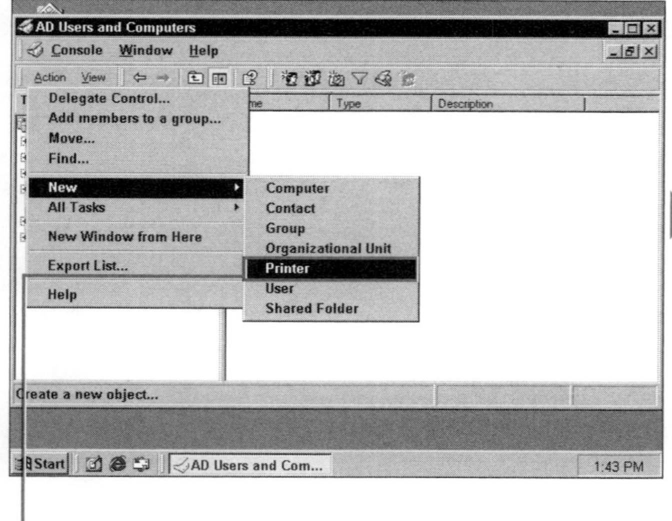

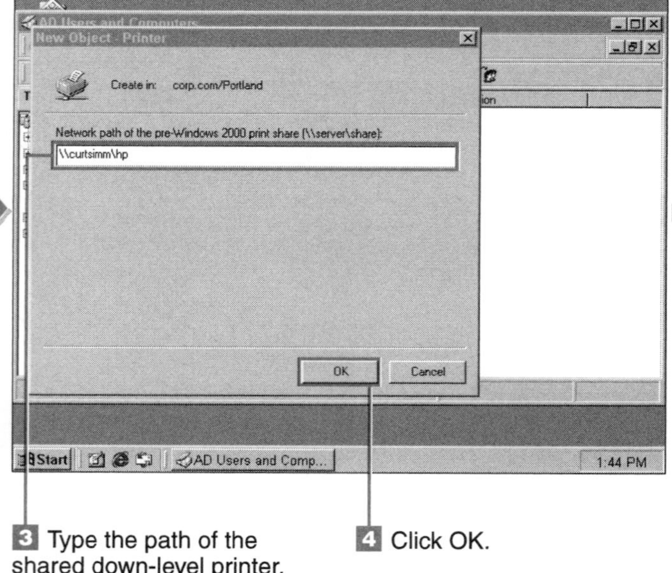

1 Open Active Directory Users and Computers and then select the OU where you want to publish the down-level computer.

2 Choose Action⇨New⇨Printer.

3 Type the path of the shared down-level printer.

4 Click OK.

Can users run a search for my printer connected to a Windows 98 computer and find it?

- After you manually add the printer to the Active Directory, users can run a search for the printer and find it.

Are drivers automatically downloaded for down-level computers sharing a printer?

- Driver files are shared with the printer, but a different operating system may have difficulty using the printer. For example, if a Windows 2000 Professional computer attempts to use a printer on a Windows 95 computer, the printer drivers may not be compatible with Windows 2000.

If I stop sharing my printer connected to a Windows 98 computer, is it automatically removed from the Active Directory?

- No. An administrator must manually remove that printer object. Users can find the printer in the Active Directory, but they cannot print to it after it is no longer shared.

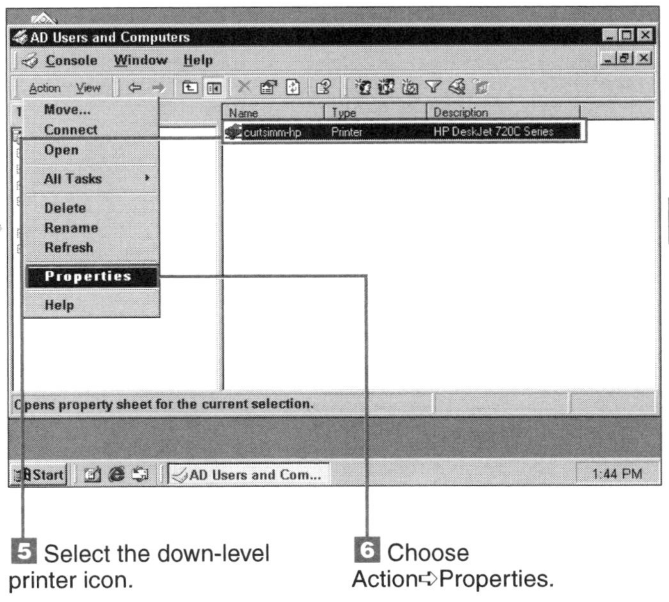

5 Select the down-level printer icon.

6 Choose Action⇨Properties.

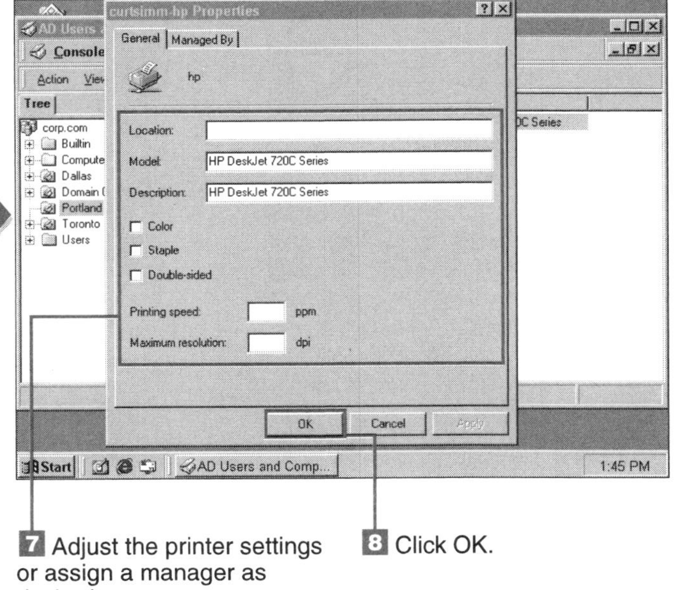

7 Adjust the printer settings or assign a manager as desired.

8 Click OK.

WHAT IS THE SCHEMA?

The Active Directory determines what can be stored through the Active Directory schema. The *schema* is a list of "definitions" that identify the kinds of objects and the information about those objects that can be stored in the Active Directory database. The schema includes the definitions for objects, such as users, computers, and printers, that are stored in the Active Directory database. For a database to function properly, a set of rules must exist to determine what kinds of objects can be stored in it and the kind of information about those objects that can also be stored.

The Active Directory schema definitions are also considered objects in the Active Directory, so they can be managed just as any other Active Directory object. This feature enables you to manage the schema in the same way you would any other Active Directory object.

Two different kinds of definitions are in the schema: attributes and classes. In terms of the Active Directory, attributes and classes are called *metadata*, which is simply "data about data." For example, a user account is considered an object, or data, and the username, password, e-mail address, group membership, and so on, for the account is metadata for that account.

UNDERSTANDING ATTRIBUTES

For each object that can be stored in the Active Directory, attributes exist for that object. An attribute defines the object in the Active Directory, and you can think of attributes as "fields" in a typical database. For example, a user account may contain attributes of username, user's actual name, e-mail address, group membership, and so forth.

Because the attributes are defined for the object, the Active Directory can effectively store the object, and users can perform LDAP search queries on attributes of an object. For example, if you know only a user's e-mail addresses, you can run an LDAP search on the e-mail address, and the Active Directory checks its database for that e-mail address. The Active Directory finds it as an attribute of a certain user account, and the user account information is returned.

Each Active Directory attribute is defined only once in the Active Directory, and the same attribute can be used in many different classes.

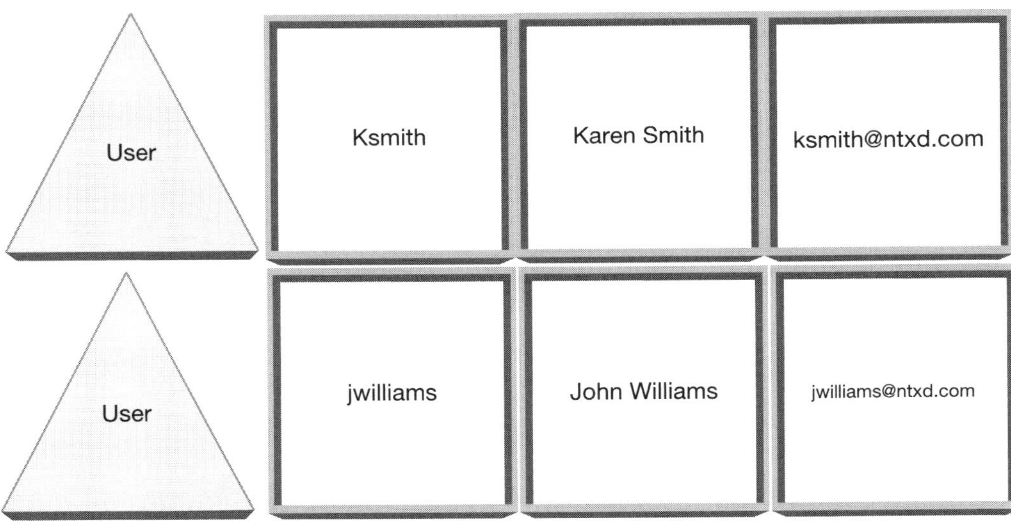

UNDERSTANDING CLASSES

Classes, also called *object classes*, define where certain objects belong. The classes group objects together that share a collection of attributes. For example, the User Class is a collection of attributes that define user accounts, the Printer Class is a collection of attributes that define the printers, and so forth. Every object in the Active Directory belongs to some class, and every object is considered an *instance* of that class.

The Active Directory comes with a set of predefined classes and attributes. In most cases, the predefined classes and attributes are sufficient for most networking environments; however, you can tailor the schema to your organization.

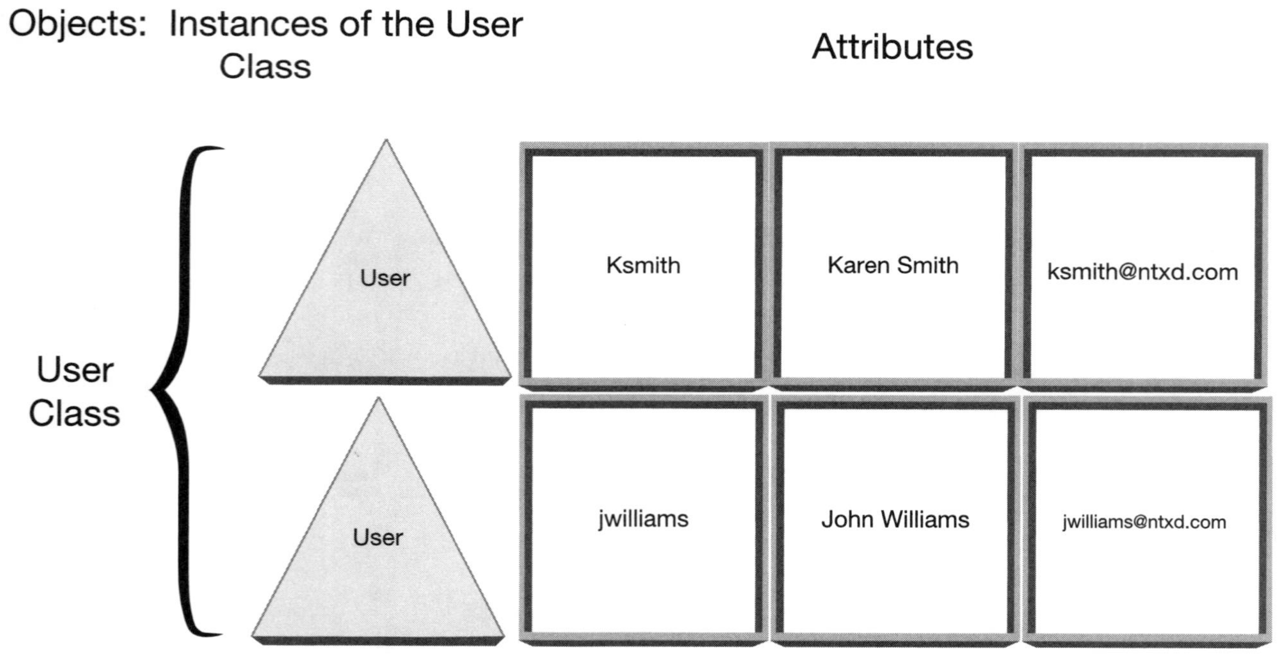

SCHEMA MODIFICATION

As an administrator, you really do not have to be highly aware of the Active Directory schema. You should understand how attributes and classes function and why they are needed, but the Active Directory schema is not a portion of the Active Directory that you administer and change as a part of your administrative duties. The schema is designed to be an internal part of the Active Directory and not something you administrate.

However, in some cases, your business may need to define new attributes or even classes. Most of the time, your needs can be met by tailoring an attribute of an object to your environment. These schema modifications are relatively simple and harmless. The most dangerous configuration would be to add a new class of objects. This process requires very careful thought and carefully planning. In fact, Microsoft recommends that only programmers or highly skilled administrators attempt to modify the schema because incorrect modification can result in Enterprise Active Directory problems and failures. Changes to the schema are automatic and they are replicated to every domain controller. If you do want to make modifications to schema, you may consider using a test network or test machine before actually attempting the modification on the network. In most cases, you can work with the schema that is already in place, so you must plan carefully to make certain that schema modification is an act that really needs to be performed. Again, great care must be exercised before making any changes to the schema.

You can modify the schema by using the Active Directory Services Interface (ADSI), which is used by developers, or you can make schema modifications using Active Directory Schema Manager, which is available in the Windows 2000 Resource Kit included on your Windows 2000 CD-ROM. The following sections introduce you to the Active Directory Schema Manager and shows you the basics of how it works. Advanced schema modification is beyond the scope of this book and is not a task that should be performed by a typical administrator.

You can use the Schema Manager to manage classes and attributes and set security permissions for them. You can also create new classes and attributes, but this action requires careful forethought and is not advisable without the help of properly trained developers.

The following section is included to give you an overview, just in case you want to experiment with the schema on a test machine.

USING THE SCHEMA MANAGER

Accessing the Schema Manager

The Active Directory Schema Manager is a MMC snap-in available by installing the Adminpak found in the I386 folder on your installation CD-ROM. Double-click the Adminpak icon, then choose to install all of the administrative tools.

After the tools are installed, you can access the Active Directory Schema Manager snap-in by manually loading the snap-in into an MMC console. After you install the Adminpak, some of the tools will be available by choosing Start⇨Programs⇨Windows 2000 Support Tools. In this location, you can access some of the tools, such as the Active Directory Replication Monitor, Security Administration Tools, and other utilities. Some tools, such as the Schema Manager are only available by manually loading the snap-in.

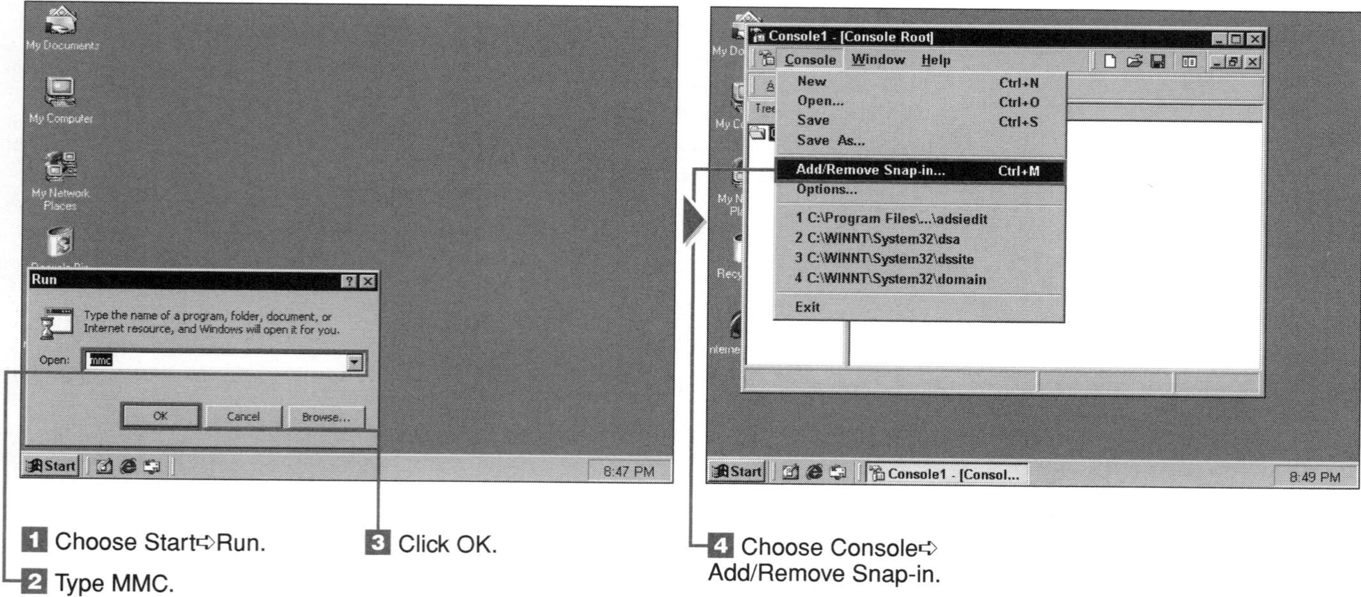

1 Choose Start⇨Run.

2 Type MMC.

3 Click OK.

4 Choose Console⇨Add/Remove Snap-in.

What does the Schema Manager do?

✔ The Schema Manager is an MMC snap-in that enables you to make modifications to Active Directory attributes and classes. From this interface, you can tailor the Active Directory to meet the needs of your organization. However, under normal circumstances, extensive changes should be performed only by highly skilled programmers. This is not a tool that you should use on a regular basis, if at all. In most cases, you can use the existing schema without altering it.

Why is the Schema Manager not included with the other Active Directory tools?

✔ The Active Directory contains three built-in administrative tools, Users and Computers, Sites and Services, and Domains and Trusts. The Schema Manager is in fact another Active Directory tool, but it is included only in the Adminpak because it is a resource tool only. The Schema Manager is not to be used as a regular management tool, and it is not installed with the Active Directory because of this purpose.

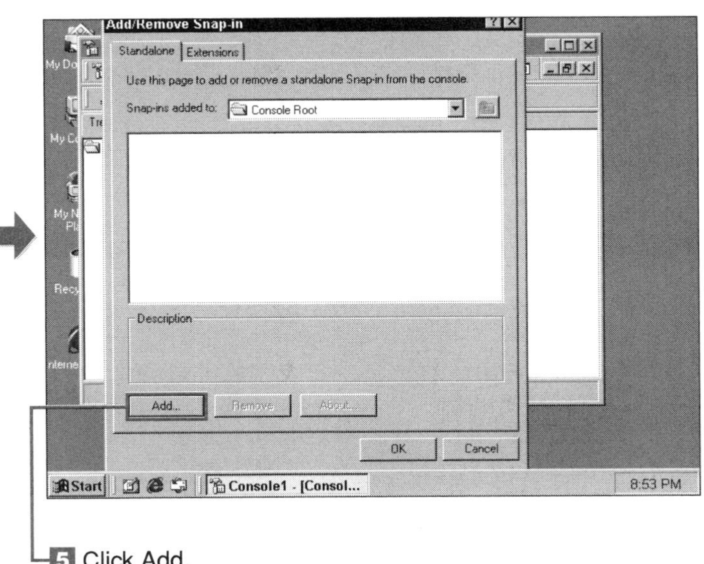

5 Click Add.

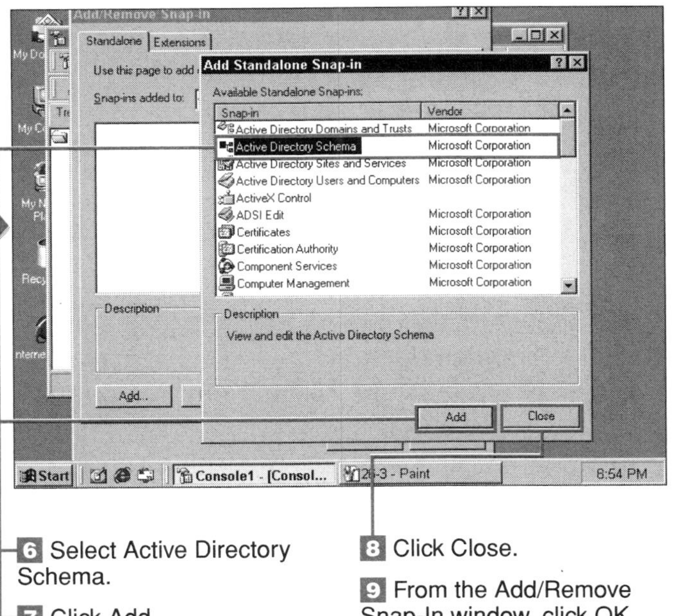

6 Select Active Directory Schema.

7 Click Add.

8 Click Close.

9 From the Add/Remove Snap-In window, click OK.

USING THE SCHEMA MANAGER

Examining class properties

The Schema Manager has containers for both classes and attributes. If you select the Classes container, a list of the Active Directory classes appear in the console. If you double-click one of them, you can see the properties sheets.

On the General tab, you see a description of the class, the Common Name (CN), the OID number, and the class type. The OID (Objected Identifiers) are unique numbers that are assigned to different object classes and objects themselves. The OID number is assigned by the International Standards Organization (ISO) and are completely unique for all directory services (such as ADS, NDS, and so on). If you wanted to create a new class of objects, you would need to apply to the ISO for an OID number. The uniqueness of the OID makes certain that different directory services follow an industry standard and are compatible.

The Category button enables you to change the category of the class in which the schema resides. Obviously, this is a feature you should carefully consider before changing.

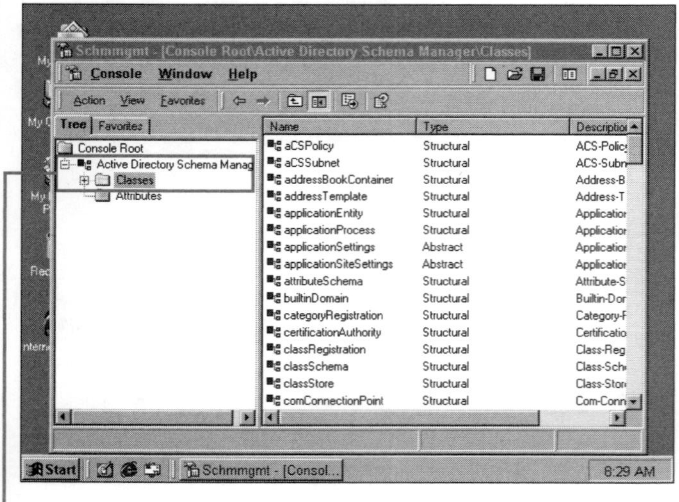

1 Expand the Active Directory Schema Manager and click Classes.

■ The classes appear in the details pane.

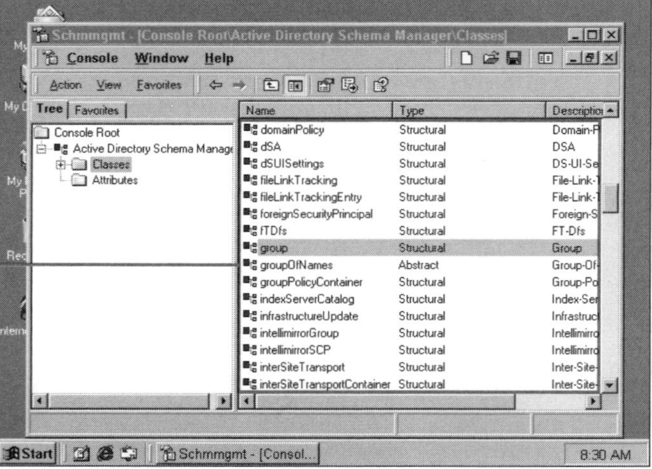

2 In the details pane, double-click a class you want to examine.

What does deactivating a class do?

- You cannot remove classes and attributes from the schema, but you can deactivate them by accessing the General tab. Deactivation marks the class or attribute as being ***unused***. The class or attribute still remains, but the Active Directory does not use it. In this case, replication of that class no longer occurs and you cannot create objects that belong to that class.

Can I delete a class?

- No. In order to prevent potential problems, classes and attributes cannot be deleted from the schema. You can, however, deactivate them so that they are not used.

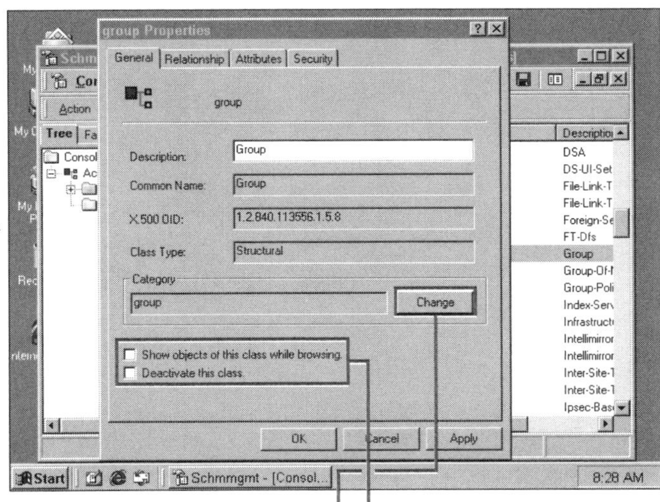

■ The class properties appear. On the General tab, you see the description, common name, OID, and category.

3 If you want to deactivate the class or show the objects in this class while browsing, click the appropriate check box.

4 If you want to change the category, click Change.

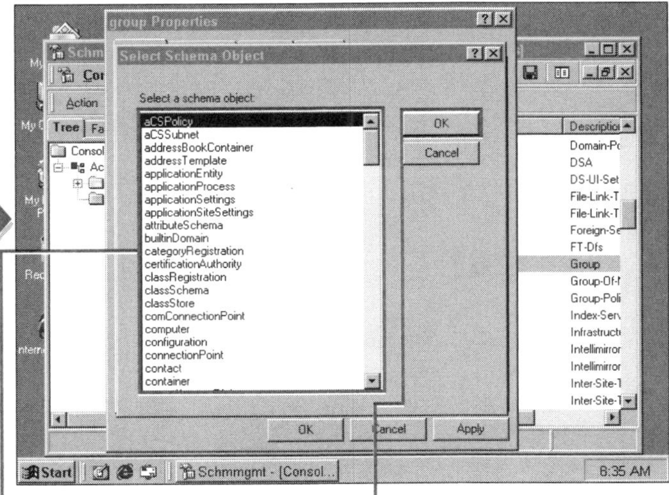

5 Select a schema object that will define the new category.

6 Click OK.

USING THE SCHEMA MANAGER

Examining class properties (continued)

The Relationship tab lists the Parent Class, Auxiliary Classes, and Possible Superior classes. You can add or remove both Auxiliary Classes and Possible Superior Classes. This feature enables you to further define the relationship between the class and other classes.

The Attributes tab enables you to define optional attributes for the class. Remember that attributes are used to define the objects residing within the class. Most class properties attributes contain both mandatory attribute(s) and optional attributes. The optional attributes further define the objects that can belong to that particular class.

You also have a typical Security tab. This feature enables you to determine which administrators have access to this particular Active Directory class. By default, account operators have Full Control, authenticated users have Read access, domain admins have Full Control, SELF has various rights, depending on your account, and SYSTEM has Full Control.

The security features within the schema manager allow you to fine-tune who can access different classes and attributes and what permissions those classes have for the classes and attributes.

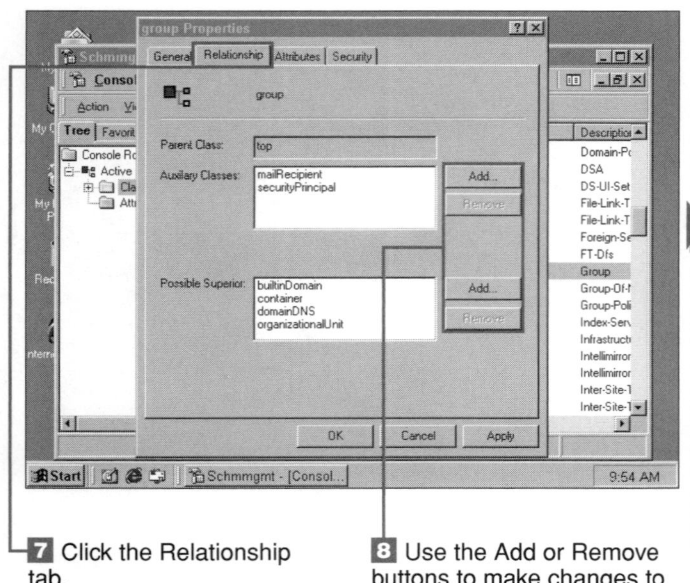

7 Click the Relationship tab.

8 Use the Add or Remove buttons to make changes to the Auxiliary Classes or Possible Superior Classes.

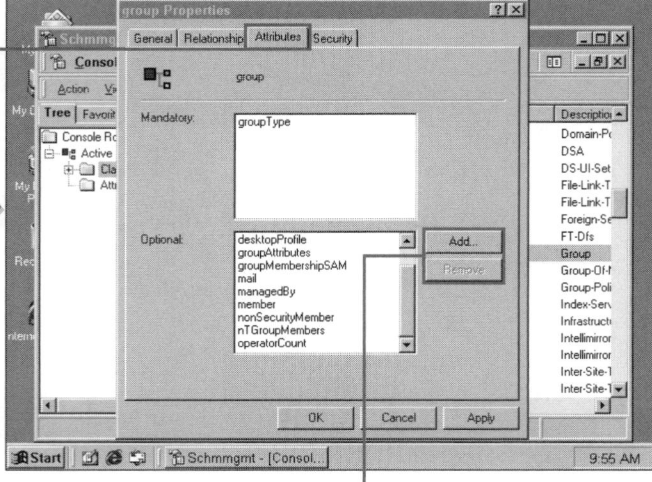

9 Click the Attributes tab.

10 Use the Add or Remove buttons to make changes to the Optional attributes.

What is the purpose of adding optional attributes?

- Optional attributes further define object attributes for a particular class. In most cases, object classes have at least one mandatory attribute that must apply to every object for the object to belong to that class. Optional attributes further define the objects in that class. You can add attributes to the class to enable you to include objects that need additional attributes defined for them. On the Attributes tab, you use the Add button to add more attributes from the list that appears.

What security changes should be made?

- You can fine-tune the security settings for each class as desired. In general, you should be very careful who you give more than Read access. However, in some cases, you may want certain users to have more control over certain classes, and the security feature enables you to make those changes as needed. As with any security policy, you should carefully plan security changes.

VIII

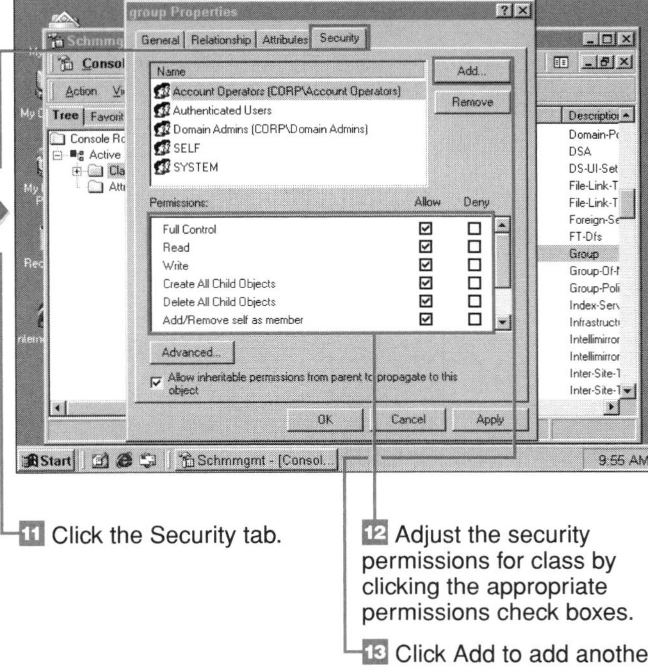

11 Click the Security tab.

12 Adjust the security permissions for class by clicking the appropriate permissions check boxes.

13 Click Add to add another user or group to the list.

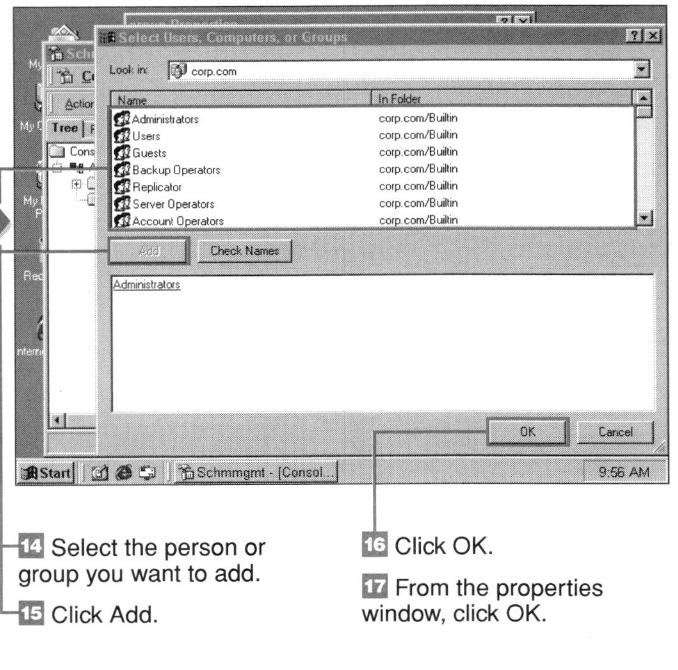

14 Select the person or group you want to add.

15 Click Add.

16 Click OK.

17 From the properties window, click OK.

USING THE SCHEMA MANAGER

Examining attribute properties

The properties sheet for all attributes consists of a General tab. On this tab, you find the description of the attribute, common name (CN), OID number, and a syntax and range field that defines how the attribute is described.

You may notice that some attributes have the statement, "This attribute is multi-valued." This means that this attribute can store multiple characteristics. For example, if a user has more than one e-mail address, the attribute that defines "e-mail address" can hold more than one e-mail address for that object.

In the bottom of the window, you see several check boxes that allow you to manage the attribute as needed.

In some classes, such as the System class, all the edits may not be allowed, depending on the attribute.

As with schema class modifications, you should be very careful before modifying attributes due to the implications in the Active Directory.

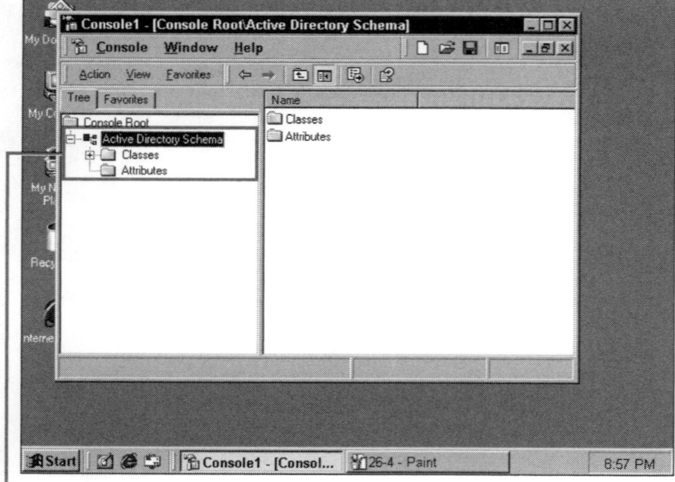

1 Expand the Active Directory Schema in the console.

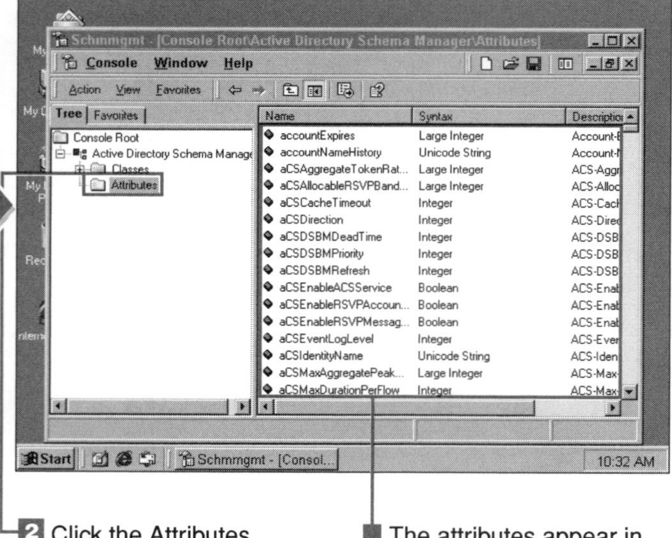

2 Click the Attributes container.

■ The attributes appear in the details pane.

Can I delete an attribute?

- No. The Active Directory does not allow you to delete either a class or an attribute. You can, however, deactivate an attribute by clicking the check box on the General tab. Make certain that you have planned carefully and understand the implications an attribute deactivation may have on the Active Directory and its functionality in your network.

What is the Replicate This Attribute To The Global Catalog check box option?

- The Replicate This Attribute To The Global Catalog check box enables you to force the attribute, and any changes you make to it, to be replicated to the global catalog server, which will then replicate the attribute to all domain controllers. Once again, these option should not be used without specific guidance or instructions from Active Directory programmers.

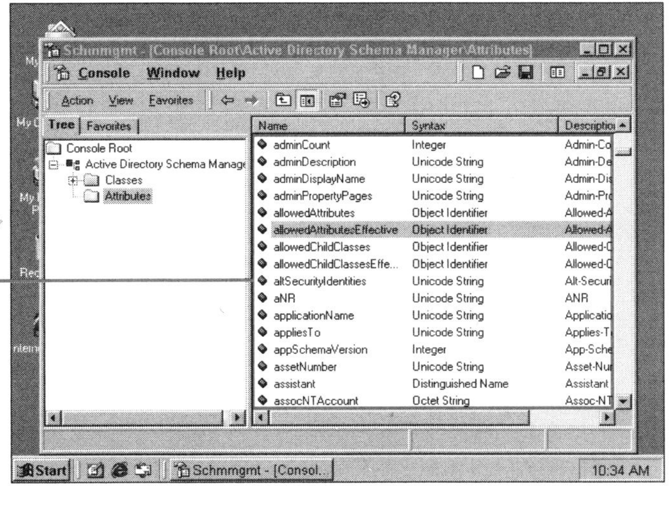

3 Scroll to find the attribute you want to view and then double-click it.

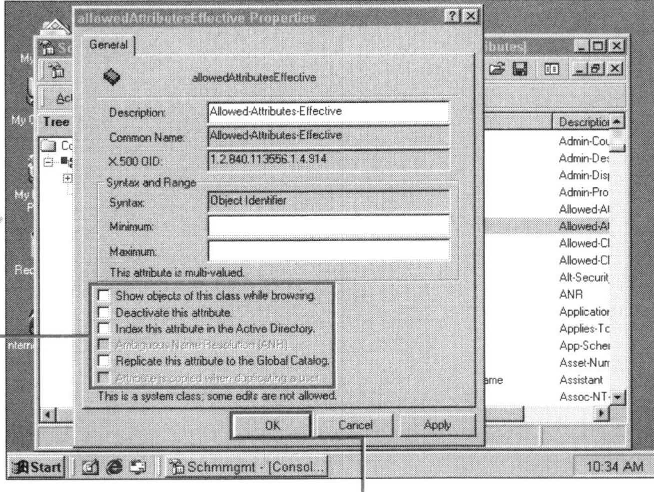

4 Click the appropriate check boxes to make changes to the attribute as needed.

5 Click OK.

BACKING UP THE ACTIVE DIRECTORY

As with any data on your computer, a good backup plan is extremely wise. The Active Directory is no exception, and you should plan a regular backup plan to ensure that you can recover your Active Directory database in case of a system error.

In general, Microsoft recommends that you store your Windows 2000 system files and the Active Directory database and transaction log files on separate disks. If one disk should fail, at least you have not lost all your data at one time. You should also plan to back up the data on a regular basis so that it can be restored if necessary.

To back up the Active Directory database and transaction log files, you use the Backup utility included in Windows 2000. When you use the Backup Wizard to back up your Active Directory, choose to back up "System State Data."

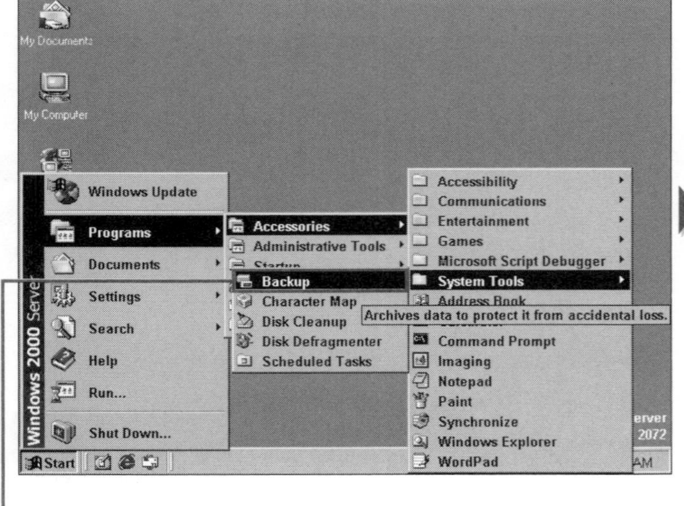

1 Choose Start➪Programs➪Accessories➪System Tools➪Backup.

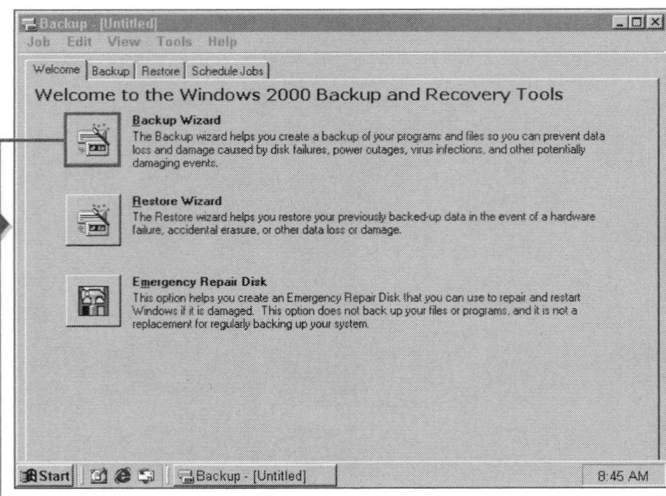

2 Click Backup Wizard.

Do I have to use the wizard to run a backup job?

- No. The wizard is provided to help you create a backup, but after you have used the wizard and are comfortable performing the backup manually, you can use the Backup tab in the Backup utility to manually run it.

What is System State Data?

- *System State Data* is a term used to describe the following data in a Windows 2000 domain controller:
  - The Registry
  - COM+ Class Registration Database
  - System Boot Files
  - Certificate Services Database (if the server is a certificate server)
  - Active Directory Services Database
  - SYSVOL Directory, which is a server copy of the domain's public files that are replicated among domain controllers

■ The Backup Wizard appears.

3 Click Next to continue.

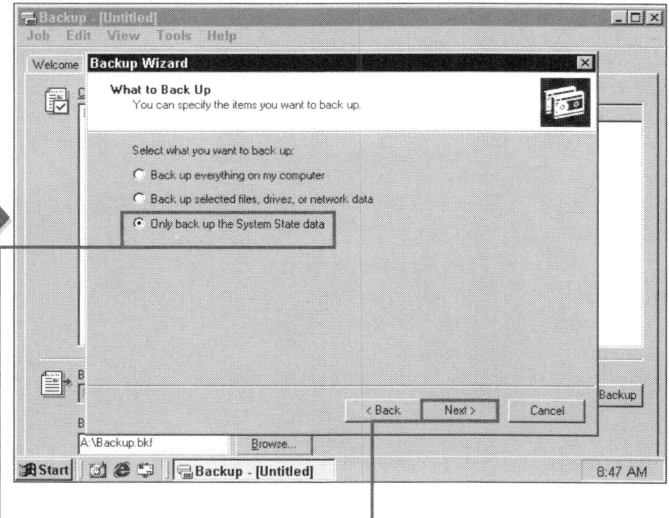

4 To back up only the Active Directory, click the Only Back Up System State Data radio button.

5 Click Next to continue

CONTINUED

BACKING UP THE ACTIVE DIRECTORY

CONTINUED

You can back up your files to a number of media options. In most cases, backups are written to a tape backup, and Windows 2000 supports all major tape back types, including digital audio tape (DAT). You can also use Zip or Jaz drives for backup purposes.

You also have the option to configure advanced backup options. First, you can choose the type of backup that you want to perform. The options are normal, copy, incremental, differential, and daily. A definition of each option is presented on the next page. Typically, most environments use a mixture of normal and incremental or differential backups. The goal is to reduce the amount of daily backup time while keeping the data that is backed up most current.

You can also back up any migrated remote storage data, which typically does not apply to an Active Directory backup. Windows 2000 has the ability to allow you to store data in remote locations on tape, CD, or Zip disk formats.

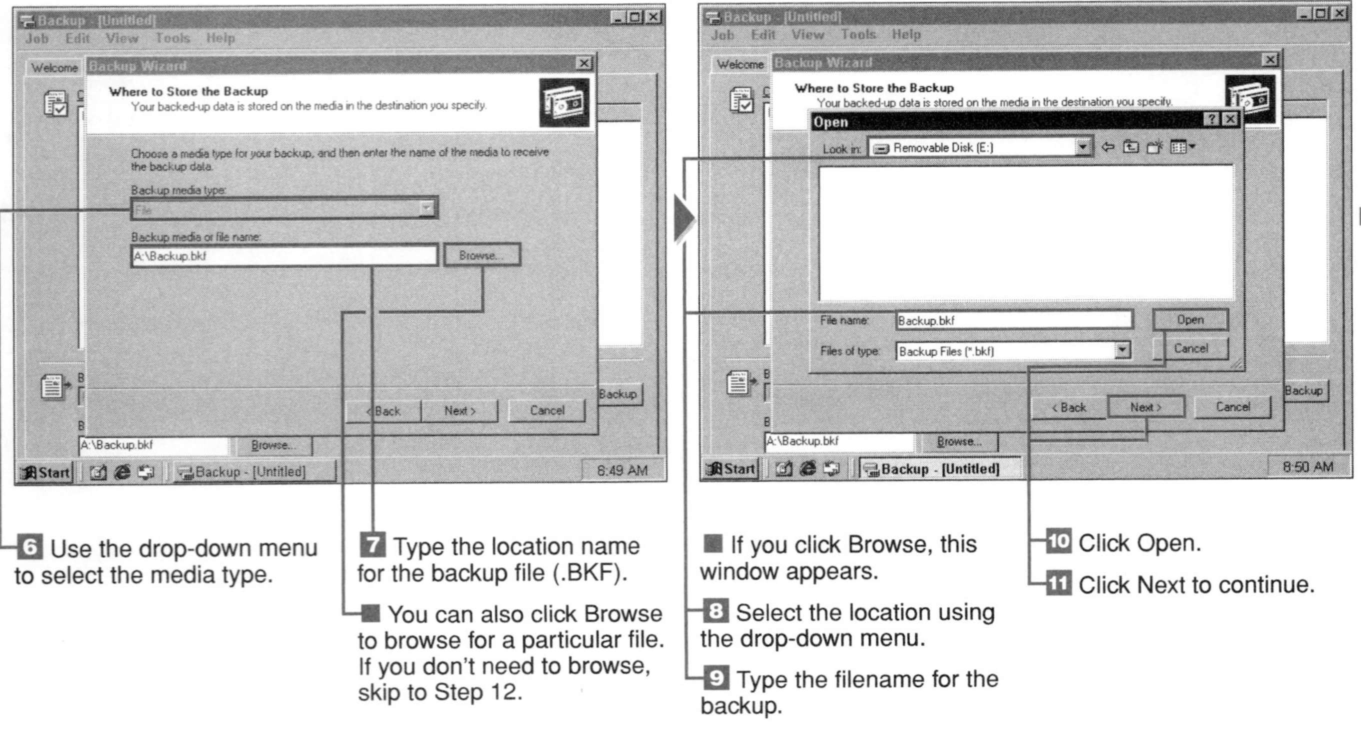

6 Use the drop-down menu to select the media type.

7 Type the location name for the backup file (.BKF).

■ You can also click Browse to browse for a particular file. If you don't need to browse, skip to Step 12.

■ If you click Browse, this window appears.

8 Select the location using the drop-down menu.

9 Type the filename for the backup.

10 Click Open.

11 Click Next to continue.

What is a definition of each backup type?

The following list describes each backup type:

- **Normal** backs up all selected files and marks each file as backed up.
- **Copy** backs up all selected files but does not mark them as backed up.
- **Incremental** backs up selected files only if they have not been backed up or have changed, and marks them as backed up.
- **Differential** backs up selected files only if they have not been backed up or have changes, but does not mark them as backed up.
- **Daily** backs up only files that have changed today, but does not mark them as backed up.

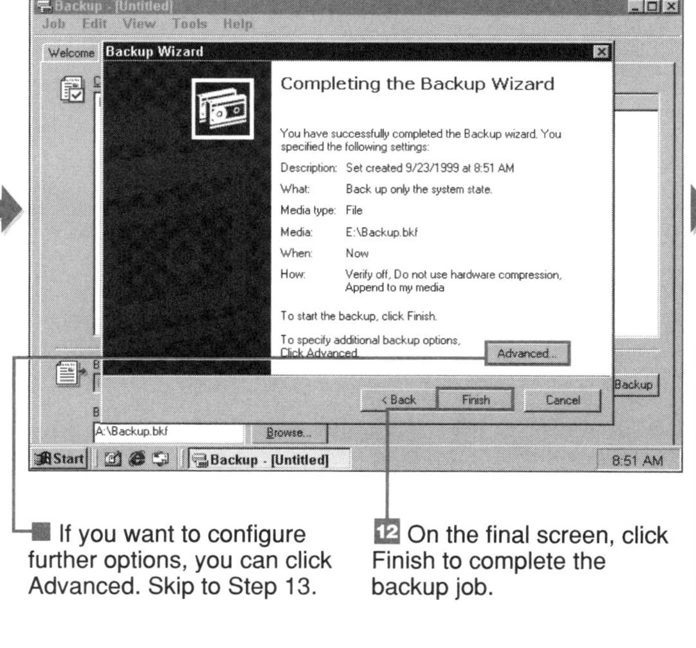

■ If you want to configure further options, you can click Advanced. Skip to Step 13.

12 On the final screen, click Finish to complete the backup job.

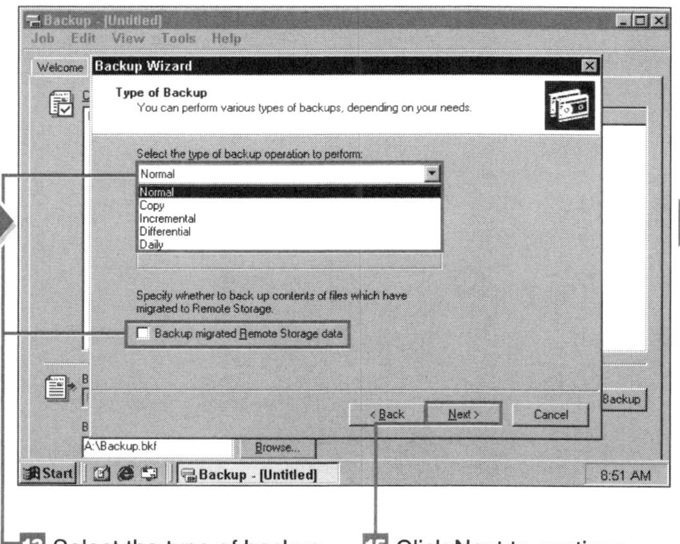

13 Select the type of backup you want to perform.

14 Click this check box if you want to back up migrated data that has been stored in a remote storage location.

15 Click Next to continue.

CONTINUED

BACKING UP THE ACTIVE DIRECTORY
CONTINUED

The wizard presents you with the option to verify the data after backup. This option allows the system to read the backed-up data to verify it. Verification can take some time, but it does enable you to make certain the data has been backed up correctly. Aside from using this option, you can also take a look at the backup log file to verify the backup job. You can also use hardware compression if it is available on the backup media. Compression gives you more space on the media, but you should make certain that all drives you may use for a restore operation can read a compressed backup job.

Next, you can choose to append the backup job to an existing job on the media, or you can choose to completely overwrite an older job and replace it with the new one.

Additionally, the wizard enables you to perform the backup job immediately, or you can choose to schedule it for a specific time.

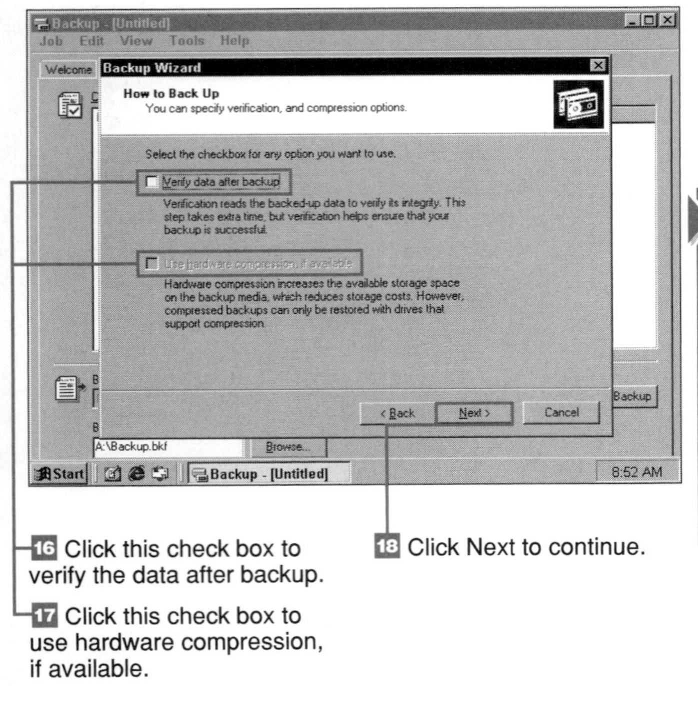

16 Click this check box to verify the data after backup.

17 Click this check box to use hardware compression, if available.

18 Click Next to continue.

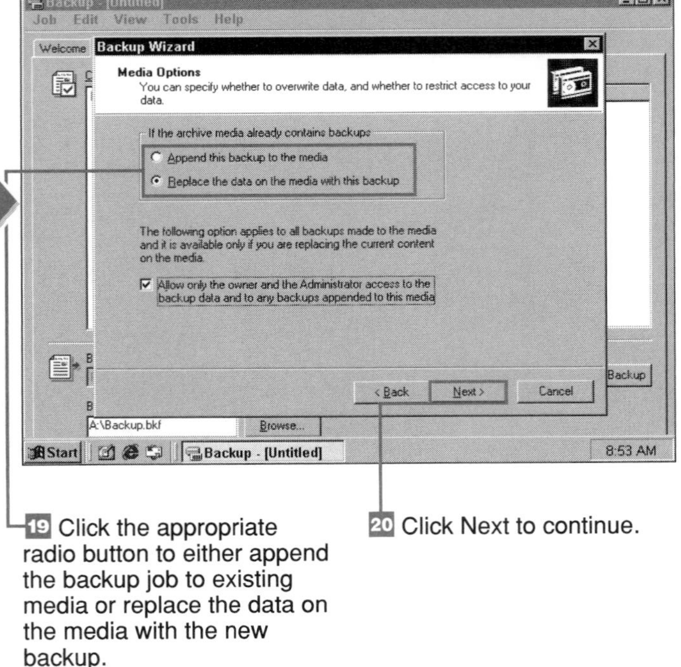

19 Click the appropriate radio button to either append the backup job to existing media or replace the data on the media with the new backup.

20 Click Next to continue.

Why does the wizard give me the option to schedule the backup job?

- The Backup utility in Windows 2000 enables you to schedule backups so that they automatically occur at a certain time every day. For example, you may want your backup jobs to run at 9 p.m. each evening after the workday is over. This automated feature allows the system to handle the backup procedures so that busy administrators can concentrate on other tasks.

What is the Backup Label?

- The backup label is simply a name that you give the backup job. In environments in which multiple backup jobs occur, you may have a particular naming convention in use so that you can easily locate different backup jobs. The Backup Wizard provides a default label that includes the date and time of the backup, but you can change this as desired.

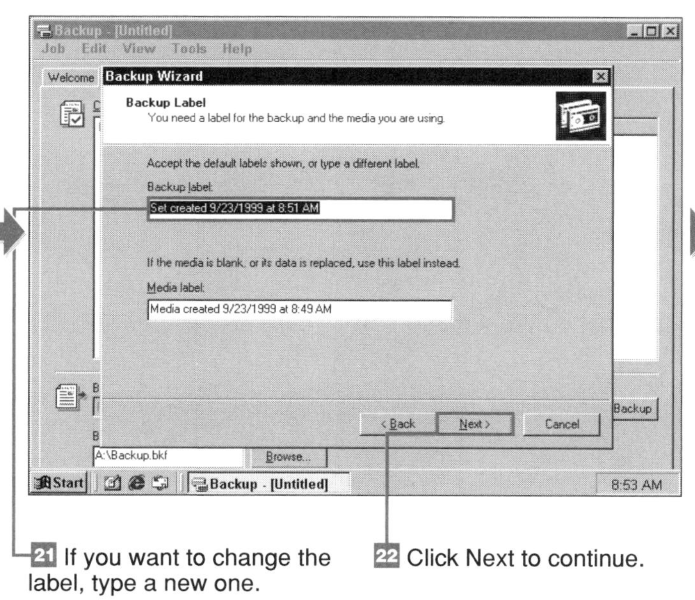

21 If you want to change the label, type a new one.

22 Click Next to continue.

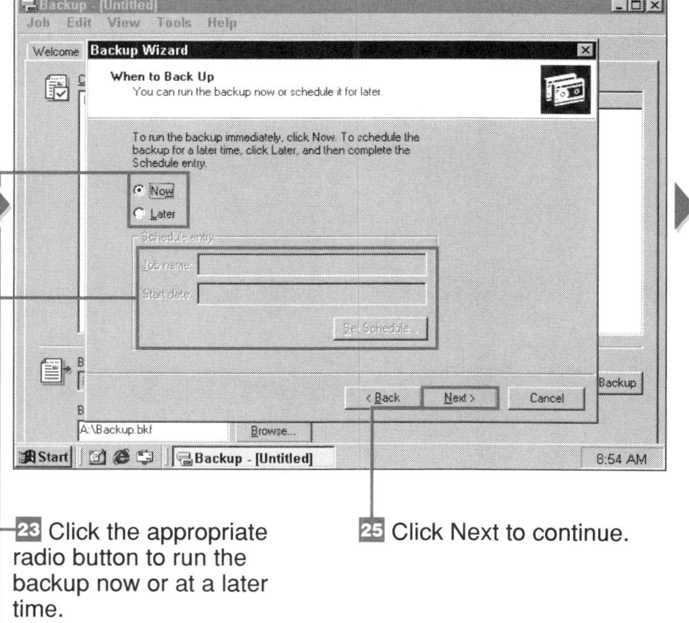

23 Click the appropriate radio button to run the backup now or at a later time.

24 If you choose to run the backup at a later time, use these boxes to set the schedule.

25 Click Next to continue.

CONTINUED

BACKING UP THE ACTIVE DIRECTORY CONTINUED

After you finish the wizard, a backup window displays the progress of the backup job. The window also tells you what is being backed up and to what media. Should you need to stop the backup job while it is in progress, you can click Cancel. However, if you cancel the backup job while it is in progress, you cannot restart it. You have to recreate the backup job and start all over to perform the backup.

As mentioned at the beginning of this section, the importance of an effective backup plan for both the Active Directory and system files cannot be understated. The backup plan lets you recover your data in case of system failure. Although a regular backup plan may take some configuration time and certainly requires storage resources, the results are well worth it in case your server goes down.

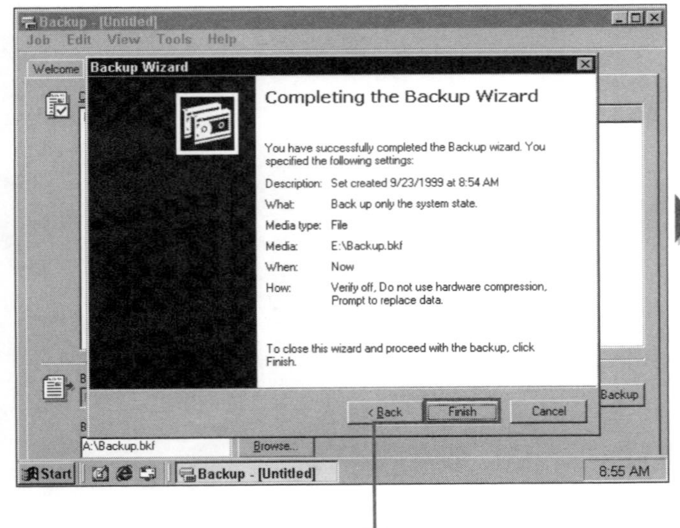

26 Click Finish to complete the wizard.

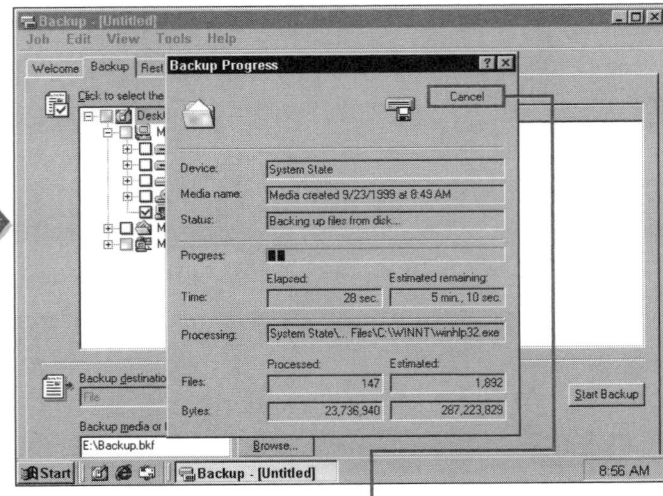

■ The backup job begins. You can click Cancel to stop it if necessary.

RESTORING THE ACTIVE DIRECTORY

If you should experience a server or disk failure, your first task is to restore the Active Directory data after the server is back online. To do this, you use the Restore Wizard in the Windows Backup utility. However, you cannot restore the Active Directory with your server running in normal mode. Instead, you must restore Active Directory in a "safe" mode called Directory Services Restore Mode.

To go into Directory Services Restore Mode, reboot your server and press the F8 key at reboot. A menu appears with several booting options. Select Directory Services Restore Mode and press Enter. The computer boots into safe mode. Log on with your administrator account, and then click OK to the message telling you the computer is running in safe mode.

After the computer boots in safe mode, you can run the Restore Wizard to restore your Active Directory.

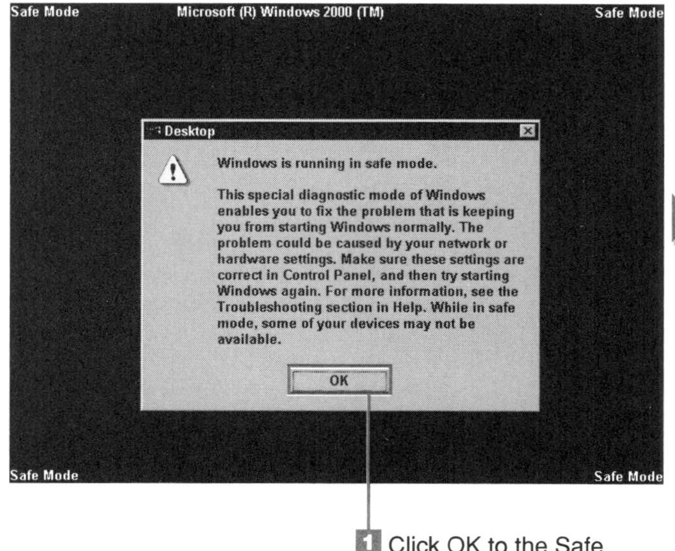

1 Click OK to the Safe Mode message that appears after you log on.

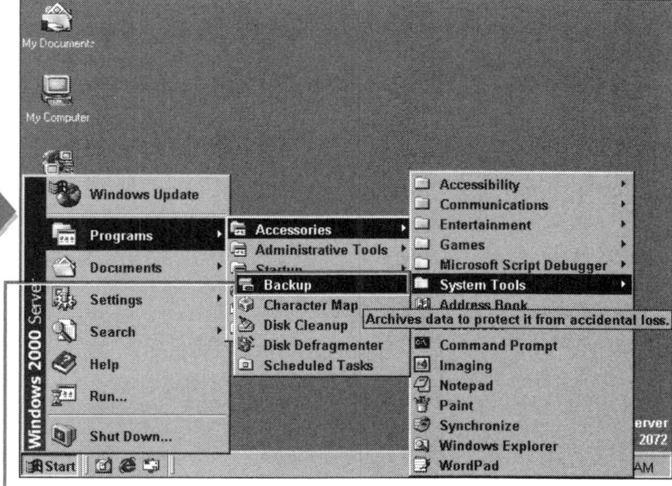

2 Choose Start⇨Programs⇨Accessories⇨System Tools⇨Backup.

CONTINUED

RESTORING THE ACTIVE DIRECTORY

CONTINUED

When you use the Restore Wizard, you select what items you want to restore. This is particularly useful if a folder is lost. You can restore the folder and the files in it without having to perform a complete restore of your entire system.

To restore the Active Directory, you choose to restore System State Data.

The wizard may prompt you for the location of the backup job, and then the restore process begins. After the restoration is complete, you can reboot your computer. When the server is back online, changes are replicated from the other domain controllers so that the Active Directory database on your computer is up-to-date.

In some instances, however, you may not wish for certain data to be updated through replication. In this case, you can choose to *authoritatively restore* that data. You can learn how to use an authoritative restore in the next section.

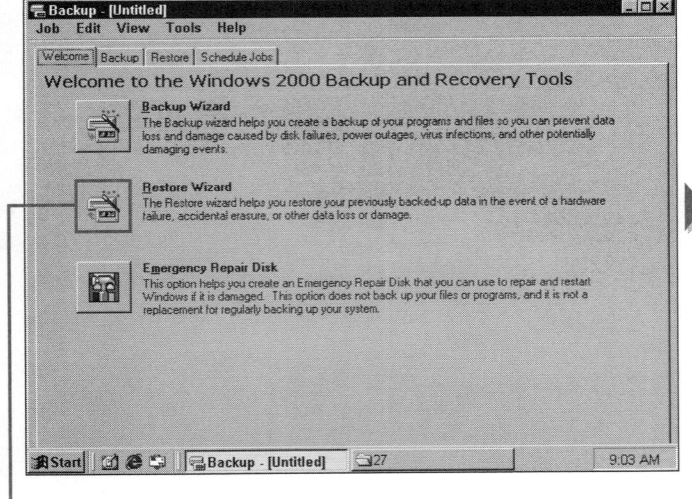

3 Click Restore Wizard.

■ The Restore Wizard appears.

4 Click Next to continue.

Can I restore other data when I am restoring the System State Data, or should I perform this task individually?

- You can restore any data that you want by selecting the desired data in the file list. The Restore Wizard then restores all the data that you select.

What happens if I leave my server in safe mode?

- Safe mode is provided so that you can repair problematic parts of your system. When safe mode is in effect, a limited number of hardware drivers are running and your server services are disabled. If you leave your server in safe mode, it is not available on the network or to service clients. Also, your Active Directory data cannot be updated through replication with other domain controllers until you reboot into normal mode.

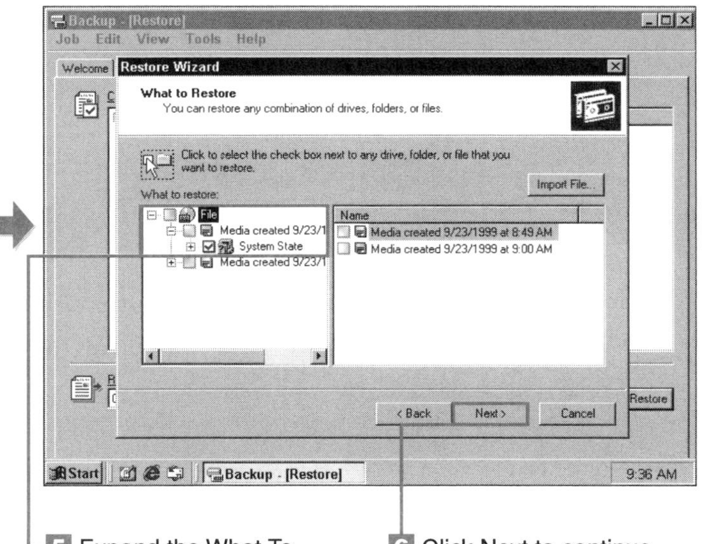

5 Expand the What To Restore File and select System State by clicking the check box.

6 Click Next to continue.

7 Click Finish to perform the restore.

PERFORMING AN AUTHORITATIVE RESTORE

After performing an Active Directory restore using the Restore Wizard, you may also need to perform an authoritative restore as well before rebooting from safe mode. An authoritative restore is used to tag certain information to prevent the Active Directory replication process from updating it. For example, say that you accidentally delete an OU. The deletion is then replicated to the other domain controllers. You can restore that OU from backup, but when you bring your server online, the other domain controllers delete it again because of replication. An authoritative restore prevents this from happening. When you authoritatively restore an object, OU, or domain, the restore is tagged as authoritative and replicated to the other domain controllers instead of the domain controllers replicating the error back to the server.

The authoritative restore is performed using the command line utility, Ntdsutil, which is accessible from the Run line. If you want to perform an authoritative restore, you must do so after the Backup Wizard restore has taken place and before you reboot your server out of safe mode.

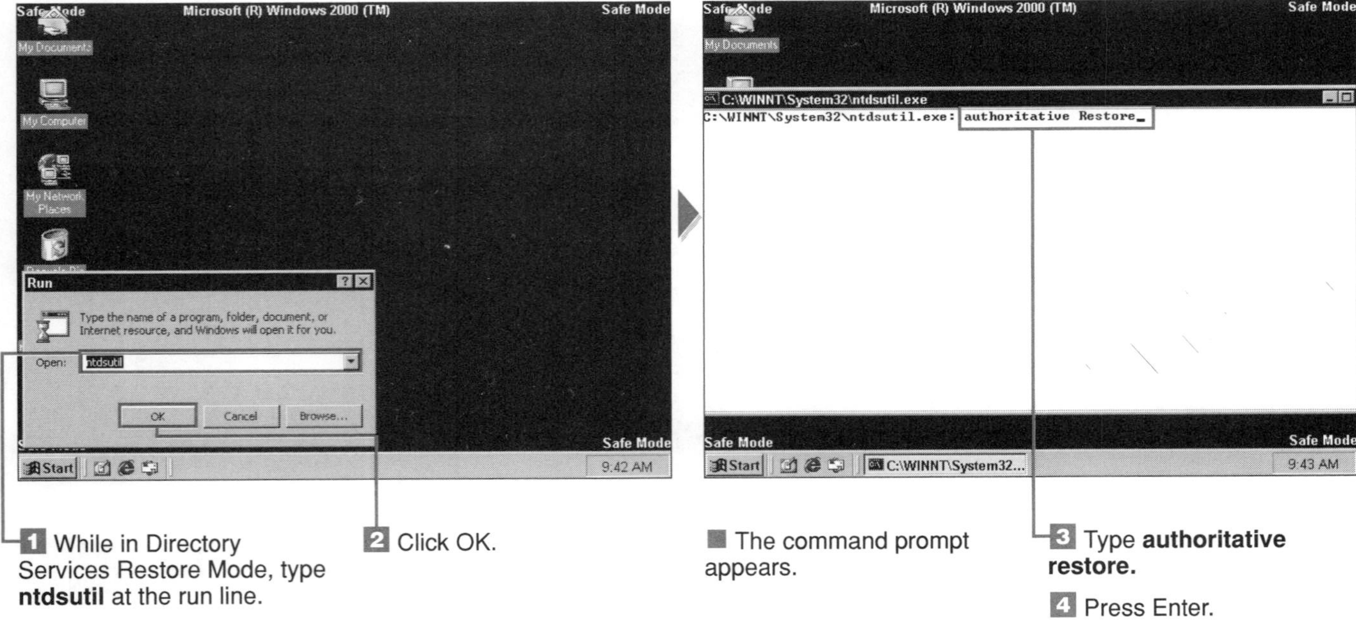

1 While in Directory Services Restore Mode, type **ntdsutil** at the run line.

2 Click OK.

■ The command prompt appears.

3 Type **authoritative restore.**

4 Press Enter.

What happens if I perform a restore and reboot my server before running an authoritative restore?

- If you reboot into normal mode before using authoritative restore, the server will be updated through replication. If you are trying to replace an accidentally deleted object or another operation in which replication should not overwrite the restore, then you must use the authoritative restore function. If not, the error is replicated back to your server and you have to go through the restore process again.

Can Ntdsutil perform other tasks?

- Yes. Ntdsutil can help you with other Active Directory management tasks. To see a list, simply access Ntdsutil at the Run line and then type **Help** when the console opens.

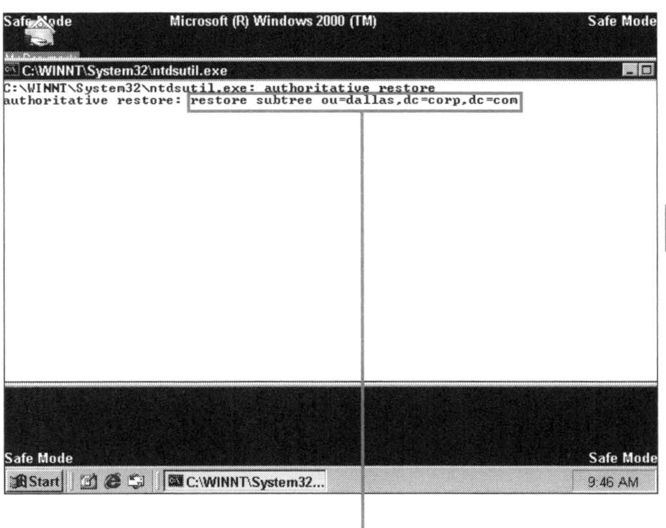

5 Type **restore subtree** followed by the correct information for the object, OU, or domain.

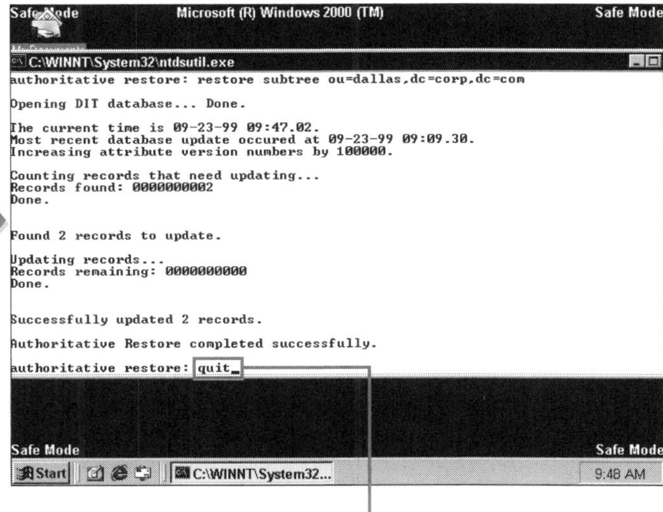

6 Review the results and type **quit** to end the Ntdsutil session.

CLEANING THE LOSTANDFOUND FOLDER

For the most part, Active Directory maintains itself. It performs replication automatically, defragments the database, and takes care of database issues. The Active Directory also performs "garbage cleanup" at 12-hour intervals to remove unneeded log files and delete old, or *tombstoned*, objects from the Active Directory.

One item you should occasionally check, however, is the LostAndFound folder. LostAndFound is a hidden container in Active Directory Users and Computer. From time to time, misplaced objects are put in the LostAndFound container. For example, say you create an object to be added to a container. At the same time, another administrator deletes the container. Now, the object has nowhere to go. Because the Active Directory cannot determine where to place the object, it is put in the LostAndFound container and held there.

As a part of your administrative duties, you should occasionally check the LostAndFound container to see if the objects residing there need to be deleted or moved to a valid container.

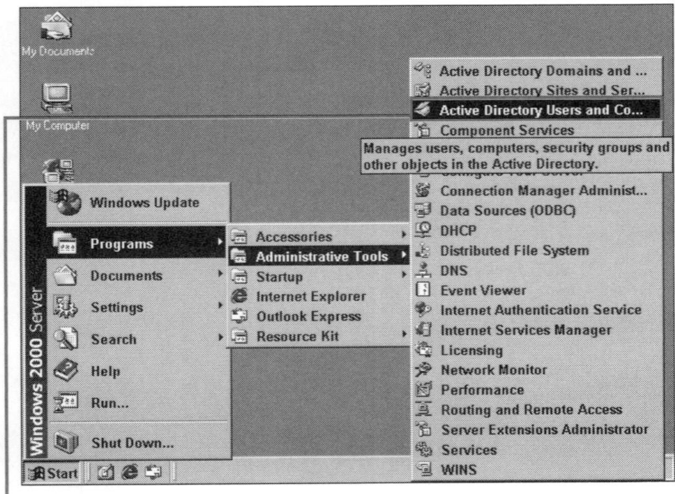

1 Choose Start➪Programs➪Administrative Tools➪Active Directory Users and Computers.

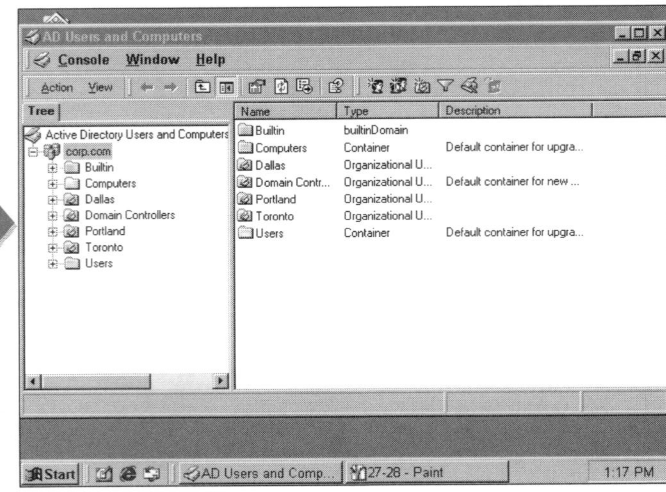

■ The Console opens.

How can I move a LostAndFound object?

- If you find an object in the LostAndFound container that you want to keep, you can move it to a different location. Select the object and then choose Action⇨Move. In the window that appears, select a new location for the object.

How often should I check the LostAndFound container?

- Objects end up in the LostAndFound container only in environments with multiple domain controllers and even multiple domains. In an Enterprise environment, you should check the LostAndFound container every few weeks because a greater possibility of misplaced objects exists. In medium to smaller environments, a once-a-month check is plenty.

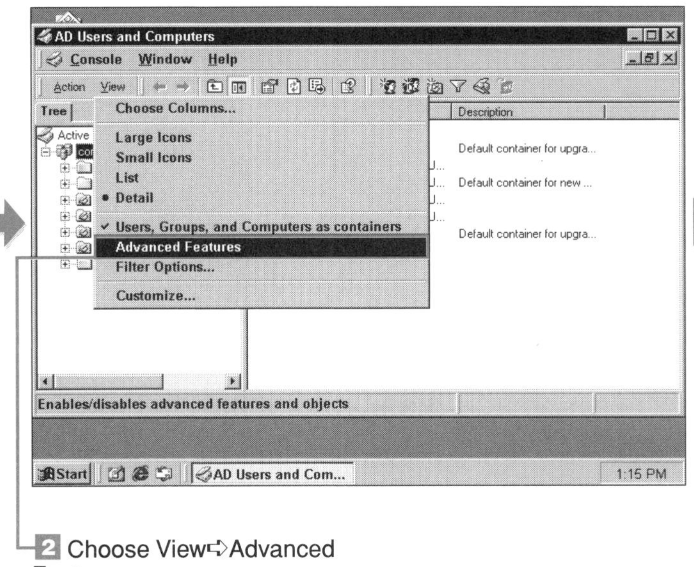

2 Choose View⇨Advanced Features.

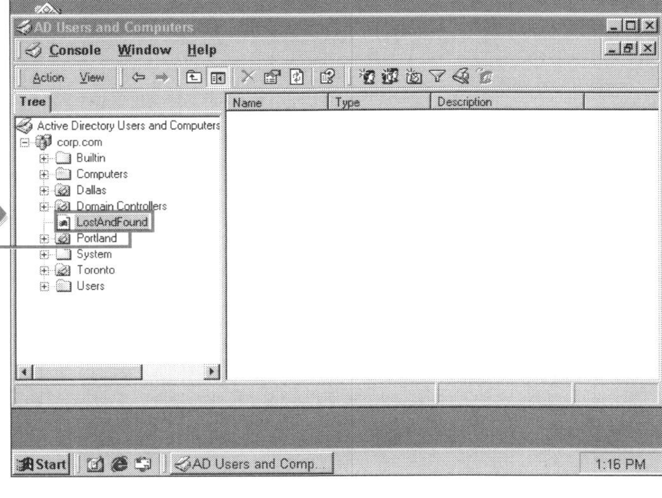

3 Click LostAndFound.

4 Review any files in the details pane and delete or move them as necessary.

RESOURCE KIT TOOLS

Installing the Resource Kit

To help you manage and maintain the Active Directory, the Windows 2000 Resource Kit contains some additional tools for Active Directory management. These tools are described in the following sections so that you can see what tools are available, what they do, and when you would want to use them.

Before you can access the tools, you must install the Resource Kit that is located on your Windows 2000 Server CD-ROM. Browse the CD, open the Support folder, and then open the Reskit folder. Double-click the Setup icon to install the Resource Kit on your server. The Resource Kit contains both tools and online documentation to assist you with a variety of Windows 2000 features and options.

You can also expect Microsoft to release updates, patches, and additional tools for the Active Directory from time to time. You can keep abreast of these updates by accessing the update Web site available at Start⇨Windows Update.

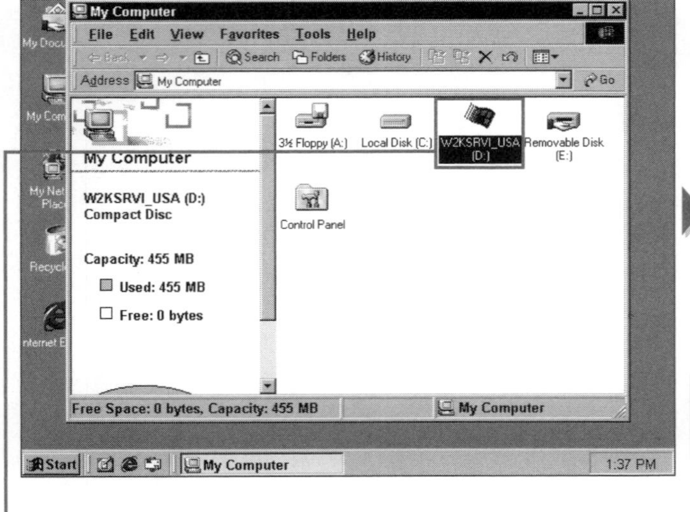

1 Open the installation CD-ROM.

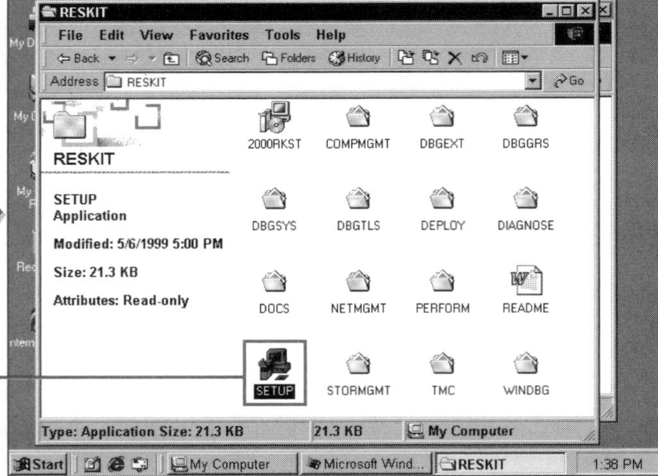

2 Open Support, Reskit, and then double-click Setup.

■ Follow the on-screen instructions to complete setup.

RESOURCE KIT TOOLS

Accessing the Resource Kit

After you install the Resource Kit, you can access it from the Start⇨Programs menu. You see from this menu that you can choose to open either the online books or the Tools Console. Choose the Tools Console.

When the console opens, you can expand the Resource Kit, expand Windows 2000 Resource Kit, and click on Tools A to Z. A list of available tools on the Resource Kit appears in the details pane.

If you are uncertain about which tool you want to use, click the Tool Categories container in the left pane so that each tool is accompanied by a short description in the details pane.

The following sections point out the tools that are useful with Active Directory management and when you should consider using each particular tool.

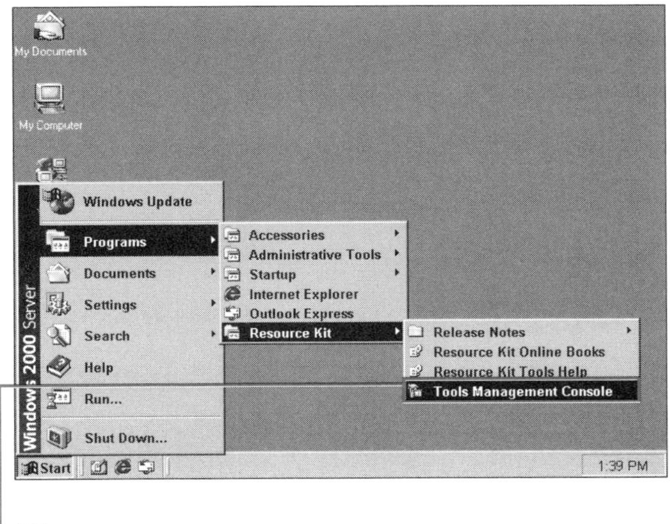

1 Choose Start⇨Programs⇨Resource Kit⇨Tools Management Console.

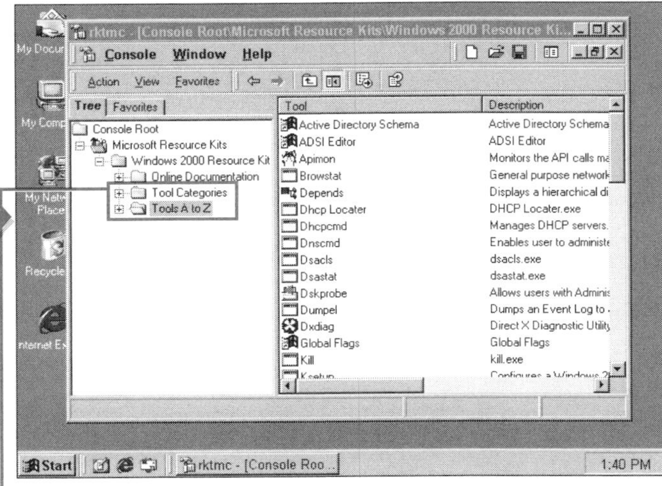

2 Expand the Resource Kit and click Tools A to Z or Tools Categories.

RESOURCE KIT TOOLS

Dsacls.exe

The Dsacls.exe (Directory Services Access Control Lists) tool helps you manage access control lists for the Active Directory. When you launch Dsacls.exe, a command prompt opens and displays information about the utility. The purpose of the utility is to display or modify existing Access Control Lists of Active Directory Objects. ACLs determine who can access what Active Directory object. With this command line utility, you can view information about the current ACLs and use the string command to modify ACLs as desired.

When the utility opens, you can see a list of switches and command line codes available to help you manage ACLs. This tool is a useful way to manage ACLs from one location, but you may face a slight learning curve to master the syntax options.

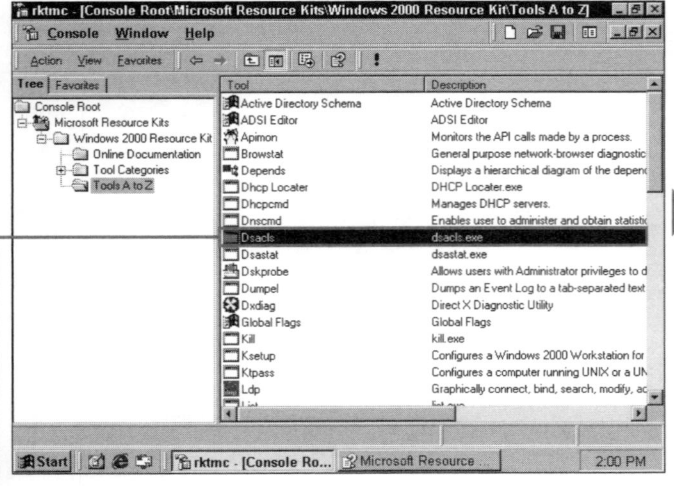

1 Double-click Dsacls.exe in the Resource Kit details pane.

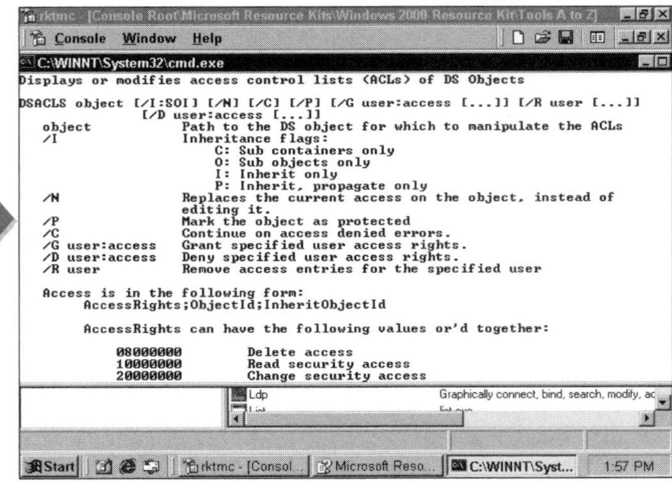

■ The utility opens with a list of syntax and switch options.

RESOURCE KIT TOOLS

Dsastat.exe

Dsastat.exe (Directory Services Status) is a command-line utility that performs diagnostic tests to detect differences between naming contexts on domain controllers.

For example, you can use Dsastat.exe to compare two different directory trees across different domains. The tool gathers statistical information about the capacity of the domain controllers, such as database size and the number of objects per server. By gathering these statistics, Dsastat.exe can determine if the domain controllers have an accurate image of their own domains.

Dsastat.exe has switches that allow you to refine its operation to specific domains, domain controllers, or global catalogs. It is particularly helpful as a troubleshooting tool.

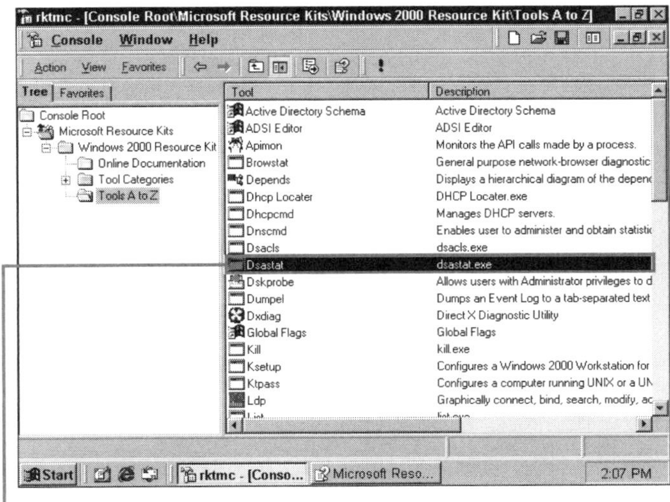

1 Double-click Dsastat.exe in the Resource Kit details pane.

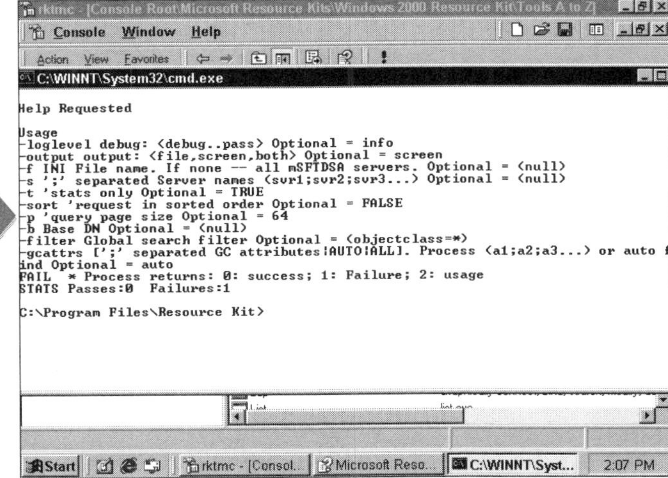

■ The utility opens with a list of syntax and switch options.

RESOURCE KIT TOOLS

Ldp.exe

Ldp.exe is a graphical tool that allows you to perform a variety of LDAP (Lightweight Directory Access Protocol) actions. You can use the tool to connect, bind, and search different servers and gain the LDAP information about different directory objects.

The most important aspect of the Ldp.exe tool is the display of *metadata*, which is information about the attributes of each object within the directory. You can search for a particular object and gain its full LDAP name, such as CN=Corpsrv, CN=Servers, DC=Corp, DC=com. This information is not displayed using a typical LDAP search for an Active Directory object. By using this tool, you can troubleshoot LDAP retrieval problems.

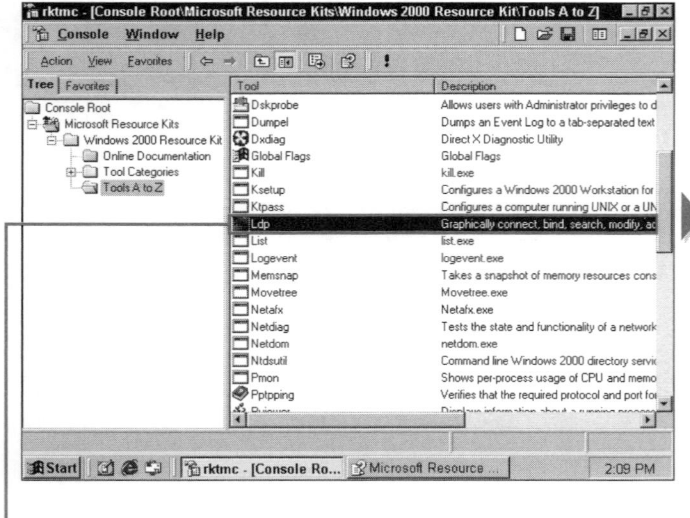

1 Double-click Ldp.exe in the Resource Kit details pane.

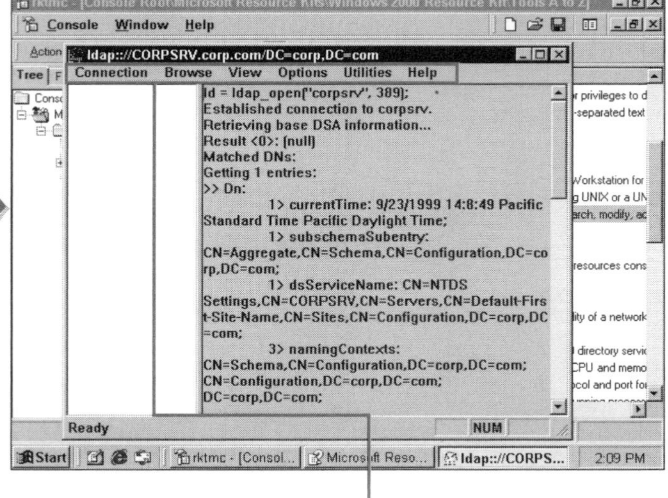

■ The window opens.

2 Use the menus to connect to different servers and gather LDAP information.

RESOURCE KIT TOOLS

Movetree.exe

Movetree.exe is a useful tool for administrators who manage Active Directory environments that are undergoing organizational changes. You can use Movetree.exe to move Active Directory objects and OUs between different domains in a single forest. This utility can be of great value if you find yourself needing to consolidate two domains or move objects and OUs between domains within a forest.

Although Movetree.exe is a useful utility, you should note that the utility does not solve all the problems with a major resource movement or domain consolidation. Some objects, due to data storage, cannot be moved, and you must perform these moves manually. As always, careful planning to attempt to avert resource movement or domain consolidation is your best action. Yet, in the case of a resource movement or consolidation, this command line utility can be of great value.

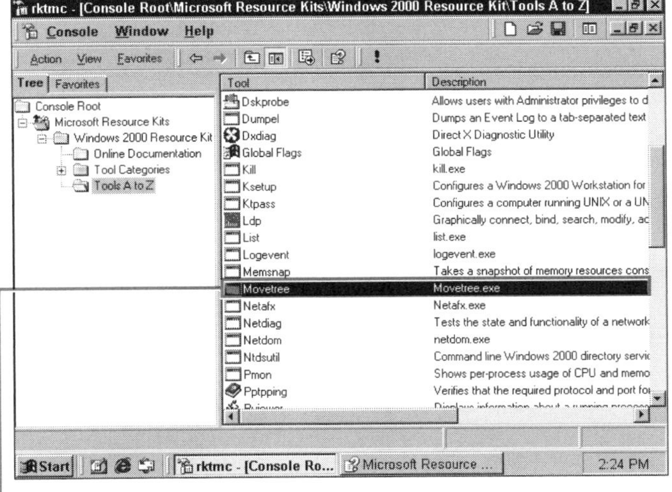

1 Double-click Movetree.exe in the Resource Kit details pane.

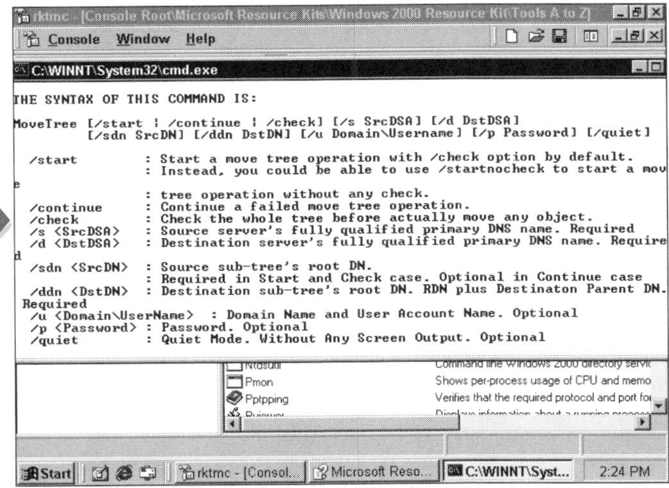

■ The utility opens and displays a list of command line switches and options.

APPENDIX A

ENFORCING PASSWORD HISTORY

Password history allows the computer to remember passwords that have previously been used on the system. By remembering passwords, the computer can tell a user when he or she is attempting to reuse a password that has previously been used.

You can determine how many passwords you want the policy to remember. The default is only 1, but you can set the system to remember as many as you like. The decision you make depends on the security desires of your organization and whether or not you allow users to reuse old passwords.

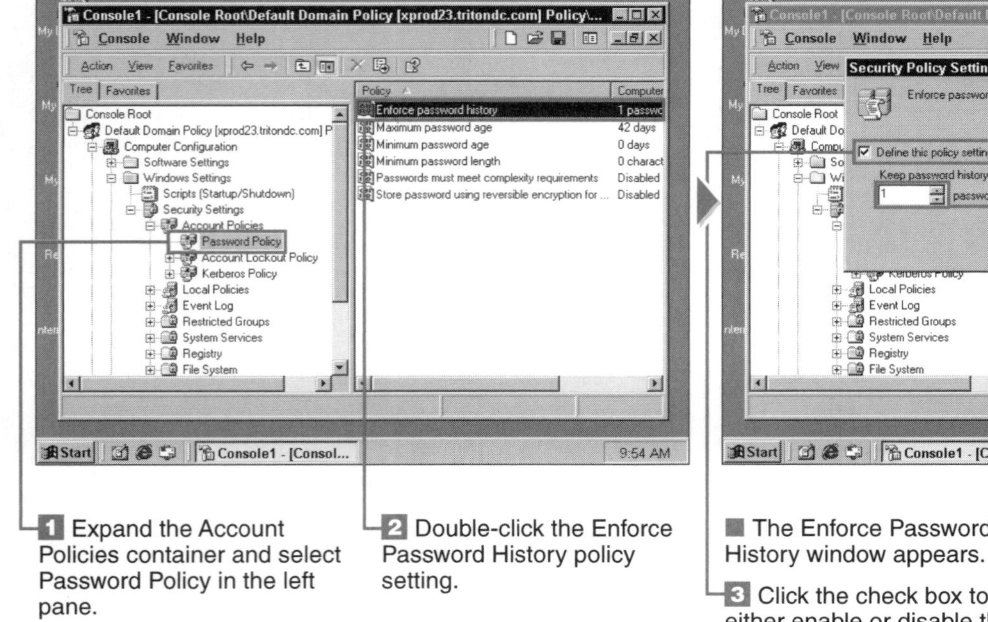

1 Expand the Account Policies container and select Password Policy in the left pane.

■ The policy settings appear in the details pane.

2 Double-click the Enforce Password History policy setting.

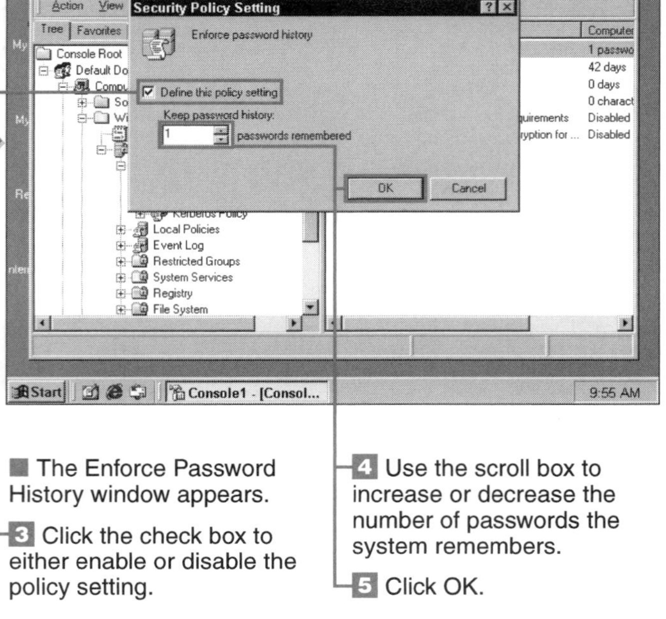

■ The Enforce Password History window appears.

3 Click the check box to either enable or disable the policy setting.

4 Use the scroll box to increase or decrease the number of passwords the system remembers.

5 Click OK.

ENFORCING MAXIMUM PASSWORD AGE

Password age is a serious security issue. Most networks do not allow a user to have the same password for an indefinite period of time. The longer passwords are used, the more likely they are to be stolen by unauthorized individuals. A good security plan limits the amount of time a password can be used. The default setting is 42 days. After the time expires, users are prompted to create a new password for their accounts. You can use a shorter or longer time if desired, but create a reasonable length of time. You do not want to force your users to learn—and remember—a new password every week, but you do not want them using the same password for six months—or longer—either.

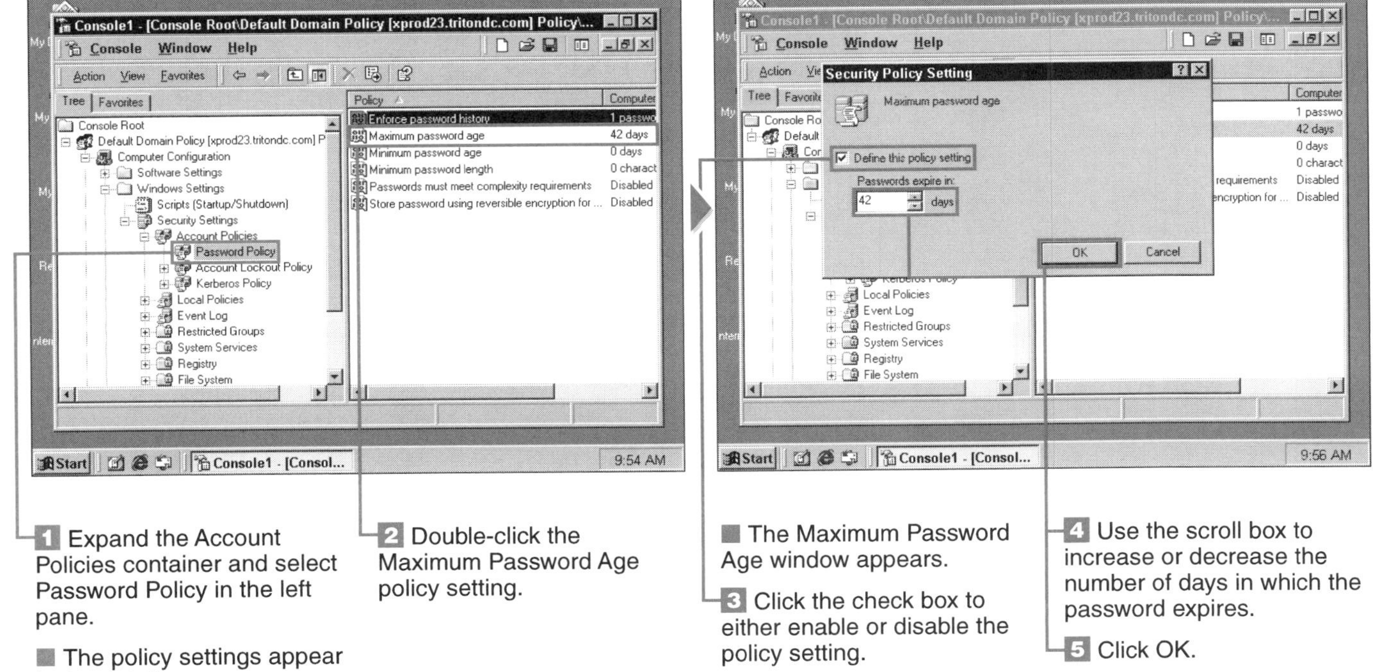

1 Expand the Account Policies container and select Password Policy in the left pane.

■ The policy settings appear in the details pane.

2 Double-click the Maximum Password Age policy setting.

■ The Maximum Password Age window appears.

3 Click the check box to either enable or disable the policy setting.

4 Use the scroll box to increase or decrease the number of days in which the password expires.

5 Click OK.

ENFORCING MINIMUM PASSWORD AGE

As with enforcing password maximum age, you can also enforce a minimum age. For example, let's say that a particular user is very worried about password security. The user changes his or her password every day, then eventually forgets the password, then the user has to get help. The minimum password age prevents users from changing their passwords too frequently by requiring a certain number of days to pass before they can change their passwords again. By default, the setting is 0 days, which means users can change their passwords any time they desire, but you can change this so that users must keep their passwords for a specified number of days before changing it.

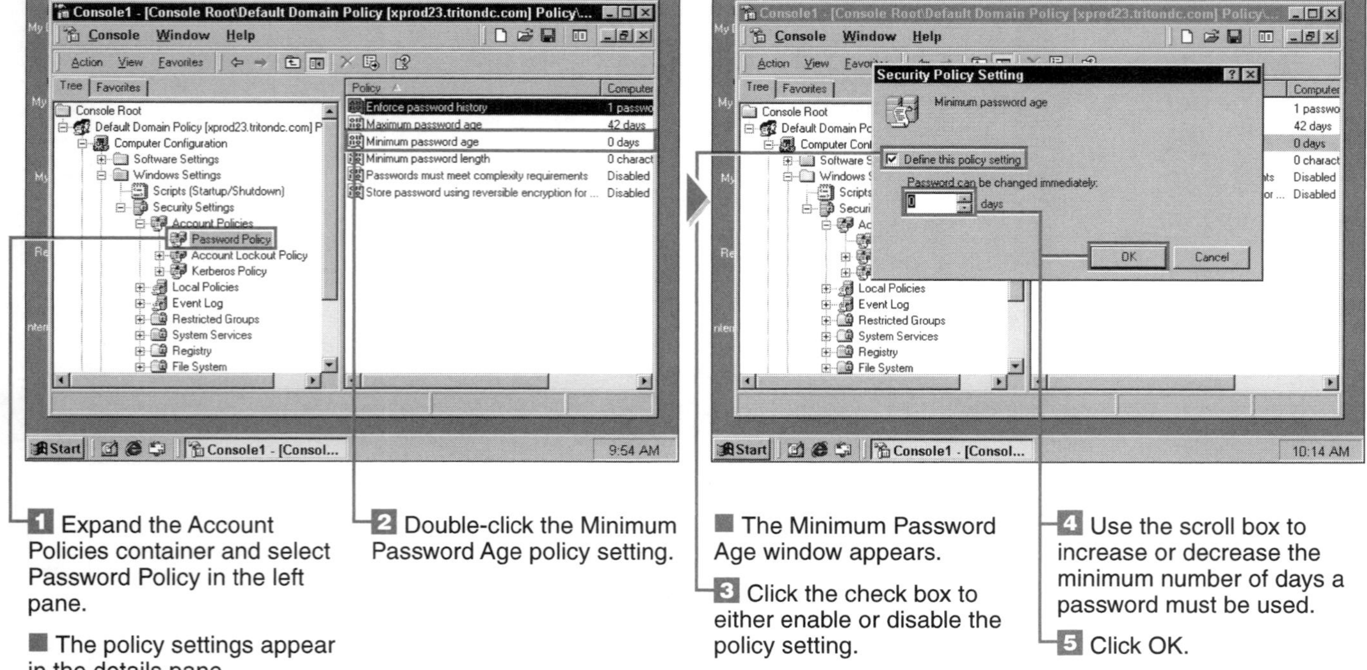

1 Expand the Account Policies container and select Password Policy in the left pane.

■ The policy settings appear in the details pane.

2 Double-click the Minimum Password Age policy setting.

■ The Minimum Password Age window appears.

3 Click the check box to either enable or disable the policy setting.

4 Use the scroll box to increase or decrease the minimum number of days a password must be used.

5 Click OK.

ENFORCING MINIMUM PASSWORD LENGTH

For security purposes, you can force users to create passwords that adhere to a certain length of characters. This is a good security policy because longer passwords are more difficult for unauthorized users to steal. As a general rule, a password character length of seven characters should suffice. By setting a length requirement, you prevent users from using simple passwords, such as "cat," or "dog," or "car," and so on. The default setting for this policy is 0, which means no length requirements exists, but for good security, you should consider implementing a password length of at least five characters, with seven being your best choice.

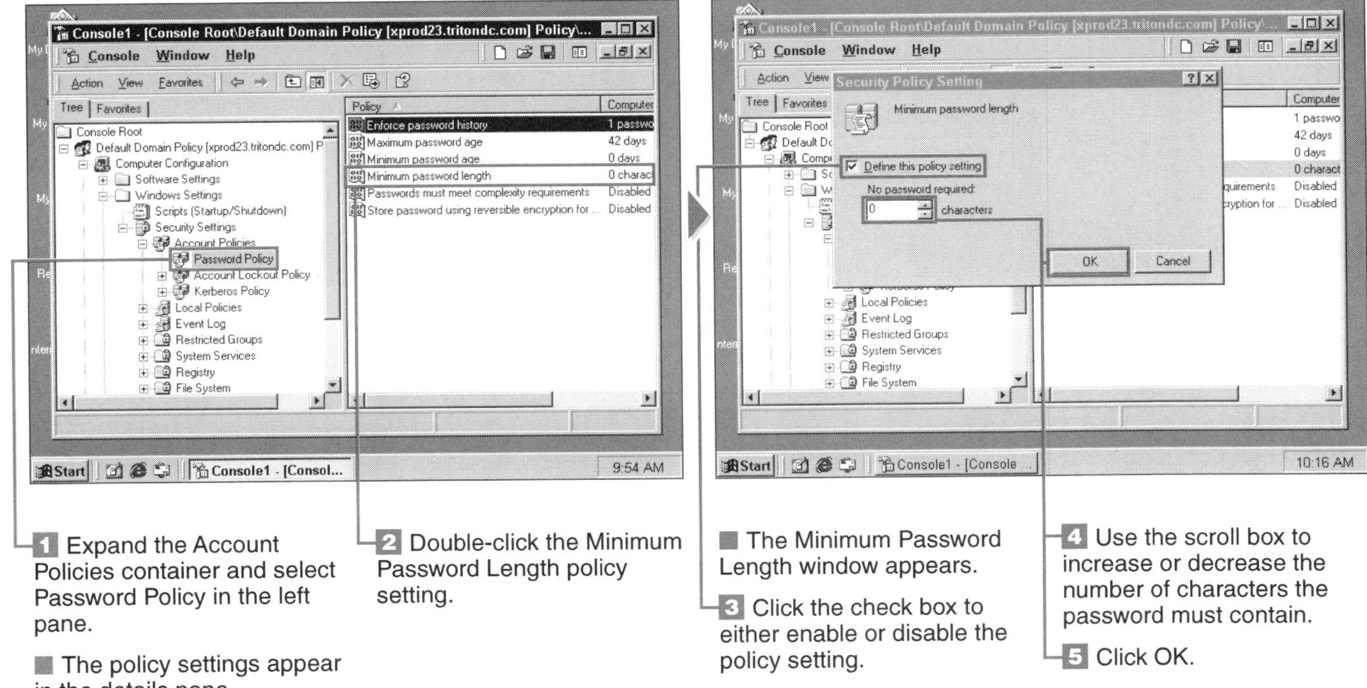

1 Expand the Account Policies container and select Password Policy in the left pane.

■ The policy settings appear in the details pane.

2 Double-click the Minimum Password Length policy setting.

■ The Minimum Password Length window appears.

3 Click the check box to either enable or disable the policy setting.

4 Use the scroll box to increase or decrease the number of characters the password must contain.

5 Click OK.

ENFORCING PASSWORD COMPLEXITY REQUIREMENTS

As with password minimum lengths, another good security measure is to require that passwords meet complexity requirements. This policy requires users to create passwords that contain a mixture of numbers, letters, or keyboard symbols. For example, under this policy, a user could not have a password of "sweetbaby," but would be required to make the password more complex, such as "sweetbaby847." Complex passwords that use a combination of letters, numbers, or symbols are much more difficult for unauthorized users to break.

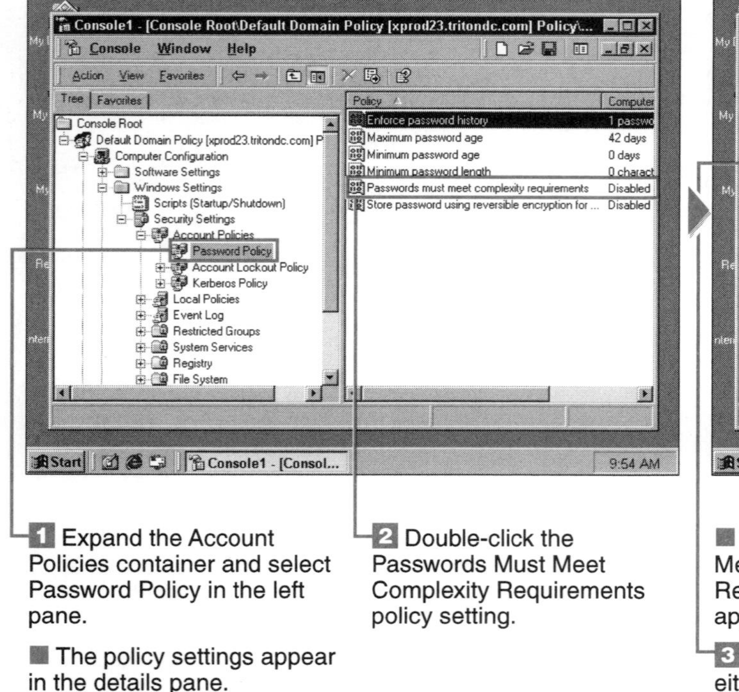

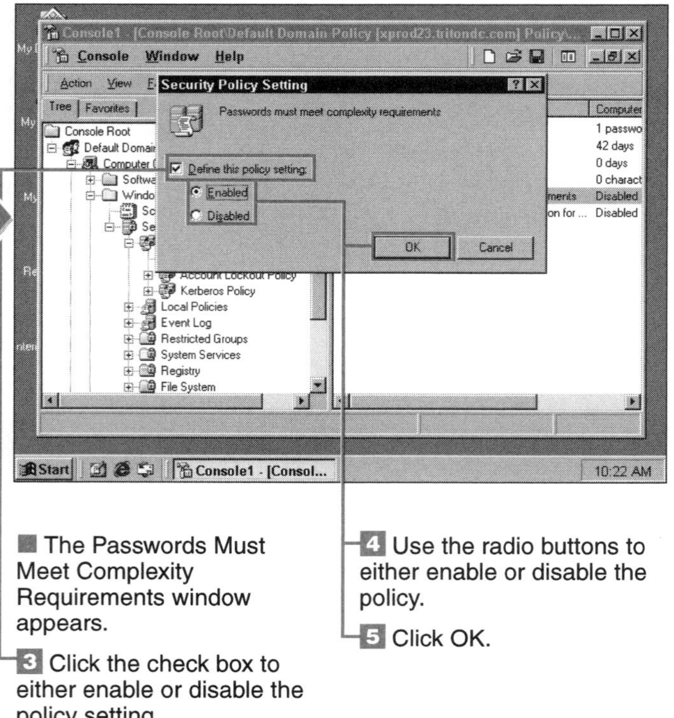

1 Expand the Account Policies container and select Password Policy in the left pane.

■ The policy settings appear in the details pane.

2 Double-click the Passwords Must Meet Complexity Requirements policy setting.

■ The Passwords Must Meet Complexity Requirements window appears.

3 Click the check box to either enable or disable the policy setting.

4 Use the radio buttons to either enable or disable the policy.

5 Click OK.

STORING PASSWORDS USING REVERSIBLE ENCRYPTION FOR ALL USERS IN THE DOMAIN

An additional security feature you can implement regarding user passwords is reversible encryption. Passwords may or may not be encrypted when in transit, depending on other security settings in your domain. This feature enables you to use reversible encryption, which basically scrambles the encrypted data in a reverse fashion in order to provide superior encryption performance. This setting ensures that passwords stolen off the network while the password is in transit cannot be read.

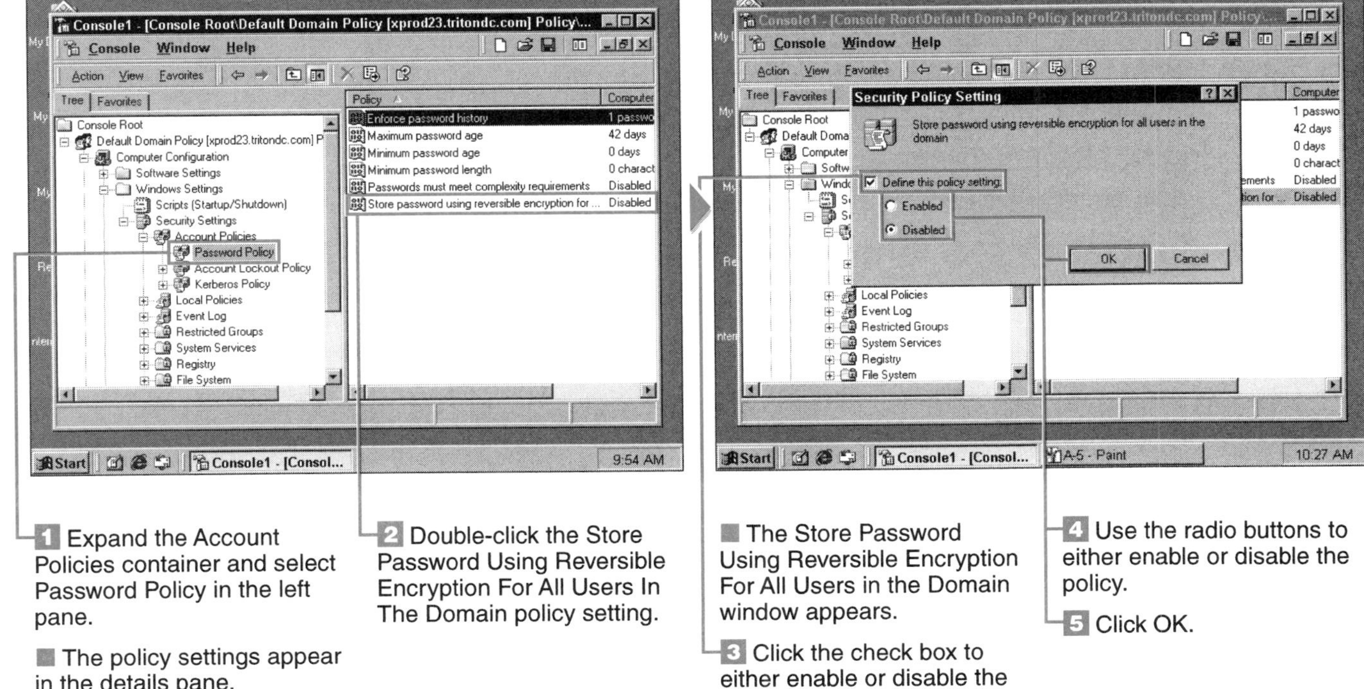

1 Expand the Account Policies container and select Password Policy in the left pane.

■ The policy settings appear in the details pane.

2 Double-click the Store Password Using Reversible Encryption For All Users In The Domain policy setting.

■ The Store Password Using Reversible Encryption For All Users in the Domain window appears.

3 Click the check box to either enable or disable the policy setting.

4 Use the radio buttons to either enable or disable the policy.

5 Click OK.

ENFORCING ACCOUNT LOCKOUT DURATION

Account lockout is a security feature that locks a user's account if the user makes a specified number of failed logon attempts. The default three failed attempts. This lockout policy enables you to define the amount of time, in minutes, that the account is locked out. For example, you can configure the account to be locked for 30 minutes. If someone is trying hack his or her way into the account, this provides a lock for a period of time, in which the hacker will hopefully give up. If you do not enter a number of minutes, then the account remains locked until an administrator unlocks it.

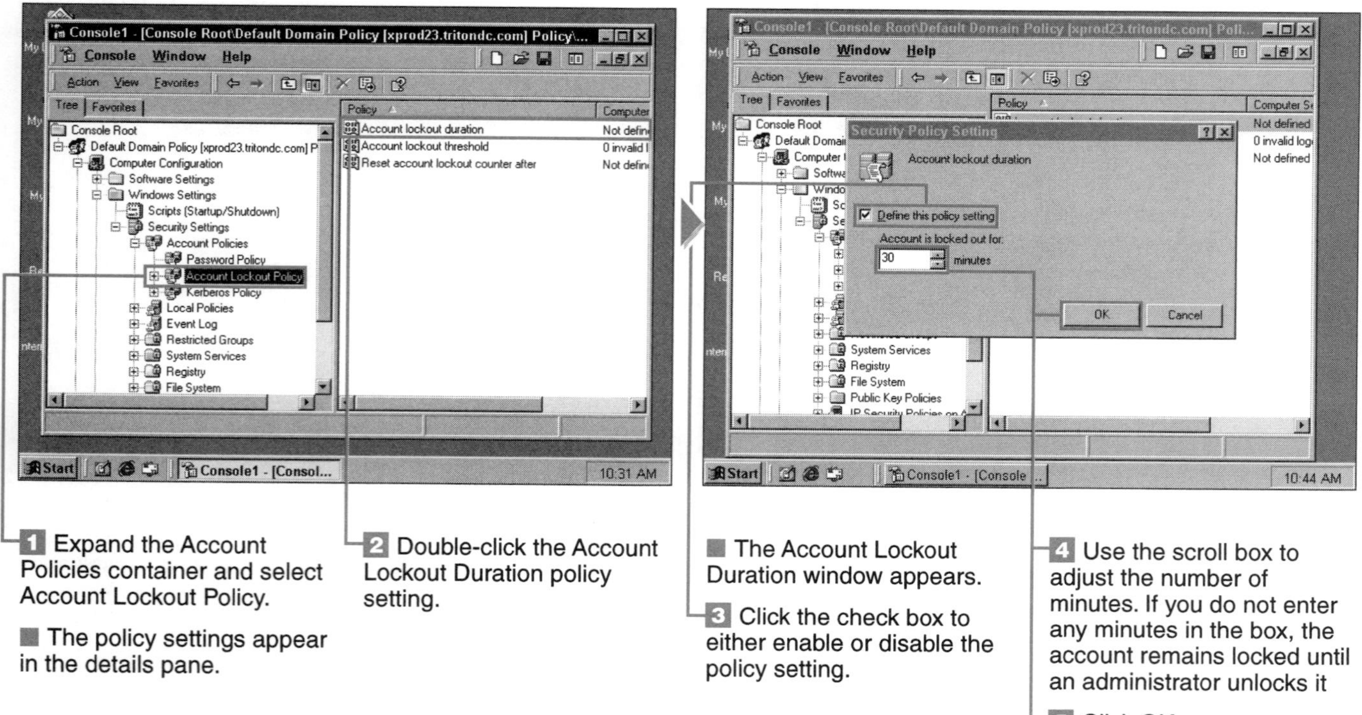

1 Expand the Account Policies container and select Account Lockout Policy.

■ The policy settings appear in the details pane.

2 Double-click the Account Lockout Duration policy setting.

■ The Account Lockout Duration window appears.

3 Click the check box to either enable or disable the policy setting.

4 Use the scroll box to adjust the number of minutes. If you do not enter any minutes in the box, the account remains locked until an administrator unlocks it

5 Click OK.

ENFORCING ACCOUNT LOCKOUT THRESHOLD

If you decide to use Account Lockout, then you need to set a threshold, which determines how many times a user can attempt to log on before the account is locked out. A good value is 3, which gives the user three chances to enter a correct password and user name before the account locks. This setting allows the user to make a spelling mistake on one or two tries, but locks after the third unsuccessful attempt. This way, if an unauthorized person is attempting to hack into the account, he or she can only try three times before the account is locked.

Also, if you specify 0 attempts, the account will not lock.

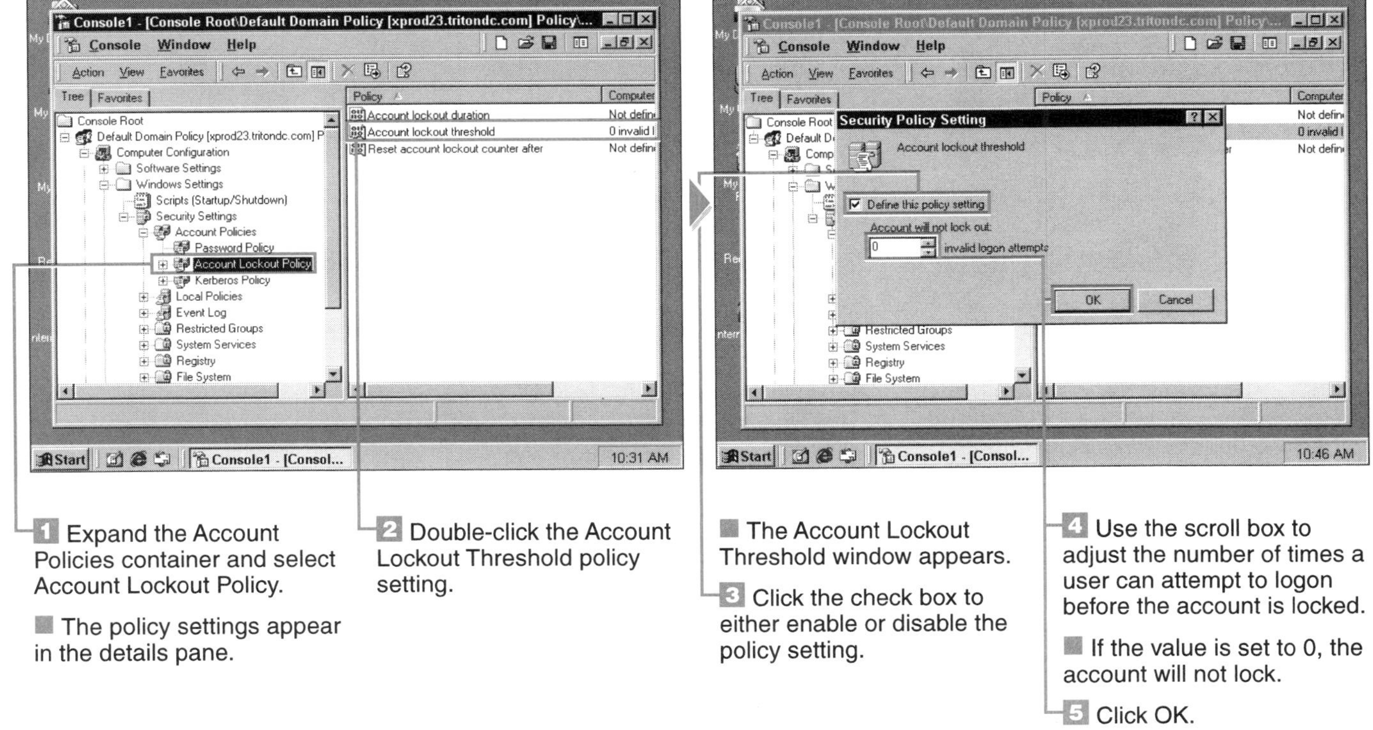

1 Expand the Account Policies container and select Account Lockout Policy.

■ The policy settings appear in the details pane.

2 Double-click the Account Lockout Threshold policy setting.

■ The Account Lockout Threshold window appears.

3 Click the check box to either enable or disable the policy setting.

4 Use the scroll box to adjust the number of times a user can attempt to logon before the account is locked.

■ If the value is set to 0, the account will not lock.

5 Click OK.

ENFORCING ACCOUNT LOCKOUT COUNTER

The computer system maintains an account lockout counter that records the number of times an account is locked within a specified time period. You can change this time period by adjusting the number of minutes that pass before the lockout counter is reset.

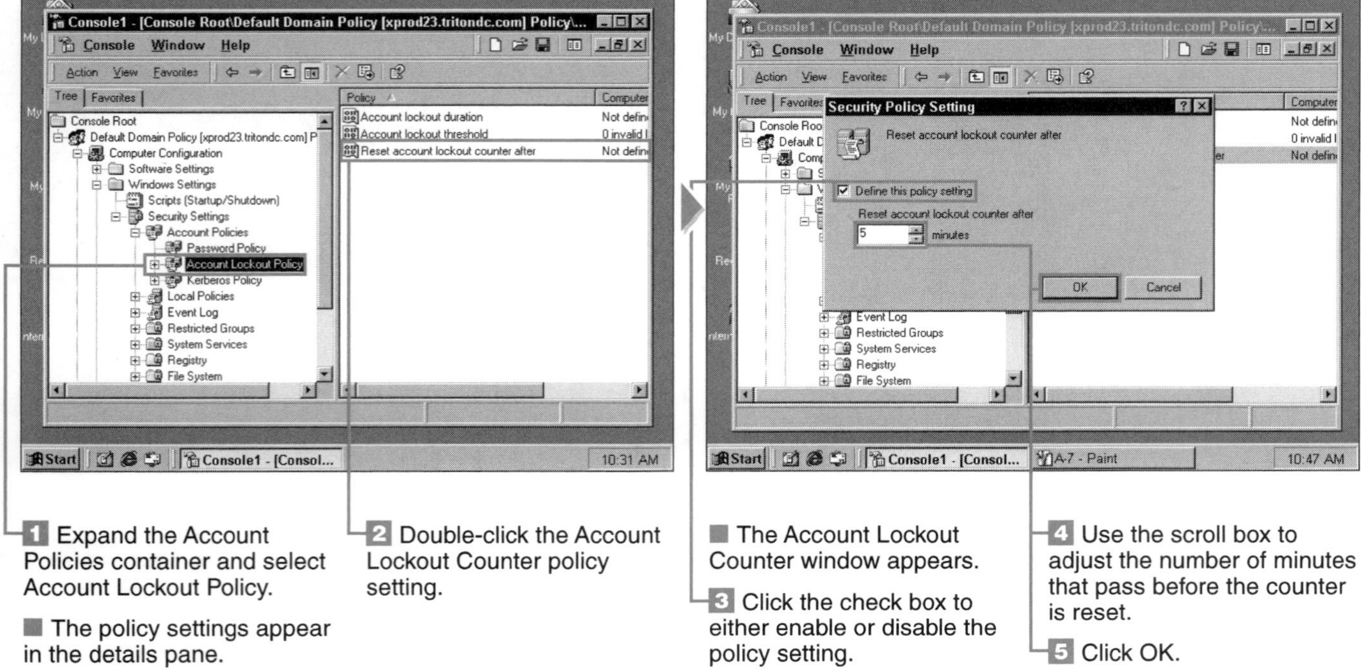

1 Expand the Account Policies container and select Account Lockout Policy.

■ The policy settings appear in the details pane.

2 Double-click the Account Lockout Counter policy setting.

■ The Account Lockout Counter window appears.

3 Click the check box to either enable or disable the policy setting.

4 Use the scroll box to adjust the number of minutes that pass before the counter is reset.

5 Click OK.

ENFORCING USER LOGON RESTRICTIONS

Kerberos is the primary security protocol in Windows 2000. By using the User Logon Restrictions policy, you can determine whether or not to enable user logon restrictions. You use this policy in conjunction with other policies found in the Kerberos Policy container. If you want to enable user logon restrictions, click the enable radio button, then use the other policies in this container to configure the desired options.

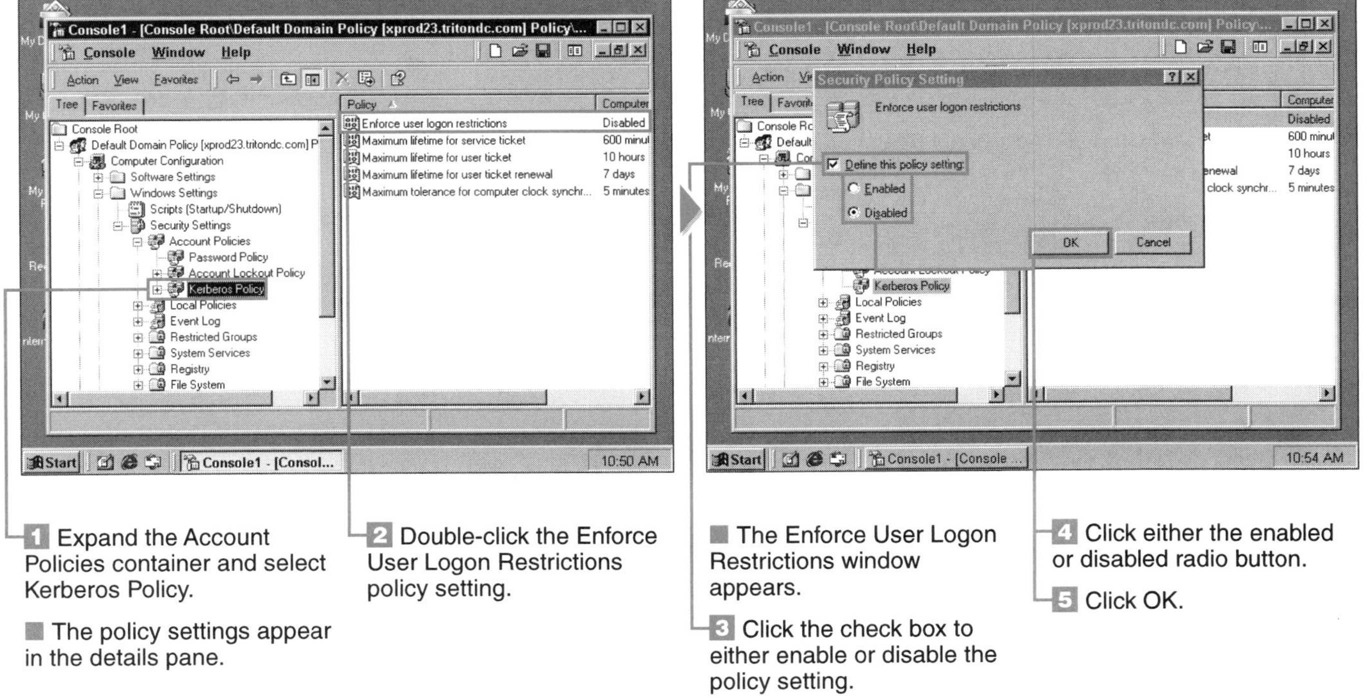

1 Expand the Account Policies container and select Kerberos Policy.

■ The policy settings appear in the details pane.

2 Double-click the Enforce User Logon Restrictions policy setting.

■ The Enforce User Logon Restrictions window appears.

3 Click the check box to either enable or disable the policy setting.

4 Click either the enabled or disabled radio button.

5 Click OK.

ENFORCING MAXIMUM LIFETIME FOR SERVICE TICKET

Kerberos authentication works by using service tickets. By enabling this policy, you can place a maximum lifetime age for the service ticket for the users' accounts. This feature requires the system to periodically generate new service tickets, which provides an additional measure of security for your network logon process.

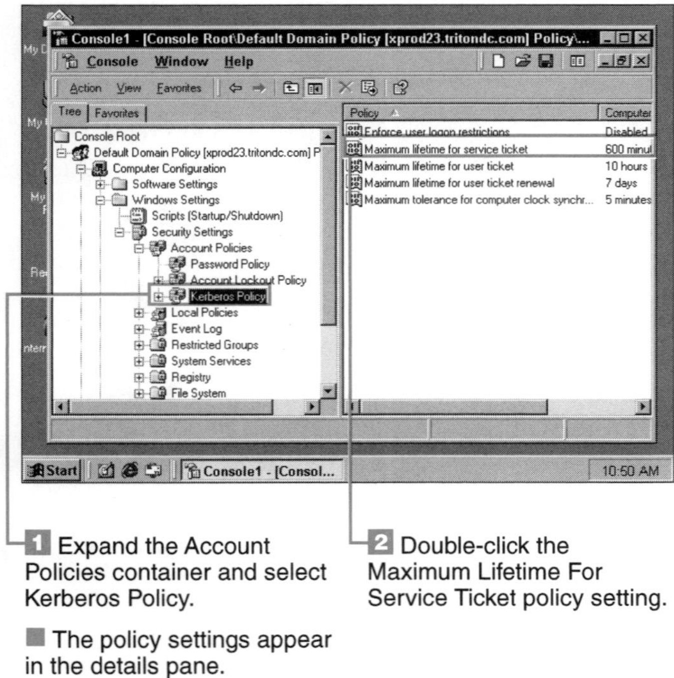

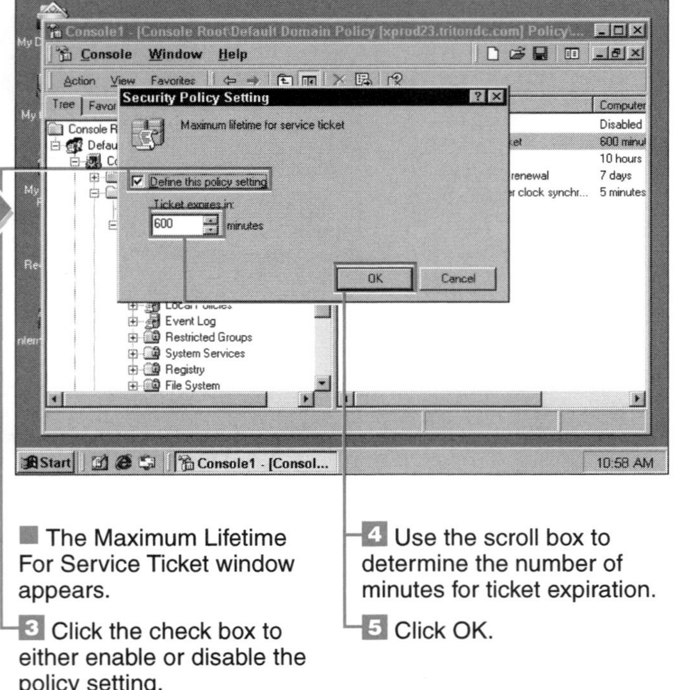

1 Expand the Account Policies container and select Kerberos Policy.

■ The policy settings appear in the details pane.

2 Double-click the Maximum Lifetime For Service Ticket policy setting.

■ The Maximum Lifetime For Service Ticket window appears.

3 Click the check box to either enable or disable the policy setting.

4 Use the scroll box to determine the number of minutes for ticket expiration.

5 Click OK.

ENFORCING MAXIMUM LIFETIME FOR USER TICKET

Just as service tickets are used for the logon service, users also have a logon ticket for Kerberos security. You can set the maximum age for the user's ticket based on hours. By default, a user's ticket expires after ten hours, but you can reduce this number for additional security. However, the default setting is typically all you need for effective Kerberos security.

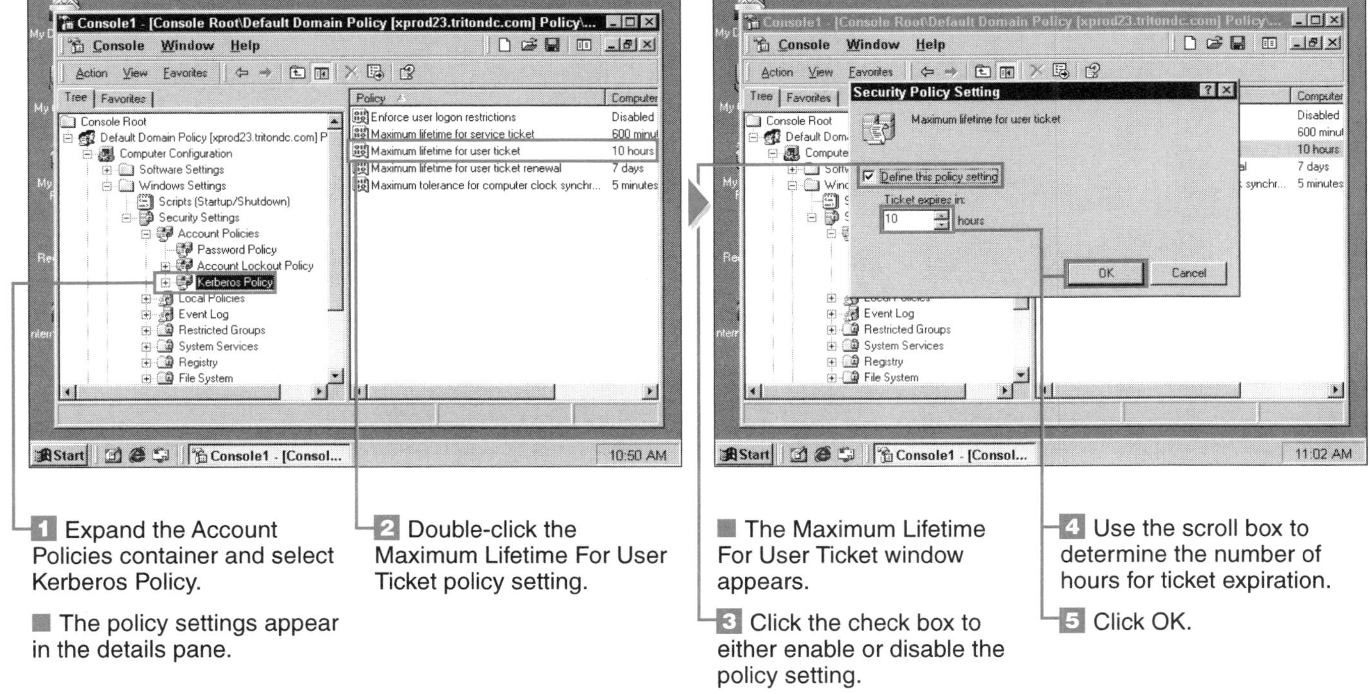

1 Expand the Account Policies container and select Kerberos Policy.

■ The policy settings appear in the details pane.

2 Double-click the Maximum Lifetime For User Ticket policy setting.

■ The Maximum Lifetime For User Ticket window appears.

3 Click the check box to either enable or disable the policy setting.

4 Use the scroll box to determine the number of hours for ticket expiration.

5 Click OK.

ENFORCING MAXIMUM TOLERANCE FOR COMPUTER CLOCK SYNCHRONIZATION

Kerberos security maintains clock synchronization with the server in order to handle ticket expirations and renewals.

The Maximum Tolerance For Computer Clock Synchronization policy allows you to adjust the amount of clock synchronization difference that is tolerated. The default setting is 5 minutes, and this is typically all you need.

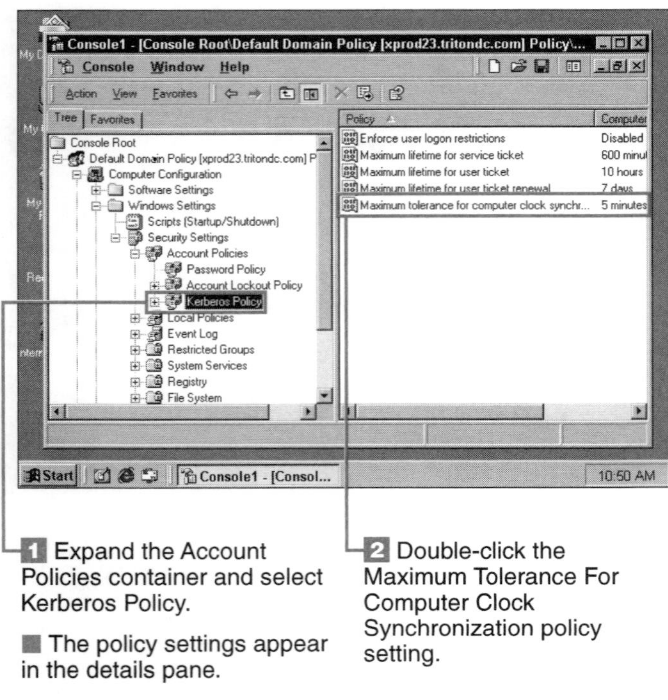

1 Expand the Account Policies container and select Kerberos Policy.

■ The policy settings appear in the details pane.

2 Double-click the Maximum Tolerance For Computer Clock Synchronization policy setting.

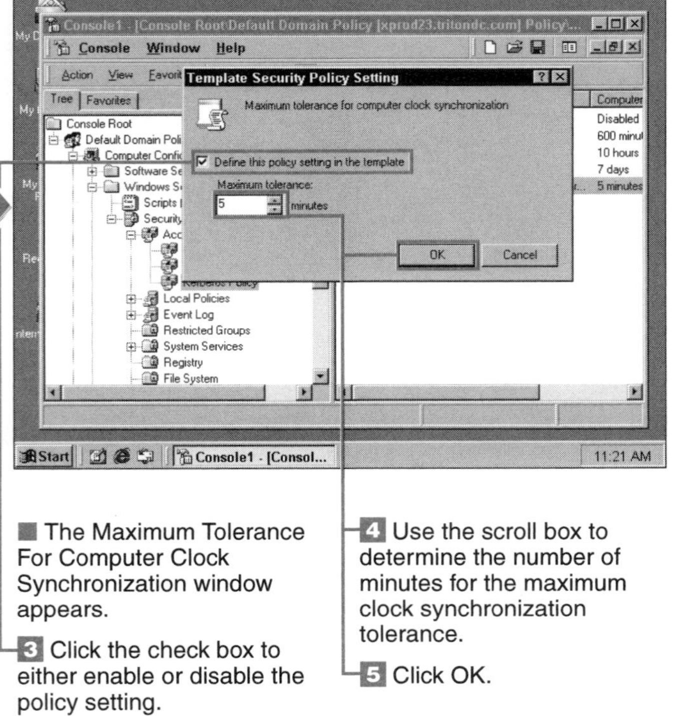

■ The Maximum Tolerance For Computer Clock Synchronization window appears.

3 Click the check box to either enable or disable the policy setting.

4 Use the scroll box to determine the number of minutes for the maximum clock synchronization tolerance.

5 Click OK.

AUDITING ACCOUNT LOGON EVENTS

Auditing is a category of local policy found under the Security Settings. These policies allow you to configure how auditing is applied on client computers and how different events are audited. Using logon auditing, you can generate a log file telling you about the successful or failed logon attempts to that computer. This information can be very helpful if you believe unauthorized persons are attempting to log on to a particular computer.

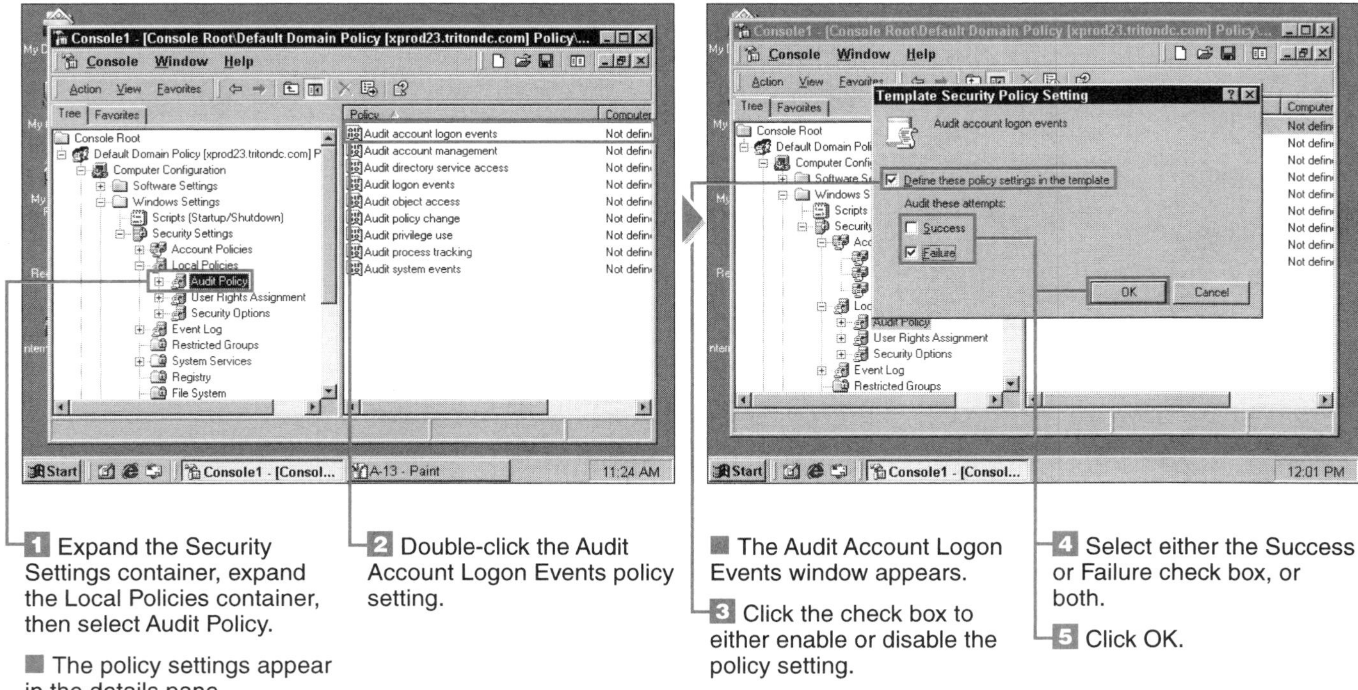

1 Expand the Security Settings container, expand the Local Policies container, then select Audit Policy.

■ The policy settings appear in the details pane.

2 Double-click the Audit Account Logon Events policy setting.

■ The Audit Account Logon Events window appears.

3 Click the check box to either enable or disable the policy setting.

4 Select either the Success or Failure check box, or both.

5 Click OK.

AUDITING ACCOUNT MANAGEMENT

You can also audit a user's account management. These events include such as items as password changes, phone number changes, and so forth. You can choose to either audit successful or failed account management actions that users may perform on the client computer.

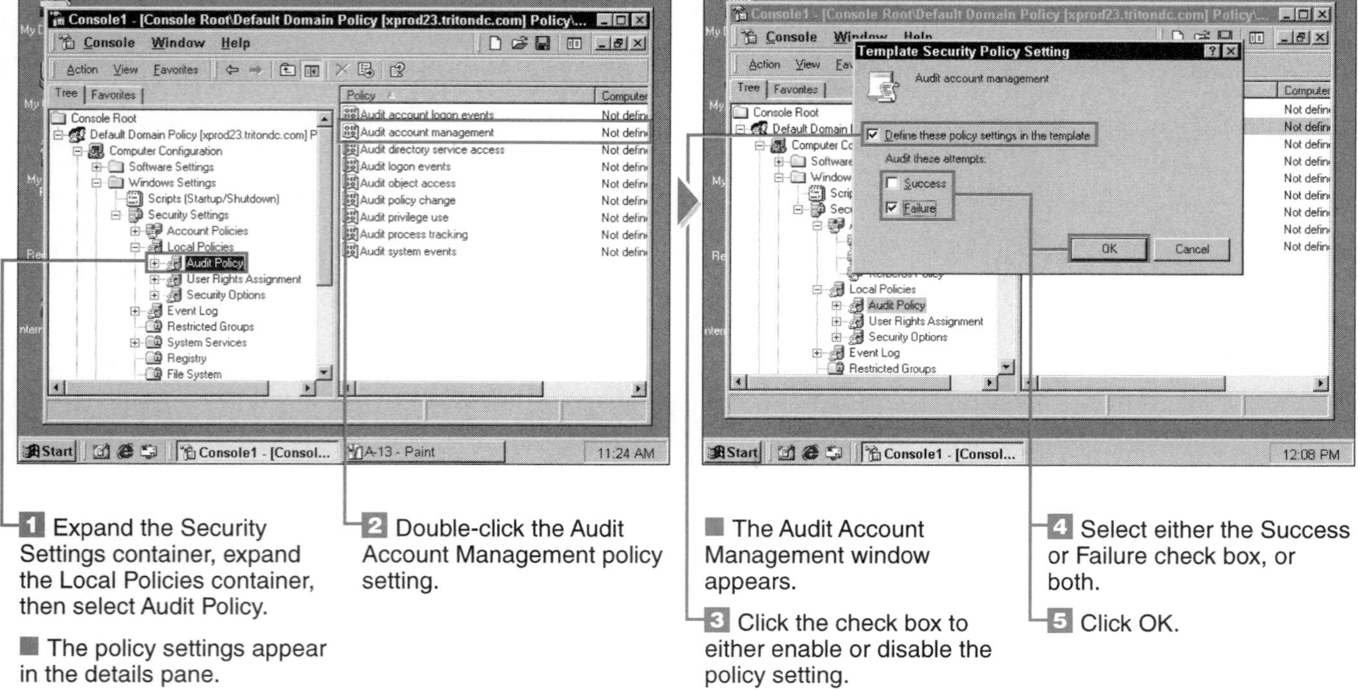

1 Expand the Security Settings container, expand the Local Policies container, then select Audit Policy.

■ The policy settings appear in the details pane.

2 Double-click the Audit Account Management policy setting.

■ The Audit Account Management window appears.

3 Click the check box to either enable or disable the policy setting.

4 Select either the Success or Failure check box, or both.

5 Click OK.

AUDITING DIRECTORY SERVICE ACCESS

The auditing of Directory Service access allows you to see a computer's success or failure when attempting to access the Active Directory. This information can help you determine if directory service access problems exist for particular computers.

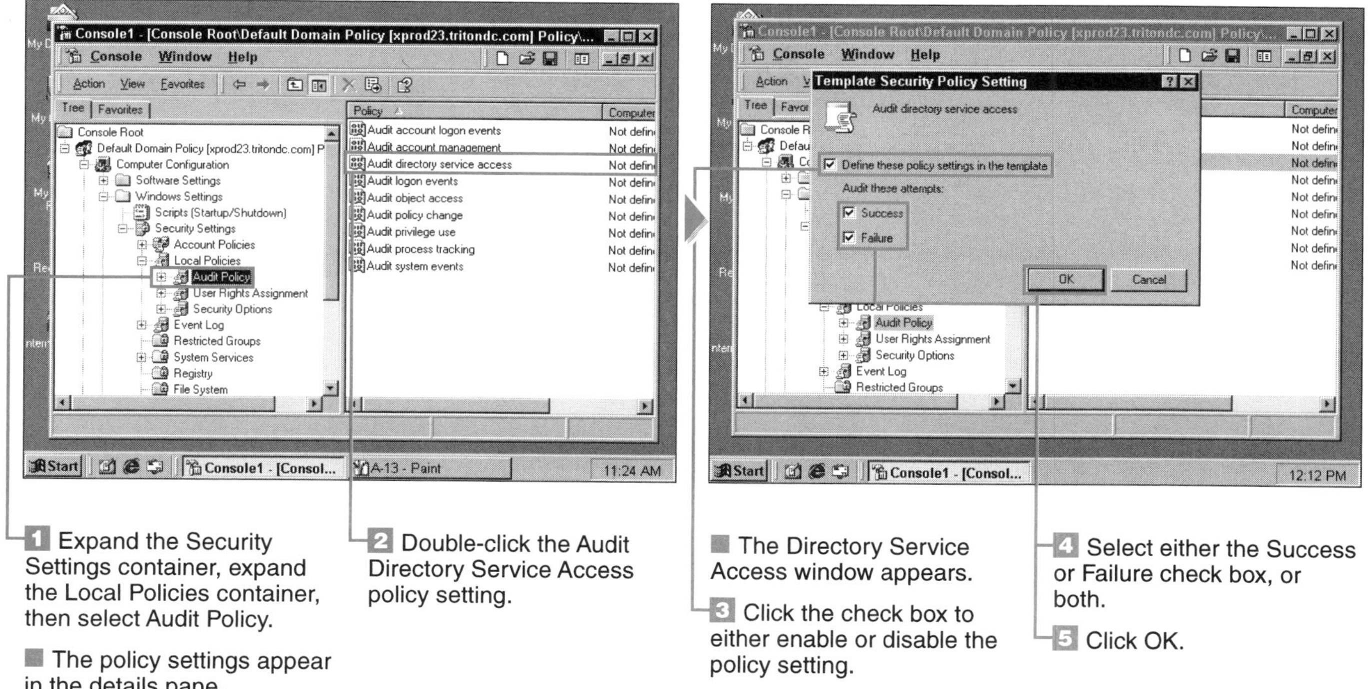

1 Expand the Security Settings container, expand the Local Policies container, then select Audit Policy.

■ The policy settings appear in the details pane.

2 Double-click the Audit Directory Service Access policy setting.

■ The Directory Service Access window appears.

3 Click the check box to either enable or disable the policy setting.

4 Select either the Success or Failure check box, or both.

5 Click OK.

AUDITING LOGON EVENTS

The audit logon events policy is much like auditing account logon events, but the logon events policy applies to any type of logon the user attempts to perform. For example, if the user is required to access a particular share or Web folder, then that logon event is audited under this policy. This policy can help you determine resource access on your network and find access problems that may exist.

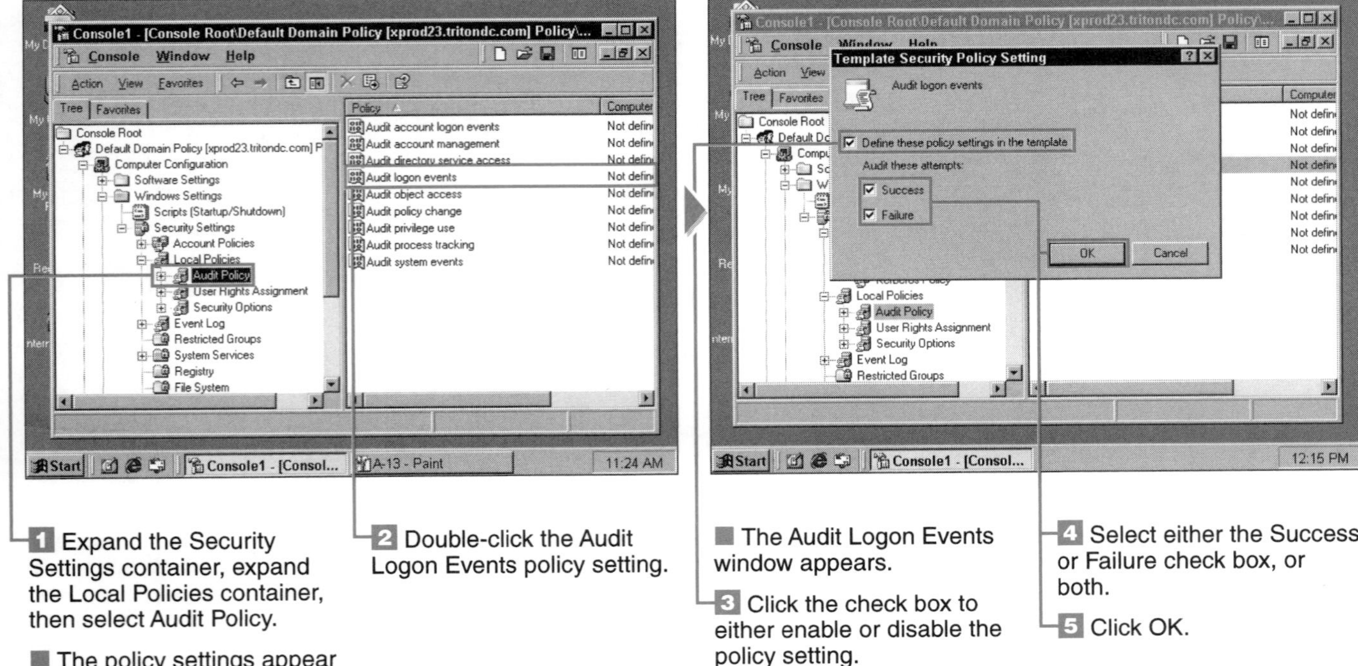

1 Expand the Security Settings container, expand the Local Policies container, then select Audit Policy.

■ The policy settings appear in the details pane.

2 Double-click the Audit Logon Events policy setting.

■ The Audit Logon Events window appears.

3 Click the check box to either enable or disable the policy setting.

4 Select either the Success or Failure check box, or both.

5 Click OK.

AUDITING OBJECT ACCESS

Object access means the Active Directory objects that users access, such as folders, shares, printer, and so forth. You can choose to audit the success or failure of object access for client computers. This information can help you see trends with access problems or help you discover when a particular client computer has a high failure rate, or when some unauthorized user may be trying to gain access to the Active Directory.

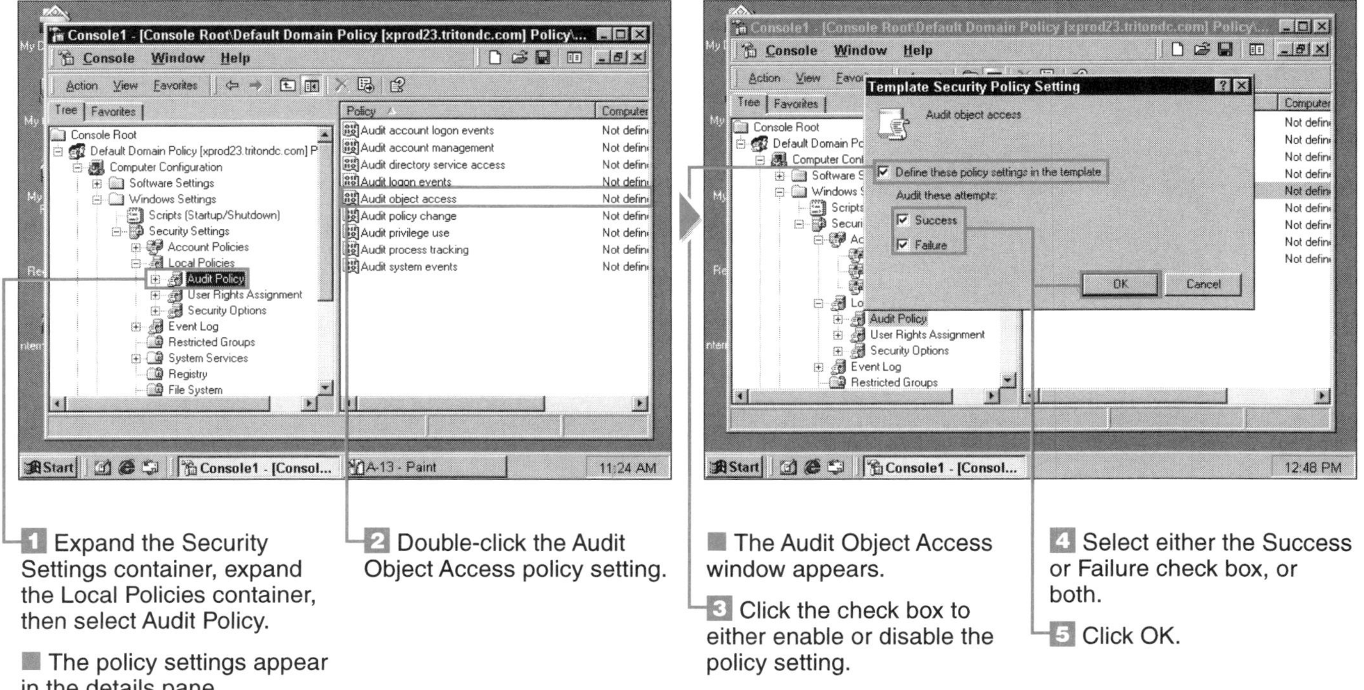

1 Expand the Security Settings container, expand the Local Policies container, then select Audit Policy.

■ The policy settings appear in the details pane.

2 Double-click the Audit Object Access policy setting.

■ The Audit Object Access window appears.

3 Click the check box to either enable or disable the policy setting.

4 Select either the Success or Failure check box, or both.

5 Click OK.

APPENDIX A

AUDITING POLICY CHANGE

You can audit policy changes that occur for client computers. This auditing process involves any changes that are made to the user's local policy by the user. You can use this information to determine if excessive change attempts are being made to the policy. This can be a clue that an unauthorized person is attempting to change configuration of the computer.

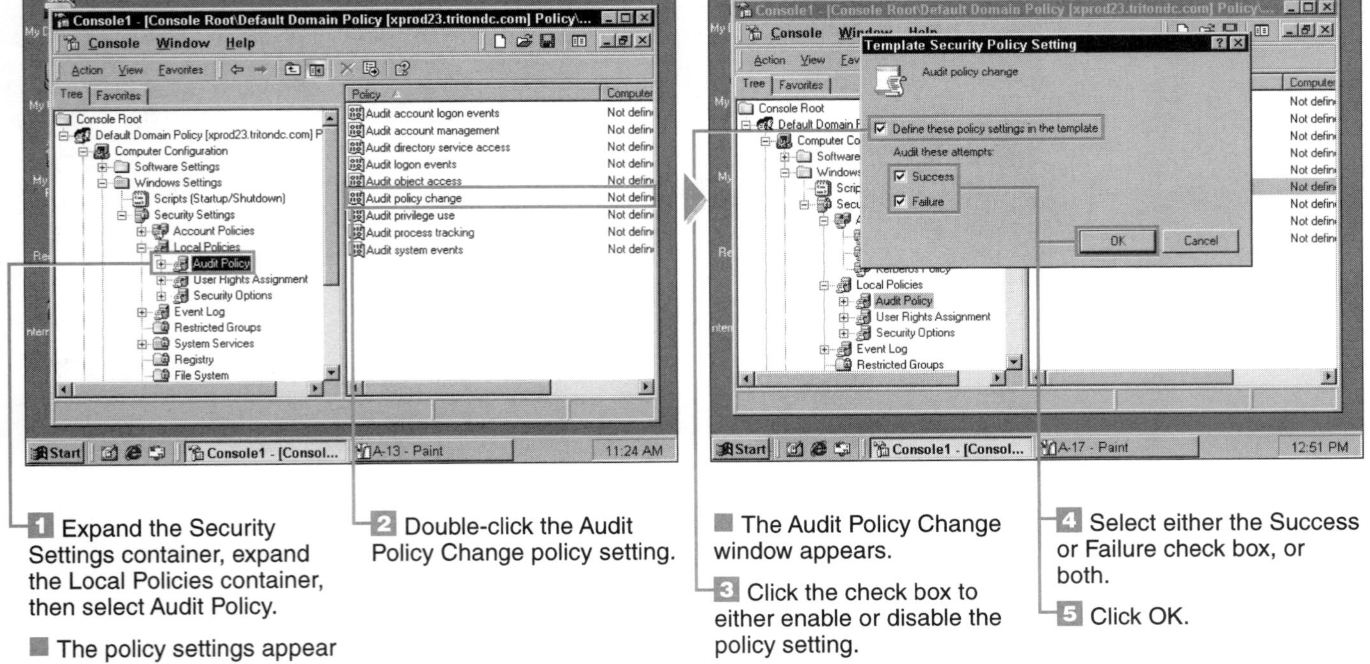

1 Expand the Security Settings container, expand the Local Policies container, then select Audit Policy.

■ The policy settings appear in the details pane.

2 Double-click the Audit Policy Change policy setting.

■ The Audit Policy Change window appears.

3 Click the check box to either enable or disable the policy setting.

4 Select either the Success or Failure check box, or both.

5 Click OK.

AUDITING PRIVILEGE USE

Privilege use audits certain events that are tied to the user's rights and privileges configured for the account. Auditing privilege use enables you to see a user's success or failure to privilege portions of the network or information. You can audit this event to determine if a high number of failures have occurred, which may signal that an unauthorized person may be trying to access information on the network.

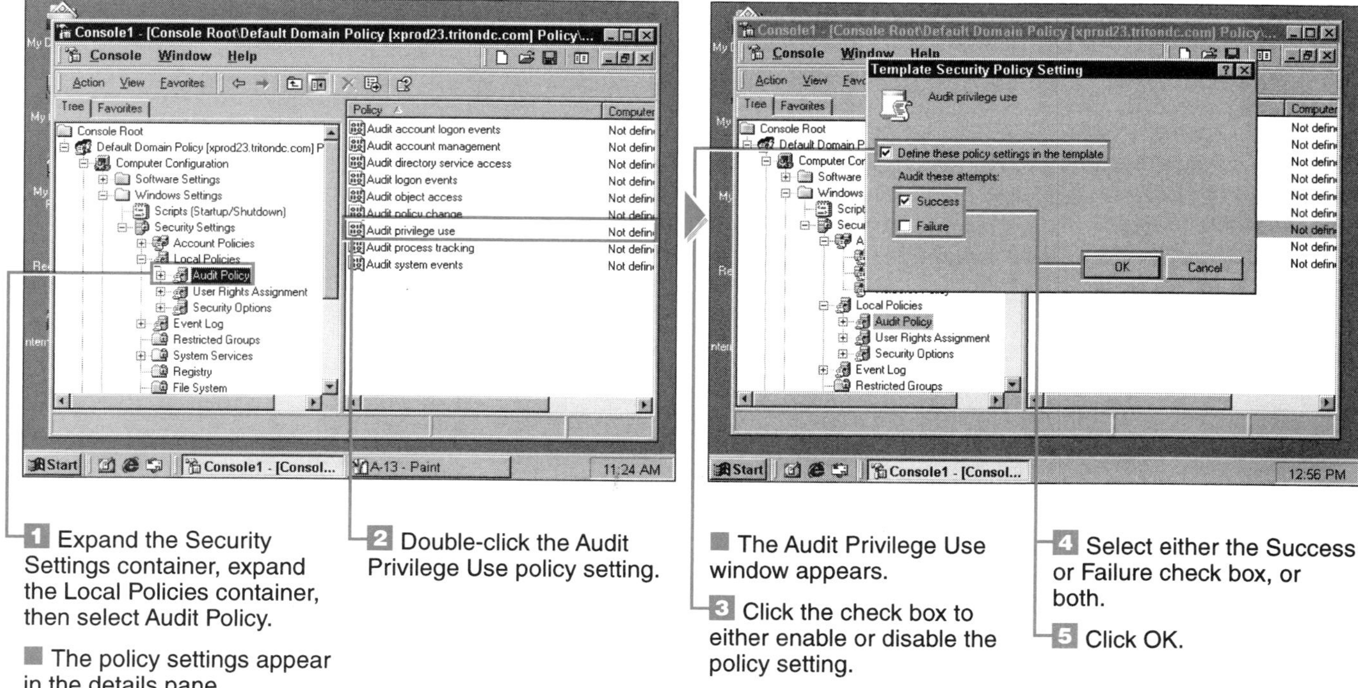

1 Expand the Security Settings container, expand the Local Policies container, then select Audit Policy.

■ The policy settings appear in the details pane.

2 Double-click the Audit Privilege Use policy setting.

■ The Audit Privilege Use window appears.

3 Click the check box to either enable or disable the policy setting.

4 Select either the Success or Failure check box, or both.

5 Click OK.

AUDITING PROCESS TRACKING

Process tracking audits success or failure of processes that occur on the users' computers and through network processes. This auditing feature enables you to view the success or failure of processes that are tracked by the system.

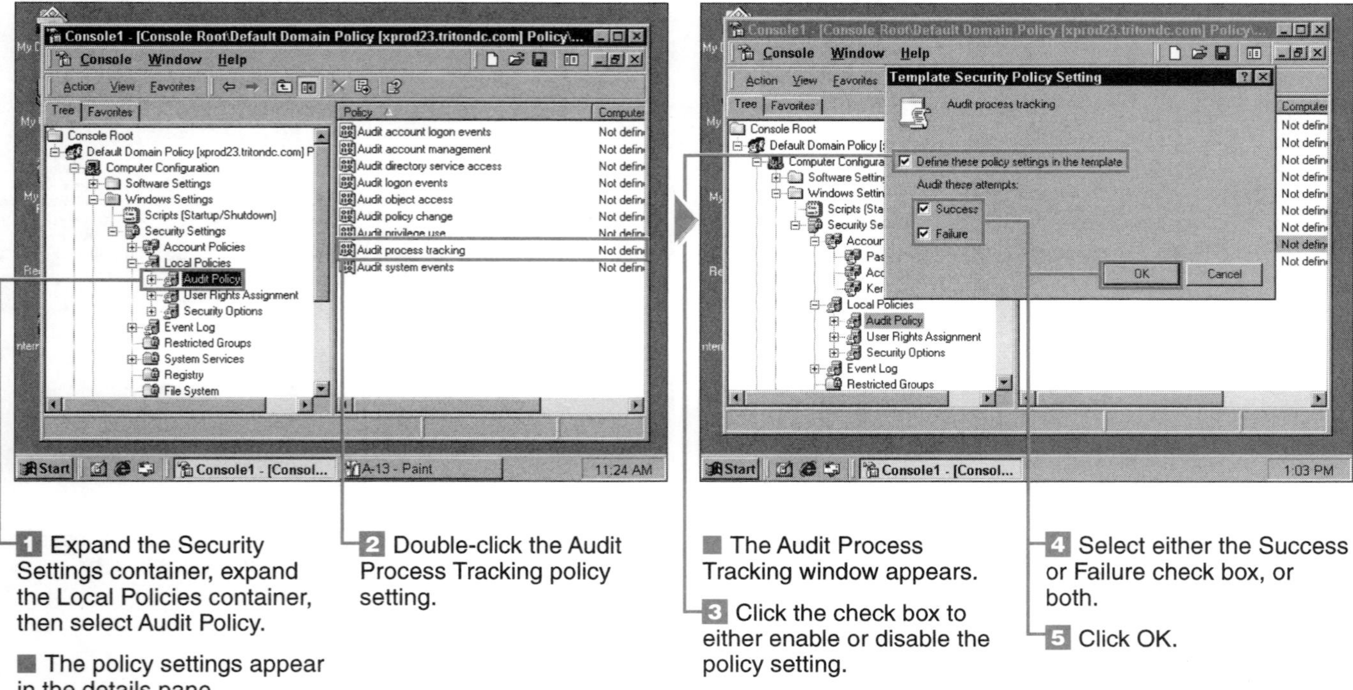

1 Expand the Security Settings container, expand the Local Policies container, then select Audit Policy.

■ The policy settings appear in the details pane.

2 Double-click the Audit Process Tracking policy setting.

■ The Audit Process Tracking window appears.

3 Click the check box to either enable or disable the policy setting.

4 Select either the Success or Failure check box, or both.

5 Click OK.

AUDITING SYSTEM EVENTS

As with process tracking, you can audit system events that occur on the user's computer both from a success or failure perspective. Typically, you would choose to audit system events based on failure. This enables you to see possible user tampering and configuration changes.

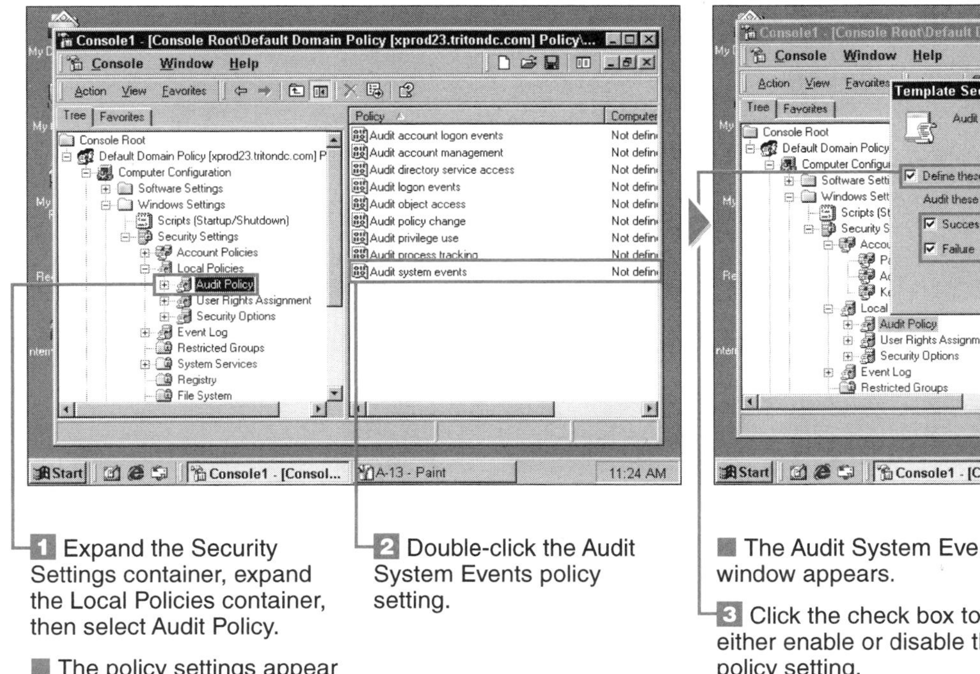

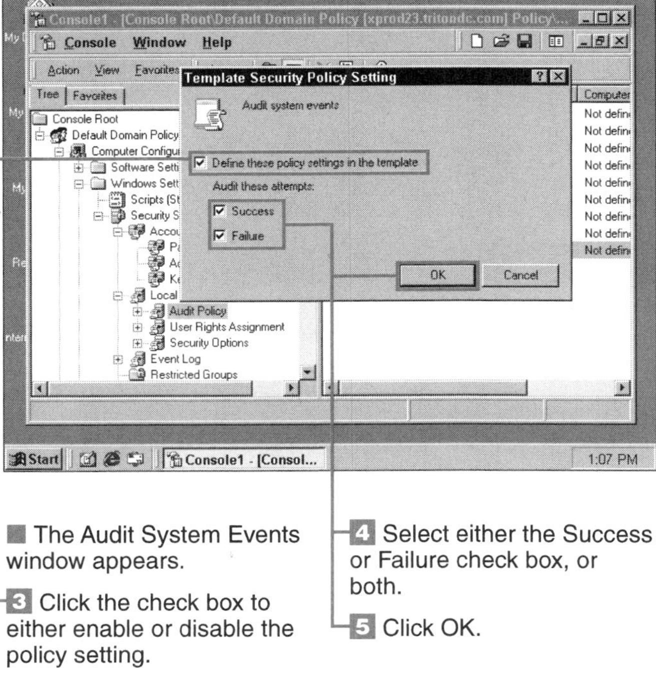

1 Expand the Security Settings container, expand the Local Policies container, then select Audit Policy.

■ The policy settings appear in the details pane.

2 Double-click the Audit System Events policy setting.

■ The Audit System Events window appears.

3 Click the check box to either enable or disable the policy setting.

4 Select either the Success or Failure check box, or both.

5 Click OK.

ACCESSING THIS COMPUTER FROM THE NETWORK

Aside from auditing events, you can also determine what rights users have for accessing and using various computers on the network, as well as other configuration options. This user right enables the groups you select to access the particular client computer through a network connection as necessary to access shared files and folders.

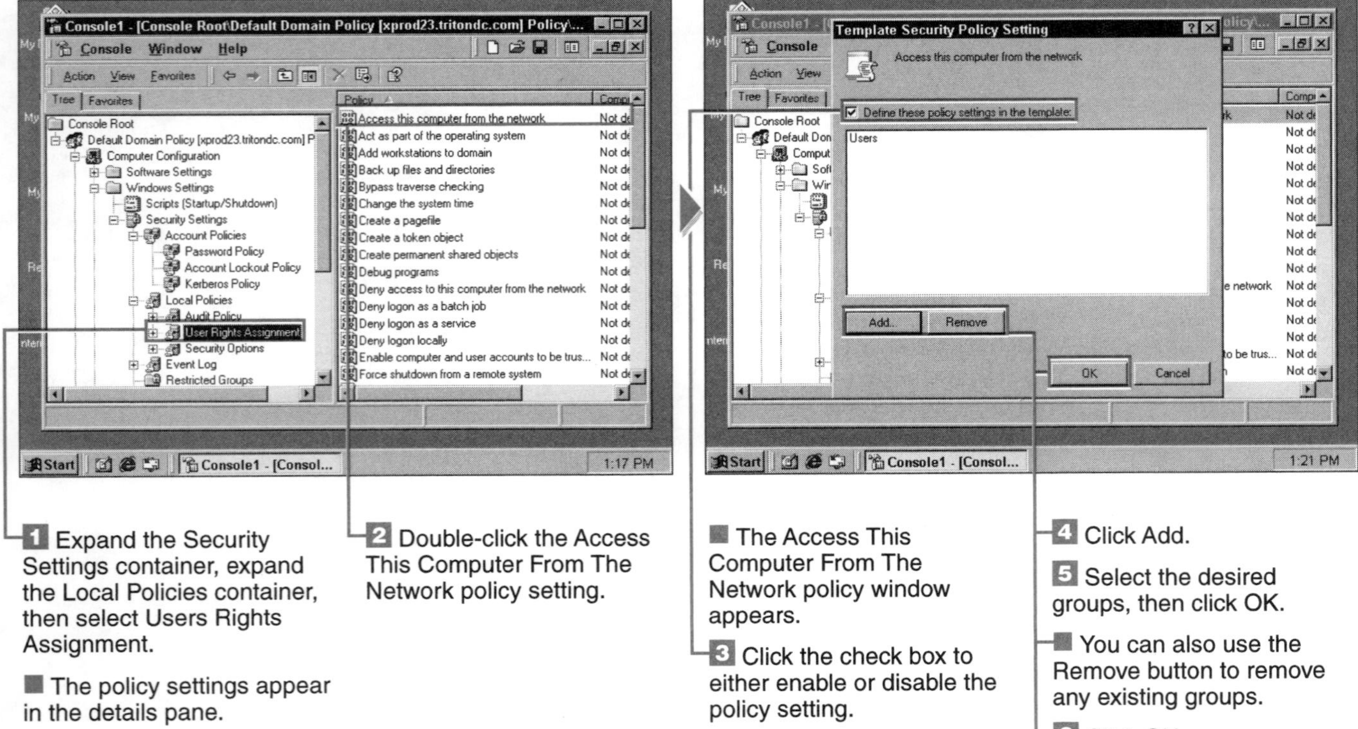

1 Expand the Security Settings container, expand the Local Policies container, then select Users Rights Assignment.

■ The policy settings appear in the details pane.

2 Double-click the Access This Computer From The Network policy setting.

■ The Access This Computer From The Network policy window appears.

3 Click the check box to either enable or disable the policy setting.

4 Click Add.

5 Select the desired groups, then click OK.

■ You can also use the Remove button to remove any existing groups.

6 Click OK.

ACT AS A PART OF THE OPERATING SYSTEM

The Act As A Part Of The Operating System policy gives users or groups the user right of being recognized by the operating system for configuration purposes. This feature enables you to restrict configuration to certain users or groups that you select.

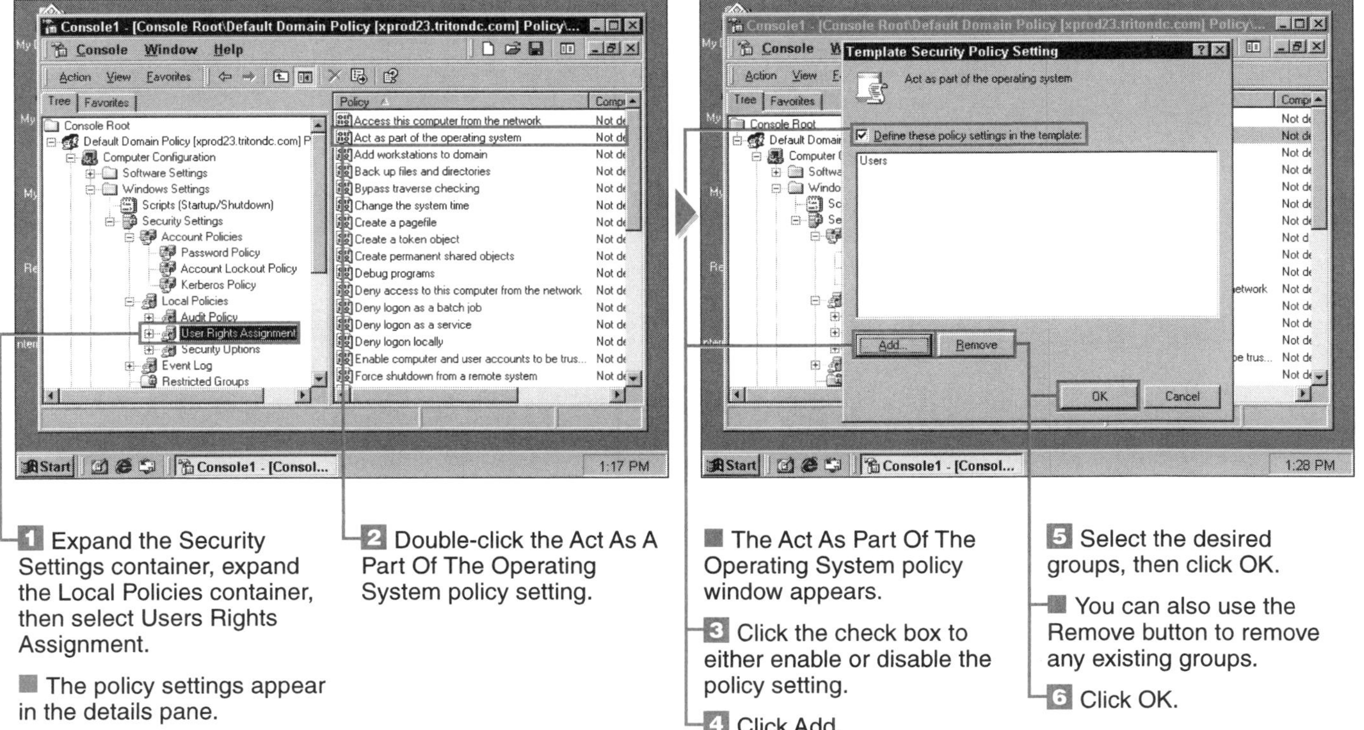

1 Expand the Security Settings container, expand the Local Policies container, then select Users Rights Assignment.

■ The policy settings appear in the details pane.

2 Double-click the Act As A Part Of The Operating System policy setting.

■ The Act As Part Of The Operating System policy window appears.

3 Click the check box to either enable or disable the policy setting.

4 Click Add.

5 Select the desired groups, then click OK.

■ You can also use the Remove button to remove any existing groups.

6 Click OK.

ADDING WORKSTATIONS TO THE DOMAIN

This policy allows users to add workstations to the domain. As with other policy settings in this container, you select which users or groups you want to have this right. Typically, you do not want everyone to be able to add new workstations to the domain, but only certain users or groups should handle this task.

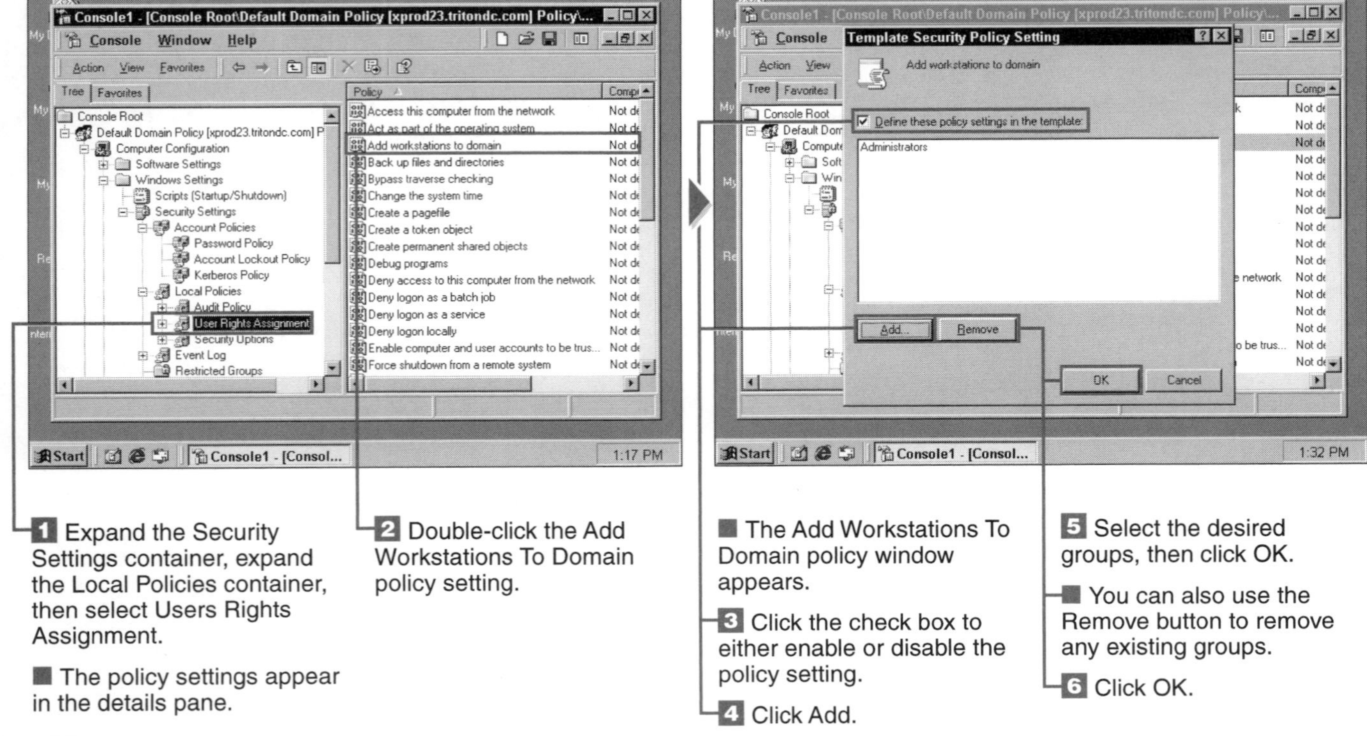

1 Expand the Security Settings container, expand the Local Policies container, then select Users Rights Assignment.

■ The policy settings appear in the details pane.

2 Double-click the Add Workstations To Domain policy setting.

■ The Add Workstations To Domain policy window appears.

3 Click the check box to either enable or disable the policy setting.

4 Click Add.

5 Select the desired groups, then click OK.

■ You can also use the Remove button to remove any existing groups.

6 Click OK.

BACKING UP FILES AND DIRECTORIES

You can use this policy setting to allow users to back up files and directories on a computer using Windows Backup, which is available on both Windows 2000 Server and Professional. As with the other user right policies, you can determine which users and groups should have this right.

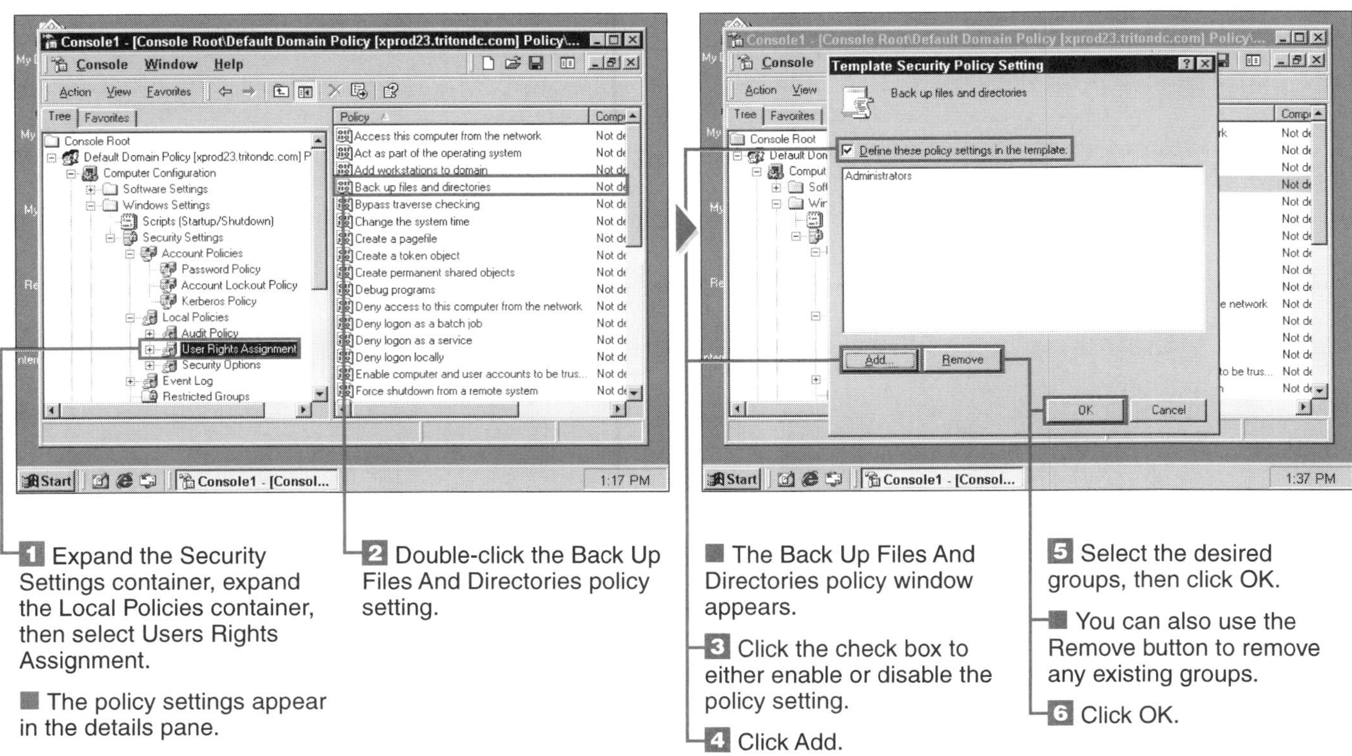

1 Expand the Security Settings container, expand the Local Policies container, then select Users Rights Assignment.

■ The policy settings appear in the details pane.

2 Double-click the Back Up Files And Directories policy setting.

■ The Back Up Files And Directories policy window appears.

3 Click the check box to either enable or disable the policy setting.

4 Click Add.

5 Select the desired groups, then click OK.

■ You can also use the Remove button to remove any existing groups.

6 Click OK.

BYPASSING TRAVERSE CHECKING

Traverse checking is a security process that determines if a user can move through a series of folders. You can use this policy to bypass traverse checking for particular users or groups. This policy allows users to traverse folder structures without having to be checked for security access.

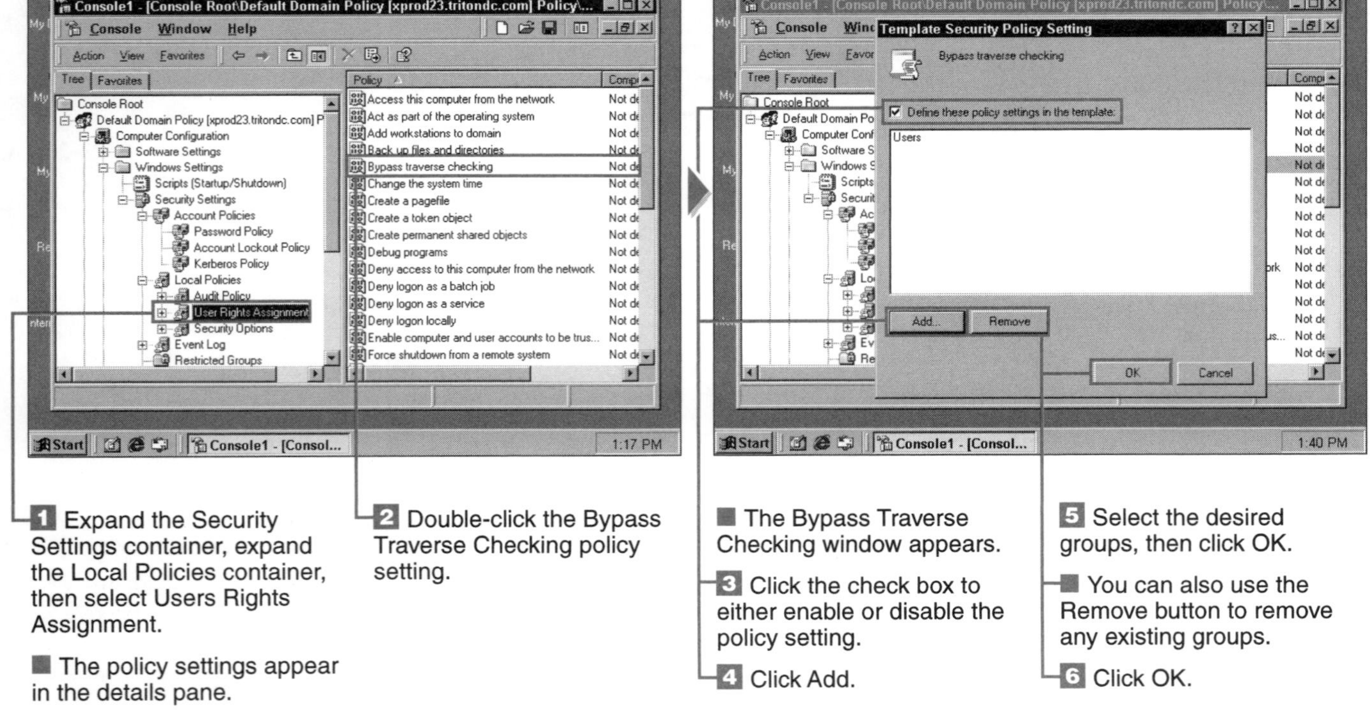

1 Expand the Security Settings container, expand the Local Policies container, then select Users Rights Assignment.

■ The policy settings appear in the details pane.

2 Double-click the Bypass Traverse Checking policy setting.

■ The Bypass Traverse Checking window appears.

3 Click the check box to either enable or disable the policy setting.

4 Click Add.

5 Select the desired groups, then click OK.

■ You can also use the Remove button to remove any existing groups.

6 Click OK.

CHANGING SYSTEM TIME

You use the Changing System Time policy to allow or disallow users or groups to change the system time on their computers. When you enable the policy, no users can change their system time unless you add the desired users and groups. As with all policies, if you do not want this policy in effect, simply do not define it.

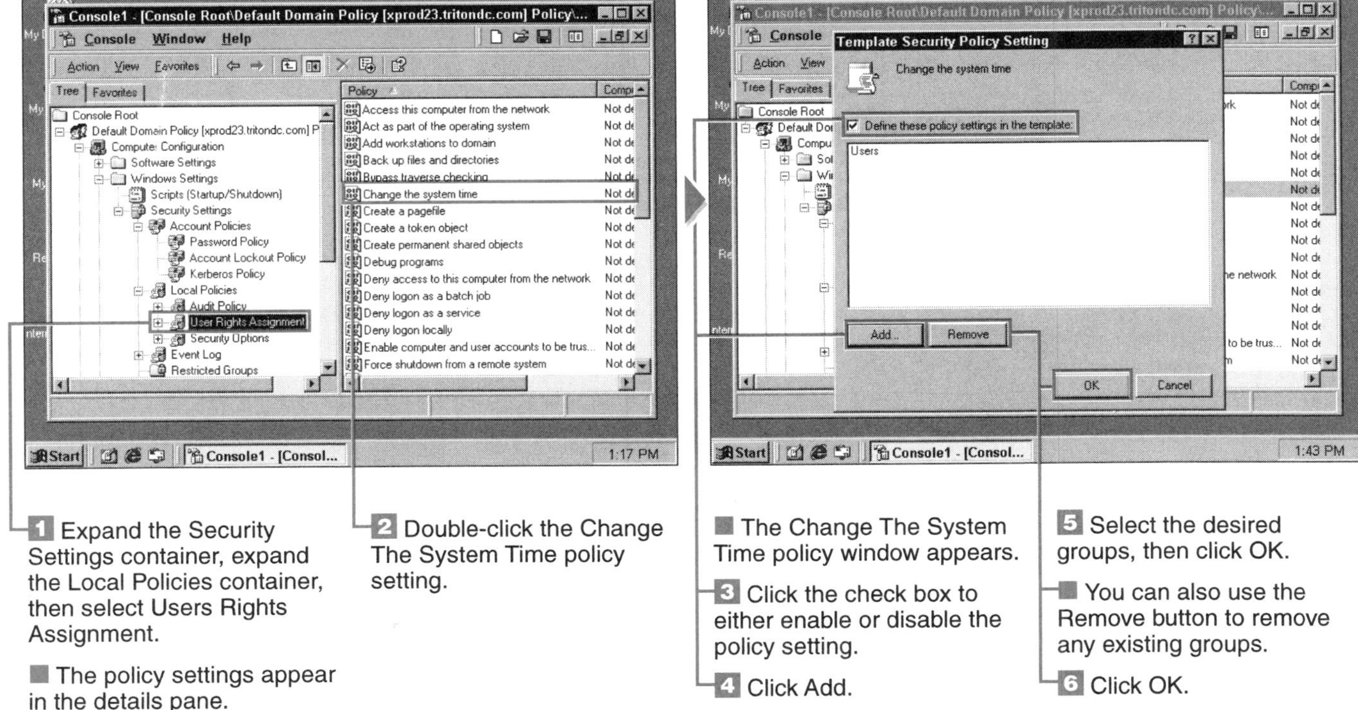

1 Expand the Security Settings container, expand the Local Policies container, then select Users Rights Assignment.

■ The policy settings appear in the details pane.

2 Double-click the Change The System Time policy setting.

■ The Change The System Time policy window appears.

3 Click the check box to either enable or disable the policy setting.

4 Click Add.

5 Select the desired groups, then click OK.

■ You can also use the Remove button to remove any existing groups.

6 Click OK.

CREATING A PAGEFILE

Windows systems use a pagefile to handle system memory. A pagefile allows the system to write temporary memory data to the hard disk when physical memory is running low. With this policy, you can determine which users or groups have the right to create a pagefile on their systems.

Typically, you want to implement a standard pagefile configuration, and this is not something end users should be tampering with.

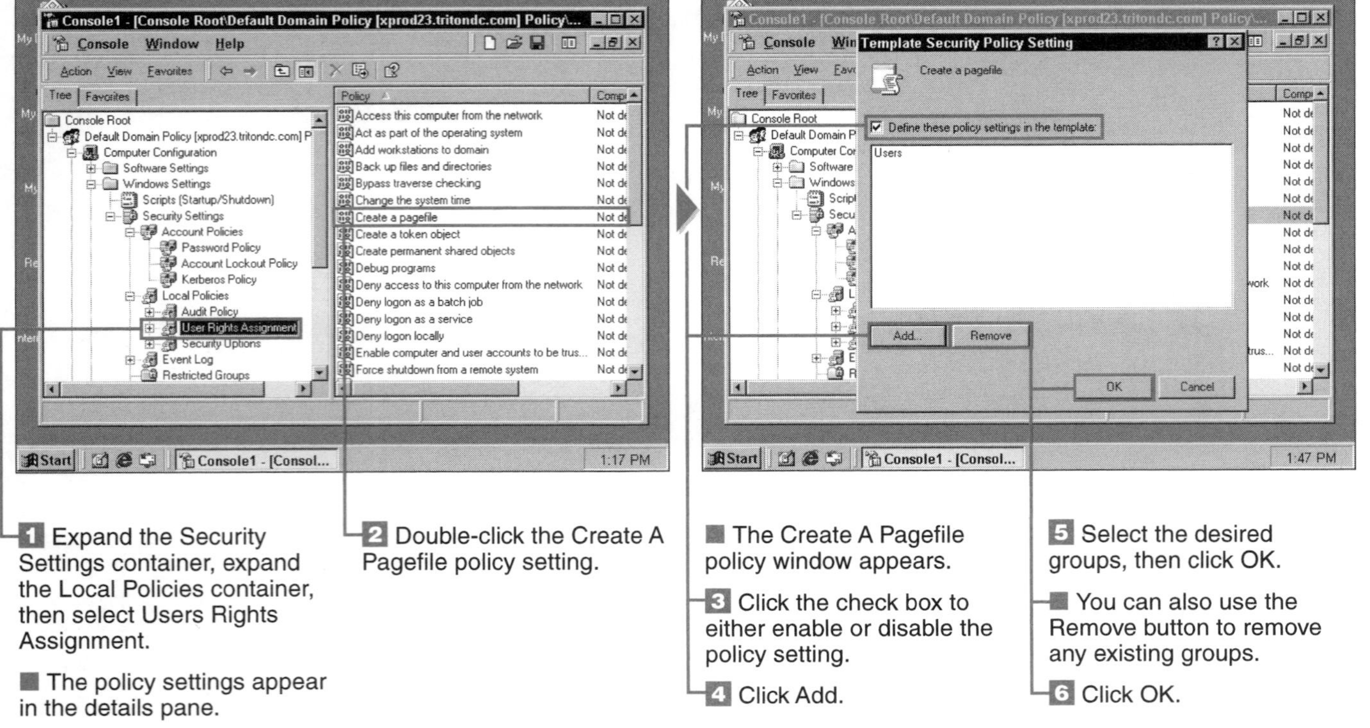

1 Expand the Security Settings container, expand the Local Policies container, then select Users Rights Assignment.

■ The policy settings appear in the details pane.

2 Double-click the Create A Pagefile policy setting.

■ The Create A Pagefile policy window appears.

3 Click the check box to either enable or disable the policy setting.

4 Click Add.

5 Select the desired groups, then click OK.

■ You can also use the Remove button to remove any existing groups.

6 Click OK.

CREATING A TOKEN OBJECT

Windows 2000 uses token objects in some security scenarios. Tokens are a part of advanced security configuration and should not be used by typical end users, so definition of the policy is a good idea.

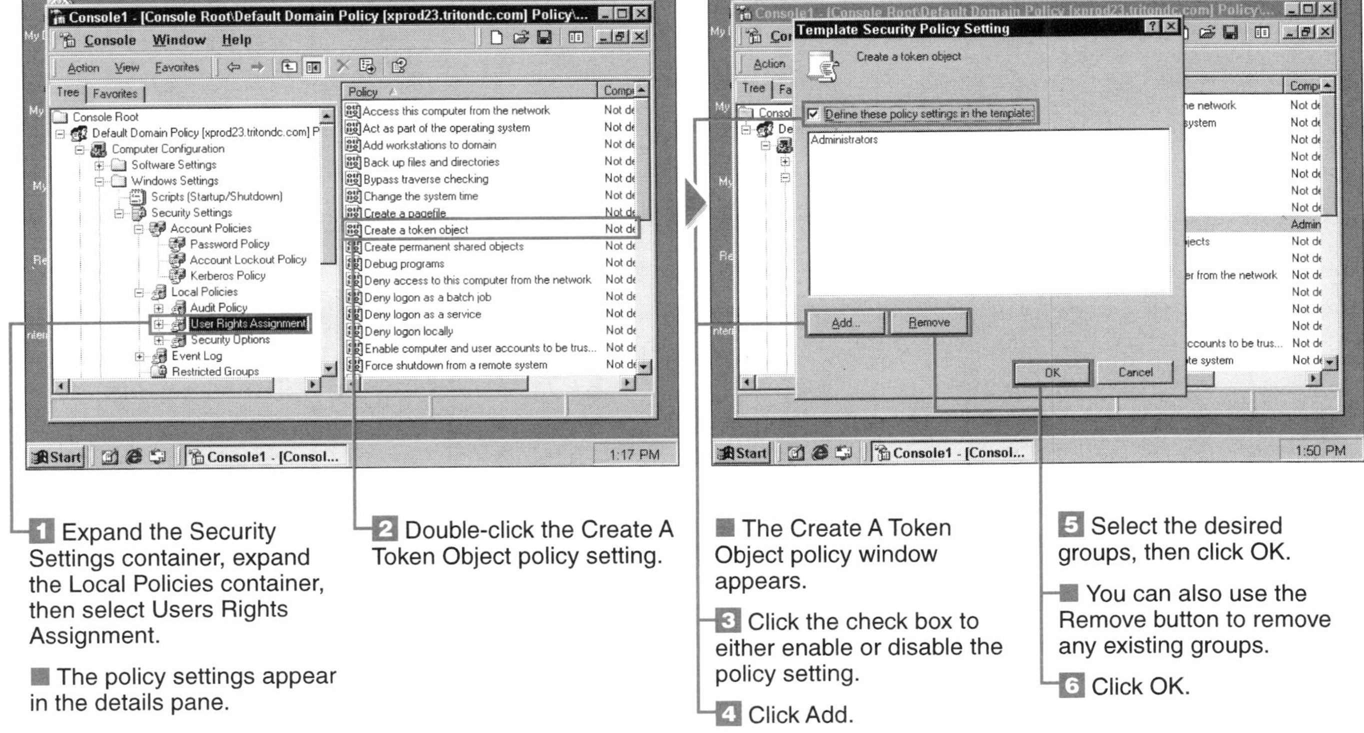

1 Expand the Security Settings container, expand the Local Policies container, then select Users Rights Assignment.

■ The policy settings appear in the details pane.

2 Double-click the Create A Token Object policy setting.

■ The Create A Token Object policy window appears.

3 Click the check box to either enable or disable the policy setting.

4 Click Add.

5 Select the desired groups, then click OK.

■ You can also use the Remove button to remove any existing groups.

6 Click OK.

CREATING PERMANENT SHARED OBJECTS

This policy enables you to define who can create permanent shared objects. This includes such items as folders, printers, applications, and so forth. If you want to define this policy, then you select which users or groups are allowed to create those shared objects on client computers.

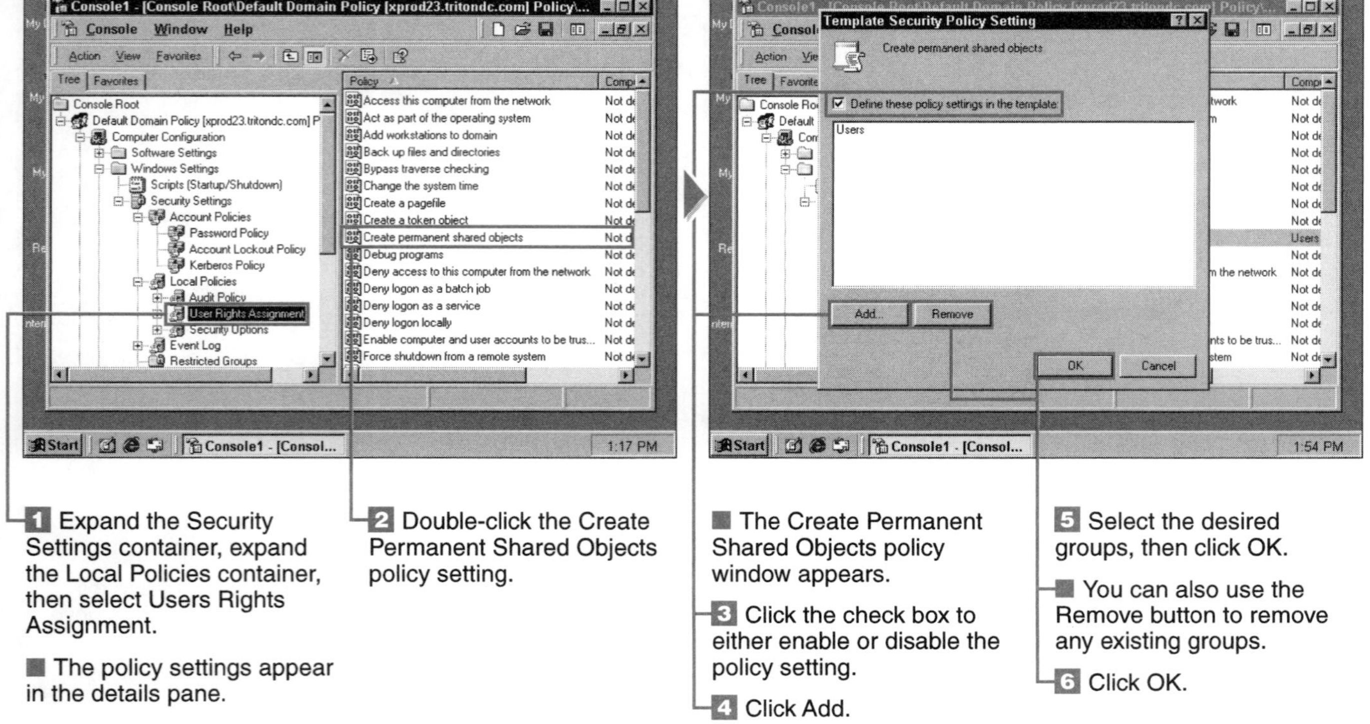

1 Expand the Security Settings container, expand the Local Policies container, then select Users Rights Assignment.

■ The policy settings appear in the details pane.

2 Double-click the Create Permanent Shared Objects policy setting.

■ The Create Permanent Shared Objects policy window appears.

3 Click the check box to either enable or disable the policy setting.

4 Click Add.

5 Select the desired groups, then click OK.

■ You can also use the Remove button to remove any existing groups.

6 Click OK.

DEBUGGING PROGRAMS

When programs malfunction in Windows 2000, you have the option to debug the program. This process generates data about the program and examines the program's code to determine what caused the problem. In many cases, the information gained is not decipherable unless you are a programmer. You can use this policy to allow certain users and groups the right to debug malfunctioning programs.

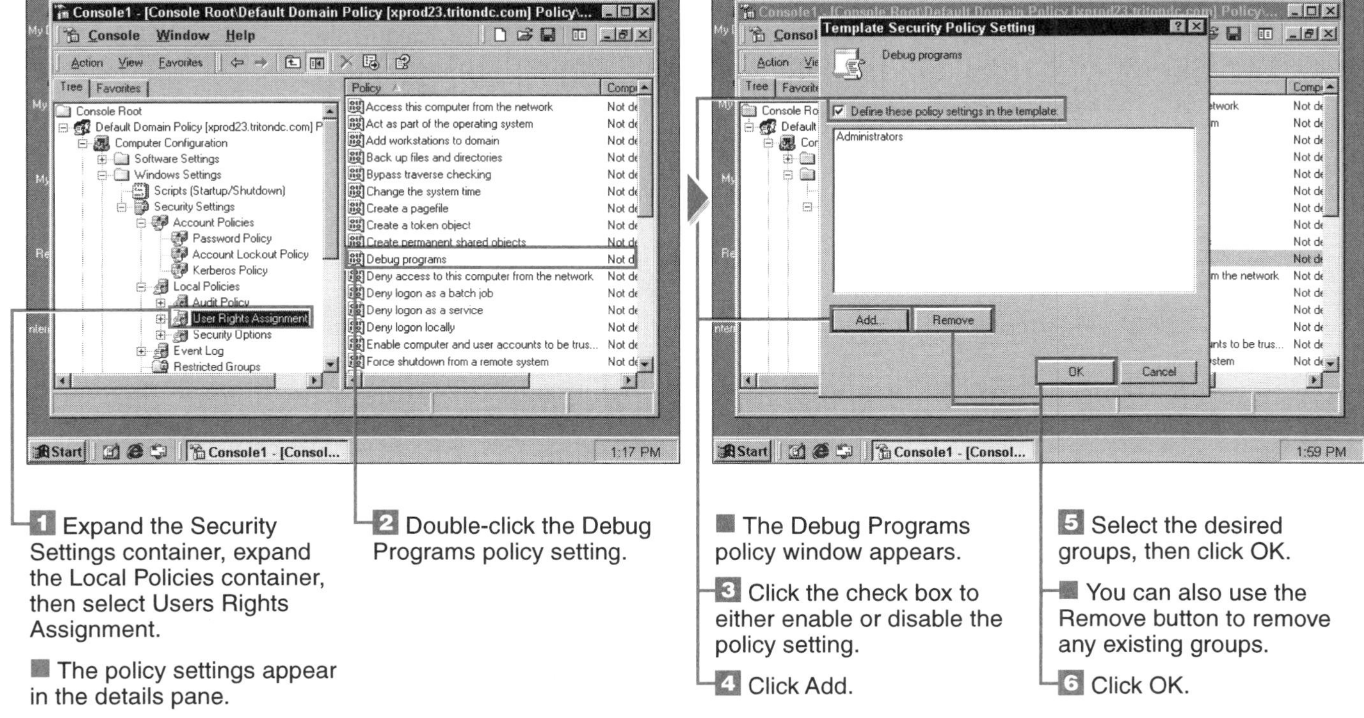

1 Expand the Security Settings container, expand the Local Policies container, then select Users Rights Assignment.

■ The policy settings appear in the details pane.

2 Double-click the Debug Programs policy setting.

■ The Debug Programs policy window appears.

3 Click the check box to either enable or disable the policy setting.

4 Click Add.

5 Select the desired groups, then click OK.

■ You can also use the Remove button to remove any existing groups.

6 Click OK.

DENYING ACCESS TO THIS COMPUTER FROM THE NETWORK

In some cases, you may have particular users or groups for whom you want to deny access to network computers. You can use this policy to configure users or groups who are not permitted to access the network computers. After they are denied access, they will not be able to connect, but other users and groups will be able to connect to network computers normally.

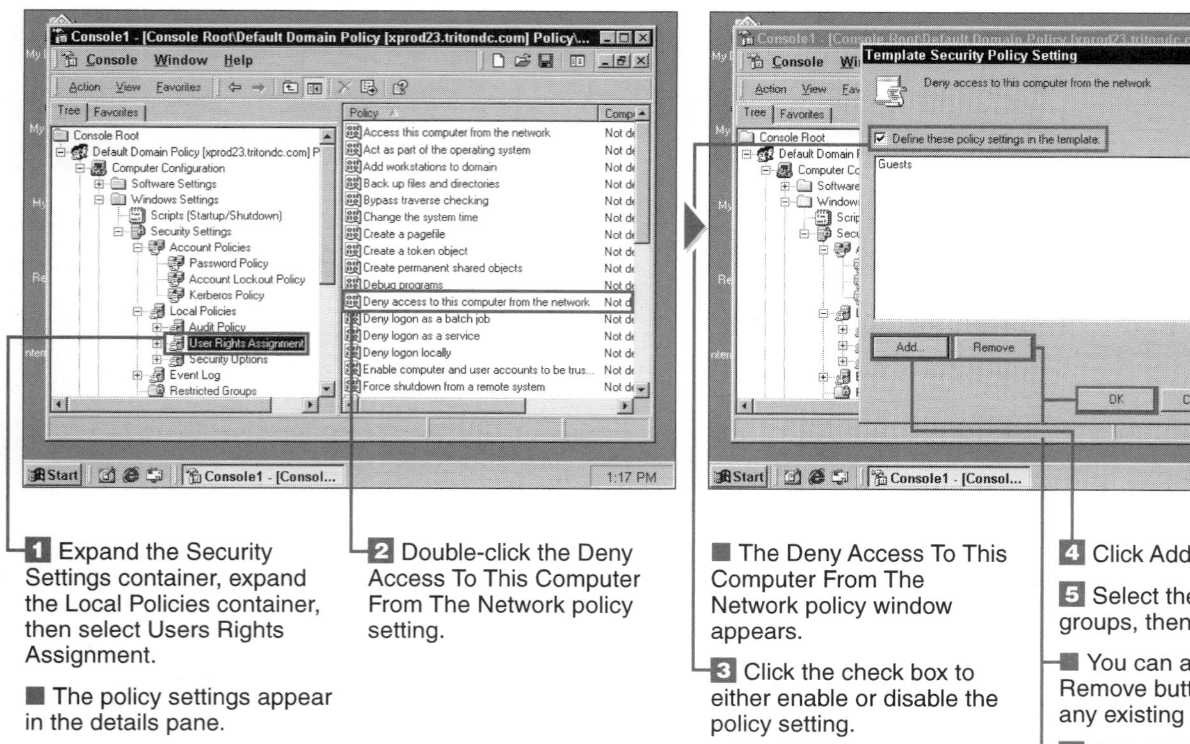

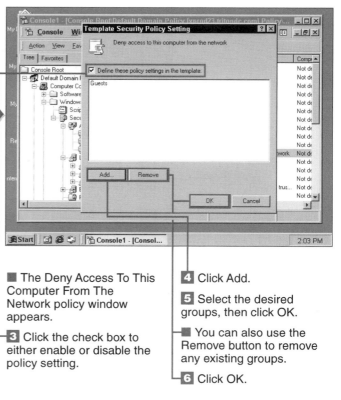

1 Expand the Security Settings container, expand the Local Policies container, then select Users Rights Assignment.

■ The policy settings appear in the details pane.

2 Double-click the Deny Access To This Computer From The Network policy setting.

■ The Deny Access To This Computer From The Network policy window appears.

3 Click the check box to either enable or disable the policy setting.

4 Click Add.

5 Select the desired groups, then click OK.

■ You can also use the Remove button to remove any existing groups.

6 Click OK.

DENYING LOGON AS A BATCH JOB

Batch jobs are scripts that are used for a variety of purposes. This policy prevents certain users or groups from logging onto a computer as a part of a batch job. This is an extra security measure and one you may want to implement, depending on the use of batch jobs on your network. This privilege is granted only to administrators by default.

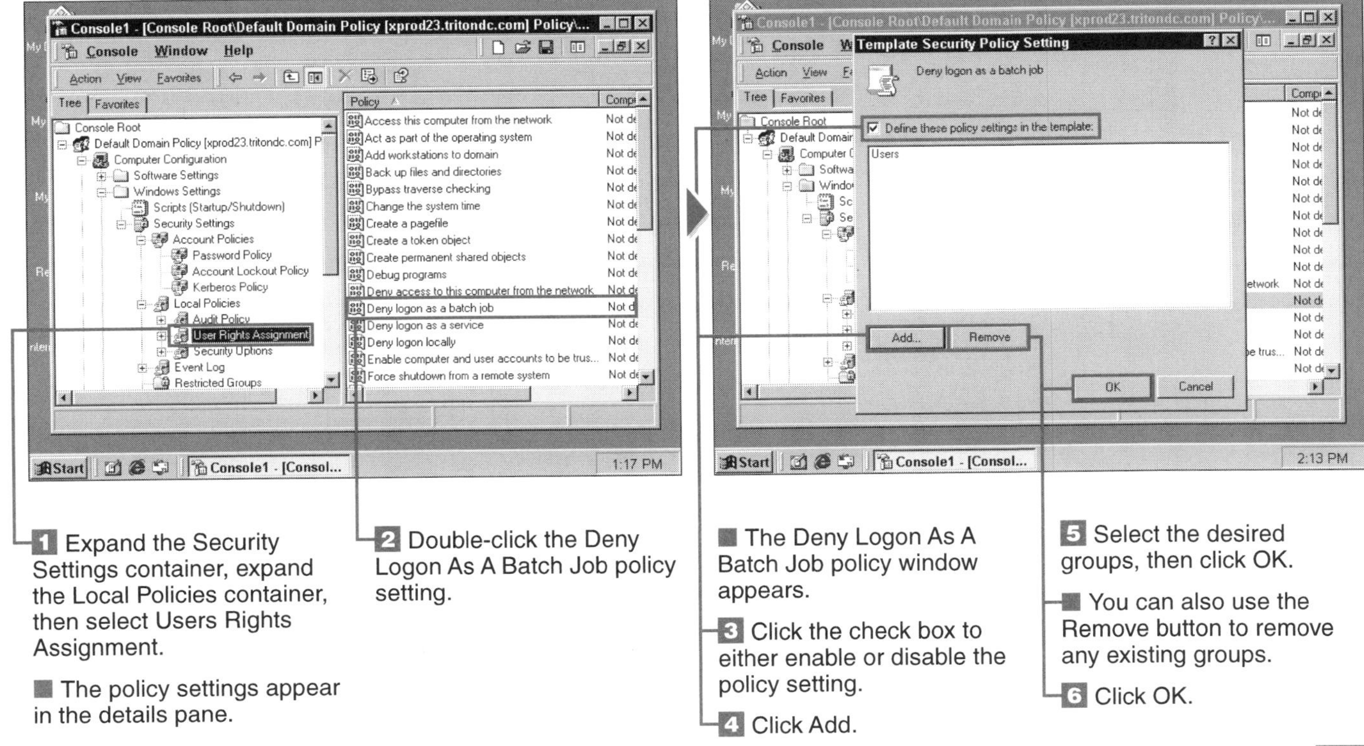

■1 Expand the Security Settings container, expand the Local Policies container, then select Users Rights Assignment.

■ The policy settings appear in the details pane.

■2 Double-click the Deny Logon As A Batch Job policy setting.

■ The Deny Logon As A Batch Job policy window appears.

■3 Click the check box to either enable or disable the policy setting.

■4 Click Add.

■5 Select the desired groups, then click OK.

■ You can also use the Remove button to remove any existing groups.

■6 Click OK.

DENYING LOGON AS A SERVICE

The LocalSystem account of a computer always retains the right to log on as a service. Logging on as a service allows the user to logon with a security principal as a service rather than a user account. This right is not granted to any user by default, but it is granted to services that require a separate account to run.

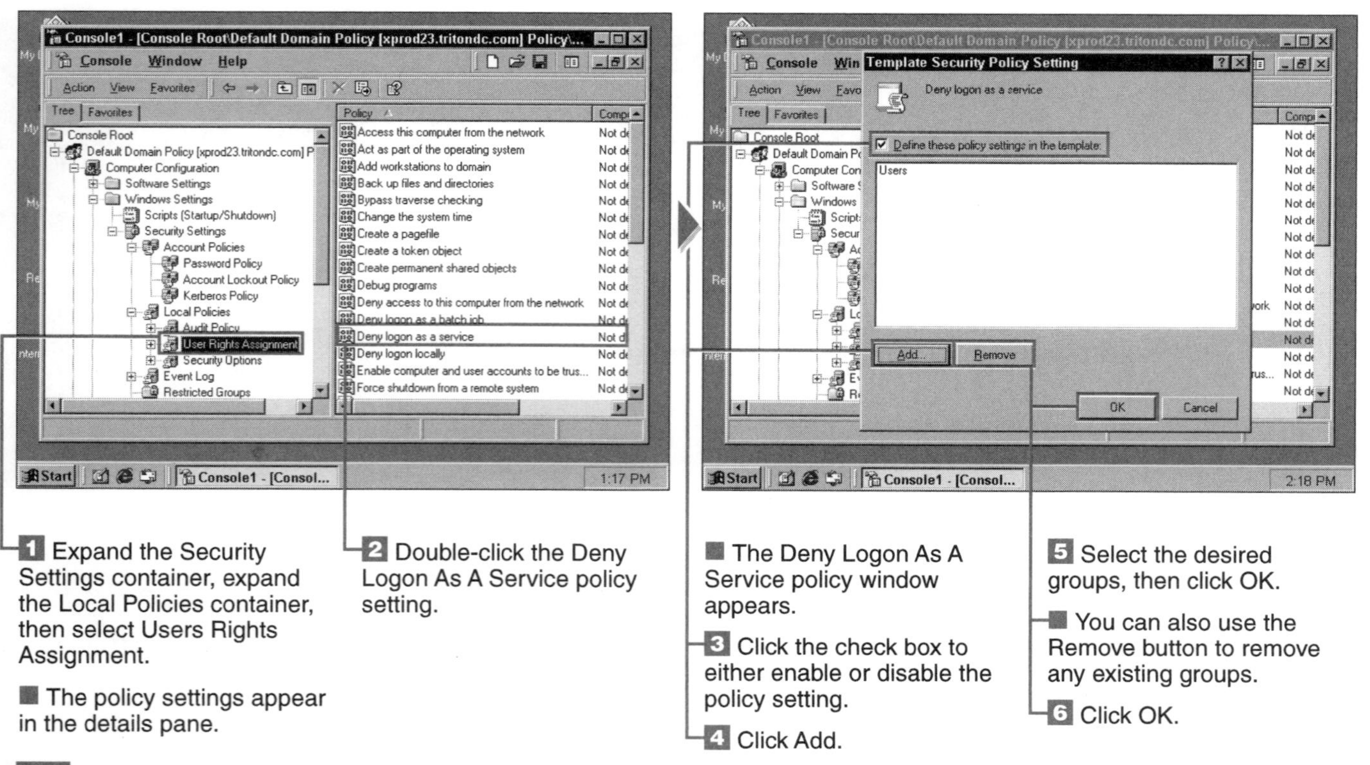

1 Expand the Security Settings container, expand the Local Policies container, then select Users Rights Assignment.

■ The policy settings appear in the details pane.

2 Double-click the Deny Logon As A Service policy setting.

■ The Deny Logon As A Service policy window appears.

3 Click the check box to either enable or disable the policy setting.

4 Click Add.

5 Select the desired groups, then click OK.

■ You can also use the Remove button to remove any existing groups.

6 Click OK.

DENYING LOGON LOCALLY

Logging on locally means that a user can sit down at a computer and log onto the machine. Whereas users may be able to logon to a computer over the network, you can choose to deny the logon locally right to various users and groups as desired. This prevents certain users and groups from physically sitting down at computers and logging onto them.

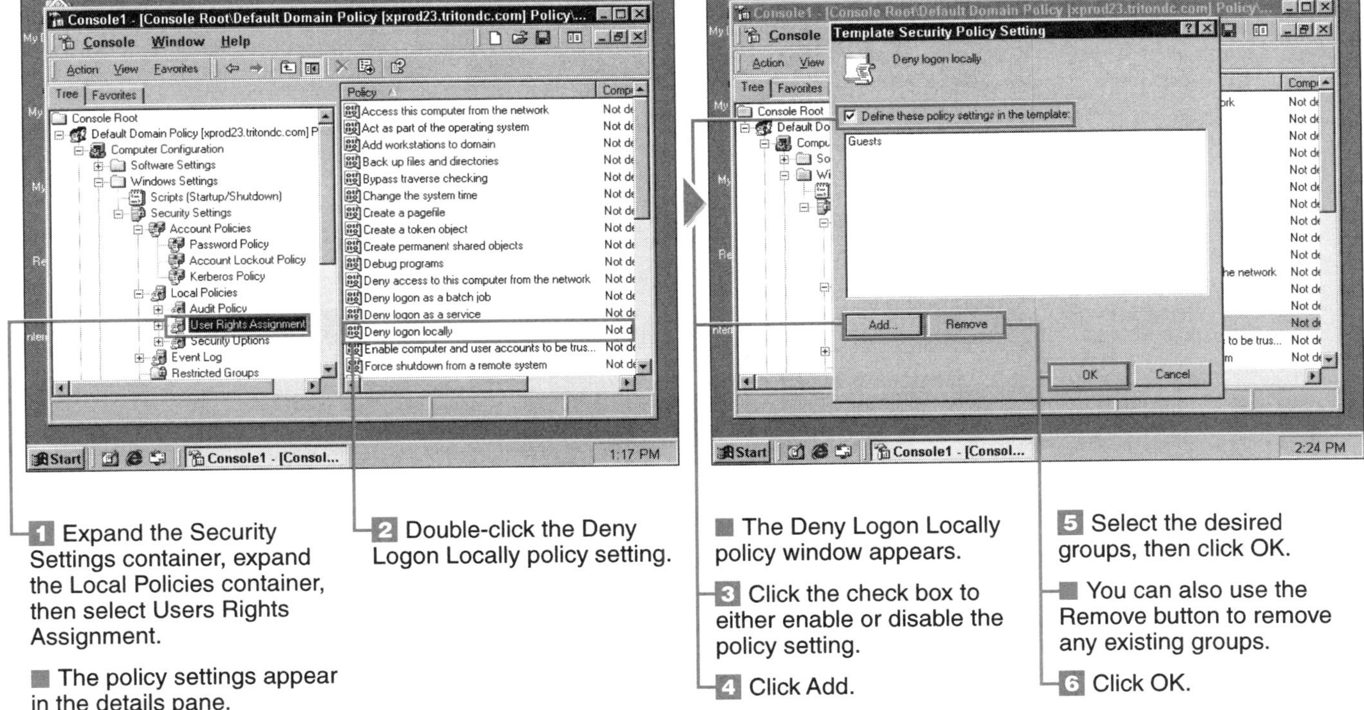

■1 Expand the Security Settings container, expand the Local Policies container, then select Users Rights Assignment.

■ The policy settings appear in the details pane.

■2 Double-click the Deny Logon Locally policy setting.

■ The Deny Logon Locally policy window appears.

■3 Click the check box to either enable or disable the policy setting.

■4 Click Add.

■5 Select the desired groups, then click OK.

■ You can also use the Remove button to remove any existing groups.

■6 Click OK.

ENABLING COMPUTER AND USER ACCOUNTS TO BE TRUSTED FOR DELEGATION

This policy allows computers and user accounts to be trusted for delegation by the users or groups that you specify in the policy. Typically, you should only allow administrators or other advanced groups, such as Power Users, the right to delegate.

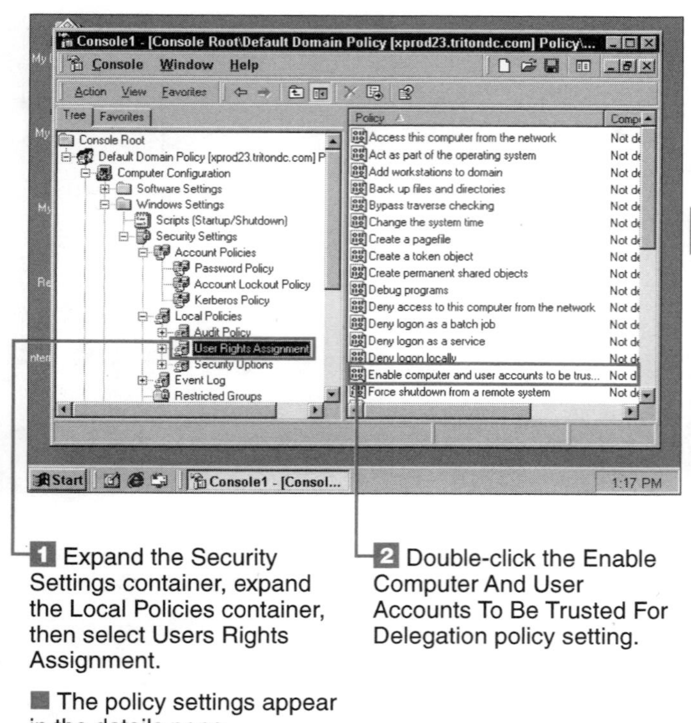

1 Expand the Security Settings container, expand the Local Policies container, then select Users Rights Assignment.

■ The policy settings appear in the details pane.

2 Double-click the Enable Computer And User Accounts To Be Trusted For Delegation policy setting.

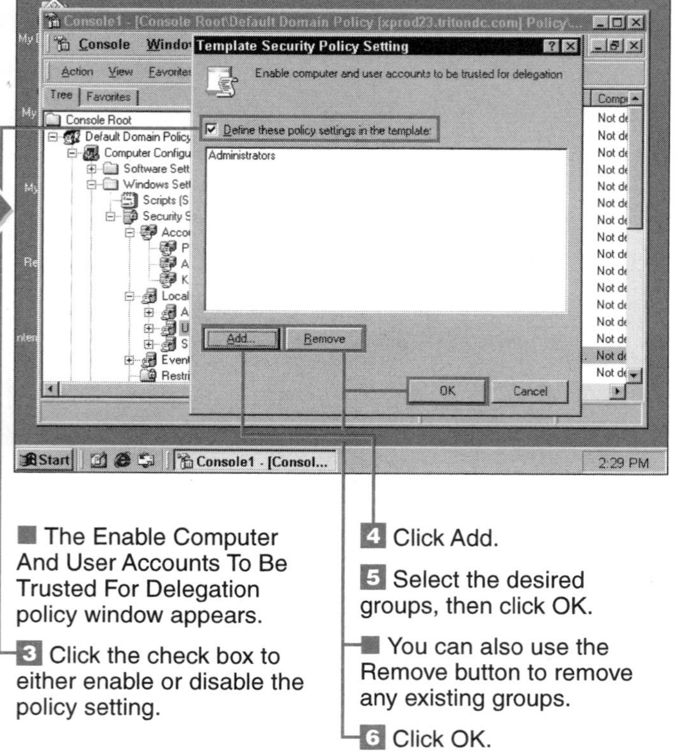

■ The Enable Computer And User Accounts To Be Trusted For Delegation policy window appears.

3 Click the check box to either enable or disable the policy setting.

4 Click Add.

5 Select the desired groups, then click OK.

■ You can also use the Remove button to remove any existing groups.

6 Click OK.

FORCING SHUTDOWN FROM A REMOTE SYSTEM

You can use this policy to allow certain users or groups to force a computer to shut down while logged on at a remote system. Administrators and other power user-type groups can use this policy so that remote management of network computers can be enabled. Obviously, this is not a policy you want to implement for typical user accounts.

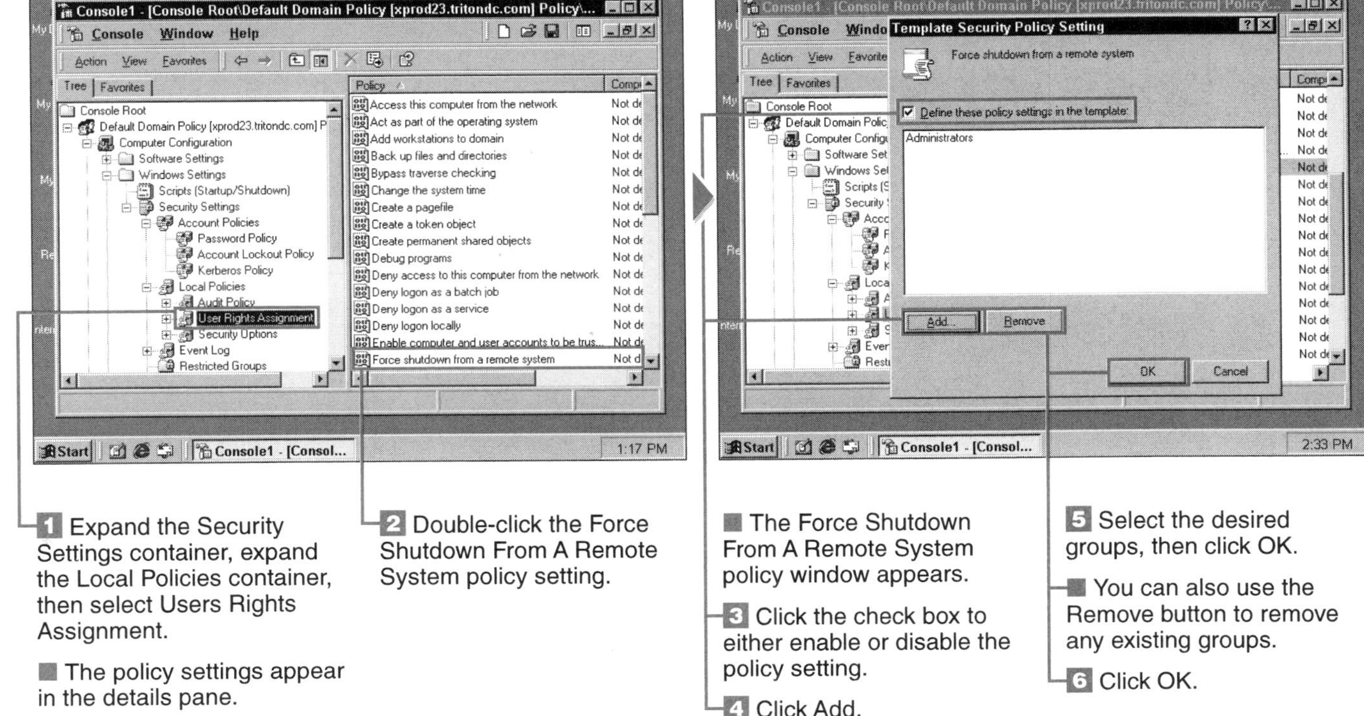

1 Expand the Security Settings container, expand the Local Policies container, then select Users Rights Assignment.

■ The policy settings appear in the details pane.

2 Double-click the Force Shutdown From A Remote System policy setting.

■ The Force Shutdown From A Remote System policy window appears.

3 Click the check box to either enable or disable the policy setting.

4 Click Add.

5 Select the desired groups, then click OK.

■ You can also use the Remove button to remove any existing groups.

6 Click OK.

APPENDIX A

GENERATING SECURITY AUDITS

Security audits are a user right you can assign to desired individuals or groups. Security auditing should only be performed by administrative groups. Security audits enable administrators to gain information about security events within the network and examine potential security problems. This is not a policy you want to enable for the general networking community.

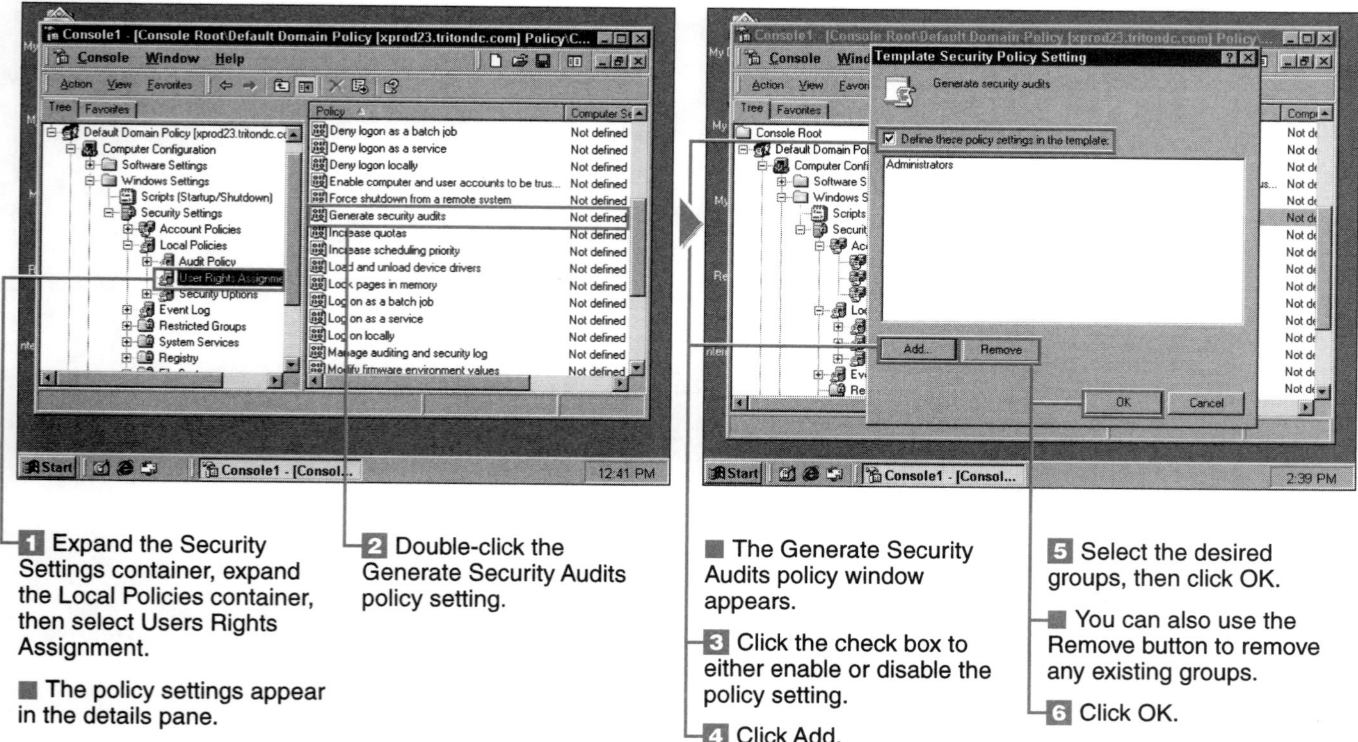

1 Expand the Security Settings container, expand the Local Policies container, then select Users Rights Assignment.

■ The policy settings appear in the details pane.

2 Double-click the Generate Security Audits policy setting.

■ The Generate Security Audits policy window appears.

3 Click the check box to either enable or disable the policy setting.

4 Click Add.

5 Select the desired groups, then click OK.

■ You can also use the Remove button to remove any existing groups.

6 Click OK.

INCREASING QUOTAS

Disk Quotas are used to provide a user a certain amount of storage space on a server. This policy enables you to give certain individuals or users the right to increase existing disk quotas. This is an administrative feature and one that should not be assigned to typical users.

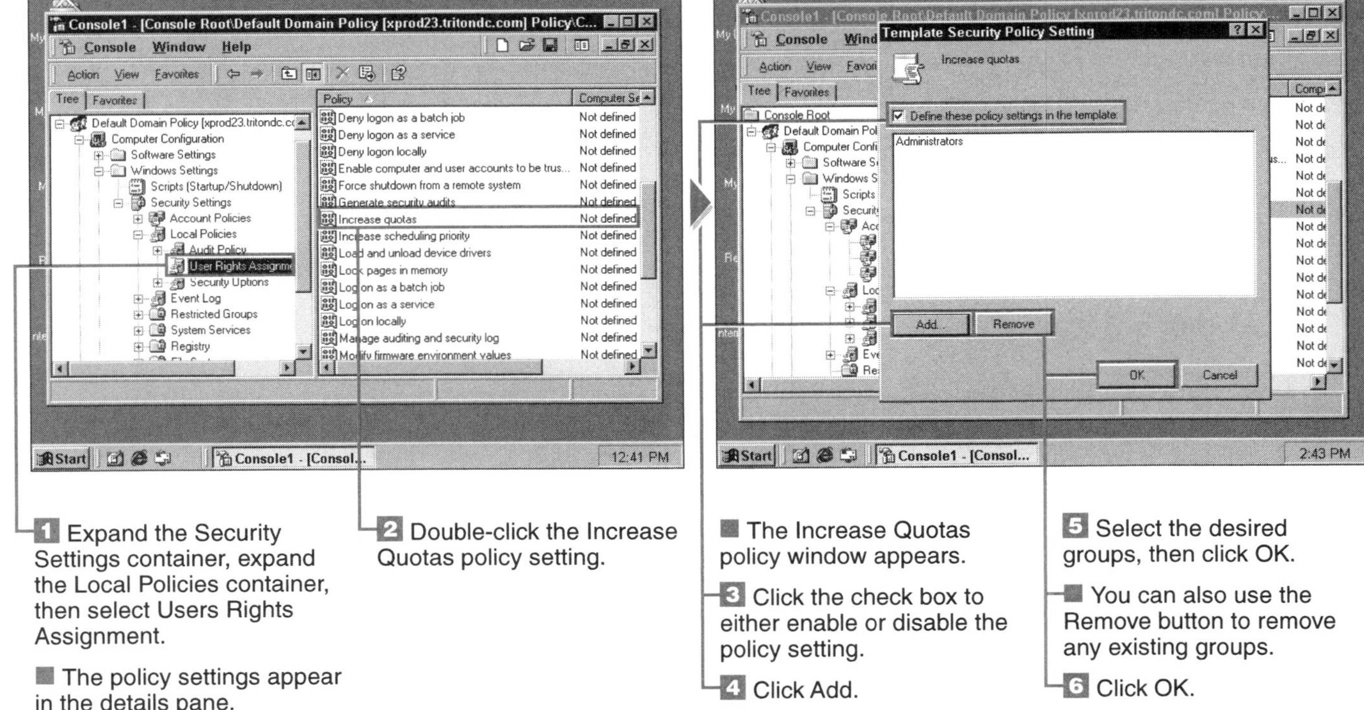

1 Expand the Security Settings container, expand the Local Policies container, then select Users Rights Assignment.

■ The policy settings appear in the details pane.

2 Double-click the Increase Quotas policy setting.

■ The Increase Quotas policy window appears.

3 Click the check box to either enable or disable the policy setting.

4 Click Add.

5 Select the desired groups, then click OK.

■ You can also use the Remove button to remove any existing groups.

6 Click OK.

INCREASING THE SCHEDULING OF PRIORITIES

This policy gives the users or groups you select the right to increase the way a computer system schedules priority processing. This action can be used to increase the productivity of a workstation, but it is an administrative task that should not be performed by typical end-users.

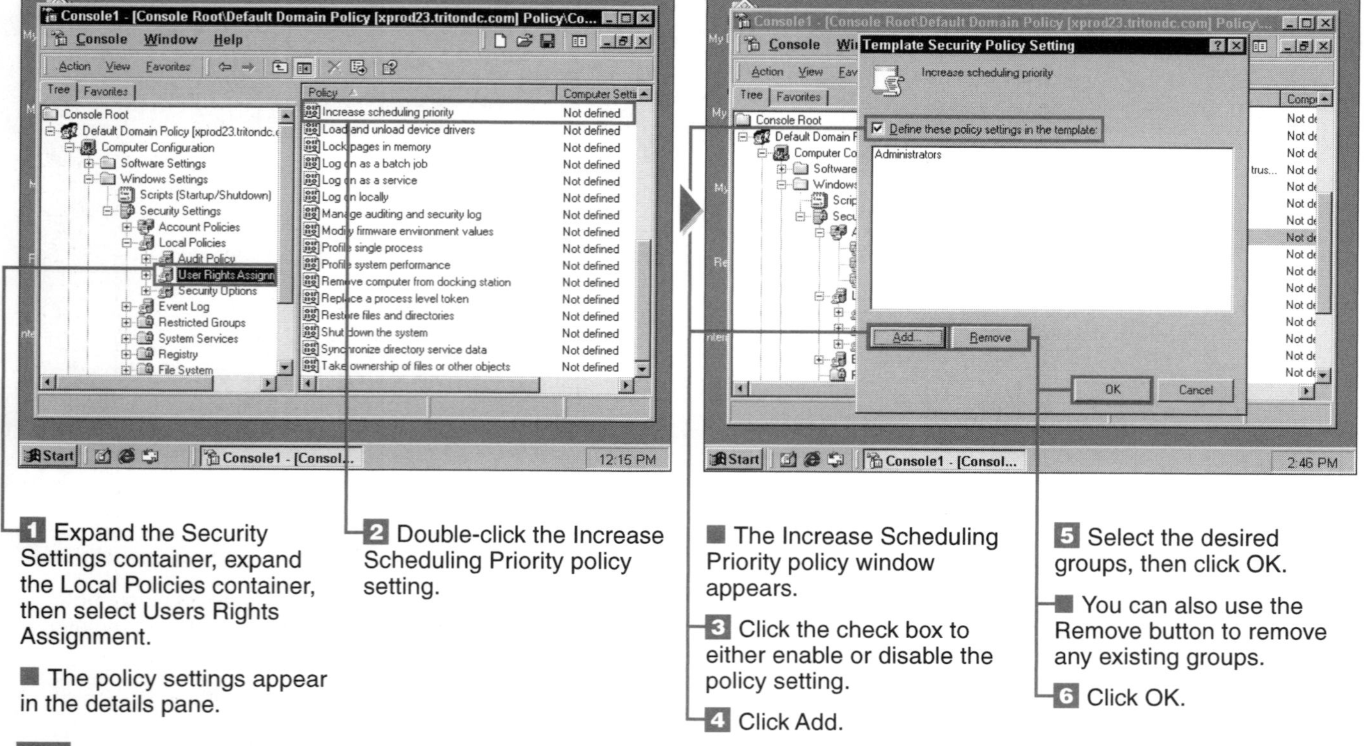

1 Expand the Security Settings container, expand the Local Policies container, then select Users Rights Assignment.

■ The policy settings appear in the details pane.

2 Double-click the Increase Scheduling Priority policy setting.

■ The Increase Scheduling Priority policy window appears.

3 Click the check box to either enable or disable the policy setting.

4 Click Add.

5 Select the desired groups, then click OK.

■ You can also use the Remove button to remove any existing groups.

6 Click OK.

LOADING AND UNLOADING DEVICE DRIVERS

This policy allows the users and groups you select to configure computers by loading or unloading device drivers. This policy can be applied to both administrative and user accounts, depending if you want your users to be able to configure their own system hardware. When a driver is unloaded, the device is essentially removed from the system. As drivers are updated for various devices, they may need to be installed on your desktop systems, and this policy allows you to determine who has that right.

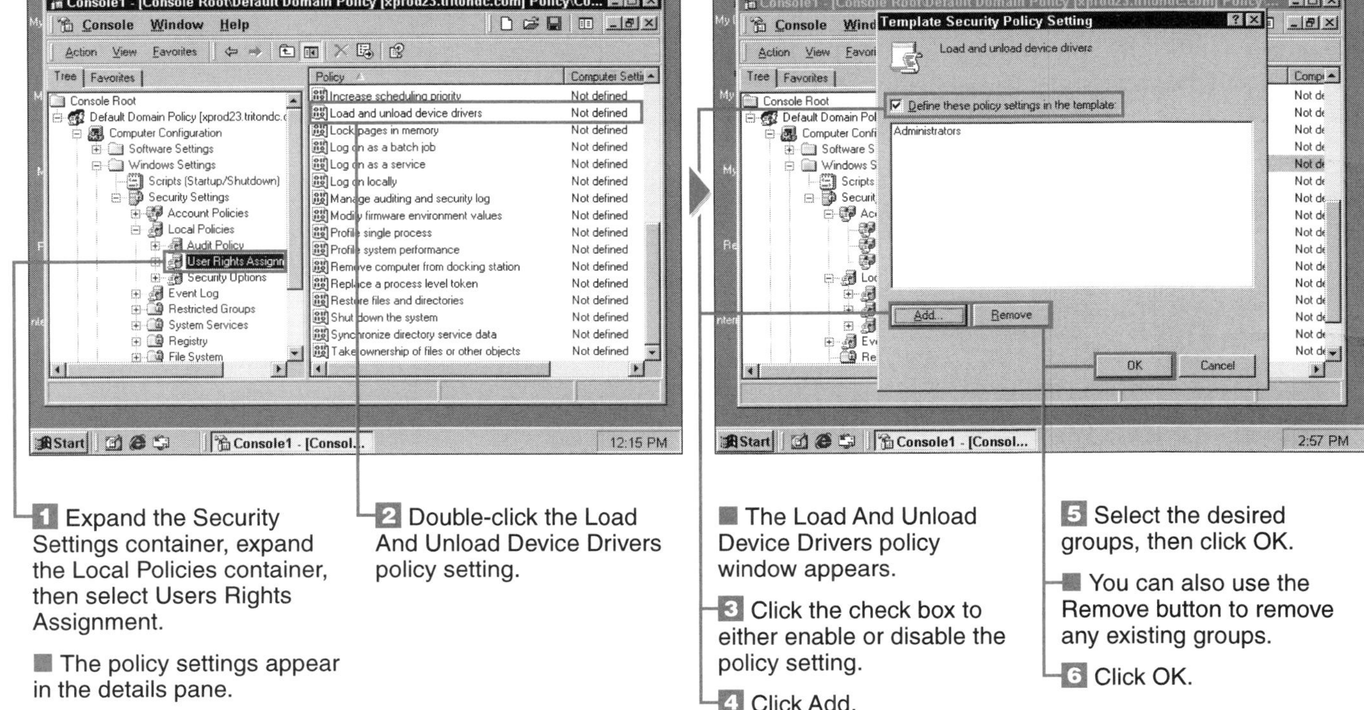

1 Expand the Security Settings container, expand the Local Policies container, then select Users Rights Assignment.

■ The policy settings appear in the details pane.

2 Double-click the Load And Unload Device Drivers policy setting.

■ The Load And Unload Device Drivers policy window appears.

3 Click the check box to either enable or disable the policy setting.

4 Click Add.

5 Select the desired groups, then click OK.

■ You can also use the Remove button to remove any existing groups.

6 Click OK.

LOCKING PAGES IN MEMORY

This policy allows the users or groups you select to lock system pages into memory. This is an advanced operation that should only be performed by administrators, and not one you should give to typical users. The lock pages option allows you to force a system to hold certain pages in physical memory instead of using a pagefile.

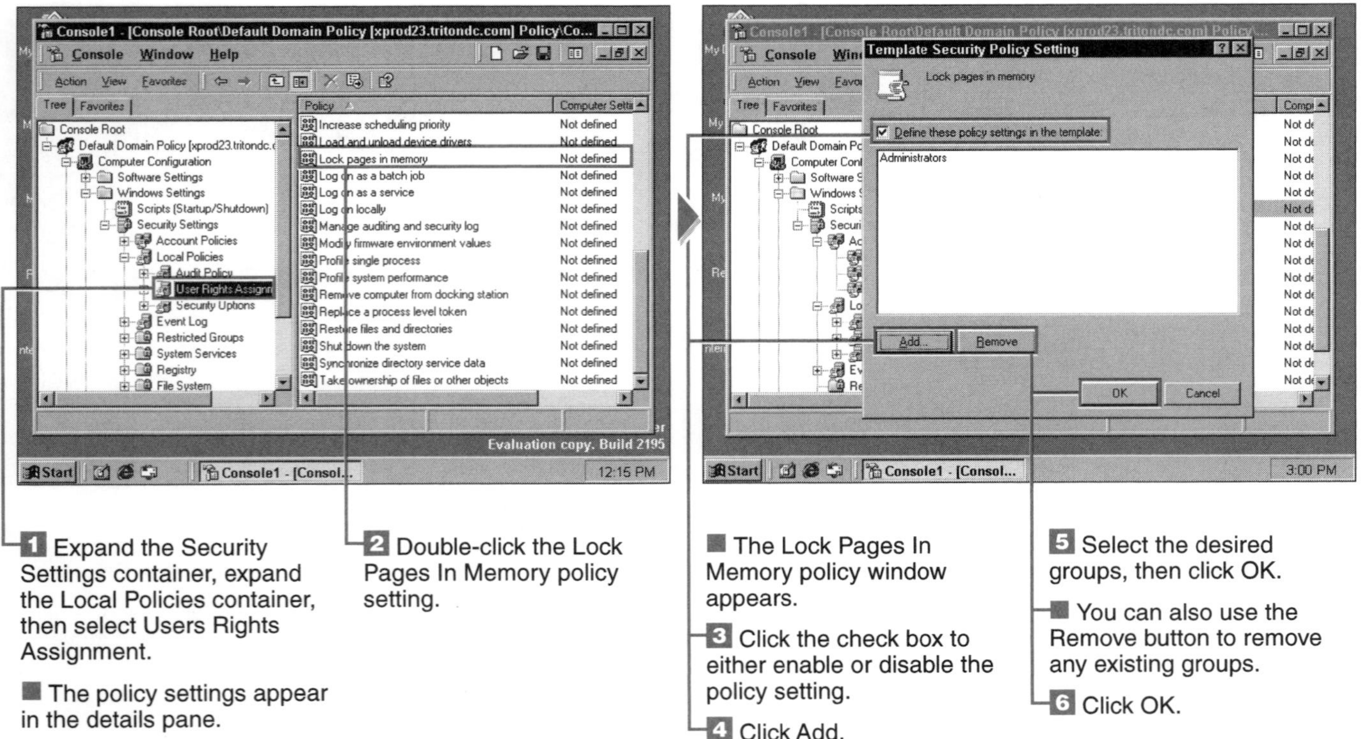

1 Expand the Security Settings container, expand the Local Policies container, then select Users Rights Assignment.

■ The policy settings appear in the details pane.

2 Double-click the Lock Pages In Memory policy setting.

■ The Lock Pages In Memory policy window appears.

3 Click the check box to either enable or disable the policy setting.

4 Click Add.

5 Select the desired groups, then click OK.

■ You can also use the Remove button to remove any existing groups.

6 Click OK.

SHUTTING DOWN THE SYSTEM

This policy gives users or administrators the right to shut down a computer system. You can use this policy to prevent certain user groups from shutting down a system and grant that right to others.

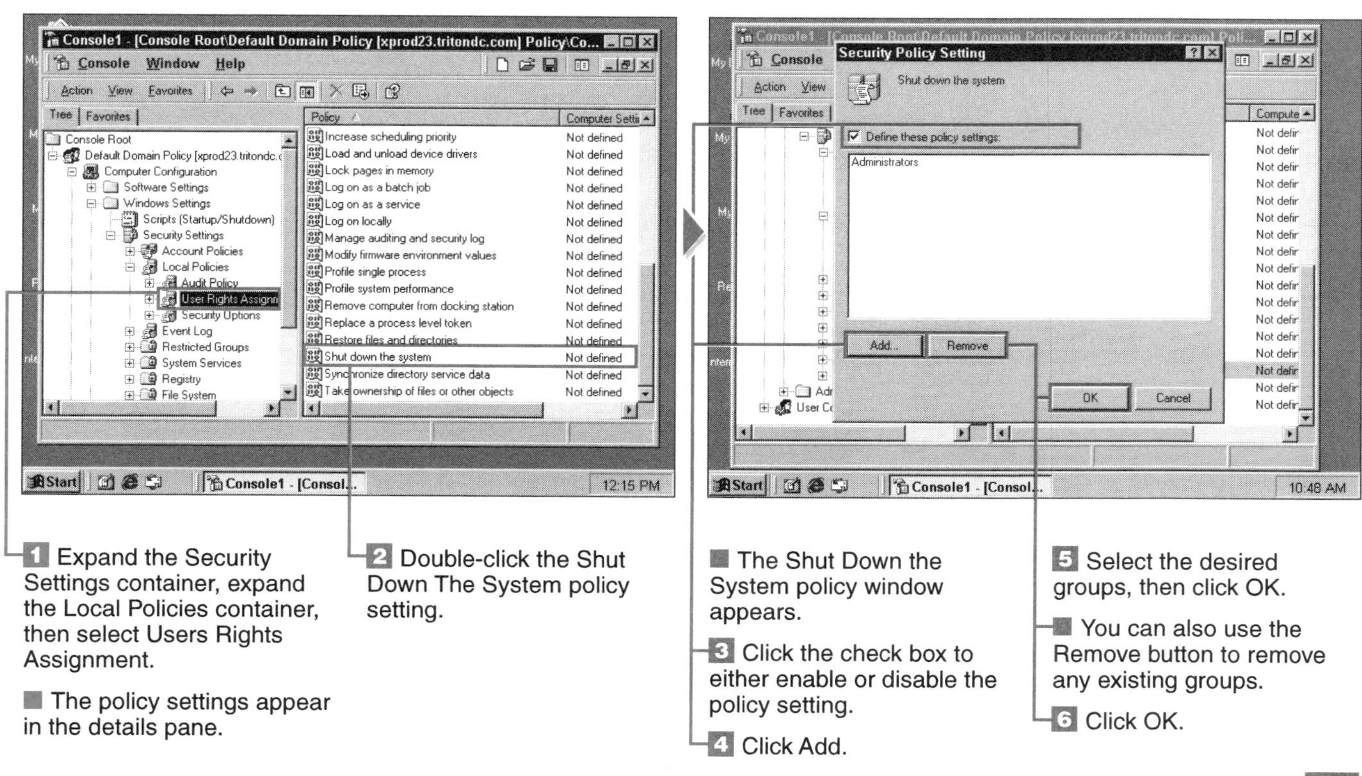

1 Expand the Security Settings container, expand the Local Policies container, then select Users Rights Assignment.

■ The policy settings appear in the details pane.

2 Double-click the Shut Down The System policy setting.

■ The Shut Down the System policy window appears.

3 Click the check box to either enable or disable the policy setting.

4 Click Add.

5 Select the desired groups, then click OK.

■ You can also use the Remove button to remove any existing groups.

6 Click OK.

TAKING OWNERSHIP OF FILES AND OTHER OBJECTS

Windows 2000 allows the taking of ownership of files and objects. This feature allows one person to create a file and another to take ownership of the file. This feature is helpful in a variety of circumstances, such as when an employee leaves the company. You determine which users or groups have the ownership right by configuring this policy. Under most circumstances, the take ownership right should be restricted to administrators or other administrative type groups.

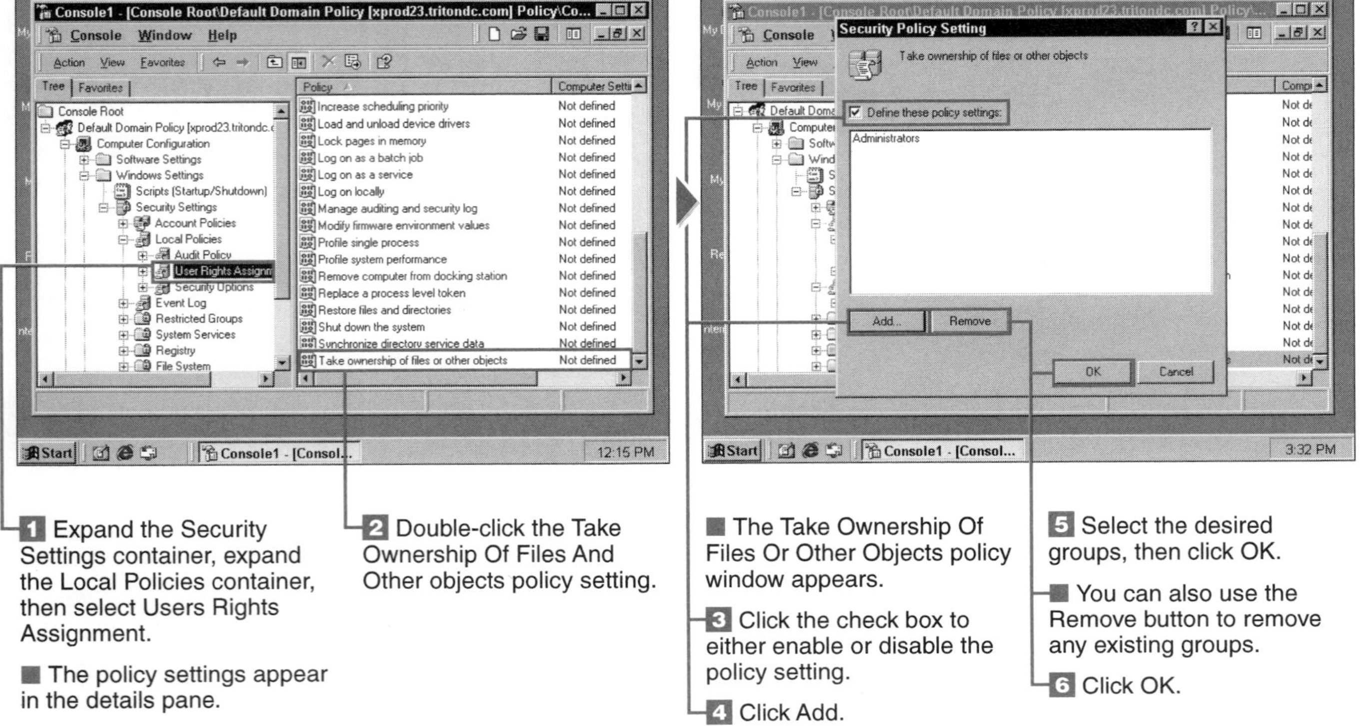

1 Expand the Security Settings container, expand the Local Policies container, then select Users Rights Assignment.

■ The policy settings appear in the details pane.

2 Double-click the Take Ownership Of Files And Other objects policy setting.

■ The Take Ownership Of Files Or Other Objects policy window appears.

3 Click the check box to either enable or disable the policy setting.

4 Click Add.

5 Select the desired groups, then click OK.

■ You can also use the Remove button to remove any existing groups.

6 Click OK.

REMOVING A COMPUTER FROM A DOCKING STATION

Portable computers, such as laptops, can be placed on docking station when they are physically connected to the LAN. This policy allows you to select users or groups that have the right to remove a docked computer from the docking station. This right can apply to any necessary users and groups.

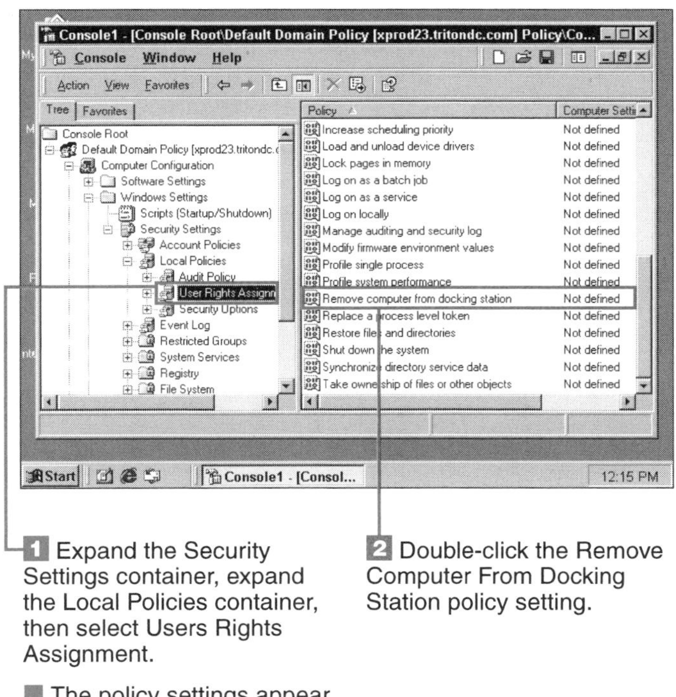

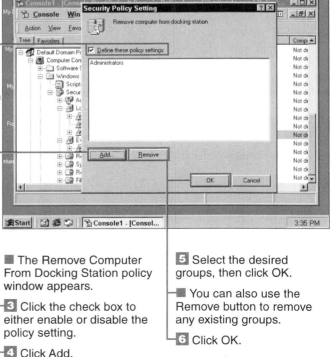

1 Expand the Security Settings container, expand the Local Policies container, then select Users Rights Assignment.

■ The policy settings appear in the details pane.

2 Double-click the Remove Computer From Docking Station policy setting.

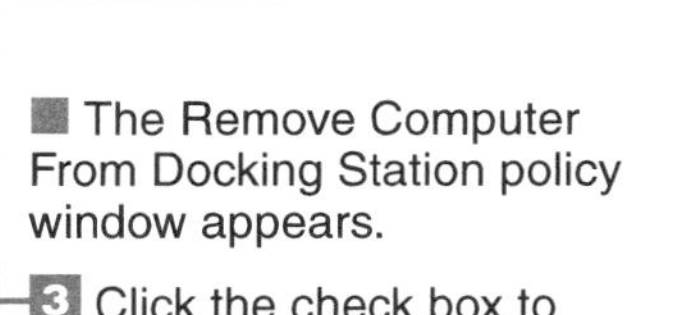

■ The Remove Computer From Docking Station policy window appears.

3 Click the check box to either enable or disable the policy setting.

4 Click Add.

5 Select the desired groups, then click OK.

■ You can also use the Remove button to remove any existing groups.

6 Click OK.

MANAGING AUDITING AND SECURITY LOG

The Audit and Security logs store audit and security information for the local machine. The logs are used by administrators to gain an understanding of how the computer is being used and who is using the computer. The Managing Auditing And Security Log policy allows you to assign rights to users or groups so that those users or groups can manage the auditing and security log. This task is an administrative or power user function.

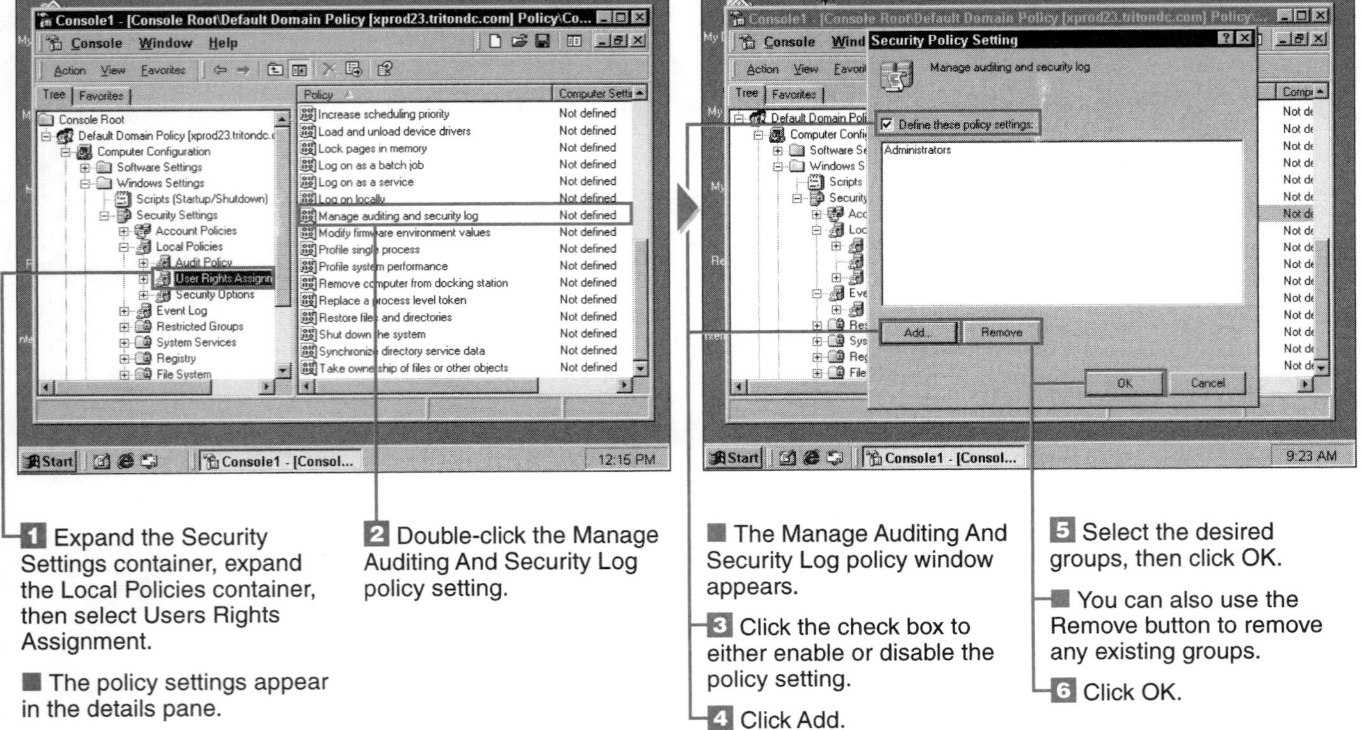

1 Expand the Security Settings container, expand the Local Policies container, then select Users Rights Assignment.

■ The policy settings appear in the details pane.

2 Double-click the Manage Auditing And Security Log policy setting.

■ The Manage Auditing And Security Log policy window appears.

3 Click the check box to either enable or disable the policy setting.

4 Click Add.

5 Select the desired groups, then click OK.

■ You can also use the Remove button to remove any existing groups.

6 Click OK.

CHOOSING THE MAXIMUM APPLICATION LOG SIZE

The Event Log container of Security settings allows you to configure how the Event Log functions for client computers to whom the policy applies. Your first option is the maximum Application Log Size. Event Logs are useful, but can use up a lot of hard disk space. You can use this policy to set the maximum size of the Application Log. The default setting is 512 kilobytes.

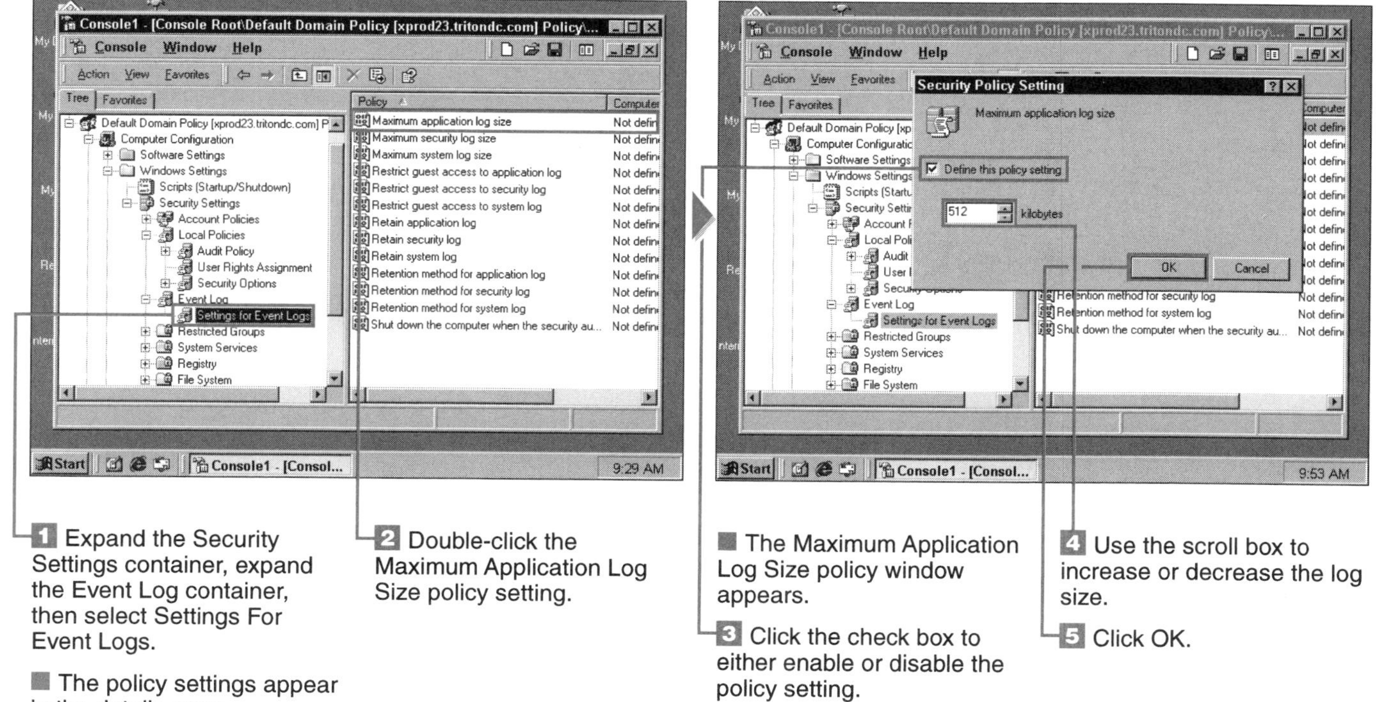

1 Expand the Security Settings container, expand the Event Log container, then select Settings For Event Logs.

■ The policy settings appear in the details pane.

2 Double-click the Maximum Application Log Size policy setting.

■ The Maximum Application Log Size policy window appears.

3 Click the check box to either enable or disable the policy setting.

4 Use the scroll box to increase or decrease the log size.

5 Click OK.

CHOOSING THE MAXIMUM SECURITY LOG SIZE

The Event Log container of Security settings allows you to configure how the Event Log functions for client computers to whom the policy applies. Your second option is the maximum Security Log Size. Event Logs are useful, but can use up a lot of hard disk space. You can use this policy to set the maximum size of the Security Log. The default setting is 512 kilobytes.

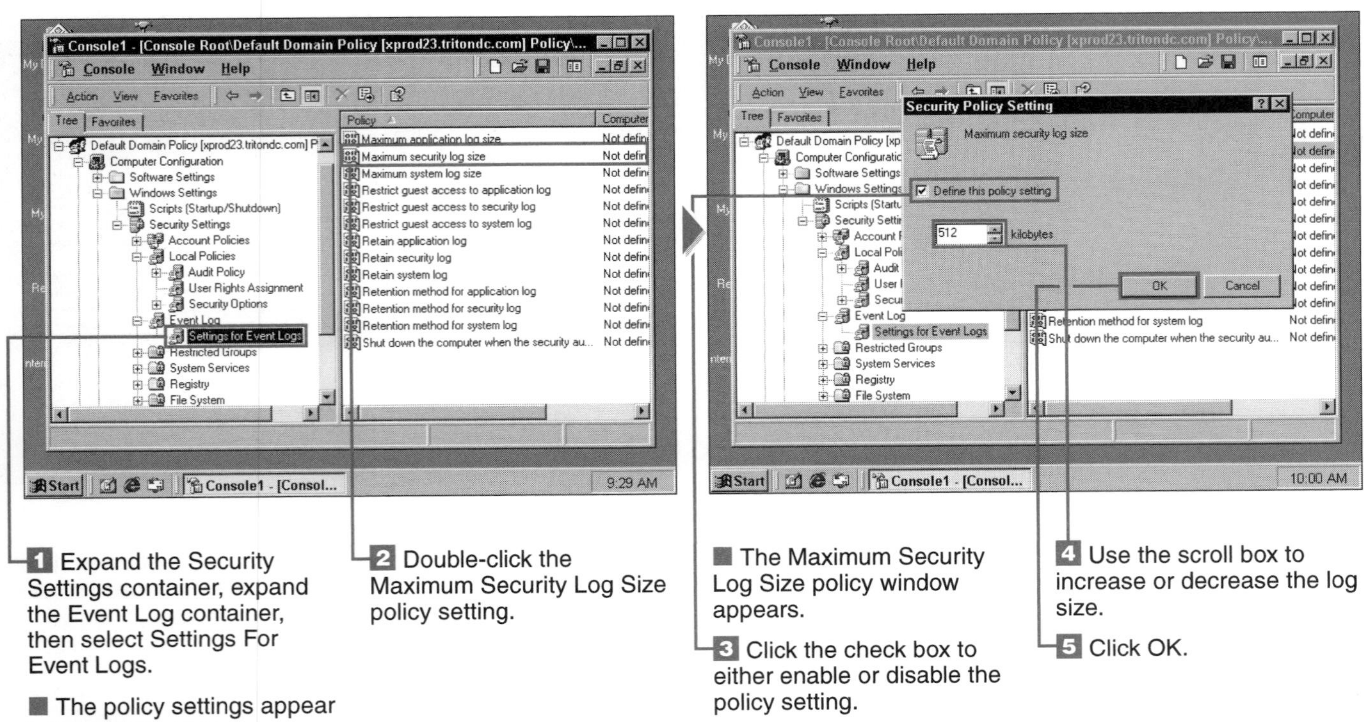

1 Expand the Security Settings container, expand the Event Log container, then select Settings For Event Logs.

■ The policy settings appear in the details pane.

2 Double-click the Maximum Security Log Size policy setting.

■ The Maximum Security Log Size policy window appears.

3 Click the check box to either enable or disable the policy setting.

4 Use the scroll box to increase or decrease the log size.

5 Click OK.

RESTRICTING GUEST ACCESS TO APPLICATION LOG

By default, users can view the application, security, and system logs in Event Viewer. As a security precaution, you can use this policy to restrict access so that users that log on with a guest account cannot access the application, security, or system logs of computers within this Group Policy.

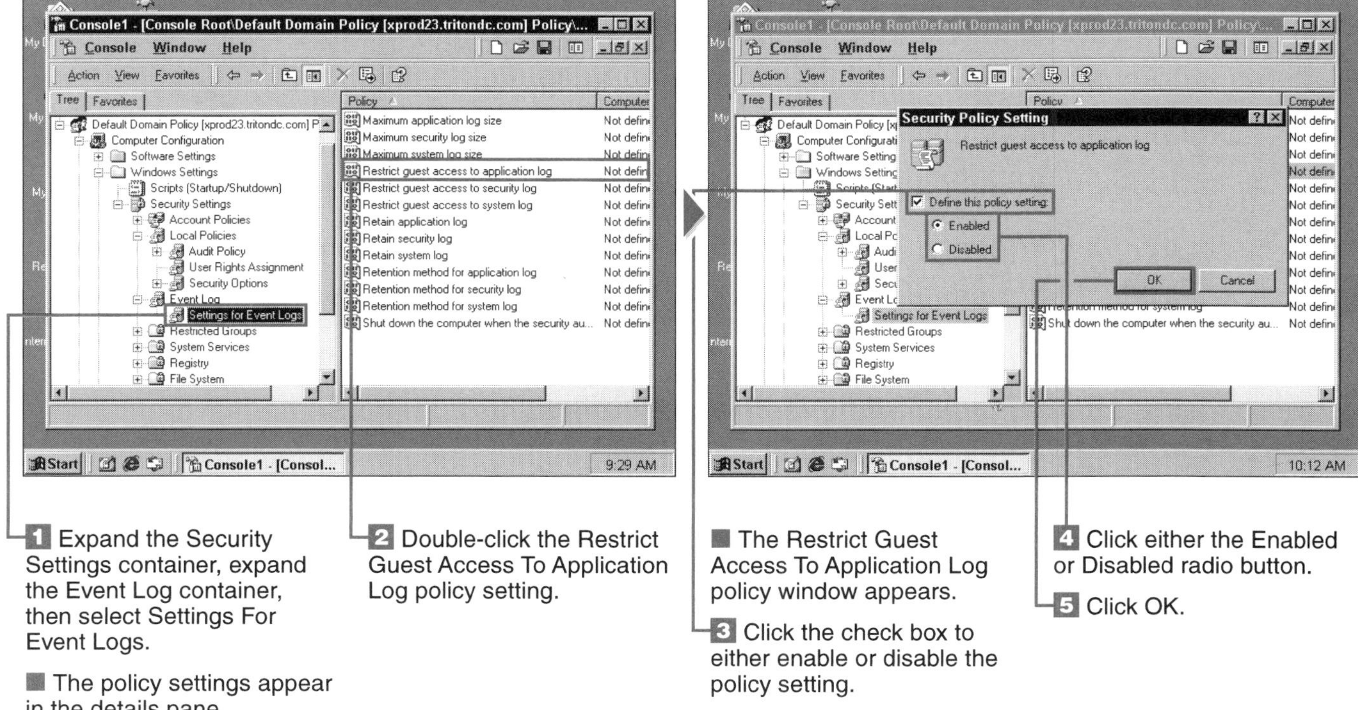

1 Expand the Security Settings container, expand the Event Log container, then select Settings For Event Logs.

■ The policy settings appear in the details pane.

2 Double-click the Restrict Guest Access To Application Log policy setting.

■ The Restrict Guest Access To Application Log policy window appears.

3 Click the check box to either enable or disable the policy setting.

4 Click either the Enabled or Disabled radio button.

5 Click OK.

RESTRICTING GUEST ACCESS TO SECURITY LOG

Users can use the Event Viewer to view the application, security, and system logs. You can use this policy as a security precaution to restrict access to users that log on with a guest account. You can specify guest users that do not have access to the application, security, or system logs of computers within this Group Policy.

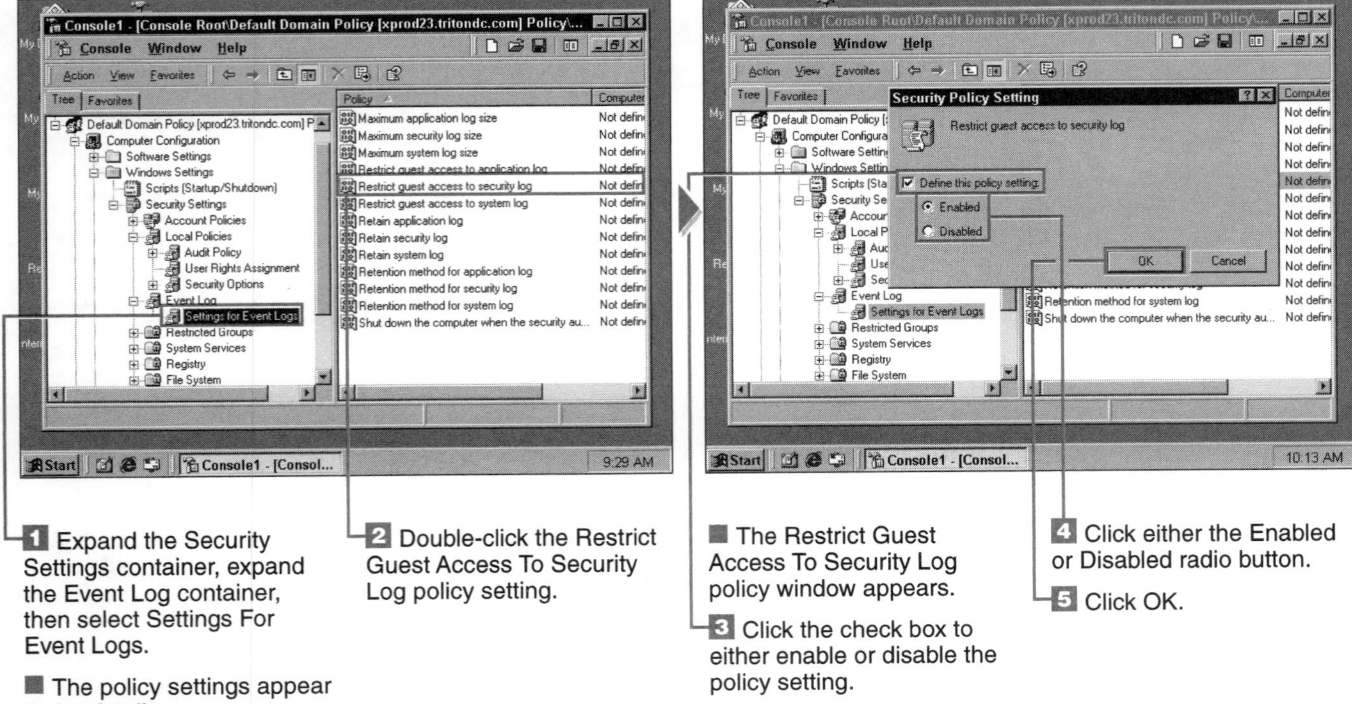

1 Expand the Security Settings container, expand the Event Log container, then select Settings For Event Logs.

■ The policy settings appear in the details pane.

2 Double-click the Restrict Guest Access To Security Log policy setting.

■ The Restrict Guest Access To Security Log policy window appears.

3 Click the check box to either enable or disable the policy setting.

4 Click either the Enabled or Disabled radio button.

5 Click OK.

RESTRICTING GUEST ACCESS TO SYSTEM LOG

By using the Event Viewer, users can view system logs as well as application and security logs. You can ensure, however, as a security precaution, that users that log on with a guest account cannot access the application, security, or system logs of computers within this Group Policy..

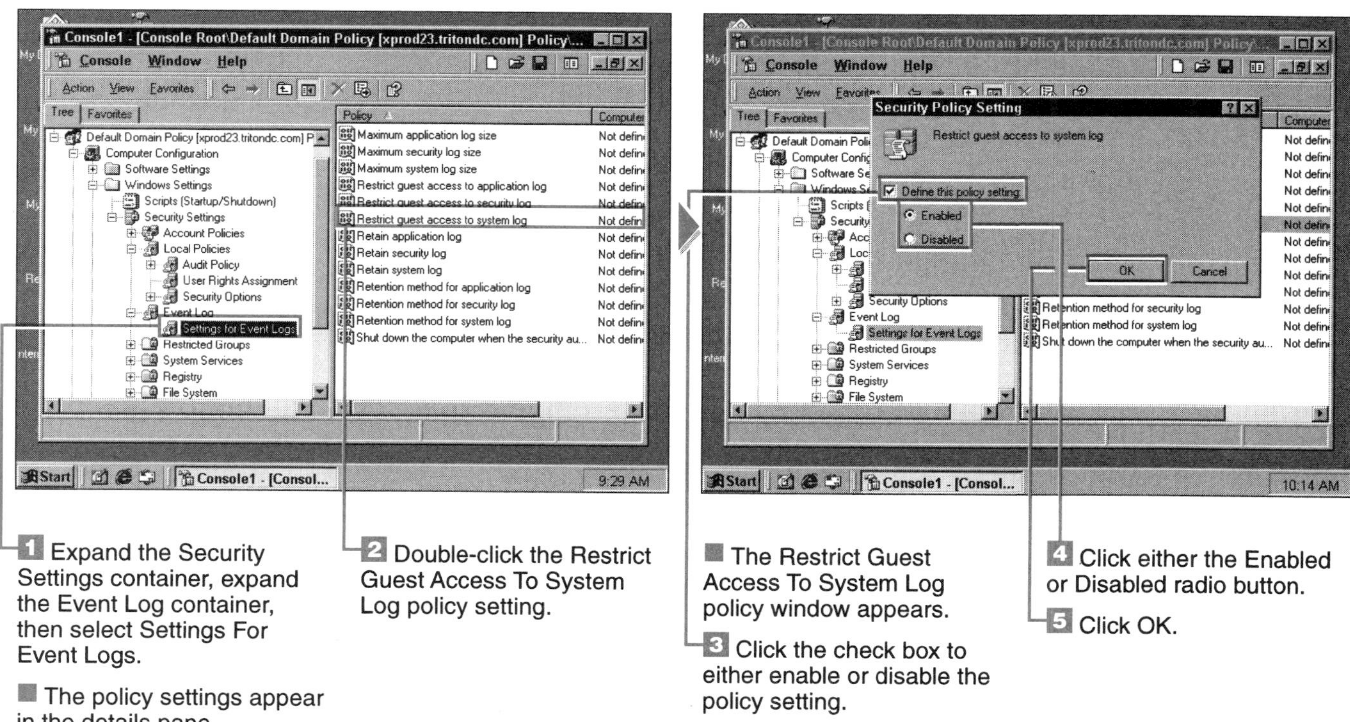

1 Expand the Security Settings container, expand the Event Log container, then select Settings For Event Logs.

■ The policy settings appear in the details pane.

2 Double-click the Restrict Guest Access To System Log policy setting.

■ The Restrict Guest Access To System Log policy window appears.

3 Click the check box to either enable or disable the policy setting.

4 Click either the Enabled or Disabled radio button.

5 Click OK.

RETAINING APPLICATION LOG

You can define policies so that log files are retained on client computers within the Group Policy for a certain number of days. The default setting is for the system to overwrite events that are older than 7 days. You can raise or lower this value to meet your needs, but this default configuration allows the computer system to retain the log file for a week. Keep in mind that if you raise the value, client computers will need more disk space to store the logs as they grow.

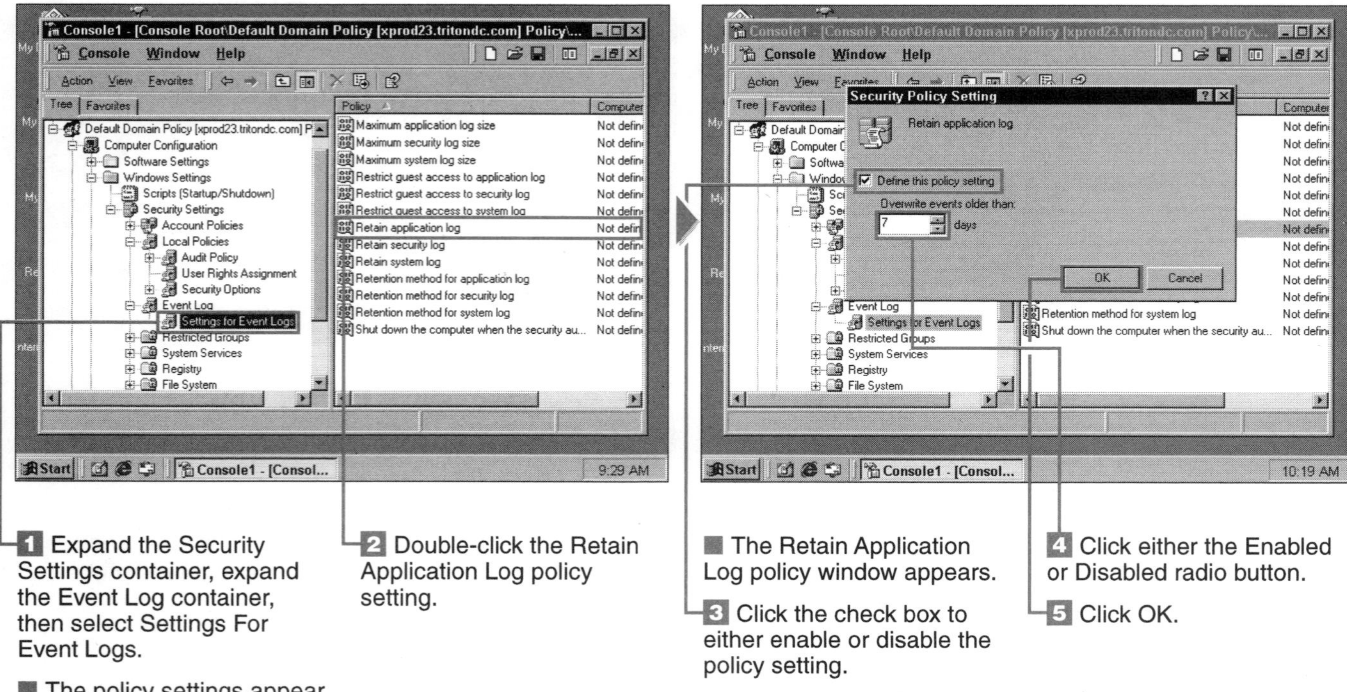

1 Expand the Security Settings container, expand the Event Log container, then select Settings For Event Logs.

■ The policy settings appear in the details pane.

2 Double-click the Retain Application Log policy setting.

■ The Retain Application Log policy window appears.

3 Click the check box to either enable or disable the policy setting.

4 Click either the Enabled or Disabled radio button.

5 Click OK.

RETAINING SECURITY LOG

You can retain security log files on client computers within the Group Policy for a certain number of days. The system, by default, overwrites events that are older than 7 days. This default configuration allows the computer system to retain the log file for a week, but you can raise or lower this value to meet your needs. Client computers will need more disk space to store the logs as they grow — something to keep in mind if you raise the value.

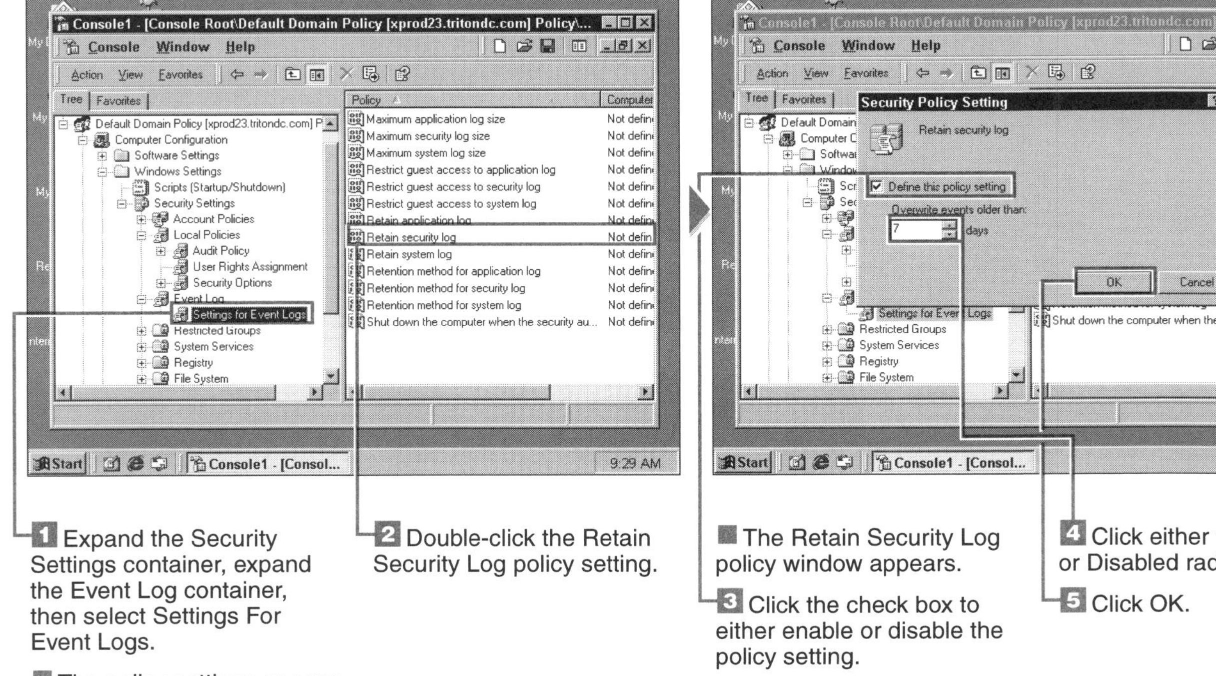

1 Expand the Security Settings container, expand the Event Log container, then select Settings For Event Logs.

■ The policy settings appear in the details pane.

2 Double-click the Retain Security Log policy setting.

■ The Retain Security Log policy window appears.

3 Click the check box to either enable or disable the policy setting.

4 Click either the Enabled or Disabled radio button.

5 Click OK.

RETAINING SYSTEM LOG

The Group Policy can be set up to retain system log files for a specified number of days. Events that are older than 7 days will be overwritten by the system (this is the default setting). Depending on your needs, however, you can raise or lower this value. Note that client computers usually need more disk space to store the logs as they grow. This is important to know if you decide to raise the value.

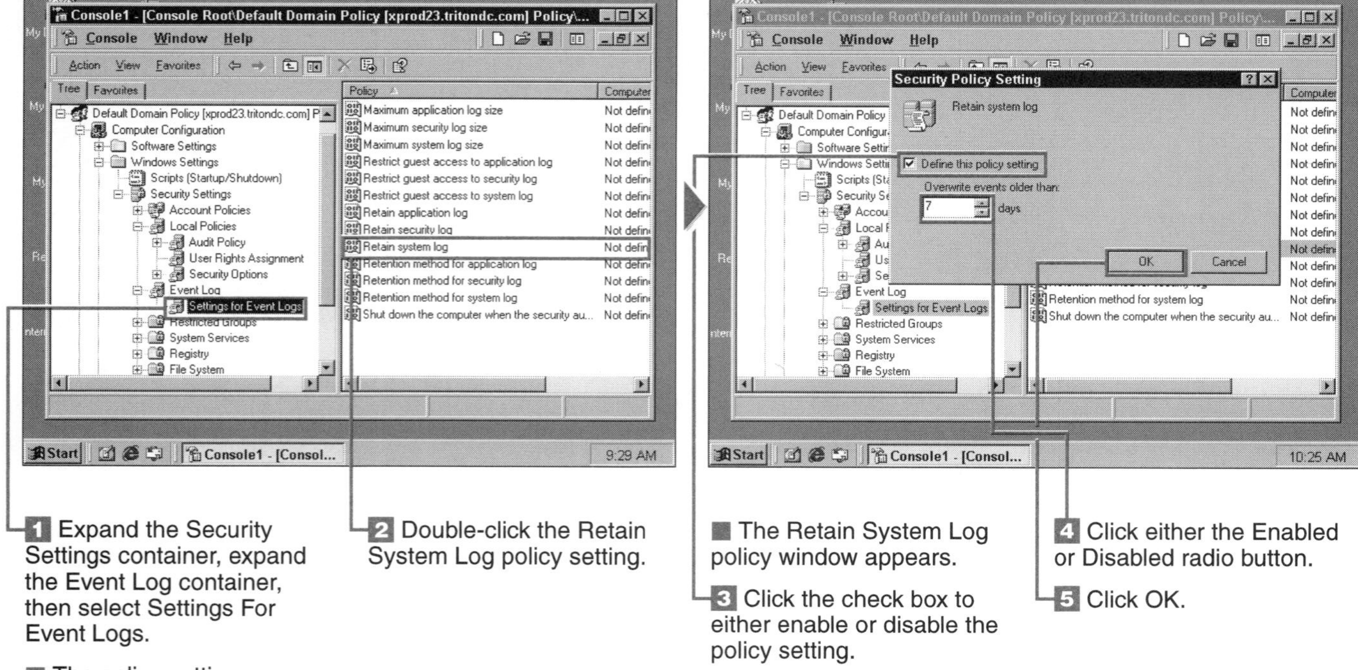

1 Expand the Security Settings container, expand the Event Log container, then select Settings For Event Logs.

■ The policy settings appear in the details pane.

2 Double-click the Retain System Log policy setting.

■ The Retain System Log policy window appears.

3 Click the check box to either enable or disable the policy setting.

4 Click either the Enabled or Disabled radio button.

5 Click OK.

RETENTION METHOD FOR APPLICATION LOG

Configuring the retention method for security logs enables you to determine how events are overwritten. You have three options: you can overwrite events by day, you can overwrite events only as needed, or you can choose not overwrite events at all. If you choose the last option, then you will be forced to manually clear the log. The most efficient setting in most circumstances is to overwrite events as needed. This ensures that you do not overwrite more events than necessary, but still allows the Event Log to create needed room.

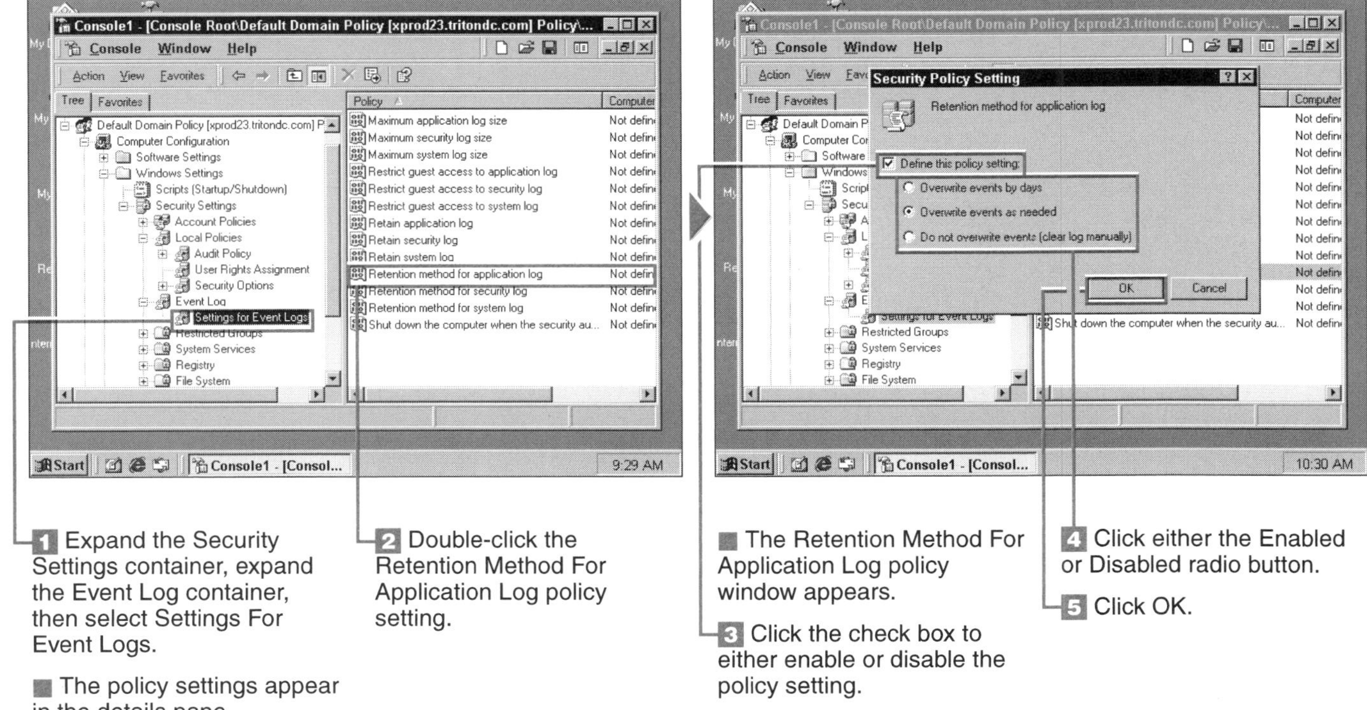

1 Expand the Security Settings container, expand the Event Log container, then select Settings For Event Logs.

■ The policy settings appear in the details pane.

2 Double-click the Retention Method For Application Log policy setting.

■ The Retention Method For Application Log policy window appears.

3 Click the check box to either enable or disable the policy setting.

4 Click either the Enabled or Disabled radio button.

5 Click OK.

RETENTION METHOD FOR SECURITY LOG

You can also configure the retention method for Application, Security, and System logs. These policies allow you to determine how events are overwritten. You have the option of overwriting events by day, as needed, or do not overwrite events. If you choose to not overwrite events, then you must clear the log manually. In most circumstances, the most efficient setting is to overwrite events as needed. This allows the Event Log to create room but does not overwrite any more events than necessary.

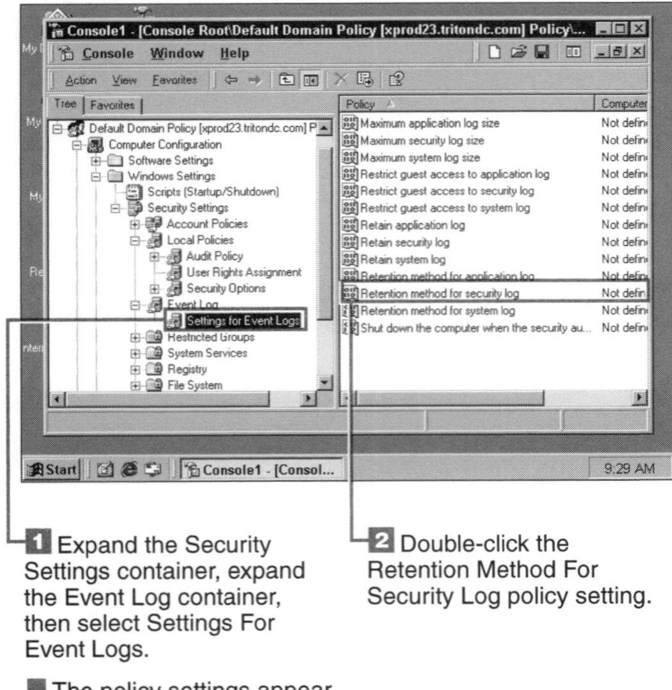

1 Expand the Security Settings container, expand the Event Log container, then select Settings For Event Logs.

■ The policy settings appear in the details pane.

2 Double-click the Retention Method For Security Log policy setting.

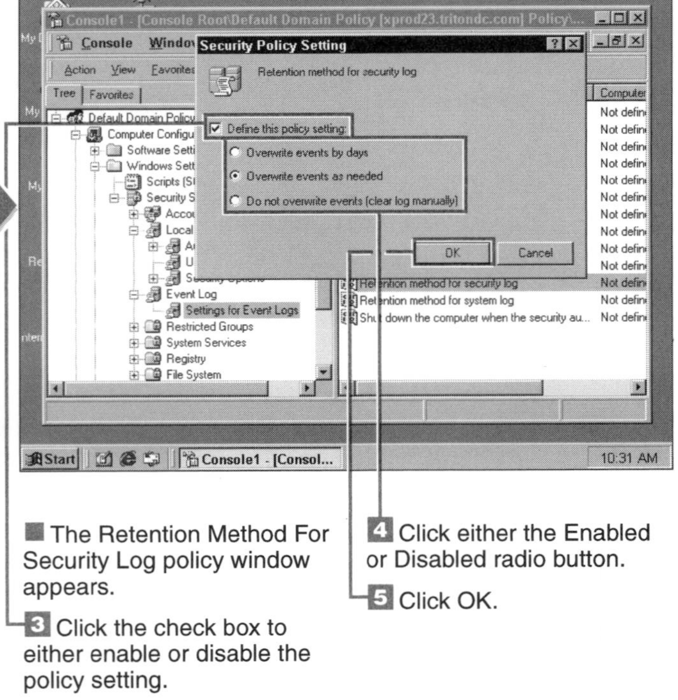

■ The Retention Method For Security Log policy window appears.

3 Click the check box to either enable or disable the policy setting.

4 Click either the Enabled or Disabled radio button.

5 Click OK.

SHUTTING DOWN THE COMPUTER WHEN THE SECURITY AUDIT LOG IS FULL

You have the option to automatically shut the computer down when the Security Audit log is full. This option can be used in cases where you do not want data overwritten and the computer has reached its maximum size. The computer will shut itself down, then an administrator can view the log before clearing it. Obviously, this is not an option you want to use on a regular basis.

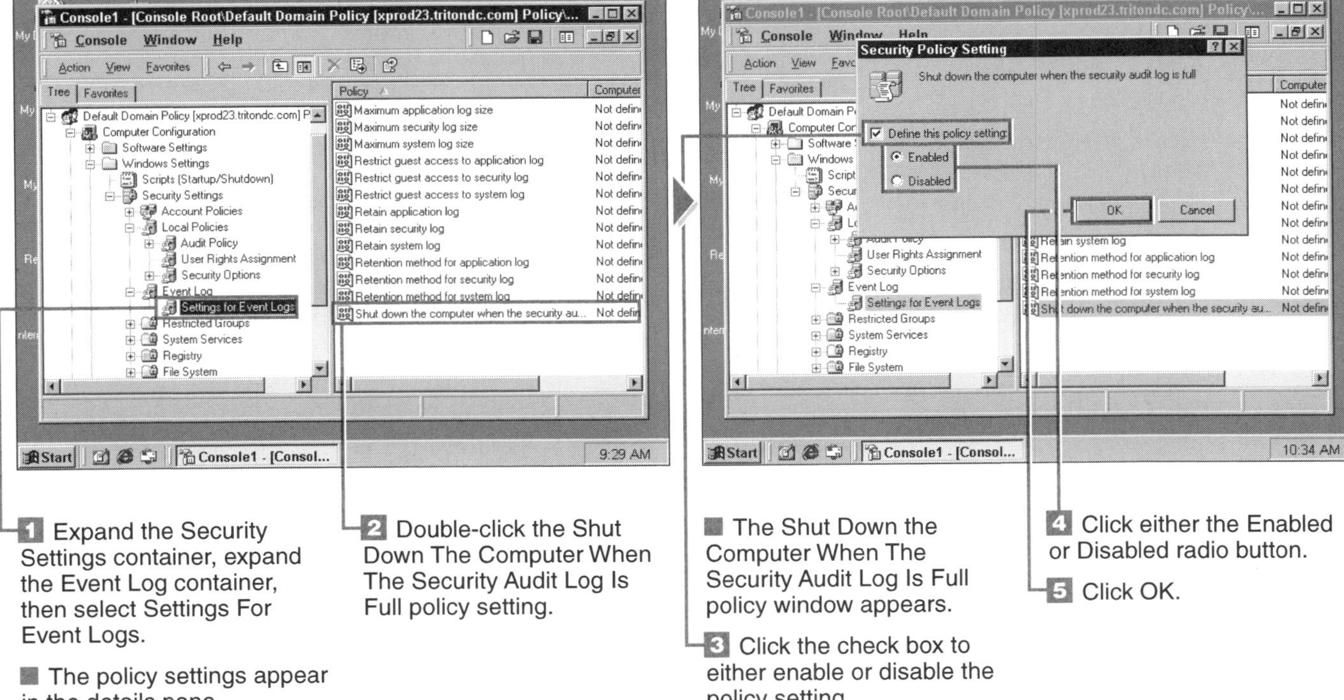

1 Expand the Security Settings container, expand the Event Log container, then select Settings For Event Logs.

■ The policy settings appear in the details pane.

2 Double-click the Shut Down The Computer When The Security Audit Log Is Full policy setting.

■ The Shut Down the Computer When The Security Audit Log Is Full policy window appears.

3 Click the check box to either enable or disable the policy setting.

4 Click either the Enabled or Disabled radio button.

5 Click OK.

APPENDIX B

WHAT'S ON THE CD-ROM

The CD-ROM found at the back of this book contains several resources you may find valuable. First, the entire text of this book, including, all screen captures is available in .pdf format so you can read the book and search for topics electronically. As you work with the Active Directory and need to reference information from time to time, you will find the electronic version of this book very useful. The CD-ROM also includes several other items that either fall under the category of "demos" or "utilities." The following two sections tell you what is available in each.

System Requirements

Make sure that your computer meets the following minimum system requirements. If your computer doesn't match up to most of these requirements, you may have problems using the contents of the CD.

- A PC with a Pentium II 300 MHz or faster processor.
- Microsoft Windows 2000 or Windows 98 with Internet Explorer 5 or later.
- At least 64MB of total RAM installed on your computer.
- At least 10 MB of hard drive space available to install all the software from this CD. (You need less space if you don't install every program.)
- A CD-ROM drive — double-speed (2x) or faster.
- A monitor capable of displaying at least 256 colors or grayscale.
- Visual C++ 6.0 with service pack 3 installed.

A word about Shareware et al

Shareware programs are fully functional, free-trial versions of copyrighted programs. If you prefer a particular program, then register with that program's author, pay a nominal fee, and receive licenses, enhanced versions, and technical support for the program. Freeware programs are free, copyrighted games, applications, and utilities. You can copy freeware programs — for free — to as many PCs as you like, but be aware that freeware programs usually have no technical support. GNU software is governed by a General Public License (GPL), which is included inside the folder of the GNU software. The only restriction for using or distributing GNU software is a big one — you can't restrict anyone else's use of the GNU software. (See the GPL for more details.) Trials, demos, or evaluation versions of are usually limited, either by time (30 days from installation, for example) or functionality (such as not being able to print or save your projects).

After examining these products, you may wish to purchase them to aid you with your Active Directory and Windows 2000 implementation.

DirectMigrate 2000

Demo version. DirectMigrate 2000, by Entevo Corp., is a tool that assists you in migrating objects from other LDAP directories into the Active Directory. This tool can be very useful if you are moving from an environment such as Novell Directory Service (NDS) to the Active Directory. DirectMigrate can also assist you in migrating Windows NT resources to the Active Directory and even enables you to test your migrations before running them. To learn more, visit www.entevo.com.

DirectAdmin

Demo version. DirectAdmin, also by Entevo Corp, contains a number of capabilities to help Active

Directory administrators. DirectAdmin can help you create, update, rename, and delete Active Directory objects and properties. DirectAdmin supports cross-platform functionality and enables you to perform many Windows 2000 functions more easily, as well as manage the Active Directory. To purchase DirectAdmin or to learn more, visit www.entevo.com.

Micro House Technical Library

Evaluation version. Micro House Technical Library contains a wealth of information about various technical topics that you can search. Micro House Technical Library is a useful asset for both learning and troubleshooting. A trial version of the library is available on the CD-ROM for your review. To purchase the product or to learn more, visit www.microhouse.com.

WS_FTP Pro

Trial version. WS_FTP Pro, by Ipswitch, is a file transfer utility for use with Windows operating systems. You can use WS_FTP Pro to manage FTP directories and perform uploads or downloads of FTP files. WS_FTP Pro on the CD-ROM is a trial version you can examine for possible use in your environment. To purchase WS_FTP Pro, visit www.ipswitch.com

MindSpring Internet Access

MindSpring Internet Access is a commercial product that gets you signed up to the MindSpring Internet service provider. If you don't already have Internet access, MindSpring is an excellent ISP that offers Internet access for a low monthly fee. MindSpring also has different Web hosting options depending on the kind of account you have. If you're already on the Internet but would like to learn more about MindSpring and the different service options it offers, you can visit the Web site at www.mindspring.com.

IMPORTANT NOTE: If you already have an Internet service provider, installing MindSpring may replace your current settings. You may no longer be able to access the Internet through your original provider.

Also note, if you already have Internet Explorer 4.0 or later installed on your computer, select the Custom Install option when you install MindSpring Internet Access, and deselect Internet Explorer. This will prevent MindSpring from attempting to replace your browser with an earlier version.

Utilities

The following shareware utilities are also available on the CD-ROM for your use.

Diskeeper Lite for Windows NT

Diskeeper Lite For Windows NT is freeware included on the CD-ROM for your use. Diskeeper Lite provides you with a high-speed, manual defragmentation utility used to defragment hard disks on Windows NT 4.0 computers. Because disk defragmentation is not offered in the operating system, Diskeeper Lite is a necessary and useful utility.

IP Subnet Calculator

Commercial Product. As you plan your Active Directory implementation, you may be faced with planning an IP subnet. The IP Calculator included on the CD-ROM can help you easily calculate digital-to-binary conversions and can be a very useful tool for use with tricky TCP/IP configurations.

Regmon

Regmon is a registry monitor that shows you real-time registry events. Regmon contains powerful sorting and filtering capabilities so you can view registry events for particular system or application processes. This tool is excellent for troubleshooting system or application problems, and is also a good way to simply learn how your system works on the "inside."

WinZip 7.0

WinZip is a shareware archiving utility you can use to compress all kinds of Windows files and documents. WinZip is commonly used to reduce the amount of disk space consumed by file storage and to reduce the size of files sent via e-mail.

How to Install the Programs on the CD-ROM

The CD-ROM accompanying this book is compatible with Windows 95, 98, NT 4.0 and later. All of the software included on the CD-ROM is contained in separate folders listed by company name. To access the software, insert the CD-ROM into your CD-ROM drive, and then follow the instructions below.

Checking Out and Installing the Software through the HTML Pages

1. Insert the CD into your computer's CD-ROM drive.

   Give your computer a moment to take a look at the CD.

2. Open your browser.

   If you don't have a browser, follow the easy steps as described in the following section, "Using the CD from the Directory Structure," to install one. For your convenience, we have included Microsoft Internet Explorer, which is an installation-savvy browser.

3. Select File⇨Open (Internet Explorer) or File⇨Open Page (Netscape).

   The browser opens.

4. In the dialog box that appears, type D:\START.HTM and click OK.

   If the letter for your CD-ROM drive is not D, replace D with the correct letter.

   You now see the file that walks you through the contents on the CD.

5. To navigate the CD interface and go to a topic of interest, simply click that topic.

   You go to an explanation of that topic and the files on the CD and how to use or install them.

6. To install a particular file or program, click its name to launch the install program.

   The program or file is automatically installed. Because you are using a browser to install this software, you will be asked to select either "Save this file" or "Run this file from its current location." Select "Run this file from its current location" when this dialog box pops up. The program you selected will now be installed on your hard drive.

   If you are installing the sample files, the procedure is the same. When you click the name of the chapter, the CD automatically copies all sample files to your hard drive in a folder called <NAME HERE>.

7. After you finish with the interface, close your browser as usual.

Using the CD from the Directory Structure

If you are using a browser that does not support software installation, you will need to follow these steps to install the software.

1. Double-click the file named License.txt.

   This file contains the end-user license that you agree to by using the CD. When you finish reading the license, close the program, most likely NotePad, that displayed the file.

2. Double-click the file named Readme.txt.

   This file contains instructions about installing the software from this CD. You may find it helpful to keep this text file open while you use the CD.

3. Double-click the folder for the software you are interested in.

   Be sure to read the descriptions of the programs in the next section of this appendix (much of this information also shows up in the Readme file). These descriptions give you more precise information about the programs' folder names and about finding and running the installer program.

4. Find the file named Setup.exe, or Install.exe, or something similar, and double-click that file.

   The installer for the program you selected now walks you through the process of setting up your new software.

Troubleshooting

The programs on the CD-ROM work on most computers with the minimum system requirements. However, your computer may differ, and some programs may not work properly for some reason.

The two likeliest problems are that you don't have enough memory (RAM) for the programs you want to use, or you have other programs running that are affecting installation or running of a program. If you get error messages such as Not enough memory or Setup cannot continue, try one or more of these methods and then try using the software again:

- Turn off any anti-virus software that you have on your computer. Installers sometimes mimic virus activity and may make your computer incorrectly believe that it is being infected by a virus.
- Close all running programs. The more programs you're running, the less memory is available to other programs. Installers also typically update files and programs; if you keep other programs running, installation may not work properly.
- In Windows, close the CD interface and run demos or installations directly from Windows Explorer. The interface itself can tie up system memory, or even conflict with certain kinds of interactive demos. Use Windows Explorer to browse the files on the CD and launch installers or demos.
- Have your local computer store add more RAM to your computer. This is, admittedly, a drastic and somewhat expensive step. However, if you have a Windows 95 PC or a Mac OS computer with a PowerPC chip, adding more memory can really help the speed of your computer and enable more programs to run at the same time.

If you still have trouble installing the items from the CD, please call the IDG Books Worldwide Customer Service phone number: 800-762-2974 (outside the U.S.: 317-596-5430).

MASTER ACTIVE DIRECTORY VISUALLY ON THE CD-ROM

You can view Master Active Directory VISUALLY on your screen using the CD-ROM disc included at the back of this book. The CD-ROM disc allows you to search the contents of the book for a specific word or phrase. The CD-ROM disc also provides a convenient way of keeping the book handy while traveling.

You must install Acrobat Reader on your computer before you can view the book on the CD-ROM disc. This program is provided on the disc. Acrobat Reader allows you to view Portable Document Format (PDF) files. These files can display books and magazines on your screen exactly as they appear in printed form.

To view the contents of the book using Acrobat Reader, display the contents of the disc. Double-click the START.htm icon. In the page that appears, click "The book in electronic format" to access the contents of the book.

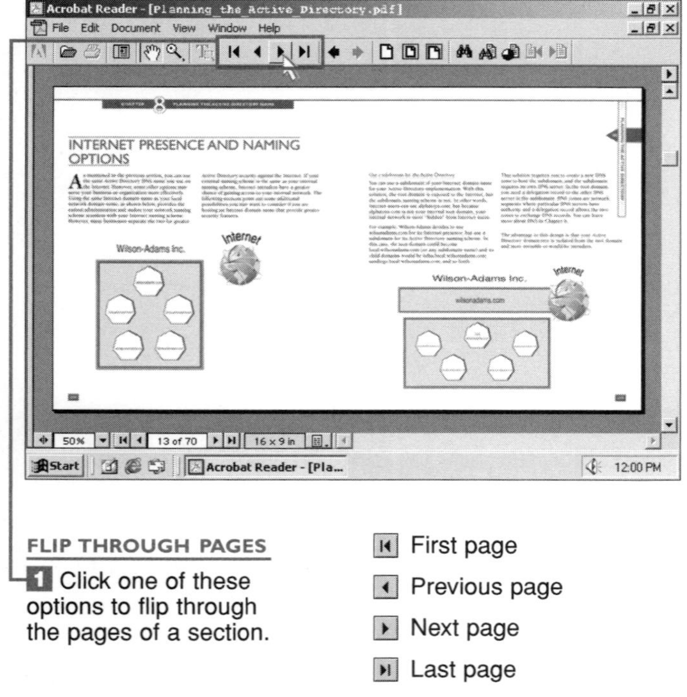

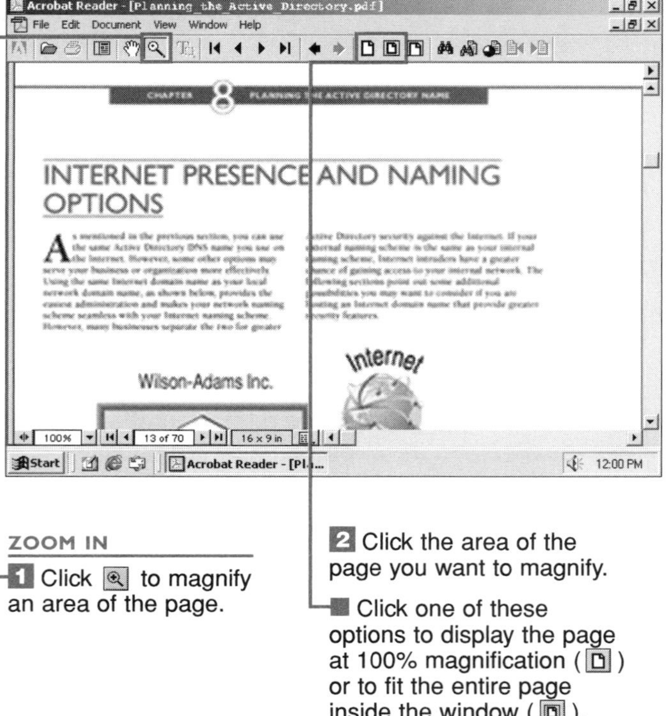

FLIP THROUGH PAGES

1. Click one of these options to flip through the pages of a section.

- First page
- Previous page
- Next page
- Last page

ZOOM IN

1. Click [zoom icon] to magnify an area of the page.
2. Click the area of the page you want to magnify.

- Click one of these options to display the page at 100% magnification ([icon]) or to fit the entire page inside the window ([icon]).

TIPS

How do I install Acrobat Reader?

✔ Open the ACROREAD folder on the CD-ROM disc. Double-click the RS40ENG.exe file and then follow the instructions on your screen.

How do I search all the sections of the book at once?

✔ You must first locate the index. While viewing the contents of the book, click in the Acrobat Reader window. Click Indexes and then click Add. Locate and click the index.pdx file, click Open and then click OK. You need to locate the index only once. After locating the index, you can click to search all the sections.

How can I make searching the book more convenient?

✔ Copy the Acrobat Files folder from the CD-ROM disc to your hard drive. This allows you to easily access the contents of the book at any time.

Can I use Acrobat Reader for anything else?

✔ Acrobat Reader is a popular and useful program. There are many files available on the Web that are designed to be viewed using Acrobat Reader. Look for files with the .pdf extension.

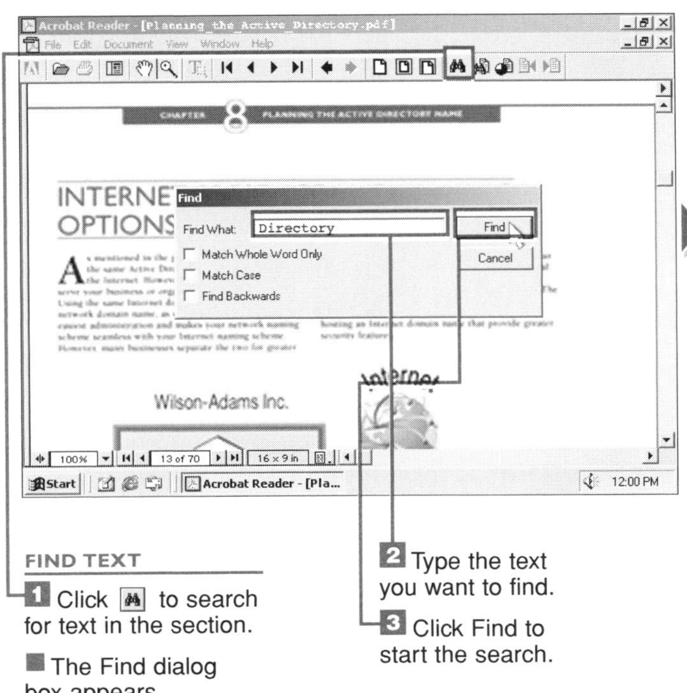

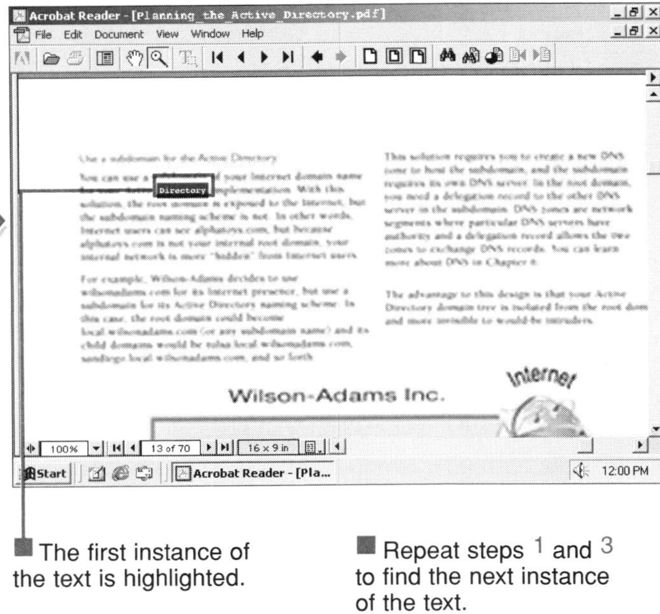

FIND TEXT

1 Click to search for text in the section.

■ The Find dialog box appears.

2 Type the text you want to find.

3 Click Find to start the search.

■ The first instance of the text is highlighted.

■ Repeat steps 1 and 3 to find the next instance of the text.

INDEX

A

INDEX

B

C

D

E

F

G

INDEX

H

I

J

K

L

M

N

O

P

Q

R

S

T

U

V

W

X

Z